Belarus

the Bradt Travel Guide

Nigel Roberts

edition
4

www.bradtguides.com

Bradt Travel Guides Ltd, UK
The Globe Pequot Press Inc, USA

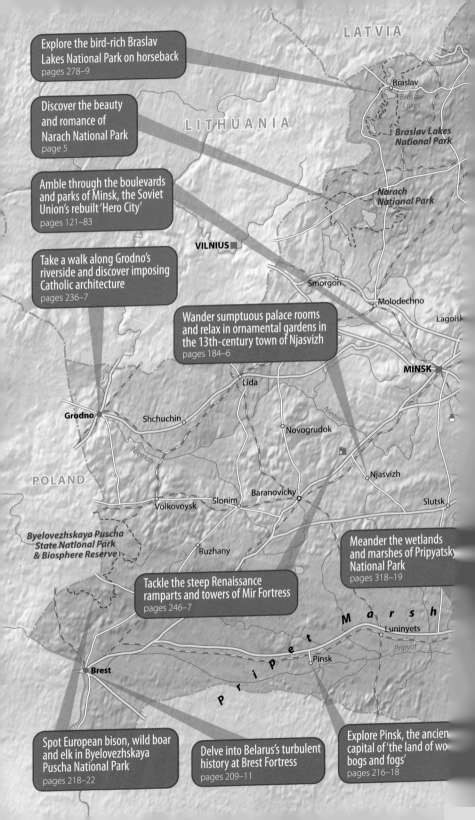

Explore the bird-rich Braslav Lakes National Park on horseback
pages 278–9

Discover the beauty and romance of Narach National Park
page 5

Amble through the boulevards and parks of Minsk, the Soviet Union's rebuilt 'Hero City'
pages 121–83

Take a walk along Grodno's riverside and discover imposing Catholic architecture
pages 236–7

Wander sumptuous palace rooms and relax in ornamental gardens in the 13th-century town of Njasvizh
pages 184–6

Meander the wetlands and marshes of Pripyatsky National Park
pages 318–19

Tackle the steep Renaissance ramparts and towers of Mir Fortress
pages 246–7

Spot European bison, wild boar and elk in Byelovezhskaya Puscha National Park
pages 218–22

Delve into Belarus's turbulent history at Brest Fortress
pages 209–11

Explore Pinsk, the ancient capital of 'the land of woods, bogs and fogs'
pages 216–18

LATVIA

LITHUANIA

POLAND

Braslav
Braslav
Lakes

Braslav Lakes
National Park

Narach
National Park

VILNIUS

Smorgon

Molodechno

Lagoisk

MINSK

Lida

Grodno

Shchuchin

Novogrudok

Nieman

Njasvizh

Slutsk

Byelovezhskaya Puscha
State National Park
& Biosphere Reserve

Volkovoysk

Slonim

Baranovichy

Nieman

Ruzhany

Pripet Marsh

Luninyets

Brest

Pinsk

Pripyat

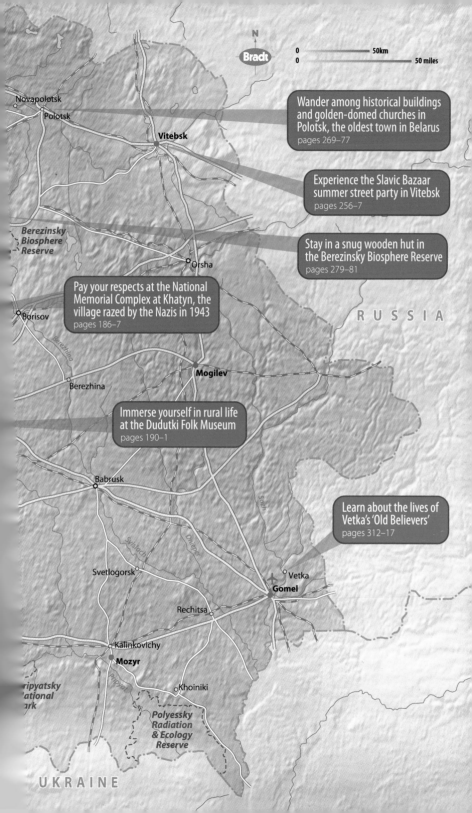

N

Bradt

0 ——————— 50km
0 ——————— 50 miles

Wander among historical buildings
and golden-domed churches in
Polotsk, the oldest town in Belarus
pages 269–77

Experience the Slavic Bazaar
summer street party in Vitebsk
pages 256–7

Stay in a snug wooden hut in
the Berezinsky Biosphere Reserve
pages 279–81

Pay your respects at the National
Memorial Complex at Khatyn, the
village razed by the Nazis in 1943
pages 186–7

Immerse yourself in rural life
at the Dudutki Folk Museum
pages 190–1

Learn about the lives of
Vetka's 'Old Believers'
pages 312–17

Novapolotsk
Polotsk

Vitebsk

Berezinsky
Biosphere
Reserve

Orsha

R U S S I A

Borisov

Berezhina

Mogilev

Berezhina

Babrusk

Svetlogorsk

Svisloch

Dnepr

Soch

Vetka
Gomel

Rechitsa

Kalinkovichy

Mozyr

Khoiniki

ripyatsky
ational
ark

Polyessky
Radiation
& Ecology
Reserve

U K R A I N E

Belarus
Don't
miss...

Russian Orthodoxy
Located within Gomel's
Rumyantsev-Paskevich
Park, the Cathedral of Sts
Peter and Paul is home to
some beautiful frescoes and
a lovely collection of icons
(RB/D) page 310

Soviet architecture
Stalinist architecture abounds in
Belarus, including the imposing
House of Government in Minsk (FS/S)
page 172

Memorials

Brest Fortress became famous for the bravery of its garrison during Operation Barbarossa in World War II, and was later made into a huge shrine (SN/S) pages 209–11

Forests and lakes

Close to the Latvian border, the sprawling raslav Lakes National Park is an enchanting mix of rolling hills, quamarine lakes and labyrinthine rivers (VM/S) pages 278–9

Minsk

e futuristic National rary is undoubtedly e most eye-catching ilding in Minsk and minates the skyline r miles around (s/S) pages 179–80

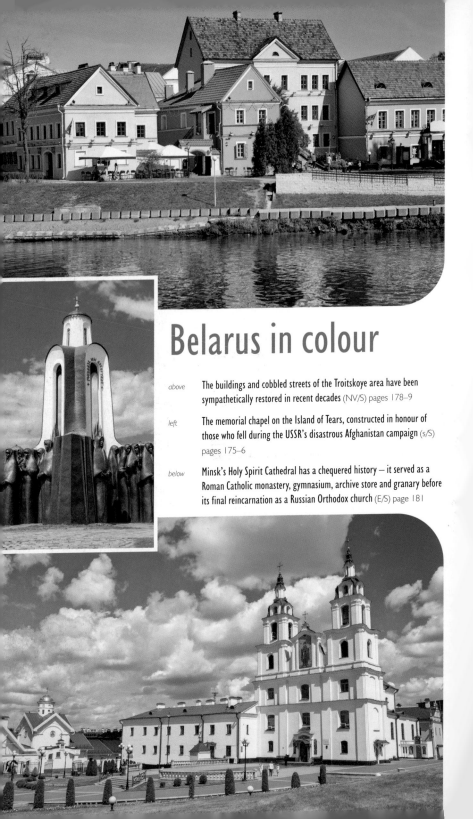

Belarus in colour

above   The buildings and cobbled streets of the Troitskoye area have been sympathetically restored in recent decades (NV/S) pages 178–9

left   The memorial chapel on the Island of Tears, constructed in honour of those who fell during the USSR's disastrous Afghanistan campaign (s/S) pages 175–6

below   Minsk's Holy Spirit Cathedral has a chequered history — it served as a Roman Catholic monastery, gymnasium, archive store and granary before its final reincarnation as a Russian Orthodox church (E/S) page 181

above The halls of the newly relocated Belarusian State Museum of the History of the Great Patriotic War house a vast collection of exhibits relating to World War II (NV/S) pages 163–4

right A sculpture of St Michael the Archangel stands outside the Church of St Simeon and St Helena, also known as the 'Red Church' (SH/D) page 180

below On the bank of the Svislach River, Gorky Park is Minsk's prime promenading and people-watching spot throughout the year (RB/D) page 169

PRIMETOUR
INCOMING TOUR OPERATOR / DMC

OPEN BELARUS. OPEN SOUL.

PACKAGE TOURS
TAILOR-MADE ITINERARIES

GUARANTEED TOURS

HOTELS

MICE

PREMIUM TRAVEL SERVICES FOR SUCCESSFUL TRAVELLING

www.belarusprimetour.com   incoming@belarusprimetour.com   +375 1

AUTHOR

Nigel Roberts first visited Belarus in 2001 and since then he has travelled extensively throughout the country. For 15 years he worked on sustainable development projects with rural communities there blighted by the Chernobyl catastrophe. A lawyer in a former life, his subsequent foray into the grocery business as a supermarket shelf-stacker failed to inspire. His interest in eastern Europe was awoken during history and Russian language lessons at school.

Visits to Moscow and Leningrad during the final turbulent years of the Soviet Union prompted further language study by night and since then he has researched and travelled widely in the area. Publication of the first three editions of this Bradt guide encouraged Nigel to write about his travels around Belarus for a number of online and print periodicals, particularly on the subject of the close relationship he has developed with communities and families in the district of Vetka.

AUTHOR'S STORY

I'm writing this vignette at the kitchen table of the Belarus home that has welcomed me as a son of the soil since my very first visit in November 2001. Here at 42 Karl Marx Street, Tanya is preparing the evening meal, Valeri is shouting at the television and Dexter the dog is sprawled across his tatty old sofa on the front porch. I've just returned from a visit to see an old schoolteacher friend at the splendid museum housed in School Number One across town and I'm a touch fazed by what just happened. As we meandered the museum's collections together, Sergei Nikolaevich invited me to close my eyes and hold out my hands, and when I did so he gently placed an item of some weight in them. It was one of the exhibits, a Bible dating from the 19th century, but it was more than just a Bible. It belonged to Old Believers, members of the Russian Orthodox Church who rejected 17th-century reforms in favour of the old ways and who suffered persecution as a result. 'This is for your work', said Sergei Nikolaevich. 'It's a present to help with your research.' When I protested that I couldn't possibly take such a beautiful treasure out of Vetka he dismissed my objection with a peremptory wave of his hand. 'We have others', he declared. The cover is wood, part bound in leather and held together with handmade clasps of metal. The printing is exquisite and the words are Old Russian, only some of which I can read. Every instinct tells me that an item of such rare potency belongs in this town, this museum, its spiritual home, but I have no idea how I'm going to convince my dear friend that I cannot accept it without causing offence.

This example of unconditional generosity of spirit may be one of the most extraordinary I have witnessed here; yet I encounter warm hospitality wherever I travel in this lovely country. Again it's a great honour for me to share with you many of the things I've seen and done since my first visit in 2001, and to open the window on Belarus for you to peek inside. The course of my life has taken an unexpected direction since I first came here. I can't promise the same for you, but I shall be surprised if you remain unmoved by Belarus and its delightful people long after you return home. Whatever your impressions, do write to tell me what you think.

PUBLISHER'S FOREWORD *Adrian Phillips, Managing Director*

When we first announced that we'd commissioned a guide to Belarus, I received a phone call from a journalist with just one question: 'Why would anyone want to go there?' I suspect his was not an unusual reaction. While other former Soviet republics looked westward, Belarus remained entrenched in the past; for most outsiders, the country represents that bleak, utilitarian 'greyness' so frequently associated with communist states. However, as Nigel Roberts passionately demonstrates, such preconceptions are hugely unfair. And it seems many of you agree, since we're thrilled to be producing the fourth edition of this trailblazing book – which remains the only standalone guide to Belarus on the market.

Fourth edition published October 2018 First published May 2008
Bradt Travel Guides Ltd,
IDC House, The Vale, Chalfont St Peter, Bucks SL9 9RZ, England w bradtguides.com
Print edition published in the USA by The Globe Pequot Press Inc,
PO Box 480, Guilford, Connecticut 06437–0480

Text copyright © 2018 Nigel Roberts
Boxed text on pages 34, 256, 266 and *By train* on page 62 copyright © Nicky Gardner
Maps copyright © 2018 Bradt Travel Guides Ltd
Minsk Metro map © 2018 Robert Schwandl (UrbanRail.Net)
Photographs copyright © 2018 Individual photographers (see below)
Project Manager: Laura Pidgley
Cover image research: Pepi Bluck

ISBN 13: 978 1 78477 602 2
e-ISBN: 978 1 78477 549 0 (e-pub)
e-ISBN: 978 1 78477 450 9 (mobi)

British Library Cataloguing in Publication Data
A catalogue record for this book is available from the British Library

Photographs Alamy: Nina Lex (NL/A); Dreamstime: Alexvalent (A/D), Ala Charnyshova (AC/D), Ryhor Bruyeu (RB/D), Dtvphoto (D/D), Natallia Khlapushyna (NK/D), Nkarol (N/D), Olga355 (O/D), Hanna Sarkisian (HS/D), Swisshippo (SH/D), Natallia Yaumenenka (NY/D); Getty Images: bruev (b/G); Shutterstock: Grisha Bruev (GB/S), Lasko Dmitry (LD/S), Soru Epotok (SE/S), ESOlex (E/S), aleksander hunta (ah/S), kosmos111 (k/S), Viktar Malyshchyts (VM/S), Mikhail Markovsky (MM/S), nodff (n/S), Sergey Novikov (SN/S), rsooll (r/S), Andrei Rybachuk (AR/S), saiko3p (s/S), Fedor Selivanov (FS/S), Lena Serditova (LS/S), Andrey Sharmanov (AS/S), udmurd (u/S), Sergey Uryadnikov (SU/S), Nickolay Vinokurov (NV/S), Katsiuba Volha (KV/S)
Front cover St Alexander Nevsky Church, Gomel (b/G)
Back cover Dudutki Folk Museum (LS/S)
Title page Mir Fortress (D/D); Traditional straw doll (GB/S); White stork (GB/S)

Maps David McCutcheon, FBCart.S

Typeset by Ian Spick, Bradt Travel Guides
Production managed by Jellyfish Print Solutions; printed in India
Digital conversion by w dataworks.co.in

Acknowledgements

When it comes to project management I'm more than happy to admit that I'm a hapless, bumbling buffoon. I'm very proud of it. In 34 years as a lawyer and public administrator the closest I ever came to actually having a career plan was to studiously avoid this darkest of dark arts. Yet by my own lamentable standards, in March 2017 I was handily placed and prepared to embark on the process of updating the manuscript for this fourth edition. Then came a visit to my GP, routine blood tests, an emergency admission to hospital in the middle of the night, eight days on a drip and (eventually) 3 hours of surgery to remove a tumour and half of my thyroid gland. Hardly the best of circumstances in which to write a book, but nonetheless a fascinating opportunity for personal development (as a management consultant might say).

That the task of updating the manuscript was completed at all and (almost) on time is entirely due to the love, care and support of Lizzie, Harriet and George at home, a debt that I can never repay. When I fell you picked me up and when I stumbled you carried me on. Without you there would be no fourth edition. And without you I wouldn't amount to very much at all. You three kept me going through the long months of struggling to get up out of the chair when I yearned to be able to meander fields and hills with the sun and a breeze on my face. Many other family members and dear old friends came to see me (often from considerable distance), telephoned, messaged (and with the blackest of humour) saw to it that I was never at risk of feeling sorry for myself. Bless you Mel, Helen, Bill, Ed, Mike, Em, Lu, Perce, Bun, Moses, Geoff, Funtime Frankie, Tim, John, Mick, Cal Doonican, Nicole, Howard, Laurence, Dave, Richard, Ian, Bryan, David, Brian, Ian and dear Jo. God bless the dear old NHS and all who sail in her say I, not least everyone at New Road Surgery, Alexandra Hospital Redditch and Wycombe General Hospital, but most especially Doctor Richard Bunsell, dear old Rick, who cleared the thorny path and then sat with me, prepped for surgery and just a bit scared, holding my hand for 6 interminable but memorable hours.

When I was back on my feet and ready to start scribbling again, my Belarusian friends once more stepped up to the mark (as they always do) with encouragement, help, support, the opening of metaphorical doors, the clearing of impenetrable fog, the pounding of streets and finally the ever-prompt answering of a thousand and one questions fired off by day and by night via the full range of communications media. Huge thanks to each and every one of you and especially to dear friends and colleagues Natalia Ovsyanko (and everyone at the Academy of Public Administration), Kirill Zemtsov, Alex Vazhnik, Joanna Vladyka, Natasha Dubrovskaya, Irina Gordienko, Alena Gourova, Irina Batsenko, Evgeniy Danilik, Anastasia Kurilenko, Tamara Vershitskaya, Alina Dmitrovich, Masha Cheriakova, Hanna Hrydziushka, Alina Krushynskaya, Oxana Prokopenko, Larissa Yatsekevich, Victor Burakov, Veronika Burakova, Liza Prostyakova, Marina Yashenkova, Vasily the Poet, Sergei Perepeluk, Oxana Kudina, Andrei Vidishev, Yalena Zabello, Natalia Suxanova, Lera Filipyeva and everyone at the Embassy of the Republic of Belarus in London, the British Embassy in Minsk, the Belarus Ministry of Sport and Tourism and the Museum of Contemporary Belarusian Statehood (both also in Minsk).

As always I am indebted to Natalya Lisovskaya and her team at the Belarus Prime Tour agency who have made such a wonderful job of collecting and verifying a huge body of data for me, as well as to Nicky Gardner and Susanne Kries of *hidden europe* magazine in Berlin, whose delightful pieces within these pages add a touch of class and quality to my inane ramblings. I am grateful also to those intrepid travellers and loyal Bradt supporters who have taken the trouble to write to me to share updates, comments, constructive criticism and experiences following their own journey of discovery to Belarus, in particular Neil Adams, Alastair Watson, Richard Madge, Olivier and Semra Umay, Colin Thomas Kirby, Adam Jones, Christopher Peters, Ted Richards, Kees Duivenvoorden, John Waller and Igor Ignatyev.

And finally, where would this book be without the support of everyone at Bradt Travel Guides? I especially thank my editor Laura Pidgley, whose imaginative eye for detail has sculpted the ragbag bundle of files I metaphorically plonked on her desk into a cohesive manuscript. I also thank commissioning editor Rachel Fielding for maintaining faith in me and the Belarus project during the grim days of my illness, when at times it felt that my beloved Birmingham City FC had more chance of winning the Champions League than I had of seeing this fourth edition to fruition. Funny old business, this life caper.

FEEDBACK REQUEST AND UPDATES WEBSITE

At Bradt Travel Guides we're aware that guidebooks start to go out of date on the day they're published – and that you, our readers, are out there in the field doing research of your own. You'll find out before us when a fine new family-run hotel opens or a favourite restaurant changes hands and goes downhill. So why not write and tell us about your experiences? Contact us on ✆ 01753 893444 or e info@bradtguides.com. We will forward emails to the author, who may post updates on the Bradt website at w bradtupdates.com/belarus. Alternatively you can add a review of the book to w bradtguides.com or Amazon.

BELARUS: STILL A RAPIDLY CHANGING COUNTRY

With each of the first three editions of this guide I expressed the view that the timing was then undoubtedly right for this delightful country to be 'discovered' some time very soon. But although there have been advances for the Belarusian tourism industry in the entirety of the intervening period (and a big leap forward in the last 18 months that has seen a significant increase in visitor numbers), it remains largely undiscovered still. Yet each succeeding visit I make reveals more changes, some small and some not so small. In Minsk, the increasing amount of neon and designer product advertising is there for all to see; more and more Western brands and international chains are in evidence; and the range of fast-food emporia continues to expand. Today the reference in the first edition to my observation in 2006 that I 'noted with resignation and a heavy heart that [Minsk] now boasts the country's first drive-thru fast-food emporium' seems absurdly naïve on my part and hopelessly out of date. The pace of change since then has not matched my original forecast, but the marked acceleration in recent times means I remain convinced that one day sooner rather than later people will come in big numbers. One significant consequence of the tourism industry sharpening up its act is that new hotels, restaurants, bars, cafés and entertainment outlets are opening in big numbers, as I noted with some alarm when wandering the streets with notebook and camera to undertake manuscript research late in 2017.

Please bear this process of change and development in mind as you embark upon your preparation for your first visit. As with each of the previous editions I have personally established and verified the accuracy of the information provided in this edition or else corroborated data through the good offices of my merry band of friends, acquaintances and business contacts on the ground throughout the country, without whom this undertaking would not be possible. Yet notwithstanding the significant work we've all put in there remains the risk of anomaly; for example in October 2017 I again visited that restaurant in Brest to find it was still advertising different opening hours on two of its windows, as it had been when I visited for the first time in 2007 and again in 2014! The primary difficulty is that the availability of data for the edification of travellers, tourists and consumers of leisure services remains at a rudimentary stage of evolution, especially in comparison with the mind-boggling array of information that is available in the West. I very much hope that nothing herein is so utterly 'off the wall' as to be unreliable, but if you have the chance to check for updates or amendments as you go, you might want to avail yourselves of the opportunity so to do. If you find that anything has changed do let me know. And I shall also be grateful if you can let me know if you find any howlers so that I can hold up my hands in shame!

Without exception the personal tales that I recount in these pages are taken from my own experiences and travels. One of the chief pleasures I derive from sharing them is the hope that those who find new experiences on their own travels may in turn be motivated to share their stories, as many of you have done already. I very much hope this fourth edition won't be the last, in which case your further feedback, comments and criticism will be most gratefully received and acknowledged (see box, opposite).

Contents

Introduction

When my dream of visiting the old Soviet Union was first realised in the late 1980s Belarus existed not as a sovereign state but as Byelorossia ('White Russia'), one of the constituent republics of the USSR. Other than to those with more than a passing interest in the politics of the area it was simply part of the vast swathe of red that formed the eastern half of the Cold War map of the world. With the fall of the Berlin Wall and the consequent disintegration of the USSR many of the former Soviet republics turned their gaze westward to embrace political and economic reform through evolution or revolution, while Belarus remained fiercely embedded in the past. It is still finding its feet in an uncertain new world. Neighbours to the west and north (Poland, Lithuania and Latvia) are now member states of the EU while those to the east and south (the Russian Federation and Ukraine) move ever closer to embracing Western commercialism and the economics of the free market. By comparison Belarus (the most westerly republic of the old USSR) seems to be taking its time to establish an identity free from its Soviet past. Though an independent nation state that prides itself on being situated in the heart of Europe, right at the crossroads where ancient trade routes from west to east and from north to south meet, it is still an unknown land. But perhaps this undiscovered box of gems is about to be opened at last.

My first visit to the country in November 2001 began with a night-time landing at Minsk Airport. First impressions were less than welcoming, with an air of mystery and an edge of danger on the icy easterly. Emerging into the darkness from intimidating encounters with a succession of humourless, stern-faced officials in khaki uniforms I was led hurriedly to the waiting transport for a 6-hour journey down to the southeastern corner of the country on unlit roads through mile after mile of silver birch forest stretching away into impenetrable blackness. As we stopped briefly to stretch our legs in the middle of nowhere the raw cold took my breath away as I gazed up into a dazzling panoply of stars, unpolluted by unnatural reflected light from below. As the first snows of winter began to fall we arrived in Vetka and over dirt tracks we came to the old part of town where wooden houses stood sentinel against the biting cold, with windows rattling in ill-fitting frames as flurries of snow danced among the eaves. The front door to the house of my hosts opened with a dazzling burst of light and heat as I was ushered into warmth and safety. My life has never been the same since that day and every time I return it is to the same family. And it always feels like coming home.

It's a cliché I know, but a visit to this delightful country really is one of those life-defining experiences. It is still relatively free of the trappings of modern tourism and Western materialism, such that it's very easy to feel a sense of having slipped into another time and dimension. In many ways the country is a 'living museum' of Soviet communism but to treat it as such would be deeply patronising, as well as a gross disservice to the resilience of its people. Decades after the catastrophic nuclear accident at Chernobyl Belarusians still feel like the forgotten people of Europe, overlooked and shunned by an international community that denies effective aid and assistance in the absence of political reform. But against all odds, a vibrant Belarusian identity is beginning to steadily emerge.

Sometime soon, I hope, I'm going to board a train at St Pancras International in London and journey to Minsk via Lille, Brussels, Cologne, Warsaw and Brest. One January I made it as far as the Polish border during the course of a trip from London via Berlin. I love traversing Europe by train and on this occasion I travelled on 28 trains in five days. One of my favourite pastimes (particularly on dark winter nights) is to take down from my bookshelves the re-launched *European Rail Timetable* (**w** *europeanrailtimetable.eu*), uncork an Irish malt whiskey and put together a pan-European journey; and with time on my side I reckon London–Minsk–London would be a breeze to organise. One day …

So it is with the greatest of pleasure that I share with you everything that I have come to love about Belarus: the natural splendour of primeval green forests, clear rivers and blue lakes; rare flora and fauna; cities that rose from the flames of Nazi barbarism as monuments to post-war Soviet urban planning; stunning museums crammed with rare artefacts; rich culture and tradition; historical sites dating from the Middle Ages to modern times; beautiful churches and the mysteries of Russian Orthodoxy; and most of all, a people whose warmth, honesty and hospitality must be experienced to be believed. Yet whisper all this softly, for we must be careful to guard and not spoil these riches.

HOW TO USE THIS GUIDE

AUTHOR'S FAVOURITES Finding genuinely characterful accommodation or that unmissable off-the-beaten-track café can be difficult, so the author has chosen a few of his favourite places throughout the country to point you in the right direction. These 'author's favourites' are marked with a ✷.

MAPS

Keys and symbols Maps include alphabetical keys covering the locations of those places to stay, eat or drink that are featured in the book. Note that regional maps may not show all hotels and restaurants in the area: other establishments may be located in towns shown on the map.

Grids and grid references Several maps use gridlines to allow easy location of sites. Map grid references are listed in square brackets after the name of the place or sight of interest in the text, with page number followed by grid number, eg: [137 C3].

BELARUSIAN AND RUSSIAN PLACE NAMES Names of major places and sights within this book are followed by their Belarusian and Russian names in Cyrillic. This editorial preference is intended solely as a means of assistance to English-speaking travellers and does not in any way intend to promote a particular cultural preference or political ideal.

TELEPHONE NUMBERS Most telephone numbers in this guide are landlines, but some venues provide only a mobile number. For dialling purposes these begin with 25, 29, 33 or 44 and in each case the relevant two digits are provided in the listing.

SEND US YOUR SNAPS!

We'd love to follow your adventures using our *Belarus* guide – why not send us your photos and stories via Twitter (🐦 *@BradtGuides*) and Instagram (📷 *@bradtguides*) using the hashtag #belarus? Alternatively, you can upload your photos directly to the gallery on the Belarus destination page via our website (w *bradtguides.com/belarus*).

BELARUS ONLINE

For additional online content, articles, photos and more on Belarus, why not visit w bradtguides.com/belarus?

Part One

GENERAL INFORMATION

Location Eastern Europe

Neighbouring countries Borders Russian Federation, Ukraine, Poland, Latvia and Lithuania. The country is completely landlocked.

Size Total state border length 2,969km; area 207,600km^2; maximum width west to east 650km; length 560km north to south

Geography Lowland terrain, with a mean elevation above sea level of only 160m, the highest point being 345m. Natural vegetation over around 70% of area, of which 38% is forest. Also 20,000 rivers and streams and 11,000 lakes, with significant areas of marsh territory.

Climate Moderately continental, with cold winters and warm summers. Average temperature January –6.25°C, July 17.8°C. Annual rainfall 600–700mm.

Status Republic

Population 9,495,800 (density 46/km^2) (October 2017)

Life expectancy Male 66.5 years, female 78 years (2015 World Health Organisation data)

Administrative divisions Six regions (*oblasts*), comprising 118 administrative districts

Capital city Minsk (population 1,974,800) (2017)

Other major cities Brest, Grodno, Vitebsk, Mogilev and Gomel

Economy Limited progression since Soviet times and currently around 80% state controlled

GDP US$47.4 billion in total, US$4,990 per capita (2016 estimates)

People Ethnic Belarusians (83.7%), Russians (8.3%), Poles (3.1%), Ukrainians (1.7%) and the remaining 3.2% comprising Jews, Lithuanians, Tatars, Azerbaijanis, Armenians, Latvians, Koreans, Germans, Georgians, Ossets, Moldavians and travelling people

Languages Belarusian and Russian have equal status as state languages

Religion Russian Orthodox, Roman Catholicism and Judaism

Currency Belarusian rouble (BYN)

Exchange rate £1 = BYN2.65, US$1 = BYN2.00, €1 = BYN2.33 (1 March 2018)

National airline/airport Belavia/Minsk National

International dialling code +375

Time GMT +2

Electrical voltage 220–240 volts

Weights and measures Metric

Flag Two broad horizontal stripes of red and green, red being double the area of green, with traditional patterning of red on a white border down the left-hand side

National anthem *Mbl, Senapycbl* ('We Belarusians')

National flower Flax

National bird/animal White stork/European bison

National sport Ice hockey

Public holidays 1 January (New Year's Day), 7 January (Orthodox Christmas), 8 March (Women's Day), Orthodox Easter, Catholic Easter, Radaunista (Ancestors' Remembrance Day) on the ninth day after Orthodox Easter, 1 May (Labour Day), 9 May (Victory Day, a glorious celebration of the end of the 'Great Patriotic War' as World War II is known here), 3 July (Independence Day), 7 November (October Revolution Day), 25 December (Catholic Christmas)

1

Background Information

GEOGRAPHY

Whether you fly over the country or drive across it, the impression you get is always the same; it's very flat and there are lots of trees. The country has no sea borders and it sits in the heart of the mid-European plain between the Baltic Sea to the north and the Black Sea to the south. It borders Poland to the west, Lithuania to the northwest, Latvia to the north, Russia to the northeast and east and, finally, Ukraine to the south. The capital of the republic is Minsk and the distances to the capitals of its neighbours are as follows:

Capital city	Warsaw	Vilnius	Riga	Moscow	Kiev
Distance (km)	550	185	470	700	580

The country covers a surface area of 207,600km^2. The maximum distance from west to east is 650km and from north to south, 560km. The total length of its borders is 2,969km. Belarus ranks 13th of all European countries (excluding Russia) in area size. In all, it is slightly smaller than the United Kingdom, more than twice the size of Portugal and Hungary and no fewer than five times bigger than The Netherlands and Switzerland. But if you look at the map, you will see that it is dwarfed by its gigantic neighbour Russia to the east, a rich metaphor if ever there was one. The plain upon which Belarus is located extends some way beyond the country's borders and in times of war this has been a distinct disadvantage, rendering it all too easy in geographical terms to invade and subjugate. In times of peace, however, this has meant that transport links, whether by road, river or rail, have been easy to establish and the trade routes that have passed in the direction of the four compass points have at times brought prosperity and multi-culturalism to these lands.

Those hills that exist here are barely hills at all, more rolling countryside; the mean elevation above sea level is only 160m, with the highest point being Mount Dzherzhinskaya in Minsk *oblast* at just 345m, although it is sufficiently elevated for there to be a modest winter sports resort there, including a ski jump. The lowest is the valley of the Nieman River in Grodno *oblast* (district) at just over 80m.

Lakes (11,000 of them) and rivers (totalling 91,000km in length) are the major features, with significant areas of marshland in-between. The area of the Polyesye, the largest of the marsh territories, runs along the southern boundary of the country and is one of the biggest in Europe. In the north is the lakeland area. Five major rivers run through the territory of Belarus: the Nieman, the Dnieper, the Berazhina, the Sozh and the Pripyat, the last of which flows adjacent to the site of the former nuclear complex at Chernobyl in Ukraine, scene of the world's worst commercial nuclear catastrophe in April 1986. Approximately one-fifth of the territory of Belarus, mostly in the southeast, continues to be affected by radioactive fallout.

Over a third of the total landscape (38%) is covered by forest, much of it forming part of the vast primeval wood that once stretched across the whole of central Europe. Not only is it a valuable source of timber, it also performs other ecological functions such as water conservation and soil protection, as well as being home to a rich variety of wildlife and shelter for copious supplies of plants harvested for medicinal and food purposes (particularly mushrooms and berries). Other natural resources include peat fields (much depleted by intensive extraction) and small reserves of oil and natural gas, although production is insignificant. There are also 63 separate sources of mineral water supplying a significant number of sanatoria and spas throughout the country.

CLIMATE

The climate is moderately continental, ranging from unforgiving winters when the mean January temperature is –6.25°C, to warm summers when the mean in July is 17.8°C. The annual level of precipitation is 550–650mm in the low country and 650–750mm at higher elevations. The average vegetation period is 184–208 days. Generally, the climate is favourable for growing cereal crops, vegetables, potatoes and fruit.

NATURAL HISTORY AND CONSERVATION

VEGETATION Natural vegetation covers around 70% of the area of Belarus, 38% of which is forest. Farmland takes up 43.9% of the land mass, which includes arable land extending to 26.8% of the total. The best way to truly understand the extent of the Belarusian forest is to fly over the country, when the clear impression gained is that mile after mile of territory is covered by a green blanket that is only occasionally broken by concentrated areas of farmland connected by ribbon-like roads. True, there are subtle variations: in the north (the area of lakes), water is a contrasting feature, while in the south, the Pripyat River is cloaked in the Polyesye marshland. But still the overriding feature is the tree. In the north, pines and other conifers predominate, yet in the south, the forests are primarily deciduous (most notably oak). Birch knows no geographical boundaries and can be found all over the country. Indeed, in those areas where active forestation has been undertaken, particularly of pine, you will see that every stand of trees is surrounded by a protective ring, square or rectangle of silver birch. This is because birch grows faster and, as it matures, it shelters the more delicate pine from the excesses of the weather, including the sun. Centuries ago, these areas of forestation together formed part of the great European primeval forest, most of which no longer exists, but here, such that remains is preserved as a natural treasure. As well as having significance as a natural timber resource, it also forms an undisturbed habitat for a rich variety of wildlife and, increasingly, it is a resource for leisure and ecological tourism.

NATIONAL PARKS Belarus is particularly proud of its national parks. In 1992 **Byelovezhskaya Puscha National Park** (340km southwest of Minsk) was included in the list of World Heritage Sites by UNESCO and one year later UNESCO granted it the status of Biosphere Reserve. This means that it is one of the sites monitored by ecologists to assess environmental changes taking place around the globe. Then, at the end of 1997, the Council of Europe recognised the park as one of the most conservation-conscious reserves on the continent. The characteristics and profile of the locality were first mentioned in *Chronicles* in AD983, while the first attempts at establishing a formal reserve on this site were made early in the 15th century. The total area exceeds 90,000ha. The largest population of European bison roams free here; once to be found in abundance throughout the forests of Europe, the species is now extremely rare and the very fact of its existence in Belarus is something of a success story for the country's conservation policies. Also to be found in this reserve are red deer, wild boar, roe deer and elk. Natural predators include wolf, fox, lynx, badger, marten and otter. Birdlife is equally diverse and includes the greater spotted eagle and the aquatic warbler. Experts have estimated that around 1,000 of the oaks in the park are between 300 and 700 years old, with some of the ash being 450 years old, certain pines being 220 and a number of junipers as old as 150. There are also white firs, spruce and pine.

Some 150km north of Minsk, **Narach National Park** boasts one of the largest (shoreline 41km) and deepest (maximum 30m) lakes in the country, bearing the same name. The country's renowned Blue Lakes are also situated here. The largest concentration of ecological resorts and recreation complexes in the whole country is situated within the wider Narach area, including a total of 18 sanatoria and recuperation centres. There are also several natural springs and the area is famed for its mineral waters. The park itself was only established in 1999. It covers 94,000ha, 37,900 of which are forest, including the country's largest concentration of pine. Its 42 lakes have a total area of 18,300ha. This is a beautiful and romantic area, steeped in mystery and legend. The lakes are said to have been created out of a tragic loss when Nara, the daughter of a forester, saw the death of her sweetheart in a magic mirror, which she then dropped in terror, the shards scattering all around. These fragments became the lakes that can be seen today. And Nara? She was turned into a white gull, and can still be seen wheeling and turning across the water, calling for her lost love …

Created in 1995 and covering an area of around 70,0000ha, **Braslav Lakes National Park** lies close to the Latvian border in the north, 249km from Minsk, where large numbers of lakes are surrounded by picturesque hilly landscapes. Brooks, rivers and channels (most of them navigable) form a water-bound labyrinth throughout which the visitor can cast off the trappings of modern life and meander undisturbed. Signs of life from ancient times, such as burial mounds, places of worship and evidence of settlements complement the natural wonders of the area. The lakes themselves extend over an area of 183km², the deepest of them, South Volos, extending to 40.4m. Lake Strusto is particularly beautiful: at the centre is the Isle of Chaichyn, which has its own small inner lake. The water ecosystems here are particularly interesting and 20 of the 800 species of plant are on the endangered list (and consequently subject to special protection measures). Of 28 species of fish, eel are the most common and are extensively farmed. Badger, lynx, brown bear, squirrel, elk, wild boar and roe deer all live in the park.

In Vitebsk region in the northeast of the country (120km from Minsk and southeast of Braslav Lakes), the 80,000ha **Berezinsky Biosphere Reserve** was created in 1925 to preserve the natural primeval landscape as well as game and other wild animals, such as the river beaver. Today, many animals and birds that are extremely rare or even extinct elsewhere live here, including the brown bear. Part of UNESCO's Biosphere Reserves World Network, much of this reserve is covered by forest, most of it pine and spruce, the remainder being largely marshland interspersed with wooded islands. The main river that flows through the reserve (for 110km) is the Berazhina.

Along the south of the country is a wide lowland area consisting of hollows, plains, forests and marshes pierced by many rivers and creeks flowing to the Pripyat River, a tributary of the Dnieper, which itself flows into the Black Sea. In the Gomel region lying between the Pripyat, Stivha and Ubort rivers is the significant marsh wetland known as the **Polyesye**, home to around 265 species of bird including heron, the rare black stork (and the more common white), grey crane, eagle owl, serpent eagle and marsh owl. Both white and black storks can be seen nesting extensively in and around villages. The first sighting of one of these birds on the wing is a memorable experience. Within the Polyesye is the 82,529ha **Pripyatsky National Park** (established in 1996), its territory extending for 64km east to west. Of particular interest here are the areas around the banks of the river. In places the spring melt causes it to rise up to 2m each year and the floodplains have their own unique vegetation, with oak and ash further from the river being replaced by black alder and willow adjacent to it. Some 826 species of plant are to be found here, including an astonishing 200 different mosses.

ECOLOGY Overall, ecological tourism is a significant growth sector of the economy, although establishing a viable infrastructure remains a work in progress if it is to be commercially competitive. As mentioned several times in a number of contexts throughout this book, the people of the country have an extremely close relationship and affinity with the land and the seasons. This theme dominates life in the rural areas and it only serves to highlight the tragedy of the Chernobyl catastrophe in 1986 and its significantly adverse consequences, which will endure for generations to come.

It would be impossible to make even a cursory and passing reference to ecological matters in Belarus without discussing Chernobyl (page 15). The shattered wreck of the stricken reactor (now entombed in its new casing) stands just 15km by road across the border in Ukraine. Prevailing weather conditions immediately after the explosion blew the deadly radioactive cloud over mainland Europe in a predominantly northwesterly direction. The region of Gomel in Belarus was directly in its path. Contamination was spread on an irregular basis as dictated by the weather. For example, there remain particularly radioactive hotspots today where rain fell at the time. Indeed, stories persist to this day that the authorities deliberately and actively dropped chemicals into cloud formations to make it rain (a process known as 'seeding') in an attempt to control the location of deposited radiation away from the largest centres of population, although this has been neither proved nor acknowledged. I know of a number of people in and around the area of Gomel oblast who to this day remember standing outside in something they describe as 'odd rain'. Whatever may or may not have happened, it is generally acknowledged that Belarus received about 60% of the fallout sustained by the Soviet Union.

Anyone interested in travelling to Belarus will be concerned to know just how safe it is in terms of radiation exposure. In the past, reliable information has not been easy to find, but it is now widely accepted as scientific fact that the risk of prejudice to health is minimal. It is even possible today to join a tour to Pripyat (in Ukraine) that takes participants around areas of the nuclear plant, though the time spent there, not surprisingly, is limited. In 2006, an Australian film crew went inside the reactor buildings to film, although for a few minutes only and even then wearing fully protective clothing. As the years have passed, more and more filming has been done in and around the plant, particularly by ecologists monitoring the impact of the disaster on the natural environment. The popularity of Chernobyl-themed tours is growing, and adventurous readers so inclined might care to browse w chernobylwel.com for an idea of what is possible.

In Belarus it is still forbidden to visit any of the hotspot areas either without permission from the authorities or unaccompanied by 'officials'. That said, the number of locations officially treated as hotspot areas is shrinking, though even now whole villages remain abandoned to the elements. They all have their own cemeteries, but only once a year, on Ancestors' Remembrance Day (the ninth day after Orthodox Easter), are the bereaved permitted to return to tend the graves of their loved ones. With the passage of time, however, the extent to which the regulation of activity within these areas remains strictly monitored is becoming open to question and today former residents, particularly the elderly, are drifting back to their old homes to live.

The perceived wisdom is that the radiation exposure experienced from a day in Pripyat is actually less than that experienced on an 8-hour plane journey. It has also been said that if you stay there for seven consecutive days, your body will absorb no more radiation than it would if you were exposed to a single medical X-ray procedure at home. Given that current radiation levels diminish incrementally as the distance from the plant increases, the danger for the short-term visitor to Belarus is negligible. Nevertheless, be cautious: do not enter forbidden areas, avoid drinking tap water and, in areas of known contamination, eat natural produce only where you can be certain of its provenance.

HISTORY

No student of modern-day Belarus can hope to gain an insight into the mystery and enigma that characterise the national psyche without first engaging in at least a rudimentary study of all that has gone before. But there is very little to be found specifically about the country in Western books, although there is much to read on the subject of Holy Mother Russia and the former Soviet Union, both of which subsumed it at various times as an integral element of their empires.

There is one theme in particular that spans the centuries: that of suffering and privation. Whether subjugated to the yoke of Lithuanian, Pole, Tsar, Frenchman, Bolshevik, Communist, Nazi, Communist again or latterly oligarch, heroism and tragedy can be found on most of the pages of the country's history, as drama and melodrama unfold in the never-ending struggle to resist pain, anguish, grief and suffering. For generation after generation, there seems to have been no sanctuary from constant oppression, with the identity of the oppressor being largely irrelevant. Further, the media of oppression are many and varied: fear, dogma, hunger, poverty, lack of education, geography, climate and, in recent times, nuclear disaster. Each succeeding generation has developed defences to resist every challenge that comes along, such that the people of today are characterised not only by an impressively stoical resilience, but also by an attitude to life that suggests more than a trace of fatalism. Reference to generalisations is always a crude and unsophisticated methodology to employ when drawing conclusions, of course, but this may go some way to explaining why there seems to be little appetite for effecting real change in any aspect of life within Belarus, whether individually or collectively. In short, history has left its mark through the long centuries of privation.

A new resource on Belarusian history has recently been published online at w map.letapis.by, where key events in timeline form are laid over a map of the country in an extremely accessible and informative way. An hour's research here makes for an exceptional introduction to the significant events that have shaped today's Belarus.

ANCIENT TIMES Indications are that early civilisations began to populate the territory that is now Belarus from the middle Palaeolithic period, or 100,000–40,000

1

years BC, while available evidence suggests that the first significant settlements emerged 24,000–27,000 years ago.

EARLY CIVILISATIONS The area was settled by the Dryhavichy, Krivichi and Radzimichy peoples between the 7th and 9th centuries AD, when the first Slavic alliances were formed. This was followed by the first state formations in the principalities of Polotsk, Turov and Smolensk. The town of Polotsk itself, founded by the Krivichi at the confluence of the Polota and Western Dvina rivers, is known to have existed since AD862 and is still regarded as the first capital of the lands now recognised as Belarus. It is also still regarded as the spiritual cradle of the country. Its first chronicled prince was Rogvolod, who ruled in the late 10th century. In the 11th the principality reached the zenith of its power and influence under Prince Vyseslav Bryachislavich, who is believed to have ruled for an incredible 72 years from 1029 to 1101. He was known as 'the magician' not only for his remarkable talents as military leader and statesman, but also because he was believed to be a literal shape-shifter, endowed with magical powers. At that time, the extent of Polotskian influence stretched from the Baltic Sea in the west and north to Smolensk in the east. This geographical location held the key to the non-aligned lands between the opulent extravagance of the Byzantine Empire in the east and the warlike Norse tribes of Scandinavia (known to the Slavic peoples as Varangians), and allowed Polotsk to gain many benefits from trade with Byzantium, the Baltic countries and Scandinavia. At the same time Byzantine Christianity began to spread across these territories, doubtless as a result of trade links, so stimulating the development of culture through the arts and literature, along with the emergence of stone-based architecture.

A golden age of creativity had begun. The Turovsky Gospels were written in the 11th century and then, between 1050 and 1070, the first major architectural structure, the imposing Cathedral of St Sophia, was built in Polotsk. It quickly became the very manifestation of the state's might and significance, for at times foreign ambassadors were officially received here, both war and peace were declared here and it was also treated as the place of safekeeping for the public purse and sacred relics. Sister (later St) Ephrosinia, the heavenly 'mediatress' of Belya Rus whose selfless labour has long since passed into legend, was born at the beginning of the 12th century, around the time when master craftsmen were known to be working at the cathedral, such as the architect Johannes and the jeweller Lazar Bogsha. In 1161, Bogsha created the 'Cross for the Enlightener St Ephrosinia of Polotsk', a unique masterpiece of eastern Slavonic applied art. And among many contemporary Christian preachers and writers of note, Kirill Turovsky was particularly well known.

THE GRAND DUCHY OF LITHUANIA The 13th century marked a key phase in the history of modern Belarus. In its first half, the foundations of the Belarusian language began to form. This coincided with the establishment of the Grand Duchy of Lithuania, which brought together a number of Belarusian lands and principalities, primarily to meet the threat of invasion from crusading Teutonic knights to the west, Turks from the south and the Golden Horde of Mongol Tartars from the east. Many famous victories were won. The core lands of the duchy at this time were the territories around Kernave, Trakai and Samogitia, together with the city of Vilnius.

The coronation of the ruler Mindaug took place in 1253 and at the same time Novogorodok (now known as Novogrudok) became the capital of the Lithuanian duchy. In 1323, this status was transferred to Wilno (now Vilnius). Under the rule of Vitautis, the duchy reached the peak of its power and influence, expanding its frontiers and gaining international prestige. On 2 February 1386, Grand Duke Jogaila was crowned King of Poland and a personal union under one single monarch was established. Then, at the famous Battle of Grunwald in 1410, the joint forces of Poland and Lithuania inflicted a crushing defeat on the Teutonic Order, an event of critical importance to the consolidation of the new state, whose power now extended all the way from the Baltic Sea in the north to the Black Sea in the south. The next significant stage of the state's development was the formation (by formal union) in 1569 of the Polish-Lithuanian Commonwealth and consequent creation of a new federative state known as Rzeczpospolita. It was ruled by the Grand Duke and Rada Polish landowners jointly, with the state being divided into provinces and administrative districts known as *povets*. The representative body of the feudal lords of the Polish gentry was known as the *sejm*, with its deputies being elected at the regional councils of the povet, although simultaneously the former Lithuanian grand duchy maintained its own government, financial system, army and emblem.

The competing struggle for influence in the eastern Baltic region had instigated the Livonian Wars in 1558 against the state of Muscovy. This war lasted until 1583. The formal settlement of the 1569 union eventually enabled the new state to win the Livonian Wars, thereby returning areas of land that had been lost and, most importantly, consolidating and securing power and influence in the eastern Baltic.

From the early 16th century, massive agrarian reform (*volochnaya pomera*) had been taking place against a background of almost constant warfare, culminating in the embodiment of the concept of serfdom in a 1588 statute, one of three during

BELARUSIAN TERRITORIES (16TH CENTURY)

KEY
Border of modern Belarus
Border of Reczpospolita

9

the century that codified the fundamental elements of the grand duchy's status, the other two having been passed in 1529 and 1566. At the same time, those towns that had assumed self-government under Magdeburg Law since the end of the 14th century were now developing at an intense rate, with the establishment of urban crafts and consequent guild protection. This was an exciting time for those engaged in commercial interests.

THE CHURCH During the 16th century, the lands that now form Belarus saw the establishment of Lutheranism, Calvinism and other Protestant doctrines under the influence of the Reformation. This was a period of considerable religious tolerance and stability, but by the end of the century the Counter-Reformation had begun. Orthodoxy and Catholicism reached a compromise that resulted in the Brest Church Union of 1596, under which the Orthodox Church of the Grand Duchy of Lithuania recognised the supremacy of Rome, while maintaining its own rites, doctrines and customs. Not surprisingly there was reluctance on the part of Orthodox believers to accept religious subjugation under the Union and this, along with inevitable economic pressures on the peasantry and the urban lower classes, resulted in considerable internal strife and opposition to feudalism.

THE RISE AND INFLUENCE OF RUSSIA Neighbouring Russia gleefully seized the opportunity to capitalise on these domestic difficulties within the state of Rzeczpospolita and launched a new war on its territory, which endured from 1654 to 1667. A large portion of modern-day Belarus was occupied and severe economic and demographic crises ensued. The population was reduced by half, whole towns fell into decay and there were many adverse consequences for all levels of society, but most notably the gentry and urban dwellers.

From 1700 to 1721, these lands formed the battleground in the North War waged by the Swedes on Russia and Rzeczpospolita. This war brought about decades of economic ruin, which only began to be overcome by the middle of the century with the revival of commerce and business in the form of a rudimentary market economy. Of more serious consequence even than warfare was the protracted political crisis that was wrought by consequent anarchy in the country and the growing power and influence of neighbouring nation states. The last single King of Poland and Grand Duke of Lithuania, Stanislas Augustus Poniatowski (1764–95), tried in vain to consolidate central power, but he was confronted by an active opposition that sought aid and support from abroad. The situation was ripe for exploitation, and the neighbouring states of Russia, Prussia and Austria capitalised on these circumstances by taking advantage of the inequality of Orthodox and Protestant believers in relation to Catholics within Rzeczpospolita. All of this led to the first division of the country in 1772, following which the land that is now eastern Belarus was annexed and incorporated into the Russian Empire. A second division was effected in 1793, as a result of which central Belarus was also annexed. There was a limited degree of patriotic resistance, culminating in the uprising led by Tadeusz Kościuszko, but in 1795 the third and final division of the country took place, with Russia subsuming the western lands of Belarus. Rzeczpospolita was never to exist again as a sovereign state and the administrative divisions, taxes and duties of the Russian Empire were finally imposed across all of its lands.

There followed a long period of Russian domination. During the Napoleonic invasion of Russia in 1812 the territory was the major theatre of war, resulting in huge losses and a significant diminution in the population. After the war, in the vacuum created by social and administrative disintegration, democratic ideas began to flourish, leading to the development of the first national liberation movement. As a consequence there was an uprising in 1830–31 to re-establish the state of Rzeczpospolita and restore the national boundaries that existed in 1772, the date of its first division. Inevitably, the uprising was suppressed, but the position of the gentry and of Catholicism had been weakened. Roman Catholic churches and monasteries were closed while the lands, estates and possessions of the rebels were confiscated by the state. Other contextual events included the closure of the University of Vilno and the annulment of the statute of 1588, which had codified the autonomous Grand Duchy of Lithuania's governance arrangements. To all intents and purposes, the lands of modern Belarus now existed only as the northwestern region of the Russian Empire.

In the 19th century, broader issues within the empire began to take effect and, as the tsars sought to cling on to power and perpetuate the subjugation of the people (in the face of increasing challenges through assertion of democracy and enfranchisement), Russian influences from the establishment grew incrementally stronger. By way of example, the compromise reached under the Brest Church Union of 1596 was reversed and the Uniate Church ceased to exist, allowing traditional Russian Orthodoxy to once more reign supreme. And while the peasants tended the fields, the landed gentry, the privileged classes and the re-established Church saw to it that any attempts to assert a specific identity for the Belarusian people were systematically suppressed, often with brutality. One of the many ways in which this suppression manifested itself was the proscription of the use of the Belarusian language in written form. Despite (and probably because of) this official denial of an independent Belarusian identity, nationalist ideas continued to flourish underground. The promotion of Belarusian literature, art, folklore and language began to take hold in the minds and consciousness of the people, notwithstanding the perpetuation of the prejudice and lack of opportunity suffered by native Belarusians in terms of access to significant administrative and governance positions of influence within the Russian Empire, as had earlier been the case for centuries across ceaseless periods of Lithuanian and Polish dominance.

Hand in hand with cultural development came increasing economic well-being, most notably in respect of the industrialisation of the country's richest natural resource (timber), although progress was only gradual and there remained painfully little change in the high rate of rural deprivation, which for the most part was worse than anywhere else in the empire. The majority of the population by far was still to be found on the land, maintained in a position of unrepresented subservience through poverty, ignorance, effective disenfranchisement and the power of privilege. Then, in 1861, peasant reform abolished serfdom. The first underground newspaper, *Peasant's Truth*, was established between 1862 and 1863, then later that year and into 1864 the national liberation movement in the empire rose up against tsarism in the lands that are now Poland, Lithuania and Belarus, although brutal suppression once more ensued and a codified legal regime was enforced that was to endure into the 20th century.

In the 1880s, however, the revolutionary organisation Gomon was established by Belarusian students who had trained at the higher-education establishments of St Petersburg. This name became synonymous with the ideals and rights of an emerging Belarusian nation, while a fledgling national identity was again assumed through the media of language, culture and literature. An upsurge in democratic and national liberation ideas and thinking was now creating real conditions for the establishment of Belarusian statehood. This century also saw an important demographic development that was to have very significant and tragic consequences for future generations and society in general. Belarusian lands were included in the Pale of Settlement, the territorial area into which Jews from all over the empire were forced to relocate their homes and communities, such that by the time of the German invasion in 1941, the population of some of the towns that fell under Nazi oppression and tyranny were up to 70% Jewish.

THE 20TH CENTURY The first national political party (the Belarusian socialist Gromada Party) was created in 1903, with the objectives of overthrowing autocracy and bringing about a Russian federation of democratic republics. Each of these republics was to be a separate nation with statehood, cultural and national autonomy and the inalienable right to independent self-determination. After the

BELARUS AND THE OTHER SSRs (1926)

LATVIA

POLAND

RUSSIAN SSR

Polotsk

Vitebsk

MINSK

Mogilev

BELARUS SSR

Babrusk

Gomel

POLAND

Mozyr

UKRAINIAN SSR

N

Bradt

abolition of serfdom in the wider Russian Empire in 1861, there had been slow but effective reform of the means of land allocation, but this did not prevent the mass displacement of the peasant classes from the lands of modern-day Belarus to Siberia. This was the fate of approximately 335,000 people between 1907 and 1914, while many more from the privileged classes dispersed further afield into western Europe and beyond to America.

As had been the case on countless occasions in the past, Belarusian territory was again a battleground when hostilities broke out in 1914, with bloody and brutal clashes between opposing armies of the German and Russian empires. After Russia's entry into the war, martial law was declared in Belarus. As with other conflicts across the centuries, there was widespread destruction and mass occupation, this time by troops under the German flag. Then, in November 1917, the armed uprising in Petrograd (formerly St Petersburg) and the homecoming to Russian territories of the Bolshevik leader Vladimir Ilyich Ulyanov (the revolutionary Lenin) hastened the end of tsarism in the empire. Political activity in Belarus intensified and the first independent Belarusian democratic republic was established on 25 March 1918, despite the continuing German occupation. The influence of the Bolshevik Revolution was acquiring significant momentum and the German occupation came to an end, but the declaration of the new republic's status could not prevent the proclamation of Soviet power in Minsk. As a result, the Belarusian Soviet Socialist Republic (BSSR) came into existence in Smolensk on 1 January 1919.

The Russians subsequently occupied much of Lithuania and as a result in February 1919 the new state became the Lithuanian-Belarusian Soviet Socialist Republic, the capital of which was Vilnius. War between Poland and the emerging Soviet Union ensued, during which the territory of much of the nascent country was under Polish occupation (including Minsk). Then, on 31 July 1920, the BSSR was proclaimed for a second time after the expulsion of Polish troops. Unfortunately for the new state, however, the 1921 Treaty of Riga resulted in the annexation by Poland of the western territories and the flickering flame of the emerging Belarusian identity was extinguished. Elsewhere, the rump of the BSSR, under Bolshevik control, continued to exist in the form of six administrative districts of the province of Minsk, with a total population of 1.5 million people. It joined the Union of Soviet Socialist Republics (USSR) on 30 December 1922 and its territories were expanded first in 1924, then again in 1926, when 17 western districts of the Russian SSR were added, the people of which were predominantly Belarusian. These districts remain part of modern-day Belarus.

In the years that followed (leading up to the outbreak of war once more in Europe in 1939), Soviet social policy made a dramatic volte-face. In a very short space of time, the USSR emerged as a massive world power, bringing together diverse cultures, races and former nation states across an enormous geographical area (and several time zones). At first the promotion and celebration of ethnicity and diversity of culture was actively encouraged throughout the Union, as if to show the world that 'the Revolution' truly was an international movement that could transcend barriers of class, language and background. The Party also saw this as the best form of protection against so-called pernicious Western influences. Against that background, traditionalism and the concept of a specific identity were allowed to flourish in the Belarusian SSR. Things proved to be very different in the 1930s. The Georgian Iosif Dzhugashvili (Stalin) had incrementally (and by design) inherited stewardship of the Revolution from Lenin as the 1920s drew to a close, and a dark period in the history of these lands ensued as the fear of internal opposition and the paranoia of the Soviet leader took hold. Millions were incarcerated, tortured and murdered across the USSR in Stalin's infamous purges. This was a time of neighbour informing on neighbour, the dreaded knock on the door in the middle of the night, false confessions obtained under torture and staged show trials in the full glare of publicity. As many times before in history, Belarusian nationalists were cruelly suppressed. The features and horrors of this dark period of world history are widely documented elsewhere, but the terrible contradiction of the huge advances proclaimed by the Soviet Union at the time in terms of astonishing economic growth against a background of mass murder and social re-engineering on a scale previously unimagined in the modern world is a grim one indeed. The new dawn of hope for Belarusian culture that had been so joyously celebrated in the 1920s proved to have been a very false one as the 1930s drew to a close.

Following the notorious and shameful 1939 pact of mutual non-aggression, German and Soviet tanks rolled simultaneously across Poland from the west and the east respectively. The state boundary that had existed immediately prior to the 1921 Treaty of Riga was quickly restored as the western territories and their communities were forcibly snatched back from Polish control and sovereignty. When the Nazis dissolved the pact in spectacular fashion by invading the Soviet Union in 1941 under Operation Barbarossa, which was designed to deliver Hitler's avowed intention to wipe the USSR from the face of the earth, the Soviet Union responded by entering the global fray. The 'Great Patriotic War' (World War II), as it is known in this part of the world, had begun. As the most westerly of the SSRs, Belarus was quickly overrun by the Nazis, in just two months. The occupation that followed was cruel and brutal. It was resisted by a mass movement of guerrilla and partisan activity throughout the republic, involving many thousands of active volunteers backed by many thousands more in reserve. The occupying forces were actively and ruthlessly opposed, but in turn this led to yet more atrocities on the part of the invaders. Almost 25% of the population were brutally murdered in hundreds of punitive operations that brought about the deaths of men, women and children through the systematic burning and destruction of thousands of villages and hamlets under the pretext of fighting guerrillas. Today, this tragic loss of life and brutal destruction of whole communities is commemorated at the memorial complex of Khatyn in Minsk province, the site of one such village burnt with its residents, a haunting and deeply moving memorial that is described on page 186.

In July 1944, amid scenes of unparalleled patriotic fervour and wild abandon, Marshal Zhukov's Red Army completed the liberation of the country following a major offensive. The cost was enormous, both economically and in terms of loss of life. The capital, Minsk, had been almost completely destroyed and today very few pre-war buildings are still standing. And of the two million Belarusian people who lost their lives in the war, many died in the concentration camps of the Third Reich across occupied Europe. In addition, almost 380,000 had been removed to Germany for the purpose of enforced labour. Incredibly, it was not until 1971 that the country's population again reached its pre-war level, although the Jewish community had been all but wiped out. Today, however, there are real signs at last that Jewish life in Belarus is returning, as actively growing communities begin to establish their identity once more. Anyone interested in learning about these communities and the history of Judaism in the country can access more information in the United Kingdom from British sustainable development charity The Together Plan or in Belarus from local NGO, Dialog (page 38).

In August 1945, under the Soviet-Polish Treaty, 17 districts of Byelostock and three of Brest (but not the city itself) were formally transferred to Poland, although the majority of western Belarus was retained by the Soviet Union. Also in 1945, the Belarusian SSR was one of the 51 signatories to the founding of the United Nations (UN). It says much about the national psyche that within the republic itself, as with others in the USSR, this act was regarded as an acknowledgement on the part of the international community of the contribution made by the USSR to the crushing defeat of Hitler's Nazi Germany. It is difficult to argue with this standpoint. Between 1941 and 1945, conservative estimates place the war dead of the USSR at an incredible 24 million people, although some place the actual figure at 30 million. This astonishing statistic is topped only by the fact that even the lower of these two figures exceeds the *total* of war dead of every other country in the world, on both sides of the conflict.

The damage and destruction of the war years was reversed in spectacular fashion and at an incredible pace by means of a rigidly enforced series of plans of regeneration through industrialisation and collective farming, all on a massive scale. A new Minsk, rising from the ashes of the old, was at the very heart of this process of rebirth and renewal. The BSSR established itself as a major centre of manufacturing within the USSR and the consequent creation of jobs brought in a huge immigrant population from the Russian Federation SSR, including into positions of influence within the government of the republic. As in earlier times, this process of mass immigration was said to be a form of 'protection'; as the most westerly of the Soviet republics, the BSSR was Stalin's first line of defence (militarily, culturally and ideologically) against the perceived moral bankruptcy of the West. But as had been the case in the 1930s, one consequence of this process of social engineering was that traditional Belarusian culture came under threat once more.

THE CHERNOBYL DISASTER The consequences of the accident that occurred in the early hours of 26 April 1986 at the Chernobyl nuclear power plant, then in the Soviet Union and now within the territory of Ukraine, have proved to be nothing short of a catastrophe for Belarus. In terms of the economic, ecological and social impacts, it is universally regarded as the worst incident in the history of commercial nuclear power, although the full impact of the disaster at Fukushima in Japan in 2011 will only emerge with the passage of time. Certainly, there is much for the Japanese authorities to learn from the Chernobyl experience.

During the course of tests to determine the ability of the fourth reactor to power safety systems if the external electricity supply was lost, a steam explosion occurred, triggering a fire, a further series of explosions and then a nuclear meltdown, in which the core of the reactor was destroyed. As the roof of the reactor was blown into the sky, the consequent inrush of oxygen reacted with the extremely high temperature of the reactor fuel to produce a graphite fire, which then hastened the spread of radioactive material. The fallout exceeded that generated by the explosion over Hiroshima in 1945 and was 16 million times greater than the release in the accident at Three Mile Island in Pennsylvania in 1978. As local people watched from the balconies of their flats in the nearby city of Pripyat, just 2km away, the explosion and the deadly cloud that billowed out in its wake (which is said to have been actively glowing) hurled nuclear fuel, intensely radioactive (but short-lived) isotopes, primarily iodine-131, and other long-lived isotopes such as caesium-137, strontium-90, americium-241 and plutonium-238, 239, 240 and 241, high into the sky and the atmosphere. It must have been quite a sight. And how chilling it is to reflect now that the onlookers can have had no understanding at all of the mortal danger in which the fates had placed them.

In 1986, Pripyat, Chernobyl and Belarus were all part of the USSR. Pripyat was once home to over 50,000 people, but today it is a ghost town, a snapshot in time, left exactly as it was when residents were evacuated later that day, with the remains of everyday life still to be seen all around.

Emergency measures that were immediately put into place succeeded in extinguishing the fires on the roof of the reactor, but the fire crews who rushed to the scene were not told of the extreme radioactivity of the smoke and debris. All of the firefighters received fatal doses and died gruesome deaths, while the fire inside the reactor was not finally extinguished until helicopter crews had dropped large amounts of sand, lead, clay and boron on to it. By the end of the year, a concrete sarcophagus had been erected over the reactor, but it was always intended to be an interim measure only. Since that time, decades of discussion and the commissioning of studies on the part of the international community, with the aim of designing a much more sophisticated tomb to effectively encase the plant, eventually came to a conclusion in 2007 with the award of a contract to build a new shelter. Thereafter (and at a cost in excess of US$1.5 billion), a giant steel arch was constructed just a few hundred metres from the reactor, before being rolled into place metre by metre over the top of the sarcophagus at the end of 2016. The sheer scale of the project is truly impressive; no engineering process of this magnitude has ever been undertaken on land. The arch is over 160m long and more than 100m tall, and the act of painstakingly wheeling it into place over the remains of the reactor and its sarcophagus took in excess of two weeks to complete. During the course of 2017 the ends of the arch were in the process of being sealed to ensure that there is no risk of any lingering radioactive material escaping into the atmosphere. This does leave outstanding, however, the question of whether or not any risk will remain of material leaching underground into the water supply. Meanwhile, the new structure is planned to endure for at least a hundred years, and probably more. Time will doubtless tell.

In the immediate aftermath of the disaster, the first response of the Soviet authorities was to say and do nothing, either by way of the release of information locally and internationally, or in terms of aid for people in the immediate area (other than enforced evacuation). This proved to be a catastrophic abnegation of social responsibility. For example, informed opinion suggests that had the authorities made supplies of non-radioactive iodine quickly available to the population, the absorption of radioactive iodine into the thyroid gland of many, with its consequent long-term deleterious health effects, would have been prevented.

In the days that followed, the evacuation of residents in the locality of the plant was stepped up, but people were not told why they were being moved. The international community began to hear rumours of a nuclear disaster, but every story was categorically denied by the authorities. Meanwhile, soldiers and workers known as 'liquidators' were sent in to mount a huge clean-up campaign. This began with the removal of debris in the vicinity of the plant, then spread to the large-scale sluicing down of buildings in an ever-increasing radius. All that this achieved, of course, was to ensure the spread of radioactive material into the ground.

Initially, several hundred people (mostly workers and liquidators) were hospitalised, of whom 31 died (28 from acute radiation exposure). Around 135,000 people were evacuated from the area and between 300,000 and 600,000 liquidators were involved in the decontamination of the 30km evacuation zone around the plant. Subsequently, hundreds of thousands more people were evacuated as the authorities began to comprehend the scale of the disaster and the area of land that had been affected.

The initial risk to health came from the concentration of radioactive iodine, which has a half-life of eight days and is readily absorbed into the thyroid gland. This happened both directly and also longer term as, for example, children drank supplies of contaminated milk. As a result, the incidence of thyroid cancer (and lesser conditions) has risen sharply over the years. Over 500,000 people in Belarus

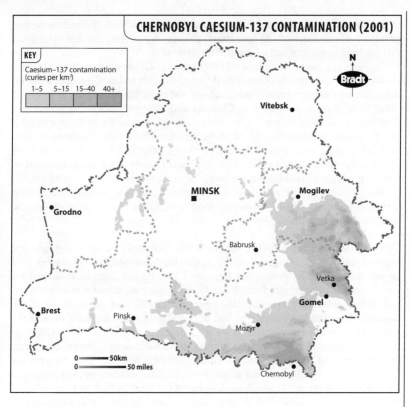

CHERNOBYL CAESIUM-137 CONTAMINATION (2001)

KEY

Caesium–137 contamination
(curies per km²)

1–5 5–15 15–40 40+

N

Vitebsk

MINSK

Grodno

Mogilev

Babrusk

Vetka

Gomel

Brest

Pinsk

Mozyr

0   50km
0   50 miles

Chernobyl

alone are thought to have thyroid pathology. Of greater impact on the infrastructure of society was the effect of contamination of the soil with caesium-137 (half-life 30 years) and strontium-90 (half-life 28 years). Indeed, 21% of the total area of Belarus is thought to have been contaminated with caesium-137. Where it is present in the soil it is absorbed by plants, insects, grazing animals and crops, and by these means enters the local food supply.

THE CHERNOBYL LEGACY The long-term effects of the catastrophe have been subject to much speculation and conflicting hypotheses. It is true that relatively few people died directly as a result of the explosion itself. It is also true that the number of cancers and birth defects directly attributable to radiation has been very difficult to measure. A report of the Chernobyl Forum (comprising a number of UN organisations, the World Health Organisation, the International Atomic Energy Agency, the Belarusian government and others) sought to minimise the consequences of the accident. This report met with heavy criticism, particularly from those organisations working directly with communities in the affected areas. A subsequent report (TORCH), commissioned by a German MEP, predicted far greater consequences. Then, in 2006, Greenpeace issued its own report to coincide with the 20th anniversary of the disaster, predicting yet more significant consequences not simply from increased rates of cancer, but also from intestinal, heart, circulatory and respiratory problems, as well as damage to the immune system.

It is also widely accepted that in addition to specific health problems of this nature, those exposed to the radiation (and indeed, some who were not) continue to exhibit many of the symptoms that commonly manifest themselves in the aftermath of trauma, such as fear, stress, anxiety, depression, physical symptoms that are hard to explain and a feeling of hopelessness.

The state has sought to address all of these issues (at very significant cost to the economy) and is particularly concerned with the health and well-being of children living in contaminated areas. Many sanatoria and rehabilitation centres in so-called 'clean' areas exist to facilitate this. Charities and non-governmental organisations have been established in many countries in western and northern Europe to offer recuperation holidays to children. Working in partnership with local administrations in Belarus, these organisations have been able to offer hundreds of thousands of children the opportunity to leave their irradiated homeland for varying lengths of time. It is widely accepted that these breaks have a very positive effect on health.

Today, however, the reality of life in Belarus is that almost two million people continue to inhabit areas that were (and still are) subject to radioactive contamination to some degree.

THE CULTURAL CHERNOBYL Later in 1986, the policies of sweeping and institutional reform instigated by the Soviet President Mikhail Gorbachev (the conventional English spelling has been used throughout this guide, although a more accurate phonetic translation would be Gorbachov) afforded the Belarusian people an opportunity to reassert their national identity and rail back against the so-called Russification policy that had been followed since the early days of the Cold War. Formal representations were made, including by way of petition, to expose and highlight the long-term suppression of Belarusian culture and heritage. In the climate of the times, social commentators dubbed this turn of events the 'cultural Chernobyl'. By now, the seeds of unrest and revolution were beginning to be dispersed on the winds all across the lands of the Warsaw Pact. In June 1988, the remains of as many as 200,000 of Stalin's victims (perhaps more) were discovered in mass graves in Kurapaty Forest on the northeastern edge of the Minsk conurbation (just beyond the ring road), although claims as to numbers, responsibility and even whether or not these murders ever occurred at all have been the subject of denial and counter-denial ever since the discovery of the site. Whatever the truth of the situation, the proponents of Belarusian nationalism used it as proof that the Soviet state did indeed engage in a deliberate policy of cultural and ethnic suppression. The socio-economic consequences of these events were such that political opposition began to achieve momentum that was ultimately irresistible during the last years and the eventual breakup of the USSR, even though Belarus was (and still is) considered to be one of the most traditionalist of the Union's republics. As the USSR lurched towards disintegration and nationalist voices began to be heard once more, the BSSR steadily began to assert its sovereignty.

The last throw of the dice for the ailing USSR was the bungled coup to remove Gorbachev (Yeltsin's finest hour!) in 1991. It failed within days and soon after, on 25 August, Belarus declared full independence. On 19 September the BSSR was officially renamed the Republic of Belarus, when the heads of the governments of the Russian, Ukrainian and Belarusian SSRs signed the Act on Denunciation of the Union Treaty of 1922. From that day, the USSR ceased to exist and a newly independent sovereign state of Belarusian peoples was born within the nascent Commonwealth of Independent States, in which it was joined by the Russian Federation and Ukraine.

On 15 March 1994 the Supreme Council of the Republic of Belarus adopted a new constitution, under which the country was proclaimed a unitary democratic legal state. On 10 July that year, Alexander Grigoryevich Lukashenko was elected the first president of the new republic. A firm opponent of the Gorbachev reforms, specialising in state farm administration, he was swept to power on a ticket to restore stability. Against a background of not inconsiderable fear for the future in rapidly developing uncertainty throughout eastern Europe in the aftermath of the fall of the Berlin Wall and the disintegration of the Soviet Union, he promised a return to the safety of a regime whose loss was already being mourned. He captured the mood of the times perfectly. He holds the position of president to this day, following sweeping victories with very large majorities in the presidential elections of 2001, 2006, 2010 and 2015, the last with 83.5% of the vote. The next election is due towards the end of 2020. Between now and then, observers within and outside the country will be interested to follow events in Belarus as European and global politics chart unknown courses in directions that are difficult to predict (page 22).

GOVERNMENT, POLITICS AND ADMINISTRATION

THE STRUCTURE OF THE ORGANS OF STATE First, the facts according to the official website of the Republic of Belarus (w *belarus.by*): the head of state is the **president**, who is directly elected by the people for a five-year term of office, although the first term that began in 1994 was effectively extended to seven years as a consequence of a presidential referendum on the part of the then (and present) incumbent in 1996, such that the next presidential election did not take place until 2001. The office holder is responsible for the sovereignity of the republic, national security, territorial integrity, and political and economic stability. The post also carries a guarantee of certain inalienable rights and institutions, including the **Constitution** and the rights and freedoms of individual citizens. In addition there is a wide-ranging portfolio of post-specific rights, including to call national referenda, dissolve parliament, determine the structure of government, dismiss the heads of judicial and other bodies, conduct negotiations on and execute international treaties, declare states of emergency, impose martial law and abolish governmental acts. The president can also issue decrees and instructions of lawful and binding force throughout the country. The office holder enjoys full immunity. Further, the Constitution provides that the 'honour and dignity' of the office is beyond question and should always be guaranteed. The head of state is also the commander-in-chief of the armed forces and head of the security council.

All functions of government are the responsibility of the **Council of Ministers**, consisting of the prime minister, his deputies and ministers of state. This body is accountable to the president and answerable to Parliament, and the parameters of its powers are set by the Constitution. The prime minister is proposed by the president and approved by the National Assembly. The Council of Ministers is the core organ of state and public administration, exercising executive power on behalf of the people in respect of the work of ministerial bodies and public agencies. This includes the activities of the KGB (still so named in Belarus) and the military (including front-line forces), as well as areas such as aviation, customs and science and technology. This mandate incorporates national budgetary control, domestic and foreign policy, economic and social development, national security and defence.

Parliamentary functions (legislative and representative) are discharged by the **National Assembly**, which consists of two chambers: a lower house (the **House of Representatives**, with 110 deputies) and an upper house (the **Council of the**

Republic, with 64 members). The people directly elect all deputies to the House of Representatives, the role of which is to scrutinise draft legislation, administer presidential elections, approve the president's choice of prime minister, monitor the 'activities' of the government, make suggestions on domestic and foreign policy, suggest constitutional amendments and propose votes of no confidence if and when required. Broadly, it has a general overview and scrutiny function. Local councils elect 56 of the 64 members to the Council of the Republic (eight from each of the six regions and eight more from the city of Minsk). The president himself chooses the final eight members. The primary role of this body is to approve or reject draft legislation that has already received the approval of the House of Representatives. It also has the power to select government officials at certain levels. Each chamber may veto any law passed by local officials if contrary to the country's Constitution. As a whole, the National Assembly serves for four years. The House of Representatives sits in session twice a year, though the president himself can call additional extraordinary sessions.

The **Judiciary** consists of the Constitutional Court and various other courts of universal jurisdiction. The Constitutional Court ensures that all new legislation complies in full with the provisions of the Constitution. It comprises 12 judges: six elected by the Council of the Republic and six appointed by the president, including the presiding judge (as approved by the Council of the Republic). The term of office for all 12 judges is 11 years. The universal courts sit in judgement on all criminal, civil, economic, administrative and military cases at all levels, including the Supreme Court of the Republic of Belarus, and courts in Minsk city, the six oblasts and towns.

THE GENESIS OF THE CURRENT STRUCTURE In the USSR, the political system was a single-party one: the Communist Party of the Soviet Union. When the system began to unravel as an unintended consequence of Mikhail Gorbachev's sweeping reform by way of **openness (glasnost) and restructuring (perestroika)**, the result was an emerging plurality on the state and political landscape as, one by one, the former constituent republics declared independence. By the second half of 1993, the Ministry of Justice in Belarus had registered 12 political parties and seven non-governmental and political movements, including (among others), the Belarusian People's Front For Revival (1989), the United Democratic Party of Belarus (1990), the Belarusian Peasants' Party (1991), the Belarusian Social and Democratic Party Gromada (1991), the Party of Communists of Belarus (1991), the Belarusian Christian and Democratic Union (1991), the Slavic Assembly Belaya Rus (1992) and the Green Party of Belarus (1992). For the most part they all had few members, pursued different political objectives and goals, followed different ways of attaining them and were organised along different lines. Many did not stand the test of time due to lack of popular support, while others joined forces. But the general characteristic of the 'opposition' as being a disparate array of disjointed and poorly organised groups was as true then as it is today.

The office of president was first established in 1994, following the adoption of a new constitution in March of that year. Six contenders for the presidency were presented to the people in June and **Alexander Grigoryevich Lukashenko** secured 45.1% of the popular vote, the highest of the six. In a second ballot run-off in July between Lukashenko and the second-placed candidate, former Prime Minister Kyebich, a self-styled 'traditionalist', Lukashenko secured more than four times as many votes as his opponent. Less than a year later, the first of a number of referenda was held, in which 83.3% of those who voted (64.8% of the electorate) agreed to the Russian language being granted official status of equality with Belarusian. A similar number agreed with the President's avowed policy of pursuing economic integration with Russia, while a lesser number (but still an overwhelming majority) agreed to adopt a new flag and to grant the President power to discontinue the Supreme Council.

The next referendum was held in November 1996, when 70% of those who voted agreed to new constitutional arrangements enabling the incumbent president's term of office to be extended to seven years and permitting the dissolution of parliament through the presidential office. Western governments questioned the legitimacy of this referendum, but allegations of electoral impropriety have always been robustly denied by the Belarusian government.

Parliamentary elections were held in 2000 and 2004, with Lukashenko securing a second term of office following the intervening presidential election in 2001. The third national referendum was also held in October 2004, continuing the theme of increasing consolidation of presidential power. Almost 80% of voters are said to have agreed with the removal of the constitutional restriction on the number of terms for which an elected president could serve. All of these ballots attracted allegations of unfair practices and widespread fraud on the part of international observers, claims that were hotly denied by the Belarusian government.

Further elections took place on 19 March 2006, including for president. The candidates were the incumbent Alexander Lukashenko, who was able to stand again following the constitutional reforms legitimised by the 2004 referendum; Alexander Milinkevich, the head of a loose federation of opposition parties; and Alexander Kazulin, a Social Democrat. Several aspects of the administration of the election and of the campaign itself led to concern among Western governments and independent election-monitoring bodies that there had been systemic failures in the process of democracy. There were allegations of intimidation and police brutality following several clashes between demonstrators and the authorities, including the forcible removal during the hours of darkness of a tented camp in central Minsk. On the other side, observers sent by the Commonwealth of Independent States declared themselves satisfied that all was in order and that the interests of transparency, lawfulness and democracy had been fully met. Senior Belarusian government sources hotly disputed claims of irregularity, entertainingly rebuffing the allegations in robust fashion by countering with claims of a similar nature in respect of the re-election of George W Bush to the White House. Whatever the reality, a landslide victory was declared for the incumbent president, with over 80% of the popular vote. Milinkevich polled just 6%. By now the theme of repeated Western allegations of fraud, corruption, illegitimacy and intimidation every time an election rolled around – with consequent rebuttal on the part of the Belarusian state, accompanied by CIS observers declaring the validity of the process and unconditional compliance in full with international standards – was becoming just a little hackneyed. There were further parliamentary elections in 2008 and 2012, split by a 2010 presidential election, in which Lukashenko secured a fourth term with a landslide victory by polling over five million votes from almost 80% of those who turned out to exercise their franchise. There were nine other candidates, the most popular of whom secured only 150,000 votes. The 2010 campaign saw significant instances of violence in clashes between opposition supporters and the police. Hundreds were arrested (including, it is said, seven of the ten candidates) when thousands took to the streets to protest against perceived irregularities on the occasion of the election itself. After the brutal clashes in 2010, there were fears that the presidential election held in October 2015 would be marked by an escalation of violence, but two key factors operated against this. First, six opposition politicians were released from prison and received state pardons in the run-up to the election, amid unofficial reports that something of a thaw in relations between Belarus and the West might be in the offing. The second factor concerned contextual matters. The country's economy was in a tailspin, with prices of basic goods and commodities rising by the day; and there was widespread concern and unease among the general public over events across the border in Ukraine, a country riven by armed conflict and insurrection. Ordinary people were feeling unsafe, insecure and uncertain about the future, such that stability and security were two commodities very much in demand. It was no surprise then that Lukashenko secured a fifth term of office, again by a landslide with 83.5% of the national vote, beating second-place Tatyana Korotkevich, who secured just 4.4%.

The Council of Europe, which monitors democracy and human rights, has barred the country from membership since 1997. At various times the European Union has also imposed travel bans on the President and other senior members of the government, along with punitive economic sanctions. Observers and international human rights groups have also persistently criticised the Belarusian government for institutional suppression of free speech and human rights in its dealings with opposition politicians and their supporters, the independent mass media and other organisations that are not state controlled. To this day, the comment made in formal testimony by former United States Secretary of State Condoleezza Rice in 2005, that Belarus had been identified by the US government as one of a number of 'outposts of tyranny' around the world, continues to be quoted. Routinely in the West, politicians, journalists, human rights activists and commentators label Belarus a dictatorship and continue to roll out the sound bite of the former Bush administration that Lukashenko is 'Europe's last dictator'. As might be expected, all of the claims of administrative, constitutional, democratic and human rights irregularities have always been vehemently denied by the Belarusian government, which seeks to draw on what it sees as the hypocrisy of the international community in its response to conflict within nation states elsewhere and its interference in areas such as the Middle East and Afghanistan. Meanwhile, the political rhetoric around the globe continues apace while, for ordinary people, life in the workplace and at home goes on as before.

TODAY'S POLITICAL CLIMATE As for opposition to the government within the country today, there continues to be very little evidence of any impact among the populace at large. This has been increasingly the case since the very first presidential election. A number of disparate groups have always existed, loosely headed at one point by Alexander Milinkevich, but they have been unable to agree on a united platform. While opposition rallies are periodically held in Minsk, no group has succeeded in calling on popular support; or at least, enough popular support to produce a groundswell of action to challenge the status quo. New potential opposition leaders emerge from time to time, but they do not remain on the scene for long, merging into the background when activism is followed by political emasculation after a period of imprisonment for tax evasion or some other irregularity; or perhaps flight from the country when the personal risks of continued opposition to the state outweigh the benefits. Occasionally dissident voices are heard, when an individual of some profile makes a pronouncement on one subject or another. But such episodes are few and far between, with no suggestion of a joined-up campaign with clear political aims. The independent news analysis agency Belarus Digest has some interesting things to say on the subject of the difficulties faced by ordinary people in sourcing information concerning opposition movements, not least in its reporting of studies on the part of a number of socio-economic and strategic institutes. In October 2013 it was noted that political opposition in the form of parties and movements certainly still existed and was functioning in various forms, notwithstanding persistent suppression, but that its presence in the mass media between April and June 2013 failed to deliver any significant level of public support, even for the most publicly known individuals. Low levels of public trust in opposition politicians and relatively high levels of mistrust were also noted. Almost all opposition personalities functioned exclusively in Minsk, with presence outside the capital in decline. Individual opposition politicians were ranked in terms of their media presence, as were parties and movements but, by the time of the next study in April 2014, new personalities and groups were emerging while others seemed to have disappeared from the scene. Further, most opposition media pronouncements appeared to be reactive in nature, rather than proactively promoting alternative policies. However, greater media presence was noted in the period from July to September 2013, which some analysts suggested might herald an attempt to bring about a higher public profile in the run-up to the 2015 presidential election. By August 2014, a number of key potential opposition leaders had declared possible interest in running for president. In the event, the 2015 election process passed with less dissent than in 2010. Once more, ordinary people were unable to identify with any individual or party of electoral credibility and it is difficult to foresee how and when this might change.

In terms of political and social unrest, demonstrations are not uncommon at certain key times, most notably significant historical anniversaries and around elections. Oktyabrskaya Square in particular has seen a number of peaceful demonstrations with violent consequences. If there is any suggestion of such an event during your visit to Minsk, avoid venturing out on to the streets at all costs. Violence leading to brutal repression almost always ensues. Two other specific events have particular significance. In July 2008, a concert in Minsk to mark the annual independence celebrations was rocked by the detonation of an explosive device that injured around 50 people. It is said that President Lukashenko was present at the event at the time of the explosion, although it appears that he was in no danger. The authorities described the bomb blast as an act of 'hooliganism', the term that is usually applied to any show of political opposition. Forensic examinations at the scene suggested that the device was crude and homemade. No individual or organisation claimed responsibility and, in spite of the fact that the state vowed to swiftly bring the perpetrators to justice, no-one stood trial in the aftermath. The fact that this event happened at all was a matter of the greatest surprise to observers of life in Belarus; incidents of this type were at that time almost unprecedented, the only other recorded events being two bomb blasts in Vitebsk in 2005 (also resulting in injuries but no deaths), which the government blamed on criminal elements within society. There was certainly nothing to suggest a political motive. Affairs took on a new dimension with the bombing of the Minsk metro in April 2011, when an explosive device packed with ball bearings and nails was detonated (apparently by remote control) at Oktyabrskaya station, right in the heart of the city and close to the organs of state. There were 15 fatalities and injuries to hundreds more, with horror and outrage not only inside the country, but also among the international community. At the time, the situation within Belarus was increasingly tense, with an economic crisis of huge proportions gripping the nation. Coincidentally I had a meeting with a government official the day after the explosion. I was assured that the event, although a terrible tragedy, was no

1

cause for alarm concerning social stability, because the government knew who was responsible and arrests were imminent. Two individuals were duly taken into custody the following day. Rhetoric at the time was suggestive of allegations of foreign involvement, but this was never proved. When confessions were obtained, a link was established between this and the earlier detonations in 2005 and 2008. No political or terrorist motive was established and although there were suggestions of mental instability on the part of one of the suspects (taking the form of an apparent lust for blood), they were both declared sane. Guilty verdicts followed the suspects' trial and sentences of death were imposed. They were duly carried out with a bullet to the back of the head. Allegations persist to this day in Western media that the process of investigation was a sham, with confessions being obtained under duress and torture. It is even alleged in some quarters that the state's own internal security services were responsible for the outrage, which remains the worst act of terrorism in the country's history.

A COUNTRY AT THE CROSSROADS OF EUROPE The reality of life in today's Belarus is that prevailing circumstances there do not encourage the development of a properly organised and credible opposition that can offer a real alternative to the present government. Indeed, ordinary people sometimes regard the opposition groups that exist as little more than agitators. Many people are distrustful of their motives and think that no change will come, no matter who is in charge. This may go some way towards explaining why there appears to be so much inertia among the population when it comes to political activism. I try very hard not to discuss politics when I'm in Belarus, whether it's in my official dealings with government departments or around the kitchen table with friends and a bottle of vodka. But I listen to what people say among themselves. The reality is that ordinary people have no time for any individual seeking a political platform. 'They're all the same' is the epithet that most sums up the common view. Despite the crackdowns on opposition media, non-government newspapers can be seen on sale in kiosks and shops, in towns and villages all over the country. And when people read them, they scoff just as much as they do when they read the official word of the state on the pages of government newspapers. And all the while, the President continues to nurture popular support from the 'old guard' with agricultural subsidies and the prompt payment of pensions and salaries (and even percentage increases) to the militia and the armed forces. To this day, there remains an almost romantic affection for what are seen as the good old days of the USSR. While statues of leaders were torn down throughout the former Soviet Union as the Berlin Wall was reduced to rubble, Lenin still stands sentinel on a plinth of concrete in every Belarusian town, city and village. Ordinary folk still yearn for ever closer relations with the Russian Federation, if not formal union with the state that many regard fondly as Mother Russia, whose President Putin continues to juggle many balls (if not flaming clubs) all at once in his pursuit of greater power and influence for Russia on the world stage. The reality is that people in this part of Europe admire and respect strong leaders.

Today Belarus finds itself with an interesting conundrum. Historically, culturally and economically, there are strong ties with Russia, the neighbour that dwarfs it in every way. The rose-tinted spectacles of those who hark back to the Soviet Union and would welcome the idea of integration or strong federation at the least are a real feature of life here. And the markets of Russia, especially oil and gas, are hugely important to the economy of Belarus. Yet the pull of the West's own huge markets is also strong. For its part, Russia needs a strong ally on its western border, but it also needs to regularly show that ally who is boss. Meanwhile, the European Union and NATO would doubtless welcome the opportunity to push the borders of their sphere of influence ever closer to Russia, though until the merest hint of a diplomatic thaw around the 2015 presidential election, there were few overtures and inducements to suggest the climate was right for any strengthening of relations without movement in accommodating the need for significant political and human rights reform. For some time now, President Lukashenko has found himself right in the middle of two giant markets run by opposing principles of governance, both of which are prepared to offer inducements in return for favours.

Events of significance close to home and on the wider global stage have impacted on the delicate balance of these affairs in recent years. Political and social unrest within Ukraine and other former Soviet states has led to increased tensions in this part of Europe, adding to the complexity of the dynamics of the relationships. First came the short-lived hostilities in 2008 between Russia and Georgia, followed by the terrible events within neighbouring Ukraine. Here tensions between the elected government in Kiev and separatists in the east backed by the Kremlin spilled into open hostility and bloodshed. International (though short-lived) condemnation followed the annexation of the Crimea on the part of Russia in March 2014. The outrage of the Malaysian airliner apparently shot out of the sky just four months later by a ground-to-air missile launched in eastern Ukraine brought home the human cost of political manoeuvering. In this part of Europe the struggle to establish national and ethnic identities proceeds unabated in the aftermath of the Cold War. Some say that the new line of the Cold War has been drawn somewhere across the fracture that has opened within the Ukrainian state. Allegations of Russian interference in the 2016 US presidential election rumble on. The future viability of the European Union is now in real question, not least as a result of the UK referendum vote to leave earlier that year. Across the continent of Europe, extremism and oppression are in evidence once more. For observers of international relations, diplomacy, society and culture, these are interesting times indeed.

Meanwhile, President Lukashenko continues to hone his political game-playing skills on the international stage, against the backdrop of the strategic and geographical significance of modern Belarus between the European Union and NATO on one side of the country and Russia on the other. Sometimes there is overt criticism of the West, and sometimes there appears to be a thaw in the form of a gesture to appease and mend fences. The purpose and intent of the rhetoric can be argued in many different ways, but one thing is certain: ambiguity is everywhere to be seen. In the run-up to Independence Day on 3 July 2014, Radio Free Europe reported that the President took observers by surprise when, during the entirety of a public speech, he addressed the nation in the Belarusian language for the first time in 20 years. Some saw this as an attempt to distance himself from Russia in the aftermath of that country's annexation of the Crimea. And yet the very next day, Independence Day itself, Bielsat TV noted that Presidents Lukashenko and Putin stood side by side at celebrations in Minsk to commemorate the 70th anniversary of the end of the Nazi occupation. The state-run news agency BelTA quoted the Belarusian leader as proclaiming, '[this] symbolises our unity. It says that we were together and we always will be.' He added, says the agency, 'as I said once when I was criticised by some people: do not worry. If need arises, we will stand shoulder to shoulder and will defend ourselves – we will fight back together as we once did.' Then later that day at the opening of the newly relocated Belarusian State Museum of the History of the Great Patriotic War, Bielsat TV reported a message for the West: 'one would assume that Western nations should appreciate the contribution

1

of our nations to the Great Victory, however, instead of gratitude we get high-handed dictate and sanctions.' Not much changes in this part of the world.

ADMINISTRATIVE AREAS In administrative terms the country is divided into six provinces, known as *oblasts*, each of which is named after the city serving as its administrative centre, with the *city* of Minsk, which is situated in the *province* of Minsk, having its own unique status. The seven administrative areas are Minsk city, Brest, Gomel, Grodno, Minsk, Mogilev and Vitebsk. The *oblasts* are further subdivided into *raions*, commonly translated as districts, with towns and villages beneath. Locally elected **Councils of Deputies** determine local issues on a four-year cycle, covering areas such as education, social welfare, health, transport and the economy, all within the framework of national state legislation. There are obvious parallels with tiers of local government elsewhere in the world, though the substance and form of locally administered affairs is a clear inheritance from the days of the Soviet Union, with key officials still being appointed by the state.

ECONOMY

FROM INDEPENDENCE TO THE PRESENT DAY The period since independence has not been an easy time for Belarus in economic terms but, in spite of difficulties that endure to this day, there are indicators to suggest stability and even a modicum of growth over the entirety of the period. As might be expected, official statistics are a constant reminder that all is indeed stable, fully resilient and in good shape to resist the vagaries of the free market. The government says that exports are up, imports are down, the trade deficit is reducing and that there are even signs of a healthy trade surplus in some sectors. In terms of exports, 66% of goods go to Russia, 9.4% to Ukraine, 2.4% to Kazakhstan and the remainder to non-CIS states (primarily within the EU).

Each of the six geographical regions has its own free economic zone (with tax breaks and incentives to stimulate and encourage new enterprise), while two specific examples of substantial government investment are indicative of the country's technological significance within and beyond its national borders. First, the establishment in 2005 of the virtual hub 'Hi-Tec Park' (the country's own version of Silicon Valley) in Minsk has enabled the technology sector to gain a foothold in global markets, particularly in the area of software development and support. Joint venture arrangements and foreign investment feature in the structure of many of the companies that are members of the hub (187 at the last count in 2017, selling to over 50 countries worldwide) and a growing reputation for excellence and innovation is delivering a significant presence in foreign markets. On a separate 8,000ha site adjoining Minsk National Airport, the Great Stone Industrial Park (a special economic zone in the course of development jointly with China) is growing at an astonishing rate. I drove past it on my way to the airport at the end of my last research trip in late 2017, and the scale of the undertaking is truly impressive. Financed by Chinese money, built by Chinese construction workers and run by a Belarus-China joint venture company set up in 2012 (60% owned by China), it boasts facilities for business, industry and engineering (both mechanical and hi-tech, including pharmaceuticals and biotechnology), research, shopping, recreation and banking, as well as residential units. Legal, tax and customs advantages feature significantly for companies locating here.

More forensic examination beyond the word of government suggests that overall, *relative* stability has been achieved against the background of the Belarusian economy having long displayed characteristics of the old Soviet Union in terms of rigid and significant state control. From the birth of the state at the time of independence this has manifested itself in two ways; first, in the form of business that is directly state owned, state run and therefore entirely state controlled, but also indirectly in the form of the massive edifice of regulations, rules, bureaucracy and red tape that faces any business in private ownership. For both sides of the economy, state and private, there is thus little de facto difference. This means that official statistics showing a steady and incremental rise in private enterprise tell only part of the story. Further, considerable reliance is still placed on the supply of raw materials from the country's gigantic neighbour Russia, while every now and again President Putin flexes Russian muscles and reminds Alexander Lukashenko who is in charge by turning off the tap on the supply of oil and natural gas. Two-thirds of goods produced in the country are exported to Russia, while the same proportion of imports come from that source. On its own, therefore, Belarus is still struggling to find the clout, money, influence and nous to muscle into the marketplace, except under the benevolence of its avuncular neighbour.

Most traditional industrial and agricultural enterprises in Belarus remain in state hands, certainly the larger ones. At various points since independence, particularly in the early days, there were experiments with more market-based ventures on an ad hoc and ill-conceived basis, but for the most part the results were spectacularly underwhelming. This was not least because the old-style Soviet mentality of the bosses and the workforce was ill-equipped to survive, let alone flourish, in global markets that were becoming ever more competitive and cut-throat. This remains largely the case, though the new high-technology industries are starting to buck the trend.

Today in Belarus, as before, collective state farming dominates agriculture, which is based on cattle and pig breeding, the cultivation of potato, beet, grain and vegetables, milk production and also the processing of timber from the vast areas of forestation in the country. Light and heavy industry features the production of plant, machinery and mechanical vehicles (tractors are a speciality), radios and electronics, chemical processing, textiles (particularly linen) and white goods for domestic use. Overall, the industrial sector accounts for 26.9% of the country's GDP. During the 1960s, heavy industry and mechanical engineering (most notably the manufacture of tractors) made a significant contribution not only to the country's own economic stability, but also to the economy of the USSR. In those terms, it was punching well above its weight, for notwithstanding its modest size, the Belarusian SSR was one of the most industrially advanced of the Soviet republics. All of that ended with the fall of the USSR. And of course, the consequential political and social upheaval came at a time when the western republics of the Soviet Union were already struggling with the crippling economic and social impact of the Chernobyl disaster.

In the post-Soviet era of the early 1990s, rudimentary market structures with non-existent governance arrangements in this part of Europe meant there was a free-for-all in state trading between the component former republics. It was all just a little like the Wild West for a while, as could be seen in Russia with the outrageous sale of huge state assets for next to nothing and the subsequent establishment of a powerful oligarchy. One of President Lukashenko's early moves in his first term was to introduce a hybrid market economy run on socialist lines. The intention was clear; take the best of both worlds to deliver not only stability but also steady growth in safe circumstances. The reality, however, was the tendency for the worst of both to come to the fore. The imposition of stifling bureaucratic and legal controls over market trading, costs and currency exchange, in a culture where the taking of responsibility and the exercise of initiative on the part of business strategists and managers simply did not exist, was never going to work effectively. As can be seen the world over, unregulated markets produce disastrous results in terms of governance and even adherence to the law, while overregulation in abundance cripples initiative and enterprise. And the world over, the search for the happy medium goes on.

Against all the odds, the traditional industries managed to deliver modest but incremental growth in the early years. At first, fledgling private enterprise was crippled by the extent to which the state could directly interfere in the running of a business. Over time this burden has been relaxed to an extent (as evidenced by the establishment of the six regional free economic zones, as well as the subsequent development of the Hi-Tec Park and the continuing expansion of the Great Stone Industrial Park) in the hope that favourable conditions would encourage foreign investment. There has been partial success. It is certainly the case that latterly, money has flowed in from abroad to deliver growth in high-technology industries and the successful completion of significant construction projects, both in the residential sector and in the leisure and tourism industry. However, not all negotiations between the government and international backers have been successful. Some joint ventures have been established (and are flourishing), but there are also reports that a number of high-profile projects have stalled and even been abandoned when foreign corporations simply would not accept the terms the government was seeking to impose. Further, the West's perception of a need for major political reform and a greater commitment to the observance of human rights means that it is not easy for foreign investment to be attracted. It's just as well, then, that even though the tap is periodically turned off, the trade in oil and natural gas with Russia delivers a valuable commodity to Belarus at a knock-down and heavily discounted price, which it then sells on the open market at considerable profit. And goodwill visits to Moscow often see President Lukashenko returning to Minsk with loans of a billion US dollars or more in his pocket. There is plenty here to keep commentators and observers of the relationship between the two countries interested. Lukashenko has not been shy in voicing criticism of Putin's stance on Ukraine and particularly the Russian annexation of the Crimea. The EU is now less public in its push for political and human rights reform in Belarus, doubtless on the basis that stability in one country in this part of Europe goes some way towards limiting the impact of the uncertainties of political volatility, nationalism and social unrest elsewhere in the region. In turn, Putin knows that a friendly Belarus is more than a useful buffer against EU and NATO expansionism. Watch this space and be careful not to blink lest you miss something.

GOVERNMENTAL STRATEGY The government will say that its financial strategy is to offer a 'socially oriented market economy' model. Without doubt, it sees the importance of competing on the world stage and significant attempts continue to be made to adapt to the ever-changing demands of international trade, as evidenced by the advantages offered in high-profile instances in the form of initiatives to relax tax and customs obligations. However, the reality for much of ordinary day-to-day business in Belarus is still that elements of the old monopolistic approach on the part of the state are underpinned by rules that appear to manifest as a toweringly bureaucratic monolith of decree, regulation and statutory obligation. Not only businesses of every size and profile but also charitable non-governmental organisations are subject to a rigorous and often debilitating regime of interference on the part of the state. In the past this took the form of random changes to the law, some of which retrospectively applied fresh requirements with little or no warning, all glued together by a burdensome process of complex inspection and monitoring. I even know of one business in the charitable sector that claims it must comply with two sets of mandatory regulations that are entirely contradictory, such that observing one set means infringing the other. Whether this says more about the reality of business life in Belarus or that element of the national psyche that sees the glass half empty and will find a million ways why something cannot happen (but not a single means of achieving it), is open to debate. I don't know the answer, but I suspect it lies somewhere between the two along the line of a broad and complex spectrum. Again, official statistics point to a buoyant economy where enterprise, hard work, initiative, lateral thinking and imaginative business practices are rewarded. This is doubtless the case for companies with a presence on the Hi-Tec and Great Stone parks. In Minsk, a mood of optimism and confidence for the future prevails. But my informal discussions with ordinary people in cities, towns, villages and homes away from the capital tell a different story. It's just another example of the ambiguity you find everywhere in this fascinating country.

In late 2008, I attended an international business symposium in London organised by the Belarusian government to extol the virtues of the country's economy. At the time, free markets all over the world appeared on the brink of meltdown following the global crisis that threatened to bring down the economies of nation states and democratically elected governments, in circumstances where the larger global corporations appeared to be exercising greater power and influence than those states and their governments themselves. At the time this particular drama still had many acts to unfold; and in the years since, further rumblings have suggested that the crisis certainly wasn't a one-off. The message from the symposium was that the prudence of the Belarusian government's benevolent stewardship of the state's economy was delivering stability, while elsewhere all was chaos and despair. It was said that Belarus was entirely protected from the world crisis. The constant theme of the conference was that these then-recent events proved without equivocation that the Belarus model represented the right course both to deliver growth and to provide effective protection from the worst excesses of the market. In broad terms this continues to be the basis for government strategy. Yet by early 2011, the model was on the brink of collapse. First came rumours of currency devaluation, followed by the inevitable panic among ordinary people to ditch the rouble in exchange for US dollars (and to a lesser extent the euro). Official devaluation by a third preceded one of my visits that spring. Everywhere I went, I saw fear that society was about to implode. People were telling me that the price of ordinary household items such as bread and milk was doubling overnight. Salaries were halved, inflation exceeded 100% and punitive rates of interest rendered borrowing impossible. Everyone was offering me increasingly extravagant rates of black market currency exchange. Signs were appearing in banks that no supplies of dollars were being held there. I particularly recall standing in line at a bank in Vetka, with people whispering to each other. 'Does he have any dollars?' was the urgent refrain. In all my visits over the years, the tension at this time was most palpable. I never once feared for my security or for the safety of my money, but I could sense desperation all around. The independence from the vagaries of the market that was being so lauded at the London symposium had turned into isolation, with no access to support from Europe and beyond. In spite of it all, both the country and the President survived. In 2015 the country's economy took another dip, with ordinary people fearing for their jobs, homes and financial viability. Today, there is stability once more and for most people things are manageable. They get by. The great divide between Minsk and the provinces endures, as it always will, but it's the same all over the world.

On 1 July 2016 a significant development occurred when a redenomination of the Belarusian rouble came into effect. For years inflation had galloped away unchecked, with the price of ordinary commodities like bread and milk listed in thousands (and tens of thousands) of roubles. Larger purchases were made on a scale of telephone numbers. Even a modest wad of notes in your pocket made you a rouble millionaire. All of this was more reminiscent of the Weimar Republic in the 1920s than a modern European state. Whether or not the range of seven new notes (from five to 500 roubles) reducing prices by a multiplier of 10,000 actually addressed the problem of rampant inflation is a matter of conjecture, but at least the perception of an economy out of control diminished. For visitors from abroad prices are much easier to calculate, the process of actually spending money being closer to that experienced elsewhere in the Western world. Only time will tell if greater alignment is actually achieved in terms of the country's relationship with global currency markets generally.

THE FUTURE In terms of support from the international development community, the most cursory examination of any international funding stream or source of aid, particularly those of the European Union, the World Bank and the International Monetary Fund, shows that compared with other countries in the region, Belarus has been treated extremely partially. At the same time, the call for political and human rights reform by those in control of the purse strings is a constant backdrop, if argued with less insistence these days. For years European Union resolutions imposed a series of sanctions, including the freezing of the assets of the President and a number of government colleagues. Travel and visa bans to EU countries were also imposed. These sanctions were a direct consequence of the EU's belief that successive elections have been unlawfully conducted, fraudulent and improper, against a background of human rights abuse, suppression of free speech and the stifling of political opposition. Yet there is nothing to suggest that sanctions and limitations on aid have any effect other than to place the people of the country themselves at the sharp end of hardship.

It is little wonder, then, that from top to bottom, all the way from the President himself to the man and woman walking village streets, there was collective belief for years and years that the very best interests of the country and its people lay in ever closer alignment with the systems and structures of the Russian Federation. This belief endures to this day for many ordinary people, but it's now less easy to call the President's position with any degree of certainty. From the very day of his election, Alexander Lukashenko made clear his avowed intention to deliver integration and he embarked on developing policies to achieve this outcome. One of his proposals was to introduce a single currency for a united Russia and Belarus. This has never happened. At the opening ceremony of the first Belarusian-Russian economic forum in Minsk on 6 September 2005, Lukashenko addressed participants using these words: 'Without losing either country's sovereignty, we aim to develop a unified legal, economic and administrative system to become the foundation for our union state.' The reality of political and social ambiguity in this part of Europe (as well as not inconsiderable potential for uncertainty and instability on the wider stage) certainly suggests a softening of old attitudes, though while the message of today's rhetoric may be less direct, there is nothing to suggest that this aspiration will suffer a major volte-face anytime soon. Only time and the course navigated by the government of the Russian Federation will determine the accuracy of its predictive foresight.

PEOPLE

Official figures show that in October 2017 the population of the country was 9,495,800, the first rise for many years (even if only a modest one – the figure had been 9,345,000 in January 2014). Until 2017 previous figures spoke for themselves in consistently confirming a pattern of negative growth rate, but happily this shows signs of being reversed at last.

Overall the population density is around 46 per km^2 and 78% of people live in urban areas – 1,974,8000 of them in Minsk, with Gomel (535,229), Mogilev (380,000), Vitebsk (378,000), Grodno (365,610) and Brest (331,000) the other major centres.

The largest demographic group is that comprising native Belarusians, who make up 83.7% of the total population. Russians come next, with 8.3%, then Poles and Ukrainians, accounting for 3.1% and 1.7% respectively. The remaining 3.2% comprises Jews, Lithuanians, Tatars, Azerbaijanis, Armenians, Latvians, Koreans, Germans, Georgians, Ossets, Moldavians and travelling people. Roughly 80% of the people are classed as belonging to the Russian Orthodox Church and around 10% are believed to be Roman Catholic, with the remaining 10% being Protestant, Jewish or Muslim. Estimates also show that the diaspora consists of 3–3.5 million native Belarusians residing outside the country's borders, most of them in the United States, Russia, Ukraine and Poland.

The halt in population decline is obviously good news and it confirms the impression I gained during my travels in 2017 when I discovered a new spirit abroad, particularly among young people in the cities. Ever since my first visit in 2001, the leading ambition of many Belarusians, particularly the young, had been to find a 'better life' elsewhere, usually in the West. But in 2017, I began to see evidence of a new pride in the life of the country and its culture. Instead of wanting to leave at the first opportunity, students and young adults told me they saw their future in Belarus. They told me they wanted to stay and to work for brighter times ahead.

Nobody exemplifies the new mood of positivity better than good friend Natalia Ovsyanko. Working with students at the Academy of Public Administration (a body subordinated to the Presidential Administration), Natalia is keen to engage young people (particularly vulnerable ones) in taking ownership of projects to promote Belarus outside its national borders. She doesn't regard herself as a businesswoman, but instead a social entrepreneur with an obligation to bring together the organs of government, civil society and academia to tackle the great societal issues of today's Belarus. Her 'We Care' project (w *wecare.by*) draws attention first to the significant contribution made to society by vulnerable people who are themselves tackling issues of mental disability and secondly to the ways in which the community at large can help those who are less fortunate than themselves to feel valued. Natalia welcomes enquiries from outside Belarus (\ *+375 44 739 80 10;* e *nat1977rus@ yahoo.com*) and will respond enthusiastically to all offers of collaborative working.

This growing sense of positive civic ownership among tomorrow's adults and their leaders in Minsk can only be good news for the future of the country, yet for now it remains in sharp contrast to the old attitudes that endure outside the main areas of population where personal ambitions for many, most of them wholly unrealistic, still revolve around a new life abroad.

As for population numbers (whether or not official), statistics are just numerals on a page. However commentators choose to interpret them, they say nothing about the national characteristics of the country's people (insofar as it is ever possible to draw conclusions from crude generalisations). Only by spending time in the heart of a community, getting to know individuals and by earning their trust and respect can this ever be possible, and then only with the broadest of brushstrokes. The features I have come to recognise during my 17 years in communities all over Belarus include resilience, self-respect, pride, self-discipline, stoicism, hospitality, warmth, generosity, humour (often dark) and wit (almost always dry). A visit to this fascinating country leaves many indelible imprints on the memory from things that are experienced and seen, but the ones that last the longest are memories of ordinary encounters with everyday people.

Belarusians who are able to do so live close to the earth, and their relationship with nature and the seasons is intense. Spring, summer and autumn are spent tending the land and in preparation for the long, dark winter. Those who live in the town will spend as much time as they can at a modest wooden cottage (*dacha*) owned by someone in their family, while rural dwellers will have their own extensive plot of land at home. The stockpile of produce from the year's labours will then be

A PINCH OF SALT

One day, hopefully soon, I shall sit down to write a travelogue by way of homage to the many delightful people I have met in 17 years of getting to know this country. Lest I forget, I have many vignettes in notebooks and diaries, scribbled on bits of paper and hastily recorded in shorthand form on my mobile phone by way of insurance. Happily, all of them nestle comfortably in my memory somewhere and periodically one will come out to play when a related thought brings a forgotten encounter back to mind. One stuffy, airless night in the midst of a Minsk summer I found myself turning the well-thumbed pages of my European rail timetable, unable to sleep or to settle. Services, destinations, trains; empty stations, lonely platforms, people. And then I was riding the rails again, on the sleeper to St Petersburg, somewhere between Gomel and Mogilev, my destination one humid and gloomy day three years earlier during the course of a research trip. I was tired and a little dispirited, knowing I had too many notes to write up, too many hand-drawn maps to correct, too many things to remember. I felt hot and uncomfortable and needed a break from speaking Russian, but I was sharing the compartment with an elderly lady who wanted to chat. I was soon glad that she did. She was courteous, friendly, interested in all I had to say and particularly kind when I asked forgiveness for the limitations of my poor Russian. She was going all the way to St Petersburg, to see her sister. We exchanged pleasantries and when conversation stuttered to a halt as I exhausted my repertoire, she settled into her book to spare my awkward embarrassment. Relieved, I turned to watch the countryside pass by, but pangs of hunger interrupted my reverie. I sorted through the bulging bag of food Tanya had given me when I left Vetka and settled on a huge, unwieldy tomato. My new friend looked up at me from her book, put it down and began to rummage around in her capacious handbag. She produced a tatty old medicine bottle, which she gave me with a smile. When I looked at her quizzically, she gestured that I should open it. It was full of table salt. Next she offered me a knife. I gave her one of my apples. She found a cucumber in the depths of her bag and passed it to me with a napkin. 'Eat, eat, take salt,' she said, 'And thank you for the lovely apple'. On we rattled towards St Petersburg, eating in silence, and we parted without resuming conversation when the train reached my stop in Mogilev, both knowing we would never meet again. For a few hours our two worlds conjoined as we rode the same rails, then our paths diverged once more. It was an encounter I shall cherish always. The generosity of strangers continues to nurture my faith in humanity. I stumble across chance meetings like this wherever I go in Belarus.

shared with family and friends. Indeed, the concept of the extended family is alive and well in Belarus. Whenever I sit down to eat at the table of my Belarusian family, the man of the house will reach for a slice of bread, close his eyes, bring the bread to his nose, inhale deeply, then look solemnly into my eyes and nod with a smile of understanding. In the villages and hamlets far removed from life in the big city, the sense of a real fondness for and dependence upon the land is a palpable one.

LANGUAGE

Russian and Belarusian have equal status as formally adopted national languages. Belarusian is one of four historic eastern Slavonic languages, all of which have most commonly been rendered in Cyrillic script. Shared elements of grammar and vocabulary can be recognised readily in each of them. And as might be expected, the cycle of development and suppression of the Belarusian language has mirrored the course of political and social upheaval across the centuries. The 1920s saw an upsurge in the promotion of Belarusian culture, language and literature, but this blossoming was brutally suppressed by Stalin's purges in the 1930s. The state's grand 'Reform of Belarusian Grammar' in 1933 was intended to ethnically cleanse the language of unwelcome historical contamination on the part of neighbouring cultures to the north and west (primarily Baltic and Polish) as well as to remove the perceived archaic colloquialisms romantically in use among Belarusian nationalists (who were seen as a counter-revolutionary threat to the solidarity of the Soviet Union). This would pave the way for greater integration between the Russian and Belarusian languages, the latter being formerly regarded as the language of the peasantry. This judgement is now largely a thing of the past, although there is a perception in some quarters today that the Belarusian language has been adopted by opposition groups and those sympathising with their cause, as well as by nationalists and intellectual thinkers seeking to establish an independent and romanticised history and culture for the concept of a separate Belarusian identity.

There was further reform in 1959, a revision that holds good today (with only modest periodic amendment since). During perestroika ('restructuring') in the final days of the Soviet Union, Belarusian and other historical languages among the constituent republics met with a significant revival as new nation states began to emerge. In 1990 it was envisaged that the language of all administrative and official documentation of the then Belarusian SSR would change from Russian to Belarusian by the year 2000. Lukashenko's election to the presidency in 1994 put a stop to this, although he did address the nation in the Belarusian language on Independence Day that year, an event not to be repeated for another 20 years. Following a referendum in 1995 that was not without controversy in some quarters, the Russian language was afforded equal status in the country.

Some commentators have claimed a de facto reduction in the significance of the Belarusian language since independence, evidenced (they say) by diminishing numbers of specific language schools, books and periodicals. My experience very much suggests that the contrary is true. Belarusian text is ubiquitous throughout the full range of communication media and can be seen everywhere on public and state buildings, street names and at tourist sites. More and more young people are choosing to speak and to write Belarusian, a trend that seems to go hand in hand with a pride in Belarusian nationhood that continues to gather strength here.

A specific example of the ambiguity around the language debate concerns the Russian word *babooshka*, which broadly translates as 'grandmother'. The Belarusian equivalent is *baboolya*, or even *baboolyechka* ('my pretty little granny'), which is often used in the countryside, where particularly the elderly are likely to be heard speaking either in local Belarusian dialects or in *trasyanka* (a mixture of Belarusian and Russian), when Russian words are often used with Belarusian phonetics and syntax. I spend a great deal of time in the rural hinterlands. My Russian is none too shabby, but I have enormous difficulty in understanding the language often in use among the elderly. In London I once knew one proud Belarusian who refused to be addressed by me in anything other than his own language and again, this always presented me with something of a challenge.

As with so much in this interesting country, the language debate contains elements of myth, cliché, revisionism and romanticism, with truth and reality spinning somewhere within the vortex of contradiction and complexity. On the streets and in homes, the untutored Western eye and ear would discern very little difference between written or spoken Belarusian and Russian. And for observers of eastern European politics and society, it will be fascinating to see which influence prevails; will there be greater linguistic convergence if circumstances force Belarus and Russia closer together socially, politically and economically, or will a tide of Belarusian nationalism see the emergence of an increasingly separate linguistic identity? This is such an interesting part of the world.

RELIGION

Across history, Belarusian lands have been at the crossroads of culture and ideology, where two worlds have often collided with tragic consequences. Both the West and the East have influenced social, political and ideological development and this applies to **religious beliefs** as much as to anything else. For most of history, there has been peace between the two major Christian churches in Belarus (Orthodoxy and Catholicism), with relations between the two being characterised by at best tolerance and peaceful coexistence and at worst a tacit acceptance on the part of both of the presence of the other. This has certainly been so since compromise resulted in the Brest Church Union of 1596, under which the Orthodox Church of the Grand Duchy of Lithuania ceded the spiritual high ground by recognising the supremacy of Rome, the price of this self-imposed subjugation being permission to maintain its own rites, doctrines and customs. Initially (and inevitably), though, there was still reluctance on the part of Orthodox believers to accept a higher authority in this way. Before the Union, the Orthodox population was very much in the majority, in contrast not only to Catholic believers, but also Jews, Muslims and Protestants. But from the 17th to the 19th centuries, most followers of the Orthodox Church were gradually converted to the Uniate, which maintained many Orthodox traditions and rites. By the end of the 18th century, in fact, Uniate believers made up almost 70% of the population, although today only a small community remains. The balance of 30% comprised 15% Roman Catholics, 7% Jews, 6% Orthodox believers and 2% Protestants and others. The Union eventually came to an end in 1839 when the Uniate Church merged with the Russian Orthodox Church, after which the Orthodox population again predominated, comprising over 60% of the population by the early 20th century.

As traditional Belarusian culture acquired a new prominence towards the end of the 20th century with the seismic changes in politics and dogma of the time, so the **Orthodox Church** came to be regarded both by people and state as a medium for the spiritual foundation of the community. Old eparchies were revived and new ones founded under the administration of a synod headed by the Minsk and Slutsk Metropolitan Filaret, the patriarchal exarch of all Belarus. And by early 2009, the doors of 1,274 Orthodox churches were open for worship, with another 152 under construction. In January 2002, there were 1,119 priests, compared with 399 in 1988.

And yet today a significant section of the Orthodox community still consists of Староверы ('Old Believers'), who first appeared on Belarusian territory in the late 17th century. They adhere to the Orthodox canons that existed in Russia prior to the major reforms of the time. Under Catherine the Great of Russia they were widely persecuted for their beliefs. Today most live in the Gomel region, with a particularly large community in the district of Vetka. I have good friends in that community, and I look forward to the day when they honour their promise to tell me all about the issues and the persecutions their beliefs have faced across the generations.

The most revered of Orthodox symbols are the saints of the Church, with nearly every place of worship claiming the body or a physical remnant of at least one, as well as prominently displaying significant numbers of icons and other holy relics. Different saints are identified as being associated with different needs or specialisms. At any hour on any day, local people will visit specific icons of particular saints in their local church, praying, incessantly crossing themselves and lighting beeswax candles before them as a sign of faith and by way of an offering. Every church will have at least one corner in which babooshkas take charge of stalls selling a huge range of relics, from candles of varying length and girth, to icons of every size and form, for the home, office and even the car.

Indeed, icons are ubiquitous and every home will have a corner of a living room opposite the door as a shrine, in which the most revered and favoured family saint is portrayed in iconic form at the highest point of the room, as close to the ceiling as possible, reverently gazing down from on high to bless the family and its home. At their most ornate, they are painted on wood and covered with gold and silver plate. Other family items of significance such as photographs of elders and of the departed are also displayed. Icons are not only revered but also treated with great deference, believers vesting them with mysterious and mystical powers. Today, most motorists (devout believers or not) will embark on their journeys with a simple icon on the dashboard or hanging from the rear-view mirror.

Orthodox churches were traditionally built in the shape of a Greek cross and even newly constructed ones bear the hallmark of the familiar onion dome embossed with gold colouring, topped by the familiar Greek cross. They were originally built of wood, and no nails were ever used in construction, the whole being held together by the intricacies of the design. Inside, the iconostasis, a sacred wall covered in icons, holy murals and other pictures of saints, closes off the public area from the section to which only priests are permitted access.

On most days of the week, churches are a hive of activity. Participating in an Orthodox service is a stirring and emotionally charged experience. Priests in flowing robes and with the deepest of baritone voices chant prayers and intonations while vigorously swinging incense holders, often with an unseen choir making rousing interventions by means of soaring responses. All the time, believers stand in rapt concentration (there are no chairs), constantly crossing themselves and joining in with the responses. This is absolutely not to be missed, but visitors must be sure to treat the occasion with the utmost respect. Without fail, men should remove hats and women cover their heads. Taking photographs is not a good idea, while purchasing and lighting a candle before an icon will always be regarded favourably.

One of the most moving sights is to witness a less formal ritual involving a junior priest and perhaps one or two babooshkas. This is a particularly common event. The priest will recite certain prayers and the ladies will respond with light, beautiful and haunting harmonies. Even sceptical hearts will miss a beat.

Given the history of **Catholicism** in the area and with Polish Catholics on the western border of the country, it is no surprise to find a significant community still in Belarus. Around 10% of the population is Roman Catholic, roughly half of whom are ethnic Poles. Not unexpectedly, the biggest enclave of Catholicism is to be found in Grodno, bordering Poland in western Belarus. In 2009, there were 467 such communities, 161 of which could be found in the Grodno region. In all, there were 451 Roman Catholic churches throughout the country, with another 35 then under construction.

Protestantism (in the form of Lutheranism, Calvinism and Evangelical Christianity) is slowly but incrementally expanding from west to east, although it remains a small community consisting mostly of ethnic Germans.

Judaism in Belarus can be traced back as far as the 9th century, with a number of sizeable communities in existence along the line of the current western border of the country by the end of the 1300s. Only a century later, the upper strata of the Grand Duchy of Lithuania's administrative functions featured Jews in prominent positions. During the 16th century, migrants from countries further west established new communities deeper into Belarusian territory.

Over the course of the next 200 years, successive Russian emperors sought to convert the empire's Jews to the Orthodox faith, on pain of expulsion if they refused. Then in 1791 Catherine the Great established the principle of the Pale of Settlement, the geographical area within which Jews were allowed to make permanent homes. Its borders were susceptible to change until the end of the Romanov dynasty in 1917 when the Pale formally ceased to exist, though the broad thrust over time was an increase in the size of the area. During its existence, one consequence of wars and diplomatic settlements with Russia's neighbours was that the location of lands available for Jews to live on was in a state of flux. At times, new areas came into

American actor **Kirk Douglas** was born in New York to Russian Jewish immigrants from Gomel, the country's second-largest city. Internationally renowned violin virtuoso **Yehudi Menuhin** was also born in New York to Belarusian Jewish parents. Hollywood film magnate and one of the original creators of the huge Metro-Goldwyn-Meyer studio, **Louis B Meyer**, was born Lazar Meir in Minsk in 1884. **Michael Marks**, joint founder of the retail giant Marks and Spencer, was born in Slonim, Grodno oblast. American fashion guru **Ralph Lauren** was born Ralph Rueben Lifshitz in New York to Ashkenazi Jewish immigrants from Pinsk. In the world of chess, Israeli International Grandmaster **Boris Abramovich Gelfand** was born in Minsk. Many notable Belarusian Jews have reached the highest elevations within Israeli politics, notably **Chaim Azriel Weizmann**, first president of the state of Israel (born near Pinsk), **Shimon Peres**, the ninth president who also served twice as prime minister and once on an interim basis (born in Minsk oblast), **Menachem Begin**, the sixth prime minister (born in Brest), and **Yitzhak Shamir**, the seventh (born in Brest oblast). And for details of the life and work of artist **Marc Chagall**, see box, page 265.

the Pale, while old ones were removed. All of modern-day Belarus was included, as was a significant portion of European Russia. Beyond the Pale (presumably the derivation of the colloquial saying), a permanent home was broadly denied, though at various times a limited number of categories of Jewish citizenship were exempt from this prohibition under the terms of a formal state dispensation, the criteria for the granting of which were arbitrary and subject to reversal. Enforced removal from certain of the bigger cities encouraged the rise of rural communities known as *shtetls*. At the time of its greatest significance, more than five million Jews lived in the Pale, then the biggest concentration of Jewish settlements anywhere in the world.

The influence of Judaism within the lands now known as Belarus was most significant early in the 20th century, when the Jewish population was in the majority (sometimes up to 90%) in many small towns throughout the country and some of the larger cities. It was common to hear Yiddish spoken all over these towns and cities. Literally meaning 'Jewish', Yiddish is a High Germanic language developed as a fusion of dialects and written in the Hebrew alphabet. Today it is written and spoken in Orthodox Jewish communities wherever they are to be found in the world.

By the end of the Great Patriotic War, the entirety of the Jewish community in Belarus had been all but wiped out as part of the Nazis' 'final solution'. Today, however, there is a new revival as small Jewish communities begin to establish themselves in towns and cities all over the country, notably in Minsk, Grodno, Brest, Vitebsk, Polotsk, Slutsk and Babrusk, as well as in other places. Once more Yiddish is beginning to be spoken and heard among elderly members of these communities, freely and without the need to hide, as new roots are laid down, Judaism is reclaimed and connections are re-established with Jewish heritage and identity. There are small but fascinating museums of Jewish heritage in Minsk and Brest, together with Jewish memorials and old cemeteries in many locations. Much of historical Jewish Belarus has yet to be rediscovered, with new finds being made all the time. There are many international organisations supporting Jewish community development that can provide in-depth information, broker meetings with members of Belarusian Jewish communities and arrange tours of culture and heritage sites (including to former cemeteries and the small number of synagogues still in existence), as well as being in a position to offer help and support in establishing and finding Jewish roots and heritage, together with assistance in obtaining invitations and visas. There are two with which I personally work. In London, contact British sustainable development charity **The Together Plan** (page 116), while partner Belarusian NGO **Dialog** (✆ +375 29 627 34 00; e *dialogorganisation@gmail.com*) is based in Minsk. Faultless English is spoken and I commend both of these organisations to anyone with an interest in Belarusian Judaism, past and present.

There was a thriving **Islamic** population at the time of the Golden Horde in the Middle Ages, but in modern times only modest numbers still live in the country, although small numbers of new mosques have opened in recent times. Today they are believed to be nine in number, serving around 30 small Muslim communities.

EDUCATION

The system of education in Belarus is state administered and funded directly from the budgets of local tiers of government, to which schools report. The structure consists of first kindergarten education, then school education and training, vocational and technical education, secondary special education, higher education, training of scientific and scientific pedagogical personnel and the retraining and self-development of adults. In 2017, almost 71% of preschool children were in full-time education in nurseries and kindergartens, although attendance there is not compulsory. Most children start school at the age of six, and by law all are required to follow the prescribed curriculum up to the age of 15. Nearly all stay on until they finish their high-school education at 18, before entering university. Indeed, Belarus has one of the highest student-to-population ratios in Europe. Most university courses run for five years. The two state languages of Belarusian and Russian are used equally for teaching and training. The whole process is overseen by the state Ministry of Education, which has developed a curriculum that consists of compulsory and optional disciplines. The compulsory modules are society and humanitarianism, nature and science, culture and the arts and physical and sports development. Within this overarching structure, there is a surprising degree of autonomy for schools locally to design their own media for teaching, based on capacity, resources and the wishes of parents. Much of the learning is done by rote. The commitment of teaching staff to the education of the state's children is admirable and beyond question, but it is clear that in terms of strategic educational planning, there is much progress to be made.

CULTURE

Across the centuries, the establishment, maintenance and promotion of 'traditional' Belarusian culture (whatever that may mean) has not been without difficulty. The first challenge is to identify the characteristics of that culture, so diverse were the founding influences, the subsequent means of suppression under various regimes and the romantic ideals that have been brought to bear in the search for a distinct identity and culture. Yet today, there is clear evidence to support the claim that interest in the promotion of Belarusian culture and language is stronger than ever. That this is particularly so among the younger generations is a very positive sign for the future; I know of many students with a keen interest in promoting their heritage. In 1995, the Students' Ethnographic Society (**w** *set.ethno.by*) was founded with the aim of encouraging young people to preserve and share the traditions of local arts and crafts. The website is in Belarusian only, but its pages give an excellent overview of activities and areas of interest. In Minsk the society regularly holds temporary exhibitions and offers classes in song and crafts, which include weaving, sewing and embroidery. This is very good news for my dear friend Joanna, who enthusiastically subscribes to the traditional singing class for just BYN15 per month. And within my broad circle of acquaintances and contacts Joanna is by no means alone in her passion for all things Belarusian. Whatever 'traditional Belarus' may be, neither locals nor visitors to the country have far to look these days to access its charms.

DRESS The origins of traditional Belarusian dress are as difficult to establish as any area of culture, and at different points in history various sources have been claimed to suit particular political expediency. Some claim that today's perceptions of the foundations owe much to incursions south by the Viking princes in the 9th century, but not surprisingly, dress also displays the influence of the neighbouring countries (Poland, Lithuania, Latvia and Russia) to which at various times throughout history Belarus has been closely linked in terms of statehood, governance, culture and society. Primarily made from wool and hand-produced linen, its key features are straight lines and red and white colouring, often with intricate patterns at the edges (as with the national flag), dependent upon the place of origin. There are many subtle variances of design from region to region and even from district to district. Historically, variances from village to village were not uncommon. The rules of society used to dictate which garments were to be worn on which occasions. For example, it was considered indecent for a man to go outdoors without wearing a particular form of jacket over his shirt. It was also prohibited for married women to go out unless wearing a headdress and apron. For both, it was also considered a minimum standard of decency for the neck, elbows and knees to be covered. Special attention was paid to female clothing at festival times, reflecting the status of women in Belarusian culture as mothers and home-keepers. Today, examples of national dress are displayed in museums up and down the country. It is most frequently worn at festivals and special occasions such as weddings, or at events promoted for the edification of foreign tourists. It remains the most prominent embodiment of traditional culture and can most often be seen at public commemorations of special events in history, in tableaux presented on national days or in state processions.

CRAFTS Traditional crafts include pottery, wood engraving, paper cutting (*vyrazanka* in Belarusian) and plait work with straw, willow, root and bark. Again, examples are displayed in museums in even the smallest of towns. The most notable and uniquely attributable example of Belarusian folk art is the *rushnik* (Belarusian pronunciation *ruchnik*), or ceremonial towel. Flaxen threads are woven together, usually on looms of historic design, to form delicate silvery white and grey geometric patterns, with ancient symbols featuring in the woven or embroidered decoration of symbolic red colouration at the edges. Each village will have its own specific design. When news of the Nazi invasion was broadcast in 1941, it is said that babooshkas in villages all over the country set about weaving rushniki in order to protect their homes from the rampaging hordes. Joanna tells me she once heard from her mother that each rushnik was to be finished within the day, to be tied around the crosses made by the menfolk that were then erected at the village entrance. Today sacred rushniki still have a very significant place in the hearts and lives of Belarusians. Not only have they long been used for practical and decorative purposes, but they also have an important role in the performance of certain rites, such as those at family meals on national holidays, weddings, christenings, funerals and for welcoming guests to the home with bread and salt. Rushniki are commonly to be found draped over icons, both in church and at home. The village of Nyeglubka, in Vetka district of Gomel oblast down in the southeast, has a traditional weaving school (page 318) where students learn the old ways of crafting this most iconic of Belarusian symbols.

CUISINE Traditional cuisine displays the same diversity of influence as dress and crafts, although the common perception is that it largely resembles that of Lithuania. Travellers who have been to other parts of eastern Europe will encounter much that they have seen before and little that they will not have seen. Great significance has always been attached to bread, both as a staple foodstuff and as an important symbol in many rituals. The potato (historically referred to as 'second bread') forms the basis for many meals and the plentiful supply of mushrooms in the forests that extensively cover the land ensures their prominence in many recipes. The best-known traditional dish is *draniki* (potato pancakes), usually served with a rich pork stew in pots. Only moderate seasoning is used in cooking.

Within families, the tradition of preserving salad items, vegetables and fruits (widely practised when it was almost impossible to find fresh fruit and vegetables in the shops) is very much alive today, as evidenced by the proliferation of vegetable gardens at dachas or the homes of parents in the countryside. Younger people, however, are less enthusiastic about this art.

A salad traditionally eaten at New Year is *shooba* ('fur coat', shorthand for 'the fish under the coat'), consisting of herring coated with shredded beetroot and potatoes, covered with mayonnaise. Also look out for *olivier* salad, a concoction of potato, carrot, egg, peas and diced sausage, again smothered in mayonnaise. These popular dishes from the days of the Soviet Union reflect the ingredients that were in plentiful supply at the time. Another New Year speciality is white toast with sprats (seasoned with lemon and garlic). And of course, no New Year (or indeed, any celebration) is complete without Soviet champagne.

For a taste of archetypical cuisine that perhaps speaks more of the Soviet Union than old Belarus, look for the sign столовая (*stolovaya*) on the streets. It translates as 'canteen' and within lies a journey by time machine that is not to be missed (see box, page 245). My experience in Lida all those years ago is typical of that still to be had today wherever and whenever you venture across the threshold of such an emporium, both in terms of food and service. Your meal will be substantial, may even be tasty, and will set you back no more than BYN7 (it may even be as cheap as BYN3!). My good friend Joanna tells me that the word on the street is that the canteen at the State Opera and Ballet Theatre in Minsk is one of the best in the city, though neither of us has yet sampled its charms.

LITERATURE The adoption of Christianity in the 10th century is likely to have been the first milestone. Early examples of literature that are known to have existed are religious works from the 11th century, while many of the chronicles written in the 12th and 13th centuries endure today both as historical records and as works of great literature in their own right. The ancient Belarusian language was granted state legitimacy when Belarusian lands were subsumed within the Grand Duchy of Lithuania, a significant event that some say made a real contribution to the development of literature in the 14th to the 16th centuries, though other observers dispute this. It's yet another example of the contradiction and ambiguity that swirl around this fascinating country. The earliest literary figure of repute was the humanist and scientist Francisk Skaryna, who was a well-known writer and translator in the ancient city of Polotsk. Between 1517 and 1519 he published his own translations of much of the Bible into the ancient Belarusian written language for the first time. This was one of the early instances of mass printing in book form in Europe. In 1522 Mikola Husovski (regarded by many as a key figure in the Belarusian Renaissance) wrote the classic work *The Bison, its Stature, its Ferocity and the Hunt* in Latin while on a diplomatic mission to meet the Pope on behalf of the Grand Duchy. It is still taught in Belarusian schools today, with children able to recite translated extracts by heart. In 1562 the philosopher Simon Budny, a renowned figure of the European Reformation as a publicist and translator, published the first printed book in ancient Belarusian on the territory of modern Belarus. In terms of milestones, the 16th century can certainly be regarded as having been something of a Belarusian golden age.

In the 1600s the Belarusian-Russian poet, playwright and enlightener Simeon of Polotsk was a prolific figure. He introduced the grand Baroque style of writing that was followed up to the first half of the 19th century, when new trends of Romanticism began to reflect the living language and folklore of the population in a sentimental homage to the perceived idyll of self-styled 'traditional' bucolic life. The most prominent figure of this movement was the great Polish-Belarusian poet Adam Mitskevich. He was born in the district of Novogrudok and dedicated his great epic poetic work *Pan Tadeush* to his homeland. At the same time, Vincent Dunin-Martinkevich, who is considered by many to be the father of modern Belarusian literature, began to consolidate his reputation with the publication of notable collections of verses. Best known today for his works of drama, he was responsible for the libretto of the very first Belarusian opera *The Village Girl* (composed by Stanislav Manyushka), originally staged in 1852 in a theatre close to the site of the Europa Hotel in Minsk today (but no longer standing). Another prominent figure at the end of the 19th century was Frantishek Bogushevich, a poet who is credited as being the first national writer of folklore and the first to write and publish his works in language that might be said to closely resemble modern Belarusian. The first nationalist newspapers to be granted lawful status, *Nasha Dolya* ('Our Lot') and *Nasha Niva* ('Our Cornfield'), served as a useful public platform to promote the works of such eminent writers as Yanka Kupala, Yakub Kolas, Eloisa Paskevich, Maxim Bogdanovich, Maxim Goretsky and others in the form of plays, prose and dramatic poetry. No longer were these forms of expression seen as the exclusive domain of the nobility. Rather, romanticism and the patriotic ideal of independent nation statehood began to appear as recurrent themes in the context of a real fondness for the rural idyll, the search for truth in the meaning of life and the juxtaposition of nationalist and revolutionary aspirations. To this day it is poet and translator Bogdanovich who remains a figure much associated with these themes, as well as those of unrequited love, loss and tragedy.

After the October Revolution in Russia in 1917, national and revivalist themes dominated Belarusian literature as part of the movement to encourage Belarusians to adopt greater self-awareness and identification of their heritage. The period 1924–28 might be said to have been marked by a process of 'Belarusisation', with the four state languages being Belarusian, Russian, Polish and Yiddish. All civil servants were required to speak Belarusian, as were members of the armed forces. Hand in hand emerged a number of new names in literature as a body of young and talented writers and poets flourished. Literary groups were formed and new magazines came into publication. Yanka Kupala is still regarded as the spiritual leader of this new wave, but 1928 saw the first arrests as the machinery of the state embarked on a series of purges. Kupala's story is a sad one, as he attempted to take his own life in 1930. The feared NKVD (secret police) employed the usual tactics of remorseless questioning and torture to force him to denounce other writers and artists in his circle, and they eventually broke him. Placing family bonds before artistic integrity, he signed a letter declaring his allegiance to the Soviet Republic of Belarus. Which of us would not have done the same? In return he was appointed 'People's Poet of the BSSR', though the rest of his life was marked by long episodes of depression. Yakub Kolas (another BSSR People's Poet) took to sleeping with his clothes on in anticipation of the dreaded NKVD knock on the door in the hours of darkness. Overall it is estimated that 99 writers in total suffered repression, with only 13 of that number later returning to creative writing. At least 22 were murdered during the night of 29 October 1937 alone (most likely in Kurapaty), when 103 scientists, civil servants and writers were shot by the security services. Many more died in miserable circumstances in Stalin's labour camps, where conditions were at least as bad as in the death camps later run by the Nazis.

Without doubt the ideological repressions of the 1930s cruelly stifled the flourishing of Belarusian creativity in language and literature but as is often the case suppression and persecution begat creativity, here in the form of a number of magnificent works of poetry and drama by artists such as Vladislav Golubok, Mikhas Charot, Vladimir Dubovka, Kondrat Krapiva and Pavlyuk Trus. During the Great Patriotic War, art and satire were particularly powerful tools, as well as poetry and heroic novels. The theme of the war (especially in the context of suffering and misery) dominated the Belarusian and Soviet literary landscape for a long time, notable examples in prose form being *Deep Flow* and *Troubled Happiness* (Ivan Shamyakin), *Unforgettable Days* (Mikhas Lynkov), *Khatyn Story* (Ales Adamovich), *Neidorf* (Ivan Ptashnikov) and *The Dead Feel No Pain* (Vasil Bykov). Classic epic poems included *Blockade* by Rygor Borodulin. Adamovich, a writer of conscience, was an early proponent of the 'documentary prose' style of writing that later inspired Svetlana Alexievich to such great achievements (page 330). Bykov, who died in 2003 (ironically on the anniversary of the day Hitler unleashed Operation Barbarossa on the Soviet Union) was a Nobel Prize nominee. He dealt with issues of warfare from an existentialist perspective, highlighting the gritty reality of what it meant to be a 'hero' in the face of stark and irreconcilable moral dilemmas. Unsurprisingly, he was no favourite of the authorities. Borodulin, who published around 70 books of poetry, was the last Belarusian poet to be awarded the title 'People's Poet', in 1992. He was also nominated for the Nobel Prize for Literature in 2006 and 2007.

As the destruction of wartime was replaced by regeneration and rebuilding in the peace that followed, the perceived idyll of rural life began to be promoted again (occasionally with an abundance of over-sentimentality), this time in the works of Melezh, Adamchik, Streltsov and others. Historical themes and heroic traditions again found a voice as well, the most famous proponent being the brilliant Vladimir Karatkievich, who reminded the ideologues that history did not begin with the October Revolution in 1917. Ivan Melezh created one of the standards of Belarusian literary culture, the masterpiece *The Polesye Chronicles*. The first book in the renowned trilogy *The People of the Marsh* is the most famous, recounting the story of village life in the region of the Polesye, the mysterious land of marsh and mist in the south of Belarus. It features young lovers who are subjugated to the will of their parents and forced to marry elsewhere for all the wrong reasons, against a background of state collectivisation threatening traditional ways of life. It works on several levels as a philosophical treatise, a celebration of folklore and as a tragic love story. My good friend Joanna tells me she read it at the age of 14 in the ninth grade and can still recall her feelings of shock at certain events described in its pages. Dramatisation of the story can be seen today at the Yanka Kupala National Academic Theatre in Minsk.

The 1950s through to the 1970s saw the emergence of many notable poets, novelists and dramatists such as Sergei Zakonnikov, Viktor Kozko and Nikolai Matukovsky, while the late 1980s and 1990s saw the rise of an avant-garde movement. After 1986, the Chernobyl catastrophe began to feature as a dark and sombre theme, most notably in the works of Shamyakin, Alexievich, Karamazov and Buravkin. The work of writer and journalist Svetlana Alexievich is known across the world, particularly following her award of the Nobel Prize for Literature in 2015. Her works of non-fiction display perceptive insight into the realities of life in the days of the Soviet Union and subsequent to its disintegration. Among the best known are *Zinky Boys: Soviet Voices from the Afghanistan War*, *Chernobyl Prayer: A Chronicle of the Future* and *The Unwomanly Face of War*. Today her relationship with the authorities in Belarus could never be described as warm. Early in 2017 I was honoured to sit with her at a round-table discussion in Minsk during the International Book Fair, where those present included a number of prominent critics of the present regime. It made for a memorable experience.

Other contemporary writers of note include Baharevich, Khadanovich, Shchur, Niaklyayev (another Nobel Prize nominee who also stood in the 2010 presidential election), Babkov, Akudovich and Rublevskaya, all of whom honour and perpetuate the country's fine literary legacy.

MUSIC Musically Belarus boasts a mixture of artists and styles. Folk music derived from the culture of the east Slavic tribes, the Krivichi, Dryhavichy and Radzimichy, is particularly prominent; consistent themes through the ages have included the adventures of dynastic families and also a celebration of farming through the seasons. *Skomorokhs* (travelling minstrels) were the first to perform secular music in the early Middle Ages, but they were also prominent in promoting ritualistic songs and chants (such as canticles and psalms), which formed part of religious ceremonies.

Some 19th-century composers of note include Michal Kleafas Ahinski, born near Warsaw but of Belarusian extraction, who became a career diplomat in the Polish-Lithuanian Commonwealth. His best-known work is the polonaise *Farewell to my Homeland* (still popular today). Napoleon Orda, born in Brest region, was a close friend and associate of Frederic Chopin.

As with so much of the tradition and culture of the Belarusian people, the historical realities of suppression and of life inextricably linked to the land have been the inspiration for many an epic song chronicling the lives of farm labourers, peasants, workers and revolutionaries. A new form of musical expression, that of the stirring melody and heroic lyric, was born out of the escapades and heroism of the partisans and guerrillas in the Great Patriotic War.

The tide of Belarusian musical culture was to ebb and flow over the course of the 20th century according to the prevailing political circumstances of the times. Since the 1960s groups such as Pesnyary and Syabry, then later Palats, Krama and Troitsa, have all injected a more modern rock feel to traditional songs, but without losing sight of their heritage. Pesnyary formed in 1969 as an art-rock band embracing Belarusian roots music (they toured the USA in 1976), even writing and performing a number of rock operas that are still performed today in philharmonia.

Another contemporary band is Stary Olsa. Originally holding true to the best traditions of Belarusian music in medieval times, they have now turned to making covers of well-known hits following their own tour of the USA in 2016. The band has a significant following within Belarus, though some believe their current popularity is a nod more to pop culture than to highbrow tradition.

Today, a number of higher-education establishments in the country are devoted to the promotion and study of the theory, history and practice of musical folklore. The number of festivals devoted to ethnic music has also increased, attracting significant popular support not only through attendance at the events themselves, but also through high-profile television networking. A number of the more prominent Belarusian performers are showcased regularly in Poland and Lithuania, where substantial Belarusian communities still exist as a result of the many changes in national boundaries in this part of Europe over the centuries.

Rock music is hugely popular among the youth of the country (as well as aged rockers of vintage), the most famous Belarusian band being Lyapis Trubyetskoi. Until they announced an intention to split in August 2014 after 25 years together the guys had been on the scene since the early 1990s, their popularity never waning during a highly successful career. One of the fathers of Belarusian rock is Lyavon Volski, former leader of the band Mroya (later renamed N.R.M.), from whom he split in 2012 and the subject of numerous bans throughout his career. My good friend Joanna tells me proudly her mother was on the spot when it all began for him; they were in the same group at art school in Minsk in the early 1980s. Still popular, every new album attracts considerable interest. Irony and satire are strongly reflected in his work, the best known of his songs being *Try Charapakhi* ('The Three Tortoises'), a popular number that can often be heard chorused whenever and wherever a sing-song gets going.

Today there is a degree of diversity on the music scene. Names you are likely to hear mentioned include Akute, Palina Respublika, Zmicier Vaitsiushkievich (often compared to Lyavon Volski), Kiwi and Vuraj (both ethnic groups), Tonqi Xod (progressive rock), Gods Tower (heavy metal), Botanic Project and Addis Abeba (both reggae bands), J-Mors and Bez Bileta (both indie-pop with a large following), Neuro Dubel (punk) and rappers Belaroots.

Of more dubious worth culturally is Belarus's enthusiastic participation in the pan-European 'Eurovision Song Contest' since 2004. The year of greatest success was 2007 (when the country finished sixth), although 2009 winner Alexander Rybak (Norwegian but Minsk-born) was acclaimed throughout the country as a son of the soil. Indeed he often returns to his homeland to perform. In 2010 Belarus ended the contest one place above the United Kingdom, who came last. In 2017 something of a milestone was achieved when indie duo Navi performed in the Belarusian language.

THEATRE AND BALLET Traditional theatre was based on folk rituals and games, relying originally upon the work of strolling minstrels to spread its influence. This is not unique to Belarus, of course; far from it. Puppet theatres were particularly popular in the 16th century, a tradition that continues to this day, with a number of cities boasting their own professional or amateur ensemble. Popularity with children here is still very high indeed. In the 16–18th centuries new Jesuit schools had a significant impact on Belarusian culture and particularly the theatre, with students encouraged to stage plays. In the latter half of the 18th century performances were regularly given by theatre companies that were established and sponsored by rich magnates and estate owners, under whose patronage many of them flourished. Some of these companies consequently acquired professional status. The National Academic Theatre was established in 1920 under Zhdanovich, followed by the second Belarusian State Theatre in 1926, in the town of Vitebsk. A third was established in 1931 in Gomel: the former travelling theatre of Vladislav

Halubok. A talented playwright, director and painter in his own right, Halubok was arrested and shot in 1937 during Stalin's purges. The theatre was subsequently dissolved but Halubok's legacy endures today with the current Gomel theatre ensemble. The 1930s saw steady progress in the staging of plays devoted to historical events, but during the Great Patriotic War most troupes suspended their theatre-based activities. State theatre groups were evacuated to unoccupied Russia, some artists were conscripted into the army and sent to the front, while others chose (or were required) to take their shows on the road wherever possible to visit active army units and to maintain focus on keeping the morale and spirits of troops and civilians alike as high as possible.

After the war state censorship continued to prevail, though one of the consequences of Gorbachev's twin initiatives perestroika and glasnost was a relaxation of control and interference. The ban on avant-garde art was lifted and experimental theatre began to emerge, but since 1994 there has been some regression. In the West, take every opportunity you can to see performances of the **Belarus Free Theatre** company (66 *The Cut, London SE1 8LZ;* \ *020 7922 2998;* e *info@belarusfreetheatre.com;* w *belarusfreetheatre.com*). Established in 2005 in Belarus and now self-styled as 'the executive arm of the Ministry of Counterculture', the company still performs underground in Minsk at risk of being raided, though the founding members left to escape persecution in 2011 (finding political asylum in London). The very informative website will tell you all you need to know.

The history of professional ballet dates back to the middle of the 18th century, and in modern times the **National Academic Bolshoi Theatre of Ballet of the Republic of Belarus** has gained an enviable reputation, notwithstanding the higher profile of its equivalent in Moscow. Today, many towns of significant size will have their own flourishing professional or amateur opera and ballet troupe. Any opportunity to attend a performance of Belarusian ballet in Minsk should be eagerly taken; the standard is high, the price of admission ridiculously cheap by Western standards and there is a degree of informality about proceedings that lends itself to a most enjoyable experience. The audience is always full of children and families, with the dress code being relaxed in the extreme. No-one stands on ceremony, but unfortunately this has a downside. It is particularly unnerving, for example, to hear the occasional ringing of a mobile phone during a performance, and then hugely irritating when the call is actually answered.

In the field of opera the most renowned performer of the past was Larisa Alexandrovskaya. The most famous today is Oksana Volkova, while in 2015 Belarusian soprano Nadezhda Kuchar was crowned BBC Cardiff Singer of the World. Vladimir Gromov, Ilya Silchukov and Yuri Gorodetsky are the best-known male performers in the genre.

FINE ARTS The history of fine art as a synthesis of cultures from the East and West can be traced back to the second half of the 14th century. The development of icon painting and the production of book miniatures were greatly influenced by the art and folklore traditions of Byzantium, including a high level of manuscript illumination art. Before the 1917 Revolution watershed there was also a grand tradition of Baroque portraits, including the so-called 'Sarmat' portraiture of the nobility. Then, after the Revolution, the town of Vitebsk, still renowned for its links with the arts, became the centre of the revolutionary avant-garde movement, enabling brilliant and talented artists to forge their reputations. Perhaps the most famous of them all was Marc Chagall. Born in Vitebsk in 1887, Chagall gained his primary artistic education in the studio of the well-known painter Jehuda

THE BATHHOUSE CULTURE

The *banya* (bathhouse) is a distinct feature of rural Belarusian life, and you should gleefully accept any invitation to partake of its riches. Traditionally made of wood, it stands in the garden of a dwelling house, perhaps close to the river or stream in the rural hinterlands, though there are also communal public bathhouses within centres of population. Inside is a wood-heated stove containing stones. The stove is fuelled up ready for use over the course of the day and when the operating temperature is reached the door to the stove is opened and water is thrown on to the stones to create intense amounts of steam. Participants throw water and sometimes beer on to the hot stove to create a fragrant, steam-filled atmosphere. To enhance the whole experience, they slap each other with a sheaf of oak or birch twigs and leaves tied together in a bundle. This is done firmly and enthusiastically in order to exfoliate the skin. Usually, the sheaf has been soaked in natural oils for a few days prior to use. This intense aroma, when added to the steam, makes for a very heady atmosphere.

Three separate activities make up a complete cycle. First, participants sit in the bathhouse, on wooden slatted benches, to begin the process of perspiration. This initial phase normally lasts for 10 to 15 minutes before everyone takes a breather by sitting in the small anteroom (which is not much bigger than a large cupboard, but considerably cooler than the steam room) and having a beer. To maintain hydration, naturally. In the second phase, guests are invited to lie across a bench, first on their front and then on their back, while the host whacks them with the sheaf. Guests then return the compliment. At this point everyone repairs to the anteroom for another gulp or two of beer. Then it's back in for the final time, to thoroughly wash and rinse your tingling body with soap and water heated by the stove and decanted into a large metal bowl. Cold water will also be at hand and you can expect your hosts to be playful with it. Afterwards, everyone relaxes together in the anteroom with more beer and occasionally vodka, in which case the sensation of intoxication, after all that perspiring, is almost instantaneous. At this point, if you are deep in the country, expect to be invited to jump in the river or lake. If you are really lucky, it will be winter and you will be encouraged to roll in the snow.

Pen, before studying in France. Upon his return to Vitebsk, he founded, lived and worked at an arts school that attracted all of the best talent of the day from around the country. Today, the house where Chagall spent his youth is a popular visitor destination (page 264). When the ideological oppression of the Soviet Union was lifted in the early 1990s, artistic life became more dynamic and much more diverse. Design, photography and computer graphics became new media for expression, while the avant-garde movement of the Vitebsk art school also found new life.

Today the art scene continues to thrive as a form of expression not only for mainstream ideas, but also as a voice for contemporary underground movements. Minsk has a number of excellent galleries where works of historical significance rub shoulders with constantly changing exhibitions showcasing the work of modern artists. It's the same in all of the major cities. Indeed, the work of artists old and new is commendably accessible throughout the country. One of my personal contemporary favourites is Vladimir Shappo, whose studio is to be found in Minsk (w *shappo.org*).

2

Practical Information

WHEN TO VISIT

The likely (and clichéd) assumption for the uninitiated is that because Belarus used to be part of the Soviet Union, the weather will always be grey, featureless and, in winter, bitingly cold. This is partly correct, though each of the four seasons is separate and distinct, and boasts its own features. **Winter** is certainly bitingly cold for the most part (with the first snows tending to fall in late November), but the temperature does not really plummet until the turn of the year. While December is often wet and slushy, come January, the thermometer can free fall to the −30°s, with long periods of snow accompanied by bitter winds. The scenery is often dramatic: clear blue skies, a watery sun, heavy frosts and thick, immovable, impenetrable ice. But these conditions tend to be the exception rather than the rule and for the most part the temperature averages around −7°C with consistent and regular snowfall. It is a time when most people remain indoors unless necessity drives them outside to work or study.

Spring is a period of intense activity in the fields. This is also the time to see storks on the wing and nesting atop the high poles that are erected in villages for this very purpose. The temperature is generally warm and welcoming. I reckon that late May is probably the best time to visit Belarus, with the ever-lengthening days affording maximum opportunity to be outdoors and exploring (whether your ambling is urban or rural). **Summers** can be extremely hot, with temperatures into the 30s, while biting insects are voracious in forests and near to water. Be sure to wear long trousers and clothing buttoned to the neck and wrists, accompanied by some form of insect repellent (particularly at dusk). But don't be discouraged: this is a time of long days, balmy evenings, glorious sunrises and sunsets, with a verdant landscape and fresh produce in the markets and by the roadside. As if to store up reserves of fresh air and sunshine for those long winter nights, people spend as much time outdoors as they possibly can. In rural areas this means tending the fields, while in the town the promenade remains a favoured pastime.

Autumn is a glorious time to be in Belarus. Summers often last well into September, but come harvest time in October the colours of the fields and forests simply take your breath away. There is no real diversity of colour but almost everywhere as far as the eye can see, a golden scene stretches into the distance. One Sunday predawn morning in October, I left Mozyr in the south by car in pitch darkness to catch a lunchtime flight from Minsk. As the first rays of the sun began to illuminate the landscape with a deep and lustrous glow, accompanied by brilliant bursts of burnished yellow, the song *Fields of Gold* was playing on the radio. OK, so I know that's a really twee story to recount, but it was a lovely moment and one that I am very pleased not to have missed.

Simply because it remains a largely unknown destination, Belarus offers much more to experience than a single visit will allow, but as a starting point, a one-week adventure makes for a fascinating, if intense, first trip. It is not possible to see all of the key centres of interest in that time, so be selective. The best advice is to visit Minsk and probably at least one other of the big towns, plus as much of the rural hinterland in-between as can be accommodated in the time available. Below are some of the top sights, in no particular order.

MINSK The capital city and living monument to the grandeur of post-war Soviet urban planning, where expansive boulevards, stretches of water and vast green areas guard the last piece of the Old Town that the Nazis could not destroy. See page 121.

NATIONAL MEMORIAL COMPLEX AT KHATYN Just 54km from the capital, this complex commemorates the hundreds of villages the Nazis razed to the ground in the Great Patriotic War. See page 186.

BELARUSIAN STATE MUSEUM OF FOLK ARCHITECTURE AND RURAL LIFE Near the village of Strotchitsa, 12km from Minsk. See page 192.

MUSEUM TOWNS Make time to visit the museums and sites of the historical towns of **Mir**, **Njasvizh** (both UNESCO World Heritage Sites), **Novogrudok**, **Pinsk**, **Polotsk** and **Turov**. See pages 244, 184, 248, 216, 269 and 320.

BREST This frontier town in the southwest of Belarus, home to the Hero-Fortress, is where religious history was made in the 16th century (page 196) and where eastern and western Europe meet at the symbolic gateway to the old Soviet Union. See page 195.

GRODNO Located near the Polish border on the banks of the Nieman River, Grodno has beautiful architecture (including the stunning Polish cathedral) and historic Lithuanian connections. See page 225.

VITEBSK The birthplace of the painter Marc Chagall, with many summer arts festivals and rich artistic traditions. See page 253.

MOGILEV With its historical centre and the beautifully restored Leninskaya Street, this is the city where the last tsar of Russia, Nikolai II, had his final residence. See page 283.

GOMEL The country's second-largest city, home to the impressive park, palace and cathedral complex founded by Prince Rumyantsev in the 18th century. See page 295.

VETKA This town and district, home to 'Old Believers', has a world-class museum of iconography, the traditional weaving school at Nyeglubka, historic churches and sites of considerable ecological interest. See page 312.

NATIONAL PARKS Be sure to visit **Byelovezhskaya Puscha** (the third UNESCO World Heritage Site in Belarus), **Narach**, **Braslav Lakes**, **Berezinsky** and **Pripyatsky**

national parks, where the wilderness and biological diversity of the country can be enjoyed in a glorious celebration of the natural world and where ecological tourism is steadily beginning to take hold. See pages 218, 5, 278, 279 and 318.

SUGGESTED ITINERARIES Although the main tourist sites (identified in the previous section) form a good basis for the structure of a visit, the best way to get to the heart of the country and its greatest treasure, its people, is to strike out alone. This requires a degree of imagination and resilience, so do be sure it's a task you feel confident about embarking upon. In particular, you will need to be comfortable with the challenges of communicating in circumstances where no English is spoken. Increasingly this is much less of an issue in Minsk, though outside the capital things are different. Further, one of the hang-ups from the days of the old Soviet Union is a complete lack of understanding of the concept of the independent traveller. It also says much for the hospitality of the Belarusians that they are keen to share their country's riches by offering personal guides to everything that there is to experience. Guided tours will certainly show you a great deal, but the level of control over the structure and pace of arranged itineraries will not suit the traveller with an urge to explore. It's all a matter of personal choice. If you want somebody else to take care of all the arrangements, use the main travel agencies. But if your own autonomy is paramount, there is plenty of information online to help you organise a bespoke visit. If you have personal contacts within the country, so much the better. A major advantage of engaging the services of a travel agency is that the process of obtaining an entry visa will be considerably simplified, though the fast-evolving relaxation in visa requirements is making this less of an issue with the passage of time (page 54). However you arrange your visit, here are some options for that first trip but be warned; there's a huge amount packed into each, with little or no downtime to catch your breath!

Five days
- Take advantage of the five-day visa-free period to get to know Minsk
- Cities, history, the arts and folklore: Minsk–Khatyn–Dudutki–Strotchitsa–Vitebsk–Polotsk–Minsk
- Cities and history: Minsk–Grodno–Brest–Minsk
- Cities, ecology and the natural world: Minsk–Berezinsky and Narach national parks–Minsk
- Cities and museum towns: Minsk–Mir–Njasvizh–Novogrudok–Minsk

One week Both of these week-long trips would include visits between cities to ecological and historical sites of interest.

- Western Belarus: Minsk–Grodno–Byelovezhskaya Puscha National Park–Brest–Pinsk–Minsk
- Eastern Belarus: Minsk–Polotsk–Vitebsk–Mogilev–Gomel–Minsk

Two weeks The following will deliver the full experience of city and nature, arts and culture, history and society, but you might just need a holiday to get over it!

- Three nights: Minsk (with day trips to Khatyn, Dudutki and Strotchitsa)
- Two nights: Grodno via Mir, Njasvizh and Novogrudok
- Two nights: Brest via Byelovezhskaya Puscha National Park
- One night: Mozyr via Pinsk and Pripyatsky National Park
- Two nights: Gomel (with day trips to Vetka and locations affected by Chernobyl)

- One night: Mogilev
- Two nights: Vitebsk (with a day trip to Polotsk)
- One night: Minsk (with a final round-up of activities, including a performance by the State Ballet Company) via Berezinsky National Park

TOUR OPERATORS AND TOURIST INFORMATION

OUTSIDE BELARUS

Tour operators The number of tour operators in the UK offering programmes for visits to Belarus (generally in small groups) is slowly but steadily increasing as the country sharpens up its act on incoming tourism. The following is a selection but not an exhaustive list, so do your own research to check the very latest situation in the marketplace. Always be sure to satisfy yourselves on the small print, including bonding arrangements and the precise detail of what is included (and excluded) in the advertised price.

Explore ☎01252 883609; e sales@explore.co.uk; w explore.co.uk. Check out the 'Belarus Explorer' tour from £1,239 for 10 days.
Intrepid Travel ☎0808 274 5111; e ask@intrepidtravel.com; w intrepidtravel.com/uk . New to the Belarus market & now advertising its 'Highlights of Belarus' package from £1,084 for 11 days.
Naturetrek ☎01962 733051; e info@naturetrek.co.uk; w naturetrek.co.uk. This wildlife specialist markets its 'Belarus in Spring' tour from £1,695 for 8 days.
Regent Holidays ☎020 7666 1244; e regent@regentholidays.co.uk; w regent-holidays.co.uk. A choice of packages includes 'Best of Western Belarus' from £1,135 for 8 days.

The Travelling Naturalist ☎01305 267994; e sales@thetravellingnaturalist.com; w naturalist.co.uk. Specialising in wildlife & birdwatching holidays, the company's 'Secret Wildlife Wilderness' 8-day Belarus tour is £2,325.
Travel the Unknown ☎020 7183 6371; e enquiries@traveltheunknown.com; w traveltheunknown.com. Options include 'Belarus Explorer' from £1,995 for 10 days.
Undiscovered Destinations ☎0191 296 2674; e travel@undiscovered-destinations.com; w undiscovered-destinations.com. See the 'Belarus – Forgotten Europe' 10-day tour for £1,799.

Independent travellers For those intent on designing a bespoke tour of their very own, the internet is now a mine of information on everything you might possibly need to know. Just point your favourite browser at 'Belarus' and settle back for a good peruse. Alternatively, check out the list of websites on page 331. The Belarusian embassies in the UK and the USA also have information on Belarusian tour operators as well as stocks of brochures, leaflets and business cards.

IN BELARUS In Belarus itself a large number of tour operators compete for incoming business, many acting under the umbrella of the **National Tourism Agency of the Republic of Belarus** (*Room 909, Ministry of Sport & Tourism, 8/2 Kirova St, Minsk;* ☎*+375 17 203 71 99;* e *info@belarustourism.by;* w *belarustourism. by*), its main outlet being its excellent and enormously helpful website, which also signposts visitors to many other related resources. The agency was established by the State Ministry of Sport and Tourism in December 2001 to promote and co-ordinate overall support for the tourism market. It aims to develop the tourism potential of Belarus, certify hotels and tourist services, and train tourism professionals, and it has made excellent progress with its PR strategy in the last couple of years with an increasing number of written materials available in English. Further, the marketplace for independent tourist agencies that are not part of the state system is flourishing and there are now hundreds of standalone organisations, with new ones opening up for business all the time. However, do take care to check credentials and bonding arrangements before making any financial or contractual commitments.

The following is a selection of the largest, longest-established and most oft-used companies in operation, both state-run and independent. They are well known, have been prominent in the sphere for a number of years and have established reputations for decent service.

AlatanTour +375 17 327 74 17; e incoming@ alatantour.com; w welcomebelarus.com. Operating since 1993, this private company continues to maintain its reputation as one of the country's leading tour operators, offering a full range of services for private & business travel, including agro- & ecotourism as well as Jewish heritage tours.

✴ Association of Rural and Ecotourism 'Country Escape' +375 17 318 04 65, +375 44 590 19 10; e info@ruralbelarus.by; w ruralbelarus. by. Active in the market for 16 years, this not-for-profit NGO is a key co-ordinating body for the development of ecological & sustainable tourism. The association maintains a database of properties that are available for hire & is best placed to facilitate all necessary arrangements & bookings, though most Belarusian tourist agencies are also now actively promoting access to rural farmsteads for visitors intent on getting back to nature.

✴ Belarus Prime Tour +375 17 302 34 02; e incoming@belarusprimetour.com; w belarusprimetour.com; see ad, 1st colour section. This is my own partner of choice in all matters concerning Belarus tourism. I have worked with the company (an independent operation) for a number of years & have recommended their services to many travellers, all of whom have been well served. I commend the company to you. The full range of services that all other agencies offer are available here, but the company will always go the extra mile in delivering beyond industry standards, including specialist activities, cultural events & individually tailored tours.

Belarus Tour Service +375 17 200 56 75; e service@welcome.by; w visa.by; see ad, page 117. Another company with a track record of long-standing service in visa support, hotel bookings, local excursions & bespoke guides.

Belintourist +375 17 226 91 00; e incoming@ belintourist.com; w belintourist.com. In business for over 55 years, Belintourist is a long-established national tour operator specialising in visa support, hotel accommodation, transport/transfers & booking a diverse range of specialist tours & excursions.

Top-Tour +375 17 228 06 06; e booking@ topbelarus.com; w topbelarus.com. Active since 1992, the company offers visa support & a comprehensive package of services within the country, including in relation to accommodation, tour programmes, day excursions & leisure/ entertainment.

Viapol +375 17 200 00 84; e belarus@viapol. by; w viapol.com. Established for over 20 years, this operator specialises in tours around the country of varying duration in English.

Vokrug Sveta +375 17 306 43 60; e incoming@vokrugsveta.by; w vokrugsveta. by. This company has grown steadily since its foundation in 1994 & now claims a substantial percentage of all incoming tourism to Belarus in both the private & corporate sectors. All services can be accessed here.

TOURIST INFORMATION In the first three editions of this guide I cautioned travellers not to expect to find anything like as much as would be available elsewhere in the developed world by way of leaflets and brochures. However, under the auspices of the Ministry of Sport and Tourism, the fledgling tourist industry has now begun to sharpen up its act in terms of marketing and public relations. The product has branding at long last and, in my meetings with senior officials in Minsk, I now discern that some imaginative and strategic thinking is guiding the future development of the travel industry within the country. The National Tourism Agency has been using the adopted logo for its range of publications in many languages for some time now, and there is a considerable portfolio of brochures and leaflets to cover a broad range of activities and services of interest to visitors, although the use of English is occasionally rather quaint. So as well as finding leaflets relating to accommodation and some eateries, mostly in hotel lobbies, you will also be well served with brochures about museums, cultural events and visitor attractions. The excellent (and free) monthly listings magazine *where Minsk* is widely available at locations throughout the city. And the concept of the 'tourist information centre' that has been adopted in the rest of Europe for so long is at last catching on in Belarus. Full listing details are to be found in the chapters for each of the six cities. There is still a little way to go, however, in terms of the service ethic. In every city, staff at the TICs are enormously helpful and will go the extra mile when offering help and assistance. In many of them, some English is spoken and varying amounts of written materials in English are dispensed. But they still close for lunch and most are shut at the weekend. Although I still say it cautiously, things are definitely continuing to change for the better and real progress is being made. Yet the most frustrating thing of all remains the fact that there is a rare and precious commodity to market in this country in terms of tourism. I maintain that this is likely to be of the greatest interest to a significant constituency of travellers from the West (who will find here much that no longer exists in other parts of Europe, all of it less than 3 hours from London by plane), but the construction of the bridge between the two has progressed little beyond its foundations. The good news with all of this remains that now *really* is such a good time to find out for yourself what this delightful country has to offer before everybody else wakes up and catches on.

SPORTS TOURISM For a small country, Belarus has performed consistently well at successive summer and winter Olympic and Paralympic games for years, with the haul of eight gold medals at the 2016 Paralympics being the high point of achievement. In Max Mirnyi, the country had one of the top men's doubles tennis players in the world a few years ago, while in the same sport Victoria Azarenka is a former world number one and singles grand slam winner.

Track cycling and ice hockey world championships have both been held in Belarus in recent years, while in 2019 the country will host not only the European Figure Skating Championships but also the second European Games (w european-games.org), a multi-disciplinary competition that includes athletics, track cycling, canoeing, boxing, gymnastics and table tennis. Both the state and the people of the country see these games as an event of enormous significance; an indication at last (they believe) that Belarus is now taking its place in the world community after decades of isolation. The PR machinery was already in full swing when I visited Minsk early in 2018, with billboards across the city displaying the games' distinctive logo. The tourism industry believes an exciting opportunity to welcome new visitors in big numbers is on the horizon, and imaginative strategies are in development to promote the country on the world stage. The Academy of Public Administration has in place an ambitious programme to train students to act not only as volunteers at the games themselves but also as ambassadors to showcase all that Belarus has to offer visitors.

President Lukashenko (a major ice-hockey enthusiast) has decreed that every town is to have its own sports palace offering a full range of sporting opportunities to the country's youth. The state claims there are 23,000 sports facilities in Belarus for general public use and for spectators, newish venues such as the capital's Minsk Arena and the football stadium in Borisov (home to Premier League champions Bate) are superbly well appointed, while the National Winter Olympic Training

Centre at Raubichi has commendably fine facilities, particularly for participants in the sport of biathlon. And when the complete overhaul and refurbishment of the national football stadium in Minsk is finished (a construction project long in the implementation and due for completion early in the summer of 2018, ready for hosting the 2019 European Games), Belarus will have an impressive range of facilities to support the growing number of international tournaments now being scheduled into the future, and which are beginning to attract interest from sports fans abroad. This can only be good news for the country's tourism industry generally, and specifically for the infrastructural facilities and services (hotels, restaurants, bars and entertainment outlets) that will be an enduring legacy for local people and tourists alike.

ECOLOGICAL TOURISM A first experience of Belarus ecotourism came my way in 2007 when I stayed down on the farm in the picturesque village of Parichi on the banks of the delightful Berazhina River. During this visit, I also witnessed a second project, the ongoing restoration of one of the country's only original working windmills (from 1924). Between then and 2014 I stayed on other rural farmsteads, all small-scale projects run by local people of immense enthusiasm and commitment, all of them struggling to get going in the absence of significant financial support. All of my visits were utterly charming, though I had a real sense that the odds were heavily stacked against the future success of these projects.

But all of this is now changing for the better, significantly and at speed. The Association of Rural and Ecotourism 'Country Escape' (page 51) has been striving for many years to develop innovative tourism and environmental projects both to enhance economic and social activity in rural areas and to promote the eco-/agro-tourism product in Belarus. I met the association's Chair Dr Valeria Klitsounova early in 2018 to hear first-hand about the current state of the industry. In 2006 34 farmsteads were registered as being open for business, but by the end of 2017 that figure had grown to 2,317. It seems President Lukashenko himself buys into the concept, for it is said he is keen to see resources being targeted to support future development. With new enterprises coming into existence all over the country, Dr Klitsounova and 'Country Escape' are riding a wave of some potency that is now contributing significantly to the range of tourism facilities available to incoming visitors. Alongside the work of the association, cultural heritage and tourism courses are now on offer to students at universities in the country, while important links are being forged to learn from markets elsewhere in the world and to promote international co-operation.

All of this is good news, not only for tourists and travellers in terms of choices available to them when considering Belarus as a legitimate destination of choice, but also for the country's communities as it establishes and strengthens the resilience of local infrastructures.

MEDICAL TOURISM In keeping with many countries of eastern Europe and the former Soviet Union, Belarus is now marketing itself as a destination for those pursuing a range of medical treatments and recuperation at the expanding portfolio of clinics, health farms and sanatoria offering services to incoming visitors from abroad. For certain medical procedures the reputation of the USSR was regarded as cutting edge, and Belarus is seeking to take advantage of this growing market. Around 160,000 foreign nationals came here for treatments in 2015, the majority of whom were from Russia, but Belarus is increasingly more open for business to the wider world in this fast-developing area. Procedures are available in the fields

2

of oncology, ophthalmology, obstetrics, gynaecology, dentistry, neurosurgery, cardiology and cosmetic surgery, all at competitive cost. Further information can be found on the website of the Ministry of Health of the Republic of Belarus (w *minzdrav.gov.by*), while the National Tourism Agency will also be able to signpost specific services and providers. One of the prime tour operators in this sphere is MedTravelBelarus (w *medtravelbelarus.com*), whose comprehensive English website is a good starting point for anyone with an interest in coming here for medical tourism. Also facilitating a range of health services for incoming visitors from abroad are BelHealthCare (w *belhealthcare.co.uk*) and Clinics of Belarus (w *clinicsbel.com*). It goes without saying, of course, that all credentials should be vigorously checked before any commitment is made.

RED TAPE

When it comes to bureaucracy, Belarus is a world leader. Inevitably, this is a relic of the old Soviet days. The level of detail, process and checking involved in the most simple of procedures is mind-boggling. Of crucial importance, however, is the ability to smile and show the utmost patience and civility when faced with process and procedure. Anger and intolerance are viewed with disdain and will always be greeted with a wry smile, a shrug of the shoulders and a process at least twice as long as the original would have been. Just don't get flustered. You're not the boss here. It will always take as long as it takes.

The monolithic wall of red tape is of course at its finest when it comes to regulating entry arrangements for visitors from abroad. From its birth as an independent nation state, Belarus adopted the requirement of the old Soviet Union that visitors with foreign passports would only be allowed entry to the country with a visa. The convoluted process of obtaining one meant this was long regarded as a significant obstacle to encouraging incoming tourism. Things started to change early in 2015 with very limited relaxation of the rules permitting 72-hour visa-free access to Byelovezhskaya Puscha National Park, followed in 2016 by the opportunity to spend five days in the western half of Grodno oblast (see box, page 228), subject of course to complying with a lengthy list of requirements; and the process of applying for exemption was every bit as complex as the visa application itself! Then in January 2017 the President signed a decree establishing a new **visa-free regime** that came into force the following month (see box, opposite). Modifications have been made since that time and further relaxation of the rules is anticipated.

With the exception of visits falling into the categories permitting visa-free entry and subject to any further changes to the rules after we went to print, the reality is that all visitors to Belarus from the UK will require a visa before entry into the country. For UK applicants, the following documents should be submitted to the consular and visa section of the London embassy. These can either be delivered personally by the applicant or on his/her behalf by a visa services company, or sent by Royal Mail or by courier.

- A valid original passport or travel document with at least two blank pages available for visas. The passport must be valid not less than 90 days beyond the date of planned departure from Belarus.
- A completed visa application, which can be downloaded in standard form via the UK embassy website (w *uk.mfa.gov.by*).
- 'Visa support documents' depending on the purpose of travel, such as an original invitation or application from a Belarusian legal entity on headed

After years of slavish adherence to an unyielding requirement for incoming visitors to first obtain a visa as a precondition to entry, the rules are at last being relaxed. Since February 2017 a visa-free regime for Minsk for stays of up to five days has been in place. In January 2018 the regime was further loosened to permit ten-day tourist visits to certain parts of Brest and Grodno oblasts, and my Ministry sources tell me these are the first steps in a series of initiatives aimed at making entry arrangements significantly easier. At the time of writing, an imminent announcement was expected to increase the visa-free period from five to ten days for Minsk (check **w** bradtupdates.com/belarus for the latest before you travel). There is even talk of subsequent extensions to 30 and even 90 days for the whole country, though the timescale for this has yet to be set.

The most significant development means that foreign nationals from 80 states (including every EU member and the USA) are now permitted to stay in Belarus for five days without a visa, subject to arrival at and departure from Minsk National Airport by air. This does not cover flights from airports in Russia. Both arrival and departure days count towards the total of five. Visitors can return for further periods of up to five days, subject to the total stay not exceeding 90 days in any calendar year.

This new five-day regime is a very significant change and throughout 2017 ministry officials regularly advised me it was likely to be the first step in an ongoing process of further relaxing the rules. 'Watch this space' was very much the key message. Even a rudimentary analysis of the statistics shows that by the end of the year the new regime was already making a difference, with large increases in visitor numbers reported. Then on 26 December 2017 came another presidential decree confirming a further change with effect from 1 January 2018 to permit visa-free tourist stays of up to ten days in several areas of Brest and Grodno oblasts, with a consequent increase in the number of permitted crossings and checkpoints for this purpose. Further areas within the two oblasts will be added to the list in due course. There will still be an application process for permission to travel without a visa, but this latest loosening of the rules is further evidence of a clear strategic intention since 2015 to overhaul the visa regime, with the pace of change quickening significantly throughout 2017 and into 2018.

At long last, this may just be the key that finally opens the door into Belarus for the mainstream travel market. With things developing quickly and in a state of considerable flux, visitors should check on the very latest rules before embarking on their travel arrangements – see **w** bradtupdates. com/belarus. The following websites will all carry up-to-date information on current requirements and eligibility:

Republic of Belarus **w** belarus.by
Ministry of Foreign Affairs of the Republic of Belarus **w** mfa.gov.by
State Border Committee of the Republic of Belarus **w** gpk.gov.by
Embassy of the Republic of Belarus to the United Kingdom of Great Britain and Northern Ireland **w** uk.mfa.gov.by
Embassy of the Republic of Belarus in the United States of America **w** usa.mfa.gov.by

notepaper in the case of a business trip, or written confirmation of a hotel booking if the visit is for tourism.
- A recent passport-sized colour photograph meeting international requirements.
- A copy of the obligatory health insurance certificate. All foreign nationals are required to hold valid medical insurance for the duration of their stay, whether or not a visa is necessary. The policy must state its validity in the Republic of Belarus and there are other minimum requirements for the detail of the cover provided.

A visa application fee must also be paid (full details of which can be found on the embassy's website), the size of the fee being dependent upon the citizenship of the applicant and the type of visa requested. There are three types: transit (valid for two days), short-term (valid for up to 90 days) and long-term (valid for up to one year for any number of visits cumulatively totalling no more than 90 days). Additionally, visas may stipulate that they are single, double or multi-entry in nature. In each case, the amount of time permitted in the country will be for the period specified in the visa within the time of stated duration and cannot cumulatively exceed 90 days in any single year. The consular officer with responsibility for granting visas will normally make his decision within five working days (two in the case of urgent applications) and may impose such conditions as are deemed appropriate. The decision of the officer is final and there is no obligation to indicate the reasons for any refusal, in which case the application fee will not be returned. For my part I have never encountered a single issue when applying for a visa for dozens of visits over a period of 17 years, but I have spoken to one eminent journalist who was told during the course of a telephone conversation not to apply, because her application would be refused. She wasn't told why. I'm also aware of one other individual whose long-term visa was cancelled without notice or explanation at Minsk Airport as he flew out of the country for a short visit home.

Visas can be issued on an individual or group basis. Full details of the specific additional documentary evidence in the form of 'visa support documents' that will be required to be produced for different categories of visa (covering trips for business, participation in sports or cultural events, study, religious purposes, tourism, journalism, implementation of humanitarian programmes and private purposes) can be found on the Ministry of Foreign Affairs website (w *mfa.gov.by*). There are four pages of closely typed script going into the minutest detail, but a period of attentive study will tell you all you need to know. And of course, one advantage of booking your trip through an accredited tourist agency is that the intense headache of applying will be taken care of for you by somebody else. Me, I've always enjoyed the challenge …

Within five working days of arriving in Belarus, visitors should report details of their temporary address and duration of stay to the local Citizenship and Migration Office. Before passing through immigration, you will be required to complete a migration form in duplicate for presentation at your point of entry. Blank copies of this form should be handed out on the plane, train or bus before you reach the border. The authorities retain one part when you enter, while the other part is returned for you to obtain the required registration stamp. Guard it as you would your passport, at all times. It will be stamped at the Citizenship and Migration Office for you to hand in when you leave the country. If you are staying in a hotel, the stamping process will be discharged by the hotel's administration services. Do not, *under any circumstances*, fail to register within the required five-day period. Checking on departure used to be arbitrary but is now rigidly enforced. Just be sure to avoid the need for 'the Platinum

Emigration Service' (see box, page 58). I haven't repeated the oversight I made then and so don't know the consequences of a similar failure to register today, but it's just not worth the risk. When arriving in the country and presenting your migration form you may also be asked to show a copy of your medical insurance certificate. This appears to be an arbitrary process. It has never happened to me personally, but I have stood in line a number of times behind others who have been asked. Keep a copy of the certificate to hand on arrival, just in case.

Finally on the subject of entry requirements is a point that only applies in very specific circumstances. If entering Belarus from Moscow or other starting points within Russia with all *Belarusian* visa requirements satisfied, don't forget that you will also need a *Russian* transit visa to permit entry into and out of Russia *en route* to Belarus. Changes to this requirement cannot be ruled out, of course, so do check carefully before you travel.

IMMIGRATION AND CUSTOMS Procedures can be irritatingly convoluted. It's no longer necessary to complete the former customs declaration form on arrival and departure, though you will still be required to fill out a migration document. And technically, it is still not permitted to take Belarusian currency out of the country at the end of a trip, although I've never been challenged on this. Your first experience of Belarusian officialdom will be to stand in line waiting for a uniformed immigration official to scrutinise every last detail of your passport, visa and migration form, apparently with the deepest suspicion, before allowing you entry. But do take heart; procedures at Minsk National Airport are now much slicker than ever before, with many more immigration officers than ever awaiting your presence from the interior of their gleaming new booths in the shiny new arrivals hall.

The maximum that a single person can import into Belarus without duty is 50kg of luggage and contents for personal use, the value of which may not exceed €1,500, or €10,000 if travelling by air. Excess baggage is liable to duty at a rate of 30% of its value, but not less than €4 per excess kg. Specific items that can be taken into the country duty-free by persons aged 18 and over include three litres of spirits or beer and 200 cigarettes, 50 cigars or 250g of tobacco, subject to the total weight of all tobacco products not exceeding 250g. There is no limit on the amount of foreign currency that can be brought in, but sums in excess of US$10,000 must be entered on the migration document presented on entry. One thing you can definitely bring into the country without having to pay duty is a very large lawnmower. I know, because I've done it. It was an experience that sorely tested my Russian, though not as much as when I took 24 full-size dummy heads through customs (resuscitation aids to help with an injury minimisation programme we were running for children

I should mention at the start of this tale that it is now ten years old and that nothing like it has happened to me since. I'm sharing it not as a representation of what to expect, but purely for its historic entertainment value, a purpose for which I'd like to think it still retains a degree of validity. You can be the judge of that. Arriving at Minsk National Airport for our flight home, I had an uneasy feeling when two militia officers strode out of the terminal. They headed for us with far too much purpose and intent for comfort. We had just paid the cab driver and were about to check in for the London flight. 'Good day. Passports please.' While one stood sentinel, the other leafed through the pages. When he found the migration document nestling at the back and turned it over to find it blank and unstamped, I'm sure a flicker of a smile played at the edges of his mouth. 'There is no registration stamp. Why not? This is a very big problem.' All of my visits to that point had been on official business and not once in the past had it proved necessary for us to register locally. But it seemed that the rules had changed and I instantly had a feeling that I knew where this was all leading.

We were instructed to follow the officer into the terminal, where he again looked at the migration document. Again, 'This is a very big problem.' He took out his mobile, spoke quietly into it and 30 seconds later, another militia officer appeared, this time with a bigger hat. He too looked at the document, shook his head and said with grave solemnity that this was 'a very big problem'. The two of them turned their backs and whispered to each other, before our new-found friend motioned for Richard and me to go with him.

As we reached the end of the terminal and passed through a small door, the turn of events that I had started to expect did indeed come to pass. 'Do you have money?' he asked. I replied that I had some roubles, but this clearly wasn't the right answer. 'No. Dollars.' Now that the likely endgame was becoming more apparent, I was able to start thinking a little more clearly about an exit strategy. My big worry had been that we would be detained until our flight had gone, which meant that we would have to stay another night, by which time our visas would have expired. Then we would have been in real trouble. We were instructed to follow the officer into a very stuffy lift, with barely enough room for two nervous travellers, two large bags and a militia man with a large hat who held every card in the deck. We descended all the way to the bottom and stepped out into a vast, gloomy and deserted area. He stood looking at me, expectant and confident of his position. I took a deep breath, apologised for the oversight, stressed that it was entirely unintended and asked what we could do to address the difficulty. 'This is a very

in schools and kindergartens). On this occasion there was a short but entertaining stand-off when the official tried to insist that duty was payable, but he soon got bored and allowed all 25 of us in without charge.

Medical insurance is required for all foreign citizens travelling to Belarus (whether visa-free or not) and, to be eligible for emergency medical care, visitors should possess a medical insurance agreement with a Belarusian insurance company, or with an authorised foreign insurance company (as will be the case for most travellers). The visa application form calls for full details of your policy and it's essential to have a copy of the policy and schedule with you for the duration of your stay. These papers will be needed to access medical care and you may also be asked to produce them on arrival at the border and big problem for you. The court will impose a very heavy fine. But I can fix it. If you give me a hundred dollars.' The endgame at last. I thought for a few seconds and then nodded. He smiled and indicated that we should join him in the lift again. Just after it began to ascend, he pressed the 'stop' button and with a judder and a bump, we came to a halt. The defining moment had come. If I didn't pay up, then it was clear that we weren't getting on our flight. But what if I did offer him money, only for him to announce that now, we were in serious trouble? Breach of immigration laws was one thing, but attempting to bribe an officer of the state was a different matter entirely.

In reality, I'm sure that it took only a few seconds to make the decision, but it felt like hours. I reasoned that US$100 in the officer's back pocket was going to be much more important to him than ensuring observance of the laws of the land. Not entirely with conviction, I reached into my wallet, counted out the last hundred that I had left (a lucky break) and handed over the wad. He smiled, folded it away (it really did go into his back pocket) and pressed the 'start' button. I thought Richard was going to faint. But as we walked back into the departure lounge the tension had palpably relaxed. Except that we still had two major obstacles to overcome. There were two official procedures to be observed in terms of checking our documents before we could leave and I was starting to envisage two more 'fees' of a hundred dollars each. And I had no more dollars. I mentioned this to my militia friend, but with a smile and a reassuring arm on mine, he told me that everything would be OK.

Bless him, he was clearly a man of honour. After a cursory word with a colleague, who went over to have a word with somebody else, we were ushered through at speed. The final check of the papers, before a stern officer in uniform, can often take 5 minutes and more. He/she will scrutinise every single page of the passport, scan the photograph, occasionally pick up the phone and sometimes summon a colleague to recheck everything, all of the time looking quizzical and glancing up to look into your face. This time? Ten seconds at most. He took my passport, turned straight to the right visa, stamped it with a flourish and handed it back. We were through and out. But Richard didn't relax until our plane had landed at Milan for our connection and he was well inside the terminal on terra firma. The moral of the tale is a statement of the blindingly obvious. Never, ever play fast and loose with bureaucracy and red tape in this country. And always have a few dollars spare, just in case you need an upgrade in services.

if making a personal application to the local Citizenship and Migration Office to register your stay within the required period of five working days. The risks covered by your policy must meet the requirements of the laws of the state and be valid on Belarusian territory. The minimum liability limit is €10,000, though most standard policies on the market will meet this requirement many times over. Should you (unwisely) be travelling without the benefit of insurance, representatives of Belarusian insurance companies will provide the necessary insurance agreements and certificates at any border-crossing point, with premiums for foreign citizens ranging from €2 for a stay of up to four days to €85 for a stay of one year. However, medical insurance is not required for tourists with transit visas crossing Belarus, diplomats and official delegations, crew members of air and rail vehicles, citizens of the CIS states or holders of travel documents issued to stateless persons and refugees.

As with the visa regime, up-to-the-minute information on the rules relating to immigration, customs, duty and insurance can be found on the official website of the Ministry of Foreign Affairs of the Republic of Belarus (w *mfa.gov.by*). See also the site of the State Customs Authorities of the Republic of Belarus (w *customs.gov.by*).

EMBASSIES Embassies for UK and US travellers are listed below, but more details on others can be found at w embassypages.com/Belarus. For a full list of Belarus's embassies abroad, go to w embassy.goabroad.com/embassies-of/belarus.

E UK 37 Karla Marksa St, Minsk 220030;
**+375 17 229 82 00; **e ukin.belarus@fco.gov.uk;
w ukinbelarus.fco.gov.uk

E USA 46 Starovilyenskaya St, Minsk
220002; ****+375 17 210 12 83/217 73 47;
e consularminsk@state.gov; **w** by.usembassy.gov

GETTING THERE AND AWAY

BY AIR

To Minsk All international flights and most of those from the other CIS countries go to **Minsk National Airport**, formerly also known as **'Minsk-2'**, situated approximately 40km east of the city on an extension of the M2 motorway. The city's other airport (**'Minsk-1'**) closed, perhaps unsurprisingly, in 2015. The terminal building was a prime example of post-war Stalinist design and flights out of it were something of an experience. Whenever I mentioned to anyone locally that I was flying out of Minsk-1 on an internal flight, the response was universally the same: 'don't do it, under any circumstances'. I was always advised that safety records for internal flights were appalling. The same is said for all internal flights within the countries of the former Soviet Union. I'm glad to be able to say that I experienced internal air travel here (and lived to tell the tale), but it's not something I would be keen to repeat.

Charmless but functional, and a glorious monument to Brutalist Soviet architecture, Minsk-2 was extensively modernised in 2005. Further significant structural works were undertaken in time for the World Ice Hockey Championships held in Minsk in the spring of 2014, with additional works since then to upgrade facilities and services to the standard to be expected of an airport serving a major European capital city. All is now (very) shiny and (very) new with announcements in English and Mandarin, while the arrivals and departures board seems to grow bigger every time I pass through. Not many years ago this airport serviced just a handful of flights each day, but things are now developing rapidly and I take this as yet another reliable indicator that visitor numbers are significantly on the increase.

A proportion of the terminal building is still a vast network of stairs, doors and unlit areas with nothing going on in the spaces between, though there are now escalators at long last. Most of the facilities are collected in and around the departure gates themselves, of which you can find details on the helpful English pages on the airport website (w *airport.by*). There is free Wi-Fi and an abundance of seating, and one good point to note is that the price of refreshments is still commendably low. The offices of all airline companies operating to and from Belarus are on the departures level, but they are often closed. For your return flight out of Minsk the duty-free facilities (found after you check through) are continuing to expand to match the increase in passenger numbers, with the usual retail outlets and café facilities at your disposal. There is also an ATM on arrival in the baggage hall. One word of caution; my correspondent Richard Madge reports that even though some airlines are encouraging passengers to check in online, the airport is not yet equipped with scanning equipment for electronic boarding passes. Do bear this in mind if you intend to use your mobile device for this purpose.

For **access to and from the city** centre, expect to pay up to BYN60 for a one-way ride by taxi, though I've heard from one traveller that there is now an agreed fixed rate of BYN30 that all taxis should offer, so do check with the driver before you get in. The journey takes approximately 30 minutes in normal conditions and more in rush-hour traffic. Buses run from outside the arrivals area of the terminal building (gates 5–6) to the city's central train and bus stations, with limited stops *en route* (*Service 300E; approx hourly between 06.00 & 23.00 (half-hourly at peak times); 1hr; BYN4 one-way*). Tickets can be purchased inside the terminal building or from the driver. If you want to feel like a local as soon as you get here look for *marshrutka* (minibus) services 1400TC or 1430TC from the same location. Journey times and cost are pretty much the same. The Ministry of Sport and Tourism told me some years ago that 2015 would see the opening of a brand new express train service connecting the airport to the city centre. Passengers are still waiting. I do hope it happens one day, because it will certainly transform access arrangements.

Airlines The number of carriers flying into the country is on the increase but none of them are budget airlines and as a result, the cost of air travel is not cheap. The unavailability of budget flights direct to Minsk is less than helpful in promoting Belarus as an attractive destination for incoming tourism, but this position is not expected to change anytime soon. The national airline is Belavia, which has direct flights from London Gatwick and Manchester. When flying to Minsk I always use Belavia, though in the past I have also flown from the UK with Lot Airlines (via Warsaw), Lufthansa (via Frankfurt) and Alitalia (via Milan). There is more choice of flights by doing it this way, but the travel time is considerably longer and there is little to choose between them in terms of cost. The main airlines serving Minsk National Airport direct are as follows:

Aeroflot w aeroflot.ru. Daily flights from Moscow; 1hr 30mins.

airBaltic w airbaltic.com. 4 flights weekly from Riga; 1hr.

Air China w airchina.com. 3 weekly flights from Beijing; 9hrs 20mins.

Austrian Airlines w austrian.com. Daily flights from Vienna; 1hr 50mins.

Azerbaijan Airlines w azal.az. 2 weekly flights from Baku; 3hrs 30mins.

Belavia w belavia.by. The national carrier. Daily flights to various European capitals and countries of the former Soviet Union. Flights from London Gatwick leave Wed, Fri & Sun; 2hrs 55mins. 1 weekly flight from Manchester; 3hrs 10mins.

Czech Airlines w csa.cz. Daily flights from Prague; 1hr 45mins.

Etihad Airways w etihad.com. 3 flights weekly from Abu Dhabi; 6hrs 5mins.

Finnair w finnair.com. 3 flights weekly from Helsinki; 1hr 20mins.

LOT w lot.com. Daily flights from Warsaw; 1hr 10mins.

S7 Airlines w s7.ru. Regular flights to Moscow (1hr 20mins), Novosibirsk (4hrs 45mins) and St Petersburg (1hr 15mins).

Turkish Airlines w turkishairlines.com. 5 flights weekly from Istanbul; 2hrs 30mins.

Ukraine International Airlines w flyuia. com. 2 flights a day from Kiev; 1hr 5mins.

UTair Airlines w utair.ru. 2 flights daily from Moscow; 1hr 20mins.

Uzbekistan Airways w uzairways.com. 2 flights weekly from Tashkent; 5hrs 15mins.

Via Lithuania
An alternative worth considering is to fly to **Vilnius** in Lithuania, and this is my route of choice if I'm not flying direct to Minsk. A number of budget airlines include this destination in their schedules, my preferred operator being

Wizz Air (w *wizzair.com*), which flies to Vilnius out of Doncaster/Sheffield (*2 flights/week; 2hrs 30mins*), Belfast (*2 flights/week; 2hrs 50mins*) and London Luton in the UK (*2 flights/day; 2hrs 45mins*). With a degree of forward planning, this is a very cheap way of getting close to the Belarusian border. There is easy access into Vilnius itself from the airport and then several fast and comfortable routes by modern train and bus every day to Minsk, with journey times between 2½ hours and 3 hours for the train, and around 4 hours for the bus, including time spent crossing the border. Minsk is only 90 minutes from the Lithuanian border by road. The only downside is that the times of trains and buses to and from Minsk are not well co-ordinated with flight arrival and departure times. Entry at budget cost via Lithuania is also possible by flying Ryanair (w *ryanair.com*) from London Stansted to **Kaunas** (*5 flights weekly; 2hrs 35mins*) and then taking the express bus from outside the passenger terminal to Minsk. The bus schedule is said to co-ordinate with the times of every incoming and outgoing Ryanair flight, but do check ahead to ensure this is the case when you want to travel. It is possible to hire a car in Lithuania for entry into Belarus by road, but it's expensive to do so.

Via Ukraine Another option is to fly to Kiev in Ukraine. Many international airlines fly there, including British Airways. You can then hire a car and enter Belarus from the southeast, again with cost implications. The drive to the border from Kiev takes around 2 hours, with the drive to Gomel on the other side taking no more than 45 minutes. Do bear in mind that whether you enter Belarus from the northwest via Vilnius, or from the southeast via Kiev, in each case there is the unknown factor of waiting times (plus bureaucratic inconvenience) at the land border crossing. It all depends on how adventurous you are feeling.

BY TRAIN TO BELARUS *by Nicky Gardner, lead author of* Europe by Rail *(w europebyrail.eu)*
The one thing you will quickly discover on any visit to Belarus is that it reshapes your view of Europe, and such a different perception of the continent will be all the more vivid if you travel overland. West Europeans heading east by train to Belarus discover that our home continent is far larger than they ever imagined. If you are starting in Britain or anywhere else in western Europe, try and make time to travel by train to Belarus. Do it just once, and you may well be seduced by the entire experience.

Direct trains to Belarus Belarus is very well connected by international trains. Indeed, there are direct year-round trains to Belarus from a dozen different countries. In Minsk, you can board trains that will take you directly to the French Riviera, the Alps or to Siberia. Comb the departure boards and you'll find trains leaving for the shore of the Black Sea, ports on the Baltic coast or by the Arctic Ocean, or even remote communities in the Kazakh steppes. Belarusians take immense pride in that connectivity deriving from the country's position at the very heart of Europe. Taking the train is an essential part of the Belarusian experience.

You can travel in style in Russian Railways' (*RZD;* w *eng.rzd.ru*) comfortable sleeping cars from cities across western and central Europe direct to Minsk and other Belarusian cities. These Russian trains will often be bound for Moscow, but it is perfectly possible to book just to cities in Belarus.

See the box opposite for a selection of rail routes across Europe. In addition to these, there are also year-round direct trains to Minsk from Genoa, Innsbruck, Linz, Poznań and Verona, as well as from over 100 cities and towns across the Russian Federation and many cities in Ukraine.

On most services all passengers are accommodated in sleeping cars

From	Frequency per week	Travel time to Minsk (hrs)	Other stations served in Belarus
Berlin	3	14–17	Brest, Orsha
Frankfurt (Main)	1	23	Brest, Orsha
Milan	1	34	Brest, Orsha
Nice	1	39	Brest, Orsha
Paris	1	30	Brest, Orsha
Prague	1	19	Brest, Orsha
Riga	3–4	11	Polotsk, Molodechno
Strasbourg	1	26	Brest, Orsha
Vienna	1	20	Brest, Orsha
Vilnius	31–34	3–5	Molodechno, Orsha
Warsaw*	9	7–10	Brest, Orsha

* In addition to the regular services from Warsaw to Minsk, an innovation for 2018 is a new fast train each morning from Warsaw to Brest (*4hrs*), where there are convenient onward connections to cities throughout Belarus. Warsaw also has a new direct daily train to Grodno in Belarus (*5hrs*). With these two new options, the Polish capital is thus now a good jumping-off point for short hops into neighbouring Belarus – see page 64 for details.

The information in this section reflects the pattern of rail services in early summer 2018, but it is always worth checking details before travel.

If you are travelling by train to Belarus from the east, you'll find excellent connections. About ten trains daily leave Moscow for Minsk, the fastest taking under 8 hours. Services from St Petersburg to Minsk are less frequent and slower (*9hrs*), although if you are bound for Vitebsk (*13hrs*) and the northeast corner of Belarus then this is a useful option.

The Trans-European Express

The classic route to Belarus from the west is from Paris, where the Trans-European Express leaves every Thursday evening for Minsk and Moscow. Despite its name, this train is hardly an express. It dawdles, and is all the better for it.

The route sticks to traditional rail lines through France and Germany rather than the new high-speed routes that defy the warp and weft of the landscape. On a spring or summer evening, it's a wonderful way to start your journey to Belarus, cruising past the vineyards of the Champagne region as you relax over dinner in the train's Polish restaurant car.

Shortly before midnight, you'll cross the River Rhine near Strasbourg, where arrival in Germany is marked by the magnificent mosque on the east bank of the river at Kehl. By next morning, your Russian train will be skirting lakes and forests on its approach to Berlin. The train slips through Poland on the second day of the journey and in the early evening it approaches Poland's eastern border. All frontier formalities are conducted on the train, with Polish officials boarding at Terespol, the last station in Poland.

The train then crosses the valley of the River Bug, which in the soft evening light can be extraordinarily beautiful. The very fact that the valley was for so long the

Amsterdam	1,739	Paris	2,129
Berlin	1,120	Prague	1,141
Budapest	1,110	Rome	2,268
Helsinki	1,148	Sofia	1,753
Kiev	580	Warsaw	550
London	2,180	Vienna	1,164
Moscow	700	Vilnius	215

western edge of the Soviet Union and still today marks the outer edge of the EU (and Fortress Europe) has given it protected status. The wetlands, reed beds and backwaters of the Bug Valley have been out of bounds to mere mortals for decades, allowing the preservation of a natural wilderness.

Next, the train crosses the valley on a long bridge. On the east side of the river, passengers are greeted by the rich red battlements of Brest Fortress and by a huge sign in Cyrillic welcoming them to Belarus – a reminder that the Bug is a fault line in alphabets as well as in politics. After Belarusian officials have completed their border checks, the train is shunted into a shed where the bogies are adjusted to suit the wider-gauge tracks that are the norm in Belarus and the Russian Federation. You can stay on board while this takes place.

This is train travel as it should be: all passengers are accommodated in comfortable sleeping cars and a restaurant car is there for passengers who want to munch their way across Europe. The Polish restaurant car, which is attached from Paris to Warsaw, serves good international dishes at reasonable prices, although the wines are pricey. A Russian restaurant car, which is hooked up to the train at Brest, serves good-value Russian fare.

The timings are such that arrival in Minsk is at an uncomfortably early hour. It's better, we suggest, to alight in Brest and let that city be your first introduction to Belarus. If you are determined to head directly to Minsk, then bear in mind that some of the direct trains from Berlin to Minsk (*14hrs; €110 one-way*) give a more civilised arrival time, reaching the capital around noon. Note that there are handsome discounts for youths, seniors and anyone travelling on or around their birthday or wedding anniversary, as on most Russian trains.

Connections from the UK An early afternoon departure from London on Eurostar gives a convenient connection for the early evening departure of the Trans-European Express from Paris's Gare de l'Est. An alternative by rail from London is to travel by day to Berlin (changing *en route* in Brussels and Cologne). In the German capital, you can connect on Saturday or Monday evenings on to a Russian Talgo train that reaches Minsk at noon the following day. The total journey time from London to Minsk is about 27 hours, and one-way fares on this route start at under €150.

Back-door routes into Belarus As the box on page 63 indicates, there are some useful back-door routes into Belarus using Polish trains that terminate at the first station after crossing the frontier. The new morning train from Warsaw to Brest is a good choice for travellers staying overnight in the Polish capital who want to arrive in Belarus at a civilised hour (*4hrs; from €10 one-way*). Another daytime route from Poland goes to Grodno, where a direct train leaves Kraków early each morning, stopping in Warsaw around 08.00, and then continuing via Białystok (in northeast Poland) to Grodno in Belarus (*5hrs; one-way €15*). This cross-border line was once used by the grand expresses from Berlin to St Petersburg, but is now reduced to the status of a minor railway with just this one daily train each day entering Belarus. The train returns from Grodno to Warsaw and Kraków in the afternoon.

The scenery on this route is very fine, with the train traversing beautiful open heath and birch woods on the run from Białystok towards the border. The Polish border checks are made at Kuźnica Białostocka (which is the last halt before the train leaves the EU). On the Belarusian side, the train pauses at an improbably remote spot in the forest just after crossing the border, where customs and immigration officials climb on board. The main immigration procedures are handled upon arrival at Grodno station.

Finally, do bear in mind that Grodno and Brest are now covered by the visa waiver scheme for travellers arriving on the trains mentioned here, subject to compliance with the specific rules of the scheme (see box, page 55).

Arriving at Minsk Station *by Nigel Roberts*

The relatively new railway station is situated right in the heart of Minsk and all international trains arrive and depart from here. As a major crossing point for services throughout the continent, it's loud, full of travellers wheeling cases, jostling and pushing, always hot and a fantastic people-watching opportunity. After disembarking, newly arrived passengers exit the platforms via ramps into the basement beneath the station, where toilet facilities, the left-luggage office, a few small shops and a café can be found. The maze of subterranean walkways also leads to the metro station situated beneath the station square, as well as to various exits by stairway into the square itself, where the lofty towers known as the City Gates dominate the scene. From the basement, stairs lead up to the ground floor, where you will find a currency exchange, small retail outlets, general enquiry windows and ticket booking offices, while postal, mobile phone and banking services are located on the first floor. The second floor has a café, bar, waiting rooms, currency exchange and more shops. A restaurant and a bar, as well as administration offices, are located on the third (top) floor. The whole of the station's frontage is glass, so the higher you go, the better the views of the world outside and through the City Gates, as well as down into the station below. For those in need of a bed on arrival, the Hotel Express is located right next to the station. It is a relatively straightforward task to reach any part of the city by metro, bus, trolleybus or taxi from the railway station square. The website for the state railway system (w *rw. by*) is very informative and now has English pages with excellent graphics telling you all you need to know about timetables, services and the country's top 20 stations.

BY COACH   A number of options exist for coach travel to Minsk and other cities within Belarus. From London, operator **Eurolines** (w *eurolines.com*) serves destinations across continental Europe, while on the continent itself **Ecolines** (w *ecolines.net*) runs a variety of additional onward routes into the country. Comparison websites such as **Check My Bus** (w *checkmybus.co.uk*) and **Go Euro** (w *goeuro.co.uk*) will tell you all you need to know about services, timetables and costs. Expect the total journey time from London to Minsk to be around 35 hours. It's the longest and the most tiring way to cover the distances, of course, and with competitive rail and air fares widely available, it may not necessarily be the cheapest.

If you are travelling on a tight budget, bear in mind that there are some very attractive fares on cross-border coach services from neighbouring countries. Several coaches each day link Vilnius with Minsk (*one-way €11*), with journey

It is 19.40 on a dark, wet and windy September night. We have been on the road north from Kiev for the last 2 hours, with only a vast panoply of stars for illumination. But we are approaching the border area and it has begun to rain heavily. We are crossing into Belarus from the Ukrainian side by car and a line of long, low buildings has just appeared out of the blackness on the treeline. Tatyana confirms they are the administration and living quarters of the border guards. Beyond them lies deep, impenetrable darkness, with mile upon mile of forest. I am immediately reminded of a black-and-white spy drama from the 1960s. The rain beats down on the roof of the car as the gloom intensifies. 'Sometimes,' says Tatyana with a deep sigh, 'people wait here for three days. The queues can be very long.'

Little by little, we inch towards the first obstacle: Ukrainian emigration. Shadowy figures drift in and out of the darkness. We reach the head of the queue and an official in uniform peers through the car window at our passports. Then we move painfully slowly to the next checkpoint, a large, purpose-built, multi-storey monument to officialdom. As we wait, I ask Tatyana about security along the length of the border. 'It's a big stretch to police,' I say. 'How is it patrolled?' She and Yura exchange views in Russian, before agreeing that most of the roads are impassable, save for the official crossing points, other than on foot. And right now, the other official crossings are closed, so this is the only means of access by road between Ukraine and Belarus.

Plain-clothes officials mingle with uniformed soldiers and militia, all under blazing arc lights. We reach the front of the queue, where two soldiers (one sporting a very large peaked hat) sit impassively at a small table, surrounded by pens, paper, ancient computer hardware and a scanning device. Out jumps Yura to hand over sheaves of passports and stamped paperwork. Another huge hat joins the first at the flimsy table. One of them scrutinises every single page of our passports and scans in the photographs, before purposefully pressing keys on his keyboard (one finger at a time), occasionally glancing up at his screen as he types. We notice with some amusement that his table, the extent of his domain, is only partly protected from the elements by the overhead canopy, so that the many wires coming out of the back of his kit are now being liberally rained upon. As we pass by, he stares wistfully at us from under his enormous peaked hat, perhaps longing to be a passenger in a car that takes him away somewhere, anywhere.

And so into no man's land. No lights, just darkness stretching into the night. Unexpected, ghostly figures emerge from the gloom. All are women, pushing bicycles with one hand, struggling with umbrellas in the other and peering through every car window as they pass by, offering coffee and food from their panniers. One by one, engines are switched off and lights extinguished. After 20 minutes, all is dark and silent. The rain stops as suddenly as it began, and overhead the vista is once more a stunning display of stars. I fall in and out of fitful sleep. 'We should be through … in the next 24 hours,' offers Tatyana and it is not easy to spot if this is irony or a cheap shot at humour. As I ponder this, the driver of the lorry next to us in the parallel queue fiddles irritably with the aerial of his compact portable television, as the screen changes from images of lurid colour to grainy black and white. Every 10 minutes or so we start to inch forward, just one car's length at a time. Now more shadowy figures criss-cross the lines of traffic, sometimes standing in small groups, their faces eerily lit by a combination of cigarette ends and vehicle tail lights.

Our progress is mind-numbingly slow. To our right, a bicycle vendor strikes it lucky, as a lorry driver beckons her over and gestures for her to pour coffee into a plastic cup from her flask. Then, much to our surprise, our progress quickens and the next booths appear closer and closer, grotesquely backlit by huge overhead arc lights. The guards seem to have decided that the lorries are going nowhere that night, for their queue has ground to a complete halt. Another very large hat appears at the driver's window and Yura tells the official he has three 'foreigners' on board, from England. Three immigration forms appear through the open window from an unseen hand. There is much more activity here; more people, more uniforms, more women on bicycles, more noise, more light. There is only one queue now and we finally reach the front. Our guard is a striking blonde woman; her friendly manner is most unexpected, but deceptive. She peers alternately at our passports and through the open door, softly speaking our names in anticipation of some recognition on our part. She motions our vehicle forward and invites us to park up, still on the exit lane, but kind of out of the way, in an 'in the way' sort of way. Yura accompanies her into the office while she scans our passports.

Ten minutes later, Yura returns and opens the door. 'She wants to see your medical insurance papers.' He scurries off with them. Then two more very big hats walk out with Yura, deep in conversation. Tatyana too is summoned to join the gathering, before she returns to open the car door to enquire sweetly of Richard as to whether or not he has any more photo ID, as the computer is unable to scan his passport photograph. He gazes imploringly into my eyes and I know at once that he has been transported back to our little adventure at Minsk Airport, when it cost me US$100 to get us out of the country (see box, page 58). 'Don't worry, this won't be a problem,' I say, as I begin to feel the first flutterings of irritation. Here we go again …

But it's all a game. Yura returns to move the car 2m forward and perhaps 10cm closer to the kerb, presumably as instructed, before returning back inside. The merry-go-round spins on. Yura keeps pacing to and fro and the hats keep scrutinising our papers. A large hat appears and gestures us forward towards the nirvana of customs (and the final control point) 100m in the distance. Our hearts lift, but the dawn is a false one. Yura does indeed drive towards the customs zone, but when we are tantalisingly close, he turns through 180° (as instructed by the hat) and parks up near to the office. He turns off the engine, climbs out and disappears. He is gone maybe 15 minutes and we begin to wonder if we are ever going to escape this scene. Then a figure appears from the inky blackness, striding purposefully forward, head down and hand clutching a wad of documents. It is Yura. He flings open the door, climbs in with purpose and we drive around a corner … and into a queue. Yura is quizzed by a large hat, but this one has the inclination neither for confrontation nor for sport and we are flamboyantly gestured forward into another queue, where another booth and another hat await. We are waved on and before we know what is happening, Yura is gunning the car into the Belarusian night, while an astonishing display of stars shines in the firmament overhead. The whole experience took 2 hours 45 minutes from start to finish and I wouldn't have missed it for the world.

times between 4 and 6 hours. A one-way fare from Vilnius to Grodno is around €8, with the journey taking approximately 5 hours. Half a dozen companies also offer direct coaches from Warsaw to Minsk (*6hrs; around €20 one-way*).

There are two main bus stations in Minsk: Tsentralny (Central) and Vostochny. Tsentralny (*6 Bobruskaya St;* ✆ *226 09 94*) serves 23 international routes to and from the terminal located close to the railway station, with only the Hotel Express between the two. It has few facilities of its own, but those of the railway station are only metres away. Vostochny (*34 Vaneyeva St;* ✆ *248 06 28*) serves primarily domestic routes, with limited cross-border services. The website Minsktrans (**w** *minsktrans.by*) has helpful English pages on routes and timetables.

BY CAR Crossing by land is an experience all of its own (see boxes, pages 66 and below). Some will see this as an enhancement to the travelling experience. I certainly do. But you will be wise to allow at least 3 hours to pass through the interminable checkpoints and, when you add this element to the time actually spent travelling, it's not a speedy way to get from A to B. And if there is a problem with your papers, or the guards are in a particularly playful mood (as they can be with nationals of another country), no man's land can be a rather lonely place, especially if you don't speak Russian or Belarusian. With a degree of hesitancy, therefore, my advice is to save the border-crossing adventure until you are comfortable with the language, or have a Belarusian travelling companion with you to assist in times of difficulty, in which case it's an intensely interesting experience that is not to be missed. Sadly, however, it is no longer possible to

THROUGH THE BACK OF THE WARDROBE

'All the arrangements are made,' said Artur. 'When you land at Vilnius, walk out of the terminal and look for a Mercedes Vito. The driver will take you to the border for 20 lita.' But when I walked into the car park, there was no Vito to be seen. 'Relax, he'll be there in 10 minutes.' He actually arrived in seven, cruising slowly up and down before finding a space to park. It was dusk. I wandered over and asked if he was going to the border. With a nod and a gesture towards the passenger door he started the engine, and within seconds we were on our way. It's no more than 20 minutes to the border crossing at Kamyeny Log, but you know you're getting close around 2.5km away, when you reach the end of the line of parked-up wagons at the side of the road. I counted well over a hundred.

The driver dropped me off at a petrol station and café 200m from a cluster of low buildings, with overhead gantries above the carriageway. I walked towards them, past a line of private cars, and up to the mirrored window of Lithuanian emigration control. A small section at the bottom opened for me to hand over my passport. It was returned after a rustle of paper and the tapping of a few computer keys. On I walked into no man's land, a broad area comprising lanes of tarmac, markings in the road, clusters of vehicles, single buildings and gantries, but very few people. Out of a hut appeared a Belarusian border guard in uniform, looking about 15 years old. He checked my passport and wrote my name in Cyrillic on a scruffy piece of official paper, handed it to me, and on I walked. There were wagons parked up everywhere, with an occasional short line of cars, none of them moving, each one occupied by a driver and passengers. I was beginning to enjoy myself. I had a very real sense of being part of a continent in transit, yet with every vehicle's journey apparently suspended and in limbo, I seemed to be the only one on the move.

replicate my experience recounted below, as the crossing point from Lithuania at Kamyeny Log has now been closed to travellers on foot.

The main pan-European route across Belarus for road transport is the E30 motorway from Paris to Moscow, via Berlin, Warsaw, Brest and Minsk. Within Belarusian borders it is delineated as the M1 motorway, and it crosses the country diagonally in a northeasterly direction from Brest in the southwest to a point south of Vitebsk in the northeast, *en route* to Smolensk in Russia and beyond. There are many border crossings into Belarus for vehicles and passengers (both private and freight) from its neighbours Poland, Latvia, Lithuania, Russia and Ukraine. If you're driving your own car, do be sure to check first that your chosen point of entry is open to private vehicles. Not all of them are. From **Poland**, the major crossing points are at Terespol, Koroszczyn, Slawatycze, Kuźnica Białostocka, Połowce and Bobrownik, the most-used being Białostocka and Terespol (the point at which the E30 European highway enters the country, with the city of Brest but a handful of kilometres away across the Warsaw Bridge). All of the crossings from **Latvia** are into Vitebsk oblast and include Urbany, Gavrilino and Lipovka. Major crossings from **Lithuania** include Privalki (for Grodno) and Kamyeny Log, the main road from Vilnius to Minsk and the point at which I crossed the border on foot in the spring of 2014 (see box, below). There is a line of crossings from **Ukraine** across the length of the southern border of Belarus, including Tomashovka, Mokrany, Vyerchny Terebyezhov, Novaya Rudnaya and Novaya Guta (where I once crossed by car, as described in the box on page 66). Travelling from **Russia**, you should know that customs checkpoints have been removed and unrestricted access on all

After another few hundred metres I reached Belarus passport control and immigration. This time the scrutiny of my passport was something more than peremptory.

On I walked. A small café appeared, followed by a tatty prefabricated duty-free shop, which was my cue to find the small piece of paper on which I had written Artur's list of requests. Purchases made, I walked on. Another uniformed border guard, who also looked no more than 15 years old, ticked off the last formality. He glanced at my passport, took the scruffy piece of paper given to me by his colleague and waved me through. And that was it. I was in. Artur's BMW was parked 100m away in the car park. The entire experience from Vito to BMW took no more than 45 minutes. And the wagons? They will have waited for hours and hours, maybe days. The queues leaving Belarus were even longer. The drive to Minsk in the darkness and torrential rain presented the perfect opportunity to reflect on the experience and just as I did when I crossed the border from Ukraine by car a few years earlier, I felt I'd been a bit-part character in a black-and-white 1960s Cold War tale, a Len Deighton or a John le Carré. The image that came to mind when I completed the walk in reverse ten days later was an entirely different one, after an eventful Belarus stay of big experiences every day, some of them positive and some of them less so. On the short drive back to Vilnius airport with the same moustachioed driver, I reflected on all that I'd done and seen. The fact of literally *walking* into and then back out of a country where the experience is so very different from anything else that happens in my life brought Narnia to mind. I'd walked through the back of the wardrobe into a different world. I can't articulate the feeling any better and I can't find the words to explain the way it made me feel actually to walk from one world to another, but I can't wait to do it again.

routes crossing the border is generally permitted unhindered, although from time to time sporadic checks and controls are enthusiastically enforced.

As might be expected, clichéd and stereotypical encounters with border guards are commonplace, particularly as a significant amount of freight carried by road haulage is still being imported even now as humanitarian aid for those affected by the Chernobyl catastrophe. Long waits are all too common, with officials taking hour after hour (and sometimes days) to authorise official papers. Travellers in groups, particularly on tours where bookings have been made through state tourist agencies such as Belintourist, will find that their party will be waved through much more quickly, effectively by jumping the queue. The same applies if you cross on foot (where that is still permitted). At certain crossings you won't be alone in doing this, and the beauty of a pedestrian crossing is that you walk straight past the never-ending line of vehicles and directly up to the various points at which papers are checked. When I last crossed on foot into Lithuania at Kamyeny Log, the walk out of Belarus across no man's land and into Lithuania took no more than 25 minutes, including four separate stops at specific checkpoints. Sadly, however, it is no longer possible to walk across the border at this point. The opening and closing of specific crossing points has a tendency to change, so do check before you travel that your crossing of choice is actually open. The English pages of the State Border Committee of the Republic of Belarus website (w *gpk.gov.by*) contain a fund of information on all you need to know regarding border crossings – even queuing times that are updated hourly! For those (like me) who are fascinated by borderlands, it's a really interesting read.

For drivers of private vehicles, a customs declaration form is required, which must also provide certain information relating to the vehicle itself. You must also be able to produce original ownership documents at customs offices at border crossings. Note that only originals of these documents are accepted. British driving-licence holders must additionally possess a valid International Driving Permit to drive legally in Belarus (available from most but not all main post offices in the UK, or via the major motoring organisations, for a fixed 12-month period). When driving anywhere abroad, it used to be the case that British motorists would need to be able to produce evidence of relevant insurance cover in the form of the mythical Green Card. With the development of EU cross-border arrangements over the course of the last 20 years or so, this is no longer a requirement for most European countries, but guess what: Belarus is one of the few that still requires it. If you have a Green Card with you, this ought to be the end of it, but don't be surprised if you are told at the border that you still need to purchase specific Belarusian cover there and then. If you don't have a Green Card you will definitely be required to buy cover. Every border-crossing checkpoint at which domestic vehicles are permitted to cross has its own insurance bureau and, in theory, according to official sources, it takes less than 10 minutes to obtain the necessary cover (although in reality it often takes considerably longer). The cost of the premium depends on the length of stay in Belarus, ranging from €5 for 15 days to €53 for one year. And do please note that in accordance with Belarusian law, your own driving licence and International Driving Permit will only permit you to drive in Belarus for three months. If you want to drive for longer, you need first to obtain a Belarusian driving licence; and to get one of those, you must first attend a Belarus driving school for three months and pass the necessary knowledge and skills tests. Really, you do …

HEALTH *with Dr Felicity Nicholson*

IMMUNISATIONS No specific vaccinations are required for Belarus, although it is recommended that travellers should be up to date with the following to remove the risk of contracting contagious diseases: tetanus, diphtheria and polio, which can be given as the all-in-one vaccine Revaxis. Other vaccines that may be recommended include hepatitis A, hepatitis B, rabies, tick-borne encephalitis and tuberculosis.

Hepatitis A vaccine (Havrix Monodose or Avaxim) comprises two injections given about a year apart. The course costs about £100, but may be available on the NHS; it protects for 25 years and can be administered close to the time of departure. This should be considered for the following: longer-stay or frequent travellers; backpackers; those staying with or visiting the local population; intravenous drug users; men who have sex with men; travel at a time of a current hepatitis A outbreak. **Hepatitis B** vaccination should be considered for longer trips (two months or more) or for those working with children or in situations where contact with blood is likely, eg: playing contact sports. Three injections are needed for the best protection and can be given over a three-week period, if time is short, for those aged 16 or over. Longer schedules give more sustained protection and are therefore preferable if time allows. Hepatitis A vaccine can also be given as a combination with hepatitis B as 'Twinrix', though two doses are needed at least seven days apart to be effective for the hepatitis A component, and three doses are needed for the hepatitis B part.

Three doses of **rabies** vaccine are needed over a minimum of 21 days as a full pre-exposure course. This then changes the post-exposure treatment, making it simpler and more readily available. While rabies vaccine is not the cheapest (typically around £57 per dose), it does last at least ten years unless you are working as a vet abroad when yearly boosts or blood tests are advised.

Tick-borne encephalitis can be encountered outdoors in Belarus and particularly in heavily forested areas, where the undergrowth is dense. It is caused by a virus and is usually spread by bites from ticks that are infected with it. The disease can be serious with a 10–15% chance of lasting neurological problems. The mortality rates vary depending on the type of virus but range from 1% to 20%.

Anyone liable to go walking in late spring or summer when the ticks are most active should seek protection. Tick-borne encephalitis vaccine (Ticovac) is available in the UK in an adult and paediatric form. Two doses given at least 14 days apart, though ideally a month, give about 90% protection. If sustained cover is needed then a third dose should be taken 5–12 months later. Whether or not you have the vaccine, preventative measures are also very important. When walking in grassy and forested areas, ensure that you wear a hat, tuck your trousers into socks and boots, have long-sleeved tops and use tick repellents containing DEET. It is important to check for ticks each time you have been for a long walk. This is more easily done by someone else. Don't forget to check your head and in particular behind the ears of children. Ticks should ideally be removed as soon as possible, as leaving ticks on the body increases the chance of infection. They should be removed with special tick tweezers that can be bought in good travel shops. Failing that you can use your fingernails by grasping the tick as close to your body as possible and pulling steadily and firmly away at right angles to your skin. The tick will then come away complete as long as you do not jerk or twist. If possible douse the wound with alcohol (any spirit will do) or iodine. Irritants (eg: Olbas oil) or lit cigarettes are to be discouraged since they can cause the ticks to regurgitate and therefore increase the risk of disease.

Go as soon as possible to a doctor as tick immunoglobulin should be available for treatment if you have not had the vaccine. Any redness around the bite should also stimulate a visit to the doctor.

As some vaccine courses take time to be given, ensure that you visit your doctor or travel clinic well in advance of your trip.

Tuberculosis (TB) is common in Belarus with an incidence of under 40 cases per 100,000 people. The disease is spread through close contact with infected sputum or through eating unpasteurised dairy products. Vaccination may be considered for those under 16 who are living or working with the local population for three months or more. Tuberculin-negative individuals under 35 years of age should be considered for vaccinating if they are at risk through their occupation. The vaccine becomes less effective with age so over-35s can only be considered if they are at very high risk of disease.

IN BELARUS Travellers to new destinations anywhere in the world inevitably encounter scare stories about risks to health.

Radiation Radiation is still present in Belarus following Chernobyl, but with sensible precautions – such as not drinking local water or eating dairy produce, mushrooms and fruits in and around the clearly marked exclusion areas most affected by the fallout – the risk of radiation-related health problems is extremely slight.

HIV/AIDS Cases of HIV and AIDS have seen exponential growth throughout eastern Europe and Belarus is no exception. The profile of the social group that is most at risk includes those who actively engage in sexual activity (not only through prostitution) or abuse drugs. The very clear advice for travellers to Belarus is no different from that which applies to travellers the world over. Don't have unprotected sex (and the best advice is to buy condoms or femidoms before you leave home to guarantee quality), avoid multiple sexual partners and don't share needles. If you notice any genital ulcers or discharge, get treatment promptly since these increase the risk of acquiring HIV. If you do have unprotected sex, visit a clinic as soon as possible; this should be within 24 hours, or no later than 72 hours, for post-exposure prophylaxis.

Rabies Animals should always be approached with the utmost caution, even in urban areas, where dogs live a very outdoor life and strays often roam the streets in packs, scavenging for food. They are prone to carry disease, rabies being the most obvious risk, and you can never guarantee that they won't attack. Instances of rabies have been steadily increasing in Belarus over the years; by way of example, the number of cases climbed steeply from 27 in 1996 to 1,628 in 2006 (when there were two human fatalities). Most cases have been reported in foxes but numbers are also increasing in racoons.

Rabies can be contracted by a bite, scratch or simply getting saliva on your skin or into your eyes, nose or mouth from any infected mammal (eg: bats, dogs, racoons, etc). The animals may look perfectly well so it is not possible to tell whether they are infected or not. First scrub the wound with soap and running water for around 10 to 15 minutes, then apply an antiseptic or alcohol if you don't have any antiseptic. Seek medical treatment as soon as possible. If you have not had the pre-exposure course of rabies vaccine then you need to have five doses of vaccine over 28–30 days and at the beginning of treatment you may also need a dose of rabies immunoglobulin (RIG). RIG is in worldwide shortage, very expensive and very unlikely to be available in Belarus, meaning you would need to evacuate as soon as possible. If you have had all three doses of the pre-exposure course then you don't need RIG at all and only two further doses of vaccine are needed to be given within three days of each other – unless you are immunosuppressed, when you would still need five doses of vaccine post exposure. The rabies vaccine is likely be available in

Belarus, but even if it is not then it will be far easier to obtain than RIG so it is still worth having the vaccine before you go. The bottom line here is not a pleasant one; if untreated, rabies is almost 100% fatal and also a terrible way to die.

Biting insects You can probably expect to contract some form of minor illness or condition at some point in your stay. During visits to rural areas from late spring to late autumn flying insects of various types can give you a very nasty bite, particularly at dusk. Take the obvious precaution of covering ankles, wrists, legs, arms and your neck, with the added protection of using insect repellent, ideally with DEET (50–55% strength is best).

Drinking water The best advice is never to drink water directly from the tap, although boiled tap water will present no risk. Bottled water, both carbonated and still, is available in abundance wherever food and drink is sold, and will be widely used in every home.

Diarrhoea On the law of averages, you are likely to pick up a dose of diarrhoea sometime, but obvious measures like thoroughly washing your hands with soap at every opportunity will help. Better still, use an alcohol hand rub, which then eliminates the risk of infection from contaminated water. If you do get it, be sure to take as much clear fluid as possible to facilitate the rehydration process. Rehydration salts in sachets or tablets are also a good idea to rebalance any salts lost in the diarrhoea. Remedies such as Imodium can be used on their own when needed, and they can also be used if you are also taking a short-term antibiotic treatment such as rifaximin, azithromycin or ciprofloxacin. These medicines are only available on prescription so you will need to consult with your GP or travel clinic expert. If you are unlucky enough to develop a fever with the diarrhoea or notice blood or slime in the stool then seek medical help as soon as possible, as longer courses of antibiotics may well be needed.

LOCAL HEALTH CARE The standard of health care available in Belarus is generally below that which might be expected in the UK and the USA. The state endeavours, under significant economic limitations, to provide comprehensive medical support to its citizens. It is usually the case that medical staff, particularly doctors, display very high standards of professionalism and commitment. They are extremely well trained, but there is a chronic shortage of equipment, materials and medicines. I have visited many hospitals boasting gifts of equipment from other nation states in Europe, where instruction manuals, if available, are in a foreign language and where post-delivery support simply does not exist. Thus no training in the use of equipment is available, no spares are supplied and repairs cannot be undertaken. Drugs and medicines supplied by donor countries are often out of date.

There is no free medical treatment for foreign visitors, so it is essential to ensure that you travel with comprehensive health cover and that you take all sensible precautions against exposure to risk. If you are normally on any medication, ensure you take adequate supplies with you to cover your trip. Be sure also to take a **first-aid and medical kit** with you, which at the very least should include the following:

- first-aid primary care guide
- antiseptic cleansing wipes
- scissors
- safety pins of different sizes

- tick tweezers
- basic hypodermic needles and syringes
- wound closure strips
- assorted plasters of various sizes
- zinc oxide tape
- assorted bandages, dressings and fabric adhesive strips
- disposable latex gloves
- paracetamol/ibuprofen/aspirin tablets (both as painkillers and also as anti-inflammatories), insect repellent, antiseptic cream, antihistamine cream and oral rehydration sachets
- antibiotics such as rifaximin or ciprofloxacin for travellers' diarrhoea

TRAVEL CLINICS AND HEALTH INFORMATION A full list of current travel clinic websites worldwide is available on **w** istm.org. For other journey preparation information, consult **w** nathnac.net (UK) or **w** cdc.gov (US). Information about various medications can be found on **w** netdoctor.co.uk. All advice found online should be used in conjunction with expert advice received prior to or during travel.

SAFETY

As a result of the highly visible militia – or police – presence on the streets there is very little crime or antisocial behaviour in Belarus, and even less that is likely to have an impact on visitors from abroad. The country is governed by a strong presidential system, with security forces that are extremely loyal to it. Historically, the authorities have shown little tolerance for opposition politicians, activists and supporters. Where events organised by opposition groups take place, there is generally heavy-handed use of the security forces to disperse and intimidate. As such, you should studiously avoid all demonstrations and rallies. At all other times, just exercise common sense and vigilance, respect people that you encounter on your way, and be alert to the possibility of mugging, pickpocketing and theft from vehicles and hotel rooms, without the need to exercise any greater care than you would at home. Don't be ostentatious with your money or place yourself in a position of vulnerability in higher-risk areas like train or bus stations and marketplaces. It is also a good idea to be on guard when drinking with people you have just met. On the streets, however, you are very unlikely to see evidence of petty crime or even antisocial behaviour such as alcohol-fuelled violence, the scourge of town centres at home. Taxis are safe, even in the suburbs and rural areas, but you should never pay up front. To put things in perspective, I have never encountered a single crime incident during all of my time in Belarus. I have never heard of anyone else, visitor or local, who has been the victim of crime. I have been out walking at night on my own and taken solo taxi rides after dark, both in well-known areas and those that are less so. Indeed, I have no hesitation in saying that you are much more likely to be treated with kindness, courtesy and unconditional hospitality than as a target for crime. If you ask for directions in the street, the likelihood is that the person you approach will go out of their way to take you where you want to go. In 17 years of visiting this country I have never felt vulnerable, at risk or insecure. So just be sensible, but don't allow feelings of insecurity to deny you the opportunity of interacting with local people.

There is much apocryphal talk and rumour about Mafia-style organised crime, which probably owes much to tales that originate in neighbouring Russia and Ukraine. Even if true, mobsters will have little or no interest in foreign travellers

Most of your encounters with local people are likely to be positive ones, because of the genuine sense of unconditional hospitality that runs through the whole of Belarusian society. I once attended the consecration of a new church in the small town of Vetka, close to the Russian border. The Metropolitan Filaret of all Belarus was there to perform the ceremony and the church was packed with local people. There was a huge surge as he entered and I was separated from my rucksack, which contained not only all of my personal belongings (passport, wallet, credit cards, cash and the like), but also a very substantial sum of US dollars. There is much poverty in and around Vetka, and the contents of my rucksack represented a fortune by local standards. I was separated from my bag for almost an hour and I am ashamed to say that I feared the worst. But I only had to report the loss to my colleagues in the local administration for things to swing into action. The Chief Executive of the local authority spoke to the Chief of Police and there was an immediate flurry of activity. Within minutes my bag and I had been reunited. It was instantly apparent that it had not been opened. It was handed to me by a militia man with the broadest grin I have ever seen, who told me with a mischievous wink that the only matter of concern was whether or not I was a terrorist with a bomb, intent on harming the Metropolitan Filaret. It was handed in by one of the locals as soon as it was spotted, and other local people had joined in the search immediately word got around that my bag was missing.

who stay well away from their 'business'. In the unlikely event that you become a victim of crime, always pause briefly before acting and think things through. If you are travelling with a tourist agency or staying in a hotel, report the crime to the agency and the hotel first. If your passport is stolen, contact your embassy immediately. Only then should you file a police report. Experiences with the local militia can be mixed and it pays to remember that, as a foreigner, you may be treated with just as much suspicion as likely miscreants, if not more.

Scams and swindles are on the increase, although again, you are unlikely to encounter any of them. But take great care every time you use a debit or credit card and never let it out of your sight. ATMs at banks are safe but as people living in the West already know, increasingly sophisticated means of reading and decoding cards are in operation in Europe and Russia, so Belarus may be next. And you should never, under any circumstances, agree to change money other than through a bank, currency-exchange bureau or reputable hotel. By Western standards, most people in Belarus have pitifully meagre financial resources at their disposal and travellers from Europe and the USA are seen as fabulously wealthy. In relative terms, they are. Bear this in mind at all times and be studiously discreet with your money, to avoid placing temptation before locals who can only dream of having the amounts routinely found in your wallet. If anything, the greatest risk of all will be encountered before you even arrive, through access to services requiring payment over the internet. Be very cautious of entrusting your personal details, financial or otherwise, to local sites that profess to be secure. Try to make all your arrangements through reputable agencies with appropriate bonding and insurance.

ROAD SAFETY The quality of driving in Belarus is erratic and motorists will find extravagant ways of avoiding obstacles and delays, including mounting the pavement if necessary. Taxi drivers are no exception. You will need to be particularly alert at night in the towns and cities, where many (but not all) junctions with traffic lights have flashing amber for all roads into the junction during the hours of darkness. The mindset of local drivers (without exception) is that, come what may, they will keep going. The concept of 'giving way' is not even an afterthought. In large numbers local drivers now wear seat belts as a matter of course, but not everyone does. It goes without saying that you should always use yours, even though you may be encouraged not to and even though some drivers will view it as an adverse comment upon their driving skills and a personal slight. I recall one journey across the country as a front-seat passenger in the care of an eminent physician. As he switched on the engine he described in vivid and gory detail a recent road traffic accident in which a mutual friend had lost his life. Instinctively I reached for my seat belt, only to be told, 'That's OK, you don't need to; I'm a good driver.'

All of this said, I have criss-crossed the country at the wheel countless times and always without (significant) incident. If you use your common sense and stay fully alert, I wouldn't expect you to encounter any difficulty. If anything, the experience puts me in mind of motoring 40 or so years ago, when the number of vehicles on British roads was a fraction of the horde that clogs up the highways and byways most days of the week now. The 'motorways' in Belarus are in name only when compared with British ones. Exceptions are the Minsk orbital road and the new sections of dual carriageway you will find within a radius of 50km or so of the cities, as well as at various other apparently random locations on main roads throughout the country. That said, the state's road-building and upgrade programme is increasing at a dizzying pace, not least in relation to the new culture of tolls (page 90). When complete, road travel all over Belarus will be much transformed for the better. For now, the significant number of roadwork sites presents its own challenge for drivers. You won't find hazard signs and mile after mile of coned-off highway with workers nowhere to be seen. Instead, don't be surprised if the highway just seems to disappear into a pile of sand, with little warning. It will probably be unlit at night. For the most part, driving speeds are considerably slower than you will be used to at home, so there is little risk. Just stay alert at all times and expect the unexpected. Subject to these caveats, driving on single carriageways, even on major routes, is a largely relaxed experience due to the low number of vehicles on the road. There are few bends, other than long ones, and for the most part, roads are flat and unendingly straight. This means that you have a good clear view of what lies ahead and can plan overtaking manoeuvres with a good degree of preparation. The busiest roads are those to and from Minsk, especially the M1, M5 and M6 between the capital and Brest, Gomel and Grodno respectively, all of which have a high proportion of long-haul freight passing through the country into and out of Russia and Poland for all points in the European Union. This means that, on certain days of the week and at certain times of the day, journeys on these roads can be of the 'white knuckle' variety … One other thing: whatever the time of year, even if the sun is beating down from a cloudless blue sky, drivers will have the heater on full, with the blower set to maximum. Be warned.

Belarus's 'A-class' highways are in average to good condition. The condition of 'B-class' roads varies considerably and some are impassable for periods in winter. Drivers should also note that cavernous pot-holes can be found anywhere. Pony-and-cart combinations are often encountered outside city limits, presenting a specific hazard for drivers in unlit rural areas.

You should observe the **speed limit** at all times. The standard speed limit is 40km/h (25mph) through villages and intensely built-up areas, 60km/h (37mph) on the fringes, 90km/h (55mph) outside built-up areas, 100km/h (62mph) on main routes and 120km/h (75mph) on upgraded motorways. These limits are rigidly and ruthlessly enforced by mobile electronic checking, especially in rural areas, where spot fines significantly swell the coffers of the local militia. But this is a country travelled by knights of the road, where the code of chivalry is routinely observed. This means that whenever any driver passes through a militia speed check, he or she will routinely flash every oncoming driver, without exception, for the next 3km or so. Just make sure you return the compliment!

As well as observing speed limits at all times, do not be tempted to drive after drinking alcohol, however minimal your intake may have been. There is zero tolerance of any trace of alcohol. Just don't do it. You should also drive with your lights on at all times between November and March. There are frequent police checkpoints on routes throughout the country. Drivers should stop at these when instructed and have all necessary vehicle papers immediately to hand, as otherwise there is a substantial risk of a fine and consequent delay. Finally, motorists entering Belarus should ensure that they do not overstay the temporary import consent for their vehicles. Violation of the exit deadline may result in confiscation of your vehicle at the Belarusian border or at a police checkpoint within the country.

WOMEN TRAVELLERS Notwithstanding the (slowly) developing tourism market, any foreign traveller continues to be viewed with considerable curiosity in Belarus, not least because of their relative rarity. This is even more true of women travellers (alone and in numbers), who are rarer still. But women travelling together should not expect to encounter harassment, as two or more local women without male company is a not uncommon sight in bars and restaurants in the big cities.

Single women should exercise caution, however. On your own you might find that you are approached for 'business' by potential 'clients'. Hotel lobbies are notorious for this, where members of staff and prostitutes who are their associates work closely together to ensure that all available 'business' comes their way. Any woman who is not known in these establishments is viewed with the greatest suspicion and even hostility. This actually happened to a Belarusian charity colleague of mine a number of years ago. We were in Minsk with a tourist group, both of us staying at the same hotel as the group. On returning to the hotel alone, my colleague was first of all told in no uncertain terms to leave on the basis that the lobby was the preserve of other working girls; then later she was again refused entry to the hotel proper, because hotel staff were convinced she was clearly touting for business!

As with everything else in a new destination, female travellers should exercise obvious caution and take the same precautions they would in their own country. It's all a matter of common sense. Avoid being on the street alone late at night, particularly in badly lit or secluded areas. Try not to take cab rides alone in the dark with small taxi firms, but instead always look for signs and phone numbers on taxis, together with formal identification papers for the driver before you step inside. Be alert in subways. Don't go out at night without being sure of where you are going to sleep and how you are going to get there. It's always best to ensure that someone knows where you are and when you expect to be back. In any situation, try to act with confidence but not aggression. A show of helplessness might be viewed as vulnerability. Be careful about accepting drinks from people that you have only just met. And it is never a good idea to accept the invitation of a lift or a coffee.

Be wary of travelling alone on overnight trains, as you will have no choice as to your companions in your allotted sleeping compartment (even in first class

HOTEL LADIES OF THE NIGHT

Each hotel will have its own regular group of working girls (I wonder what the most appropriate collective noun would be?). They meander around the lobby in heels and short skirts, gently smouldering and oozing availability. Every man who passes, whether or not accompanied by colleagues, family, spouse or partner, receives the sultry look and 'come hither' stare. Sometimes the bait is taken, the line is reeled in and the parties repair to the bar to close the deal. Occasionally the deal is struck much more quickly, in hushed and whispered tones. Then with a nod to the lobby staff, the players stroll arm in arm to the lifts. The security guards also receive their cut of the takings. It is their job to ensure that no interlopers are allowed to muscle in. And so it is that every female who enters the lobby, no matter how respectable and whatever the company she keeps, is given the once over. Some nights, business is slow and the girls are underemployed. So when male visitors take their key from reception staff and it is obvious that they are are going to bed, their room number will be passed to one of the girls, who will then give the occupant a respectable time to get into bed before she comes to call on them. The tap on the door is generally a soft one and she will not persist, although the phone will always ring 10 minutes later if the knock is unanswered. If the visitor then picks up the phone, they will be offered 'company', but a polite refusal will be an end to the matter. Male visitors won't be harassed. But to avoid any embarrassment, just don't answer the phone. Then the following night and every night after that, the merry-go-round in the lobby will spin all night long.

you will not have the luxury of sleeping alone). But again, Belarusian hospitality is likely to come to the fore. You will most likely encounter interesting and sociable companions (male and female), without there being any question of an uncomfortable, claustrophobic or threatening atmosphere. And there are clear rules of etiquette that are universally followed. For example, women can expect absolute privacy to change clothing and prepare for bed. In addition, you will always be offered the lower berth for sleeping.

TRAVELLERS WITH DISABILITIES Wheelchair users will find that Minsk is not the most accessible of cities, and other cities and towns even less so. Things are slowly changing for the better, but staff in the tourism trade are generally not used to taking care of visitors with specific needs. You will find that increasing numbers of hotels, restaurants and museums have disabled access and facilities, but you should not assume that this will be so. Always check ahead and don't expect people to proactively anticipate the support you might require. Sadly, disability awareness still has some way to go and staff are likely to be caught unawares without prior knowledge of a visitor's specific needs. But if you are travelling with one of the major tourist agencies and they are advised of your requirements in advance, you can expect to have your needs accommodated. On the metro system, only the newly constructed stations are wheelchair-friendly.

A word on **travel insurance**: these days, consumers have a huge variety of insurance providers from which to choose, most of whom offer a broad range of cover to anticipate most situations that might arise (subject, of course, to exceptions and caveats). All of us have insurers of choice, which probably means that we have existing policies to cover our individual needs. It always pays to shop around, of course, and in addition to the obvious big players there are also a number of bespoke providers specialising in the provision of insurance for disabled and older travellers or to cover pre-existing medical conditions. In the UK they include All Clear Travel Insurance (w *allcleartravel.co.uk*), Atlas Direct (w *atlasdirect. co.uk*), Direct Travel Insurance (w *direct-travel.co.uk*), En Route Insurance (w *enrouteinsurance.co.uk*), Free Spirit Travel Insurance (w *freespirittravelinsurance. com*) and Freedom Insurance Services Ltd (w *freedominsure.co.uk*). In the USA, consider Travelex Insurance Services (w *travelexinsurance.com*).

ETHNIC MINORITY TRAVELLERS Belarusian society likes to think it is tolerant and embracing of multi-culturalism, but the reality is somewhat different. In modern times the ugly face of racism is never far from view throughout eastern Europe (as elsewhere, of course) and sadly, incidences of racism are not uncommon in Belarus. Less overt but just as insidious is the fact that institutional racism is endemic throughout society in this part of the continent, although the younger generation is as enlightened and tolerant here as elsewhere. Minority ethnic travellers are likely to be stared at and viewed with great curiosity, but of itself this should not be regarded as evidence of racism. Rather, it reflects inquisitiveness on the part of local people towards anyone who is viewed as a foreigner.

LGBT TRAVELLERS Notwithstanding its own view of itself as an inclusive culture, intolerance and homophobia remain present in Belarusian society. Since March 1994 the law has acknowledged same-sex relationships between consenting partners, but there is no support for LGBT initiatives or organisations, which remain largely underground. It will come as no surprise that as youth culture strives to break free from the shackles of state oppression, LGBT rights are increasingly embraced, although this has yet to permeate more widely through other sections of Belarusian society and culture, as evidenced by the extraordinary statement on the country's official website that gay couples are advised 'to avoid public displays of affection and to book twin rooms rather than doubles'. Meanwhile, the powerful Russian Orthodox Church, which claims that 68% of the population are active followers, considers homosexual relationships as among the 'gravest of sins'. Interestingly and on its own admission, however, this proportion of active followers is significantly down from the figure of 80% claimed in 2014.

TRAVELLING WITH KIDS As there is universal acceptance in Belarusian culture that heterosexuality is 'the norm' (as are distinct stereotypical gender identities for men and women) a husband, wife and children travelling together will be broadly welcome wherever they go. There are no specific obstacles for families and no inconveniences that cannot be encountered elsewhere in the world. In practical terms, essential items for infants such as nappies, formula milk, general toiletries and medicines for paediatric pain relief are widely available in towns and cities. Don't expect to find imaginative concessions to the challenges of getting around with pushchairs (eg: on public transport), but with a spirit of adventure, patience and a sense of humour, few places will be out of bounds.

A number of years ago I helped a British family with two young children to arrange a holiday in Belarus. All went smoothly and the feedback I subsequently received was extremely positive: 'We are so glad we went. We found the people friendly and accepting of us. Our children enjoyed the trip too. We found plenty to entertain them and the food is easy enough for them to adapt to, which helped. We found quite a few things to do with the children. We found there to be a surprising safety culture, eg: strapping children on to the horse of a carousel at a funfair, which would probably go against most people's stereotypes.'

WHAT TO TAKE

In the big cities you will of course find the enormous range of consumer goods you would expect to find at home. This means that it is no longer necessary to pack for a trip to Belarus as though you're preparing to enter another dimension. When travelling in the old Soviet Union the shops were always empty and it was universally the case that you would need your own bath plug in every hotel, no matter how swish. Today, the issue of availability of goods seems to relate more to quality. This means that when you buy cosmetics, sanitary products, clothes, gadgets (such as torches, radios and corkscrews) and all the trappings of modern living, don't expect local goods to last very long. That said, things *are* changing, and it is now possible to purchase a broader range of higher-quality essentials, in Minsk at least. Before you go, though, do make a list of all essentials you may want to buy or replace, as well as specific items that will need to be of decent quality. As with anywhere you might travel, one thing that's very useful to have with you is a large packet of antiseptic wipes, which are very versatile and serve a number of purposes. And given that photography is an important medium for capturing your experiences, be sure to take more batteries and memory cards than you think you will need. You will encounter many more things that you will want to record than you expect.

Most importantly of all, find room in your luggage and day baggage for two rolls of toilet paper. Hotel rooms will have adequate supplies, but elsewhere you should not rely on expecting to find anything at all, including in restaurants, bars and other public places. Things are definitely improving in the major tourist areas, particularly in Minsk, but do be warned that toilets elsewhere in Belarus can be smelly, require you to squat instead of sit and have a wastepaper basket for used paper, which is deposited rather than flushed. That's one use for those antiseptic wipes. Conveniences in public spaces such as parks and at railway stations are quite an experience. There is always an attendant on hand to charge a fee (usually around BYN0.50) and although facilities are often basic, you will always find a vase of flowers (sometimes plastic) and pictures on the walls. Finally, don't forget to take a first-aid kit (see page 73 for details of what it should include), plus a sewing kit for emergency repairs.

CLOTHES Belarusians are very conscious of status. They take great pride in their appearance and will take every opportunity to wear their most fashionable items of clothing whenever they can. The best advice is to take things in which you will feel comfortable, but have with you at least one smart outfit. For men, this need be no more than pressed trousers, smart shoes, a laundered shirt and a tie. Don't worry about a jacket unless you feel underdressed without one. It's all a case of personal preference. For women, a dress or skirt and formal blouse are a good idea. Attendance at a formal event is always on the cards and first impressions go a long way towards establishing cordial relationships with your hosts. But ostentatious gear with exclusive designer labels and accompanying 'bling' will have the opposite effect. For outdoor wear, bring practical clothing with several pockets and a pair of sturdy shoes.

Summers can be very hot. Shirts, trousers and long flowing skirts made of light cotton will help you to be more comfortable. Button-down sleeves and button-up collars minimise the risk of overexposure to the sun. By contrast, winters can be freezing. Anyone visiting Belarus from November through to March will need lots of warm clothing. Being outdoors in winter is a wonderful experience if you're prepared for it, but it can be extremely uncomfortable if you're not. It's better to wear a large number of thin layers, which allow you to adjust your body temperature more easily. In all probability, you will be going in and out of buildings and using public transport on a regular basis. It is here that the importance of being able to shed layers comes to the fore, because cars, buses, trains and buildings are like furnaces in wintertime. Whenever you enter a public building, you will be expected to check in your overcoat, hat and any baggage you have with you at the cloakroom. Winter means snow, so strong, warm, waterproof footwear is a must. Take the thickest overcoat that you possess for extra warmth, but also a waterproof jacket for when it rains. An insulated hat, scarf and gloves should also be considered essential.

BOOKS AND MAPS Authoritative and up-to-date guides and maps for Belarus are still few and far between outside its national borders. Those that exist are stocked in specialist travel bookshops such as Stanfords (**w** *stanfords.co.uk*), Daunt Books (**w** *dauntbooks.co.uk*) and the Map Shop (**w** *themapshop.co.uk*), or are available online from the usual outlets. Books play a huge role in Belarusian culture and when you get there you will find that, even in small stores, there are lots of glossy paperbacks and hardbacks on the history, culture and ecology of the country. English-language books are increasingly available. The best on the market is *Heta Belarus Dzietka!* (*That's Belarus, Babe!*) by Masha Cheriakova and Marta Chernova, two young Belarusians with a passion for promoting their country to an audience outside its borders. Written in a chatty, witty style (in English alongside Belarusian) with a lovely line in self-parody, there is no better introduction to today's Belarus, its culture and its people. I can't recommend this publication enough. See page 330 for more details.

A decent number of maps covering the whole of Belarus are now available for purchase in the UK, while in Belarus itself, the government produces its own 1:800,000 map via its agency Belkarta (**w** *belkarta.by*). It is easy to read, has English translations of place names and sites, contains key pieces of information and, best of all, it incorporates plans of the six major cities on the reverse side. One of the best and largest-scale maps available in Europe appears to be the 1:600,000 version sold by the Canadian company International Travel Maps and Books (**w** *itmb.com*). Inevitably, the most detailed maps are only available for purchase with Cyrillic script in Belarus itself. The tourist industry there still has far to go, but it has begun to sharpen up its public relations strategy of late, so that decent-quality hand maps and pocket guides are now starting to be distributed for free in some hotels and transport hubs. Just don't count on it, because you might very well find the dispenser empty when you need it most. The very best advice is to be prepared for any eventuality by taking your own with you.

SPEAKING THE LANGUAGE You will be surprised at how many metaphorical doors are opened for you if you try a few words of Russian, so as a basic 'must do', take a pocket phrasebook with you. It's worth trying to learn the Cyrillic alphabet in advance, because it makes no end of difference if you can sound out letters and thereby read place names. For those without even a rudimentary knowledge of the alphabet or how to pronounce the letters, it can be a very intimidating language. But trust me on this: when you can sound out letters, then you can sound out words as well and you will be surprised, first at how easy it can then be to sound out quite long words and second, by how many of them you can actually take a good guess at translating. And if you can learn a word or two of Belarusian to drop into a conversation you will be regarded with awe as a polyglot!

There are many **phrasebooks** on the market: my two favourites are those published by Rough Guides and Lonely Planet. There's not much to choose between them, as both have basic but useful dictionaries within the text, along with practical sections designed to help you get by in the most common everyday situations. When it comes to **basic language courses for self-study**, the market is saturated and you will be spoilt for choice, particularly when it comes to online resources. And if you have a smartphone, the number of apps available for downloading seems to grow by the week. In a competitive and expanding market, well-known tutors such as Memrise (**w** *memrise.com*) and Duolingo (**w** *duolingo. com*) have their fans, but my own personal favourite is Babbel (**w** *uk.babbel.com*). Language study is an entirely personal and subjective activity, so do your research and pick whichever provider best suits your preferred method of learning. Those (like me) who love books are still well served. I find the *Teach Yourself* series (**w** *teachyourself.co.uk*) particularly useful, because they publish an extensive range of materials to enable the student to prepare through different learning disciplines. Passing no comment on the choice of descriptive term in the title, *Russian for Dummies* (**w** *dummies.com*), in audio and book form, is an excellent way to prepare for practical experiences. The layout is imaginative and the style of teaching effective. I also like the *New Penguin Russian Course* (**w** *penguin. co.uk*), which packs a lot of learning into one portable volume. Nowadays, there are a number of books and CDs on the market that profess to be more effective because they use so-called 'new ways of learning'. My own view is that there is no substitute for learning the basics of the alphabet, pronunciation and grammar in the traditional way, if you want things to stick in your mind. This isn't everyone's view and it may very well be that new and different ways of learning suit you best, in which case just go with whatever meets your preferred style.

A word about **online language courses**. One of the best I have seen is *Master Russian* (**w** *masterrussian.com*). The resources available on this site are comprehensive, including a number of online multiple-choice tests for you to take and submit, with instant feedback on your results. This isn't the only site, of course, and time spent web-browsing to find one that suits your own tastes best will never be wasted.

When you are ready to take your study to the next stage, you will need to acquire a more technically based **grammar book**. My personal preference is the set of volumes produced by Barron's Educational Series in the United States (**w** *barronseduc. com/foreign-languages-russian*). The company's books on verbs, grammar, idiom, vocabulary and pronunciation are especially good. And for a single volume to slip into your pocket that is compact but full of essential learning, take *Oxford Russian Grammar and Verbs* (*Oxford University Press;* **w** *oup.co.uk*).

Finally on books, my view is that you cannot do without a **dictionary** once you have moved beyond the elementary stage of study. If you're serious about your learning, then a weighty tome to keep at home or in the office (or wherever you study) is indispensable, in which case the *Oxford Russian Dictionary* is difficult to beat. I also recommend that you acquire a smaller, pocket dictionary to take with you on your travels. My own preferred choice to slip into a pocket is the *Langenscheidt Pocket Russian Dictionary* (*Langenscheidt;* **w** *langenscheidt.com*), although equally good are the *Oxford Colour Russian Dictionary* and the *Berlitz Russian Phrase Book and Dictionary* (**w** *berlitz.co.uk*).

If you are only able to acquire one learning tool both for home study and to take with you, then buy the *Oxford Beginner's Russian Dictionary*. The dictionary section itself is more than comprehensive, but in the same tome you also have a 'learning and lifestyle kit', which includes a great deal of useful tips, as well as some essential background information on lifestyle, etiquette and culture.

My own view is that the very best way to learn any language is to attend a **language school**. If you ensure that your teacher is a native speaker (usually the case, but not always), you will have the opportunity not only to hear the language as it is truly spoken, but also (and just as important) to learn with others in an interactive manner. Many course providers will give you the opportunity to enjoy at least a week's learning at a school in Russia, but naturally this comes at a cost. Listen and Learn (w *listenandlearn.org*) offers individual and group courses at many locations throughout the United Kingdom. And if you make enquiries of your local school or college, you will probably be surprised at how easy it is to find a course close to where you live. In my experience, one of the best course providers is Brasshouse Languages at the Library of Birmingham (*1st Flr, Centenary Sq, Birmingham B1 2ND;* \0121 303 0114; e *brasshouse@birmingham. gov.uk;* w *brasshouse.ac.uk*). Part of Birmingham City Council, it is the largest adult education centre in the country specialising in languages. Over 30 can be studied here (including Russian) and fees are extremely competitive. Courses commence at beginner's level and progress upwards from there. I know this place is good, because I studied here for two years in evening classes and I highly commend it to you.

If you have a burning desire to maintain your interest in this country and its people after you return home from your first visit, then I seriously recommend that you embark upon some study of the language. It will call for a degree of commitment, certainly in terms of your time, but the task is one that will give you great satisfaction as your learning develops. And you can do it in the comfort of your own home if you wish! Just don't set your sights too high to begin with.

ELECTRICITY

As in Russia, electricity in Belarus is 220–240v, 50Hz (alternating current). All plugs are symmetrical two-pin, typical of those used in western Europe. It's a good idea to take at least two international adaptor sets with you. For safety, always unplug appliances that are not in use, as random power cuts and subsequent reconnections causing surges are not uncommon.

MONEY AND BUDGETING

The national currency is the Belarusian rouble (BYN), divided into kopeks, with 100 kopeks to the rouble. It is not fully convertible, such that you are unable to purchase currency until you arrive in Belarus. Before redenomination by presidential decree on 1 July 2016, Belarusian currency always put me in mind of the Weimar Republic in the 1920s, with notes beginning at 50 roubles and going all the way to 200,000. It didn't require a particularly large sheaf of notes in your own pocket for you to be a rouble millionaire. On that day, however, four noughts were removed from the equation overnight and BYR10,000 became BYN1. Whether this made any actual difference to rampant levels of inflation at the time is a moot point, but the new denominations are considerably more user-friendly. This is particularly so for visitors from abroad, who are now able to calculate cost and price in a scale that is much more closely aligned to home currencies in the West. Banknotes are available in denominations of 5, 10, 20, 50,

100, 200 and 500 roubles, with coins to the value of 1, 2, 5, 10, 20 and 50 kopeks, plus 1 and 2 roubles. As of June 2018, US$1 was worth BYN2.00, while £1 equated to BYN2.65 and €1 would buy BYN2.33.

EXCHANGING MONEY Foreign currency should only be exchanged at banks or official currency-exchange bureaux, which includes the currency desks at hotels, the airport and train stations. In the cities and towns, even smaller ones, you will have no difficulty in finding them. It is best to change money from US dollars, euros, UK pounds sterling or Russian roubles, as travellers may encounter difficulties with other currencies. If you have booked on a tour through Belintourist or another recognised tour operator then accommodation, transport and meals will already have been paid for, so large amounts of spending money are not necessary. The US dollar is still the most desired currency, with euros and UK pounds sterling next. You may have difficulty exchanging your money if your notes are not new and crisp.

CREDIT CARDS All major credit cards are widely accepted in hotels, shops and restaurants in cities and large towns, though you should err on the side of caution and have cash with you when purchasing goods or services in smaller towns (and certainly in rural locations). Visa and MasterCard are most widely recognised. Plastic fraud has not yet taken a hold but doubtless will one day soon, so try not to let your card out of your sight when you pay. Always check your receipt and keep it until you have been able to compare it with your next statement when you return home.

ATMS ATMs can be found all over Minsk and in the other cities, and in increasing numbers in towns big and small. Most of them in the major areas of population will dispense US dollars as well as Belarusian roubles. I've occasionally encountered random problems with my cards not being recognised by machines, though not often or to a significant degree. You won't need to have a wide selection of cards with you, but one alternative to your main card of preference will be a good idea. Just bear in mind that your bank is likely to charge a fee (and perhaps more than one) for the use of your card abroad.

PREPAID CASH CARDS A number of these are now available on the market, and in security terms they represent a much safer alternative to cash. And they can of course be topped up from home by those you leave behind! With recognised backing for your cash card of choice (eg: from Visa and MasterCard) you should not have any difficulty in withdrawing cash from an ATM. Just check before you buy that the one you choose will be valid in Belarus.

CASH Exercise common sense with your money and you won't go far wrong. It's best to take a supply of crisp US dollar bills or euros, a debit card to access the local currency from an ATM and one credit card to use in hotels, shops and restaurants, perhaps with one additional card to use in the unlikely event that you encounter any technical difficulty with the others. Keeping each of them in a separate pocket decreases the risk of total wipeout by theft. Flourishing a large wad of cash is never a good idea, even in roubles. The pocket money that you have with you is likely to be more than the average Belarusian earns in a month.

BUDGETING The question of how much currency to take with you depends on your tastes and how much you plan to spend. If you are travelling with a party booked through an agency such as Belintourist, most of your payments will be made up front before you travel. If you are going solo, it will still be easy to comfortably get by spending only a little if you are so minded. You can eat and drink very cheaply by avoiding the flashy joints, as you would in any capital city, and getting around by car, bus or train is astonishingly inexpensive. Entrance fees to museums and theatres are also amazingly good value, particularly given the wealth of treasures to be experienced.

If you are travelling independently and solo, very much as a 'finger in the air' exercise it will be possible to stay in a comfortable (but not luxury) hotel, eat well (but not lavishly), take in a museum or two and cover your transport costs, all for US$200–225 per day. If so minded you can do it considerably cheaper, but you can also pay substantially more. It's all a matter of personal taste and budgetary management. This range of figures may not hold true for much longer, however. As soon as the local economy begins to realise that the number of foreign visitors is on the increase (as will inevitably be the case), prices will start to rise. The largest item of additional expense is likely to be the purchase of transport and accompanying guides on specific excursions. If you don't understand the language then self-guided tours will be of little use, as facilities for English-speaking visitors are still not yet comprehensive at museums and historical sites, although things are markedly improving as the tourism industry gets better at welcoming incoming visitors from abroad.

The import and export of local currency is prohibited and all remaining banknotes must be reconverted at the point of departure. That said, I have never encountered any difficulty in taking out cash left over at the end of a trip for use on the next one. The import of foreign currency is unlimited, subject to declaration, while the export of foreign currency is limited to the amount declared on arrival.

As for tipping, most restaurants will include an element for the service charge in the bill (generally 10–15%), although it always goes down well if you leave something extra, but always in roubles. To leave US dollars on the table after your meal would be viewed as the height of arrogance.

Here are three tentative budgets for a week (eight days and seven nights) at the luxury end of the scale, living comfortably (but not extravagantly!) and as economically as possible. There is one huge caveat to all of this: prices are changing virtually by the day and although this information is current at the time of writing, things may well be different when you come to travel. Just do your research before you go. You will see that these tables *exclude* air fares, as well as internal travel from city to city. And if your trip is arranged with a tour operator, then much of the expenditure will be included in the basic tour price. So for the purposes of this exercise, my assumptions have been that you are travelling independently and staying in one city, probably Minsk. Prices are given in US dollars per person:

Expenditure (type)	Luxury	Comfortable	Economical
Hotel (including breakfast)	2,100	840	245
Lunch and dinner	500	210	160
Urban travel	150	40	15
Museums, sights and excursions out of town	400	175	25
Theatre and culture	125	50	25
Souvenirs and gifts	300	100	25
Total	**3,575**	**1,415**	**495**

GETTING AROUND

Travellers planning a first trip to Belarus must ask themselves: do I go it alone, or should I book through an agency as part of a group? Each experience will be different and each has its pros and cons. As a former Soviet republic, the country still finds it difficult to cater for independent travellers (other than in respect of the main train and bus routes between the six major cities), because in the old days the state would want to know exactly what locals and tourist groups were doing at any given time. As was the case then, significant state control remains an aspect of everyday life. If you are part of a group hosted by one of the state travel operators, the clear instruction given to your guide will be to chaperone you every moment of your stay. Virtually the only time you will be alone will be in your hotel room.

On the up side, the time you spend waiting around at immigration, customs, restaurants, hotel check-ins, theatres and museums will be considerably less. You will also have the services of an English-speaking guide. But essentially, you will only see what the authorities want you to see. Nowadays this probably has as much to do with Belarusian hospitality as it does state control: people want to show tourists everything of which they are proud. They want you to have a good time and they want you to be impressed. Independent travel has the advantage of allowing

ON THE ROAD

Olya was fed up with her lot. She had finished university early in the summer, had just started her first teaching job at the school where she herself had studied and she was working extremely hard. Life was just a little tough. So when I told her that I wanted to visit the west of the country (along the Polish border) she jumped at the chance to join me. We borrowed a car from the brother of a very good friend of a very good friend of mine (that's how things are done here) and set off on a beautiful autumn morning.

The road from Gomel to Brest is a delight. It runs east to west in a virtually straight line for 538km, through the low-lying marshland of the Poleysye. It carries little traffic, so the drive is actually very relaxing. The road stretches to the horizon without bend or hump and overtaking is a joy. The only slight inconvenience is that you have to stop periodically to clean the windscreen of ex-mosquitoes, in their hundreds. And even though it is a thriving border town of some 300,000 residents, driving through the city of Brest itself is also a delight. The signs are good (if you can read Cyrillic), the layout of the roads is easy to fathom and your fellow motorists are generally courteous. Driving techniques are occasionally quirky, but there is very little aggression or competition and certainly not the vaguest hint of 'road rage'. You just need to be careful to avoid the pot-holes around town, which can be alarmingly deep.

I also love the back roads from Brest to Grodno, where there are usually very few cars for company. But, however hard I try, I can never find the right road out of Volkavuysk. The signs are less than helpful and I always seem to be heading in the direction of the opposite point of the compass to the one I intend. It's clearly a Belarusian version of the Bermuda Triangle.

My first night behind the wheel on the streets of Grodno was a bit of a challenge. We had been on the road all day and arrived to find no hotel rooms available. We secured an apartment for the night in one of the suburbs, but try as we might to find it we couldn't hit the right street (let alone the right block). In exasperation we phoned the landlord and he agreed to come out to meet us. He was a very young man with a very fast car. As dusk approached, he took off into the gloom like a bat out of Hades, leaving me to pursue him as best I could, all the while watching the you to do what you want, when you want. And you have greater control over your budget. But if you can't speak the language, you will be at quite a disadvantage. The Cyrillic alphabet bears very little resemblance to that of Western languages and without a rudimentary understanding, communication (especially written) will be difficult in the extreme. Some of the people that you are likely to encounter as you travel around (and with whom you will need to communicate) are going to speak at least rudimentary English, but this is not something to be expected as a matter of course. Young people generally have enviable language skills, but staff in train and bus stations, hotels, restaurants and shops do not. Very few museums have comprehensive information available in English, and the same applies to menus in restaurants. Things have been slowly but steadily developing for a number of years, and the last 18 months or so have seen a sharp rise in preparedness for English-speaking visitors, though more still needs to be done. Some will not be fazed by this and may even see it as an enhancement to the adventure. I certainly do if ever I'm travelling with little or no local language. As with so much else, it's all a matter of personal preference.

road (Grodno drivers are more excitable than their counterparts in Brest), reading the map and checking the signs. In Cyrillic text.

The only dodgy moments of the trip came on the following day. I was clearly tired. Driving around town, I couldn't understand why the car was a little sluggish. And why there was a smell of burning. Then my hand slipped to the handbrake. It was, of course, fully engaged. Please don't tell my mate's mate's brother. The second episode was more scary. It's interesting the way your thought processes work when you're tired and when the evidence of your own eyes doesn't seem to compute in your head. On the road to Minsk we hit another long, straight stretch and I counted a line of nine huge wagons heading in our direction for Poland, maybe a kilometre ahead. Then all of a sudden, I couldn't see the path of our side of the carriageway ahead. This confused me, because only a second ago, everything had been perfectly clear. I was even more confused when it seemed that one of the wagons was side by side with another. Then it dawned on me. He was overtaking. I felt like an extra in the Circus Maximus, standing in the path of the onrushing chariot race in *Ben-Hur*. By this point in the journey we were on single carriageway. With a yank to the right on the steering wheel we were into the dirt by the side of the road, great clouds of dust billowing behind us as we bounced along. The wagon made it back in, just in time, but it wasn't a risk I was prepared to take. Olya wasn't in the least bit concerned. She slept through it all.

Overtaking can be challenging if the road is busy and there is a long line of cars, wagons, bicycles, tractors and horse-drawn carts on each side of the road, because everyone seems to be pulling out at the same time and trying to overtake the car in front, which has already started its own overtaking manoeuvre. And when I pulled out from behind a truck on the road to Gomel to take a quick look myself to see if it was safe to overtake, I'm not sure who was more surprised, me or the driver of the oncoming militia car.

For the most part, though, it's stress-free motoring. You can relax, enjoy the scenery and wait for the exotic Beamers, Mercs and 4x4s with blacked-out windows to glide effortlessly by and away into the distance. Ah, the joys of the open road.

BY AIR Although a number of regional airports remain open, their business is almost exclusively in the transportation of freight. There are currently no internal passenger flights, and although there has been talk for years that the state airline Belavia is planning to open up routes within the country, this remains to be seen.

BY RAIL I should make my position abundantly clear from the outset. I *adore* travelling by train in this country. Actually, I adore train travel anywhere. I've ridden the rails all over Belarus by night and by day. I've met so many interesting people and I've watched the landscape roll by for countless hours. It was always a cliché that under Soviet dictators the one thing upon which absolute reliance could be placed was that the trains always ran on time. In its day, the Soviet rail system was the largest in the world, crossing 12 time zones. In common with its neighbour Ukraine, Belarus inherited its share of the network when the Soviet Union collapsed. Nowadays as then, trains between major cities are frequent and relatively cheap, but slow. If you have the time to spare, this is no problem at all; gazing out of a train as it lazily meanders across the country is an excellent way to get a feel for the terrain and the environment. And taking the overnight sleeper from Minsk to Gomel, especially in the dead of winter, is an experience not to be missed. This said, booking train tickets can sometimes be problematic, as it is not uncommon to find that timetable information doesn't match what you are told at the booking office.

Although some parts of the rail network have been modernised to significantly reduce journey times (with gleaming new rolling stock – comfortable, sleek and well-appointed – to match), many of the trains are still fairly old, particularly those running on local services. These older trains have a distinct charm, with wooden frames and white curtains around the windows. Carriages are heated in the winter, though they can be draughty. Overnight trains usually have traditionally designed compartments with closing doors, with a bench seat on each side and fold-down berths above. If you get to choose, always go for the lower-level berth, as the top berths slope outwards (away from the wall) and there's a good chance you'll fall out in the middle of the night. I did once, fast asleep somewhere between Minsk and Gomel, and it hurt. Bed linen is available for hire at a ridiculously cheap price. The carriage attendant will even offer bedding on long daytime journeys. A restaurant car will be available, and your attendant will also periodically come round taking orders for coffee, tea and snacks. There will be a menu on the window table in each compartment. You will not be allowed to board without first showing your ticket, and as the attendant will be providing your bedding and refreshments, and the nights can be very long, it's best to greet him/her with a smile and a few words of basic but welcoming Russian. If you strike up an early rapport, the journey will be much more pleasant.

There is a certain code of etiquette relating to travel by **overnight sleeper**. Unless you are travelling in a group of four, you will be sharing your compartment with strangers. When you enter your allotted compartment, be sure to introduce yourself. If you have your own food and drink with you, share it around. And if you have beer or better still, vodka, you'll find your new companions won't be strangers for very long. Just don't expect to get much sleep. If you are male, remember to offer the lower bunks to female companions and don't forget to excuse yourself from the compartment to permit them the privacy of changing their clothes for bed.

Intercity services are in the course of being upgraded. In some cases journey times are being halved, the rolling stock is new and levels of service are close to that which can be expected in other parts of the continent. In many ways service is actually better, with staff eager to please in the new age of customer service that is still a novelty here.

Many carriages on **day trains** consist of either old-style compartments with doors or the usual open-plan arrangement with rows of seats. It is normally possible to order tea, coffee and snacks. Local vendors with fresh produce may also be waiting as each train pulls into the platform for scheduled stops. Toilets are located at the end of each carriage, but they may be closed while the train passes through urban areas or as it crosses a national border. And don't forget to take your own roll of paper, just in case.

To access more rural areas, shorter local lines run through small stations that are little more than a platform, seemingly in the middle of nowhere. These trains are often packed in the early mornings and evenings (mostly with country dwellers travelling to sell their own produce in local markets) and just a little uncomfortable, with people crammed on to bench seats of only rudimentary comfort.

Buying train tickets is tricky if you don't have the language. Ticket windows are not difficult to identify, but don't expect to be greeted with an overabundance of patience on the part of either ticketing staff or those in the queue. **Left-luggage facilities** are available at the stations serving the six major cities and many of those in smaller towns. They will either be automatic, in which case you will need to buy a token from the nearby booth, or a room with shelves attended by a member of staff, most likely a babooshka. These are quite secure, but don't lose the scrappy piece of paper that the attendant gives you, because 'jobsworths' are everywhere to be found in officialdom in this country. No ticket, no luggage!

For all relevant information, the state railway website (**w** *rw.by*) is useful and practical, with lots of photographs and a significant number of English pages.

BY BUS Generally travel by bus is a little cheaper and sometimes quicker than by train, although you may be compromising on comfort. For longer journeys, your coach might be relatively plush, but if you're unlucky it could be old and rather rickety (and almost certainly will be for local travel, especially in rural areas). Crammed and claustrophobic minibuses also operate on local routes. The timetable is always fairly flexible – again, more so in rural areas. Try not to rely too much on forward planning and if you have the luxury of time on your side, just turn up at the bus station and see what time the next one leaves. When on board, don't be surprised if your bus stops wherever it is flagged down. This makes it a true community facility, but it also makes overcrowding much worse. According to official statistics, 4.3 million passengers travel by bus each day along 4,290 routes – so you'll be pretty unlucky not to find a bus to take you where you want to go. Just don't be surprised if it feels like all 4.3 million are travelling on the same bus as you.

BY CAR The supposed difficulties and risks associated with driving in Belarus are frequently exaggerated. Various travel websites will tell you that you'll have to contend with bad roads, on-the-spot fines from traffic police and speeding maniacs in blacked-out BMWs, not to mention that all signs are in Russian or Belarusian. You will read that every other road user drives excessively fast and recklessly, that they ignore pedestrians and traffic lights, that the roads, even the main arterial ones, are full of cavernous holes and that snow, ice and fog in the winter are a major hazard. The last two points have far more truth to them than the first two, but you're unlikely to have any trouble if you keep your wits about you, exercise common sense, observe the rules of the road and act with courtesy at all times. True, I've witnessed some extravagant (and dangerous) overtaking manoeuvres on most of the motorways, which are generally single carriageway except for the sections extending 80km out of Minsk and less for the other cities, but you are unlikely to run any risks if you stay alert. That said, you might want to bear in mind the experiences I recount in the box on page 86.

The state is currently funding a massive road-improvement programme. When complete, the network will have been substantially upgraded and motoring will be all the better for it. For now, however, expect to come upon substantial roadwork sites anywhere with little notice in advance. Hand in hand with a newly modernised road system comes the advent of a state-of-the-art electronic system for the collection of tolls ('BelToll'). Introduced in July 2013 and initially in operation on the main national M1 motorway (the pan-European E30 route) and a number of specific sections elsewhere, including the M2 spur to the airport, it replaced the old system of toll gates that used to operate on certain of the main routes. Phase 1 of the roll-out, covering around 815km of national roads, is now complete. Phase 2 is in the course of being introduced and by November 2016 125 sections of road covering 1,614km were subject to toll payment, including most of the motorway network (significant parts of the M1, M2, M3, M4, M5, M6 and M7), as well as large parts of the P1, P21, P23 and P99 roads. Drivers are required to register on the system's website (w beltoll.by) and having paid the necessary deposit, they receive the dashboard unit applicable to their grade of vehicle, which then transmits data to digital receivers at toll stations positioned at various points on the network. Automatic collection of the relevant toll from the registered account then ensues. On-board units can also be acquired at BelToll Customer Service Points at selected border crossings and other locations throughout the country. Up to 16 specially equipped vehicles will also be patrolling the network checking for non-compliance. At the time of writing, domestic vehicles less than 3.5 tonnes registered in countries of the Customs Union (Belarus, Russia, Kazakhstan, Kyrgyzstan and Armenia) were exempt from payment. Other exemptions include motorcycles, emergency vehicles and buses. For all other vehicles the tariff depends on weight and ranges from €0.04 to €0.145 per km. For further information see the extensive English pages of the system's helpful website, which include a useful map indicating the entirety of the road network covered by the scheme.

The good news is that because of the low population density, traffic queues in Belarus are few and far between, even in the big cities (although you might want to avoid being downtown in any of the six big cities, especially Minsk, in the traditional rush hours), and out of town there is a real feeling of liberation and a sense of being back on the open road. In the country, you can drive for hours without passing another vehicle. The final piece of good news is that fuel is much cheaper than elsewhere in continental Europe (and approximately half the price payable in the UK). And Belarus is at last catching on to the concept of service stations, with new ones opening all across the network. Only a handful of them are open 24 hours, but the rest will be open for business early in the morning and late into the night.

Car hire The concept of commercial car hire has become considerably more accessible over the course of the last few years and facilities are now easy to find, predominantly at Minsk National Airport and at all the major hotels in the city (particularly the new ones) or other central locations. Rates vary considerably and different conditions apply. Big international companies ply their trade side by side with the Belarusian outfits. You can afford to be choosy, so undertake your research before you arrive, but do book ahead. This is even more important if you will be arriving over the course of a weekend, because the offices of most hire firms are only open between 09.00 and 18.00 Monday to Friday. Many advertise extended hours (including at weekends) but this may only be for collection/drop-off and not for new business, so don't take the risk. And of course, when you are standing at the desk without any transport you are a captive market and the price is susceptible to adjustment upwards, sometimes outrageously so. But if you do the deal before you leave home, pay up front and are content with a modest vehicle such as a Skoda Rapid, Ford Focus or Volkswagen Polo, expect to pay anything from £200 to £400 (including all extras) for a week's hire. Daily rates are also available, and some companies offer unlimited mileage. Always check the insurance arrangements in advance and don't forget to bring your International Driving Permit. On arrival at Minsk National Airport, most of the hire companies ply their trade at gates 3, 4, 5 and 6.

One word of caution: although car crime is not common in Belarus the company details on the vehicle will mark you out as a wealthy foreigner. Park in public places and not in secluded locations. Exercise common sense and take the obvious precautionary measures with valuables and possessions.

The following listings are a selection only of the biggest international hire firms and others are available, particularly Belarusian outfits; exercise your own judgement on the merits of each.

🚗 **Avis** Minsk National Airport; 📞+375 17 334 79 90; also Bldg 2, Room 516, 11 Nyezalyezhnastsi Av (rear of Hotel Minsk), Minsk; w avis.com

🚗 **Europcar** Gates 3–4, Minsk National Airport; 📞+375 29 133 65 53; also at Bldg 2, Room 319, 11 Nyezalyezhnastsi Av (rear of Hotel Minsk), Minsk; w europcar.com

🚗 **Rhino Car Hire** Gates 5–6, Minsk National Airport; 📞in advance from the UK 0845 508 9845 & from the USA +1 888 882 2019; w rhinocarhire. com

🚗 **Sixt** Gates 5–6, Minsk National Airport; 📞+375 29 604 44 82; w sixt.com

HITCHHIKING Although hitchhiking is not common, because there is no concept of a free ride from strangers just for the sake of travelling around, you might still find that as a driver you are flagged down in urban streets and on main highways by people looking for a lift as an entirely practical and expedient means of getting from point A to point B. Your would-be travelling companion will expect to pay, but the best advice is not to take any risks at all by picking up strangers. Interestingly, you will rarely see a car that is not full to bursting with passengers. This is not just because the strong sense of community means that friends and relatives will be offered lifts by a car owner, the driver timing his own arrangements to fit in with those of his passengers, but also because motorists will look to supplement their income by giving lifts to those in need, particularly around transport hubs such as coach and rail stations (and even bus stops). I cannot recommend Belarus as a destination for hitchhikers, but if you need to get from A to B and know where you're going, if you're feeling adventurous and you want a real alternative to bus or train travel, this is a great way to interact with local people. They will be fascinated to learn that you are a foreigner and will treat you with respect and affection if you try out a few words of Russian on them. The driver will probably take whatever you offer by way of payment so be generous, but not flash. He might even refuse to accept anything when he knows you are a visitor from abroad, but persist inventively without being overbearing. Suggest that he uses the money to buy something for his wife, children or mother. You may even be offered the hospitality of his home for a meal and a bed. Just be fully aware of the potential danger of climbing into a car without knowing anything about your travelling companion. Or companions.

BY BICYCLE Within Belarus the infrastructure for cycling enthusiasts remains at a rudimentary stage of development, but this is not to say that ambling on two wheels is a non-starter for visitors to the country. Pedalling for leisure is not an activity enjoyed universally by locals, though travel by bike as a means of conveyance from A to B does serve a practical purpose for many. This is particularly so in small towns, villages and rural areas, where contraptions of the 'sit up and beg' variety are not uncommonly seen on highways and byways.

In Minsk bikeways and cycle paths are beginning to be established in significant numbers, with the design of new districts reflecting the need to accommodate cyclists. Of the urban routes that currently criss-cross the city, the longest traverses the capital for 27km in a northwest–southeast diagonal line. Bikes are available to hire along this and other routes during the summer months from pop-up traders, as well as at Minsk Arena velodrome and specialist bicycle stores. Compared with prices elsewhere in Europe and beyond, the cost of cycle hire here is remarkably cheap. It is unlikely that the needs of cyclists were under consideration when the architects and planners designed a new Minsk to rise from the ashes of the Great Patriotic War (with its huge areas of parkland and expansive boulevards boasting broad areas of pavement and walkway), but the reality today is that the urban landscape easily lends itself to leisure cycling. Against that background, the NGO Minsk Cycling Community (**w** *bike.org. by*) exists to develop and promote cycling within the city and greater region, while on the wider stage, route 2 of the project EuroVelo (**w** *eurovelo.com*), a framework of cycle routes across the continent established under the aegis of the European Cyclists' Federation and financed by the European Union, will one day run uninterrupted east–west for 5,500km from Moscow to Galway (including a route through Belarus). A number of sections are still in the course of development, including much of the route here, though this is clearly a statement of good intent. Meanwhile, competitive track and road cycling attracts a growing following of enthusiasts, not least within the ranks of the Belarusian Cycling Federation and Minsk Cycling Club (**w** *minskcyclingclub. by*). For now, however, few facilities to support and encourage sustainable urban cycling can be found in other Belarusian cities outside the capital.

An unspoilt, natural environment exists in abundance outside the main areas of population, which means that cycling through forests, by rivers, around old villages and along minor roads largely devoid of traffic is a joy. Infrastructure and facilities are not ubiquitous, but things are gradually changing for the better. Bike routes and hire facilities already exist in a number of the country's national parks (including Byelovezhskaya Puscha), as well as along the line of Avgustovski Canal in Grodno region, where a range of outdoor leisure activities can also be accessed. Outside the country a number of tour operators market cycling holidays to Belarus, including adventure travel specialist Explore (**w** *explore.co.uk*).

In summary, cyclists are welcome in Belarus and an inchoate infrastructure is starting to develop. But a word of caution: don't expect to find the same level of facilities and support that can be sourced elsewhere in Europe; and when in the saddle always takes the very greatest of care. There is little in Belarus society that could be identified as a 'think bike' culture and consequently fellow road users should not be expected to give cyclists the due attention and consideration that is both necessary and appropriate to ensure required standards of personal safety.

ACCOMMODATION

Your accommodation costs will easily be the biggest expense of your visit and at the higher end they can be substantial. **Hotels** in Belarus now fall into three broad categories. First, the clichéd relics of the former Soviet Union (monolithic concrete blocks), many of them still in state ownership; next the new breed of private establishments, often boutique in style; and finally the big boys, the international chains at the top of the market with their vast, gleaming monuments to capitalism and free enterprise. In the first category, a star system ranging from one to five is in operation but it bears little resemblance to anything that you will have seen before. The older Soviet-style hotels have a bewildering variety of rooms of different class and status, with prices to match. You can expect to be offered, for example, a room that is economy, standard, business, semi-suite or deluxe, with daily rates starting at US$60 and going all the way up to US$900 and beyond. You will be encouraged to indulge yourself at the top end of the range, but if all you want is somewhere to rest your head, then rooms at the bottom end will be more than adequate. In the second category, facilities and standards of service match those to be found outside the country. And in the third you will find pretty much all that each particular brand offers across its worldwide portfolio. Whatever your choice you can usually find a reasonable deal on a decent hotel room if you have the time and confidence to shop around online.

All of that said, you don't have far to look if you crave a taste of the old-style Soviet experience. In the 1960s and 1970s, when the first intrepid European tourists pioneered holidays to the Soviet Union through the only medium that was available (the state tourist agency Intourist), they all returned home with tales of having stayed in soulless, monolithic concrete buildings where the awfulness of the food was matched only by the surliness of the staff, there was no hot water, every fitting was hanging off, there was never a plug for the bath, the windows didn't fit their frames and guests were kept awake into the early hours by the cockroaches. Today things are different in the throwback emporia you can still find in Belarus: the food is pretty good, the staff try to smile (some of them, sometimes), you don't need to bring your own bath plug and perhaps most important of all, the cockroaches seem to have gone. Nevertheless, the soulless monolithic buildings are still there, as is the concrete, both more crumbly and neglected than they were back then.

Wherever you stay, other than in extreme circumstances of misfortune, you are going to have a fairly comfortable bed, unlimited hot water, clean sanitation, central heating, a television and a lockable door for your room. You'll also have the services of a concierge on your floor (although these services are usually limited to the shrugging of shoulders when you complain that something in your room is either missing or not working), at least one bar and one restaurant, a newspaper stand, currency-exchange facilities and staff with a smattering of basic

ACCOMMODATION PRICE CODES

Accommodation listings are laid out in decreasing price order, under the following categories: upmarket, mid-range, budget and shoestring. The following key gives an indication of prices, which are based on a double room per night in high season, including any taxes.

Upmarket	$$$$	BYN170+
Mid-range	$$$	BYN90–170
Budget	$$	BYN35–90
Shoestring	$	<BYN35

English. And free entertainment in the hotel lobby during the hours of darkness (see box, page 78).

When you **check in**, you will be asked to present your passport and migration form, which you can expect to be stamped immediately by way of registration and returned to you straight away. State regulations require that every visitor is formally registered and the stamping of your form by hotel staff completes the process. Look after this form as diligently as you take care of your passport, because you are required to hand it in when you leave the country. At your point of exit it will be checked for proper registration as a matter of course. Behind the lobby desk will be secure safe-deposit facilities, although each room in the more upmarket hotels will have its own safe. Don't be too paranoid. Things left in your room will almost always be safe. Just be sensible, lock valuables away or keep them with you, and don't put temptation in anyone's way.

If your hotel booking has been made through one of the country's tourist agencies, they will usually act as the middle man and take payment from you in advance, so you won't need to pay the hotel other than for items purchased during your stay and charged to your room account. Just be sure to check in advance what is included in the stated price (eg: breakfast). If you have to settle an account when you leave, check it scrupulously. Nearly all hotels (even those at the bottom end) have facilities to take payment by credit or debit card. There will usually be an ATM in the lobby if you prefer to pay by cash, but you will only be able to do so in Belarusian roubles.

Of course, not everyone wants to stay in a hotel. In recent times, a new breed of **hostels** have opened for business in Minsk and other large cities. Well appointed and with high standards of service, they represent excellent value for money. Competitively priced **private apartments** are available for rent in all of the big cities and many of the towns, with the advantage that you can self-cater. In times gone by, I have arrived in both Brest and Grodno in the early evening without booking accommodation in advance, to find there was not a single hotel room to be had in either town. It's a good job I was travelling with Olya. For the cost of a local newspaper and a few calls we rented an excellent apartment in Brest (5 minutes from the city centre) for US$30 a night and another in Grodno, equally well located but to a higher specification, for US$70 a night. In Minsk I have access to a charming, well-appointed flat with two double bedrooms in a superb location, all for US$50 per night. Bed linen, towels, cutlery and crockery are always provided. And you have the advantage of feeling right at home when you return after a day or evening out. In some parts of the country, **health sanatoria** have opened their doors to tourists, offering bespoke programmes lasting from one to ten days.

Since 2004, following a presidential decree, there has been a real move to promote **ecological and agro-tourism** in rural areas, giving visitors the opportunity to stay 'down on the farm' or in private homesteads, where they can live the good life and engage in various ecological activities. Resourceful homeowners outside towns are beginning to see that here is an opportunity to supplement their income, particularly as the decree from the President conferred certain tax advantages. One of the key co-ordinating bodies in Belarus is the Association of Rural and Ecotourism 'Country Escape' (page 51). Accommodation is also available in lodges and tents for those interested in activity holidays in the national parks.

EATING AND DRINKING

DRINK It will come as no surprise that this section begins with a few words about **vodka** (водка). Virtually all of the countries in this part of the world lay claim to being the first to distil this spirit of mythical status, each claim probably having as much validity as the others. Whatever the truth, it's an inescapable fact that vodka distillation is big business. Every supermarket and shop has row upon row of vodka bottles of all shapes and sizes, varying widely in quality and price. It's usually colourless and free of flavourings, although there is a huge market around the world for spirits flavoured with so-called complementary additives such as pepper, honey, grasses and fruit (eg: lemon, raspberry or cranberry). Most people in Belarus drink it straight and unflavoured, as do I. There is an active market in home-distilled vodka and people out in the country are particularly inventive when it comes to making use of organic material for this purpose, usually potatoes. It often tastes surprisingly smooth but can be astonishingly high in alcohol content, so if offered, by all means give it a try but do treat it with extreme caution and absolute respect. I've experienced a few terrible hangovers after a night of *domashnaya* ('home') vodka. But I have never drunk it without knowing its source or being able to trust the founder of the feast.

It's very important to understand how and why people here drink vodka. They don't do so for recreational purposes, sipping from a tumbler at home or in a bar as they socialise with friends and family. Vodka has a much more important role than that in the culture of Belarusian society. Every holiday, birthday, wedding, christening and funeral is celebrated with traditional toasts. Family events and social gatherings, particularly to welcome new friends and visitors, would be unthinkable without the presence of a half-litre bottle on the table, with plenty more in reserve should (when!) the need arises. To give an indication of the ubiquity of the vodka toast in Belarusian culture, I have drunk it with the Metropolitan Filaret of All Belarus, with a state lawyer at 09.30 (in his office) to celebrate his birthday, with a headmaster in his office during the school day, at breakfast with the father of my host family, and by night on a farm next to a roaring fire with rural elders gathered around, singing songs and exchanging stories, all accompanied by toast after toast after toast. And although it's a cliché to say that vodka is a reflection of the fire and passion of the Russian soul, as well as an enduring image of 'Holy Mother Russia', there is nonetheless a degree of familiarity to this statement that those who know Belarus will recognise.

All of that said, however, there is also a dark and dangerous story to be told. The tragic reality is that vodka has destroyed many lives and, to this day, its effect on family and community life is as pernicious as it has always been. In the rural communities that I know so well, I am acquainted with a number of individuals who pass each day in a state of abject intoxication. For them, it is the only antidote to 'life'. I know families deprived of a father through alcoholism; and I have visited many state institutions for children abused by parents of both sexes because of drink. Capable of being a sociable companion, it can also be a cruel master.

Beer (пиво) is popular as a staple alcoholic drink for recreational consumption. Much of it is bottled or cask-conditioned, but there is a growing trend for local micro-breweries to produce their own diverse range of craft beers of high quality. If you're an aficionado, you will have no difficulty in sourcing an increasing number of excellent examples and 'beer bar' or 'beer pub' are signs you will find in increasing numbers around towns and cities as the country reaches out to welcome incoming visitors from abroad as well as offering a different type of night out for locals. Don't be surprised to find many of the beers you will recognise from home or elsewhere in Europe on draught, though my own preference is to search out the product of a small local micro-brewery.

No **wine** (вино) is produced in Belarus, but decent Georgian and Moldovan reds are widely sold and are popular. Also available cheaply is 'Soviet champagne' (Советское шампанское), a sickly, sweet, gaseous and hideous drink that bears no resemblance to the French original. As an alternative to vodka (not that one is needed), **cognac** (коньяк) from Armenia is very popular. It is also very competitively priced and of a high standard.

In terms of non-alcoholic beverages, *kvas* (квас) makes a great alternative to the usual branded soft drinks that can be bought here as easily as in the rest of the world. Made by fermenting bread baked with wheat, rye or barley, it is sometimes flavoured with herbs, fruit or berries. Many homes produce their own but it is also made commercially and widely distributed in shops and supermarkets in bottled form. It has a malty taste and is very refreshing when served chilled on a hot day. In the summer months, vendors are ubiquitous in the city and even in a plastic cup it's an especially satisfying (and cheap) thirst-quencher in the heat and the dust.

People also bottle *compote* (компот), a rich essence of home-grown fruit (usually red berries), sugar and boiled water. It's absolutely delicious. A full range of fruit juices is available in shops, restaurants and bars, but most are made from concentrate. The usual international varieties of bottled **mineral water** (минеральная вода) are commonplace. Also served is a Belarusian variety that is highly carbonated and tastes salty and mineral-rich. It's definitely an acquired taste, but I think it's delicious.

Coffee (кофе) and **tea** (чай) are drunk throughout the country. Tea is normally taken with lemon and sugar (or even jam or honey), so you can expect a quizzical look if you ask for milk.

FOOD The cuisine of Belarus derives from the same historical and cultural sources as those of its neighbours and is an articulation of the people's relationship with the land. So if you've travelled in Russia, Ukraine, Poland and the Baltic states you will recognise dishes and recipes that are common to each. For generations, local people have grown their own produce, particularly potatoes, root vegetables and fruits. This is no surprise, for to do so reflects some of the key historical features of life here across the centuries: long and unrelenting winters, short but intense growing seasons, political and social tyranny, the intensely physical and demanding workload of the peasantry and periodic famine. The resilience needed to combat all of these privations has to be fuelled by hot, nourishing and restorative food. For generations it was a simple question of survival.

As has been discussed elsewhere in this book, one of the consequences of the political and societal changes over the last 125 years in this part of Europe as first the Russian Empire crumbled, then the Soviet Union, leading to the emergence of an independent Belarusian state, has been a cyclical process of first denial then rediscovery (and even reinvention) of traditional Belarusian heritage. This has related as much to cuisine as to anything else. Today, the fond remembrance (or perhaps rewriting?) of that heritage has its metaphorical roots firmly in the land and in the seasons. The post-independence phase has seen acceleration of the 'rediscovery' of lost traditions. But if you ask a sample of the people themselves where their preference for cuisine lies or if they are even bothered about their culinary heritage, a significant proportion will probably say that they are more interested in sampling and getting to know international dishes. This will certainly be so for those living in the big city. For the people of provincial towns and villages, however, the connection to the land will be more direct. This is certainly so in Vetka homes, where for 17 years I have been treated to the wonderful home cooking of simple but delicious dishes of high nutritional value and intense natural flavour. But on my last road trip with Olya around the country (it was only a flying visit of three days' duration) our evening meals were curry, pizza and pizza, in that order!

The staple diet of those in rural communities was always related to the **potato** and other root vegetables because for those living close to the land, this type of dish made good use of produce that was grown locally. Historically, the timing of meals for those working the fields always depended upon the beginning and end of their working day. A big breakfast, around dawn, based on boiled potatoes and baked pancakes, was followed by the main meal of the day around noon. Often served in the fields, the first course would consist of *borsch* (beetroot soup) laden with vegetables, potatoes, mushrooms and occasionally meat. In fact, to call this dish 'soup' does it something of an injustice, for it is a meal all of its own. The second course would be a dish based on cereals and more potatoes, washed down with kvas, kompote or sour milk. When the sun was at its height, it was a nourishing, filling meal, packed with energy-fuelling nutrients to keep the workers going until dusk. Supper at home after dark would inevitably be more potatoes, this time with some form of stock. There was always a plentiful supply of bread, cereals and meat in the autumn and winter. Spring was the hungriest season of all, simply because last year's store of produce would have been consumed during the harsh winter.

Like Ukrainians, Russians and Poles, Belarusians are still fond of borsch with a very large dollop of sour cream (*smyetana*) and it is particularly warming and nourishing in the depths of winter. A thinner chilled version in the summer is hugely refreshing. Borsch is still omnipresent today on every menu, whether in a restaurant or at home. And given the historical context for modern life, it is no surprise that wherever 'Belarusian cookery' is found, whether homage to the past or invented cliché, it is based on traditions which have steadfastly survived turbulent political times. Whoever is in power, the land must be worked and mouths must be fed, whatever the privations of the people. For this reason, many dishes still are based on the potato. One particular and popular favourite is draniki, pancakes prepared from shredded potatoes, often fried with mushrooms and served with sour cream. It's absolutely delicious.

Historically, **meat** was often in short supply and was only really eaten on the occasion of significant Christian festivals. Pork has always been a favourite, along with salted pork fat, which is regarded still as a great delicacy. One of the most popular pork dishes is *machanka*, a personal favourite of mine. It is said to date from the 18th century and consists of chunks of meat in a rich and thick gravy, served in a stoneware pot with fried pancakes. You can expect to find it on every restaurant menu. On a recent visit, my family introduced me to the concept of eating (wait for it) *frozen* pork – smoked, placed in the freezer and then eaten straight from it. Your senses will tell you that everything is wrong about this curiosity, but when it (literally) melts in your mouth as you chew it, the experience is unexpectedly tasty. If it's ever offered, do give it a try.

As for **fish**, modern Belarus has no sea borders and, even historically, there is no tradition of seafaring or farming of the oceans from the days when the country was included with other lands bordering the Baltic and Black seas. Much more common are lake and river fish, notably perch and carp. They are particularly tasty when served stuffed with vegetables and mushrooms. At home, river fish (locally caught, naturally) are often baked or boiled without seasoning and occasionally fried. Fish is also served in thick chunks in soup. Eel, smoked or

stuffed, is the speciality of the northern lakeland territories. I have eaten eel with
Eduard Voitekhovich at Komorovo, close to the border with Lithuania, freshly
caught (and still alive when we got there), heavily salted, barbecued at dusk and
absolutely delicious.

The intense relationship that people in rural hinterlands still have with the
land is reflected in an almost spiritual fondness for **mushrooms and berries**.
Harvesting them is one of the great activities of late summer and autumn. Many
dishes include fresh, salted and pickled mushrooms, together with berries of
many varieties, some of which will be unfamiliar to Western visitors. Mushrooms
are also often used in stuffings, sauces or fillings. Most households preserve and
pickle fruits and vegetables for the winter months when there is a shortage of
fresh seasonal produce.

Eating out If you eat in a **restaurant** outside Minsk at lunchtime you may well
be the only customer and, even in the evenings, your fellow diners will most
likely be the local nouveaux riches, foreign diplomatic staff (in Minsk) and
businessmen. At weekends, however, it's different, with families celebrating
birthdays, anniversaries and other special occasions. If a particular restaurant
takes your fancy, do book in advance to avoid disappointment. For example, the
most popular restaurants may well be closed to paying guests because of wedding
parties.

Restaurants are increasingly offering international cuisine and traditional dishes
on the same menu (the latter mainly for tourists on group tours). There are also
more and more fast-food restaurants all over Minsk. In plentiful supply is the
Soviet-style eatery with synthetic disco music and décor to match, and dubious
cabaret entertainment. Menus are largely in Russian and Belarusian only, although
restaurants are increasingly attempting English translations (often with hilarious
results). They are frequently the thickness of a magazine – not because of the range
of dishes on offer, but because each part of a meal is priced separately by weight.
And don't be surprised to be told that several alternatives of your choices are not
available! It's all part of the fun, I say.

Café culture is considerably more egalitarian in its patronage than restaurants.
Coffee bars are plentiful in the larger towns and cities, where students and young
people meet to hang out and look disdainfully superior.

A cheaper but less pleasant alternative to the cafés are the shacks with outdoor
seating where loud disco music is played, young waitresses wearing far too much
make-up and little else lean on the counter looking very bored and the fare on offer
is gassy tasteless beer and tired open sandwiches.

PUBLIC HOLIDAYS AND FESTIVALS

1 January	New Year's Day
7 January	Orthodox Christmas
8 March	Women's Day
(movable)	Orthodox Easter
(movable)	Catholic Easter
9th day after Orthodox Easter	Radaunista (Ancestors' Remembrance Day)
1 May	Labour Day
9 May	Victory Day, a glorious celebration of the end of the 'Great Patriotic War'
3 July	Independence Day
7 November	October Revolution Day
25 December	Catholic Christmas

The intensity of the Belarusian people's relationship with the land (and by association, with the seasons) means that holidays and festivals are imbued with heavy symbolism and significance, though increasingly there is crossover between the festivities of the Gregorian and Julian calendars around Christmas. Western-style **Christmas** is beginning to be celebrated in city homes on 25 December (with attendant partying to see in the New Year on the 31st), though this practice has yet to extend into the rural hinterlands with any degree of popular engagement. Orthodox Christmas is still celebrated on 7 January, when traditionally Grandfather Frost (the eastern Slavic equivalent of Santa Claus) brings presents and sweets for children. In recent times, fireworks have become a widespread feature on the evening of 6 January, though safety precautions sometimes leave a little to be desired. I once spent an interesting 6 January night in Vetka's Red Square with people igniting them all over the place. This holiday used to be followed on the night of 13 January by observance of the symbolic passing of the old year, or *Kaladya*, with young people parading in fancy dress, often as animals, singing traditional Kaladya songs as they walked from one house to another, homeowners treating them to edible delicacies as they passed through. Today this is more of a fond remembrance from a romanticised version of life in Belarus than reality, though the tradition is still observed by some over the Orthodox Christmas/New Year period. Historically, Kaladya represented a ritualistic celebration of the coming and passing of the winter solstice.

By tradition, late February or early March used to see the symbolic observance of the passing of winter (**Maslenitsa**) in the run-up to Orthodox Easter. Again, observance is much less widespread today than it used to be and, like Kaladya, it speaks more of homespun cliché than of reality. In rural parts of the country you are more likely to see the tradition upheld. In times gone by, people would bake pancakes, the shape and colour of which symbolised the growing strength of the sun with the coming of spring.

Orthodox Easter is the biggest festival in the religious calendar. In rural communities especially, the woman of the house will spend all day on Easter Saturday preparing food to be blessed by the local priest, before taking it by hand (and generally on foot) to church. Stalls selling cakes and delicacies are often to be found at the church door for those wishing to short-circuit the process. At midnight, families congregate at their local church and parade three times around the outside of its perimeter in solemn procession behind the priest, carrying beeswax candles and thinking reverent thoughts for future blessings. After returning home in the

2

Vetka, Easter Sunday, 02.00. In the UK it's midnight. For my kids Harriet and George back home, Saturday night will still be in its infancy. Here, all of us have risen from our beds for the early morning church service to have our food blessed for this holiest of holy days. Then it's back home to eat, and, I very much hope, to sleep. Tanya is getting ready and will wear her finest (her place at God's right hand is secure), while Valeri and I are wearing yesterday's clothes. He and I have found just one TV channel still on-air, broadcasting inane rubbish. We're both muttering darkly and exchanging glances as we slowly shake our heads. It's the middle of the night and we're going to church. What sorcery is this?

It's 03.00 and now I'm standing outside the house in the middle of the road. The sky is Bible-black and far from starless, with a sliver of crescent moon. No other household seems to share our devotion, but after all, this is Karl Marx Street. We set off on foot and as we get to the top of the road, I see why our walk in the darkness was a solitary one. Everyone is here already. A shuffling mass is heading right to left towards the church. I scan the crowd for *Zhivago's* Tanya but she isn't here. Perhaps 2,000 other folk are though, lined up around the church (two deep) and along the street in both directions. Everyone has a basket, tin or plastic bag, and everywhere there are cakes, cucumbers, meats, sweets, pickle jars full of water and boiled eggs by the thousand. And lit candles in every bundle.

It's cold now. Breath condenses by candlelight. We leave our basket with our friends and head into church. A homeless man, unkempt, head bowed and stinking of alcohol stands at the top of the steps, clutching a wad of filthy notes (maybe 50,000 roubles, though little more than a quid) in small denominations. We enter, crossing ourselves furiously, and light candles. As we head back out and down the steps I peel away to walk and to watch and to listen.

It's 04.00. There are so many people here. I just make it back to our little family huddle as the priest emerges from the church, fully robed, acolytes bearing buckets

early hours, sometimes as dawn breaks, the matriarch will prepare the table for presentation of the sumptuous family feast that has by then received the solemn blessing (see box, above).

The first day of May (**Labour Day**), 9 May (**Victory Day**) and 3 July (**Independence Day**) are celebrated exuberantly with all the pomp and ceremony that used to be associated with the Soviet Union (especially Victory and Independence days). Town and village centres are taken over by parades of young people, war veterans, local dignitaries, the emergency services, the army and every conceivable representative body of civic society. Traditional costumes, singing and dancing are everywhere to be seen. The long days of summer then form the backdrop to many outdoor festivals celebrating the folklore and traditions that are the bedrock of modern Belarus (or at least, its own vision of its past). **Kupalye**, celebrated over the night of 6–7 July, is the most mysterious of them all. It represents an acknowledgement of the significance of the summer solstice in the same way that Kaladya observes its winter cousin. There are clear parallels with the observance of pagan festivals and rituals on the longest day the world over. Legend has it that at midnight on this date and no other, the flower of a particular variety of fern unfolds and that the one who finds it will be blessed with eternal youth, happiness and the gift of foresight. In rural areas, young men still set off into the forests hoping that this is the year when a miracle will occur and they will find the of holy water, a small gaggle of babooshki muttering incantations. Every basket, tin and plastic bag is blessed. From time to time an unrobed attendant shouts 'Christ is Risen!' Three times he intones, each call louder than the previous one. 'He is risen indeed!' we answer. As the priest passes by, people pick up their food when blessed and head off home. Quickly the line of candles becomes but a trail of holy water. He blesses all in the circle around the church then heads back inside. On we wait.

It's 04.30 now. In the east the sky begins to soften, the dawn chorus heralding the new day with a single chirrup. Other birds join in, cocks begin to crow and, all across town, dogs add their voices to the choral performance. We've picked the wrong spot. A junior priest has the task of blessing all of us still waiting in the street. We're standing to the right of the church, but he chooses the line to the left and it's a full 30 minutes before he reaches us. It's worth the wait, because this fellow has a sense of humour. Every so often he looks up as he blesses, smiles, loads his brush and swishes water across the face of a chosen one. There are chuckles. He's more than a priest. He's a music hall act.

Now blessed and dripping with water, we pick up our bundles and head homewards for our feast. Tanya asks Valeri to place our lit candle high in the icon corner in the lounge (it will burn there all day) and we sit at the kitchen table to watch her empty the basket of provender. We eat, we drink holy water and we chat. There is *samagon* (home-distilled vodka), though I politely decline. A night on samagon to celebrate Valeri's birthday earlier this week preceded a nightmare day that ended with me in the hospital.

And now to bed. Daylight has come and the birds are very busy. The potency of all I witnessed this night is beyond words. In Russia, all over Belarus and greater eastern Europe, in every village, town and city district, the same scene will have been enacted. When the Nazis came in 1941 and Stalin needed the people to resist as one, no wonder he threw open the church doors.

mythical flower. Meanwhile, girls pick field flowers, bind them into wreaths and float them down streams for single young men to collect them, thereby enabling the girls to discover their destiny and learn of the one whom they will marry. It's all about fertility, you see; and although it all sounds incredibly kitsch, the reality is that some young people in villages and small communities really do engage with this festival.

SHOPPING

In the 1970s, it was always said that in the Soviet Union shop windows were full of tempting things to buy, but that when you went inside there was nothing on the shelves. For the most part, this was true. No self-respecting Russian would be seen out on the street without an old and tatty plastic bag, whatever the hour of day or night, just in case they came across something to buy somewhere, whether or not they actually needed or wanted it. But now, especially on the streets of Minsk, there are new designer stores selling exclusive Western labels and pharmacies selling top-range cosmetics, all with flashy billboards to match. By night, the glare of neon is beginning to light up the sky on street corners and at major road intersections. Vast, glitzy shopping malls with piped mindless muzak and supermarkets (including 24-hour hypermarkets) are springing up all over the suburbs of major cities and on the streets of towns big and small. This even includes provincial Vetka, which now has its own national chain hypermarket.

For a more intriguing shopping experience that will take you back to the days of the Soviet Union, try the GUM department store in Minsk. It's a fascinating slice of post-war Soviet social history. Typical goods that make decent souvenirs include lacquered inlay caskets and trinket boxes, laminated wooden spoons, framed straw animals, ceramic plates, decorative amber incorporated into pictures of rural scenes, wooden carvings, religious artefacts, decorated wooden eggs, cheap metal badges with grand Soviet slogans under a portrait of Lenin, traditionally embroidered blouses, linen tableware, original samovars and the ubiquitous wooden *matryoshka* doll (many of which have the face of modern politicians instead of the traditional peasant woman). It's also fascinating to browse the departments of homeware, white goods, shoes, clothing, music and toys to see what's available for locals to buy.

Elsewhere on the streets, particularly in suburban neighbourhoods, you will find small metal kiosks selling newspapers, magazines, sweets, chewing gum and beer. The vendor will hardly be visible through a tiny hatch opening, while the walls and glass frontage are literally plastered with the goods that are available for purchase.

Indoor markets are huge, inexpensive and offer more choice than the shops. Wherever you find yourself, do try to look out the nearest one. And if you can, it's worth visiting an open-air market, particularly in the smaller towns and villages. Locals will often ride to market in a horse and cart, with the man of the house (usually elderly) up front with a large stick and a babooshka at the back, precariously perched among piles of turnips, potatoes and beetroot. Dress down as much as possible, try to be inconspicuous and be prepared for some lively haggling. In both types of market, be aware that 'designer' items and CDs/DVDs sold at very cheap prices will be fakes, and that pickpockets may be about, so keep one eye on your wallet and valuables at all times.

Shops are open seven days a week but some will still close on Sundays, or at least operate reduced hours. Opening times for most shops are generally from 09.00 (occasionally from 08.00) until 18.00 and sometimes later. With the advent of more and more shopping malls and supermarkets comes a steady pushing back of opening hours, such that late-night shopping is on the increase. You will even find new hypermarkets that are open 24 hours.

ARTS AND ENTERTAINMENT

In all the countries of the former Soviet Union, the fine arts (whether classical or avant-garde) play an important role in everyday life. On Saturday nights, concert halls and theatres across Belarus are filled with the elderly, families and young people, there to celebrate the best of Russian and Belarusian culture. Even the smallest community will have its own theatrical troupe and modest concert hall.

The price that locals pay for tickets is very low (even for the best seats at a performance given by one of the state companies in Minsk), though as a tourist you may have to pay considerably more. Don't be put off, as the price is still far less than you would pay at home. Audience knowledge of the arts is impressive and, more often than not, the quality of the performance will be very high. It's a special moment to be sitting in a theatre in Minsk as the orchestra strikes up the overture to a Tchaikovsky **ballet**, then to witness the colour and splendour of the set and the athleticism of the dancers. At the end, members of the audience will vie to be the loudest to shout bravo as awestruck little girls in their finest clothes nervously hand bouquets to the principal dancers.

Among the best performances are those of the National Academic Bolshoi Opera and Ballet Theatre Company and the Belarusian State Philharmonic. Do try to take in a performance given by one of these companies. If you are travelling with one of the main tourist agencies, this will probably be included as a matter of course, but even if not and you have to book yourself, ticket availability should not be a problem (see page 182 for details).

Puppet theatres and **circuses** are still very popular with children of all ages (even grown-up ones). The state circus regularly draws large crowds, but although the tumblers, jugglers and clowns are highly polished entertainers, for me the whole experience is marred by degrading animal acts such as 'flying bears', which may make you feel extremely uncomfortable. I've only been once and it's not something I'd care to repeat, much though the acrobats impress me.

In the larger towns, **live music** can be enjoyed most nights of the week, ranging from ethnic folk and jazz ensembles playing in intimate, smoke-filled venues to the latest Belarusian group hammering out stadium rock. Many restaurants have live acts, especially at weekends, the style of music reflecting the restaurant's image. Trendy places will put on a cabaret show, 1970s style, while the 'traditional' venues aiming at the tourist market will showcase folk acts, usually solo performers or duets, strumming guitars and singing of unrequited love, historical melodrama, the glory of the peasant lifestyle or the celebration of the potato harvest (and often all of them at once).

Every town will have at least one **cinema** and in Minsk there are dozens, including an open-air drive-in, together with several cinemas with surround sound, state-of-the-art digital projection and air conditioning. The latest releases are regularly shown, although they may be dubbed (badly).

Even in the smallest towns, **museums** display impressive collections of historical artefacts that tell the story of the locality through the ages. There will be exhibits focusing on the earliest settlements, the evolution of agricultural and industrial practices, folk art and ecology. These can be fairly dry, especially for children. Museum staff will be readily available to chaperone visitor groups and to offer detailed commentaries on the displays. Babooshkas are often on hand to collect your admission fee and to jealously guard endless rooms of exhibits.

The post-Soviet era has also led to the growth of some less family-oriented distractions. The shadier *biznizmyeni* in all six cities (and especially Minsk) have bankrolled numerous casinos, nightclubs, strip joints and lap-dancing clubs, usually adjacent to or incorporated within the larger hotels. The prostitution industry, always lucrative in the past, is still booming.

PHOTOGRAPHY

Always have with you more digital memory space than you think you are going to need. You will be able to find cards in shops in the cities and larger towns, but they won't be cheap and shops won't supply much of a variety of specialist equipment. It's also worth bringing spare camera batteries.

People you meet will usually allow you to take photographs, though you should always ask permission first. Even if they readily accept, people will often pose in very stiff and formal ways, with very serious facial expressions. Elderly people in particular will stare fiercely into the lens. If you can, make arrangements to send on a printed copy and be true to your word. The photo will take pride of place in a modest home and will be a conversation piece for guests. It's also a good idea to take photos with you of your family and children, as people will take great interest in them.

Don't be tempted to take pictures of military facilities, soldiers, militiamen, policemen, offices of the KGB (still omnipresent) or government buildings. The first sight of a camera will be greeted by a shrill blast on a whistle from a member of the militia who you did not even know was there, and your film or camera may be confiscated.

MEDIA AND COMMUNICATIONS

MEDIA Ever since the date in 1991 when Belarus came into existence as an independent nation state on the disintegration of the Soviet Union, there have been claims that state control of all forms of media communication (newspapers, journals, periodicals, websites, email, mobile telecommunications, radio and television) has been all-encompassing, just as it was in the days of the USSR. Ironically, this followed a period of relative freedom in the final years of the Soviet Union, when President Gorbachev essayed in vain to bring about real reform of the system through glasnost ('openness') and perestroika ('restructuring'). But since that time there has been sustained criticism on the part of human rights and 'media watch' organisations that freedom of speech has been universally suppressed in Belarus and that the state-controlled media outlets have enjoyed privileges that have been denied to independent ones. Against all the odds, some independent publications appear to have survived, but life is not easy for them. Increasing regulation of their activities makes it all too easy for them to run the risk of non-compliance, with closure being an ever-present threat. Meanwhile, everywhere you look, on television or in newspapers, the state's view of things is omnipresent. Suppression of freedom of speech is firmly denied by the government. The universal mandate given to the president in successive elections is cited as authority for the claim that the people are happy with things as they are. Doubtless, the small and poorly organised opposition see things differently. The context to all of this is that the United States of America and the European Union continue to cry 'foul' and to impose economic sanctions on Belarus both directly and indirectly. By way of example, the European Parliament passed a resolution under reference C157/465 in July 2005 in which it 'strongly condemns the Belarus regime's indiscriminate attacks on the media, journalists, members of the opposition, human rights activists and any person who attempts freely to voice criticism of the President and the regime'. This and all other criticism has met with robust and withering rebuttals on the part of the Belarusian government, along with suggestions that Western democracies might care to reflect on their own policies and human rights records, domestic and foreign. All the while, the Russian Federation sits impassively in the ambivalence of its own relationship with Belarus and the West. It's as though the Cold War had never ended. Inevitably, the truth lies somewhere along the great divide. Certainly, there are many pertinent questions to be asked and answered, but the same can be said for many political regimes around the world, including some very close to home. Perhaps the best indicator is the view of the human rights and 'media watch' charities that have critically reviewed the substantial body of evidence of state control and suppression of freedom of speech that is said to exist in abundance. You must make up your own mind from all that you read and see. The official website of the Republic of Belarus is w belarus.by. The President's own website is w president. gov.by. For an alternative view, you might continue your research on the website of Charter 97 (w *charter97.org*), an independent organisation campaigning for human rights and democracy in Belarus. The websites of NGO Human Rights

Watch (w *hrw.org*) and not-for-profit organisation Reporters Without Frontiers (w *rsf.org*) are also an interesting read.

An information portal that I follow by email subscription and on social media is the excellent *Belarus Digest* (w *belarusdigest.com*). Launched in 2008, the digest has a team of contributors headed by Yarik Kryvoi. As an online provider of non-aligned analysis on all matters pertaining to Belarus specifically aimed at an English-speaking audience, it publishes articles that are extremely readable and accessible. The website's homepage commendably states its position thus: 'the conduct and poor reputation of the Belarus regime provides fertile ground for all kinds of myth and speculation. Belarus Digest tries to demystify Belarus and write about what is actually going on in the country.' On this very point, one of the most interesting pieces of journalism that I have ever read from within Belarus concerning this much-misunderstood country appeared on the *Belarus Digest* website on 19 February 2014. Entitled *Is Belarus a European North Korea? – Top Three Myths about Belarus in Western Media*, it was written by Artyom Shraibman, an analyst and political observer working for an independent news agency in Minsk. It should still be available to read in the archive section of the website and I do commend it to anyone interested in looking beyond sound bites and strap headlines. Generally, the internet is of course a treasure trove of information and a few hours spent on detailed research through the medium of your favourite search engine before you visit will be time extremely well spent.

Press The country's official website (w *belarus.by*) asserts that as of 1 January 2017, 729 newspapers and 829 magazines were in publication, two-thirds of them in private ownership. Readers may be interested to note the following direct quotation from that official site:

'The Constitution of the Republic of Belarus guarantees the freedom of thought, belief and expression, and prohibits the monopolisation of the media and censorship. The Law 'On Mass Media' formalises the basic principles of the mass media's activity: accuracy, equality, respect for human rights and freedoms, diversity of views, protection of morals and observance of the norms of journalists' professional ethics.'

The state-controlled news agency is The Belarusian Telegraph Agency *BelTA* (w *belta.by*), the largest agency in the country. In terms of print media, the English-language paper *Belarus Today* (w *belarustoday.info*) is published weekly. The principal dailies are *Sevodnya Belarus*, *Sovyetskaya Belarusya* and *Respublika* (all w *sb.by*), all official state newspapers. Printed in Belarusian only is the daily *Zvyazda* (w *zviazda.by*); PDF versions can be downloaded from the website. One of the most important private daily newspapers (often critical of the authorities) was *Belaruskaya Dyelovaya Gazeta* (w *bdg.by*), which has suffered closure after closure throughout its history, and is currently only available online. *Belaruskaya Gazeta* (w *belgazeta.by*) is a weekly private publication primarily in Russian, as is *Nasha Niva* (w *nn.by*), this one bilingual, that has periodically felt the hand of the state on its shoulder. Unfortunately the English pages of the website are no longer being updated, though the archive is still worth a look. Also look for *Argumyenty I Fakty* (w *aif.by*); sadly not available in English, it's a source of comment on the stories behind news and current affairs. Regional newspapers published in each of the major cities are available in each oblast. Most towns will have their own district newspaper, which will often be a single folded sheet containing local news of a parochial nature.

Television According to the state, as of 3 January 2017, 99 television stations were broadcasting daily, 59 of them in private ownership. The state-controlled Belarusian National State Television and Radio Company Belteleradio (**w** *tvr.by*) broadcasts six national channels within the country and produces the internationally available 24-hour satellite channel Belarus 24, providing a wide range of content that includes news, analysis, films, history, culture, cuisine and tourism. Its portfolio of channels within the country consists of Belarus 1 (primarily news), Belarus 2 (directed at the youth audience), Belarus 3 (social and cultural), Belarus 5 (sport), ONT Belarus (national television) and STV (capital city television). Belteleradio additionally broadcasts the regional channel Belarus 4, with locally focused programmes for each of the six regions. It's also easy to pick up a large number of stations broadcasting from Russia, and the usual global stations are available via cable and satellite. Broadcasting in the Belarusian language, independent satellite and cable station Belsat TV (**w** *belsat.eu*) is based in Poland and can be picked up within Belarus on television sets that have the appropriate hardware. Programmes can also be streamed online. The state is not one of its biggest fans and it's no surprise that the authorities do not include it in the package of channels made widely available to Belarusian homes.

Radio The state also says that as of 3 January 2017, 174 radio stations were on air daily, 25 of them private. The state-run company Belteleradio broadcasts five stations: 1st Channel (the flagship station for news, information and culture, the largest in the country), Radio Belarus (**w** *radiobelarus.by*), which broadcasts in Belarusian, Russian, German, Polish, French, Spanish, Chinese and English; Culture, promoting national and international culture, primarily in the Belarusian language; Stolitsa (**w** *radiostalica.by*), the first FM station in the country broadcasting in the Belarusian language only; and Radius FM (**w** *radiusfm.by*), which delivers news and popular music 24/7. Belteleradio also broadcasts regional stations from the five major cities outside Minsk, as do a range of other service providers. Many other state-controlled stations broadcast special-interest programmes. Non-state broadcasters include the popular 24/7 Euroradio FM (**w** *euroradio.by*), which is aimed at the 15–35 market and broadcasts nationally. Stations broadcasting from outside Belarus can also be received, some of them specifically targeting Belarusian listeners, such as Radio Svaboda (**w** *svaboda.org*), with links to Charter 97 (**w** *charter97.org*) and Radio Free Europe (**w** *rferl.org*).

Internet All of the media organisations listed above have their own websites packed with informative pages of news, comment and data. In each case, just bear in mind the identity of whoever is running the site. And do please note that those I list represent only a selection. Your browser will take you to a whole world of alternatives. As mentioned on page 105, I follow the work and output of *Belarus Digest* (**w** *belarusdigest.com*). You might also want to see what the organisation Charter 97 has to say (**w** *charter97.org*)

POST The state post Belpochta (**w** *belpost.by*) offers the usual full range of postal services. Do please note, however, that mail that's not in Cyrillic script, either posted in Belarus for destinations outside the country or posted outside for delivery within Belarus, may very well not reach its destination. If you are sending mail home to the UK or US, then at the very least write ВЕЛИКОБРИТАНИЯ ('Great Britain') or СОЕДИНЕННЫЕ ШТАТЫ АМЕРИКИ ('USA') at the end of each address; that should at least guarantee that your correspondence gets to the UK or USA at some point in time, though not necessarily until after you return home.

The English pages of the company's website are a mine of information and will tell you all you need to know before you travel about services and postal rates. Branches and kiosks are everywhere throughout the country in cities, towns and villages. When you're in Minsk be sure to visit the splendid building of the central post office and don't forget to look out for the Soviet-style clock above the entrance as well as the sumptuous interior décor.

TELEPHONE SERVICES The state-controlled National Telecommunications Operator of the Republic of Belarus, Beltelecom (**w** *beltelecom.by*), provides a full and varied range of modern telephony services to domestic and business users. It is widely believed within the country that telephony services are routinely monitored by the state. No different from the rest of us, then …

The country code for calls from outside Belarus is +375 and the relevant code for each of the six cities and regions of the country is as follows:

Minsk	+375 17	Grodno	+375 152	Mogilev	+375 222
Brest	+375 162	Vitebsk	+375 212	Gomel	+375 232

To make an **international call to Belarus**, dial 00 (or +) 375, followed by the city/region code, and the subscriber's number, though any leading zero should be omitted. To make an **international call from Belarus**, dial 8, wait for the continuous dialling tone, dial 10, the country code, the city code (minus the first zero), followed by the subscriber's number. To make a **landline to landline call within Belarus,** dial 8, wait for the continuous dialling tone, then dial the city/region code followed by the subscriber's number. If making a **landline to mobile call within Belarus,** substitute the relevant mobile code (either 25, 29, 33 or 44) for the city/region code. To make a **landline call within the same town in Belarus,** dial 2, then the subscriber's number only.

Cellular (mobile phone) services are supplied by Velcom (**w** *velcom.by*), MTS (**w** *mts.by*) and Life (**w** *life.com.by*), all of which provide international roaming services. Like everywhere else in the world, mobile telephony is a hugely expanding market in Belarus and by Western standards it's an extremely cheap means of communication within the country's national borders. If you are going to make significant numbers of calls to local numbers within Belarus from your own mobile you will save pots of money by purchasing a local SIM card when you arrive. These are available at any retail outlet of the three mobile operators; you will need to show your passport and pay a modest registration fee. You can also obtain credit there and then. It's very easy to subsequently top up your balance online by calling an automated number, or at a bank or mobile phone outlet. It's also a very cheap way of staying in touch with mobiles at home by way of SMS (text) messaging. A single message costs no more than a handful of pence, but it's not a cheap way to make voice calls. Your credit will disappear before your very eyes at a rate of knots. Consumer website **w** finder.com will tell you all you need to know about services, terms and conditions, coverage and packages offered by each of the country's cellular providers. For **international calls to subscribers of Belarusian mobile networks**, dial +375 then the relevant mobile code (as above) followed by the subscriber's number.

Emergency telephone numbers within Belarus

Emergency services ☏112		**Police** ☏102	
Fire ☏101		**Ambulance** ☏103	

INTERNET As with telephones, the state-controlled Beltelecom oversees and runs the country's servers, a role that includes managing every connection to and from the outside world. The control of the state is, therefore, all-encompassing. In Minsk connections are fast and Wi-Fi is widely available, though public areas are not secure. Outside the capital connection to the internet in homes is still by dial-up in some instances, and is thus very slow. Many hotels and other public spaces throughout the country advertise the availability of secure wireless facilities. Do ensure, however, that your antivirus and security software is the best it can be.

BUSINESS

Usual **business hours** for offices are 09.00–18.00 Monday–Friday; for banks 09.00–17.00 Monday–Friday; for general stores 09.00–21.00 Monday–Saturday, 09.00–18.00 Sunday; and for food shops 09.00–20.00 daily (with many of the newer supermarkets and hypermarkets open 24 hours in the city suburbs and malls). That said, a growing commitment to the adoption of standards of business services you might recognise in the West means that opening hours generally are being extended, although these hours will be more unpredictable and unreliable outside the big cities. Wherever you are, closure for lunch between 13.00 and 14.00 is fairly common and should probably be assumed unless you confidently know to the contrary in specific instances.

If you are in Belarus on business, remember that **bureaucracy and red tape** is a frustrating and omnipresent obstacle to speed, efficiency and flexibility in any transaction, so do plan ahead as much as you can. And do try very hard not to show frustration at legal or administrative requirements and bureaucracy in general. If you do, then things will always be slowed down and another obstacle placed in your way. There's nothing wrong with persisting if you think you're being fobbed off, but this can be done with courtesy, respect and a smile. If you are unsure of your ground it's preferable not to try to blunder on unaided in the search for a way forward. You will always be able to engage the services of a local lawyer or other business consultant to help smooth the way. Belarusians are used to functioning within an impenetrable miasma of contradictory rules and regulations, which means they will generally reserve judgement on an issue or question until they are sure of themselves in any situation.

At first meeting, you can probably expect a brief but very firm handshake and a curt nod of the head by way of introduction. Don't expect effusive enthusiasm and open doors at the outset of negotiations. It's then a question of deporting yourself with all the usual niceties and common courtesies of civilised **business behaviour**. Listen closely, never interrupt or patronise anyone, always acknowledge the other person's point of view, then put your own arguments quietly, respectfully and without histrionics. A touch of dry humour usually goes down very well. Don't try to suggest that your position is in any way stronger than anyone else's or seek to impose your point of view with conduct that might be viewed as bullying. If you do, the shutters will come up and there will be no progress. Bureaucracy and red tape here is difficult enough without you making it easy for someone to shrug their shoulders and tell you that something cannot happen because 'it is not permitted' (a phrase oft used and heard). If you stay calm throughout with a smile on your face, then you can expect to be listened to respectfully, especially if you are also prepared to make concessions in an effort to move things along. And it helps to show that you regard your counterparts as being of equal status to you in every way.

If and when a decision is made on an issue that is acceptable to all sides, the matter does not end there. Decisions are made in stages, upwards through a hierarchy, so even if you manage to gain agreement at one level of an organisation it does not automatically follow that superiors will agree. Generally speaking the higher up you go, the easier it is to get a 'yes', but it is not uncommon for matters to proceed a very long way (and right to the point of conclusion), only for everything to be called off without explanation. So always have an alternative plan ready. And as with negotiations the world over (in business or life in general) if you can make the other side think that the outcome was all their idea in the first place, so much the better.

Overall there are continuing signs that in economic terms, the country is beginning to open up internally and to look outside its borders to encourage trade, business and commerce. The obvious caveat here is the all-encompassing nature of state control. The economy continues to be run on a rigidly planned basis, and even though a growing number of entrepreneurs are looking to imaginatively transact business across national borders, all private operations are subject to registration, detailed scrutiny, regulation and bureaucracy. Whether private or state, the control of every enterprise is absolute. The government is ever more keen to encourage foreign investment into the country, and there are many examples of significant joint enterprise ventures to be seen, although it's usually on the basis that strategic and practical decisions on the way all monies are spent remain fully in Belarusian hands. This has led to a number of high-profile deals running into the sand.

Today Belarus is keen to show the world that it is open for business in markets around the globe, though it remains to be seen how much further the country will extend its hand towards the economic markets of Europe and beyond. It's not an agenda Belarus can control unilaterally, however. At one level, neither the European Union nor the United States of America believe that conditions are favourable for businesses in their countries to trade here. In advance of this point being reached, de facto sanctions operate extensively in the absence of the significant political reform and evidence of a commitment to free speech and the unconditional observance of human rights that the West deems both necessary and appropriate. Meanwhile, business and trade relations with the markets of China are developing at speed. Against that background President Lukashenko shows no sign of embracing political reform or abandoning the state's commitment to a planned and controlled economy in favour of more free-market principles. Yet the language of every public statement continues to be about opening up trade with the rest of Europe and beyond. There are many agendas at work here. Previously, the message from Belarus has been to push for greater co-operation and ultimately perhaps even formal union with the Russian Federation while on other (notable) occasions, criticism of Russia (particularly its foreign policy) is loud and unequivocal. Events across the border in Russia are particularly interesting in this context, where President Putin's position as head of state appears to grow ever stronger. His approach to making Russia a world economic and political player are interesting: one might say that his methods (in domestic and foreign policy terms) fail to attract universal approval. In 2014 relations between Russia and the West steadily worsened as the crisis in Ukraine sank to the edge of the abyss and, since that time, many observers have found it easy to conclude that the old days of the Cold War have returned. In 2017 persistent allegations of Russian interference by electronic and digital means in a number of Western elections refused to go away. Subplots, subtexts, allegations, counter-allegations and 'fake news' are everywhere to be seen. It is very difficult to forecast how things will go from here.

BUYING PROPERTY

Type 'buying property in Belarus' into a search engine and you will immediately gain access to several websites telling you how easy it is to become a property owner in Belarus. Don't be fooled. Although the voracious international market in land and property deals is focusing increasingly on the countries of the former Eastern bloc as the latest source of cheap investment, Belarus is firmly closed for business in this sphere. Other than for the 'new money' classes, there is no real concept of proprietorial land ownership as there is in the West. Many people rent their homes from the state. In the country there is no zeal for being ostentatiously seen as lord and master of the land, as evidenced by a distinctly laissez-faire attitude to the delineation of property boundaries. People here just aren't in the least bothered about being seen as land and property owners. They have far more important things to occupy their time and thoughts.

CULTURAL ETIQUETTE

The characteristics of the Belarusian people are hard to generalise and in any event it's hugely difficult to give a view without sounding monumentally patronising. The general adage that you can only 'speak as you find' is as true with this as with anything else. The comments that follow, therefore, are an articulation of the impressions I have gained from interacting closely with a broad range of people over a period of 17 years, including ministers, diplomats, senior government staff, journalists, business people, teachers, academics, public officials and perhaps most importantly of all, everyday folk of all ages in their homes and communities. If I have to generalise I would say that I have often observed a calm demeanour, tolerance and a wicked sense of dry humour during my time in Belarus. On first meeting, people are unfailingly respectful, courteous and polite. Be sure to reciprocate. Don't mistake a degree of shyness or reserve for offhanded behaviour. If you take the lead it doesn't take long for any initial reserve to be relaxed. Generous gestures of unconditional hospitality almost always follow and open conversation will soon flow. People here can get very passionate when debating the big issues of the day, which often happens around the kitchen table. You will be expected to play your part in the debate and will be asked a great many questions about life where you come from. Be honest, but be very careful about how you comment on Belarusian society. Derogatory statements will not go down well. Never be critical of the government or of the president, because you never know who might be listening. The banya, or Belarusian sauna, can be a great way to bond with hosts and friends (see box, page 46). There are communal banya in many towns with nominal entrance fees. The format is largely the same as with private banya, but the anteroom will be much larger and will contain communal shower facilities, while cold water will be available in a plunging pool outside the steam room. You will inevitably be in the company of strangers here, so the bonding experience of the more intimate private banya shared with friends may well be supplanted by macho posturing.

TRAVELLING POSITIVELY

When I talk to people about how unspoilt and uncommercialised Belarus is and about how that makes it a destination of rare interest for the visitor, the response is always the same: that nobody will go until budget flights are available. That is a very depressing supposition. Put bluntly, there is a very persuasive argument that the footprint we leave as we depart a country has considerably greater importance than the intentions and aspirations we have for our visit when we arrive. Budget flights anywhere do not necessarily encourage such an altruistic aim, and the very opposite can sometimes be an unfortunate consequence.

Since the Chernobyl catastrophe, much of the aid that has been targeted at Belarus and its people has been by way of humanitarian assistance. Yet for a number of years, sustainable development programmes have been on the increase, with the purpose of transferring skills and experience to help build an infrastructure for local people to develop local solutions to their own problems.

Your presence in Belarus and the interest you show in the people you meet and all that you see will be a very good start. To give you a few ideas about continued involvement on your return home, you might want to have a look at the websites listed on page 330, which will give you a broad feel for the types of project that are being supported by the international community. I shall be very surprised if you do not return from your first visit with a burning resolve to put something back into this wonderful country and its people. Plenty of

HOW TO CHAPERONE GEESE

One of the early projects that the West Oxfordshire Vetka Association (WOVA) chose to support in its infancy was the establishment of a goose-farming co-operative in the village of Svetilovichy, right in the heart of the contaminated zone in southeastern Belarus. A beautiful (but very hot) summer's day saw me standing by a dusty roadside on the edge of the village, waiting to chaperone a flock of goslings to their new homes. After an hour or so, a battered and beaten saloon pulled up. Out clambered the driver, extremely hot and bothered. When he opened up the back I could scarcely believe my eyes, for crammed in from floor to roof was tray after tray of two-day old goslings, 750 of them. They had travelled all the way from Minsk, a 7-hour journey, without water or fresh air. Miraculously, all survived. After a cursory examination of the precious cargo, we led the saloon through the village to a small farmstead, where local villagers had been waiting patiently for over 2 hours in the heat of the midday sun. They formed an orderly queue to the rear of the saloon and each family or individual took charge of 20 inquisitive and noisy birds, many of the villagers stuffing them into wicker baskets for transportation home. The aged babooshkas had tears of gratitude in their eyes and flowing down their cheeks as they headed slowly home with their new charges. Witnessing this scene of real community engagement, it was impossible not to be moved and deeply humbled. The local co-ordinator Anna wept as we stood side by side and hand in hand to watch the distribution process. I drive through this village regularly on my travels. On one such occasion our car pulled to the side of the road and there stood Anna, overjoyed to see me again and tearful as ever, to give extravagant hugs and kisses and to press a plastic carrier bag of gifts into my hand for my wife and children, before pushing me gently but with purpose back into the car. The whole encounter took no more than 30 seconds, but she had heard I was in the locality and had waited by the roadside for my car to pass through to give me presents for my family. As for the fate of the geese and the co-operative? Ah, that's another story for another book ...

David and I are spending the day at the Children's Correction Centre in Vetka. We walk into a small room, where soothing music is softly playing. It has simple, basic furniture and ordinary décor. At a table in the middle of the room sits 14-year-old Zhenya. When he first started coming to the centre, all he could do was walk and lie down, but not sit. As he rocks slowly backwards and forwards, his head on his chest, the face of teacher Galina glows with pride as she tells of the great progress he is making, and how it is a wonderful achievement for him to be able to sit unaided. Sometimes he lifts his head, mutters indistinct sounds and smiles. He is the eldest child of four in his family, and lives in a village 30km away, where there are still hotspots of radiation following the Chernobyl catastrophe.

Zhenya is doubly incontinent, and sometimes his family has no nappies for him. With love and devotion, Galina works with him every day to develop his basic motor functions. She begins each session by gently massaging his hands. He is unable to hold a pencil, and wouldn't know what to do with it anyway, but with Galina's guiding hand he becomes an artist. She smothers his palm and fingers with bright red paint and then gently makes a handprint on a sheet of paper. Today he has a cold. He sneezes and snuffles, and sits and rocks.

In a corner of the same room, held on a rudimentary couch of cushions by a single harness attached by velcro, lies Nina, who is also 14 years old. Her mother sits quietly in another corner, hands in lap, patiently watching all that transpires in this room of calm, loving care. Nina has profound and very significant needs, the most pressing of which are caused by acute hydrocephalus. Mum says that inside her head, which teacher Tatyana gently strokes, 20% is brain and 80% is water. Elsewhere in the world the condition is treated by the application of a routine procedure to drain the fluid. Here in Belarus, it seems that no such procedure is available.

Nina can see and hear and she smiles a great deal, especially when she is spoken to and when you hold her hand. She has the most beautifully radiant smile, which lights up the room and makes everyone's heart sing. She adores music and she loves to be touched and stroked. When David and I sit by her side and hold her hand, in slow and deliberate motion she turns her head towards us, and she beams that dazzling smile. Tatyana and Mum release the harness and together they lift her into a semi-upright sitting position, which is no easy task; she also has little or no motor function. But when you hold her hand, she hangs on for dear life. For many moments, this girl is the centre of the universe for us all.

Mum tells us that she is able to sound out simple words – 'mum', 'dad', 'give' – and that she has very discerning taste. At every meal, Mum chews Nina's food

options exist, certainly in the UK and Ireland, and the best thing of all is that you can get involved quickly in your own locality and pretty soon you will have the chance to play a direct and active role. My own view is that while humanitarian assistance can certainly help to alleviate some of the hardship that exists in this country, it does little to stimulate growth and development within the regions in sustainable terms. And it is only by this means that communities and individuals will be able to build confidence and self-respect in the search for ownership and control of their own destiny. The development projects that I had the opportunity to personally implement with Belarusian communities and then transfers it into her mouth. If she doesn't like it, she spits it out. We hear that she particularly likes chocolate. Not for the first time today, I think of my own kids.

It is at this point that Galina whispers to our translator Oxana that she would like to ask her a personal question outside. When they come back into the room, Oxana quietly says that Galina is worried we might be upset by today's experience, that we might find it 'distasteful'. Nobody ever comes to the centre to show even the slightest passing interest, so to have someone from outside the circle of family and carers sitting with the children, holding their hand and talking to them is an event of extraordinary potency. Such a small gesture, but one of such significance to those who believe that nobody cares about them.

Nina is yawning now and we leave her to rest for a while. In his corner, Zhenya snoozes fitfully, his hands behind his head. Over a cup of tea the centre's Director, Elena, tells us more about the two children, and also about Vanya. His hydrocephalus is severe and specialists attend him at home, because he cannot be transported to the centre. He is blind and has only limited hearing. November will see his 16th birthday. Support to his family includes a significant psychological element for his mother. She cries a great deal.

Today is our third consecutive visit. Each time, around lunchtime, we have taken tea with Elena. And on each occasion, as we look out of the window, the centre's bus draws up outside. Galina and Tatyana hold a hand each to walk Zhenya out for the ride home. Cradling her precious child carefully in her arms, Nina's mum carries her to the bus and climbs aboard to sit with her on her lap. There is no harness and no seat belt. Today I see them to the bus and wave as the door is closed. Nina smiles and she is gone. Every day, the driver covers 360km of Vetka's roads, some of them dirt tracks, to collect the children and then take them back home.

Later, as we emerge into the spring sunshine for a walk, we ask if Elena and Oxana will do us the honour of allowing us to buy them lunch. Our offer is politely declined. Then with the trace of a mischievous smile, first Elena says that she likes red roses before Oxana tells us she prefers black ones. Later, as we walk back through town, Elena announces that she has changed her mind. It would please her greatly if we could buy nappies. Zhenya has no need for red roses.

The next day, David and I go to the market. We buy nappies, washing powder and food for Nina, Zhenya, the others and their families. We spend less than £20. A measly 20 quid. A fast-food meal for four at home. A third of a tank of fuel for a family car. Three packets of cigarettes. So who or what really needs correcting here?

For Part II see box, page 114.

over a period of 15 years under the umbrella of the charity I helped to found and run, the West Oxfordshire Vetka Association (WOVA), were *absolutely* the most rewarding and fulfilling activities I have ever pursued outside the environment of my home and my family. At the outset I had no specialist skills in the field but by learning with people themselves in their own communities as they progressed their own learning and experience, I was fortunate indeed to feel that it really is possible to make a difference to (and have a positive impact on) the lives of real people. The work was never easy and was sometimes intensely frustrating, yet in terms not only of the outcomes delivered in Belarus but also my own personal

For Part I see box, page 112.

There is an inevitably depressing reality about every block of flats in Belarus, and in every former Eastern bloc state that I've been to for that matter; the concrete is archetypically Soviet and almost always crumbling, the condensation on the windows is impenetrable, there's usually an overweight topless bloke leaning over a balcony somewhere smoking a cigarette, and the common areas are unremittingly grim. And as we mount the stairs to the top floor of this particular block on Sverdlova Street in the town of Vetka, deep in the heart of the Chernobyl radiation zone, I feel nervous. Elena asked us to think very carefully before we agreed to meet Vanya. His mother cries a lot. We might be upset, or offended, she says.

We reach the top floor and knock on the last door. We are welcomed inside and we enter a world of calm, peaceful order. The weather is really hot this week and inside the flat all is rather airless and oppressive (or is that just our nervousness?). I feel clumsy as introductions are made, and in my haste to remove my shoes I tread on the phone and send it flying. But Vanya's mother Natasha greets us warmly. She is anxious that we meet her son.

He lies on a covering on a rubber sheet on a short bed in a small room, where Belarusian folk music gently plays on a small music system. Vanya likes music, you see, and he especially likes Belarusian folk. The first thing I notice is the size of his head. His face is turned in our direction and his eyes are open, but I know at once that he doesn't see us. Those sightless, unfocused eyes roll in their sockets as we gather round him. His breathing is steady. A blanket covers him from the neck down (it's the mosquito season), but we can tell at once that his small body is motionless and locked in the foetal position.

Natasha talks to him gently. He recognises her voice. His carer Anna says that he likes to be touched (just like Nina). She delicately taps the side of the wardrobe above Vanya's head, and his mouth opens into an enormous smile. Even though he cannot see and can only slightly distinguish between dark and light, his hearing is good and he adores that knocking sound.

As I hold Vanya's hand, which is grotesquely locked in an unnaturally awkward position, Anna gently unfurls two of his fingers, which are long, and slim, and quite beautiful. The fingers of a musician, we all agree. Later, after we have gone, Anna will dab paint on his finger, just as Galina and Natasha do with Zhenya and Nina at the centre, then she will gently press it to the paper on which is drawn a beautiful tree in springtime, with long branches and nascent greenery; for it is Vanya's job to add the finishing touch of blossom. That beautiful picture will be framed when we get home, and prominently displayed. David and I want people to know about Vanya.

It is time to let him rest, and Natasha ushers us into the living room. She has 'English tea' for us, as well as freshly baked buns. With something of a flourish, she reaches into the sideboard behind her, produces a bottle of vodka, and presents it

development, I wouldn't change a single moment of it. My colleagues and I made plenty of mistakes, but I'd like to think we learned from all of them and did our very best to put the experience of that shared learning into positive outcomes in our subsequent project work.

In 2009, I was taken to see the grimly named 'Children's Correction Centre' in Vetka. It supports children and their families across a full spectrum of special to me to take home. While I'm saying thank you, she reaches for another bottle. This time it is Russian champagne. We raise our glasses and drink to Vanya. Natasha tells us all about him. Everything about his birth was normal and for the first few weeks of his life there were no indications that anything was amiss. Then one morning, as she stood over his crib, he woke. She watched as his eyes opened and then slowly rolled to the top of their sockets. Natasha's own eyes are now watery as she tells us that with each day that passed, his head began to swell; how he would cry every day, and that he was inconsolable. They didn't know what to do. No-one could help. It has been a long, steady process of decline and degeneration since then. Natasha tells us how lucky she is that Vanya's father, Kolya, is so devoted to him. Every day, he carries Vanya to the bath, climbs in first with the boy in his arms, and lowers him slowly into the water as he sits down beneath him, a feat of formidable endurance and strength. The dignity and strength and love and endurance of this family leave all of us in awe, and the living room is very quiet now.

Natasha turns to the sideboard again, rummages in a box of papers, and pulls out two documents. Vanya has not only a civilian passport issued by the government, just like everybody else, but he also has an army one. We hear of Natasha's pride, and also of her anguish, the day the military came to tell the family they wanted Vanya to play his part in the defence of the Motherland. He would never be able to, of course, but the bestowing of such revered status was nonetheless a source of great honour. This boy has the authority of the state and of the military to go anywhere in the world, but his condition is so severe that he cannot leave his home, not even to go to the centre; his world is his bedroom, the bathroom and the living room of this top-floor flat. He has no motor function, must be carried everywhere, and his whole body, especially his head, must be fully supported at all times.

Natasha's tears flow again as I squeeze her hand.

Later in the week, David and I would meet the local Director of Education, and give our pledge not to abandon Zhenya and Nina and Vanya and the others. As I hold Natasha's hand now, I look into her eyes and give the same pledge. She is grateful that we have come, and that we have listened. Some visitors from elsewhere in Europe came last year, she tells us; they took photographs and tea, and smiled and laughed, then left. She hasn't seen or heard from them since.

Footnote: Over the next two years, David and I got to know Kolya, Natasha and Vanya really well. We spent many hours in their company. Then one Friday night in March I was at a football match in Doncaster with my son George when I received an unexpected and very distressed phone call from Natasha. Vanya was unwell, she told me, and was in hospital. The doctors said there was nothing they could do. After a short illness, Vanya Agophonov died on 30 March 2012. He was 17 years old. Our dear Vanya was laid to rest the very next day.

needs, from slow learning and speech therapy at one end all the way to profound physical and mental disability at the other. That first visit made it very clear that the centre itself had many needs and when I went back in 2010 to spend the week there, I could see this was the project that WOVA had been waiting to find. For starters, half of the centre's buildings were derelict and in need of major works of structural repair. We developed a detailed project plan and a strategy for sourcing offers of expertise, funding and support to put in place the facilities that the children, their families and the devoted staff so richly deserve. Delivering positive outcomes proved to be a difficult and frustrating journey, but the good news is that by the spring of 2014 the vast majority of the necessary works had been completed, with the building handed back to the centre's Chief Executive and staff, duly refurbished and newly equipped to provide better services for vulnerable children and their families. I was invited to attend the grand opening that was due to take place later that year, but I politely declined. Neither I nor WOVA embarked on the project for public acknowledgement, gongs, awards or a high-profile media presence. We were happy to leave all of that to the ex-politicians now playing a public role in the higher strata of international organisations who fly into areas of need by helicopter and fly out a few hours later after being photographed with local dignitaries and posting self-publicising material on their Twitter, Instagram and Facebook accounts. This happened on numerous occasions in the areas where WOVA worked, but I'll save the articulation of my frustrations on this for my blog and other publications beyond the remit of this guide. For now I'll climb off my soapbox and close on this subject by saying that development and charity work should never be about personal gain, recognition, reward or award. You can read more about some of the remarkable children I met and a little of my encounters involving the centre in the boxes on pages 112 and 114.

All of the projects I worked on (even those less successful than others) enriched my life beyond measure. And to feel that I have been taken into the hearts of people in a very different community from my own, a long way from my home, is truly humbling. Every time my plane touches down at Minsk or I cross the border, it feels like coming home. Getting involved couldn't be easier. Over to you now to play your part.

INTERNATIONAL CHARITIES

Chernobyl Children International

w chernobyl-international.com. Based in Ireland, this organisation has undertaken an astonishing amount of work over the last 26 years or so, raising around €100 million of direct aid to regions affected by the catastrophe & arranging recuperation breaks in Ireland for approximately 25,000 children from areas affected by radiation fallout.

Chernobyl Children's Project w chernobyl-children.org.uk. An umbrella charity with regional groups in England, Scotland & Wales working with children, families & young people in the aftermath of the nuclear disaster. Support is given to children's cancer treatment, hospices, orphanages & holiday camps within Belarus, while every year recuperative holidays in the UK are offered to groups of children living in the areas blighted by radiation. This is a very fine charity delivering effective & practical support to the most vulnerable in Belarusian society.

The Together Plan w thetogetherplan.com. A London-based charity working closely with partner organisation Dialog in Minsk. Its aim is to help & support Jewish communities in Belarus to develop & realise their potential, including the Minsk Jewish Ghetto Survivors Association (see box, page 177).

United Nations Development Programme w by.undp.org. This website is dedicated to the United Nations Development Programme in Belarus. The entirety of the programme has a global application in the field of sustainable development. There are many initiatives presently under way in Belarus.

LOCAL CHARITIES A brief word now about local charities and NGOs operating in Belarus that are not related to the alleviation of Chernobyl consequences. They certainly do exist and, indeed, I have many Belarusian friends and colleagues undertaking splendid work in the field of community development and the promotion of family health and well-being, but if you type 'charities in Belarus' into your internet search engine, page after page will appear with a Chernobyl theme. I know of many small individual NGOs operating in the regions and indeed, I have worked closely with a number of them on locally focused projects designed to benefit particular communities, or parts of them. State rules and regulations applicable to NGOs in this country are comprehensive (that's a euphemism) and life can be difficult for them. The best way to gain access to their areas of activity is via the United Nations and its constituent bodies, such as UNDP or UNICEF. An hour or two spent on the relevant websites will enable you to locate projects of specific application, including details of local partner NGOs and charities in Belarus itself.

Alternatively, all of the charities whose objectives are related to the alleviation of problems and consequences for Chernobyl children and their families have locally based activities and functions throughout the UK, Ireland and many other countries in western Europe. Offers of help and assistance, particularly with regard to hosting Belarusian children on recuperative holidays, are always gratefully received. Wherever you live, a local branch is unlikely to be far away. I have met many families who have offered their homes to children in this way and entirely without exception, the experience has always been described to me as a life-affirming one. Irrespective of this being a wonderful opportunity for you to 'give something back', it will also greatly enhance your own personal development and that of your family members, particularly children. Kids are rarely burdened with the baggage that only comes with adulthood and to see deep friendships flourish between youngsters, notwithstanding language barriers, is an experience not to be missed. And this can be the door that leads you to other community-based activities for the benefit of families and individuals in Belarus. There are opportunities to support any number of projects that are designed to build capacity and well-being, from investment, funding and monetary donations on the one hand, all the way to more direct contributions on the other, including for example, offering skills and expertise for building projects, driving vehicles bearing humanitarian aid or collecting plant and equipment in your own country for transportation to Belarus. Among other things, I have taken through customs a computer modem, medical equipment, toys, books, writing equipment, resuscitation dummies, clothes and a coffee jug. Oh and that lawnmower, of course. Opportunities to make a contribution really are boundless and you won't regret a single moment or a single penny.

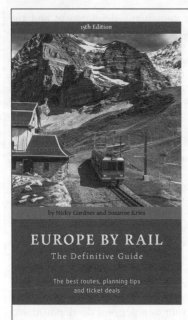

Part Two

THE GUIDE

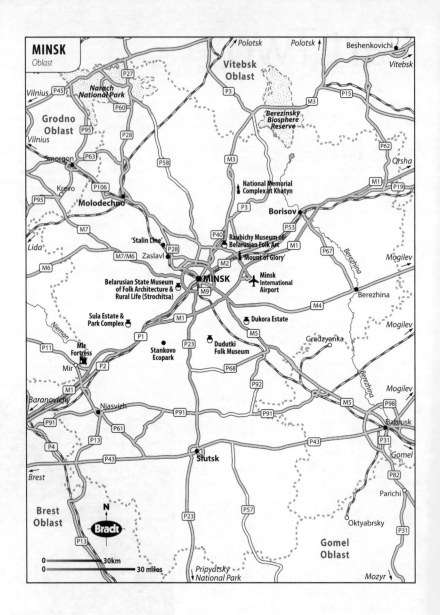

MINSK
Oblast

Polotsk → *Polotsk* ↑ Beshenkovichi

Vitebsk

Vitebsk
Oblast

P27

*Narach
National Park*

Vilnius P45 P60

P3 M3 P15

*Berezinsky
Biosphere
Reserve*

Grodno
Oblast

P95 P28

P62

Vilnius

Smorgon P63 M3 M1 *Qrsha*

P106 P19

Krevo National Memorial
Complex at Khatyn

Molodechno

P95 P3 Borisov

M7 P53

'Stalin Line' Raubichy Museum of
Belarusian Folk Art

Lida P40 M1 P67 *Mogilev*

P28

M7/M6 Zaslavl 'Mount of Glory'

M6 M2

Belarusian State Museum MINSK Minsk
of Folk Architecture & International
Rural Life (Strochitsa) M9 Airport

Nieman M1 Dukora Estate M4 Berezhina

Sula Estate & P1 *Mogilev*
Park Complex

P11 Mir M5
Fortress Stankovo Dudutki Gradzyanka
Mir Ecopark Folk Museum

P2 P23 P68 *Mogilev*

M1 P92

Baranovichy Njasvizh M5 P98

P91 P91 P91 Babrusk

P61 P43 P31

P4 P13 *Gomel*

P43 Slutsk P82

Brest Parichi

Brest
Oblast P23 P57

P13 Oktyabrsky P31

Bradt Gomel
Oblast

0 ——— 30km
0 ——— 30 miles

*Pripyatsky
National Park* *Mozyr*

3

Minsk City and Oblast
Мінск/Минск

Telephone code 17

Minsk is the capital and largest city in Belarus, with a population of 1,974,800 in 2017. As the national capital, it has special administrative status in the country and it is also the administrative centre of Minsk oblast. Perhaps surprisingly, given the geographical size and metaphorical significance of its giant neighbour, the Russian Federation, Minsk is also the headquarters of the Commonwealth of Independent States (CIS), which was formed on the breakup of the Soviet Union. In truth, however, the significance of this status is minimal. The CIS has always been a fluid federation, honoured more in concept than in reality.

First reference to a settlement here appeared in the *Primary Chronicle* of 1067 (acknowledged as an authoritative work of written Kievan Rus history). Situated on one of the most significant trade routes connecting the Baltic and Black seas, today this reconstructed city of expansive boulevards, wide streets, modern and Classical architecture, huge shaded parks, fountains and monuments to heroism on the banks of the Svislach River has an appeal all of its own that it will take you some while to articulate, even though you feel it as soon as you set foot here. It has long been regarded as one of the most impressive cities in all of the republics of the former Soviet Union. Almost completely destroyed by the Nazis in World War II (still referred to in the former Soviet republics as the 'Great Patriotic War'), Stalin ordered it to be rebuilt after the conflict ended in a manner that would stand as a testament to the rest of the world of the might, resilience and ingenuity of Soviet communism. As such, it remains the best example of post-war Soviet urban planning on a grand scale (and the only one of the western Soviet republics' capital cities largely untainted, for now, by Western commercialism, though the balance is tipping ever more quickly). Herein lies its appeal and idiosyncrasy, for after a short while here you begin to realise that it is unlike any other capital city that you have visited before.

Minsk is the sort of place where you can feel relaxed and at ease without even knowing it. Most capitals of the world are characterised by a high level of ambient noise and a jumble of activity wherever you look. Not so Minsk. For a city of nearly two million people, the atmosphere is universally calm. Outside rush hour, when there is gridlock at major junctions and drivers are impatiently leaning on car horns, ten-lane boulevards are often devoid of traffic. In many cities of the world, there is a feeling of claustrophobia as buildings close in on top of each other. But in Minsk, the skies are huge and there is a real sense of open space. Wherever you meander, vast and sweeping panoramas unfold before your gaze, all with a host of different sights. At times it feels you can stroll for ages in areas of parkland and not see another soul, but without feeling nervous in the process. The streets are spotlessly clean and free from crime or even antisocial behaviour. Access to all areas of interest to the visitor by public transport is simple and uncomplicated, not to say impressively efficient. Many of the sights can be reached on foot and in so doing, you will rediscover an activity that is largely lost in the West these days: that of promenading. This is because walking is seen as so much more than simply a mechanical act of propulsion from A to B. Rather, it is an art form to be savoured, with every footstep to be relished. Everywhere you look, even in the depths of winter and no matter what the time of day or night, you will see people strolling, apparently aimlessly, but locked in conversation and arm in arm. Here in Minsk (and indeed, everywhere in Belarus), teenagers mingle with families, young children, older people and young women on their own or in twos, just taking the air, enjoying the sights, chatting and relishing the fact that they have, for a short while, stepped off the merry-go-round of life.

My favourite time to be in Minsk is on a Sunday, before breakfast. I always set the alarm early and get out on the street as soon as I can lever myself out of bed, just to walk and walk. The grandiose buildings and particularly the monuments to the heroism of the city and its people during the privations of war are all the more impressive if you can enjoy them in solitude and in silence. Often I ride the metro for hours with a multiple-journey card, picking stations at random and alighting to wander. My favourite treat to myself is to get out at Traktorny Zavod (Minsk Tractor Works), emerging from the subway a time traveller, launched back 50 years into the heyday of the Soviet Union. Monuments, flags, banners, billboards and the Stalinist architecture of the factory itself proclaim the glory of labour under Lenin's authoritative gaze. And on Sunday you will have the whole place to yourself to meander as you please. Inner peace, serenity, a feeling of security and a rare connection with the soul, all on the streets of a major capital city? Count on it!

GEOGRAPHY AND CLIMATE

As your plane banks and gradually descends on its approach into Minsk, you may be surprised to find relatively dense forest not that far from the airport. It's true that Minsk National is a little way out of town, but the drive into the city centre through the suburbs also reveals pockets of dense woodland either side of the main routes. They have been ingeniously incorporated into areas of parkland, but the whole effect is to give a very clear impression of the great swathe of primeval forest that once covered the entirety of the central European plain.

The hills across which the city has spread over the centuries and through which the Svislach River gently meanders can hardly be called hills at all, for the mean altitude above sea level struggles to reach 200m. And whether you approach Minsk by land or by air, from any direction, the impression gained is always the same: it's pretty flat.

A cursory glance at the map of Europe shows that Belarus is situated right in the middle of the continental land mass, with the capital city itself at the heart of the country.

All of these factors combine to produce a continental climate that is both moderate and temperate. Prevailing winds are westerly, northwesterly and southwesterly, a consequence of which is the relatively frequent incidence of moist air masses from the Atlantic. So it is that average temperatures for each season and the annual level of precipitation (falling as rain and snow) sit in the middle of the average for the whole country.

HISTORY

It does not overstate the issue to say that the entire history of Minsk (and indeed, of greater Belarus) is characterised by conflict, invasion and subjugation. It is a quirk of fate or the whim of the gods that it just happens to have been in absolutely the wrong place at entirely the wrong time on so many occasions, caught between the envious gaze of warring and expansionist neighbours on all sides. This is reflected in the history of the city. First mentioned in *Chronicles* as Menesk in 1067, it was founded on the banks of the Svislach and Nyamia rivers, when the population of an older settlement, now the village of Gorodische, 16km away on the Menka River (from which Minsk derives its name) moved to a more favourable location, the site of the present city. The first settlement was no more than a fortified wooden fortress incorporating the homes of the townspeople, the whole being surrounded by earthen ramparts. It came under the protection of the state of Polotsk, widely regarded as the first ever independent Belarusian state. The first structures of stone appeared by the middle of the 12th century, by which time the significance of the town was incrementally rising as a consequence of the separation of Polotsk into a smaller number of independent jurisdictions, each under the control of its own prince. Before the split, the territory of the town and the entirety of the area had been scarred by the violence of warfare as opposing princes sought supremacy. Its geographical location at the heart of the European continent, situated on important trade routes by road and by river, ensured its significance as a conquest to be prized.

THE 13TH TO 18TH CENTURIES When the Grand Duchy of Lithuania acquired it in 1242, key members of the local elite quickly began to enjoy privileged rank and status in the state's hierarchy and in society. As a consequence, the town soon became one of the largest and most significant in the whole of the duchy. Prince Vasily is mentioned as being ruler in 1325 and then in 1387 Prince Yagyela gifted the town and its surrounding settlements to his brother Skyrgal, who passed them to Prince Vitovt just five years later. Around this time, Minsk was added to the Wilno (now Vilnius) province of the grand duchy, before gaining greater significance as the centre of its own administrative area later that century. The emerging status of the city was recognised further in 1499 when the great Lithuanian prince Alexander bestowed Magdeburg rights of self-determination upon it. By this time, the population was around 4,000. Warfare and conflict returned again in 1505 when the town was burned and looted by the Mongol Golden Horde, although the fortified castle held out. Two years later, it came under siege again, this time by troops under the command of the Moscow prince Mikhail Glinsky. But in 1569, it became the capital of its own province upon the formation of the mighty Rzeczpospolita state (when the Treaty of Lublin united the Grand Duchy with the Kingdom of Poland). It quickly became the largest city at that time in the territory of modern Belarus, incorporating 60 other towns and villages. The union brought about the first significant societal development of the city for some while, as a significant Polish community settled there and quickly began to influence its culture and administration.

The struggle for supremacy over this important settlement proceeded unabated. Surrounded by the three mighty states of Poland, Lithuania (which by then had joined into one) and Russia, this is hardly surprising. The Livonian Wars with Russia under Ivan the Terrible (which had begun in 1558) did not end until 1583, although the city's position as a powerful seat of government was further recognised in 1580 when the Grand Duchy's Supreme Court of Appeal was relocated there, alternating every two years with Wilno and Novogrudok. All the while, the cultural, commercial and spiritual development of the city was proceeding apace in spite of the constant threat of warfare. As significant architectural features began to spring up all over town, its civic status was recognised when it was granted its own coat of arms (in 1591). Again, armed conflict exacted its price and significant structural damage was suffered in the war between Russia and Rzeczpospolita that began in 1654. Russian forces occupied the city in 1655 and very few houses survived, with the population halved (to around 2,000) by the time they were expelled. In fact, the city was under Russian administration until 1667. More hardship was to follow. The extensive works of restoration and rebuilding that were put in train thereafter were wiped out during the Northern Wars between Russia and Sweden, first under the occupation of Swedish forces in 1707, then again when the city was retaken by Russian troops under Peter the Great.

A period of relative stability followed throughout the remainder of the 18th century, but the long period of destruction had left its mark and Minsk was by now little more than an insignificant provincial settlement of some 7,000 people. But the days of the once-mighty state of Rzeczpospolita were numbered and upon the occasion of its Second Partition in 1793, Minsk became part of another mighty state, this time the Russian Empire. It quickly acquired the status of capital of a Russian province (in 1796) and under the patronage of its powerful new rulers it began to grow and develop exponentially. The original blueprint for the modern city is still recognisable from this time; for example, the line of the main Zakharyevskaya thoroughfare remains as originally laid out. It subsequently became known as Francysk Skaryny Avenue, then Nyezhavizhimosty (Russian for 'Independence') and today is known as Nyezalyezhnastsi (Belarusian for 'Independence'). At this time, the city's buildings were still predominantly wooden structures, but three major fires in the period up to 1835 had enabled the pace of redevelopment to quicken. With inevitability, civic and architectural progress had again been interrupted by warfare when the 1812 invasion by French troops under Emperor Napoleon decimated the city's population (from 11,200 to just under 3,500). During the war Minsk was used by the French army as a major base for munitions and weapons, as the front line moved eastward towards Moscow.

It is quite a thought to muse on the inherent contradiction of a city striving to grow and develop through the centuries against a backdrop of almost ceaseless destruction and bloodshed. As discussed elsewhere on these pages, this contradiction and its consequential privations have gone a long way towards shaping the national psyche of the country and its people that is still so in evidence today.

19TH-CENTURY PROGRESS As the decades of the 18th century passed, the march of progress proved irresistible. Minsk was rebuilt as a network of streets and boulevards was established. The first library was opened in the 1830s, and the city's first fire brigade was commissioned. This was followed by the establishment of the first theatre company. Broadsheet newspapers began to appear. The population grew to around 30,000 by the middle of the century as trade, commerce and civic administration helped to bind and strengthen the community. Not even armed insurrection on the part of nationalists in 1830 and then again in 1863 was able to halt this progress. The significance of the ancient trade routes through the city was emphasised with the construction of major road and rail links, from east to west linking western Europe to Moscow, and from north to south linking the Baltic and Black seas. Developments in the commercial infrastructure quickly followed as supplies of water, telephone, electricity and urban transport were established, along with new factories. In turn, this led to greater community and societal development as churches, schools and places of entertainment sprang up all over town. As the 20th century approached, the population of the city climbed steadily towards the 100,000 mark.

WORLD WAR I AND ITS AFTERMATH Just when people were getting used to stability and relative affluence, the spark of revolution was fanned into flame throughout the Russian Empire as social and political emancipation gathered pace. In Minsk, major industrial development saw the rise of worker militancy, while the nationalism evidenced by the armed risings of 1830 and 1863 continued to smoulder. Then the fires of destruction burned again as the continent was ravaged by battle and bloodshed during World War I. During 1915 Minsk once again found itself a battle-scarred city on the front line in a major theatre of warfare (Germany's Eastern Front). It was chosen as the location for the headquarters of the Imperial Russian Army (although the Tsar and the chiefs of staff were away to the east in Mogilev), with large infrastructure facilities (such as munitions bases and military hospitals) close by. As before, the city suffered structural damage and a significant diminution in the population as citizens became refugees on the long road east in search of safety in the arms of the Motherland. The revolutionary movement sought to exploit these difficulties and a massive campaign to undermine the morale of the troops proved to be successful. The Bolsheviks promised bread and peace to soldiers, workers and families alike in the internationalist fight against the global oppression of the ruling classes. Matters came to a head when Lenin swept into government following the November Revolution of 1917. A Soviet of Workers was immediately established in the city as military lines of command imploded, with disillusioned soldiers deserting in their tens of thousands and trudging home eastward. At the end of December, the National Belarusian Congress made a formal declaration of the birth of the Belarusian People's Republic, an independent nation state. As a result of the negotiated Treaty of Brest-Litovsk (a staggering piece of exploitative and politically expedient diplomacy on the part of Lenin), which delivered Russia's withdrawal from the war, Minsk fell under the occupation of German troops in February 1918. Then on 25 March, the declaration of independence made in December was formally adopted and the city was pronounced capital of the nascent state. Independence lasted less than 12 months though, and in December 1918 the Red Army marched into town. The status of Minsk as a capital city was reaffirmed in January 1919, but this time of the brand new Belarusian Soviet Socialist Republic (BSSR). A new order had begun, although further destruction and loss of life followed in the war between the emerging USSR and Poland as Lenin sought to unite many territories under the red flag. The war was not formally ended until the Treaty of Riga, under the terms of which Minsk became capital of the BSSR (one of the founding republics of the newly proclaimed USSR). It held this position until the breakup of the Soviet Union in 1991, when it became the capital of the newly independent Republic of Belarus.

Throughout the remainder of the 1920s and the 1930s Minsk benefited from exponential development on a startling scale, in keeping with the rest of the Soviet Union. An ambitious programme of industrialisation and reconstruction began as soon as hostilities ended and within a short space of time, it had gained pace and momentum never before seen in the Western world. In a few short years huge new industrial complexes were in full production to deliver the state-controlled objectives of successive Five Year Plans, while workers and citizens began to benefit from ambitiously established social welfare and community facilities in the form of new schools, hospitals and places of entertainment. But nothing was as it seemed, of course. It was only decades later that the true story of ideological, ethnic and artistic persecution perpetrated by Stalin's brutality in the name of protecting 'the Revolution' began to emerge.

THE GREAT PATRIOTIC WAR History so often repeats itself and it was again the city's destiny that one yoke of oppression was replaced by another. The rise of Nazi barbarism in Germany throughout this time was a cause of great anxiety throughout Europe. Prior to the outbreak of hostilities in September 1939 the population of the city was around 300,000, but after Germany unexpectedly tore up the notorious Molotov–Ribbentrop Pact of Non-Aggression by launching Operation Barbarossa on the Soviet Union on 22 June 1941, Minsk again found itself back on the front line of battle as it had so many times before in its history. The city suffered the horror of aerial bombardment by Blitzkrieg on the very first day of the invasion as Hitler sought to subjugate the population through terror, and it was no surprise when it fell to the invading German army just six days later. The occupation was to endure for 1,100 days. Stalin's policy had been to retreat and fall back to throw every resource into the defence of Moscow and as a result, a great deal of plant and machinery from the majority of the factories in the city, along with tens of thousands of people from the civilian population and the most precious of museum and gallery artefacts had already been shipped eastward deeper into the Motherland for protection and security and to be preserved for future use.

The Nazis immediately declared Minsk the centre of a new Eastern Reichskomissariat and local people were treated with merciless and abject brutality. The context for this was Hitler's absolute belief that the Slavs were a 'subhuman' race that needed to be eradicated from the face of the earth. So it was that communists, so-called 'sympathisers', partisans and ordinary men, women and children were imprisoned, tortured and murdered in huge numbers. Public parks became the site of mass hangings. Many more from the local population were pressed into slave labour, both within Belarus and also following transportation to all corners of the Reich. Food became scarce in the extreme as supplies were requisitioned to feed the occupying forces and thousands of civilians starved to death. The worst of the barbarism was inflicted on the Jewish community (see box, page 177 and page 176). It is not widely known that the city became one of the largest of the Nazi ghettos throughout all of Europe in the war, with up to 100,000 Jews imprisoned there. But by early 1942, the city and its people had begun to fight back, as Minsk became the focal point and pivotal administrative centre of the entire Soviet partisan resistance movement, driving forward the struggle against oppression in Stalin's Great Patriotic War.

LIBERATION AND THE SOVIET UNION Minsk was eventually liberated by Soviet troops amid scenes of unbounded joy on 3 July 1944 (now celebrated as the Republic of Belarus National Independence Day, a national holiday), but the German army had clung on tenaciously throughout the first six months of the year and the destruction of the city was almost total. Most of the houses, factories and administrative buildings had been flattened, while much of the road, rail and bridge infrastructure had been bombed out of use. When the Red Army re-entered the city, it was to find that its population had been decimated from 300,000 at the start of the war in 1939 to little over 50,000 at the cessation of hostilities. Over 70,000 of Minsk's residents had been murdered. When those who lost their lives in the surrounding districts are taken into consideration, the total rises to more than 400,000 people.

At first, serious consideration was given to leaving the ruins of the city untouched, abandoning it and moving the national capital east to Mogilev, but with the final defeat of the Nazis in 1945 the process of rebuilding began. Every effort was made to restore as much of the old city as could be saved. Sadly, precious little was left and today only a small part of the Classical architecture remains, concentrated mostly in Old Town (Старый Город), close to the city centre. Throughout the late 1940s and 1950s, a new city centre rose from the rubble and ashes of the old one, as imposing new buildings in the grand design that became synonymous with Stalin appeared alongside expansive boulevards and within huge squares. Once more, the city grew and began to flourish under a process of massive and unprecedented industrialisation, the undertaking exceeding even that seen in the 1920s and 1930s. Hand in hand with the re-establishment of the social and administrative infrastructure was exponential population growth, as young people moved to the 'big city' from the rural hinterland. There was also a rigidly planned and controlled state policy to migrate skilled workers into the region from other parts of the Soviet Union to finally deliver regeneration. To meet the consequent housing need, Minsk spread outwards beyond its former city boundaries and upwards in the form of archetypical, high-density and high-rise concrete apartment housing.

But in spite of this fundamental transformation, a grateful nation never forgot the sacrifices made by the people of the city in wartime and, with others elsewhere in the USSR, Minsk was bestowed the honour of being officially recognised as 'Hero City (Город Герой) of the Soviet Union' in 1974.

THE POST-SOVIET REPUBLIC After the fall of the Soviet Union in the early 1990s the city's evolution continued, though in a different direction. As the new state sought to establish its credentials on the European and global stage, Minsk began to assume the status and the adornments of an international capital city. Embassies and consulates were opened in abundance as governments worldwide sought to present their credentials and establish their interests, while the administrative buildings that formerly supported the Soviet machine now became centres of national republican government. But as the new republic struggled to find its feet in the wake of the consequences of the Chernobyl catastrophe and the large-scale collapse of the institutions of the former

MINSK Overview
For listings, see pages 139–57

Where to stay

1	40 Let Pobyedi	D4
2	Beijing	D6
3	Belarus	B3
4	Express	C6
5	Hampton by Hilton	B6
6	MyHostel	B6
7	Planyeta	A3
8	Renaissance Marriott	A6
9	U Fontana	A4
10	Victoria	A2
	Victoria & Spa	(see 10)
11	Yubileiny	B3

Off map

Aparthotel Comfort	B6
Beltransgaz	H1
Bonhotel	A4
East Time	E6
Green City	A4
Internationale Bildungs- und-Begegnungsstätte	A6
Marriott	A2
Orbita	A4
Postoyalets	H5
Slavyanskaya	A4
Smile	A6
Sport Time	A2
Sptunik	B6
Turist	E6
Victoria Olimp	A2
Viva	B6
Zvezda	A6

Where to eat and drink

12	26 Coffee Bar	C6
13	Astara	D5
14	Bella Rosa	E3
15	Berezka	D3
16	Bergamo	C1
17	BierKeller	D4
18	Chaihana Lounge	D1
19	Chumatsky Shlyakh	B5
	Clever Irish Pub	(see 27)
	Craftman	(see 27)
20	Doo Dah King	B5
21	Druzya	C1
22	Dyepo	D6
23	Enzo	D6
24	Falcone	B5
25	Fresh	D3
26	Golden Coffee	C3
27	Gvozd	E3
28	Hooligan	D6
29	Jomalungma	E3
30	La Scala	B5
31	Lafka	D6
32	Lido	D2, E2
33	Moby Dick	D6
34	Netto	D3
35	Olivo	D3, E1
	Panorama	(see 3)
36	Royal Oak English Pub	C3
37	Shtolle	E2
38	Taj	B4
39	Tempo	F2
40	Tiflis	F1
41	Traktir Na Parkovoi	B4
42	Vasilki	E1
43	Verba	B2
44	Zerno	D3

Off map

Bastion	F1
Dejavu	C6
Erivan	A4
Matchbol	A3
Natvris Khe	H2
Wood and Fire	H1
Westfalia	A6

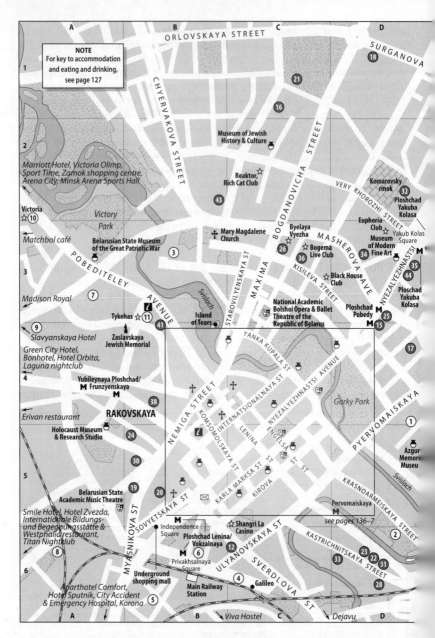

USSR, economic instability was everywhere to be seen. Yet since the turn of the century, things have begun to change for the better. The drive into the city from out of town used to be categorised by the sight of half-built and long-abandoned building projects, but today there is a marked change. Just inside the orbital motorway on the outskirts of Minsk, many new mini-suburbs (some of them extremely affluent) have sprung up and metro lines have been extended. Today there is huge redevelopment within the city centre itself, and more metro

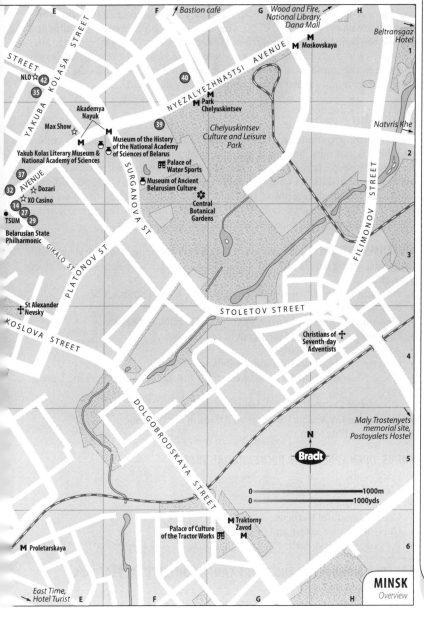

MINSK
Overview

stations have been opened. There is talk that the motorway ring road (which today marks the furthest boundaries of the city) will become an inner orbital, with a new outer ring road to be constructed further afield. The occasion of the World Ice Hockey Championships in the city in May 2014 saw new hotels and infrastructural development appearing all over town. Even before the current proposals, the road system (including the existing Minsk orbital motorway and inner ring road) had been improved dramatically. Much of the city is under government-financed development, but money from sources all over the world is also pouring in, a sure sign of growing economic confidence both within and outside the country. And the march of Western commercialism threatens to alter the landscape irretrievably, with more and more neon on every street corner and increasing numbers of drive-through fast-food emporia and new designer stores. Some might say the barbarians are at the gates again.

HIGHLIGHTS

There is a strong commitment throughout Belarusian society to promoting culture and the arts, not only in terms of governmental public and social policy, but also for ordinary people in their leisure time. Allied to this is a national passion for sport and outdoor pursuits. It's no surprise, then, to find that history, fine art and sport are well represented in terms of public facilities, with something to please every taste. The best of the attractions for the first-time visitor include the following, further information on which can be found later in this chapter.

MUSEUMS AND GALLERIES A top ten list to whet the appetite of any visitor, with additional listing details on these and other museums and galleries in the city on page 163:
- Belarusian State Museum of the History of the Great Patriotic War
- National Historical Museum of the Republic of Belarus
- Museum of Nature and Environment of the Republic of Belarus
- National Art Museum of the Republic of Belarus
- Azgur Memorial Museum
- Government Historical Museum of Belarusian Literature
- House Museum of the First Congress of the Russian Social Democratic Labour Party
- Museum of Contemporary Belarusian Statehood
- Museum of the Ministry of Internal Affairs of the Republic of Belarus
- Strana Mini Museum

PARKS, OPEN SPACES AND RECREATIONAL AREAS
- Gorky Park
- Alexandrovsky Public Garden
- Yanka Kupala Park
- Central Botanical Gardens
- Chelyuskintsev Culture and Leisure Park
- Pobyedy (Victory) Park

SQUARES, MONUMENTS AND SIGNIFICANT ARCHITECTURAL FEATURES
- Privakhsalnaya Square
- Nyezalyezhnastsi (Independence) Square
- Oktyabrskaya Square (increasingly known by its Belarusian name Kastrichnitskaya)
- Pobyedy (Victory) Square
- Island of Tears
- Jewish Minsk
- Upper Town
- Troitskoye (Trinity) suburb
- The urban art of the former industrial landscape around Kastrichnitskaya Street

- The National Library
- The buildings of Nyezalyezhnastsi Avenue

CATHEDRALS AND CHURCHES
- Church of Sts Simeon and Helena
- Holy Spirit Cathedral
- Mary Magdalene Church
- Maryinsky Cathedral of the Holy Virgin Mary
- St Alexander Nevsky Church
- Cathedral of St Peter and St Paul

THEATRES AND CONCERT HALLS
- National Academic Bolshoi Opera and Ballet Theatre of the Republic of Belarus
- Yanka Kupala National Academic Theatre
- Belarusian State Academic Music Theatre
- Belarusian State Puppet Theatre

ENTERTAINMENT AND NIGHTLIFE The energy, bustle and joie de vivre of Zibitskaya Street, Minsk's very own party district.

GETTING THERE AND AWAY

As you might expect, Minsk is the geographical focal point for all means of transportation into and out of the country. It is the main (and for the most part only) entry and exit point for air travel to Belarus. Major European road and rail links converge on the city from all points of the compass. Details of air routes, carriers and airport facilities can be found on page 60, together with key information on rail travel, access by coach, roads, border-crossing points and a few tips on independent travel by car.

GETTING AROUND

BY METRO, BUS, TRAM AND TROLLEYBUS Public transport in Minsk is extremely cheap and unfailingly reliable, though somewhat overcrowded (as might be expected in a capital city). If you want to feel like a local, however, then you must give it a try. Other than walking (and most of what you will want to see is accessible on foot) you have considerable freedom of choice, given that any of the options (metro, bus, tram and trolleybus) are all user-friendly. Each journey costs just BYN0.55 – 0.60 if you buy a bus, tram and trolleybus ticket from the driver or a metro ticket from a metro station. **Tickets** can be bought from kiosks (at all major stops), post offices and stores all over town (in singles or multiples) and, in the case of **metro tokens**, at every station (BYN0.60 for every journey, no matter the length); and if your stay is for a few days or more, consider the **contactless smart cards** that are available for periods of 3, 5, 10, 15, 20, 30, 60 or 80 days in multiples of 10, 20, 30, 40, 50 or 60 journeys (and even unlimited numbers of journeys in the case of some time-limited tickets). They can be used on any form of public transport (including overground services operated by Belarusian Railways within the city limits), but this must be specified at the point of purchase. Public transport is exceptionally cheap, and smart cards represent even better value. This is easily the most convenient way to use the city's public transport system, which is of itself by far the best way to get around. Hopping on and off is a terrific way to get your

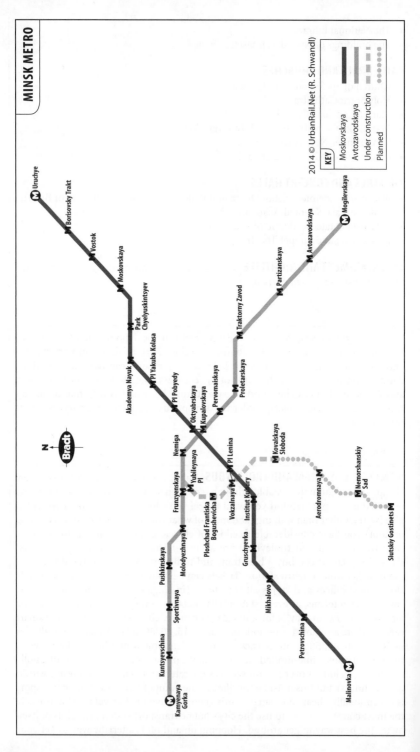

MINSK METRO

2014 © UrbanRail.Net (R. Schwandl)

KEY

Moskovskaya
Avtozavodskaya
Under construction
Planned

Uruchye
Borisovsky Trakt
Vostok
Moskovskaya
Park Chyelyuskintsyev
Akademya Nayuk
Pl Yakuba Kolasa
Pl Pobyedy
Oktyabrskaya
Kupalovskaya
Pervomaiskaya
Proletarskaya
Traktorny Zavod
Partizanskaya
Avtozavodskaya
Mogilevskaya

Nemiga
Yubileynaya Pl
Frunzyenskaya
Molodyezhnaya
Pushkinskaya
Sportivnaya
Kuntsyevschina
Kamyenaya Gorka

Ploshchad Frantiska Bogushevicha
Pl Lenina
Vokzalnaya
Institut Kultury
Gruschyevka
Mikhalovo
Petrovschina
Malinovka

Kovalskaya Sloboda
Aerodromnaya
Nemorshanskiy Sad
Slutskiy Gostinets

N Bradt

132

bearings and acquire a feel for the buzz of the city. It's one of my very favourite Minsk pastimes.

With just two intersecting lines, the **metro system** is very easy to work out. The lines bisect at Kristichnitskaya/Kupalovskaya station. It's the same location but is known by two names, one for each line. Where a sight in this chapter makes reference to it as the nearest stop on the metro, I give the station name that is relevant to the sight's closest point. Just be sure to follow direction signs carefully as you exit. The service runs daily from 05.30 until 00.40. During the morning and evening commute (07.00–09.00 and 17.00–19.00) the service runs every 2½ minutes, with only modest changes for the rest of the day until 23.00, when you will wait 10–12 minutes between trains. To access the network, buy your smart card/tokens (or *jetons*) from a window near the barriers (or in advance; see box, page 135).With tokens, insert one into the slot adjoining the barrier and walk through when the green arrow is lit. Alternatively, touch in with your smart card. Don't forget your jeton or card and don't try to ride the system for free: if you attempt to walk through without inserting a token or touching in with your card, then the seemingly open barrier will slam shut with a vengeance, attempting to cut you in two. I've seen it happen; I can't speak for the poor miscreant, but it made *my* eyes water and I was only a spectator. See the map opposite for details of the two lines and all stations.

Buses run between 05.30 and 00.30, while **tram and trolleybus** services, like the metro, finish 10 minutes later. And if travelling by bus, tram or trolleybus, don't forget to punch your ticket at the machine on board to validate it. Announcements are in English throughout the entirety of the metro system and on certain of the buses in the city centre, when passengers are alerted to the proximity of tourist sites of interest.

BY TAXI Taxis in Minsk are fairly cheap and reasonably reliable but like any city in the world, as a foreigner you are at risk of being ripped off by operators with an eye for maximising their income, and perhaps more so in Minsk on account of the language difficulty. Only ever use officially licensed cabs. You will recognise one when you see it. Look for a yellow car; some have a light on top of the roof and/or decals of black-and-white patterned squares, but all have a number prominently displayed. Some of the more common services are 135, 152, 157, 252 and 7788, but English is not often spoken (whether by dispatcher or driver). If you must use taxis, best practice is to seek the advice of a local you trust, and then to stick to the same driver for all your needs. I rarely take a taxi, but if I do I've used the same driver for years. Full details on application!

TOURIST INFORMATION

This is the right point in the narrative to remind readers of the caveat on page 51, relating to the shortage of information on opening hours, telephone numbers and prices for restaurants, bars, clubs, museums and the like, at least when compared with other world locations. And don't forget that in some instances, conflicting information can be provided by different sources. That said, every effort has been made to personally establish and corroborate every last detail. The fact that things are still developing so rapidly in this country is another challenge for the visitor. I do remain convinced, however, that all of this *will* change for the better. Every year I meet with senior officials at the Ministry of Sport and Tourism, and each time I encounter infectious enthusiasm and a willingness to learn new and better ways to present this country's tourism product. In any event, there should be real comfort for you in the knowledge that if you are on an organised visit, then you are bound to find that places on the tour *will* be open! And for my part, I always find that a modest degree of ambiguity (and even contradiction!) adds to the value of the adventure and of the experience. There are always times, of course, when you need to be able to rely on the absolute accuracy of up-to-date information. New listings websites (as well as apps for your smartphone) are appearing in increasing numbers all the time, so let your search engine and mobile device do the work for you. In other words, come to this city prepared and bring your own downloaded information with you.

When you do find yourself in Minsk, head for the centrally located **tourist information centre** (TIC) [136 B4] (*13 Revolutsionaya St;* \ *203 39 95;* e *infotourcenter@tut.by;* w *minsktourism.by;* ⏱ *08.45–13.00 & 14.00–18.00 Mon– Thu, 08.45–13.00 & 14.00–16.45 Fri*), although it isn't easy to find. Head along Revolutsionaya from Lenina, cross over Komsomolskaya, then look for the small sign on the left-hand side as you head towards Gorodski Val. The TIC is located at the rear of the building. And as if the task of tracking down the primary source of tourist information were not quaint in itself, it shows that the tourist industry here still has work to do when the city's premier information hub for visitors closes for lunch, finishes early on Fridays and is closed at the weekend. That said, when it *is* open the staff are helpful and accommodating, English is spoken and all of the usual bookings can be made for you, including hotels, theatres, restaurants, day excursions and trips of longer duration. Brochures, leaflets, maps and guides in English are also available.

GUIDEBOOKS AND MAPS Additionally, more and more English guidebooks and maps are now finding their way on to the shelves of bookstores, hotel lobby shops and newspaper kiosks. Easily my favourite city publication is the *Minsk Belarus Local Guide* ✻ produced by HiFive Belarus! (w *hifivebelarus.com*). The work of a co-operative of more than 30 young and energetic local people, this book and website together are a mine of up-to-the-minute information and hot tips on everything you might want to know when you're in town, all delivered in a chatty, streetwise style. Also look out for the excellent panoramic city map of Minsk showing each building drawn in 3D (BYN3.70), which provides an exceptionally useful pictorial representation of the city and is thus a most useful aid to navigation, as well as the very good local guidebook *Minsk in One Day* (text by Chrystaphor Khilkevich, photographs by Sergei Plytkevich, published by Riftour). It contains more pictures than text, but it still has a great deal of interesting information as well as its own excellent panoramic map. For general listings information the best periodical by far is *where Minsk* magazine. Produced monthly with a circulation of 25,000, it is distributed free of charge in hotels, restaurants, the TIC and public places generally, and you will have no difficulty in sourcing a copy all over town. Most of it is in Russian, of course, but the English pages are very informative and there are useful maps at the back. The magazine's website (w *whereminsk.by*) is also an excellent source of listings data, though it is only in Russian at present.

CITY TOURS As more and more visitors from abroad begin to catch on (at last) that Belarus is open for tourism, a cottage industry of small-scale visitor services is gaining an important foothold in the market, particularly in the capital. Usually run by individuals or very small groups of local people with expert knowledge, they offer bespoke services of quality that are tailored to individual need, often at competitive prices. As ever, word of mouth is the best way to access such services, so if you have existing contacts in Belarus do check for any recommendations, or else ask around when you get here. There are two in particular that I have used in recent times for walking tours of Minsk and whose services I can recommend. I have meandered the streets of the capital for hours with both **Belarus Travel** ✱ (*Natalia Dubrovskaya;* 📞 *+375 29 666 45 39;* e *dubrik80@gmail.com*) and **White Wings** ✱ (*Alina Dmitrovich, office 16, 23 Svobody Sq;* 📞 *+375 44 539 83 06;* e *freetourinminsk@gmail.com, info@whitewings.by;* w *freewalkingtour.by; 2hr guided walk in English at 11.00 every day from outside City Hall, free of charge, with a range of themed walks at other times inc Soviet Tour, Minsk Pub Crawl & Jewish Minsk, fee payable*). Flawless English, excellent local knowledge and a fund of fascinating tales come as standard. If you want to feel like a local yourself in the company of individuals who actually are locals, do avail yourself of their services. My own view is that to practise the art of the *flâneur*, meandering the streets of a city on foot, is easily the best way to feel its beating heart. But not everybody agrees. If your choice is to get acquainted with the sights through the window of mechanised transport, two bus tours now operate in Minsk. With four departures a day (rising to eight between May and August), **Minsk City Tour** (*19B Oktyabrskaya St;* 📞 *+375 17 360 02 40;* w *citytourminsk.by*) and their red buses will convey you past the main sites of interest with an audio guide in English, though the 100-minute tour is fixed and it's not possible to hop on and off. If you prefer your buses yellow, choose **Tour Open Minsk** (*8 Moskovskaya St;* 📞 *+375 29 344 59 99;* w *openminsk.by*) with four daily departures from the stop on Yakuba Kolasa Square. The ride lasts about 75 minutes but sadly the commentary is in Russian only.

WHERE TO STAY

The biggest percentage of your budget is going to be blown on accommodation costs, so be sure to do your research. It used to be the case that the industry standard was a monolithic tower block incorporating varying amounts of crumbling concrete, 1970s décor, a smart (if sterile and soulless) lobby, basic (if functional) facilities and old-style Soviet service that well-travelled visitors would instantly recognise from the days of the USSR. This has changed in recent years, with a significant number of new hotels being built to meet perceived demand from the business community and incoming tourism from abroad, not least around the time of the World Ice Hockey Championships in 2014 (when plush new hotels seemed to be springing up

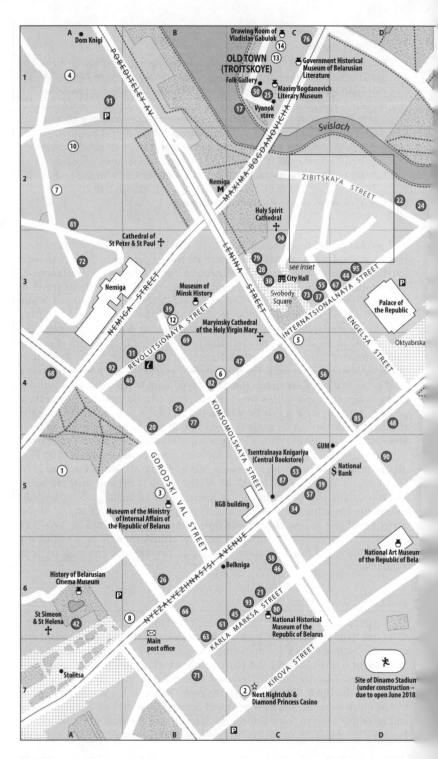

A
B
C
D

Dom Knigi

POBEDHELEY AV

OLD TOWN
(TROITSKOYE)

Drawing Room of
Vladislav Gabulok

76

14

13

Government Historical
Museum of Belarusian
Literature

1

4

91

P

10

7

81

72

Nemiga
M

Cathedral of
St Peter & St Paul ✝

Nemiga

Museum of Minsk History

39

12

69

Maryinsky Cathedral
of the Holy Virgin Mary ✝

31

83

92

ℹ

40

Folk Gallery

50 25

Maxim Bogdanovich
Literary Museum

17

Vyanok
store

Svislach

ZIBITSKAYA STREET

22 24

Holy Spirit
Cathedral ✝

94

79

28

38 City Hall

Svobody
Square

73 37

5

55

67

95

44

37

see inset

INTERNATSIONALNAYA STREET

ENGELSA STREET

P

Palace of
the Republic

Oktyabrska

2

3

MAXIMA-BOGDANOVICHA

LENINA STREET

NEMIGA STREET

REVOLUTSIONAYA STREET

47

43

56

85

48

6

82

29

77

20

GORODSKI VAL STREET

KOMSOMOLSKAYA STREET

Tsentralnaya Knigariya
(Central Bookstore)

53

87

GUM

$ National
Bank

19

57

90

1

3

Museum of the Ministry
of Internal Affairs of
the Republic of Belarus

KGB building

34

National Art Museum
of the Republic of Bela

4

5

History of Belarusian
Cinema Museum

P

St Simeon
& St Helena ✝

42

8

Main
post office

NYEZALYEZHNASTSI AVENUE

26

Belkniga

58

46

21

93

80

National Historical
Museum of the
Republic of Belarus

66

45

61

63

KARLA MARKSA STREET

National Art Museum
of the Republic of Bela

🏃

6

Stolitsa

71

KIROVA STREET

2 Next Nightclub &
Diamond Princess Casino

Site of Dinamo Stadium
(under construction –
due to open June 2018

7

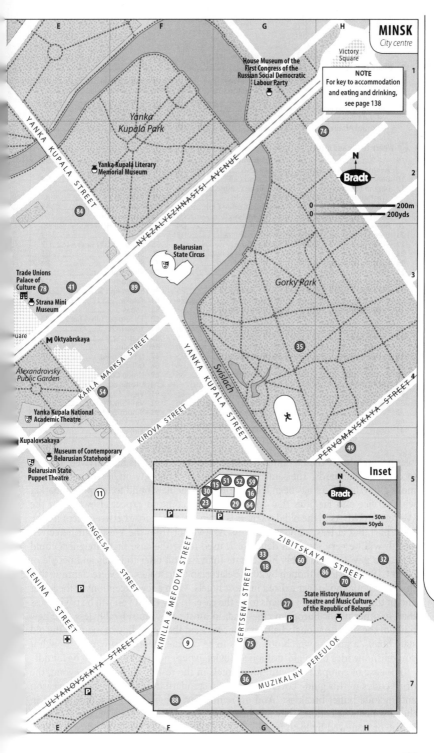

everywhere). Since then a number of high-end internationals have arrived in town to drive up standards. The same old atmosphere of sterility often still pervades, if more glitzy, but there has been a big effort with the new build to tempt the market with service and facilities that consumers have come to expect elsewhere in the Western world. As in the old days there is often little to choose between them for the most part, but at least standards are up. As a visitor from the West your perceived wealth will be very much in demand. It used to be the case that foreigners could expect to pay a considerably higher rate than was on offer to locals and people of other CIS countries, although by 2010 Belarusian tourist agencies were claiming that this differential no longer existed in most hotels. With a few exceptions at the lower end of the market this now seems to be the case. In any event you will be paying less than in other major European cities and, in most cases, considerably less. The new build of the multi-national chains has encouraged the upgrading of many of the old state hotels, a process which now seems to be constant work in progress, though if you relish the idea of an old-fashioned Soviet experience it's still there to be found!

For ease of comparison with other hotels in the rest of Europe and beyond, the price codes in this guide cover the cost of a standard double room in high season and include buffet breakfast. And do remember: these are not the only hotels in the city, just a selection. They are, however, ones that have been personally tested by me or reviewed by local friends and colleagues in the tourism industry whose judgement and objectivity I trust. And of course, you'll find a wealth of information yourself via your favourite internet search engine to help you make your choice.

HOTELS
Upmarket

🏨 **Beijing** [128 D6] (163 rooms) 36 Krasnoarmeiskaya St; 📞329 77 77; e beijinghotel@beijinghotelminsk.com; w beijinghotelminsk.com. Located close to the Svislach River, facilities inc the Seasons Chinese restaurant (🕐 11.30–14.30 & 17.30–23.00 daily; $$$$), Style Slavic restaurant (🕐 08.00–21.00 daily; $$$$), Oasis café (🕐 07.00–21.00 daily; $$$), fitness health & beauty centre, on-site parking & airport transfers. **$$$$**

🏨 **Buta Boutique** [136 A5] (35 rooms) 7 Myasnikova St; 📞366 55 55; e reservation@hotel-buta.by; w hotel-buta.by. A decent option if you want to avoid large & corporate. The location is reasonably central & each category of room in a broad range is well appointed. Facilities inc Buta restaurant (🕐 24/7; $$$), bar, free Wi-Fi & AC in all rooms, sauna, swimming pool, fitness centre, casino & free parking. Special offers & deals a permanent feature. **$$$$**

🏨 **Crowne Plaza** [136 C7] (151 rooms) 13 Kirova St; 📞218 34 00 (call centre), 200 93 53 (reservations); e info@cpminsk.com, reservation@cpminsk.com; w cpminsk.com. Situated directly opposite the Dynamo Minsk national football stadium & with most of the city's sights easily accessible on foot, this significant chain hotel, part of the Princess Group International, opened for business in May 2008. Self-assessed as 'a 5-star international hotel' & aimed at the business market. The facilities are comprehensive & doubtless match those to be found in every other of the 200 Crowne Plaza venues across the world, but the real plus here is the quality of the staff, who are consistently praised for the highest standards of service. Rooms are well appointed, all with mod cons, & facilities inc fitness centre, gym, jacuzzi, swimming pool, Diamond casino, Next nightclub, 2 restaurants (Dolce Vita & Empire), Star café/bar, dry cleaning & laundry. Some of the facilities are accessible to those with disabilities. **$$$$**

🏨 **DoubleTree by Hilton** [136 A1] (193 rooms) 9 Pobediteley Av; 📞309 80 00; e doubletreeminsk.info@hilton.com; w doubletree3.hilton.com. Centrally located in a vast new-build shopping, entertainment & dining complex with delightful views over the river, parkland & Old Town, the rooms are described as 'standard', for which read 'luxury standard'. As befits this high-end international, everything here oozes top quality. Each bedroom is superbly appointed & you pay only a modest premium for a river view. Free Wi-Fi, AC, HD plasma TV & espresso machine in every room. All is very shiny of course, but expect the best in service & facilities (& also expect to pay for it). My tourism contacts rate this as the best hotel in town. Ember restaurant (🕐 07.00–23.00 daily; $$$$), 21st-floor Sky Lounge & Bar (🕐 noon–16.00 & 18.00–01.00 Mon–Fri, 18.00–02.00 Sat–Sun; $$$) & Beans & Leaves Lobby Café (🕐 09.00–22.00 daily; $$$), plus ballroom, 3 boardrooms, state-of-the-art 24hr business support & fitness centre. **$$$$**

🏨 **Europe** [136 C4] (68 rooms) 28 Internatsionalnaya St; 📞229 83 39; e reservation@hoteleurope.by; w hoteleurope.by. Right in the heart of the city, on the corner of Lenina & Internatsionalnaya sts & close to a number of key sights, this imposing 7-storey hotel opened in Sep 2007 on the spot where a hotel has existed since 1841, although the original was completely destroyed in the Great Patriotic War. The country's 1st genuine 5-star establishment until the President Hotel opened in 2013, it was considered before then to have overtaken the Minsk as the swankiest hotel in town, a privilege in status for which visitors should still expect to pay, & in no uncertain terms. The best rooms enjoy impressive panoramic views over Old Town. All are extremely well appointed & those at the top of the range are the very latest in luxury. Some of the rooms are non-smoking & there are also facilities for the less able. The shiny lobby oozes money, although every time I've been there it's been close to empty. Even if you're not in residence, wander in off the street & take a look at the lovely central atrium. Don't forget to look up. In addition to the exclusive Avignon restaurant (page 149), 5 opulent bars & a nightclub, there is a business centre, conference & meeting rooms, library, secure underground parking, car-hire facilities, laundry, beauty parlour, gift shop, currency exchange, fitness centre, gym, sauna & pool. **$$$$**

✳ 🏨 **Garni** [136 B4] (49 rooms) 11 Internatsionalnaya St; 📞229 76 00; e info@

hotel-garni.by; w hotel-garni.by. Well located in the centre of town in an attractive 19th-century building, this small but charming hotel opened for business in 2012. It's part of the Minotel group that also inc the Belarus & Sputnik hotels in town. The design is elegant & the décor is of a good standard, with each of the AC rooms comfortable & well appointed. Staff are very professional & courteous. Good English is spoken. Facilities inc a decent restaurant, together with conference & full business services. There are lots of really nice little touches about the service here & many have contacted me to let me know how good this place is (both friends in Belarus & visitors from abroad). When I stayed here myself on a subsequent research visit I could see why. $$$$

🏠 **Hampton by Hilton** [128 B6] (120 rooms) 8 Tolstova St; 📞 215 40 00; e msqhx.hampton@ hilton.com; w hamptoninn3.hilton.com. Proximity to the main railway station (moments away) is this hotel's chief selling point; that apart it's a corporate box. The all-round spec is decent & facilities inc free Wi-Fi, hub with 24hr snack counter & bar & fitness centre. Accessibility generally good. Consider it an option if in town on business but if not, you can do much better elsewhere. $$$$

🏠 **Marriott** [128 A2] (217 rooms) 20 Pobediteley Av; 📞 279 30 00; w marriott.com. uk. Just as swanky, glitzy & shiny as the other international chain new-builds, but its location midway between Park Pobyedy & Minsk Arena puts it further out from the sights of the city centre (though still riverside). Lower rise & with an external elevation more pleasing on the eye than many. All bedrooms are well appointed, some with balconies. Modest premium for river views. Decent accessibility & non-smoking throughout. Fornello restaurant (🕐 *10.00–23.00 daily; $$$$*), Barrel Bar (🕐 *24/7*), VIP executive lounge (🕐 *10.00–23.00 daily*) & lobby bar, plus free parking, ATM, currency exchange, fitness centre, pool, 10 meeting rooms & business support. $$$$

🏠 **Minsk** [136 B6] (252 rooms) 11 Nyezalyezhnastsi (Independence) Av; 📞 209 90 62/75/78; e hotelminsk@pmrb.gov.by; w hotelminsk.by. Until the arrival of the Europe & latterly various top-end internationals, this was the only truly 4-star hotel in the whole country & it's still a fairly opulent base for your stay in town, if a little behind the competition. Located

downtown on the main drag & on the edge of the imposing Nyezalyezhnastsi Sq, within easy walking distance of many of the sights, this former Soviet hotel was given a major facelift in 2002 with a marble lobby, state-of-the-art conference facilities for 50, business services, fitness centre, sauna, casino, ATM, currency exchange, tourist agency, secure car parking, car-hire facilities, shops & 'vitamin bar'. All rooms are elegantly furnished & have the usual mod cons you would expect to find in a hotel of this quality. It also boasts 2 restaurants (inc Seventh Heaven on the 7th floor with fine panoramic views of the city – page 147), 2 bars, a nightclub & a banqueting hall. Some of the rooms are classed as 'non-smoking' & there are limited facilities for the less able. Europcar & Avis have desks in the lobby, though often unmanned. If so, walk through the back of the lobby, left across the car park & into the hotel's business centre. On the ground floor here is a bank, further ATMs, another travel agency, small café & access to the adjoining supermarket. Take the elevator to the 4th floor for car hire. $$$$

🏠 **President** [137 E5] (154 rooms) 18 Kirova St; 📞 229 70 00; e info@president-hotel. by; w president-hotel.by. On the site of the old Oktyabrskaya Hotel & still relatively new, this was intended to be the jewel in the crown of Minsk's hotels, but luxury competition from the new kids in town has caught up. All is very glitzy & shiny, with staff going the extra mile to provide high-quality service. The conference hall seats 600 & has state-of-the-art equipment & services. After a few initial teething issues, everything here is now 1st rate. There are 3 very good restaurants, a 'wellness centre', spa, gym, 25m swimming pool, sauna & shops. There's also a VIP presidential suite with its own pool, sauna & elevator. Every room comes with AC & disabled facilities are good. There's parking underground too. It's well located for all the sights, but the real excitement value here comes from its position right next to the Office of the President of the Republic, so security is high & the atmosphere extremely businesslike. Whatever you do, don't be tempted to take the opportunity to photograph the office building. Instead, confine yourself to watching out for the President's heavily guarded motorcade leaving at high speed. $$$$

🏠 **Renaissance Marriott** [128 A6] (266 rooms) 1e Dzerzhinsky Av; 📞 309 90 90;

w marriott.co.uk. Part of the worldwide Marriott chain. The location on a major road junction southwest of the city centre is not ideal but I've always enjoyed a stay here. The staff are friendly & standards are high. Good accessibility throughout. Facilities inc free Wi-Fi, Arborea restaurant (⏰ 07.00–midnight daily; $$$$), lobby bar, swimming pool, health & beauty centre, currency exchange & free on-site parking. $$$$

🏠 **Victoria** [128 A2] (168 rooms) 59 Pobediteley Av; ☎ 239 77 77, 204 88 44 (24hr information line 204 88 55); e reservation@hotel-victoria.by, info@hotel-victoria.by; w victoria1.hotel-victoria.by. This top-of-the-range 4-star hotel ('Victoria 1'), aimed clearly at the business market, received a visit from the President himself shortly after opening in 2007, an event that signified the importance that the state places on the success of the venture. Indeed, the vast new presidential palace is nearby on the edge of Pobyedy Park. Situated on the banks of the Svislach River not far from the city centre & with lovely views over the park's Komsomolskoye Lake (but not as close to the city centre as the blurb would have you believe!), this hotel seeks to combine state-of-the-art business facilities with luxury accommodation. It still looks sparkly & is very 'new money'. The brand has been massively expanded in recent times to inc the new Victoria & Spa next door ('Victoria 2'), as well as the Victoria Olimp Hotel further up the road. Two other new Minsk hotels, the Na Zamkovy & the Monastyrski, are also inc in the portfolio. All bedrooms are fully AC, with LCD interactive sat TV, internet access & minibar. Facilities also inc nightclub, casino, 2 restaurants, pizza & sushi lobby bar, 24hr on-site underground car parking, beauty centre (with spa), solarium, massage facility, sauna, hairdresser, laundry, currency exchange, ATM & souvenir/newspaper stand. If the PR hype is to be believed (some think so), then this place is something special, but for the traveller without business interests its appeal is likely to be limited. $$$$

🏠 **Victoria & Spa** [128 A2] (256 rooms) 59a Pobediteley Av; ☎ 309 50 00; e reservation@hotel-victoria.by; w victoria2.hotel-victoria.by. This latest glitzy hi-tech hotel ('Victoria 2') has been open since April 2014, adjoining the Victoria as part of its portfolio. It comes as no surprise then that the 2 are pretty much interchangeable (so the same comments as above apply). High spec

throughout with AC & free Wi-Fi in every room. Facilities inc Platinum restaurant (⏰ 07.00–05.00 daily; $$$$), banquet hall, spa, pool & treatment rooms. $$$$

🏠 **Victoria Olimp** [128 A2] (238 rooms) 103 Pobediteley Av; ☎ 308 75 55; e reservation@olimphotel.by; w olimphotel.by. Also included in the Victoria chain & another example of the significant redevelopment along Pobediteley Av (this one further out of town & near to Minsk Arena). Facilities inc the Olympia restaurant (⏰ 07.00–05.00 daily; $$$$), café-pizzeria, lobby bar, gym, spa, sauna & health & beauty centre. $$$$

Mid-range

🏠 **Belarus** [128 B3] (427 rooms) 15 Storazhevskaya St; ☎ 209 71 00, 209 71 06; e secretary@minotel-belarus.com; w hotel-belarus.com. An imposing 22-floor concrete high-rise, this hotel dominates the skyline around Pobyedy Park & Komsomolskoye Lake, towers over the Minsk Hero City monument & the recently relocated Museum of the Great Patriotic War & has spectacular views across parkland & the Svislach River towards Old Town & the Island of Tears, particularly by night. Subject to complete renovation & only opened again in the spring of 2014 as part of the Minotel group of hotels. The view from the high-quality top-floor Panorama restaurant is stunning (page 150). Many of the rooms have their own balcony & all of them are now reasonably well appointed. There are several bars & eateries, a conference hall, business centre, sauna & shops. $$$

🏠 **Bonhotel** [128 A4] (124 rooms) 2 Pritytskava St; ☎ 389 73 89; e info@bonhotel.by; w bonhotel.by. Not far from Pushkinskaya metro station. Facilities inc the Bonbistro restaurant (⏰ 07.00–22.30 daily; $$), lobby bar, tourist booking services, ATM, car hire, parking & airport transfers. $$$

🏠 **Green City** [128 A4] (56 rooms) 156 Pritytskava St; ☎ 317 50 32; e hotel.greencityminsk@gmail.com; w greencityhotel.by. Located in an emerging shopping, business & entertainment complex well to the west of the city centre & close to the ring road (but with Kamyenaya Gorka metro station nearby), this smart new hotel has décor that suggests it is keen to establish its green credentials. Facilities inc free

3

Wi-Fi & climate control in all rooms, restaurant, bar, free parking & airport shuttle (separate charge). Proximity to the ring road & motorway system is handy if you're driving but otherwise a disadvantage. **$$$**

🏠 **Gubernski** [136 A2] (11 rooms) 9 Osvabozhdenya St; 📞 226 88 80; e info@gubernski. by; w gubernski.by. Tucked away between Nyemiga & Frunzyenskaya metro stations in the city's business district, this small hotel prides itself on a bespoke service to guests. The 19th-century building is pleasing on the eye both inside & out. All rooms have free Wi-Fi & AC. Facilities inc small restaurant for private dining by arrangement, car hire & shuttle transfer (air & rail). **$$$**

🏠 **Internationale Bildungs-und-Begegnungsstätte** [128 A6] (40 rooms) 11 Gazety Pravda Av; 📞 270 39 94; e hotel@ibb. by; w ibb.by/hotel. This slick business facility, incorporating state-of-the-art conference facilities in 5 seminar rooms & a function hall seating 350, was constructed in 1994 in partnership with a German venture. Not quite as swish as it once was, it's in danger of being overtaken by the new kids on the block who are taking conference & business facilities to a new level in this city. That said, it still feels classy & has a relaxed & calm ambience, not least because it is around 10km from the general brouhaha of the city centre, in a suburb to the southwest. Facilities inc sauna, bar & the excellent Westphalia restaurant (🕐 07.00–23.00 daily; **$$$**). **$$$**

☀ 🏠 **Monastyrski** [137 F7] (48 rooms) 6 Kirilla & Mefodya St; 📞 329 03 00; e reservation@ vtroitskaya.by; w monastyrski.by. This gem of a hotel (inc in the Victoria stable) is ideally located for the sights of Old Town & is steps away from the bars & restaurants of Zibitskaya St. A former Bernardine monastery (recently renovated & extended), everything here is of course faux-medieval, but it's well done. Staff are friendly & standards of service are high. All rooms have free Wi-Fi & AC. Facilities inc Lavski restaurant (page 147), bar (🕐 16.00–midnight daily), sauna & fitness centre. Zibitskaya St is the city's party district & this is the obvious place for party-goers to stay. One slight drawback is that the area is now fully pedestrianised, so there's a walk when checking in & out. **$$$**

🏠 **Na Zamkovoy** [136 A2] (26 rooms) 25–27a Zamkovaya St; 📞 329 04 05; e hotel.nazamkovoi@ gmail.com; w nazamkovoy.by. Another hotel in the Victoria portfolio, this one stands in the business district (not far from the Gubernski). Free Wi-Fi & AC in every room. Facilities inc restaurant (🕐 07.00–midnight daily; **$$**), bar & parking. **$$$**

🏠 **Orbita** [128 A4] (278 rooms) 39 Pushkin Av; 📞 206 77 81; e reservation@orbita-hotel.com; w orbita-hotel.com. Opened in 1991, this 14-storey high-rise is home to a restaurant (🕐 noon–midnight daily; **$$**), pizzeria (🕐 16.00–05.00 daily; **$$**) & a banqueting hall, together with several bars, conference facilities, sauna, casino, nightclub & parking. **$$$**

🏠 **Planyeta** [128 A3] (277 rooms) 31 Pobediteley Av; 📞 226 78 53; e booking@ hotelplaneta.by; w hotelplaneta.by. Extensive renovation has placed this hotel on a slightly higher-quality threshold than the others in this category, although the wall-to-wall pseudo-marble in reception is a little gaudy. Located within a few mins' walk of the Belarus & Yubileiny hotels, all rooms are clean & comfortable. Facilities inc business centre, currency exchange, Hertz car-hire office, restaurants, bars, sauna & casino. **$$$**

🏠 **Slavyanskaya** [128 A4] (126 rooms) 6 Narochanskaya St; 📞 359 15 00; e booking@ slavyanskaya-minsk.by; w slavyanskaya-minsk. by. Near to Minsk Arena (5mins on foot) & not far from Sport Time hotel (so a distance away from the main sights), this is one of the new breed that opened early in 2014 to welcome the World Ice Hockey Championships to the city. If this is your choice in town try to get a room on the upper floors, where the views are impressive. Facilities inc free Wi-Fi, restaurant & bar (🕐 07.00–midnight daily; **$$**) & free parking. **$$$**

🏠 **Sputnik** [128 B6] (135 rooms) 2 Brilyevskaya St; 📞 220 36 19; e info@sputnik-hotel.com; w sputnik-hotel.com. Now part of the Minotel group. The hotel's location south of the city centre is not great & it's a rectangular concrete box. Directly validated information is scarce & difficult to find, but the website is helpful & this hotel is always busy. Facilities inc free Wi-Fi, restaurant (🕐 07.00–midnight Mon–Fri, 07.00–02.00 Sat–Sun; **$$**), bar, sauna & parking. **$$$**

🏠 **Turist** [129 E6] (215 rooms) 81 Partizansky Av; 📞 295 40 31; e office@hotel-tourist.by; w hotel-tourist.by. Located close to large-scale shopping facilities, this is a functional but comfortable 15-storey high-rise. Amenities inc restaurant (⏰ *07.00–midnight daily*; **$$**), bar, summer pavement café and casino, currency exchange, ATM, hotel transfers & paid parking. The staff are friendly & a stay here represents good value for money. If you want basic facilities & rudimentary comfort without the frills, this is the place for you, although the location is not that convenient for visitor attractions or restaurants. **$$$**

✴ 🏠 **Yubileiny** [128 B3] (239 rooms) 19 Pobediteley Av; 📞 226 90 24; e info@yhotel. by; w yhotel.by. Overlooking the Svislach River & built on the site of a former mosque close to Pobyedy Park, this is a very busy hotel, full of hustle & bustle. Rooms at the lower end of the scale are a little shabby, while the higher-grade ones have been recently decorated. For sheer value for money, this hotel takes some beating. Maybe it's just familiarity, but if I need a hotel in town it's the one I always use. It's nothing special, but all is dependable at this cosy old sweater of a place. Facilities inc restaurants, bars, sauna, ATM, bowling & casino. **$$$**

Budget

🏠 **40 Let Pobyedi (or '40th Anniversary of Victory Day')** [128 D4] (119 rooms) 3 Azgura St; 📞 294 79 63; e 40hotel@tut.by; w 40hotel.by. You get what you pay for in this 12-storey Soviet-style apt block, situated behind Gorky Park & within walking distance of most sights. Owned by the Ministry of Defence, it's cheap & functional & the staff are friendly; there is also a small café/coffee shop. Ask for one of the refurbished rooms when booking. **$$**

🏠 **Beltransgaz** [129 H1] (25 rooms) 4 Francysk Skaryna St; 📞 215 69 50; e hotel. mag@btg.by; w btg.by. Established primarily for travelling executives of the state gas company. A stay here will give you a different experience, but the location is some way off the main drag. That said, the rooms are big & well appointed, & there's a café, bar & shop on site. There is a general air of freshness about the place, & it's different! Pay extra for b/fast in the café. **$$**

🏠 **Department of Finances and Logistics of the Ministry of Internal Affairs** [136 A3] (20 rooms) 9 Gorodski Val St; 📞 327 25 60; e gostmvd@ mail.ru; w mvd.gov.by. Next door to the Ministry of Internal Affairs ('Serving the Law, People,

Motherland!') stands its own hotel, on the same block as the KGB's Dzherzhinsky Club (I kid you not). When I wandered in off the street on my last research trip late in 2017 I asked whether visitors from abroad were welcome. The receptionist told me yes, but doubted they would want to come. 'Prices here are democratic', she told me. I think she meant 'cheap'. Read into this as you will, but it has to be worth a try, doesn't it, to slightly tweak the semantics & say you've sampled KGB hospitality? Most rooms are twin without bathroom, though there is a small number of 'suites' with TV, fridge & kettle. Facilities inc 24hr reception, free parking & free Wi-Fi. (On the KGB's network? Perhaps not.) To complete the experience, pay the ministry's quirky museum a visit, located behind the hotel (page 166). **$$**

🏠 **East Time** [129 E6] (134 rooms) 5 Velospedny Lane; 📞 330 24 00; e info@ easttime-hotel.by; w easttime-hotel.by. Close to Vostochny bus station, services inc café, lobby bar & car hire. **$$**

🏠 **Sport Time** [128 A2] (133 rooms) 2 Myastrovskaya St; 📞 279 39 60; e info@ sporttime-hotel.by; w sporttime-hotel.by. Just 10 mins from the Minsk Arena sports, concert & shopping complex. Services match those at sister hotel East Time (see above). **$$**

🏠 **U Fontana** [128 A4] (18 rooms) 4 Amuratorskaya St; 📞 203 58 18; e u-fontana@ bk.ru; w ufontana.by. This small hotel is a decent walk from the sights, but it's comfortable enough if your budget is tight. Facilities are modest but perfectly acceptable, & there is free parking. The restaurant has a sports theme, with trophies on display & signed shirts & other memorabilia on the walls. Interestingly, the menu boasts 'exclusive recipes from Belarusian & Russian sports stars'! During the summer months, there is a pleasant dining area outside, where *shashlik* on the BBQ (a version of shish kebab ubiquitous in this part of the world) & a cold beer come recommended. There is also a sauna, (very) small pool & games room. **$$**

🏠 **Zvezda** [128 A6] (102 rooms) 47 Gazyety Zvezda Av; 📞 366 74 85; e admin@hotelzvezda. by; w hotelzvezda.by. Built in 1982, this establishment (a joint Belarusian-American venture) is a good bet if you are travelling independently & with your own transport. Located in a southwestern suburb of the city, it is a 15min drive from the cultural & business centres. There is an Italian café, sauna, hairdresser & small meeting room. This hotel does not appear to be widely used by visitors from abroad, though a selling point that will be familiar to Westerners is the availability of guest packs, inc toothbrush, toothpaste, soap & shampoo, with complimentary bottled mineral water on a daily basis. Just bear in mind the relative remoteness of the location, although it's well placed for public transport. **$$**

Shoestring
⌂ **Express** [128 C6] (56 rooms) 4 Privakhsalnaya Sq; ☎ 225 64 63; e hotel-express@tut.by. Adjacent to the main railway station on the right as you exit the main hall, this is the place for the budget traveller on a shoestring arriving tired by train with nothing booked. Just keep your expectations low & don't expect to be able to book in advance. There are sgl, dbl & trpl rooms, but you should expect to share. There are no English-speakers among the staff. **$**

⌂ **MyHostel** [128 B6] (1 dorm & 1 family room) 1–72 Kirova St; m 29 539 82 25; e myhostel.by@gmail.com; w myhostel.by. Conveniently just metres from the railway station (cross the road & head through the City Gates to find it on the left-hand side), everything here is clean, cheerful & very cheap. Photographs on the website show all you need to know, inc the precise location. Free Wi-Fi. Airport shuttle negotiable. **$**

⌂ **Postoyalets** [129 H5] (5 dbls & 4 dorms) 147 Partizansky Av; ☎ 543 49 81; e book@hotel-ru.com; w hotel-ru.com. Located 500m from Mogilevskaya metro station, this is one of the new breed of decent & reliable hostels that fit the bill. It's cheap, friendly, cheerful & comfortable, with a range of good facilities to enhance the value of your stay. Great value if you're on a tight budget. **$**

⌂ **Revolucion Hostel** [136 B3] (2 sgls, 1 family room & 8 dorms) 16 Revolutsionaya St; ☎ 394 78 55; e booking@revolucion.by; w revolucion.by. Only open since 2013, this hostel has an excellent location, 400m from Nemiga metro station, next to a cinema in the heart of the historic area, with many of the sights only a short distance away, as well as cafés, bars, nightlife & shopping. Inside, the décor pays homage to the heroes of the Revolution. Like Postoyalets (see left), it's one of the new breed of hostels & is a decent option. My personal favourite in town for this type of accommodation. **$**

⌂ **Smile** [128 A6] (3 dorms) Door 8, 131 Dzherzhinskova Av; m 29 771 94 14; e smile.minsk@mail.ru; w smileminsk.by. In the southwest of the city centre & almost on the ring road (but only a 10min walk from Malinovka metro station), this friendly & tidy hostel offers excellent value, although you can get the same thing right in the city. **$**

⌂ **Trinity** [136 C1] (4 dbls, 2 twins, 7 dorms) 12 Starovilyenskaya St; m 29 311 27 83; e hosteltravelerbelarus@gmail.com; w hostel-traveler.by. In a superb location at the bottom of Old Town & metres from the Island of Tears monument (easily my favourite part of town for an overnighter), this decent hostel has much to commend it. Facilities inc free Wi-Fi & bicycle hire; staff are friendly, welcoming & very helpful. The free city map is useful. The **Riverside Hostel** at 14 Starovilyenskaya [136 C1] is part of the same organisation & shares check-in here. **$**

⌂ **Viva** [128 B6] (4 dorms) 4 Zhukovskova St; m 29 627 11 33; e hostelviva.by@gmail.com; w hostelviva.by. Another good hostel option with a range of decent facilities & services on site, just a 7min walk from Centralnaya bus station & the railway station, with metro station Institut Kultury close by. **$**

RENTING APARTMENTS Without question this is my accommodation choice of preference. It's now an increasingly viable and attractive option, particularly if you are looking to stay for a weekend or longer (although rental by the night is also possible if you need it). In those circumstances, there is simply no comparison on cost and this is much the best way to do it if you want to live like a local for the duration of your stay. You also have the opportunity to very much please yourself as to your comings and goings. As a resident of the city, albeit a temporary one, you're going to feel much more part of the landscape than as a hotel tourist. Just exercise common sense with your enquiries and negotiations: this market is developing rapidly and there does not appear to be much of a safety net (if any at all) to regulate the activities of agents who may charge a significant fee just to put you in direct contact with unknown property owners. It is to the owners that the actual rental will then be payable. So be careful out there: constantly check costs and look diligently for hidden charges. Make sure you know what you are getting for your investment, and do please satisfy yourself as to how you're going to register your passport with the authorities as required by national immigration laws. Some agencies will offer a registration service as part of the deal, as well as transfers to and from the airport. Just point your favourite internet search engine at 'apartment rental Minsk' and away you go. As with so many markets and services, word of mouth is the best medium for securing a good deal on a rental. There's no substitute for acting on personal recommendation and if you can make your arrangements with the help and advice of someone who's been there, done it and bought the T-shirt, so much the better. Ask around and find someone who knows where to go for the most reliable deals. For my part I'm fortunate to be able to stay with friends these days when I'm in Minsk, but I often prefer to stay in the city alone or with people from home I'm showing around town. In those circumstances I rent locally on personal recommendation and I always go for the same place. I have yet to find it unavailable, even at short notice. It's a two-bedroom apartment in a prime location on the edge of Old Town with fabulous views overlooking the Island of Tears monument and two balconies for people-watching over coffee or a beer. It's decorated to a high specification and bars, restaurants and a small supermarket are metres away on foot. Rental for just US$50 per night is one phone call away. In other European capital cities the same flat would be charged out at 10 or 20 times as much. Full details and the phone number are available on request. I've never encountered a single problem with this or any other apartment rental anywhere in the country. There's simply no substitute for feeling like a local, so get out there and find yourself a deal.

As well as local agencies within Belarus, a number of American and European companies operate international rental agencies in the city; some of them claim to have access to their own apartments in Minsk, but a lot of these companies seem to be little more than intermediaries to facilitate contact with the real owners. If you can speak the language with confidence and don't mind being in town without having anywhere booked, the best way to avoid the attention of agents is to buy a local newspaper when you get here and browse the classified ads section. Dozens and dozens of rental apartments will be listed and the phone number provided will almost always belong to the landlord in person. I did this a number of times around the country in my early days of coming to Belarus, before my network of contacts became established. I never had any difficulty in finding an apartment, even for one night, and I never encountered a single problem. Just don't forget to register your passport within the necessary period, as the law requires.

To dip your toe in the water and as a compromise between a hotel stay at one end of the scale and going solo with renting an apartment at the other, a decent option you might want to try is **Aparthotel Comfort** [128 B6] (*48 1-room studios, 48 2-room apts & 4 3-room apts; 1 Schorsa St;* m *44 575 08 00;* e *info@comforthotel. by, reservation@comforthotel.by;* w *comforthotel.by*). Open since 2012, this mixed development of apartments over nine floors is 3.5km out of the city centre, but near to Institut Kultury metro station. The quality of décor and facilities is decent and guests can have a buffet breakfast in the café on site.

WHERE TO EAT AND DRINK

The restaurant trade is another of the rapidly expanding markets in this fast-developing country, with new eateries opening up all the time as the tourism industry begins to sharpen its act. Many of the places listed here are some kind of throwback to the 1970s, particularly in terms of gaudy Soviet-style décor, but the last two years in particular have seen an explosion of new restaurants, cafés and bars, such that the range of cuisine now available is diverse, with high standards of service and culinary expertise to match. Overall, prices are lower than in other European cities, but Minsk is catching up fast. With so much choice available, you can afford to experiment and be adventurous. Most establishments will have menus in English, though not very informative ones, and the majority of places will have someone who can speak at least rudimentary English. The price code covers the average price of a main course, but do remember that things are changing very rapidly. Do your research in advance if you can. One last point; many of the establishments listed under *Cafés & coffee bars* (page 151) might just as easily have been listed in the *Restaurants* category, so do check both sections before choosing where to have lunch or dinner.

RESTAURANTS
Traditional Belarusian

✕ **Berezka** [128 D3] 40 Nyezalyezhnastsi Av; m 29 140 43 43; w berezka.by; ⏱ noon–02.00 daily. Located on Pobyedy Sq, this serves good-quality Belarusian & international cuisine in pleasing surroundings. Competent & attentive staff. **$$$$**

✕ **Cheburechnaya** [136 B6] 9 Voladarskava St; ☎200 42 78; ⏱ 10.00–23.00 daily. Traditional food amid rustic (& a tad gloomy) décor. This makes the list not because the food is particularly better than at other Belarusian emporia in town, but for its historical significance; it is said to be one of the locations closely associated with the declaration of independence of the first (& short-lived) Belarusian republic on 25 March 1918. Thus to dine on this spot is to walk in the footsteps of history (a phrase to make the eyes of my children roll skywards, even today!). Come on the anniversary, but be sure to book. **$$$$**

✕ **Gostyny Dvor** [136 A3] 17 Sovyetskaya St; ☎328 64 27; ⏱ noon–midnight daily. Centrally located close to the Red Church, this serves 'Old Russian' cuisine with an open fire & live music to complete the experience, along with suits of armour & medieval drapes on the walls. Think Middle Ages & castles, but it's all done with style, service is excellent (if a little slow) & the food is very good. You might even have it all to yourself; on my last visit with a small group of friends midweek we were the only ones there. **$$$$**

✳ ✕ **Grunwald** [136 C6] 19 Karla Marksa St; ☎210 42 55; ⏱ 08.00–midnight Mon–Fri, 10.00–midnight Sat–Sun. Belarusian, Polish & Lithuanian

cuisine in a relaxed & friendly atmosphere. It's intimate, classy & reminiscent of Old Europe, but don't expect speedy service. Come prepared to stay for the whole evening & just people-watch while you eat. I first came here in 2002 & it's still one of my favourite haunts in town to while away a few hours enjoying good food. **$$$$**

✕ **Kamyanitsa** [137 H5] 18 Pervomayskaya St; ☎294 51 24; e cafcam@tut.by; w kamyanitsa. by; ⏱ noon–23.00 daily. The proprietor is keen to stress that the food here is prepared to recipes from the days of the Grand Duchy of Lithuania & of the mighty Rzeczpospolita state. It might be hype, but everything is done with style here; the medieval setting is classy, staff are helpful & well presented & the food is good, complemented by live roots music in the evening. A number of my friends rate this place. **$$$$**

✳ ✕ **Karchma Starovilyenskaya** [136 C1] 2 Starovilyenskaya St; ☎335 45 02; ⏱ 09.00–midnight daily. Located in a prime position on the banks of the Svislach on the edge of Old Town, this place serves Belarusian & Italian cuisine within décor that represents a worthy attempt at recreating a historical setting, if a little twee. Food is good & in the summer the atmosphere is relaxed, & the view over the river is quite splendid. My flat is only metres away & I often come to sit outside over coffee. My favourite lunch here consists of quiet reflection over red caviar flatbreads, black olives & a beer. **$$$$**

✕ **Kuchmistr** [137 E4] 40 Karla Marksa St; ☎327 48 48; ⏱ noon–23.00 daily. Well placed in the heart of town, there's nothing flash about this place but it has a good reputation for traditional food served with a touch of panache, yet without fuss or pretension. There's an easy charm about the service & the ambience is relaxed. Good English is spoken, & a group of Geordies & Scousers have written to me to confirm they had no difficulty in being understood! Also served here is a variety of home-distilled spirits, inc a fiery horseradish concoction. Everything about this venue is classy & understated, which puts it high on my own list. $$$$

✗ **Lavski** [137 F7] 6 Kirilla & Mefodya St; 329 03 20; w monastyrski.by; ⏰ 07.00–midnight daily. Located at Hotel Monastyrski (so relatively new), this is perfect if you're around Zibitskaya, as the food here is good, with service to match. Open to non-residents. $$$$

✳ ✗ **Rakovsky Brovar** [136 A3] 10 Vityebskaya St; m 44 733 93 39; w brovar.by; ⏰ noon–midnight daily. Located in the historical part of the city, this classy restaurant has its own micro-brewery, with décor that is a cross between a Belarusian hunting lodge & 19th-century Scandinavia. Think wood panelling plus drapes & tapestries in abundance. On entry, you will be greeted by a huge sturgeon in a tank, but don't be put off. Behind is a sports bar with big screens backing on to the brewery itself. Alfresco dining is well served by a cosy patio downstairs & a terrace on the top floor. The beer is excellent & the food superb, with service to match. One other venue bears the same name in town (& is under the same ownership), but it's a café-bar & not a restaurant. Do give this one a try, but be sure to book or at least get here early, as its high reputation means it's popular with locals & tourists alike. I've been coming here for years & it's still one of my favourites in the city. $$$$

✗ **Seventh Heaven** [136 B6] 11 Nyezalyezhnastsi Av; 209 90 87; ⏰ noon–midnight daily. Located on the top floor of the classy Hotel Minsk (page 140), this offers splendid views over the city, while the cuisine is only a short way behind. There is live music at w/ends. $$$$

✗ **Skif** [137 H2] 34 Nyezalyezhnastsi Av; 284 75 41; w cafeskif.by; ⏰ 09.00–midnight Mon–Thu, 09.00–01.00 Fri–Sat, noon–midnight Sun. Yet more medieval castle-like décor, but the food is good here (with plenty of choice) & the location right outside one of the gates to Gorky Park is excellent. The main restaurant is rather heavy on the historical accoutrements for my liking & I much prefer the ambience in the covered veranda.

Service could be a little slicker too, but it's worth a visit. $$$$

✗ **Stari Gorod** [136 C1] 19 Maxima Bogdanovicha St; 286 05 08; ⏰ noon–midnight Sun–Thu, noon–02.00 Fri–Sat. Located in the reconstructed Old Town, this place might be aimed at the tourist market but it doesn't cut corners on quality. The cellar is cosy in the winter & the terrace inviting in the summer, while the food is always good & well presented. Give this one a try. $$$$

✗ **Talaka** [136 A2] 18 Rakovskaya St; 203 27 94; ⏰ 10.00–06.00 daily. Another basement establishment where the theme is clichéd Belarusian village home, but there's something a little out of the ordinary here & it's all been put together with thought & some quirky touches. The food is consistently good & it's a popular venue, especially with locals. $$$$

✗ **Traktir Na Parkovoi** [128 B4] 11 Pobediteley Av; 203 69 91; ⏰ noon–midnight daily. Only a stone's throw from Hotel Yubileiny, this serves Belarusian & Slavonic cuisine in a setting that is modelled on a traditional Belarusian farmstead, with a courtyard boasting a huge open fire for cooking. Shashlik is a particular speciality. Romany music is played by a fiddler or accordionist wandering from table to table & it's impossible not to be seduced by the romance of it all, even though you know it's tacky & clichéd. The only downside is that tourists love it & they all seem to know about it. Just to say you've been once, though, give in to it & indulge yourself. I still go periodically & I haven't been disappointed yet. To keep that warm glow going, each diner receives a complimentary liqueur upon leaving. $$$$

✗ **U Frantsiska** [136 C5] 19 Nyezalyezhnastsi Av; 664 09 34; w brovar.by; ⏰ noon–23.00 daily. Part of the Rakovsky Brovar stable (a good sign in itself) & right in the middle of town, this offers decent traditional Belarusian food amid reasonably attractive olde-worlde décor. $$$$

✗ **Vyerkhny Gorod** [137 G7] 4 Svobody Sq; 321 20 89; ⏰ 10.00–23.00 daily. An indicator that you can expect good things at this fine restaurant is that close friends running a travel business not only recommend it to visitors, they dine here themselves. The location in this lovely square is perfect, with excellent views of the Holy Spirit Cathedral & beyond. The best dishes are the Belarusian ones, service is professional & the décor is classy. $$$$

Lido [129 E2] 49/1 Nyezalyezhnastsi Av; m 29 302 59 59; w lido.by; ☺ 08.00–23.00 Mon–Fri, 11.00–23.00 Sat–Sun. Less of a fine-dining experience (it's self-service) & more a safe option for families with children, this chain emporium has cheerful staff & the cuisine is better than you might expect. There's an imaginative children's menu & themed events for little ones. Trouble is, once you've seen the interior of one medieval recreation, you tend to be less impressed by the others. Maybe one to avoid unless you have your children with you (in which case they will love it). It's also a little out of the centre just off Yakuba Kolasa Sq, but it has many fans (including a good number of my Minsk friends!). Make up your own mind. Also at 5a Kulman St [128 D2]. $$$

Vasilki [129 E1] 37 Yakuba Kolasa St; ☎706 70 34; w vasilki.by; ☺ 11.00–23.00 Sun–Wed, 10.00–02.00 Fri–Sat. Traditional Belarusian cuisine & décor; it's a particular favourite of Minsk friend Alena. Come prepared for a potato fest with friendly service, though the menu is hugely varied. The draniki here are particularly tasty & prices are very competitive. One of a chain, with other outlets in the city, inc 2 on Nyezalyezhnastsi. Pizza Tempo is in the same stable. $$$

Eastern European & ex-USSR

Astara [128 D5] 37 Pulikhova St; ☎299 97 61; ☺ 10.00–23.00 daily. A big experience in every way awaits in this corner of Azerbaijan. Don't go if you're looking for understatement & a quiet night, but I'm told that the food is excellent. Much favoured by a good friend who lives close by; I'm still waiting for him to take me, though he tells me it's worth the wait. $$$$

✳ **Chaihana Lounge** [128 D1] 61 Surganova St; m 29 325 45 45; ☺ 11.00–02.00 Sun–Thu, 11.00–04.00 Fri–Sat. This fine Uzbek restaurant is well regarded & it's easy to see why. Good service, cosy atmosphere & interesting dishes. Also superbly located in my favourite part of town at 4 Starovilyenskaya St [136 C1] (m 29 325 65 65), where my correspondent Alastair Watson tells me the lamb *pilaf* is 'simply delicious' (& it comes in 3 portion sizes). $$$$

Chumatsky Shlyakh [128 B5] 34 Myasnikova St; m 29 190 77 77; w barbaris.by; ☺ 10.00–23.00 daily. Traditional Ukrainian recipes served in a bright, rustic interior by staff in national dress. Live music is played at w/ends & a delivery

service is available. Sample Belarusian cooking elsewhere first, then come here to compare notes. Part of the group that owns the Malt & Hops pub (page 156) & Doo Dah King bar (page 155). $$$$

Dejavu [128 C6] 6 Volodka St; ☎124 24 90; ☺ noon–midnight Mon–Thu, noon–05.00 Fri–Sat, noon–01.00 Sun. So you've sampled the cuisine of the constituent republics & now it's time for the glory of the CCCP. The food is decent, the décor is unashamedly retro-Soviet with some splendid accoutrements & there's a nice touch of irony to the service. There's even a bust of Lenin in the corner. Loud & lively, especially at the w/end, so only come if you're in the mood. $$$$

Erivan [128 A4] 3 Pyervy Zagorodny St; ☎170 08 08; ☺ noon–midnight daily. To complete your culinary tour of the Caucasus, try this lively Armenian restaurant. It's another big night out & the floor show is extravagant. $$$$

Natvris Khe [129 H2] 4 Svyazistov St; ☎385 02 55; ☺ noon–midnight Tue–Sun. A truly authentic Georgian experience can be had here, all to the accompaniment of live roots folk music. The setting is beautiful & the food is good, but it's a long way out in the suburbs. $$$$

Tiflis [129 F1] 3 Tolbukhin St; ☎385 64 74; ☺ 11.00–23.00 daily. It's another Georgian experience & one that's worth the trek out of the centre, especially as the location close to Chelyuskintsev Park & the Botanical Gardens makes this a decent shout for lunch on a day of meandering among the greenery. The food is excellent. $$$$

Tovarisch [137 E2] 21 Yanka Kupala St; ☎327 34 35; w tovarisch.by; ☺ noon–midnight daily. There's another full-on Soviet Union experience to be had here. As with Dejavu, the retro décor is impressive & it's particularly lively at the w/end. Many of my Minsk friends rate this place. Both food & service are good. $$$$

Verba [128 B2] 51 Kropotkina St; ☎334 69 95; ☺ 11.00–23.00 daily. Very much a local neighbourhood restaurant, this fine venue specialises in Caucasian food free of tourist trappings. The soup *piti* with lamb, potatoes & hummus is a delight, as are the *lyula* kebab & pork shashlik. There's a main dining room, which has a touch of the 'Soviet' about its style & ambience, a bar & several discreet, well-appointed private rooms seating up to 6. I like this one, as do many of my correspondents. It's unpretentious & knows that it's a hip venue, so it doesn't have to try. **$$$$**

✳ ✘ **Xinkalnya** [136 D3] 25 Internatsionalnaya St; **m** 29 667 47 47; ⊕ noon–midnight daily. Only open since July 2017, this Georgian restaurant already enjoys a fine reputation. The décor is simple but classy & the food is good, with friendly service to match. Especially note the impressively proportioned bread oven on the ground floor. I came here for splendid Georgian dumplings one evening last winter with the temperature outside at −20°C. Booking essential for evening dining. **$$$$**

European haute cuisine

✘ **Avignon** [136 C4] 28 Internatsionalnaya St; ☎ 229 84 31; **w** hoteleurope.by; ⊕ 07.00– midnight daily. Fine dining in elegant surroundings at Hotel Europe (page 139) with high-quality service & prices to match. **$$$$$**

✘ **Bistro de Luxe** [136 B4] 10 Gorodski Val St; **m** 44 789 11 11; ⊕ 08.00–midnight Mon–Fri, 11.00–midnight Sat–Sun. On the bottom corner of Internatsionalnaya. Come for elegant French dining in a classy setting. Quiet by day for b/fast & lunch, but booking is essential for the evening, when Minsk society arrives for dinner. Now one of the best dining experiences in town, with excellent food & superb service. **$$$$$**

✘ **Falcone** [128 B5] 9 Korolya St; **m** 29 377 77 76; **w** falcone.by; ⊕ noon–midnight daily. Without doubt this fine Italian restaurant is the real deal. With a kitchen formerly run by Michelin-starred head chef Domenico Acampora, it's no wonder that this is the haunt of the city's elite. All is elegant here, from the décor to the service, & the menu is a culinary delight. There's even a children's playroom to keep the little ones entertained so you can relish every pampered moment of the dining experience. Don't miss out, but expect to pay for the privilege. **$$$$$**

✳ ✘ **Grand Café** [136 C4] 2 Lenina St; ☎ 703 11 11; ⊕ noon–midnight daily. Fine dining at its best, this is the favourite restaurant of many in Minsk, inc a number of my close friends. The food is exquisite, the décor elegant & the service highly professional. The location is central, across from Hotel Europe on the opposite side of Lenina. It's not cheap, but you get what you pay for. If you're a non-smoker the only downside is that the smoking & non-smoking areas are 2 halves

of the same room, but overall this is a very classy establishment. Highly recommended if your budget can take the hit. If not just come for a drink, take a raised stool at the bar or one of the window tables & spend a glorious hour observing Minsk's nouveaux riches preening themselves & each other for ostentatious public display. It's one of my favourite Minsk activities & you won't be required to dress up yourself. **$$$$$**

✘ **La Crete d'Or** [136 C4] 3 Lenina St; **m** 29 105 05 03; **w** grebeshok.by; ⊕ 11.00– 23.00 daily. Classic French cuisine is on offer here in a very elegant setting, where the standard of service is second to none. Most of my friends prefer Grand Café for fine dining, but this classy restaurant is not far behind in their estimation. I can't decide between the two, which are almost opposite each other on Lenina. Either way there's an air of refinement here. Next door is a coffee shop of the same name serving decent coffee & snacks, plus a branch of Belarusbank with an ATM. You're going to need it! **$$$$$**

✘ **Renaissance** [136 C3] 23 Svobody Sq; ☎ 327 09 91; ⊕ noon–midnight Sun–Thu, noon– 02.00 Fri–Sat. This is another elegant venue in a splendid location serving excellent cuisine, where the décor is classy & the service understated & professional. On my first visit here everything was the epitome of laid-back refinement, with mellow live jazz. It was also empty … **$$$$$**

✳ ✘ **View** [136 A1] 7a Pobediteley Av; **m** 44 702 88 88; **w** view.nrg.by; ⊕ noon–23.30 daily. Located next to the DoubleTree by Hilton & with an enviable reputation for fine dining. A number of my Minsk friends come here for special occasions; it's easy to see why. The views are indeed spectacular, so try to secure a window table & try to come at dusk as the lights of the city come on. Free parking is a bonus. **$$$$$**

✘ **Wood and Fire** [129 H1] 1 Francysk Skaryny St; ☎ 268 83 55; **w** woodfire.by; ⊕ noon– midnight Sun–Thu, noon–02.00 Fri–Sat. Northeast of the city centre & not far from the National Library (spectacularly illuminated by night as a backdrop to your meal), high standards of service accompany fine dining here. I have yet to try this one, but colleagues in the tourism industry & a number of friends recommend a visit. The location is a drawback & the locale is not as green as it used to be; a great deal of development is taking place in the vicinity. But if you're out this way visiting the library, lunch here is an option, & the terrace is lovely in the summer. $$$$$

✕ Panorama [128 C3] 15 Storazhevskaya St; ☎198 16 85; ◷ noon–midnight Sun–Wed, noon–02.00 Thu–Sat. Located on the 22nd floor of the fully refurbished Hotel Belarus (page 141). The panoramic views of the city are unsurpassed (look out especially for the National Library, lit up by lasers like a Christmas tree), while the food, from an international menu, is of a consistently high standard. Having survived a long period of closure throughout the hotel's massive overhaul, this restaurant is back to its best. I love it for the view alone. Service is helpful & professional. $$$$

✕ Westfalia [128 A6] 11 Gazyety Pravda Av; ☎172 00 00; w westfalia.by; ◷ 07.00–23.00 daily. Some way out of town in the joint Belarusian-German venture IBB hotel & conference complex (page 142), this restaurant is well worth a visit nevertheless. It's been open for years & has thus stood the test of time, especially as it's off the main drag. The food is exquisite, the service slick & the wine list (inc cocktails) comprehensive. There is live music Wed–Fri. Excellent value for money. $$$$

Italian

✕ Bella Rosa [129 E3] 3 Gikalo St; ☎284 53 03; w bellarosa.by; ◷ noon–midnight Sun–Thu, noon–02.00 Fri–Sat. This is a classy Italian with food of high quality & prices to match. $$$$$

✕ Bergamo [128 C1] 37 Kulman St; ☎334 45 56; ◷ 10.00–midnight daily. Quality Italian food in a decent setting & much frequented by the Italian community in town. Enough said? Expensive, though. $$$$$

✕ La Scala [128 B5] 36 Nemiga St; m 29 311 99 99; e info@la-scala.by; w la-scala.by; ◷ noon–midnight daily. This new kid on the block is rapidly acquiring a fine reputation for quality dining. The imaginative menu is courtesy of Executive Chef Ignazio Rosa, a Sicilian by birth with an impressive CV listing 30 years' experience around the restaurants of Europe. Reasonably central, good service, decent food. $$$$

✕ Milano [136 B6] 19 Voladarskava St; m 44 762 11 11; w uhg.by; ◷ 08.00–midnight Mon–Fri, 09.00–midnight Sat–Sun. Part of the Union Hospitality Group that also includes Café de Paris, Union Coffee (page 154) & Paul Bakery (page 153) in Minsk. Food & service here are good, & decent

English is spoken. Come for a meal or a coffee with friends. Good friend Alena recommends this place & that's good enough for me. $$$$

✕ Tempo [129 F2] 78 Nyezalyezhnastsi Av; ☎278 56 80; w tempo.by; ◷ 08.00–23.00 daily. It's a chain restaurant with branches all over town, but if you're in a hurry for fast sustenance while you're ticking off the sights, give it a try for Italian standards cooked well. The website will tell you where the others are, as well as all you need to know about what's on offer. Always busy, always lively, service is slick & it does the job. A delivery service is also available. $$$$

✕ Freski [136 C3] 19 Internatsionalnaya St; ☎327 81 72; ◷ 10.00–midnight Sun–Thu, 10.00–03.00 Fri–Sat. Decent food, OK service, good location. $$$

✕ Il Patio [136 D4] 22 Nyezalyezhnastsi Av; ☎327 17 91; w ilpatio.by; ◷ 11.00–midnight Sun–Thu, 11.00–01.00 Fri–Sat. Still a very popular venue among locals & visitors alike. The decent-quality food is served competently & without fuss. Not spectacular, but good value. $$$

Mediterranean

✕ Tapas [136 B4] 9 Internatsionalnaya St; m 29 399 11 11; ◷ 11.00–midnight daily. Central location, decent tapas, fine paella & good service. The summer terrace is a great place to hang out with friends. Locals like it here, including a number of my acquaintances. Often busy. $$$

Oriental

✳ ✕ Jomalungma [129 E3] 7 Gikalo St; ☎280 53 88; ◷ noon–02.00 Sun–Thu, noon–05.00 Fri–Sat. Still one of my favourites after all these years. A 5min walk from Ploshchad Yakuba Kolasa metro station & close to Bella Rosa Italian restaurant, it serves Indian, Tibetan, Nepalese, Japanese, Chinese & Thai cuisine, with limited hotel delivery service. I love this place. The décor is fabulous, the food is of a high standard & service is good, with the proprietor in constant attendance. He drives the staff incredibly hard & isn't fussy about closing the kitchen door before tearing them off a strip. The 1970s cabaret floor shows are more than a little incongruous! There is also a 'hookah' bar (◷ noon–02.00 daily) & a tearoom here, but you might want to give the karaoke bar a miss. The dining outlet at Minsk National Airport is now a Jomalungma. $$$$

✕ Taj [128 B4] 26 Romanovskaya Sloboda St; ☏711 11 10; w taj.by; ⊕ noon–midnight daily. I have yet to try this one, but Minsk friends have been urging me to do so for some time. They tell me the excellence of the food is matched by the service & that everything here is impressive. Where Jomalungma has familiarity on its side, the reputation of the Taj is continuing to grow. $$$$

South & Central American

✕ Cantina Mexicana [136 D2] 25 Yanka Kupala St; m 29 609 66 66; ⊕ 08.00–midnight daily. Standard Mexican fare with few frills. $$$

CAFÉS & COFFEE BARS

☕ 26 Coffee Bar [128 D6] 26 Sverdlova St; m 29 371 50 31; ⊕ 08.00–23.00 Mon–Fri, 09.00–23.00 Sat–Sun. Close to the railway station & a number of higher-education institutions, this place can get rammed, but the buzz is good & if you pick your moment, all is calm here. The architecture in this part of town will interest students of Stalinist Neoclassicism.

✳ ☕ Barzha floating restaurant [136 C1] Riverbank mooring, Svislach River, Troitskoye suburb; ☏355 00 22. Easy to spot on its mooring at the bottom of this popular tourist area, it's never busy & the standard of food & service is always high. Given the location & the quality of the views across the water, it's well worth a visit for a coffee, drink or meal. I like it here.

☕ Bastion [129 F1] 35 Volgogradskaya St; ☏280 17 67; ⊕ noon–23.00 daily. Cheap & cheerful ethnic Slav dishes in a traditionally styled environment. Pleasant but uninspiring.

☕ Beze [136 C5] 18 Nyezalyezhnastsi Av; ☏328 64 09; ⊕ 11.00–01.00 daily. Quaint & charmingly retro. The richest of desserts are served here, so this is the place if you have a sweet tooth. The apple & cherry strudels are delicious.

✳ ☕ Bread and Wine [136 C6] 21 Karla Marksa St; ☏327 00 10; ⊕ 10.00–22.00 daily. Primarily an emporium for purchasing wine, but you can also drink by the bottle on the premises. Simple food (bread, ham, cheese & olives) accompanies the quaffing. Very relaxed, this place is especially popular in the evening, when booking is essential.

☕ Bufet [136 D2] 2 Zibitskaya St; m 44 701 90 00; ⊕ noon–02.00 Sun–Thu, noon–05.00 Fri–Sat. At the top end of the Zibitskaya drag, all

is calm & relaxed here by day, then buzzing by night. Good friend Lera & I very much enjoyed our excellent salads & puds when we came for late lunch on my last visit.

☕ Coffee Berry [137 G5] 6 Zibitskaya St; m 29 639 43 81; ⊕ 11.00–23.00 Sun–Thu, 11.00–02.00 Fri–Sat. Come for coffee or juice, but as with Bufet at the other end of Zibitskaya, come here anyway for alcohol-free recuperation & rehydration. Handily located for taking a break from all the beach-themed excitement at Na Plyazhe next door. Also at 5 Internatsionalnaya St [136 B4] & in the underground Stolitsa shopping centre on Nyezalyezhnastsi Sq [136 A7].

☕ Dôm [136 B4] 26 Revolutsionaya St; m 29 384 11 33; ⊕ 11.00–midnight Mon–Wed, 11.00–02.00 Thu, 13.00–02.00 Fri, 13.00–midnight Sat–Sun. A night out on Revolutsionaya is a decent alternative to the bustle & energy of Zibitskaya. Opposite the TIC, this unpretentious bar & eatery with its lovely balcony comes recommended by a number of my Minsk friends.

☕ Doner King [137 H6] 2 Zibitskaya St; m 44 544 66 22; w donerking.by; ⊕ 24/7. I bow my head in shame for including a doner kebab take-away. Actually, I don't. When I'm out drinking with friends on Zibitskaya, it absolutely hits the spot. Also at 4 other locations in the city.

✳ ☕ Dyepo [128 D6] 23 Kastrichnitskaya St; m 29 663 40 88; ⊕ 11.00–23.00 Sun–Thu, 11.00–01.00 Fri–Sat. Next door to Lafka in the trendy urban art district (& also now at 6 Zibitskaya St [136 D5]), this top café on the site of the old tram depot is one of the first names I hear when I ask my student friends for new recommendations. Both locations are hugely popular. Great coffee & very good food (pancakes a speciality).

☕ Elyana [136 C5] 18 Nyezalyezhnastsi Av; ☏227 00 03; ⊕ 08.00–02.00 Mon–Sat, 08.00–midnight Sun. The usurper of my former favourite café in town on this very site (Union Coffee, happily now relocated). I may not be the most objective of evaluators, but the coffee & menu are good & the transition seems to have been seamless. The mid-town location is perfect for refreshment & a break from your wanderings. I may yet return to use this place as my base for book updates & scribbles, as once I did.

✳ ☕ Enzo [128 D6] 23 Kastrichnitskaya St; m 29 177 00 88; w enzo.by; ⊕ 11.00–midnight Sun–Thu, 11.00–01.00 Fri–Sat. Sharing the same address as Dyepo & Lafka (& also one of the first names on everyone's lips when I ask about trendy venues). The burgers & steaks here are already famed. Very popular.

❋ 🍵 **Family Club** [137 G4] Gorky Park; ☎620 20 35; ⊕ 11.00–22.00 daily. As the name & location suggest, this is one for families. It's also one of my own favourites in town. Right in the middle of the park, it offers an oasis of calm to escape the hustle & bustle of the city. The food is good (especially the pizza) & service is always excellent. Rarely busy (though it's very popular for wedding parties), it comes recommended.

🍵 **Ferz Coffee** [137 G7] 1/2 Muzykalny Pereulok; ☎226 50 45; ⊕ 10.00–23.00 daily. At the top of Gertsena, this is another option for caffeine therapy while you party on Zibitskaya. Or come here for a quiet night out. Decent coffee & puds, inc to take away.

🍵 **Fresh** [128 D3] 42 Nyezalyezhnastsi Av; ☎284 54 04; ⊕ 10.00–23.00 Sun–Thu, 13.00–01.00 Fri–Sat. 'Fresh' indeed, if unremarkable, but handily placed for a break from your sightseeing. Also at 2 Khmelnitskova St (⊕ *10.00–23.00 daily*).

🍵 **Golden Coffee** [128 C3] 26 Maxima Bogdanovicha St; ☎756 21 17; w goldencoffee. by; ⊕ claims to be open 24hrs, but seems to close 06.00–08.00 for a 'technical break'. One of a chain that features widely across Latvia, Lithuania & Ukraine, serving decent tea & coffee. Very lively & good value, but lacking charm. The new roof bar is now open. Also in the Expobel shopping mall (⊕ *10.00–23.00 daily*).

❋ 🍵 **Green Cuisine** [136 D3] 23 Internatsionalnaya St; m 29 177 11 44; ⊕ noon–23.00 Mon–Thu, noon–midnight Fri–Sun. Serving vegetarian dishes of the highest quality, this is a real find. Good friend Lera first brought me here early in 2017 & I keep coming back. The menu is never less than interesting & the friendly staff are charming & eager to please. Soups here are a joy. The closest I've come to being persuaded to give up meat.

🍵 **Guru Coffee Club** [136 C6] 34 Komsomolskaya St; m 29 150 22 55; w gurucoffeeclub.by; ⊕ 09.00–23.00 daily. Right next door to the charming Lozhki café, Guru is also a delight. Quiet, friendly & relaxed; book lovers will feel very much at home here. Also at 3 other locations in the city.

🍵 **Il Grottino** [136 C4] 13 Internatsionalnaya St; ☎226 63 33; ⊕ 11.00–23.00 daily. Modest but with a loyal following among local people; pizza here is very good & very cheap. You're going to be meandering hereabouts (it's just around the corner from Lenina), so it's a top shout for a pit stop to catch your breath or for quality street food on the go.

❋ 🍵 **Kommunarka Lakomka** [136 C5] 19 Nyezalyezhnastsi Av; ☎310 35 18; w kommunarka.by; ⊕ 09.00–21.00 Mon–Fri, 09.00–20.00 Sat–Sun. Another Minsk institution & fine example of retro Soviet chic, Kommunarka has been producing confectionary in the city since 1905 & there are outlets all over town (& throughout the country). This store, in a delightfully renovated building on the main drag next to Tsentralnaya Knigariya, has a dazzling array of sweets & cakes, plus cafeteria seating for indulging on the premises. The hot chocolate here is glorious. My friend Natasha reckons the cakes are the best in town & it's hard not to agree, with prices among the cheapest. While pounding the streets updating this manuscript we regularly called in for a sugar rush & to download. Recommended both for self-indulgence & for buying souvenirs to take home.

❋ 🍵 **Lafka** [128 D6] 23 Kastrichnitskaya St; m 29 132 20 88; ⊕ 24/7. Already a Minsk institution among students & the young, this tiny café is a must visit. Urban chic at its finest, with decent coffee & an excellent choice of street food/snacks/sandwiches to match, at great prices. I have yet to test its 'we never close' credentials, though I hear there are 2 30min breaks around b/fast & mid-evening. Come for no other reason than to say you've been. It's that trendy.

🍵 **London** [136 D5] 18 Nyezalyezhnastsi Av; ☎289 15 29; ⊕ 10.00–midnight Sun–Thu, 10.00–02.00 Fri & Sat. A cosy venue offering a huge selection of teas & coffees, with cakes & sweets to match. Long popular with the locals; you'll have to ignore the tacky London décor & paraphernalia, however.

❋ 🍵 **Lozhki** [136 C6] 34 Komsomolskaya St; ☎327 07 72; ⊕ 10.00–23.00 daily. My correspondent Jill Flanagan once told me there's a good range of decent beer, teas, coffee, milkshakes & pastries here. Bizarrely the walls are decorated with spoons, cups & saucers, while the ceiling has a spoon chandelier. On Jill's recommendation I visited for the first time in 2017 with good friend

Alena, to discover that it's one of her favourites in town. I concur with their judgement.

🖥 **Manufaktura** [136 B6] 17 Karla Marksa St; m 29 152 07 89; ⏱ 09.00–23.00 daily. Tucked away just off a busy street (so an oasis of calm for a few moments of quiet reflection), this fine café is uncomplicated but classy & serves excellent coffee. The ambience here is relaxed & elegant. A particular favourite of my very good friend Natasha, who reckons the coffee is among the best in town.

🖥 **Matchbol** [128 A3] 40 Zhudra St; 📞 312 18 53; ⏱ 11.00–23.00 Sun–Thu, 11.00–midnight Fri–Sat. A Vietnamese café specialising in national dishes & snacks. It's a long way out of the city centre (& a 20min walk from Sportivnaya metro station), which is a pity, because it has a simple charm all of its own.

✴ 🖥 **Maya Angliskaya Babushka** [137 E5] 36 Karla Marksa St; 📞 327 22 24; ⏱ 09.00–midnight daily. Its location just across the road from the British embassy might have something to do with its name, which translates as 'My English Granny'! It's tiny, but cosy & rather romantic, & also easy to miss, as you need to descend steps from street level to enter. Assorted teas & delicious pastries are served to customers on comfortable sofas in a Victorian setting. Full meals (inc b/fast) are also available until 17.00. Many of my Minsk friends come here. Recommended.

🖥 **Moby Dick** [128 D6] 16 Kastrichnitskaya St; m 29 640 03 03; w mobydick.by; ⏱ 08.00–22.00 daily. One for a pit stop while you're meandering the hip streets to admire the urban art of this former industrial district. The buzz is good here. It's part of a gym complex, but don't feel you have to work out first to earn your coffee break. Take out if you want to keep walking.

🖥 **Netto** [128 D3] 13 Krasnaya St; 📞 668 13 13; ⏱ 09.00–23.00 Sun–Thu, 09.00–02.00 Fri & Sat. Located 5min walk from Ploshchad Pobyedy metro station, this is a very popular establishment where the ambience is good, the food decent & the service top drawer. Those of my friends who like it all remark that it's a comfortable & relaxing venue.

🖥 **News Café** [136 D5] 34 Karla Marksa St; m 29 103 11 11; ⏱ 08.00–midnight Mon–Fri, 11.00–midnight Sat–Sun. Close to Maya Angliskaya Babushka & the British embassy, this has a reputation as one of the most glamorous places in the city; indeed, luxury motors, bling & the glitterati

are to be seen in abundance here. Not my scene, I'm afraid, but the coffee is good & service is first class, I'm told. Good friends in town rate it highly.

🖥 **Olivo** [136 B6] 13 Voladarskava St; 📞 327 81 47; ⏱ 11.00–23.00 Sun–Thu, 11.00–01.00 Fri–Sat. This is a decent place for a pit stop, with good coffee & lots of snacks on offer. Trendy, popular & relaxed, all at the same time. Do bear this place in mind if you're dashing around & need a quick break. Also at 46 Nyezalyezhnastsi Av [128 D3] (m *29 688 29 41;* ⏱ *10.00–23.00 Mon–Thu, 10.00–01.00 Fri, noon–01.00 Sat, noon–23.00 Sun*) and at 35 Yakuba Kolasa St [129 E1] (📞 785 58 30; ⏱ *11.00–midnight Sun–Thu, 11.00–01.00 Fri–Sat*).

🖥 **Paul Bakery** [136 D3] 21 Internatsionalnaya St; m 29 177 22 12; ⏱ 08.00–midnight daily. Part of an international chain owning other cafés in town & only open since June 2017, this French-style bakery is a very popular meeting place. I often come here to work with laptop & notebook over b/fast or excellent coffee & pastries. Extensive English menu.

🖥 **Perfetto** [136 A4] 1 Romanovskaya Sloboda St; 📞 200 24 10; w perfetto.by; ⏱ noon–midnight daily. Opposite McDonald's on the corner of Nemiga St, all is very shiny & very Italian here. One to try if you want more than just coffee; the food is consistently good.

🖥 **Shtolle** [129 E2] 53 Nyezalyezhnastsi Av; 📞 331 10 00; w stolle.by; ⏱ 10.00–23.00 daily. One of a chain; there are 7 of these in prime locations in the centre of the city. Think pies & pasties, both savoury & sweet, with a delivery service if you need. Otherwise it's a great way to access tasty food on the go. Consistently decent standards. My friend Olga, who is a regular patron, thinks so too.

🖥 **Stories** [136 B4] 14 Internatsionalnaya St; m 29 614 17 14; ⏱ 08.30–22.00 Mon–Thu, 08.30–23.00 Fri, 10.00–23.00 Sat–Sun. Quality coffee & pastries in a central location. Relaxed & friendly, so ideal for recharging batteries during your meanderings hereabouts.

✴ 🖥 **Svobody 4** [136 C3] 4 Svobody Sq ; m 29 144 47 14; w svobody4.com; ⏱ 08.00–midnight Mon–Thu, 08.00–02.00 Fri, 10.00–02.00 Sat, 10.00–midnight Sun. Good friend Lera first brought me here for lunch early in 2017 & I've been back many times since. Loud & buzzing in the evening, calm & relaxed by day, with a location, on the edge of this lovely square in the midst of the sights, that cannot be beaten. Food & service are slick but quietly understated. The first choice of many Minsk friends. A visit here is highly recommended.

✳ ☕ **Tsentralny** [136 D4] 23 Nyezalyezhnastsi Av; 📞 226 12 89; ☺ 08.00–23.00 daily. To feel the beating heart & glimpse the soul of Minsk, a visit here is a must. Centrally located at the junction of Nyezalyezhnastsi & Lenina (absolutely the point at which everything in the city converges), this cafeteria is a slice of 1950s Soviet chic. The food is average (sandwiches & snacks) but incredibly cheap. My dear friend Joanna particularly likes the cheese & tomato sandwich, though my favourite here is smoked salmon, ham & salad. Just grab a drink & something to eat, lean on the counter facing the street & take it all in. People come & go at speed (it's especially busy as offices empty in the evening & workers grab a beer on the way home) so there's no finer spot for people-watching. Be sure to look up & around; the Soviet décor (particularly the murals) is a joy. Perhaps most important of all, it's the perfect antidote to American giants TGI Fridays & McDonald's opposite & next door. Whenever I'm in Minsk no day passes without me paying a visit to Tsentralny. I can't recommend this place too highly.

☕ **Union Coffee** [137 F3] 17 Yanka Kupala St; **m** 29 615 13 13; **w** unioncoffee.by; ☺ 08.00–midnight daily. I was crushed on my last visit to Minsk to find that my favourite coffee bar on Nyezalyezhnastsi was no more, but now I'm comforted to know that it has merely relocated to new premises on Yanka Kupala. I haven't been yet, though Minsk friends have. It seems to have survived the move with standards intact. Also at 6 Bobruskaya St [128 C6] in the Galileo shopping mall there.

☕ **Utopia 60** [136 D5] 9 Lenina St; 📞 328 66 74; ☺ 09.00–23.00 daily. Right in the middle of town, the location could not be better. A number of my Minsk friends call in here to graze & catch up. I have yet to visit, but their assessment of its charms is a positive one.

☕ **Zerno** [128 D3] 46 Nyezalyezhnastsi Av; 📞 271 32 63; ☺ 07.00–23.00 daily. A little way from the main sights (it's almost as far as Yakuba Kolasa Sq), but locals like this place & the coffee is good. Hop on the metro & take a look.

BARS 'Zibitskaya'; Ask anyone in town where to go for a good night out & the reply is always the same. The compact area around Zibitskaya St at the bottom of the Upper Town (on the south bank of the Svislach) has an astonishing collection of bars & restaurants cheek by jowl. Right in the heart of the area, the sprawling new Mercure Hotel was close to opening when I was last here & the urban landscape hereabouts is developing fast. So Minsk now has its own 'party street' to rival any drinking quarter elsewhere in Europe &, with the temptation of visa-free travel to Minsk for 5 days, I'm convinced there will be a significant influx of visitors very soon. Get here before everyone else catches on. There are dozens of drinking emporia within a radius of 100m, with 15 alone in one small block! Many are listed below, though I have deliberately kept descriptions brief & modest. With notable exceptions there is little to choose between them; & in any event, evaluation is an entirely subjective issue. Come to Zibitskaya for a loud & large night out, but come prepared. Remember where your bed for the night is located, know how to get back there, be alert & stay streetwise; then join the party. Wander at will, dip in & out (a kebab from Doner King (page 151) will take care of the munchies) & over time decide which bar is your own personal favourite. Do bear in mind that you don't have to go large. Instead of drinking until you drop, you'll find some classy drinking emporia & eateries here for a less frenzied but equally satisfying night out. Perhaps come by day in the first instance to do your research. Either way, do please share your thoughts, experiences, stories & pictures to help us build a database for those who follow.

More generally & beyond Zibitskaya, many of the places described earlier as restaurants & cafés also double as bars, with most of them readily serving drinking clientele as well as diners. There are lots of others out there that don't get a mention in these pages, with more & more opening all the time. Minsk is currently experiencing exponential growth in entertainment, eating, drinking & leisure-time activities, with both locals & visitors now spoilt for choice. So wherever your meanderings take you in this delightful city, embark on a voyage of discovery & when you find somewhere new, be sure to tell me about it.

🍷 **4-4-2** [137 G5] 6 Zibitskaya St; **m** 29 672 44 42; ☺ 17.00–01.00 Mon–Sat, 17.00–midnight Sun. Sports aficionados will have no trouble guessing the theme. Buzzing on big match nights & very popular generally, with a continuous backdrop of screened live sport. Beer & football works for me, but it doesn't for everyone.

♀ **Banki i Butilki** [137 G5] 6 Zibitskaya St; m 29 322 35 35; ⊕ 17.00–02.00 Mon–Thu, 17.00–04.00 Fri–Sun. At 'Jars & Bottles' it won't take long to spot the theme, both in terms of décor & drinking/eating receptacles. Popular & trendy, loud & busy, long & narrow; many of my student friends come here, not least for the sorrel shots I haven't yet been brave enough to try.

✷ ♀ **Beercap** [137 G6] 10 Gertsena St; m 29 630 02 10; ⊕ 17.00–23.00 Sun–Thu, 17.00–01.00 Fri–Sat. Located in the Zibitskaya zone, this is now one of my favourite bars in town. Lively & hugely popular, the vaulted cellar & outside yard make for a top place to work your way through an impressive selection of craft beers. The tunes are good, too, & you can also buy to take away. This is where good friend Alex Vazhnik & I meet en route to the football in Borisov, or just to console each other over the latest calamity to befall our beloved Birmingham City FC. To the best of my knowledge, Alex is the only Birmingham fan in all Belarus.

♀ **BierKeller** [128 D4] 12 Voiskovoi Lane; ☎286 00 39; ⊕ noon–midnight daily. Not surprisingly it's very German in every way (food, beer, décor, costumes). The food is decent & the pavement terrace ideal for people-watching in the summer. My good friend Artur who lives round the corner was keen for me to sample the impressive range of beers & I wasn't disappointed. Close to Gorky Park; useful if you're thirsty after a meander.

✷ ♀ **Calvin Coolidge** [137 F5] 6 Zibitskaya St; m 29 695 50 00; ⊕ 16.00–02.00 Mon–Thu, 16.00–04.00 Fri–Sat, 16.00–midnight Sun. An oasis of cool & detachment within the mania of Zibitskaya, this is one of my very favourites in town. Cool & classy, hip & sassy, laid-back & refined, it's a great place for listening to late-night, smoky jazz while you sip your favourite cocktail. It's an Old Fashioned for me, every time.

♀ **Cherdak** [137 G6] 9 Zibitskaya St; m 29 189 09 09; ⊕ 17.00–02.00 Sun–Thu, 17.00–05.00 Fri–Sat. Above the rooftops, this relaxed & classy cocktail bar with its delightful attic décor is not easy to find but is well worth the search. Come also for the lofty outdoor terrace. Be very careful descending the wooden stairs down to ground level after a few drinks.

♀ **Clever Irish Pub** [129 E3] 5 Gikalo St; m 29 109 22 22; ⊕ 16.00–02.00 Mon–Thu, 16.00–04.00 Fri, noon–04.00 Sat, noon–02.00 Sun. You know what you're going to get here, but it's an especially good shout for a beer or 2 if you're on this street for a meal at my long-standing favourite Jomalungma (page 150). Even if not, come for the craic & the football.

♀ **Craftman** [129 E3] 5 Gikalo St; m 29 607 05 05; w craftmanbar.by; ⊕ 18.00–midnight Mon–Thu, 17.00–02.00 Fri–Sat, 17.00–midnight Sun. I have yet to visit this craft beer paradise & I feel I've really missed out. It's first on my list for my next visit. Great choice of quality beers, I hear, knowledgeable staff & decent, uncomplicated comestibles to accompany the quaffing. Everyone I ask around town nods sagely about this place. Let's go.

♀ **DIY** [137 F5] 6 Zibitskaya St; ☎241 91 97; w diy-bar.by; 18.00–02.00 Tue–Thu, 18.00–04.00 Fri–Sat, 18.00–01.00 Sun. A hookah bar on the Zibitskaya run, so a good option for mellowing out as the night wears on. Non-smokers should look elsewhere.

♀ **Doo Dah King** [128 B5] 14 Bersona St; ☎103 10 00; ⊕ 17.00–05.00 daily. Loud, raucous & popular. A good night out is to be had here, with live music nightly. Part of the Barbaris group that also includes the Malt & Hops pub (page 156) & Chumatsky Shlyakh (page 148).

♀ **Druzya** [128 C1] 40 Kulman St; ☎396 58 58; w druzya.by; ⊕ noon–02.00 Sun–Thu, noon–03.00 Fri–Sat. North of the city centre on the edge of the 'People's Friendship Park', this vast beer restaurant with its own brewery (hugely popular with the locals) has a less than pleasing exterior & a cavernous feel inside as soon as you cross the threshold. Put that to one side. The craft beer brewed on the premises is excellent & the food is decent too, especially outside on the grill in summer. Good beer & top shashlik. What's not to like? Just think carefully before diving into the karaoke.

♀ **El Pushka Bar** [137 G6] 12 Gertsena St; m 29 999 09 39; ⊕ 18.00–02.00 Sun–Thu, 18.00–04.00 Fri–Sat. In the heart of the Zibitskaya zone & just below one of my favourites (Beercap, see left); come here for cocktails & the South American vibe. Small, popular & very crowded (or if you prefer, intimate).

✷ ♀ **Gambrinus** [136 C3] 2 Svobody Sq; ☎388 00 02; w gambrinus.by; ⊕ noon–midnight Sun–

3

Thu, noon–02.00 Fri–Sat. An old favourite. All of my Minsk friends who come to this splendidly located place in this lovely central square do so for the beer (which is excellent), though the food is decent too. Lively & popular, the ambience makes this one for your list. Expect it to be busy. It's the first choice of my good friend Natalia. I've been eating & drinking here regularly for a number of years & I'm never disappointed.

✴ ♀ **Gaststätte** [136 B3] 16 Revolutsionaya St; ☎306 20 62; ◷ noon–midnight Sun–Thu, noon–02.00 Fri & Sat. With a second entrance around the corner at 9 Komsomolskaya St, this is one of the new breed of 'beer restaurants' in town. The location in the heart of the city is excellent, as is the experience here. As you might expect, it's done out like a Bavarian bierkeller. There's a fine choice of quality beers & an extensive menu of GDR-themed sausages & salads (whatever that means) with all the trimmings. My warm beef salad was delicious when I came midweek & it was very busy. Many of my friends in town think this is the best of its kind, though new kids on the block are pushing it hard. Live music most nights of the week from 21.00. Come for a few beers, a sausage or 2 & immerse yourself in the Latin rhythms of live flamenco guitar (it's kind of fusion, this place). A downside is that there is only one toilet each for boys & girls, so expect to queue.

♀ **Godzhi Cocktail Bar** [136 B4] 17 Revolutsionaya St; m 29 660 22 88; ◷ noon–02.00 Sun–Thu, noon–04.00 Fri–Sat. Another bar worthy of your attention during a night out on Revolutsionaya. Come to dine or just for cocktails.

♀ **Gosti** [137 E3] 25 Nyezalyezhnastsi Av; ☎677 79 99; ◷ noon–01.00 Sun–Thu, noon–03.00 Fri & Sat. Opinion is divided among my Minsk friends & views are either very positive or at the other end of the scale. I think it's OK, but standards of customer service do need an overhaul. Live (& very loud) music if that's what you need.

♀ **Gradus** [137 F5] 6 Zibitskaya St; m 44 576 25 45; w gradus-bar.by; ◷ 10.00–01.00 Sun–Thu, 10.00–04.00 Fri–Sat. More cocktails on Zibitskaya. None of my friends have been. You'll be road-testing in the vicinity anyway, so give it a try.

♀ **Gvozd** [129 E3] 5 Gikalo St; ☎606 03 97; w pubgvozd.by; ◷ noon–midnight Sun–Thu, noon–02.00 Fri–Sat. Good food, great choice of beer, friendly staff, chilled ambience & decent live music at the w/end, all with my dear old friend

Jomalungma restaurant just up the road. It ticks all the right boxes & is popular with locals & visitors alike. My Minsk friend Olga says it's the best in town.

✴ ♀ **Hooligan** [128 D6] 16 Kastrichnitskaya St; ☎327 10 45; ◷ 08.00–midnight Sun–Thu, 08.00–04.00 Fri–Sat. In the same building as Moby Dick (page 153), the décor & vibe match the urban art & industrial landscape of the area. Popular & very trendy.

♀ **Khoroshi God** [137 G5] 6 Zibitskaya St; m 29 136 37 38; ◷ 17.00–midnight Mon–Thu, 11.00–02.00 Fri–Sat, 11.00–midnight Sun. Next door to 4-4-2 (page 154), so also facing the river. Decent wine bar with a strong local following.

♀ **Klumba** [137 G5] 6 Zibitskaya St; m 29 157 43 57; ◷ 18.00–01.00 Mon–Thu, 14.00–04.00 Fri–Sat, 14.00–01.00 Sun. Dance, shout & drink downstairs then chill & drink upstairs. The staff here like to experiment with their mixing, but I prefer to keep things simple. I'm way too old for this place.

♀ **Kurilka Bar** [136 C4] 23 Svobody Sq; m 29 604 32 32; ◷ 18.00–04.00 nightly. Interesting & almost as sassy as it likes to think it is, but come just for a drink or 2 first before committing to a longer stay. Also home to the city's Harley-Davidson Club, though arriving on one is optional.

♀ **Mad Rabbit** [137 G5] 6 Zibitskaya St; ☎338 88 50; ◷ 16.00–02.00 Mon–Thu, 16.00–04.00 Fri, 15.00–04.00 Sat, 15.00–02.00 Sun. Slightly unnerving décor (especially after a drink or 2) but people like the cocktails here. Gin is a speciality & it's the first choice of many of my Minsk friends, particularly outdoors in the summer.

♀ **Malt and Hops** [137 G6] 9/24 Zibitskaya St; m 44 599 90 11; w barbaris.by; ◷ noon–midnight Sun–Thu, noon–02.00 Fri–Sat. Pub-style with British & Irish beer & whiskey in abundant choice for those who are missing home (including my own favourite, Fuller's London Pride). Many other brands are here also, so do be ambitious & go international. Popular.

♀ **Na Plyazhe** [137 G5] 6 Zibitskaya St; m 29 333 22 89; ◷ noon–02.00 Sun–Thu, noon–04.00 Fri–Sat. Facing inwards towards Old Town at the bottom of Gertsena St. You'll believe you're in a tropical paradise (almost). Very loud & very popular, & Coffee Berry is right next door when you need a break.

♀ **Pinky Bandinsky** [136 B4] 13a Komsomolskaya St; m 29 630 33 95; ◷ noon–

01.00 Sun–Thu, noon–03.00 Fri–Sat. There's a lot happening on this part of Komsomolskaya, which was mostly a building site on my last visit. The fin-de-siècle architecture was in the course of renovation, with new boutique shops about to open. In the middle of it & slightly tucked away sits this decent bar with elegant décor. A number of Minsk friends come here.

✳ ♀ **Private House** [137 H6] 9 Zibitskaya St; m 29 324 10 10; w p-h.by; ⏰ 16.00–04.00 Mon–Fri, 14.00–04.00 Sat, 14.00–midnight Sun. Something a little different on Zibitskaya & I do like this one. Classy & laid-back, with a small cinema room in the rear. Also live music, dancing, hookah & digital gaming. Pleasing outdoor terrace for the summer.

✳ ♀ **Royal Oak English Pub** [128 C3] 20 Kisileva St; m 44 774 46 67; ⏰ 08.00–midnight Mon–Thu, 08.00–01.00 Fri, 10.00–01.00 Sat, 10.00–midnight Sun. Good friend Natalia brought me here for dinner after a night at the opera; it's one of her favourites. Obvious English touches are quite well done, but there's more here than just a taste of home. It's popular, the beer is well kept & the menu is decent. Live music & Fuller's London Pride? Sold.

♀ **Staramestsky Beer Bar** [137 G7] 4 Gertsena St; m 29 396 96 66; ⏰ noon–midnight Sun–Thu, noon–02.00 Fri–Sat. Just up the hill from one of my favourites (Beercap), there's a good choice of beer at this decent micro-brewery with an impressive commitment to the art of brewing. Also on Revolutsionaya & Karla Marksa.

♀ **Sweet and Sour** [136 C6] 14 Karla Marksa St; m 29 628 25 93; ⏰ 16.00–02.00 Mon–Sat. Next to the National Museum of History, this classy, understated bar is popular with local people (including a number of my friends). Grab some culture late in the afternoon then come here for pre-dinner cocktails.

♀ **The Pub** [136 B7] 6 Karla Marksa St; m 29 368 22 22; ⏰ noon–midnight daily. Down at the Sverdlova end, it is what it says it is. Not on the list of any of my Minsk friends, though more than one tell me they hear the choice of beer is good & the food decent.

♀ **TNT Rock Club & Bar** [136 B4] 9 Revolutsionaya St; ☎ 655 55 55; ⏰ noon–midnight Sun–Thu, noon–05.00 Fri & Sat. Next to the TIC in a very central location among a number of bars & restaurants, this is a really friendly place (according to correspondent Jill Flanagan), with live music, decent food & quality cocktails. The critique of other friends is that rock fans will love it, particularly the more mature ones. Very loud & in-your-face, so get yourself warmed up with German beer & sausage at Gaststätte beer restaurant just up the road (see opposite), then come here for some serious head-banging. A frighteningly good night out & much praised by Minsk friends, but keep the next day free.

♀ **Tumani** [137 H6] 9 Zibitskaya St; m 29 319 29 10; ⏰ 18.00–05.00 Sun–Thu, 18.00–06.00 Fri–Sat. Come for cocktails while on the Zibitskaya run. Good buzz here. Perhaps a precursor to something a tad mellower later in the evening at Private House next door (see left).

♀ **U Ratushi** [137 F7] 1 Gertsena St; ☎ 226 06 43; ⏰ noon–02.00 daily. Handily placed in Old Town above the Zibitskaya zone, this venue has long been popular with its loyal following. I first came around 10 years ago & I think it's now looking a little tired, not least the food, but I'm one of those loyal supporters & I'm willing it to pick up. A number of my Minsk friends still come, too.

♀ **Vinii Shkaff** [136 A4] 30 Revolutsionaya St; m 29 166 60 88; ⏰ noon–midnight Sun–Thu, noon–05.00 Fri–Sat. Close to Dôm & a little beyond the city's TIC on the other side of the road (down towards Gorodski Val), this decent wine bar (relaxed & popular with locals) has a pleasing outdoor area. It may not be Zibitskaya, but a night out on Revolutsionaya without the mania is a good alternative.

♀ **Vinum Gastrobar** [136 C6] 21 Karla Marksa St; m 29 633 32 02; ⏰ noon–23.00 Sun–Thu, noon–02.00 Fri–Sat. Just along from Grunwald, one of my favourite restaurants in town, this place is also worthy of your attention. Food, ambience & service all decent.

3

ENTERTAINMENT AND NIGHTLIFE

If you read the publicity blurb aimed at enticing would-be punters in search of hedonistic pleasure, you would be led to believe these are the only places in town for aspiring socialites, sophisticates and the well-to-do to be seen. True it is that the country's nouveaux riches biznizmyeni and their glamorous escorts are to be found at leisure here, often until dawn (it's the same the world over, after all), but some of these places are also the haunt of the seedy underside of society. In particular, prostitution is rife and ladies of the night can be seen plying their trade among the tables. But if you exercise common sense and street wisdom then the art of people-watching can be served richly here. Stay sober, keep a tight hold on your wallet, keep your wits about you and you won't go far wrong. Guys will need to pay an entrance fee ranging from BYN15 to BYN25 for standard club venues just to cross the threshold. It's less for girls (and sometimes free). A more sophisticated and chic experience in the 'classier' locations will cost more. In terms of what each place offers there is little to choose: DJs, parties, themed nights, live music, karaoke and the like are ubiquitous, and all are well versed in coming up with new and exciting ways to part you from your money. Qualitative judgement depends on which are 'in' and which are 'out' at any given point. If clubbing is your bag go to w minsknightlife.net for a broad overview of the night-time scene in Minsk, then ask around when you get here for local advice on the best place to go.

NIGHTCLUBS

☆ **Black House Club** [128 C3] 12 Kisileva St; m 29 697 66 11; w blackhouseclub.by; ⏱ 23.00–07.00 nightly. I hear this place fancies itself as a cut above. I haven't been, so can't say.

☆ **Bogema Live Club** [128 C3] 17/1 Masherova Av; ☎ 650 65 65; ⏱ 20.00–09.00 nightly. Parties, DJs & themed nights, plus karaoke to live accompaniment.

☆ **Dozari** [129 E2] 58 Nyezalyezhnastsi Av; m 29 345 22 33; ⏱ 23.00–06.00 Wed–Sun. Popular on opening a few years ago, this still appears to be the place to be seen for night-time activities, an accolade held for some while. Hugely popular.

☆ **Euphoria** [128 D3] 1a Very Khorozhi St; ☎ 162 20 10; ⏱ 19.00–06.00 nightly. Another karaoke club.

☆ **Madison Royal** [128 A3] 9 Timiryazheva St; ☎ 619 00 40; ⏱ 23.00–06.00 Thu–Sun. Following a major process of refurbishment that included adding the accolade 'Royal' to its title, this club continues to be regarded by many as the premier night spot in town. It's certainly one of the longest established, modestly asserting that it's the only luxury club in the city, though aficionados must judge for themselves. Expect the usual facilities & distractions.

☆ **Max Show** [129 E2] 73 Nyezalyezhnastsi Av; ☎ 292 00 38; w maxshow.by; ⏱ 22.30–06.00 nightly. More non-stop erotica with all the attachments.

☆ **Next** [136 C7] 13 Kirova St; ☎ 718 77 77; w nextclub.by; ⏱ 23.00–06.00 Wed–Sun. Part of the Crowne Plaza Hotel complex & regarded as glamorous, though the majority of the clientele appear to be young Belarusian women escorted by more mature foreign businessmen. Enough said, I suspect.

☆ **NLO (the UFO)** [129 E1] 37 Yakuba Kolasa St; ☎ 290 20 80; w nlo.by; ⏱ 18.00–05.00 Tue–Fri, 16.00–06.00 Sat, noon–06.00 Sun. This place reckons it has the best sound system in all of Minsk. Electronic music, live acts & original themed party nights make it popular with the young crowd.

☆ **Reaktor** [128 C2] 29 Very Khorozhi St; ☎ 333 38 88; w reaktorclub.com; ⏱ 23.00–06.00 nightly. Pulsating music aimed at the teenage market. Themed on the nuclear age, it also reckons to have its own reactor. Perhaps not. Now marketing special events, underground concerts & non-mainstream performances.

☆ **Rich Cat** [128 C2] 29 Very Khorozhi St; ☎ 333 38 88; w richcat.by; ⏱ 23.00–06.00 nightly. Live bands, DJs & themed nights.

☆ **Titan** [128 A6] 104 Dzerzhinskava Av; ☎ 709 10 10; ⏱ 23.00–06.00 daily. Reckoned to be the largest club & entertainment complex in the city, but it's a long way out, beyond IBB hotel.

☆ **Tyekhas** [128 B3] (attached to Hotel Yubileiny) 19 Pobediteley Av; ☎ 226 99 04; ⏱ 20.00–05.00 nightly. A small & uninspiring venue offering adult entertainment.

☆ **Versus** [136 B6] 11 Nyezalyezhnastsi Av; ☎ 200 25 20; ⏱ noon–05.00 nightly. Erotic shows & all the trappings at Hotel Minsk (page 140).

CASINOS

☆ **Byelaya Vyezha Casino** [128 C3] 17 Masherova Av; ☎284 69 22; ⏰ 24hrs daily. Once the most popular nightclub in the city, with a state-of-the-art dance floor equipped with 9m-high video plasma screens. Only the restaurant & casino on the ground floor remain, though it still attracts a large crowd of serious punters.

☆ **Casino Royal** [136 B6] 11 Nyezalyezhnastsi Av; ☎111 55 55; w royal.by; ⏰ 24hrs daily. The casino at Hotel Minsk (page 140).

☆ **Diamond Princess Casino** [136 C7] 13 Kirova St; ☎218 34 45; w worldofprincess.com; ⏰ 24hrs daily. Like Next nightclub, this gambling emporium is part of the Crowne Plaza Hotel complex (page 139). Princess Group International has a number of casinos in the city, so you have more than one chance to enrich the company's shareholders.

☆ **Shangri La Casino** [128 C5] 8/3 Kirova St; ☎321 20 22; w shangrila.by; ⏰ 24hrs daily. Just up the road from Crowne Plaza Hotel.

☆ **Victoria** [128 A2] 59 Pobediteley Av; ☎305 58 58; w casino-victoria.by; ⏰ 24hrs daily. This casino at the rapidly expanding Victoria Hotel complex opposite Pobyedy Park is said to have the largest number of gambling tables in the city.

☆ **XO Casino** [129 E2] 56 Nyezalyezhnastsi Av; ☎777 77 51; w casinoxo.by; ⏰ 24hrs daily. Another addition to the city's nightlife, with every encouragement to part with your cash. Floor shows & live music are the backdrop.

SHOPPING

DEPARTMENT STORES AND SHOPPING CENTRES There is a whole world of discovery by way of retail therapy just waiting for you. Should anything catch your eye in a shop window as you promenade along the boulevards, just step off the pavement and take a look. Shop browsing is a real art in this city and the best thing of all is that you won't be hassled by manic assistants eager to secure their commission on a sale. It's a stress-free experience and a great way to observe another interesting slice of Belarusian life.

Western designer goods are becoming increasingly available from new boutiques that are springing up all over the city, but why shop for things that you can get back home? The main drag for shopaholics is **Nyezalyezhnastsi Avenue** and, in particular, the section northeast of the Hotel Minsk. The two large state department stores can be found here: **GUM** ✳ [136 C5] (*21 Nyezalyezhnastsi Av;* ☎ *226 10 48;* ⏰ *09.00–21.00 Mon–Sat, 10.00–20.00 Sun;* 🚇 *Kastrichnitskaya*); and **TSUM** [129 E3] (*54 Nyezalyezhnastsi Av;* ☎ *389 00 15;* ⏰ *09.00–21.00 Mon–Sat, 10.00–21.00 Sun;* 🚇 *Ploshched Yakuba Kolasa*). Shop here for all things Belarusian, including ethnic souvenirs and books. Just browsing is an experience in itself. GUM in particular is a must for those on the trail of Soviet-style memorabilia, especially cheap lapel badges which all seem to show Lenin's profile against a variety of backdrops. Part of the massively expansionist building programme at the end of the Great Patriotic War, the architecture and décor are classically Stalinist, even down to the trademark red stars in the glass of the windows and the grand statuettes in heroic poses on the staircases inside. With hammer-and-sickle motifs all around you, it's like a 1950s time warp. Many other specialist stores can be found on this avenue. Window-shopping is also a fine complement to the art of promenading, particularly when accompanied by an occasional diversion to a pavement café. **Nemiga department store** [136 B2] (*Na Nemiga; 8 Nemiga;* ☎ *227 62 93;* ⏰ *09.00–21.00 Mon–Sat, 10.00–20.00 Sun*), with its ancillary outlets and food supermarket, is located at the junction of Lenina and Nemiga streets, close to the Nemiga metro entrance. It's all rather tired and drab, but still worth a browse. Further along the street is the inevitable McDonald's restaurant where Natalia and I took my daughter Harriet and her friend Daniel after a night at the ballet. They were in need of a slice of balancing Western culture, you see. In front of us in the drive-through queue were two teenagers on bicycles. The throng here is always massive and the enterprising youngsters had worked out that this was the quickest way to get served.

Gleaming new malls, shopping complexes and hypermarkets (each bigger and brighter than the last) are under construction and opening in many other locations all over town. The extent of new development in this city is astonishing, with no sign that the rate of expansion is slowing. Quite the reverse. Look for the following:

Arena City [136 A2] 84 Pobediteley Av; ⊕ 10.00–22.00 daily. Home to a Prostore (⊕ *09.00–midnight daily*) & the splendid 15,000-capacity Minsk Arena Sports Hall, one of the country's prime sporting venues.

Dana Mall (under construction) [129 G1] 11 Mstislavets St; ☎269 32 79; ⊕ 09.00–23.00 daily

Galileo [128 C6] 6 Bobriuskaya St; ☎566 11 20; ⊕ 10.00–22.00 daily

Galleria [136 A1] 9 Pobediteley Av; ☎309 81 81; ⊕ 09.00–23.00 daily

Green City [128 A4] 156 Pritytsky St; ☎317 50 76; ⊕ 09.00–23.00 daily

Korona [128 B6] 24 Kalvariyskaya St; ☎226 52 19; ⊕ 09.00–midnight daily

Stolitsa [136 A7] ⊕ 10.00–22.00 daily. This major underground shopping centre opened beneath Nyezalyezhnastsi Sq a couple of years ago.

After stumbling around the hazards of the largest building site I have ever seen for as long as I could remember, it was quite a surprise to see it open at last. As you enter the complex it looks just like any other soulless mall in the West, with piped muzak & shiny fittings. Most of the units are now filled, but it hasn't managed to attract Western designer-label outlets &, if you peek beneath the glossy veneer, the goods on offer are pretty second rate. But like Nemiga, it's worth an hour of your meandering time to experience life as the locals see & live it, especially as it's pretty quiet whatever the time of day. There's seating in the central atrium, with natural light from the cupola above to remind you of the real world outside retail land.

Zamok [128 A2] 65 Pobediteley Av; ☎309 54 50; ⊕ 10.00–02.00 daily

MARKETS The biggest market in town is **Komarovsky rinok** [128 D2] (*6 Very Koruzhey St;* ☎*292 66 08;* ⊕ *09.00–19.00 Tue–Sun;* 🚇 *Ploshchad Yakuba Kolasa*), a vast covered hall where all manner of goods are available for purchase, including an astonishing array of fresh produce. This is a fantastic place to meander and people-watch, but do keep your wits about you and be on the lookout for pickpockets. Don't allow your carelessness to spoil a truly authentic slice of archetypical Belarusian life. The market at **Dynamo Stadium** [136 D4] (*8 Kirova St;* ☎*227 26 11;* ⊕ *08.00–17.00 daily*) was still closed on my last visit, the significant refurbishment and rebuilding programme at the stadium now long beyond the originally scheduled completion date. **Smaller markets** are to be found in the suburbs all across the city.

BOOKS Probably the best bargains of all by way of souvenirs are books. Glossy pictorial guides are available very cheaply and although many of the tomes are in Russian, there is a significant (and growing) number of English works. But to my mind, Cyrillic printing is a work of art in itself. In any event the pictures and maps will bring fond remembrance of your visit. There are many bookstores all over town and every one is well stocked, but my personal favourite is **Tsentralnaya Knigariya** (**Central Bookstore**) ✳ [136 B3] (*19 Nyezalyezhnastsi Av;* ☎*327 49 18;* ⊕ *09.00–21.00 Mon–Fri, 10.00–20.00 Sat–Sun;* 🚇 *Kastrichnitskaya*). This shop has the largest stock of books in the city, with an ever-growing selection of Belarus guides and maps (some in English) as well as a fine range of postcards and Soviet-style posters and calendars. Also along this section of the avenue on the opposite side (towards the main post office) is the **Belkniga bookstore** [136 B6] (⊕ *10.00–20.00 Mon–Fri, 10.00–18.00 Sat, 11.00–17.00 Sun*), where you will find a good selection of pictorial guides. On my last visit I asked if they had an English–Belarusian dictionary. 'That's a very good question' was the reply; 'no, but we have an English–Polish one ...' Some 250m further along and directly opposite the KGB building is a smaller branch selling a wide selection of maps and atlases, while another branch is situated on Karla Marksa Street next door to My English Granny café. I also like **Dom Knigi** ✳ ('**House of Books**') [136 A1] (*11 Pobediteley Av;* ☎*203 15 03;* ⊕ *10.00–21.00 Mon–Fri, 11.00–20.00 Sat, 11.00–19.00 Sun*). The favourite of my bookworm friend Roni Karsai from Budapest, it's not as big as the Central Bookstore but the quality of its material is high and I've always found it less crowded, making browsing more relaxed. If you're searching for mementos of your visit or gifts for those back home, you can choose from fridge magnets, flags and tacky souvenirs galore in these book emporia, but for something a little out of the ordinary they also sell notebooks and other stationery with images of the country and of the Soviet Union that make really good presents and souvenirs at a fraction of the cost.

OTHER PRACTICALITIES

BANKS Banks and booths offering money-exchange facilities are in plentiful supply everywhere (but particularly in the city centre). Travellers report no exchange controls when leaving the country (and this is certainly my experience), although it is nonetheless worth holding on to your receipts just in case. Money can also be changed outside normal banking hours in the shopping centres springing up all over town. With more and more outlets opening in increasing numbers you won't encounter any difficulty with currency exchange.

Below are the main head office addresses for a selection of major banks, most of which also have branches scattered throughout the city offering the usual banking, currency and exchange services (see websites for details). Standard opening hours are 09.00–17.00 Monday–Friday, but these may vary by 30 minutes to an hour either way, with some closing early on Friday. All will have at least one ATM. Machines can also be found in ever more plentiful supply elsewhere, such as the lobbies of the larger hotels, and of course in the new shopping centres and hypermarkets.

For all information concerning banking and finance generally, go to the English pages of the website of the **National Bank of the Republic of Belarus** (*20 Nyezalyezhnastsi Av;* ☎*306 00 02;* w *nbrb.by*).

$ **Absolutbank** 95 Nyezalyezhnastsi Av; ☎237 07 02; w absolutbank.by

$ **Alfa-Bank** 70 Myasnikova St; ☎217 64 64; w alfabank.by

$ **Belagroprombank** 3 Zhukov Av; ☎218 57 16; w belapb.by

$ **Belarusbank** 18 Dzherzhinskova Av; ☎218 84 31; w belarusbank.by

$ **Belarusky Narodny Bank** 87a Nyezalyezhnastsi Av; ☎309 73 09; w bnb.by

$ **Belgazprombank** 60/2 Pritytskava St; ☎229 16 16; w belgazprombank.by

$ **Belinvestbank** 29 Masherova Av; ☎239 02 39; w belinvestbank.by

$ **Belpromstroibank ('BPS')** 6 Mulyavin Bd; ☎289 46 06; w bps-sberbank.by

$ **BelSwissBank** 23/3 Pobediteley Av; ☎306 20 40; w bsb.by

$ **BTA Bank** 20 Very Khoruzhey St; ☎334 54 34; w btabank.by

$ **Fransabank** 95a Nyezalyezhnastsi Av; ☎389 36 36; w fransabank.by

$ **Home Credit Bank** 129 Odoyevskava St; ☎229 89 89; w homecredit.by

$ **IdeaBank** 25 Karla Marksa St; ☎328 63 02; w ideabank.by

$ **Moskva-Minsk Bank** 49 Kommunisticheskaya St; ☎237 97 97; w mmbank.by

$ **MTBank** 6A Partizansky Av; ☎229 99 99; w mtbank.by

$ **Paritet Bank** 77 Nyezalyezhnastsi Av; ☎171; w paritetbank.by

$ **Priorbank** 31a Very Khoruzhey St; ☎289 90 90; w priorbank.by

3

$ RRB Bank 18 Krasnozvezdnaya St; ☎306 02 02; w rrb.by

$ Technobank 44 Kropotkina St; ☎283 28 28; w tb.by

$ VTB Bank 14 Moskovskaya St; ☎309 15 15; w vtb-bank.by

COMMUNICATIONS Free public access Wi-Fi is widely available all over the city. For information on telephone, see page 107.

Post and courier The main post office is situated at 10 Nyezalyezhnastsi Avenue [136 B6] (☎ *200 04 06; call centre* ☎ *154;* w *belpost.by;* ⊕ *08.00–20.00 Mon–Sat, 10.00–17.00 Sun*), offering all the usual services. It's a delightful building inside and out, with hammer-and-sickle motifs everywhere to be seen. Look especially for the archetypical Soviet-design clock on the front façade. One of my correspondents tells me about a delightful experience here thus: 'I wandered into the post office for some stamps and the first (elderly) lady I approached behind the counter took me under her wing, marched me to the front of the queue and then personally stuck all of our stamps on our postcards with glue and a lovely big smile!' You can post mail from hotels or any post offices and it is processed regularly.

Express delivery services are available from the following:

✉**DHL** 70 Myasnikova St; ☎200 11 55; w dhl. com. The company also has a number of other offices & outlets throughout the city, inc at the main post office.

✉**EMS** 10 Nyezalyezhnastsi Av; ☎200 03 87; w belpost.by. This is the state service located at the main post office.

✉**FedEx** (via its nominated contractor M&M Militzer & Munch) Office 902, 1 Melyezha St; ☎268 41 11; w mum.by; also at 19 Pobediteley Av; ☎226 99 09

✉**TNT** 10 Platanova St; ☎284 90 44

✉**UPS** 3 Muzikhalny St; ☎327 22 33; w ups. com

MEDICAL
Hospitals & clinics
✚ **City Accident & Emergency Hospital** 58 Kizhevatova St; ☎212 76 21; w bsmp.by

✚ **Dentko Dental Clinic** 58 Nyezalyezhnastsi Av; ☎284 45 11; w dentko.by

✚ **Minsk City Clinic Number 1** 64 Nyezalyezhnastsi Av; ☎331 92 58; w 1gkb.by

✚ **Minsk City Clinic Number 2** 25 Engelsa St; ☎327 50 29; w 2gkb.by

✚ **Minsk City Clinic Number 3** (Klumov Ophthalmology) 30 Lenina St; ☎327 61 88; w 3gkb.by

✚ **Minsk City Clinic Number 4** 110 Rosa Luxemburg St; ☎208 75 70; w 4gkb.by

✚ **Minsk City Clinic Number 5** 9 Filatova St; ☎296 49 63; w 5gkb.by

✚ **Minsk City Clinic Number 6** 5 Uralskaya St; ☎245 26 21; w 6gkb.by

✚ **Minsk City Clinic Number 8** (Gynaecology) Bldg 3, 53 Senniskaya St; ☎205 42 30; w ggb.by

✚ **Minsk City Clinic Number 9** 8 Semashka St; ☎272 70 91; w m9gkb.by

✚ **Minsk City Clinic Number 10** 73 Uborevicha St; ☎345 30 46; w 10gkb.by

✚ **Minsk City Clinic Number 11** 4 Korzhenevskova St; ☎225 88 14; w 11gkb.by

✚ **Minsk City Clinic Number 12** (Dental) 28 Kedyshka St; ☎268 84 71; w 12stom.by

Pharmacies
All are open 24hrs daily, unless otherwise stated.

✚ **Belfarm Centre** 12 Chkalova St; ☎224 04 82; also at 43/1 Yakuba Kolasa St; ☎222 84 82

✚ **Belfarm Pharmacy** 44 Nyezalyezhnastsi Av; ☎284 93 81; ⊕ 08.00–22.00 Mon– Fri, 09.00–20.00 Sat & Sun; also at 78 Nyezalyezhnastsi Av ; ☎280 60 21; ⊕ 09.00– 21.00 daily

✚ **Belfarmatseya Pharmacy Number 7** 62 Partizansky Av; ☎295 01 03

✚ **Belfarmatseya Pharmacy Number 13** 16 Nyezalyezhnastsi Av; ☎227 08 54

✚ **Belfarmatseya Pharmacy Number 32**
87 Nyezalyezhnastsi Av; ☎292 05 31
✚ **Belfarmatseya Pharmacy Number 36**
11 Shevchenka Bd; ☎288 97 43; ⊕ 24hrs Mon–Sat
✚ **Belfarmatseya Pharmacy Number 58**
25 Korzanevskava St; ☎398 27 21
✚ **Belfarmatseya Pharmacy Number 78**
78 Gazety Zvezda Av; ☎277 28 48
✚ **Belmedinfarm Pharmacy Number 12**
153a Maxima Bogdanovicha St; ☎288 47 34
✚ **Doctor Do Pharmacy Number 6** 30 Nemiga
St; ☎211 06 75; also at 118 Maxima Bogdanovicha
St; ☎237 53 68
✚ **Doctor Do Pharmacy Number 13** 20 Karla
Marksa St; ☎220 28 44
✚ **EuroPharmacy Number 5** 1 Pobediteley Av;
☎306 26 98; ⊕ 08.00–22.00 daily
✚ **Panagiya Pharmacy** 8 Nemiga St; ☎327 54
00; ⊕ 09.00–21.00 Mon–Sat, 10.00–18.00 Sun

✚ **Pharmacy Number 1** 25 Maxima
Bogdanovicha St; ☎334 00 34; ⊕ 08.00–22.00
Mon–Sat, 09.00–21.00 Sun
✚ **Pharmacy Number 19** 2 Kirova St; ☎225
61 81
✚ **Pharmacy Number 28** 48 Nyezalyezhnastsi
Av; ☎284 85 68; ⊕ 08.00–22.00 daily
✚ **Pharmacy Number 1 (Healthplanet)**
18 Nyezalyezhnastsi Av; ☎226 17 81; ⊕ 08.00–
22.00 Mon–Fri, 10.00–21.00 Sat–Sun
✚ **Pharmacy Number 8 (Healthplanet)**
147 Maxima Bogdanovicha St; ☎335 24 77;
⊕ 09.00–22.00 Mon–Sat, 10.00–22.00 Sun
✚ **Pharmacy Number 14 (Healthplanet)**
2 Glebki St; ☎507 89 61; ⊕ 08.00–21.00 Mon–Fri,
10.00–19.00 Sat–Sun
✚ **Rosfarm Big Pharmacy** 58 Nyezalyezhnastsi
Av; ☎331 06 87; ⊕ 08.00–22.00 Mon–Fri,
09.00–21.00 Sat–Sun; also at 3 Kirova St;
☎328 47 05

WHAT TO SEE AND DO

MUSEUMS
Azgur Memorial Museum ✴ [128 D5] (*Мемарыяльны музей-майстэрня З.І.
Азгура/Мемориальный музей-мастерская З.И. Азгура; 8 Azgura St; ☎308 06 32;
⊕ 10.00–17.00 Tue–Sat; 🚊 Ploshchad Pobyedy; admission BYN3*) My Hungarian
friend Roni Karsai describes this museum as 'simply magnificent'. It is certainly
unique. Ten minutes' walk from Pobyedy Square, it is housed in the studio of
the renowned Belarusian sculptor Zair Azgur (1908–95), a member of the USSR
Academy of Arts who completed a portfolio of sculptures of heroes, statesmen,
soldiers, generals, partisans and civilians during the Great Patriotic War. A
lifetime's work is displayed in the huge workshop here, where Roni experienced
an uncanny sense of being watched. She describes the workshop as 'a huge portion
of history crammed into a single space', with hundreds of familiar and unfamiliar
faces, including politicians, waiting to greet you.

Belarusian State Museum of the History of the Great Patriotic War ✴
[128 A3] (*Беларускі дзяржаўны музей гісторыі Вялікай Айчыннай вайны/
Белорусский государственный музей истории Великой Отечественной
войны; 8 Pobediteley Av; ☎203 07 92; e museumww2@tut.by; w warmuseum.by;
⊕ 10.00–18.00 Tue–Sun (last entry 17.00); 🚊 Nemiga; admission BYN8/3.50 adults/
students & schoolchildren, additional BYN2 to take photographs, entry free every
3rd Tue of the month*) The massive logistical task of moving the vast collection of
exhibits forming the basis of this magnificent museum from its former location in
Oktyabrskaya Square to its new home here in Pobyedy Park was completed on the
occasion of a hugely symbolic opening ceremony in the presence of none other
than heads of state Lukashenko and Putin on 2 July 2014, the eve of Independence
Day and the 70th anniversary of the country's liberation from Nazi occupation.
Quite rightly, the President and the country as a whole regard the events of the
Great Patriotic War with enormous significance, to the extent that they dominate

the national psyche even today. The gleaming new museum is even more impressive than the old one, which was itself a truly sombre record chronicling the terrible events of World War II from the perspective of the USSR (and for many years, the only one of its kind in the whole of the Soviet Union). Around 8,000 artefacts out of a collection in excess of 145,000 are displayed in 28 exhibits over ten rooms, each of which is crammed with memorabilia. Documentary films are on a constant loop and from time to time war veterans are present to recount their experiences. Audio guides and comprehensive information boards (including interactive digital displays) in Belarusian, Russian and English recount the story of the Soviet Union's war.

Navigation is easy, as visitors are guided from room to room via a curving walkway that follows the natural contours of the land until it reaches the astonishing Hall of Victory in the style of the glass dome atop the Reichstag building in Berlin (designed by renowned British architect Norman Foster). Students of history will recall the enduring image of Red Army soldiers raising the hammer-and-sickle flag above the ruins of the old Reichstag building in the final days of the war. The website is particularly informative, both on the museum and on the broader context of the conflict, though the text is sadly only in Russian. Everything is fully accessible, with a café and a number of souvenir kiosks (where you can buy an excellent guidebook for BYN2.50). When I came here in autumn 2017, Natasha and I virtually had the whole place to ourselves. A visit here is highly recommended and could rightly claim top spot on your list of Minsk must-see experiences. Expect to be deeply moved by all that you find.

Government Historical Museum of Belarusian Literature [136 C1]

(Дзяржаўны музей гісторыі беларускай літаратуры/Государственный музей истории белорусской литературы; 13 Maxima Bogdanovicha St; ☎ 334 56 21; e bellitmuseum@tut.by; ⊕ 09.00–18.30 Mon–Fri; ☒ Nemiga; admission BYN3) Located on the edge of Old Town, this is one of the most significant literary museums in the country, with a unique collection of manuscripts, first editions, rare books, photographs, artwork and personal mementos of many of the most renowned Belarusian literary giants. In all, it contains over 50,000 items, some of them dating from the 11th century. There are also paintings, sculptures and exhibits of regional everyday life through the ages. And if you're in literary mode, it's worth knowing that it's a stone's throw from the Maxim Bogdanovich Literary Museum.

History of Belarusian Cinema Museum [136 A6] (*Музей гісторыі беларускага кіно/Музей истории белорусского кино; 4 Sverdlova St;* ☎ *327 10 75;* e *cinema@ museum.by;* w *cinema.histmuseum.by;* ⊕ *11.00–18.30 Tue–Sun;* 🚇 *Ploshchad Lenina; admission BYN2*) Not easy to find, this small but quaint museum is located in a small yard between the Hotel Minsk and the Red Church (page 180). Ask for directions at the reception desk in the lobby of the hotel. The subject matter will of course primarily appeal to those with an existing interest in cinematography, but first-timers will also appreciate a glance at a specific aspect of the country's social history. There are displays of photographs, posters and sketches representing the history and art of Belarusian cinema through the ages, as well as artefacts and exhibits featuring articles of cinematic equipment. Given that the location is central to many of the things you are likely to be visiting, don't overlook this one.

House Museum of the First Congress of the Russian Social Democratic Labour Party [137 G1] (*Дом-музей I съезда РСДРП/Дом-музей I съезда РСДРП; 31 Nyezalyezhnastsi Av;* ☎ *290 68 47;* e *domusmuseum@gmail.com;* w *domusmuseum.histmuseum.by;* ⊕ *11.00–19.00 daily;* 🚇 *Ploshchad Pobyedy; admission BYN3*) An interesting museum, often overlooked, covering the history of Minsk at the start of the 20th century and the role played by the First Congress of Social Democrats (held in 1898). The museum is set in the house in which the first congress was held and notable visitors over the years have included Fidel Castro, Ho Chi Minh, Leonid Brezhnev and Mikhail Gorbachev. Its symbolic importance to the history of the state endures.

Maxim Bogdanovich Literary Museum [136 C1] (*Літаратурны музей Максіма Багдановіча/Литературный музей Максима Богдановича; 7A Maxima Bogdanovicha St;* ☎ *334 42 69;* e *bogdanovich@tut.by;* ⊕ *10.00–18.00 Mon–Fri;* 🚇 *Nemiga; admission BYN1.50*) Housed in a beautifully restored 19th-century building with ironwork and balconies, close to the Svislach River in Old Town, this collection is dedicated to the famous Belarusian poet and includes original manuscripts, books of collected verses printed during the poet's lifetime, photographs and personal belongings. There is also a recreation of some of the rooms of the house where he was born. Romance, drama and tragedy abound here. Both general and themed tours are available with the services of a guide, but not yet in English. Literary recitals and musical evenings are also held here. The web pages in English are most informative and really interesting.

Museum of Ancient Belarusian Culture [129 F2] (*Музей старажытнабеларускай культуры/Музей древнебелорусской культуры; 1 Surganova St;* ☎ *284 18 82;* ⊕ *09.00–16.00 Mon–Fri;* 🚇 *Akademya Nayuk; admission free*) As might be expected from the title, the exhibits here are primarily archaeological, including the remains of a Palaeolithic boat excavated from the mud of the Sozh River in the southeast of the country (there is a very similar exhibit in the museum in Vetka; see page 315). There are also collections of traditional folk art, household items, clothes and religious artefacts (including icons) from areas affected by the Chernobyl disaster. Everything is presented in a very traditional, not to say old-fashioned manner, so this is probably one for the specialist. Hands-on and interactive it isn't.

Museum of Contemporary Belarusian Statehood ✳ [137 E5] (*Музей сучаснай беларускай дзяржаўнасці/Музей современной белорусской* *государственности; entrance 4, 38 Karla Marksa St;* ☎ *327 46 11;* e *msbg@tut. by;* w *msbd.histmuseum.by;* ◷ *10.00–17.00 Mon–Thu, 10.00–16.00 Fri–Sat, last ticket 1hr before closing;* 🚇 *Kupalovskaya; admission BYN4/3/2/free adults/students/ schoolchildren/under-7s & those with a disability, free entry for all 1st Mon of the month, BYN6.50 for a guided tour*) I'm not sure I've ever been anywhere quite like this before. This little-known museum, located in the presidential office building, opened in August 2012. Established on the instructions of the President himself, the museum seeks to showcase the country's national identity, with the principal goal of creating an attractive image. It covers the period from the establishment of the republic in 1991 to the present day. Over 22 hours of film are shown on a loop, and there are many photographs of the President in a range of different situations. To gain access, head for the door to the library at the rear of the Presidential Palace next to the President Hotel. Entry procedures are strict. It is now possible to turn up without prior notice (this wasn't always the case), but visitors must show a passport, ID card, driving licence or any other document displaying full name and photograph, details of which are copied down into a ledger. There is airport-style electronic security and all bags are thoroughly searched. Books are even opened for reading. Thereafter a lift speeds you up several floors to emerge into a lobby, followed by room after room dedicated to the glory of the state, including its foundation, industry, natural resources, sports, art, culture, gifts to the President from heads of state, international relations, currency, stamps, medical advancements and even space exploration. Other than Natasha and myself, it was completely empty of visitors when last I came. Do come to see for yourself. The staff are unfailingly helpful and knowledgeable.

Museum of the History of the National Academy of Sciences of Belarus [129 F2] (*Музей гісторыі Нацыянальнай акадэміі навук Беларусі/ Музей истории Национальной академии наук Беларуси; 66 Nyezalyezhnastsi Av;* ☎ *284 14 52;* e *nasb@presidium.bas-net.by;* ◷ *09.00–17.00 Mon–Thu, 09.00–16.00 Fri;* 🚇 *Akademya Nayuk; free of charge for groups by appointment*) This specialist museum, situated within the grand and imposing National Science Academy of Belarus, is dedicated to the academy's history and achievements throughout all aspects of Belarusian history, life and culture. The collection is certainly impressive and science academics will find much of interest here. I'm not a scientist, but even I was thoroughly engaged.

Museum of the Ministry of Internal Affairs of the Republic of Belarus [136 B5] (*Музей Міністэрства ўнутраных спраў Рэспублікі Беларусь/Музей Министерства внутренних дел Республики Беларусь; 7 Gorodski Val St;* ☎ *227 82 66 or 327 09 70 to arrange a guided tour;* ◷ *10.00–19.00 daily;* 🚇 *Ploshchad Lenina; admission free*) Located behind the ministry's own hotel (page 143), the display of police and militia vehicles through the ages outside the museum's building heralds a journey into the history of law enforcement. Waxwork figures modelling uniforms from the past pose with weaponry and other paraphernalia. The second floor has displays devoted to the victims of the Great Patriotic War and to the heroes of the Chernobyl catastrophe. Well worth a visit.

Museum of Minsk History [136 B3] (*Музей гісторыі горада Мінска/Музей истории города Минска; 10 Revolutsionaya St;* ☎ *321 24 30;* e *muzejminska@gmail. com;* w *minskmuseum.by;* ◷ *11.00–19.00 Wed–Sun;* 🚇 *Nemiga; admission BYN1.50*) Relatively new and located in a lovely late 19th-century building in a central location. The architecture itself is as much a part of what's on show as the exhibits themselves,

a good proportion of which are artefacts from archaeological digs in the vicinity of Old Town, where the original castle (now long gone) was built. Four of the ten rooms are used for temporary exhibitions, concerts and performances.

Museum of Modern Fine Art [128 D3] (*Нацыянальны цэнтр сучасных мастацтваў Рэспублікі Беларусь/Национальный центр современных искусств Республики Беларусь; 47 Nyezalyezhnastsi Av;* \284 86 21; e *artmodernmuseum@ gmail.com;* ⊕ *11.00–19.00 Tue–Sat, last entry 18.30;* ⍟ *Ploshchad Yakuba Kolasa; admission BYN5*) Located on the edge of Yakuba Kolasa Square, this is another splendid museum and gallery that is worthy of your attention. It's a vibrant celebration of the creative arts, with 4,500 exhibits comprising paintings, graphics, sculptures, decorative art and posters. Do check before you come for details of the latest exhibitions and events. There's a lot happening here.

National Art Museum of the Republic of Belarus ✳ [136 D6] (*Нацыянальны мастацкі музей Рэспублікі Беларусь/Национальный художественный музей Республики Беларусь; 20 Lenina St;* \327 71 63; e *nmmrb@bk.ru;* w *artmuseum. by;* ⊕ *11.00–19.00 Mon & Wed–Sun, last entry 18.30;* ⍟ *Kupalovskaya; admission BYN5, plus additional charge for specific exhibitions*) Plundered by the Nazis during the Great Patriotic War, this is still the country's largest museum of Belarusian and foreign art, with over 25,000 works on display in 13 halls. It's a magnificent collection, but don't expect to find any of Chagall's works here. The fate of the vast majority of its original contents remains a mystery to this day but little by little, its collections were painstakingly reassembled during the post-war years and now include Belarusian art, icons, manuscripts and books from the 12th to the 20th centuries, western European art from the 16th to the 20th centuries and oriental crafts from the 15th to the 20th centuries. The website's English pages are extremely informative.

National Historical Museum of the Republic of Belarus [136 C6] (*Нацыянальны гістарычны музей Рэспублікі Беларусь/Национальный исторический музей Республики Беларусь; 12 Karla Marksa St;* \327 43 22; e *pryroda@histmuseum.by;* w *pryroda.histmuseum.by;* ⊕ *11.00–18.30 daily;* ⍟ *Kupalovskaya, Ploshchad Lenina; admission BYN5, plus additional charge for specific exhibitions, free to all last Wed of month*) Some regard this as the foremost historical and wildlife museum in the whole country, but as with the Museum of Ancient Belarusian Culture (page 165), everything is displayed in a rather dreary and unimaginative way. Still, if you're a traditionalist when it comes to museums, you won't be disappointed. The bare facts show that there are an incredible 338,000 exhibits grouped into 45 collections that include archaeology, religious relics, weapons, fine arts, icons, photographs, manuscripts, historic printing and much, much more. On the ground floor is the **Museum of Nature and Environment of the Republic of Belarus**, telling the story of the country's wildlife, where tens of thousands of exhibits are stored, including a rib and shoulder blade of a mammoth, a horn of an auroch, and a giant mushroom. There was once also a quaint display of potatoes (I kid you not), but correspondent Zo Hoida tells me this is no more. Pity. Two smaller museum collections are displayed at 177 Kazintsa Street and 9a Bogdanovicha Street.

State History Museum of Theatre and Music Culture of the Republic of Belarus [137 H6] (*Дзяржаўны музей гісторыі тэатральнай і музычнай культуры/Государственный музей истории театра и музыки Республики*

Беларусь; 5 Muzykalny Pereulok; ✆*220 26 67;* e *mhtmc@tut.by;* w *theatre-museum. by;* ☉ *10.00–17.30 daily;* 🚇 *Nemiga; admission BYN2*) Also located in a lovely 19th-century building, the so-called 'House of Masons' (where the masonic lodge 'Northern Torch' held its meetings), this showcases 14,000 exhibits, including collections of costumes, music scores, gramophone records and posters, together with musical instruments, playbills, programmes, personal documents, sculptures, drawings and paintings. Events to commemorate significant anniversaries relating to notable personalities of theatre and music are also held here. Also worth a visit is the other branch of this museum, the **Drawing Room of Vladislav Galubok** [136 C1] (*14 Starovilyenskaya St;* ☉ *10.00–17.30 daily; admission BYN2*), two rooms telling the story of the life and acting career of this founder of the Belarusian national theatre, stage director and the first 'People's Artist of the BSSR'.

Strana Mini Museum ✳ [137 E3] (*Музей мініяцюр Беларусі «Краіна міні»/ Музей миниатюр Беларуси «Страна мини»; 25 Nyezalyezhnastsi Av;* m *29 15 15 670;* e *info@belarusmini.by;* w *belarusmini.by;* ☉ *11.00–20.00 daily;* 🚇 *Kastrichnitskaya; admission BYN14/10 adults/students, schoolchildren & seniors, BYN8 for a guided tour for up to 7 persons, 8 or more free*) Only open since December 2016 and situated downstairs in the Trade Union Palace of Culture building on Oktyabrskaya Square (enter by the main doors, turn left and follow the signs down), this charming private attraction is absolutely delightful. Still a work in progress, it currently displays 18 fully interactive models of famous Belarusian sites and landmarks. When finished there will be 70 exhibits. Each is beautifully crafted and a wealth of key information is presented in user-friendly digital format (including in English) on what to see, where to stay, where to eat, how to get there under your own steam and how to book an excursion. There is a well-stocked souvenir shop, small café, meeting/workshop rooms and event space to encourage learning about the country and to enable youngsters to develop and showcase their creative talents. Audio guides are available in English and there is even a hugely informative app for your smartphone so you can do your homework in advance! Museum founder Eugene Danilik and his knowledgeable and helpful staff are on hand to enhance your visit. Locals love it and it's very popular with tourists. Considerably more than just a display of models, the museum provides a wealth of fascinating information about the country and is highly recommended as a starting point when you first get here.

Yakub Kolas Literary Museum [129 E2] (*Дзяржаўны літаратурна-мемарыяльны музей Якуба Коласа/Государственный литературно-мемориальный музей Якуба Коласа; 5 Akademicheskaya St;* ✆ *284 17 02;* e *muzeykolas@yandex.ru;* w *yakubkolas.by;* ☉ *10.00–17.00 Mon–Sat;* 🚇 *Akademya Nayuk; admission BYN2, free to all last Sat of month*) Situated a short distance from Nyezalyezhnastsi Avenue in the grounds of the National Academy of Sciences, this attractive pale-blue stucco building was the national poet's home from 1944 until his death in 1956. It's a charming museum that recreates his life in the form of the restored drawing room, dining room, office and bedroom as they were between 1947 and 1952, when the house was a focal meeting point for many of the intellectuals and artists of the time. Other rooms contain collections of additional exhibits, mementos and artefacts.

Yanka Kupala Literary Memorial Museum [137 E2] (*Дзяржаўны літаратурны музей Янкі Купалы/Государственный литературный музей*

Янки Купалы; 4A Yanka Kupala St; ☎ *327 78 66;* e *kupalamuseum@mail.ru;* w *kupala-museum.by;* ⏰ *09.45–17.30 Mon–Sat;* 🚇 *Kastrichnitskaya, Ploshchad Pobyedy; admission BYN6, free to all last Mon of month*) Situated in a beautiful location in Yanka Kupala Park, close to the Svislach River where once stood his home, this is another specialist but charming literary museum, this time telling the story of the life and work of the famous Belarusian poet, playwright, translator and author through the medium of recreated rooms, exhibits, works and personal artefacts. Readings of the great man's works are regularly given here.

PARKS, OPEN SPACES AND RECREATIONAL AREAS

Gorky Park [137 G/H3/4] (*Цэнтральны дзіцячы парк ім. Максіма Горкага/ Центральный детский парк им. Максима Горького; 22 Nyezalyezhnastsi Av*) Or to be more precise and to give its full name, 'Central Children's Gorky Park'. Here for over 200 years and originally the oldest of the governor's gardens in the city, this lovely park is situated on the banks of the Svislach River. The main entrance is through a large and imposing gate off Victory Square, next to Café Skif. There are many attractions for children, together with an observatory and planetarium, a covered skating rink and a stage for summer concerts. Horseriding and boating are available and the big wheel has fine panoramic views of Minsk from its 56m high point. Installed in 2003, it has enclosed cabins, unlike its rather ramshackle predecessor. For those with a head for heights, it also has open seating, with nothing between your legs except a lot of fresh air. A ride in a closed cabin costs BYN1.50, while adventure seekers pay BYN1 to sit out in the open. One circuit takes 9 minutes. I haven't ridden it though it looks reasonably high-tech and secure, unlike the one in Gorky Park in Moscow that I did ride in 1990 in the last days of the USSR, but that's another story for another day.

The abundance of manmade entertainment features are clearly designed with children in mind (particularly those at the top of the park by the Ferris wheel, where you will find rides, candy floss, ice cream and cheap toy stalls), but don't think that there's nothing for adults here, as its generally attractive and relaxed ambience has more to do with the natural environment. There are groves of lime and maple trees that have stood for a hundred years or more, along with rare cedars and pines. While you're here, look out for the statue of Maxim Gorky in comfortable repose on a bench near to the central gate (erected in 1981). With three cafés within its boundaries (including Family Club (page 152), one of my personal favourites in town), this is the ideal location for promenading and people-watching, whatever the season.

Alexandrovsky Public Garden [137 E4] (*Аляксандраўскі сквер/ Александровский сквер; Nyezalyezhnastsi Av*) Originally laid out in 1872, this attractive green space closer to the city centre along Nyezalyezhnastsi Avenue (on the south side of Oktyabrskaya Square) is more an open public area and less of a formal park and garden these days (locals may even look at you blankly if you ask for directions!), but I always find it pleasing to walk here. It contains the city's oldest public fountain, A Boy and a Swan, together with a number of significant sculptures, both Classical and modern. Immediately following its opening, it became a favourite place of rest and relaxation for intellectuals and writers, which is why a theatre was built in its southwestern corner in 1890. It was never popular with locals, not least because plays in Belarusian, Polish and Hebrew were banned there until 1905. Today, it is the National Academic Theatre, bearing the name of the famous poet Yanka Kupala. Stand on the pavement with your back to the front entrance facing the crossroads before you, a crossing point of symbolic significance.

Diagonally opposite is an excellent bookshop with the children's puppet theatre above, the line between these points representing the arts, culture and literature. On the other diagonal stands the presidential building (and Communist Party headquarters in the days of the Soviet Union) at one end to your left, with the British Embassy at the other to your right, the line between connecting two vast imperialist powers of old. Before you move on, look for an enduring symbol of the Great Patriotic War: mounted on a plinth is one of the first T-34 tanks to enter the city when it was liberated by the Red Army in 1944.

Yanka Kupala Park ✳ [137 F1–2] (Парк імя Янкі Купалы/Парк имени Янки Купалы; Nyezalyezhnastsi Av)

Yanka Kupala, a politically active poet and writer, is a favourite son of the Belarusian nation. He and his contemporary Yakub Kolas are widely regarded as the most significant figures of modern Belarusian literature and language. Designed in 1962 (20 years after his death) and situated just across the avenue from Gorky Park, it is home to the Yanka Kupala monument and museum (page 168), along with many other sculptures. Its broad central walkway slopes gently down to the Svislach River, which forms a boundary on two sides and is 120m wide on one of them, with fine views towards the lovely buildings on Kommunisticheskaya Street where Lee Harvey Oswald rented an apartment in 1960. Over 4,000 trees and many more shrubs were planted when this park was laid out, making it an oasis of green in the heart of the city (especially as there are few cafés within its boundaries other than summer ones by the river) and a splendid place for an afternoon's stroll. Less manufactured and smaller than Gorky Park, it actually feels bigger, with more room to breathe and to appreciate the greenery. With considerably fewer people around, it's possible to amble for ages and not feel that you're in a major capital city at all. The Yanka Kupala museum within the park stands at the location of the wooden house where once he lived. The house itself (containing much of his work) was flattened by bombing in the Great Patriotic War.

Central Botanical Gardens [129 F2] (Цэнтральны батанічны сад НАН Беларусі/Центральный ботанический сад НАН Беларуси; 2 Surganova St; e office@cbg.org.by; w cbg.org.by; ⊕ 23 April–31 Oct 10.00–20.00 daily; admission BYN6)

Founded in 1932 and now under the stewardship of the National Academy of Sciences, the gardens display many varieties of plant life, all in a setting that is most pleasing on the eye. The rose garden, alpine garden and landscape park are particularly attractive, and in spring the rhododendrons are a delight. It is a very popular place of relaxation for the city's residents and, because it's a little way out of the city centre, you should find that there are fewer tourists than elsewhere. The English pages of the website are a treasure trove of interesting and practical information. Opening times are rather ad hoc, dependent largely on the weather, so do ring in advance to avoid the risk of a wasted journey.

Chelyuskintsev Culture and Leisure Park [129 G2] (парк Чалюскінцаў/Парк Челюскинцев)

Opened in May 1932 and adjacent to the Central Botanical Gardens, this boasts a children's amusement park and a delightful miniature railway. There's a large slice of Minsk life to be experienced here, with lots of places to sit and watch the world go by, along with summer cafés where the shashlik comes highly recommended. There is also a large area of urban forest, which gives a clue to the former ecology of the land on which the city now stands. As with the Botanical Gardens next door, the location a little way out of the city centre and closer to the suburbs means that it's frequented by many more locals than tourists, a huge point in its favour in my view. Nearly all of my Minsk friends with families agree. For my good friend Artur, there's no question about it: he always brings his family here for leisure time, even though Gorky Park is just minutes away from their apartment on foot.

Pobyedy (Victory) Park ✳ [128 A2–3] (Парк Перамогі/Парк Победы)

Founded in 1945, this enormous wooded area contains the huge Komsomolskoye Lake and is a very popular location for promenaders. It's certainly one of my favourite haunts for an early morning stroll on a Sunday. Significantly redeveloped in recent times and now benefiting from major enhancement, it is also now the home of the Belarusian State Museum of the History of the Great Patriotic War, the iconic hammer-and-sickle flag of the USSR flying proudly from its cupola in glorious homage to the perceived golden days of yore and the heroism of the ultimate victory over the Nazis. The imposing Minsk Hero City monument on Pobediteley Avenue marks the main entrance to the park and the war museum is immediately behind it. Walk through the main gate and uphill along the avenue to Victory Fountain at the top, where a delightful panorama across the lake and beyond awaits. This is a lovely spot. You are likely to share it with elderly folk holding hands, children rollerblading with their mothers and couples promenading. If you live in one of the many high-rise developments that surround the park, it's a wonderful garden to have right outside your building, all at your boundless disposal and free of charge. Head on down to the side of the lake and track left towards Bird Island with its boardwalks and nature trails through the woods. From the edge of the island there are fine views across to the suburbs beyond the lake, with the BelExpo exhibition centre and the President's huge and ornate office and residence in the foreground. Retrace your steps off the island across the wooden bridge festooned with the padlocks of lovers and head lakeside to your right, where you will find seating galore and a summer café to enhance your appreciation of the view. At this point you will be alongside the massive redevelopment at Hotel Victoria. At the weekend, there are families at leisure as far as the eye can see here, and the sweetest public lavatories you will ever encounter can be found in the park, directly in front of the main BelExpo hall, complete with a lobby, ornaments, artificial flowers galore and two elderly attendants waiting to charge you the princely sum of BYN3 to avail yourself of the services there. As you walk on past the new presidential complex it just seems to get bigger and bigger until it fills your field of vision. Look out particularly for the design of the glass panels matching the edging on the country's national flag. You can then complete your circumnavigation of the lake and park through picnic areas with sunshades and outdoor showers, beaches with delightful children's play areas complete with a mini-lighthouse and jetties and a fitness trail, before you reach the grand entrance gate where your exploration began.

At this juncture in your ambling I have one more thing for you to do. Walk out of the park at the main gate on the corner of Masherova Avenue, cross over the road and head uphill along Drozd Street for 200m, turn round, and take in the vista laid before you. To my mind, it says *everything* there is to say about this city, this country and the national psyche. The glory of the Victory monument, with the gleaming Great Patriotic War Museum behind it, the hammer-and-sickle flag of the old USSR fluttering in the breeze; eight-lane boulevards carrying very little traffic, with hardly anyone walking the scene; block after block of Soviet-style concrete in a 360-degree panorama; wide open spaces and grand utopian town planning on a massive scale; trees and concrete under huge open skies, where the eye is always drawn up and away to the horizon. It's quite a view and a rare treat for the senses.

SQUARES, MONUMENTS AND SIGNIFICANT ARCHITECTURAL FEATURES – A CITY
WALKING TOUR The following entries from Privakhsalnaya Square to Victory Square predominantly follow a straight line, bisecting the city in a northeasterly direction along Nyezalyezhnastsi Avenue. Here lies the heart of the city and a day's amble to take in the sights as listed comes highly recommended. *En route*, you will pass a host of bars and eateries to keep you fortified, as well as any number of diverse shops for a little retail therapy and souvenir hunting along the way.

Privakhsalnaya Square [128 B6] (Прывакзальная плошча/Привокзальная площадь) Originally home to the city's first railway station (constructed of intricate red brick in the 1870s), this square now holds the impressive replacement, built here in the 1990s. All around the sense of space, air and grandeur is impressive and it's a very busy spot, full of hustle and bustle, noise and motion. Archetypical Stalinist granite buildings on a grandiose scale can also be found here, including the two lofty towers known colloquially as the 'City Gates'. Consisting of 11 storeys on three tiers in the style of a wedding cake and positioned at the corners of two five-storey blocks of flats, they form an impressive entrance to this open and sweeping public space, which itself forms an integral part of the post-war spatial planning of the city. Begun in 1948, the towers were finished in 1956 under the watchful gaze of chief architect Rubyanenko from Leningrad (now St Petersburg). At the time of construction, these two dwelling units were something of an exception in social-planning terms for they were entirely self-contained, incorporating their own shops, restaurants, pharmacies, school and medical facilities. When originally built, the two towers were topped with spires, while sculptures stood on the corners of the first tier. Façades were decorated with ornate stucco. Sadly, all of the apocrypha concerning Soviet concrete are true and these adornments are long gone, their crumbling demise a portent of the collapse of the system that created them. All that remains is the country's biggest clock (diameter in excess of 3.5m and over a hundred years old), along with the country's former coat of arms. The new railway station faces you on the other side as you enter the square through the City Gates. The concept of imaginary twin gates replicates in fond homage the design of the original station, which itself featured double-tier pavilions either side of its entrance. But the new structure extends horizontally rather than vertically, with the onlooker's gaze drawn between the imaginary gates to the soft and rounded lines of the central access, which is topped by a simple but impressive pyramidal roof skylight. The whole effect is set off beautifully by the reflection of the entire square in the mirror-like walls of the spacious foyer, giving the visitor the perception of a grand city entrance through triumphal portals. Walk out of the square through the City Gates, turn half left at the first junction along Sverdlova Street, and into Nyezalyezhnastsi Square.

Nyezalyezhnastsi (Independence, formerly Lenin) Square ✴ [128 B5]
(Плошча Незалежнасці/Площадь Независимости) If the sense of space and air in Privakhsalnaya Square is impressive, here it is breathtaking. A number of pre-war Stalinist buildings survive and of course there is also yet another imposing statue of Lenin, master of all he surveys. The best panoramic view of the square can be seen through the arch in Leningradskaya Street, when the buildings on the north side, dominated by the **House of Government** (with Lenin in the foreground) and the red Catholic **Church of St Simeon and St Helena** (page 180), stand open to the eye in all their glory. Government House is a monument to simplistic symmetry, with several buildings of different heights overlooking the central ten-storey structure, the whole being recessed from the square at a distance of 50m,

just to add to its imposing and monumental appearance. Built between 1930 and 1934 as a manifestation of civic power and influence, in architectural terms this building was originally intended to be the blueprint for the whole of the city. The eastern side of the square where Nyezalyezhnastsi Avenue begins is flanked by the Neoclassical lines of the magnificent **Hotel Minsk**, built in 1957, and the impressive **Central Post Office**, built in 1953. The southern side consists of the **Belarusian State University** (1962), the **Minsk City Executive Council buildings** (1964) and the **Metro Administration building** (1984). This magnificent square has survived military occupation by a cruel oppressor, has been the sight of countless processions to celebrate revolution and freedom, hosted demonstrations in the era of perestroika as the Soviet Union breathed its last and then, finally, was the location from which the birth of the newly independent republic was proclaimed on 19 September 1991. For many years latterly, the whole experience of standing in this symbolic and visually arresting place was ruined by the presence of a huge and cavernous building site right in the very middle of the square, as an underground shopping complex slowly took shape. Happily, all of the remedial work in the square has at last been completed. Do try to spend a little while in this impressive location and focus your attentions on the splendour of all that can be seen around you.

Nyezalyezhnastsi Avenue ✳ The city's main thoroughfare, which runs away from Independence Square down through Victory Square, is the axis around which the great works of reconstruction were designed after the war. In 1944, a documentary film was shot to give a bird's-eye panorama of the centre of Minsk. To view it now (especially with the benefit of a visit to the city as it currently stands) is a sobering and sombre experience. Of the 825 major buildings that stood at the outbreak of hostilities, only 60 of stone and 20 of wood survived. One cannot but marvel at the resilience, commitment and civic pride of a country and people who set about the task of regeneration with such gusto. This imposing avenue, built anew with geometric precision on the site of the former Sovyetskaya Street, is said by many to resemble the famous Nevsky Prospekt in St Petersburg, not only for its architectural prominence but also for its human side, represented by a café-style culture. Promenaders stroll hand in hand in an ambience of relaxed sophistication. Join them! Amble at leisure and let the charm of the environment seduce you. Release your senses and most of all, let your surroundings draw you in.

The spell is not even broken when you reach an enormous building of pale yellow stucco and Neoclassical design, with a grandiose entrance flanked by enormous pillars on the left-hand (northwestern) side of the street, the **home of the KGB** [136 B6]. Pause here to gaze up. Ordinarily you would expect buildings of this size and significance to present a symmetrical frontage around the entrance. But in this case, the right-hand corner boasts a round observation tower that is not replicated on the left. Legend has it that a former Head of the Soviet KGB who was a football fanatic (it may even have been Nikita Khrushchev himself, though many locals don't think so) had this observatory constructed specifically so he could gaze over proceedings at the national football stadium down the hill at the bottom of Komsomolskaya Street, an attractive thoroughfare leading to the present building site that has the remains of the **Dynamo Stadium** [136 D7] at its centre. Currently in the process of being massively overhauled, it was originally constructed in 1931 on the site of an old Jewish cemetery. The graves were bulldozed and the stones used for hardcore in road construction. Along the centre of Komsomolskaya Street are pleasant gardens, with the bust of much-feared Felix Dzerzhinsky in the foreground. Born in territory that is now part of Belarus, and of Polish extraction, he was one of Lenin's closest acolytes and founder of the hated Cheka, the forerunner organisation to the KGB.

Moving on down Nyezalyezhnastsi, first towards Oktyabrskaya and then Victory Square, look for the **National Bank** [136 D5] building on the right of the street directly opposite a Minsk institution, the **GUM state department store** [136 C5]. Built on the corner of Lenina Street in 1951, 'this shoppers' paradise' (as the official description has it) boasts exquisite external décor that is best appreciated from the National Bank side of the street. It is said that on conclusion of the first day's business (which exceeded all expectations), two lines of policemen formed a safe passage across the lines of traffic from the store to the bank so that staff could take the day's takings there for deposit. The junction of Nyezalyezhnastsi and Lenina is a major crossing point in the city. There's so much going on here! It's a good point to take in the sumptuous view. Be sure to take time to look all around you and especially to look up, then when you're ready, cross through the underpass and on down Nyezalyezhnastsi.

Oktyabrskaya (formerly Central) Square (Belarusian name Kastrichnitskaya) [136 D4] This square probably suffered more architectural damage during the war than any other part of the city. There is yet more Stalinist architecture here, including the imposing **Trade Unions Palace of Culture** [137 E3] (built in 1954). One example that has not survived is the statue of Stalin himself, which only stood for five years or so. Rough justice you might think, because the siting of the statue necessitated the demolition of the former Roman Catholic Church of St Thomas Aquinas here. It is said that the statue's sculptor (Zair Azgur himself, no less) was so distressed when it was blown up that he kept and coveted for the rest of his life the only chunk that remained intact; a button from the dictator's tunic. The square was made complete by the construction in 2001 of the dominating **Palace of the Republic** [136 D3], which put the finishing touches to the original post-war plan to connect the historical heart of the city with its new administrative centre, high on a plateau above the Svislach River. In recent years this square has been the site of a number of significant political demonstrations and sit-ins, including in 2010 when there were scenes of violence and bloodshed as the authorities broke up the camp established by demonstrators there. On the south side of the square is **Alexandrovsky Public Garden** (page 169), behind which is the imposing edifice of the pre-war Communist Party of Belarus Central Committee building, which today is the location of the Office of the President. Be very careful when taking photographs here. If spotted by the militia, you will have some explaining to do. Continuing along Nyezalyezhnastsi, you pass **Yanka Kupala Park** (page 170) to the left and **Gorky Park** (page 169) to the right, both bounded by the Svislach River. Just after the river on the left is one of the most picturesque thoroughfares in the entire city, Kommunisticheskaya Street, with grandly opulent buildings on one side and the landscaped riverbank opposite Yanka Kupala Park on the other. Building number 4 is where Lee Harvey Oswald lived.

Pobyedy (Victory) Square ✴ [137 H1] (Плошча Перамогі/Площадь Победы) Situated further downtown on Nyezalyezhnastsi Avenue and downhill from Oktyabrskaya Square in the valley of the Svislach River (where this main route out of town in the direction of Minsk National Airport meets a number of attractive thoroughfares) stands Victory Square. It used to be round but is now elliptical, such that it alarmingly resembles the chariot scene from the movie *Ben-Hur* in rush-hour traffic. I've driven it several times and it's not for the faint-hearted. That said, being a front-seat passenger in a car driven by a local is considerably worse, but that's another story. The whole is dominated by the imposing **monument** to

commemorate the nation's losses in the Great Patriotic War. Many Minsk residents still refer to the square as the 'Circus', as it was formerly called before the great obelisk was erected in 1954. At 40m tall, it is topped with the 'Order of Victory', the trademark Soviet red star. On 3 July 1961, an eternal flame was lit at its base. Wedding bouquets are commonly to be seen here, for it is an accepted feature of wedding ritual in this country that the bride and groom (with their full entourage) will pay homage to those who have fallen in war at memorials such as this. It's a necessary and essential photo opportunity for them as part of the day's proceedings and indeed, you can expect to see a wedding party at any number of locations in the city, arriving at speed in a motorcade, windows down and horns blaring.

At the design stage for this imposing and solemn monument many of the best-known Belarusian sculptors of the time were commissioned to contribute to the scenes shown in bas-relief on the four facets at the foot of the column. They are named *9 May 1945 Victory Day*, *Soviet Army During the Years of the Great Patriotic War*, *Belarusian Partisans* and *Glory to the Fallen Heroes*. If you look carefully here, you will find a neat microcosm of Soviet revisionism. Stalin was already dead by the time these reliefs were sculpted and his profile, not surprisingly, was added to the fresco, originally appearing on the flag next to Lenin's portrait. But as the years passed and Stalin's legacy hastened his fall from grace, his profile was quietly and without ceremony transformed into Lenin's ear. The dominance of the column has its best perspective from a distance, but a closer view lends greater appreciation to the scenes depicted at the base.

At the same time, take a look around you. The classically constructed houses on the south side, each with beautiful entrances and neat towers, are connected by handsome rows of columns. There is also an underground hall containing a commemorative memorial that is well worth a visit. And if you have the energy for further exploration, you might carry on up Nyezalyezhnastsi to **Yakub Kolas Square** [128 D3] for one last slice of architectural splendour. One of a number of attractive sculptures in the central area of gardens is that of the national poet and writer himself, deep in thought and contemplation. Retrace your steps back to Privakhsalnaya Square on foot if you want to view all that you've seen again but from the other direction, or else jump on the metro and head for some sustenance at your favourite café or bar. You've earned it!

OTHER NOTABLE MONUMENTS AND ARCHITECTURAL FEATURES

Island of Tears ✴ [136 B4] (Востраў слёз/Остров слез) Situated on the Svislach River directly opposite Old Town and inaugurated on 3 August 1996, this is a commemorative memorial to the fallen in the USSR's ill-fated and disastrous Afghanistan campaign (1979–88). The central feature is a chapel upon the walls of which bleak and harrowing images of bereaved widows and mothers are sculpted, all waiting in vain for their loved ones to return. Inside are four altars bearing icons, together with small shrines dedicated to the fallen from each of the country's administrative oblasts, their names listed on the walls. In the centre, memory bells have been lowered into a sunken recess containing soil from a number of graves, along with a sealed capsule containing soil from the fields of battle in Afghanistan where some of the nation's sons fell. This is a highly symbolic and ritualistic gesture, often to be found at memorial locations in this country. Nearby is the statue of a doleful angel in mourning, weeping because he could not save the boys' lives.

The Afghanistan fiasco matches the American misadventure in Vietnam for mind-numbing folly. For years after the war ended, veterans received no recognition either from an ungrateful state or from the party machine. The authorities simply looked away to pretend the madness had never even happened. Access to the chapel is via a short footbridge from the Troitskoye suburb, or Old Town (page 178), but beware the street vendor waiting to accost you at the bottom of the footbridge with tacky souvenirs, including out-of-date calendars. He has an interesting collection of badges from the old Soviet Union though, most of them featuring Lenin's gaunt face atop a party slogan exhorting the workers to ever greater achievements. The short written guide to the Island of Tears memorial is also worth buying for the photographs alone as a reminder of your visit.

Jewish Minsk Perhaps the most widely known of the historic sites of Jewish Minsk is the **Zaslavskaya Memorial** ✴ [128 B4]. This moving, bleak and harrowing sculpture of a line of terrified men, women and children seen descending a steep slope marks the very spot where on a single day in March 1942, 5,000 Jews from the Minsk ghetto were shot to death by the Nazis. This number included 200 children from the ghetto's orphanage. Around 500 of the bodies were dumped in the pit that was dug here. The bronze obelisk at the bottom is inscribed in Russian and Yiddish. This is the boundary of **Rakovskaya suburb**, the location of one of Europe's largest ghettos between 1941 and 1943. It is thought that only 13 individuals survived to the Soviet liberation out of the community of over 100,000 who endured the Nazi occupation in the most barbaric and inhumane of circumstances within the confines of the ghetto.

Nearby, on the site of the old Jewish quarter, is the **Holocaust Museum and Research Studio** [128 A5] (*Музей Халакоста і гістарычная майстэрня/Музей Холокоста и историческая мастерская; 25 Sukhaya St;* ✆ *380 37 17;* e *kozak@ibb. by;* w *gwminsk.com;* ⊕ *09.00–16.30 Mon–Fri*). Located in a Jewish house over 100 years old, directly opposite the site of a former Jewish cemetery, it has no external sign to acknowledge its significance. The museum entrance houses a memorial to the 33,000 Jews transported to the Minsk ghetto from all over occupied Europe. In the first pogrom, 10,000 Minsk Jews were murdered to make room for 10,000 more arriving by train from other locations. Each room houses a number of exhibits, the most moving of which are the display boards telling the story of individual families. Images of lives brutally snatched away can be seen all over the rooms here. At long last, the stories of the Jewish victims of Nazi oppression in this country are beginning to be translated into English (see box, opposite), although sadly there are no English display boards at the museum. The exhibits include a German military map of Minsk marking the area of the ghetto, as well as photographs of the Maly Trostenyets concentration camp, now itself a memorial site (see below). Across the road from the museum, the site of the old Jewish cemetery bears a number of memorials (including a symbolic broken table) with inscriptions in Russian, German and Yiddish. The only other evidence that this was once a cemetery is the broken gravestones scattered all around.

Minsk also has a **Museum of Jewish History and Culture** [128 C2] (*Музей гісторыі і культуры габрэяу у Беларусі/Музей истории и культуры евреев в Беларуси; 28 Very Khoruzhey St;* ✆ *286 79 61;* e *jewish_museum@mail.ru;* ⊕ *09.00–18.00 Sun–Fri; free of charge, but admission by prior appointment is required*). Situated on the Minsk Jewish Campus, more than 10,000 artefacts have been collected for display (including documents and photographs) to promote the history and culture of the Jewish community. Educational and research facilities are available here, and a number of specific exhibitions are also featured.

Opened in 2015 by the President himself, the **Maly Trostenyets memorial site** [129 H5] (Мемарыяльны сайт Малага Трасцянца/Мемориальный сайт Малого Тростенеца) is situated southeast of the city centre, just beyond the bottom end of Partizansky Avenue (between the ring road and the intersection of the M4 and M1 motorways). The centrepiece is the deeply affecting 10m-high sculpture in bronze, 'The Gates of Memory'. Granite memorials either side of a paved access 'Road of Memory' provide statistical information about atrocities committed at sites of

FRIEDA'S STORY

It's a cold Thursday morning in Minsk. I'm standing in the snow with five Jewish families from London, in an open area between apartment blocks close to the city centre. This is the site of the Minsk ghetto, first established in 1941 during the Great Patriotic War. We're on the edge of an enormous hole in the ground with steps descending to the bottom, along the line of which stands a doleful memorial to the dead of the ghetto. This is the pit into which the Nazis threw the bodies. We're here to listen to Frieda Wulfovna, a ghetto survivor. For years she couldn't talk about the things she had seen as a young girl. She didn't think people would believe her. Then one day, while visiting the Jewish Centre in Minsk that had been established to record all that happened here between 1941 and 1944, she opened a book written by a fellow survivor and began to read about all the terrible things she had witnessed for herself as a child. Screams, executions, rivers of blood. From that moment she finally realised that people would believe her own story and she began to find the words to articulate her memories. This is an extract from that story, in her own words and transcribed as translated, recalled and told on the site of the former ghetto as the snow came down, on the edge of the pit of death. The full transcript of Frieda's story appears on my website (w *nigelroberts23.wordpress.com*).

I remember a terrible pogrom that lasted four days. People were desperate to find hiding places between buildings and behind false walls, ceilings and floors. I can recall hiding in one such place, between buildings, for all of those four days. Sixty of us were crammed into a tiny, confined space. I could barely move. A little girl of four years was there. Like all of us, she hadn't eaten for four days and she began to cry. To save the rest of us, that child's mother placed her hands over her mouth and suffocated the life out of her.

Before the ghetto, there used to be a Jewish market within the area. The Nazis used it as a place of execution. I remember being there one day when the Nazis took only young girls. I can recall a group of 20 to 25 of them, some barely 18, all with their eyes covered. The Germans chose this occasion to test out new experimental bullets that exploded on impact. It was raining that day. The streets ran red.

The Nazis didn't just murder people. They were cruel and perverted. They would take people as they walked through the streets near to their homes, so their families watching from their houses would see. People were shot indiscriminately. Lorry loads of drunken soldiers used to arrive by night and open the gates, randomly butchering entire households. There were three mobile gas chambers within the ghetto. The local Nazi commander asked for more, so that more people could be killed faster. Himmler came to Minsk one day in 1942 to formulate a plan for getting rid of Jews more quickly. The screams I heard every single day in the ghetto I still hear now, as I walk the streets where once it stood.

Frieda Wulfovna has travelled all over Germany with other survivors to recount the events that happened in the ghetto. Their story is beginning to be told at last.

3

mass murder elsewhere in Belarus by the Nazis. Further work is planned here as indicated on the information display board (with text in Belarusian, Russian and English), but this site is already a place of poignant pilgrimage for many visitors.

Now 75 years on, the brutality of the Nazi occupation has left wounds that are open and raw. No community was left unscathed and to this day, deeps scars remain etched on the national psyche of the country. Recognising this is the key to understanding so much about this part of Europe. To help with your learning do try to visit the memorial sites at Zaslavskaya and Maly Trostenyets as well as the Khatyn National Memorial Complex (page 186) and preferably in that order. These are sobering experiences with resonance even today. We ignore the lessons of history at our peril.

For further information on anything concerning Jewish Minsk, to arrange access to memorial sites and to meet members of the current community, including Frieda Wulfovna, or to arrange museum visits or tours of Jewish Minsk with Russian- or English-speaking guides, contact British sustainable development charity **The Together Plan** (page 116) or Belarusian NGO **Dialog** (page 38).

Upper Town ✳

Located in and around the delightful **Svobody Square** [136 C3] (Плошча Свабоды/Площадь Свободы), many of the lovely buildings here are reconstructions, including the impressive **City Hall** [136 C3] (completed as an exact copy in 2006), but it's a splendid spot for an amble nonetheless. A symbol of municipal government has existed on this spot since the 16th century and today's monument to civil governance, modelled on the last incarnation of City Hall before total destruction in the 19th century, is but the latest in a long line of them. Outside in the square, the sculpture of the governor's carriage presents a photo opportunity that many are unable to resist. It's another example of the delightful work of Vladimir Zhbanov, whose street statuary appears all over town and elsewhere in Belarus. The **Holy Spirit Cathedral** (page 181) and the **Maryinsky Cathedral of the Holy Virgin Mary** (page 181) are on the fringes of the square, while elsewhere you will find Hotel Europe (page 139) and a number of high-quality restaurants and bars. The view down to the Troitskoye suburb over Komsomolskoye Lake and beyond presents an irresistible vista by day and by night. Even though most of what you see in and around the square is a reconstruction, there is an easy charm here that is pleasing to the eye. If you continue down towards the river (behind and to the right of Holy Spirit Cathedral) you come to Mink's very own 'party district' in and around **Zibitskaya Street** (page 154), with its proliferation of bars and restaurants.

Troitskoye (Trinity) suburb ✳

(Траецкае/Троицкое) Famous for its bars and taverns since the 13th century, this attractive historic area down by the Svislach River (and on the opposite bank to Upper Town) is known as 'Old Town'. It's mostly a reconstruction, although there are those in this city who will tell you indignantly that what you see is wholly original. The truth is likely to lie somewhere between the two, so let's say that the original buildings here have been substantially and sympathetically renovated. Certainly, the works undertaken to the brightly coloured two- and three-storey buildings during the 1980s and subsequently have been tastefully accomplished, enabling the visitor to experience the city as it existed a century or so ago. Then, the dwellings were of stone and the streets were cobbled. This was a non-aristocratic part of the city, housing factory workers, peasants, craftsmen, traders, low-rank civil servants, military personnel and the petty bourgeoisie. Today, their successors are the owners of the offices, shops, cafés, bars and restaurants that occupy the buildings here (along with the flat in a charming 19th-century fin-de-siècle building that is my accommodation of choice when I'm in town).

To wander the cobbled streets at will is a pleasing diversion from the noise of the city. To orientate yourself first walk down to the water's edge of the Svislach beside Starovilyenskaya Street to take in the view of the Island of Tears (page 175) and the water beyond, then amble along Starovilyenskaya with the river on your left and Trinity suburb on your right. You can dip in at will to find cobbles, corners and steps. It's not a large area and you won't get lost. In the centre you will find the **Maxim Bogdanovich Literary Museum** (page 165), whose work is not popular among Belarusians, Natalia tells me, 'but I think his words are so beautiful'. Behind Karchma Staravilyenskaya restaurant is the **'Folk Gallery' store** [136 C1]. Focused exclusively on the tourist trade, it sells 'traditional' souvenirs and trinkets, all of them priced as you might expect. Right next door is the **'Vyanok' store** [136 C1] with an interesting and unusual selection of very reasonably priced antique books. Also look out for the **Barzha floating restaurant** (page 151) moored on the riverbank in this locality. Overlooked by many as a probable tourist trap, it's never busy and whenever I've stopped off for lunch the food and service have always been consistently good. Even the staff seem surprised that someone actually wants to eat there. Then while you are in the vicinity, walk back over the river and across to the entrance to Nemiga metro station at the junction of Maxima Bogdanovicha Street and Pobediteley Avenue (on the Palace of Sports side of the road). In May 1999 on the day of a local festival a terrible tragedy occurred when hordes of excitable youngsters ran into the pedestrian underpass here to shelter from torrential rain: 53 of them were trampled to death. A plaque commemorates this awful event. All these years later, you will still find personal mementos and reminders left by family and friends. In a country where loss and tragedy are commemorated everywhere, this is a particularly poignant spot and many who pass by are given to pausing for quiet reflection. You will too.

Kastrichnitskaya (Oktyabrskaya) Street ✳

Walk south along Lenina Street to the junction with Ulyanskova Street, turn right towards the Dynamo Stadium then take the first left to cross the river; Oktyabrskaya Street. It has been known by this name since 1961, though increasingly it is referred to as Kastrichnitskaya, its Belarusian name. Once a red-brick industrial heartland (some of the factory buildings hereabouts are more than 100 years old), most of the machinery may have fallen silent but this is now one of the trendiest spots in town. 'You have to see Minsk's hipster street!' said Natasha, and she was right. It's well worth an amble. Vibrant urban art on the grandest of scales is everywhere to be seen, and thanks largely to the annual street festival Vulica Brasil (w *vulica-brasil.by*), this area is now one of the city's top must-visit sights for locals and tourists alike.

The former metalworking plant (once one of the largest in production throughout the country), the tanneries and the tram depot may no longer function as originally intended, but now they hum to the music of cafés, bars and creative spaces. Visit Dyepo for pancakes, Enzo for burgers, Lafka for 24-hour coffee and Hooligan to party, then look to find the Old Fellah himself (Lenin), no longer the master of all he surveys, now just a feature of the tableau on display.

The National Library ✳

[129 H1] (*Нацыянальная бібліятэка Беларусі/ Национальная Библиотека Беларуси; 116 Nyezalyeznnastsi Av;* 266 37 02; e *inbox@nlb.by;* w *nlb.by;* 10.00–21.00 Mon–Fri, 10.00–18.00 Sat–Sun, with shorter opening during the summer schedule; tours by prior arrangement; Moskovskaya)

Opened by the President himself on 16 June 2006, this most unusual building makes for a really eye-catching sight in all of its futuristic splendour. The correct term for its geometric shape is (apparently) a rhombicuboctahedron. Whatever the technicalities, it's quite a sight. Located on Nyezalyezhnastsi Avenue and a little out of town on the main thoroughfare into the city from Minsk National Airport, it dominates the skyline for miles around, particularly when it is illuminated in a dazzling display of colour at night, although the construction of new developments in the vicinity is beginning to encroach upon it. For the geometrically uninitiated, the architects based the whole concept on the shape of a diamond; the problem is that at first glance it appears to be perched precariously at ground level on little more than one of its points and there is an apocryphal rumour locally that it is dangerously unstable in its design. Some 14 million books have now been moved here. The English pages of the library's website are extremely informative, so undertake some research on this quirky feature in advance then stop off on your travels (it's a 5-minute walk from the Moskovskaya metro station) for some great photo opportunities (while it's still standing). There is an indoor observation platform on the 22nd floor (⊕ *noon–23.00 daily, last entry 22.30*) and it's also possible to venture outside although, at 73m above the ground, you will need a head for heights. It's well worth it, because the views over Minsk by night and by day are unsurpassed.

All in all, this institution provides an impressive array of public services. Facilities include 20 reading rooms, a theatre, a 22nd-floor coffee bar, ground-floor restaurant, museum, art gallery, children's room, exhibition space, internet centre with free access at 20 terminals and even a fitness centre with sauna. Anyone presenting a passport (including nationals of other countries) is given a reader's ticket for five years (*BYN3.50*). It's an impressive commitment to public education and enlightenment. Also here is an interesting **book museum** (✎ *293 25 85;* ⊕ *10.30–19.00 Tue, Wed & Fri, 10.00–18.00 Thu & Sat–Sun, subject to changes & 1 Jul–31 Aug; admission BYN1.50*). Exhibits cover the history of book printing in Belarus, modern publishing internationally and the history of the library itself. There are 400 rare books and manuscripts from the 15th to the 20th centuries on display, the most precious of which is the Bible published by the first Belarusian printer, Francisk Skaryna, in 1517.

CATHEDRALS AND CHURCHES
Church of St Simeon and St Helena [136 A6] (*Касцёл святых Сымона і Алены/Костёл Святого Симеона и Святой Елены; 17 Sovyetskaya St*) Erected and consecrated between 1908 and 1910, this imposing structure, with its 50m-high bell tower, is known locally to residents simply as the 'Red Church'. See if you can guess why! One of the city's iconic landmarks and an ever-present feature of its publicity blurb, it is situated on the north side of the vast Independence Square. Lenin stands on his plinth just along the way. After the October Revolution it was used first as a theatre and then as a film studio. It even survived the massive development of the square in the 1960s, when the city's planners wanted it to be pulled down and replaced by a widescreen cinema. I'm glad it saw this plan off. The impressive buildings all around are fine examples of post-war Soviet planning on the grandest of scales, but there's something special about the endurance of this single building. There are daily services at 09.00 and 19.00, plus 10.00 and noon on Saturdays and 11.00 and 13.00 on Sundays. Outside and within its curtilage, look first for the symbol of Good triumphing over Evil, the sculpture of the Archangel Michael, wings outstretched, 4.5m tall, slaying the dragon; then find the poignant Nagasaki memorial bell erected in September 2000, a powerful symbol uniting two communities ravaged by the elemental power of nuclear energy gone wrong.

Holy Spirit Cathedral ✻ [136 C2] (*Кафедральны сабор Сашэсця Святога Духа/Кафедральный собор Сошествия Святого Духа; 3 Kirilla i Mefodya St;* w *minskcath.anitex.by*) Another of the city's iconic landmarks, this splendid Eastern Orthodox Baroque cathedral on the edge of Svobody Square was originally constructed between 1642 and 1687 as a Roman Catholic monastery of the Bernardine Order, and part of the monastery complex remains. Ravaged by warfare and long in disuse through damage and disrepair, it was eventually passed to the Russian Orthodoxy and consecrated to Saints Cyril and Methodious in 1860. After the 1917 Revolution it first became a gymnasium for the fire service, then a repository for documentary archives and later a grain store. It is also said that it was used as a political prison. During the entirety of its chequered history it has benefited from many phases of renovation following damage and periods of closure. It is now one of the last surviving monuments of Old Minsk and an enduring image of its history. It houses a number of impressive icons, including that of Our Lady of Minsk, which is said to have miraculously appeared on the bank of the Svislach River in 1500. It is an essential 'must-see', with a good souvenir shop. Evening services are held at 18.00 every day except Monday. Outside there are fine views to Pobyedy Park over the Svislach River and Komsomolskoye Lake, but expect to share them with vast numbers of tourists and pigeons; this is probably the city's most frequented go-to place for visitors.

Mary Magdalene Church ✻ [128 B3] (*Царква Святой роўнаапостальнай Мары Магдалíны/Церковь Святой Равноапостольной Марии Магдалины; 42 Kisileva St*) This lovely church is my favourite in all the city, not least because it's just a little off the main tourist track so you're likely to have it all to yourself. Located above one of Minsk's main roads, the matte black of the cupola studded with golden stars and of the lovely bell tower contrasts beautifully with the white stucco of the façade. It was built in 1847 to replace an earlier church here, while the delightful Starovezhskaya Gate on the edge of the grounds was added later. In recent times the entirety has been beautifully maintained. Inside is a dazzling array of icons and relics, the air heavy with the scent of incense. As I sat outside taking it all in on my first visit, I watched as a young mother wheeled her pram to the main door. She asked my companion to mind her baby while she went inside to fill three plastic bottles with holy water. At the same time, a family was standing outside with their tiny baby wrapped tightly in blankets, waiting for the time of the child's baptism. This is a beautiful place of living worship.

Maryinsky Cathedral of the Holy Virgin Mary [128 B3] (*Марыінскі кафедральны касцёл/Мариинский кафедральный костёл; 3 Svobody Sq*) Located across the street from the City Hall and sandwiched tightly between buildings constructed later, what you see today is all that remains of the Jesuit monastery built here in the 18th century. A Baroque masterpiece, it's a wonder that anything at all remains. The two bell towers were rebuilt in recent times after the Communists blew them up in 1951, the building having suffered extensive damage during the Great Patriotic War. The interior is exquisite. Hemmed in by adjoining development, it's easy to walk past and leave this delightful cathedral unnoticed, but do find the time to pause and take a look. Just inside are display boards with interesting photographs showing the history of this holy place. Evening services are held at 19.00.

St Alexander Nevsky Church [129 E4] (*Царква Святога Благавернага Князя Аляксандра Неўскага/Церковь Святого Благоверного Князя Александра*

Невского; 11 Kozlova St) Worthy of a short detour when you tick Pobyedy Square off your list, this small but imposing red-brick construction with the archetypical domes of gold is most pleasing to the eye. It has been opened and closed time and again during warfare and in peacetime, according to whichever political circumstances have prevailed during its 120-year existence. Consecrated on 2 February 1898, it replaced the original wooden church on this spot. During the Great Patriotic War it survived (perhaps with divine intervention?) when a Nazi bomb crashed through the central dome from on high to land near to the St Nicholas icon but failed to explode. There is also a military cemetery here. Evening services are held at 18.00 and 20.00.

Cathedral of St Peter and St Paul [136 B3] *(Сабор святых апосталаў Пятра i Паўла/Собор святых апостолов Петра и Павла; 4 Rakovskaya St)* Located next to the Nemiga department store and built between 1611 and 1613 with donations from 52 nobles and inhabitants of the area, this lovely 'yellow church' (so named colloquially because of the colour of its pale stucco façade) is said to be the oldest of the city's functioning places of worship. It's had a chequered history, however; a cycle of disrepair and neglect followed by renovation under the patronage of the Russian nobility played out over three centuries before Stalin closed it down in the 1930s, since when it has served variously as a fish store, residential dwellings and a document archive, only being restored as a place of worship in the 1970s. Evening services are held at 18.00.

THEATRES
National Academic Bolshoi Opera and Ballet Theatre of the Republic of Belarus ✳ [128 C3] *(Нацыянальны акадэмічны Вялікі тэатр оперы i балета Рэспублікі Беларусь/Национальный академический Большой театр оперы и балета Республики Беларусь; 1 Paris Commune Sq;* ☎ *334 80 74;* e *ticket@ belarusopera.by;* w *bolshoibelarus.by (an excellent website in Russian & English);* 🚇 *Nemiga; buses: 24, 38, 57 & 91; trolleybuses: 12, 29, 37, 40, 46 & 53)* Built in 1938 and located at the bottom end of Yanka Kupala Park, on the edge of Old Town, the theatre building itself recently underwent three years of substantial and significant reconstruction (during the course of which unexploded munitions laid by the Nazis during the Great Patriotic War before the Red Army liberated the city were uncovered and rendered safe). During that period, performances of ballet were generally held in the Great Hall of the Palace of the Republic (*1 Oktyabrskaya Sq*). Now that the old theatre has been restored (and beautifully so), all performances start at 19.00 and generally feature popular ballet classics such as *Swan Lake, Sleeping Beauty, Giselle* and *Don Quixote.* Opera buffs will not be disappointed either, with regular performances of well-known works such as *La Traviata, Aida, Carmen, La Bohème* and *The Barber of Seville.* Throughout the year, the theatre also presents a very broad repertoire of work by lesser-known composers. Tickets can be purchased from the theatre box office at 1 Paris Commune Square (⊕ *10.00–14.00 & 15.00–20.00 daily*), or from the following locations: one of two theatrical booking offices at 19 Nyezalyezhnastsi Avenue (near to the entrance of the flower shop) and the TSUM central department store (*54 Nyezalyezhnastsi Av*), on the third floor, next to the dry cleaners; the ticket office on the second floor of the GUM department store; and the subway adjoining one of three metro stations: Ploshchad Yakuba Kolasa, Institut Kultury or Kastrichnitskaya/ Kupalovskaya. Compared to Western prices tickets are astonishingly cheap (BYN10– 20), while the standard of performance is exceptionally high. This is an experience not to be missed, but do be sure to book ahead and as early as you can.

above left   The 16th-century Mir Fortress is now one of only four UNESCO World Heritage Sites in Belarus (D/D) pages 246–7

above right   The Kholmsky Gate, pockmarked by bullet-holes and shell craters, is testament to the severity of the attack on Brest Fortress during World War II (r/S) page 211

below   Although the palace at Njasvizh dates from the 16th century, it displays features of the Renaissance, Baroque, Neo-Gothic, Rococo, Classical and Modernist periods (KV/S) pages 184–6

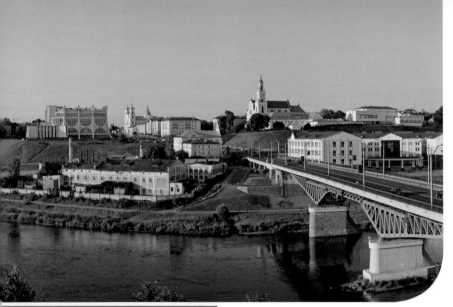

top

On the banks of the Nieman River, Grodno is renowned for its lofty feel and unique architecture, including the Drama Theatre (r/S) pages 225–43

left

The magnificent Cathedral of St Sophia is Polotsk's crowning glory (AS/S) page 273

bottom

Located at the confluence of the Pinya and Strumen rivers, Pinsk was once the ancient capital of the mysterious Polyesye lands (AR/S) pages 216–18

top   Although heavily damaged in World War II, the exquisite Rumyantsev-Paskevich Palace in Gomel has been impressively reconstructed to its former glory (LD/S) page 311

right   Mogilev's town hall is a reconstruction of the original 17th-century building that was damaged during World War II (MM/S) page 291

bottom   The Surrealist painter Marc Chagall is Vitebsk's most famous son, and is commemorated with a statue at the heart of the city (NL/A) page 264

above 18th- and 19th-century rural life is recreated at the Dudutki Folk Museum, which features workshops in traditional wooden buildings (O/D) pages 190–1

left National holidays often feature parades of children and young people, traditional costumes, singing and dancing (NV/S) pages 99–101

below left The _rushnik_, or ceremonial towel, is the foremost example of Belarusian folk art, and each village has its own specific design (KV/S) page 39

below right Home-distilled vodka can be found all over Belarus, and is often smooth-tasting but remarkably high in alcohol (AC/D) pages 94–5

above   Vetka's Folk Arts Museum showcases the historical and cultural features of the Gomel region (HS/D) pages 315–17

below left   Orthodox Easter is the biggest festival in the religious calendar; at midnight, families congregate at their local church and light beeswax candles (RB/D) pages 99–100

below right   At the Belarusian State Museum of Folk Architecture and Rural Life, *Kaladya* customs mark the passing of the old year (NY/D) page 192

bottom   Historical re-enactments often take place in the summer; here actors participate in the commemoration of the Battle of Grunwald (RB/D)

above   A UNESCO Biosphere Reserve, Berezinsky covers around 85,000ha of primeval forest, marshland and lakes (n/S) pages 279–81

left   Traditional, single-storey wooden houses are one of the iconic images of Belarus and can still be seen all over the country (N/D)

below   Known for the stunning Blue Lakes, Narach National Park is home to the country's highest concentration of eco resorts (NK/D) page 5

above left   The European brown bear is common in many of the country's parks and reserves (SU/S) page 5

above right   The largest population of European bison roam free in Byelovezhskaya Puscha National Park (ah/S) page 218

right   You're likely to spot roe deer at Braslav Lakes National Park (SE/S) page 278

below   The white stork is the Belarusian national bird (GB/S)

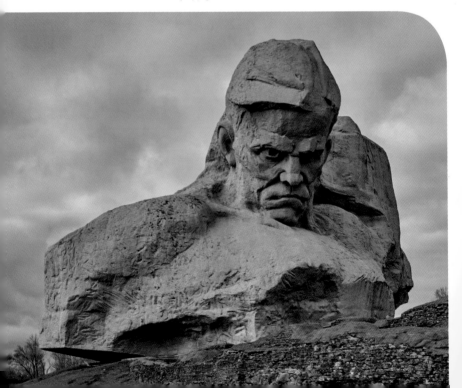

Even if a night of high culture fails to appeal, a visit to this lovely theatre and its gardens is highly recommended. Meander at leisure to inspect the charming statuary, including the monument to poet Maxim Bogdanovich, erected in 1981 to commemorate the 90th anniversary of his birth. Born just across the street from here, he was only 26 when he died. Stand by the fountains and admire the splendour of the theatre's entrance (ticket windows are to be found either side of the main doors), then walk up the steps, turn and pause to take in the view over the fountains towards the Cathedral of the Holy Spirit and former Bernardine Monastery in Upper Town. Allow your gaze to scan right of centre, past the ugly modern buildings in the foreground, to spot the pale pink stucco that marks the boundary of Troitskoye suburb. Further to your right is the impressive architecture of the Minsk Military Academy, named after Russian general Alexander Suvorov, who was prominent in the 18th-century invasion of the country. This is a fact that troubles my dear friend Natalia, who thinks the academy should be named after a Belarusian hero, not someone leading an occupying force. Quite right too.

Yanka Kupala National Academic Theatre [137 E4] (*Нацыянальны акадэмічны тэатр імя Янкі Купалы/Национальный академический театр имени Янки Купалы; 7 Engelsa St;* ✆ *327 60 81, 327 42 02;* w *kupalauski.by;* 🚇 *Kupalovskaya*) Situated on the corner of Alexandrovsky Public Garden and built in 1890, this theatre was used as a congress hall after the 1917 Revolution. It was here that, in March 1918, the All-Belarusian Congress made the declaration of independence of the first (and short-lived) republic. It was restored to use as a theatre in 1920, and today performances are held daily (except Saturday) at 19.00, in the Belarusian language only. Tickets can be purchased from the theatre box office or at the ticket booth in the subway adjoining Oktyabrskaya/Kupalovskaya metro station (🕐 *10.00–19.00 daily*).

Belarusian State Academic Music Theatre [128 A5] (*Беларускі дзяржаўны акадэмічны музычны тэатр/Белорусский государственный академический музыкальный театр; 44 Myasnikova St;* ✆ *200 81 26;* w *musicaltheatre.by;* 🚇 *Ploshchad Lenina;* 🕐 *box office 09.00–21.00 Mon–Fri, 10.00–20.00 Sat–Sun; performances at 19.00 Tue–Sun*) Established in 1970, the theatre was originally known as 'The State Musical Comedy Theatre of the Republic Of Belarus' until the year 2000. The diverse programme here is largely mainstream and features operetta, musicals, musical comedy, musical review, ballet, rock opera, music concerts, children's shows and the occasional experimental review. With a talented and energetic troupe, performances are always popular. Tickets can be bought online, at the theatre box office and at the usual city outlets.

Belarusian State Puppet Theatre [137 E5] (*Дзяржаўны тэатр лялек Рэспублікі Беларусь/Государственный театр кукол Республики Беларусь; 20 Engels St;* ✆ *327 05 32;* w *puppet-minsk.com;* 🕐 *box office 10.00–20.00 Tue–Fri, 10.00–17.00 Sat–Sun & 13.00–20.00 on the days of evening performances; tickets BYN5–10;* 🚇 *Kupalovskaya*) This delightful Belarusian institution (originally founded in Gomel 80 years ago, before moving to Minsk in 1950) performs just across the road junction from the Yanka Kupala theatre. The troupe spends much of its time on tour and only a limited number of performances are held here. If you're lucky enough to be in town when there's a show on, don't miss it. Adults will be just as entranced as children.

3

NJASVIZH ✳ (Нясвіж/Несвиж) Situated 120km southwest of Minsk and only half an hour by road from Mir and its charming castle (in Grodno region) is the delightful historic settlement of Njasvizh, one of the oldest in the country. Thought to have first been established as a settlement in the 13th century, historians believe that the town itself was founded around 1446. Though the new town is without charm, many of the oldest buildings have been retained in the historical area, and the former home of the Radzivili family is widely regarded as the most attractive palace that the country has to offer. It is surrounded by a large park boasting a number of ornamental lakes and sumptuous gardens. The family's ownership of the town began in the middle of the 16th century and was to last for more than 400 years, during which time it gained great fame for its prosperity. In 1586, the town was granted Magdeburg rights of self-government and determination, which was a catalyst for rapid economic development. Many trade guilds were established and it was no surprise that at the end of the 16th century it was almost completely rebuilt, the chaotic and haphazard layout of its medieval streets being replaced by the geometric design that remains to this day. The main street crosses the town from east to west. It was originally surrounded by earthen walls that were constructed to make the town a fortress. Some of them, most notably in the southeast, can still be seen. Over the centuries, many severe trials (such as plunder, fire and war) took their toll on the town but, through it all, the mighty Radzivili dynasty survived. The line finally ended in 1939, but not until it had first seen off not only the Great Lithuanian Principality, but also the might of the Russian Empire.

Getting there and away By car take the same M1 motorway from Minsk towards Brest as if bound for Mir, then take the left turn on the P11 road to the south signposted Njasvizh, 10km after the turn on the right for Mir, and continue for around 20km. Upon leaving Minsk, the terrain very quickly becomes much more reminiscent of western Europe, with rolling wooded hillsides of oak and beech replacing the silver birch that is omnipresent elsewhere in Belarus. Halfway to Mir on the right-hand side and adjoining the carriageway, look for the gleaming new **Westa Hotel** (✆ *165 44 86;* w *westa.by;* **$$**) with its lake, health care and sports facilities. I haven't stayed there, but it looks to be a decent bet if you're in need of out-of-town accommodation while on the road. Njasvizh is situated on a main bus route from Minsk (departing from the central bus station), the ride taking around 3 hours. As with Mir in Grodno region you should set aside a full day for Njasvizh to see all there is to see at leisure, but both can be combined in a single (though tiring) day trip from Minsk if time is at a premium.

What to see and do In addition to the palace and only a short walk away from it are the stunning Corpus Christi Roman Catholic Church (designed in early Baroque style by the 16th-century Italian architect Bernardoni, who also designed the palace), the tower of the castle gates, the remains of the town gate (this is the only one of the original four still standing) and the Benedictine monastery. A further short distance away is the town square, where the trade hall and market houses are situated, all of which date from the 16th century. Representations of and artefacts from the life of this historic town are collected in the compact but engaging museum on Leninskaya Street. The outstanding Belarusian Renaissance thinker and humanist Symon Budny is known to have worked in the former printing house where in 1562 he published a number of significant works. His nearby statue marks this key point in the history of Belarusian literature.

The first stone in the construction of the palace was laid in 1584. It was rebuilt many times and to this day displays features of the Renaissance, early and late Baroque, Rococo, Classicism, Neo-Gothic and Modernism. The complex once numbered around 170 rooms, with a series of underground passages connecting it to the town's monasteries. It was originally encircled by ramparts, ditches, four towers and a cluster of ponds and also boasted valuable collections of fine art, weaponry, books and family archives. Today, the only resident is the ghost of the Black Dame, who is said to restlessly wander the corridors on moonless nights. In fact, legend and mystery continue to dominate both this palace and the fortress at Mir. The treasures of the Radzivili family have never been found, although many locations at the two castles have been searched. The dungeons are so large that parts of them are as yet unopened. One of the most intriguing legends is that a cavernous underground passage (35km long) was constructed between the two, large enough for two coaches to pass side by side. Needless to say, it also has never been found. The beautiful park and garden around the palace (which include some delightful ornamental ponds) were not laid out until the late 19th century. The total area is around 100ha, with a number of different styles and appearances to be seen, including a Japanese garden and a Russian wood.

The road through the town from the direction of Mir follows a straight line and, as you breast a small rise, the old town is ahead and slightly below, affording a first teasing glimpse of the treasures that await. If there is space, park in the small square by the Symon Budny statue, where you will also find **Corpus Christi Church**. The exterior is attractive, but inside it's exquisite. Do go in for a look – the magnificent Baroque friezes are simply stunning.

On leaving Corpus Christi, turn right and walk through the palace car park, past the tacky souvenir stalls and along the path to reach the information and ticket building on the right, just before the start of the walkway to the **palace** itself (❧17 70 2 06 02; ⊕ 09.00–18.00 Wed–Mon; admission BYN14). The path is a tarmac one and is raised above the level of the lake, so the views all around are delightful. Just before you reach the end of the path, bear right to see the Great Patriotic War memorial and eternal flame. This is a good photo opportunity, with the palace itself in the background, while the view of the palace from the rear of the memorial is simply beautiful. Now walk through the entrance archway (pausing to admire the unusual waterspouts), show your ticket and head on into the impressive courtyard. The self-guided tour starts at door 15 in the right-hand corner. Proceed up the stairs, availing yourself of the café facilities if in need, then through the door on the right to begin.

The first room contains informative display boards in English, while all of the rooms beyond contain items of interest, the last of them being an exhibition room. Exit down the stairs then cross the courtyard to enter the door marked 'Palace Interiors'. Here you will find a sumptuous exhibition. First leave your bags in the cloakroom and take a peek in the shop, where the goods on sale are less tacky than outside the palace. Don't forget to put on your over-slippers, then amble through room after room of sublime décor containing fascinating exhibits. Audio guides are also available. There is a most glorious fireplace in the large dining room, while the small dining room beyond and the ballroom are equally lovely. The next floor has rooms displaying Slutsk woven belts, before you pass through the splendour of the Knights Golden Hall and the Hunting Hall. Not to everyone's taste, the trophies here will certainly grab your attention. Following the signs will take you back to the beginning of the tour, where you exit the turnstile at the main gate. There are yet more tacky souvenir stalls here and a number of basic but adequate cafés. If you have time, turn right to walk around the perimeter of the palace, where you gain a real perspective on its size and grandeur. Keep looking into the delightful gardens on your left as you amble and, if time permits, dip in for a promenade. The grounds and lakes are extensive and really beautiful. On my last visit in spring, the birdsong, the breeze through the trees and the carpet of new living green were irresistible. It's now a short stroll back across the walkway as you contemplate the delights of your day here.

All in all, this splendid site is one of the finest in the country and, although many of the historic buildings are still undergoing great works of restoration, it's well worth a day of your time to meander and to take in the beauty of all there is to see. For years, the historical significance of this place went unnoticed beyond the country's national borders, but it was finally recognised in 2005 with its inclusion on the UNESCO World Heritage List. If you can, try to visit during one of the medieval cultural festivals that are held here. The biggest is called 'Ancient Njasvizh', which usually takes place in July, when the streets and parks are full of scenes from centuries long gone, including jousting tournaments, battle recreations, dancing, juggling and displays of ancient crafts. It can be crowded, of course, but it's a small price to pay, while the advantage of a visit out of season is that you can have the place to yourself (my very favourite time of all). Make your own decision when to go, but make sure you go all the same.

OUT-OF-TOWN MEMORIAL SITES
National Memorial Complex at Khatyn ✳ (*Мемарыяльны комплекс Хатынь/Мемориальный комплекс Хатынь; Logoysk region;* ❨ *745 57 87 (to arrange guided tours, but in Russian only);* e *khatyn@mail.ru;* w *khatyn.by/en; site ⊕ 24hrs daily; guided tours & photography exhibition 10.00–16.30 Tue–Sun; admission free, but there is a charge of BYN8 for the museum*) If you take only one out-of-town trip while in Minsk, then do try to make it this one. Only 75km from the capital, this memorial complex bears witness to the horrors of Nazi barbarism during the Great Patriotic War. It was constructed on the site of the former village of Khatyn, which was razed to the ground in the spring of 1943 and its inhabitants brutally butchered. At the centre of the complex is a truly astonishing bronze sculpture, the 6m-high *The Unconquered Man*. Before you go, do visit the excellent English-language website for a full description of the terrible events in 1943 and for further details of the memorial complex that exists today.

The tragedy of Khatyn was not just an isolated episode in this tumultuous war, for the experience was replicated many times over on the territory of the Soviet Union. It is said that the inhabitants of 618 Belarusian villages were burned alive during the occupation in SS punishment operations against partisan groups. Of these villages, 185 were never rebuilt and have simply vanished from the face of the earth. Overall, every fourth Belarusian perished during the war: a total of 2.2 million people. This figure includes the 380,000 who were deported to Germany as slave labourers, never to return home. A staggering 209 cities and townships and 9,200 villages were destroyed. So catastrophic was the impact on the population that it did not recover to its pre-war total until 1971. Every visitor to Belarus is struck by the large number of war memorials that exist and the extent to which the conflict continues to dominate the national psyche to this day. A visit to Khatyn helps to place all of this into the right context.

So it is to the memory of all of these communities that the vast complex at Khatyn is dedicated. Covering a total area of 50ha, the memorial has 26 symbolic chimneys, each with a mournful, tolling bell, to mark the site of each of the 26 houses, the boundaries of which are delineated by low concrete walls with gates, all of them depicted as being open as a metaphor for the hospitality of Belarusian people. Also marked are the sites of the village wells. On the face of each chimney is a plaque bearing the names of each family member who lived there, from aged grandparents to babes only a few weeks old. In itself this is a truly sombre metaphor, for only the brick chimneys were left standing when the Nazis torched log houses in Belarusian villages.

As you approach the complex from the car park, the lie of the land slopes gently down to *The Unconquered Man*, who stands facing you. A broad concrete path leads right up to the base of the sculpture, with its centre line planted with flowers. It is only when you visit at flowering time that you appreciate the significance of this, for the pattern of planting was very deliberately designed to display a long, meandering line of vivid red blooms all the way to the statue: a river of blood.

On your right as you first set foot on this path are two enormous granite plates at an angle. This is the location of the barn in which the villagers were murdered and they represent its collapsed roof. Elsewhere is a mass grave containing the remains of the villagers. There is also a separate cemetery for the other villages that were burned to the ground and are now lost, the symbolic graves bearing an urn containing soil from each one. There is a 'Wall of Grief' to commemorate concentration camp victims, with niches containing memorial plaques detailing the loss of life at each camp. Then set among three silver birches symbolising life burns the eternal flame to keep alive the memory of all who lost their lives in the conflict.

By presidential decree in 2004 further enhancements to the site were undertaken to mark the 60th anniversary of the country's liberation, including the establishment of a small museum and photo montage to document both the occupation as a whole, this specific atrocity and the history of the memorial complex.

The memory of my first visit here will stay with me forever. As we walked into the complex on a chilly early spring morning, a rifle shot cracked out in the distance. It was probably hunters in the nearby woods. But the effect on us all was both immediate and startling. I have visited a number of times since and I have never failed to be deeply moved. I have taken several Belarusian friends there for their first visit; all were moved to tears. The mournful monotone of the tolling bells in the silence that pervades all around acts as a summons, inviting you to look, learn and never forget.

There are two important contextual points to bear in mind in all of this. First, following the liberation of the Soviet Union, a rampant Red Army took terrible and brutal revenge on the civilian population of Germany as the Nazi forces were driven back over the Oder River; then secondly – and with huge irony – this memorial complex at Khatyn should not be mistaken for the Katyn Forest memorial, located east of here (and 20km outside Smolensk in Russia), where in 1943, German forces uncovered the mass graves of more than 22,000 Polish officers and civilians shot by the NKVD on Stalin's orders. Only after the disintegration of the Soviet Union was vicarious responsibility for this atrocity accepted by Russia.

Getting there and away By car, take the M3 motorway north out of Minsk in the direction of Vitebsk. After 70km, take the right turn signposted Хатынь. The complex is located 5km along that road. There is no reliable access by means of public transport, although I know of one small and enterprising group of visitors who travelled there by pre-booked taxi from Minsk. The driver waited in the car park for 2 hours while the party explored the site at their leisure, before taking them back to Minsk. The total cost was US$100, which represents good value.

'Stalin Line' Historical and Cultural Site (*Гісторыка-культурны комплекс «Лінія Сталіна»/ Историко-культурный комплекс «Линия Сталина»*; \512 12 33; e *tourism@stalin-line.by*; w *stalin-line.by*; ☉ *10.00–18.00 Tue–Sun; admission BYN14; parking BYN3*) As Europe stumbled towards conflict in the 1930s and paranoia gripped the national psyche of countries across the continent, the foreign policies of most governments became increasingly obsessed with defence and self-protection. The Soviet Union was no exception. All along the western border of the USSR, from the Baltic to the Black Sea, Stalin ordered a network of defensive military fortifications to be built. In all, 23 fortified zones were constructed, four of them within the territory of Belarus. At that time the border was a mere 40km from Minsk. In concept and design, it matched the Maginot Line along France's eastern

MASSACRE AT KHATYN

Khatyn was once a small but thriving community in a picturesque wooded area, but this hamlet no longer appears on even the most detailed map today, other than as a memorial. The atrocity took place on 22 March 1943, when troops of the occupying German army completely encircled the village. Earlier that day, a skirmish had occurred in the vicinity, when partisans attacked a motor convoy on the highway just 6km away. A German officer was killed in the engagement. Whether or not anyone in the village knew anything about this is a matter of conjecture, but what then happened is beyond understanding even to this day. All of the villagers, young and old, healthy and infirm, women, children and babes in arms, were driven from their houses at gunpoint and herded into the barn. No mercy was shown. Among them were Joseph and Anna Baranovsky with their nine children. So too were Alexei and Alexandra Novitsky with their seven children, along with Kazimir and Elena Lotko with their seven children, the youngest of whom was only 12 months old. Vera Yaskevich was also driven into the barn with her seven-week-old son Tolik. Vera's other daughter, little Lena, first tried to hide in the family home, but then she decided to run for the woods. At first she was successful in evading the trailing bullets, but the soldier who ran after her and overtook her showed no mercy, callously gunning her down before the eyes of her helpless and horror-struck father. Among those who found themselves in the wrong place at the wrong time were two people from other villages who by chance were in Khatyn that day.

When everyone was inside the barn the doors were barred, the roof covered with straw and the building doused in petrol. After setting it alight, soldiers positioned themselves on all sides of the conflagration to machine-gun any of the suffocating people who managed to break out. The village was then looted and the 26 homesteads burned to the ground.

The whole scene is unimaginable. Terror-struck parents hopelessly striving to save their wailing children, throwing them through windows into the murderous gunfire, or else just sheltering them in their arms and with their bodies, helpless and powerless, themselves crying and overcome by panic. People stumbling from the building, their hair and clothes ablaze, straight into a hail of bullets. Choking smoke everywhere, the smell of burning and the deafening screams of despair.

In total, 149 people, including 75 children, were burned alive. Only one of the adults of the village survived; his tale could not be more harrowing. Only three children – Volodya Yaskevich, his sister Sonia and another boy, Sasha Zhelobkovich – had been able to hide from the murderers and would escape death. And by a miracle, two girls from two different families – Maria Fedorovich and Yulia border and it was intended to serve the same purpose, although it was nowhere near as imposing. The Nazis outflanked the Maginot Line, of course, while Stalin's equivalent was breached with little difficulty.

This network became known as the 'Stalin Line' and on 30 June 2005, a precise reconstruction of a section of the historical layout covering 40ha was ceremonially unveiled at this site, on the P28 road 6km beyond the town of Zaslavl (30km from the capital), in the presence of the President himself, resplendent in full military uniform. Incorporating authentic equipment from the time (complete with dents from shells and bullet holes), it is an open-air museum of military fortifications, including the defence line itself with trenches, anti-tank obstacles and ditches, anti-personnel obstacles and machine-gun pillboxes. Today, visitors can walk around

Klimovich – were also spared from death in the barn. Somehow, they managed to escape the fire and crawl to the nearby wood, where they were later found by the inhabitants of the neighbouring village of Khvorosteny, barely alive. But after having survived this horror, the village of Khvorosteny was itself also burned to the ground later in the war. This time, the two girls did not survive. It beggars belief that fate can be so cruel.

Two other children not only escaped from the barn, but also survived the war. They were seven-year-old Viktor Zhelobkovich and 12-year-old Anton Baranovsky. Viktor's mother Anna was holding him firmly by the hand as she staggered through the smoke and flames of the burning barn. Mortally wounded by gunfire, she covered her son's body as she fell. Viktor had been wounded in the arm. He lay on the ground under his mother's corpse until the Nazis finally left the smouldering ruins of the village. Anton Baranovsky was wounded in the leg and also lay motionless to avoid detection.

As the inhabitants of the neighbouring villages and hamlets later picked their way through the ruins, they discovered the two stricken boys, wounded and badly burned. After tending to their wounds they took them to the orphanage in the small town of Pleshinitsy, where they were raised after the war.

The only adult witness to the massacre at Khatyn was the 56-year-old village blacksmith Joseph Kaminsky. Wounded and severely burned, he did not regain consciousness until late at night when the fascists were already long gone. As he meticulously searched through the ruins of his village and the bodies that lay there he came across his injured son among the corpses. The poor boy had received bullet wounds to his abdomen and he was severely burned. Joseph tended to his wounds as best he could, but his son died in his arms as he cradled him.

And so it is that the only human sculpture of the Khatyn memorial complex, *The Unconquered Man*, tells the tragic story of Joseph and his son. It is a doleful and harrowing metaphor for the suffering not only of the villagers of Khatyn, but also of all who were bowed under the yoke of oppression and tyranny. When you see this sculpture of bronze for the first time, particularly if you have some prior understanding of what took place here, the power and impact of the image is staggering in its effect.

After the war Joseph Kaminsky lived for many years in the nearby village of Kozyry. He often returned to the ruins of Khatyn, where passers-by would see him cutting the grass and tending the site of his former home. He died in 1973 and is buried in Logoysk.

some of those pillboxes and sit in a gun emplacement, stroll along the trench system (although much of what remains is rather overgrown) and clamber over a tank. There is also an exhibition of other military hardware featuring tanks, helicopters, fixed-wing aircraft and the iconic 'Katyusha' mobile rocket launcher that so often features in black-and-white newsreel film from the Great Patriotic War. Escorted tours are available from guides dressed in uniforms of the day. It goes without saying that this is an excursion for dry weather. The excellent website now has a decent range of informative pages in English with useful photographs and maps, all of which are extremely interesting.

If travelling by car, head northwest out of Minsk city centre on the P28 road, cross the orbital ring road and stay on the P28 to find the site 6km north of the town of Zaslavl. Alternatively, a half-day local excursion can be booked through a travel agency for around US$50 per person for groups of 2–3 (excluding the entrance fee and any extras), with a proportionate per capita reduction for larger groups dependent upon numbers. A single traveller booking a one-person excursion will pay around US$100.

'Mount of Glory' (*745 57 87;* ⊕ *site access 24hrs; admission BYN1*) To honour the glorious victory of the Red Army over the fascist invaders, this monument, atop a manmade hill consisting of scorched earth and soil brought from the nine 'hero cities' of the USSR and battlegrounds of the Great Patriotic War, is visible for miles around. Created to mark the 25th anniversary of the liberation of the country from the Nazi occupation, it is located 21km out of the city centre at the side of the main highway to Moscow (where it joins the road to Minsk National Airport). It stands an imposing 70m off the ground at its zenith and is situated in the vicinity of the last battle in the war to take place on Belarusian soil. It consists of four titanium-covered bayonets pointing directly to the sky, representing the four fronts on which divisions of the Red Army, partisans and members of other underground organisations successfully completed the liberation of the country. At the base of the monument itself is a golden circle upon which images of the faces of soldiers and partisans have been sculpted, along with heroic inscriptions to the glory of the Red Army.

A row of tanks and other assorted military hardware lines the car park at the base of the mound and there is also a café selling the usual refreshments (with an outdoor barbecue area for national holidays and special commemorations). A concrete path winds around the mount to give access on foot to the obelisk itself and the entirety of the memorial stands in 26ha of parkland, in which are displayed sculptures of wood depicting folk art.

Ceremonies of symbolic significance take place here on key anniversaries and over the years there have been many notable visitors, including Fidel Castro. Legend has it that when descending from the top he disdainfully refused to take the concrete path, instead striding away and down the grassy mound itself, pursued by his entourage and the remainder of the guests (dressed in their finery and in some cases, high heels). No authoritative corroboration of this story exists, but it's a lovely tale nevertheless. And Fidel's reputation lives on. None of us would be surprised if it were true, would we?!

OPEN-AIR MUSEUMS
Dudutki Folk Museum (*Музейны комплекс Дудутки/Музейный комплекс Дудутки;* ☎ *132 11 77;* e *info@dudutki.by;* w *dudutki.by;* ⊕ *10.00–17.00 Tue–Sun; admission BYN12*) Located 35km south of Minsk (near to the village of Dudutki

on the banks of the Ptich River) stands this former country landowner's estate, where life as it was lived in the 18th and 19th centuries is affectionately recreated. Both an open-air museum and a working farm, it includes an original working windmill and other functioning workshops (located in traditional buildings of wood) displaying carpentry, pottery, braiding and other handicrafts, together with a blacksmith, a bakery and a cheese-maker. The craftsmen will be very happy to show off their skills and you will be invited to have a try! Vintage cars are also on display and visitors can take advantage of the banya, as well as taking part in horseriding, sledging and horse-drawn cart rides. Additional charges apply. There is an outdoor animal enclosure in which wild boar roam (reasonably at leisure) and there is also an ostrich pen plus runs for standard farm animals such as pigs and goats. For the children, there are horses and rabbits. The atmosphere is extremely relaxed and you can wander around at will. The riverside paths and farmland tracks make for an inviting backdrop to your lazy meanderings. Various guided tours are also available lasting approximately 3 hours, the cost being dependent upon numbers.

After your exertions, you can visit one of two excellent **restaurants** (where you can sit outdoors in good weather) for a splendid meal of locally produced and traditionally cooked fare, accompanied (of course) by vodka that is legally distilled on the premises. Bread, cheeses, butter and many meats are all sourced on site. Expect to pay around BYN20 per person for your meal. There is also a small **hotel,** but there are only four double bedrooms and inevitably tour companies make bookings well in advance. To round off your visit, spend some time in the shop, where you can buy high-quality goods manufactured on the spot at eminently reasonable prices. 'Gypsy performances' and concerts of traditional music are regularly performed, but the best time to visit is during one of the traditional festivals to celebrate, for example, the winter solstice, the arrival of spring or harvest time, when the whole place is alive with colour and activity. You could easily spend a whole day here. A good friend who runs a successful tour agency in Minsk thinks it's all very twee and tourist-focused, aimed at those looking for a rose-tinted view of rural life as once it was in this country. I tend to agree, but that's not to say that a visit is without worth. Just bear in mind that much of what you see may be as much a cliché as historical accuracy. Refer to the very informative website to view excellent photographs and videos and for a full background briefing on the history of the site, as well as comprehensive details of the modern-day activities on offer here.

Getting there and away By car, take the P23 road from Minsk, then follow the signs east for 12km. The village is on the bus route from the capital to Ptich, but the nearest stop to the museum is some 2km away. If you are visiting on a local tour through an agency, you'll find that most companies allow a half day here, but you will be pushed for time if you want to see and do everything.

Raubichy Museum of Belarusian Folk Art (Музей беларускага народнага мастацтва ў Раўбічах/Музей белорусского народного искусства в Раубичах; \507 44 68; w artmuseum.by; ⏲ 10.00–17.00 Wed–Sun) Located only 24km from Minsk, this ethnographical museum is situated in the former Krestogorskaya Church. It has numerous displays of folk art from all over the country, including costumes, fabrics, weaving, pottery, carved wood, earthenware and straw goods. Only 10km away is the idyllic **Minsk Lake**, dotted with numerous islets and surrounded by forests of dense pine. Also nearby is the **International Sports Complex**, incorporating ski jumps, shooting grounds, tennis courts, football pitches and an international biathlon course, together with two hotels and a number of

eating establishments. Again, organised excursions from Minsk are available. If travelling from Minsk by car, take the M3 motorway north out of the city from the ring road for around 12km, before turning right on to the P80 road for 3.5km. At the crossroads turn left on to the H9059 road, then slight left again on to Ivanovskaya Street. There are daily bus and marshrutka services from the city.

Belarusian State Museum of Folk Architecture and Rural Life ✳

(*Белорусский государственный музей народной архитектуры и сельской жизни/Беларускі дзяржаўны музей народнай архітэктуры і сельскага жыцця;* ☎*507 69 37;* e *museum@etna.by;* w *etna.by;* ⊕ *1 May–31 Oct 11.00–19.00 Wed–Sun; 1 Nov–30 Apr 10.00–17.00 Wed–Sun, last entry 1hr before closing; admission BYN3*) In the style of Scandinavian Skansen museums devoted to the history of architecture, where buildings that have been carefully deconstructed and then removed from their original location are then painstakingly rebuilt brick by brick on the exhibit site, this outdoor museum of century-old buildings from different regions of Belarus is located near to Strochitsa, 15km southwest of the capital in a very picturesque spot at the confluence of the Ptich River and its tributary the Menka. It features around 100 buildings, including peasant dwellings, taverns (one serving delicious traditional meals), three windmills, a country school and a church, and many guided tours are available, together with demonstrations of traditional crafts, including bee-keeping, fishing and weaving. There are also thousands of exhibits including kitchenware, tools, earthenware and national costumes. Here visitors have the chance to learn about regional folk architecture, as well as the country's myths, legends and fairy tales. In the opinion of my good friend who thinks that the Dudutki experience is somewhat hackneyed, a visit here presents an altogether more authentic recreation of village life. I think she's right. The informative website will tell you all you need to know about what to expect. If you visit just one historical recreation of traditional rural life then make it this one. By car from Minsk city centre head southwest and take the road towards the village of Ozertso for 7km beyond the ring road. There are several bus and marshrutka services a day from the city.

Stankovo Ecopark (*Центр Экологического Туризма Станьково/Цэнтр Экалагічнага Турызму Станькава; Stankovo village, Dzerzhinskava region;* ☎*599 34 88;* e *stankovo@inbox.ru;* w *ecopark.by;* ⊕ *10.00–19.00 Wed–Sun; scale of admission fees payable for individual attractions BYN3–5, toddlers & war veterans free*) This relatively new centre for ecological tourism is located 1.5km from the village of Stankovo and around 40km southwest of Minsk. Neither I nor anyone I know in Minsk have been there yet, but I list it here for information purposes. The attractions include a recreation of a wartime partisans' camp, 'fortified Minsk' (displays of weaponry), shooting galleries (including archery), zoological garden, children's rides and play areas, horseriding and apparently the house of Grandfather Frost, though surely he lives in Byelovezhskaya Puscha National Park (page 218)? Facilities include chalet-style overnight accommodation, a restaurant, cafés and a bathhouse. By car from Minsk city centre, take either the P23 road south for 23km beyond the ring road then turn right on to the P65 for a further 15km; alternatively leave the city centre along Dzerzhinsky Avenue, cross the ring road and take the P1 road southwest to Dzherzhinsk for 27km then follow the P65 south for 12km. From the centre of Stankovo village follow signs to the Ecopark (a further 1.5km). There is a direct and regular bus shuttle service to the Ecopark itself from Minsk city centre during the day, as well as bus and marshrutka services to the village.

Dukora Estate (*Дукорскі маёнтак/Дукорский маёнтак; 15 Shkolnaya St, Dukora agrotown, Pukhovichy region;* ☎ *707 77 64;* e *zakaz@dukora.by;* w *dukora. by;* ⊕ *10.00–18.00 Tue–Sun; admission BYN6/free adults/under-6s*) Situated 40km southeast of Minsk on the M5 motorway to Gomel, it is too early to judge whether or not this manor and park complex, the 'new Dudutki', will prove to be a hit. Time will tell. But if Dudutki is a cliché, you are unlikely to find any greater rural authenticity here than at Disneyland. It is certainly difficult to see the upside down house as anything other than a gimmick. A full range of activities is on offer to help visitors dip into the life of old Belarus, including traditional music, dance, culture and cuisine, a bathhouse, rides for children, animal pens and historical recreations, as well as overnight accommodation. At least it is located on the territory of a genuine 18th-century manorial estate, though the original manor house was destroyed by bombing in 1944. The very informative website only has Russian pages, but it will give you a good idea of what to expect. By car from Minsk city centre take the M4/ M5 link southeast from the ring road in the direction of Mogilev/Gomel for 14km, then follow the M5 to Dukora for 20km and head into the centre of the village. Take the P69 road north towards Smilovichy and, 600m after leaving Dukora, take a turn to the right where indicated and proceed for 1.5km to the estate car park. Marshrutka and bus services depart Minsk city regularly during the day for the village of Dukora, with the estate a further 2.5km away on foot.

Sula Estate and Park Complex (*Парк-музей Інтэрактыўнай Гісторыі «Сула»/Парк-музей Интерактивной Истории «Сула»; Sula Village, Litvenskiy district;* ☎ *613 77 01;* e *zakaz@parksula.by;* w *parksula.by;* ⊕ *10.00–18.00 Mon–Fri; admission BYN6/free adults/under-12s*) Almost 50km southwest of Minsk and to the west of the P1 road, this example of the traditional recreation genre, self-styled as 'the first Belarusian interactive history park-museum', at least has the advantage of manor house buildings that were still standing as ruins prior to very extensive renovations that took ten years to complete. The Sula River meanders gently through the parkland and the grounds are pleasing, with most of the attractions and sites of interest (including the 'exposition of Old Slavic cults and beliefs', the Viking quay, the 'Megalithic exposition' of stones, the weapons smithy, the museum, two hotels, a distillery and a restaurant) clustered between the river and Sulskoye Lake, though the scent of Disney is unmistakable. The availability of quad-bike hire and a helicopter tour from the lakeside helipad perhaps sets the scene. Yet apparently, 'boundaries between the material and the spiritual are non-existent' here, something I have yet to put to the test. By car from Minsk leave the city centre along Dzerzhinsky Avenue, cross the ring road and take the P1 road southwest to Dzherzhinsk for 27km, then follow signs for the estate west along minor roads for around 18km. A word of caution: I have yet to visit this attraction so haven't put the existence of comprehensive signage from Dzherzhinsk to the test. My advice is to take a local navigator or else be very confident you can rely on your satnav. Regular bus and marshrutka services leave Minsk for Dzherzhinsk, but onward travel to the estate by public transport will be very hit and miss. A separate bus service leaves Minsk for the village of Rubezhevichi (11km from the estate) but there is no public transport to complete the journey.

BELARUS ONLINE

For additional online content, articles, photos and more on Belarus, why not visit w bradtguides.com/belarus?

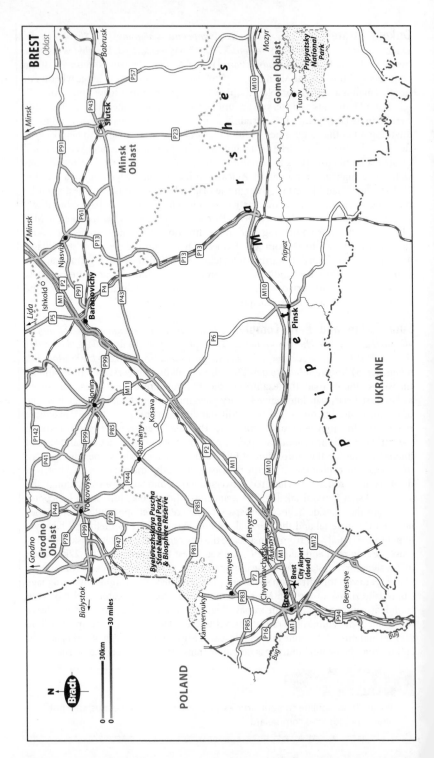

4

Brest City and Oblast
Брэст/Брест

Telephone code 162

Located in the southwestern corner of Belarus, Brest region has borders with both Poland and Ukraine. The administrative and cultural capital of the oblast is the city of Brest itself, which has a population of around 331,000. Only a short distance from the Polish border at the confluence of the Western Bug and Mukhavyets rivers, Brest is actually significantly closer to Warsaw than to Minsk and its geographical position on the main Berlin–Moscow railway line and on the major intercontinental highway from west to east, together with its historical location as the crossing point on which trading routes from all points of the compass converged, has afforded the development over time of a unique environment for different cultures to meet and evolve together. It is very much the case, though, that Western influences predominate here. There's a bounce in the step of the locals and a degree of self-confidence hinting at a more outward-facing view of life, with a greater affinity to the West than can be found further east in the country. Furthermore, the position of the city, right on the western extremity of first the Russian Empire, then latterly the Soviet Union, has bestowed upon it enormous strategic importance in times of war and peace. Today, Brest is not only a principal border crossing, but also a bridge: in cultural terms, between eastern and western Europe and politically, between the European Union and the Commonwealth of Independent States.

All in all, this city really does feel like a major border crossing with a great deal of energetic hustle and bustle, but at the same time there is also a calm and relaxed side that speaks of charm, grace and elegance. There are many delightful avenues that are just right for promenading in this splendid city, with cosmopolitan restaurants, bars and cafés where you can stop and watch the world go by.

The establishment of the free economic zone over 50 years ago has helped to create an environment in which trade can flourish with confidence. Poland's entry into the European Union in 2004 will also have helped support trade, but the city's greatest claim to fame is its fortress, sited on an island and made legendary by the great heroism and deeds of sacrifice of its defenders during the Great Patriotic War.

Although not on the grand scale of Minsk, there is much to interest the visitor in the architecture of the city. A number of examples of the imposing Neoclassical style so favoured in the last decades of the Russian Empire can be found here (especially in and around the central station square). Not surprisingly, there is also much that is reminiscent of Poland, particularly the Roman Catholic churches, while a number of Orthodox churches are particularly pleasing on the eye. Also worth an hour or two of your time is a slow stroll along the bank of the Mukhavyets River, a pastime much favoured by promenaders of all ages. Just beware of the mosquitoes, so be sure to button up. The river runs east–west and is parallel to Masherova Avenue,

Brest City and Oblast

195

half a kilometre to the south of this main thoroughfare. There are pleasant gardens and walkways on the northern bank.

The whole southern part of this region has its own natural and cultural identity as the Belarusian Polyesye. The main waterway flowing through it from west to east (as far as Chernobyl in Ukraine and beyond) is the Pripyat River and its many tributaries. This is a unique natural environment and 12 reserves and 29 other protected areas have been set up here with the objective of affording it as much protection as possible. Pride of place goes to the world-renowned state national park and biosphere reserve of Byelovezhskaya Puscha, a unique medieval woodland area 65km to the north of the city (page 218).

HISTORY

THE CITY'S EARLY ORIGINS The city of Brest has long been regarded as the traditional western gate of the country, a city with a glorious and valiant history across the centuries, complemented by a vibrant and hopeful present and future. It was first mentioned in the *Story of Temporal Years Chronicle* in 1019 as Beryestye, in the context of the struggle for the crown of Kievan Rus between Duke Svyatopolk of Turov and Duke Yaroslav the Wise of Novgorod. A number of theories exist as to the original derivation of its name. Some believe that it comes from one or two Slavic words meaning either 'birch bark' or 'elm', while others are of the opinion that it is Lithuanian in origin, from the word meaning 'ford'. The preponderance of forest and the confluence of two major rivers here mean that either is possible. Brest developed over time as a frontier town and trading centre on the western fringes of Kievan Rus, a wooden castle being built there in the 12th century on the site of the current fortress. The historical chapters of this book repeatedly show how, for many hundreds of years, the territories of Belarus have been the rope in a tug-of-war between powerful and aggressive states on its borders. The strategic location of Brest ensured that it was a regular target for subjugation and it featured heavily in a number of bloody engagements. Early in the 13th century it was part of the Grand Duchy of Lithuania, having formally been a Polish town, before being sacked by the Mongol Horde in 1241. Then in 1390, it became the first city on Belarusian territory to be granted self-determination and government under Magdeburg Law, only a short period after suffering significant structural damage at the hands of the Teutonic Order.

As its cultural and social influence grew, it became more and more the location for key events. Meetings of certain of the state's most significant sejms, or parliamentary bodies with limited powers of local self-determination, were held here; and in 1553, a Calvinist cathedral and printing house were established under Duke Nikolas Radzivili the Black where, in 1558, one of the best-known of all Renaissance books was printed, the Brest Bible. In 1569, it became part of the mighty Polish-Lithuanian Commonwealth. In 1596, it hosted the historic council that established the Eastern Catholic (or Uniate) Church to reconcile (or perhaps forge a compromise between) Roman Catholic and Eastern Orthodox believers. Conflict returned in the 17th century, when Brest was first invaded by Russia (in 1654) and then all but destroyed in a series of wars involving Sweden. It was eventually restored to Russian hands in 1795 and renamed Brest-Litovsk on the occasion of the further partition of the Polish-Lithuanian Commonwealth.

THE WORLD WARS AND THEIR AFTERMATH The mighty fortress was constructed between 1836 and 1842, not only as a citadel for the protection of this frontier town, but also as a major component in the defensive structure of the giant Russian Empire. Unfortunately, however, it wasn't enough to protect the city and when the flames of World War I engulfed much of Europe it fell to the Germans in 1915.

In March 1918, in a ceremony as heavy with symbolism as the fortress itself, Lenin's Bolshevik government concluded the Peace Treaty of Brest-Litovsk with Germany, bringing the war to an end on the Eastern Front. In this treaty, Lenin gave up vast swathes of territory (the lands of the Baltic, Poland and large chunks of modern Belarus and Ukraine), including, of course, Brest. This was a masterstroke of political compromise and expediency on the part of the newly installed Bolshevik government, which was struggling to impose authority back home. On the face of it, the deal appears to have been a major defeat, but Lenin had little choice: quite simply, the enormous and so-called 'invincible' army of the Russian Empire had collapsed in anarchy. In tens of thousands, ordinary soldiers had given up the fight and were trudging home. Mutiny was everywhere. Domestically, all was in chaos and disarray following the Revolution in November 1917. But crucially, the peace gave Lenin enough breathing space to establish and consolidate Bolshevik control over the organs of the state.

The victorious Western powers overturned the German-Russian treaty as part of the settlement that came out of the Versailles Conference in 1919. Under the Treaty of Versailles, the restored but fledgling Polish state took control of Brest that year from the Germans, although during the conflict that ensued between Poland and the Soviet Union, the fate of the city was for it to move from the control of one state to another several times. At the conclusion of the war, Brest became Polish and the 1921 Treaty of Riga formally ratified this position. It remained so until the outbreak of World War II.

The fortress suffered very heavy damage during World War I but still retained its strategic importance and, after the conclusion of the 1921 treaty, it housed a significant Polish military presence. The garrison was pressed into service during the Nazi invasion of Poland in the early days of September 1939, when only four battalions stood shoulder to shoulder to defend the city against the formidable and overwhelming motorised force of the 19th Panzer Corps commanded by highly respected general Heinz Guderian. An intense and bloody battle ensued over four days, before the Poles withdrew. For a while, the focus of attention was diverted from the city, but Brest was annexed by the Soviet Union later that year under the secret (and shameful) Molotov–Ribbentrop Pact. In this unholy alliance of diametrically opposed totalitarian dogma, the USSR and Nazi Germany callously carved up the sovereign Polish state for themselves, as the democracies of western Europe turned their backs and looked away in the climate of appeasement that prevailed at the time. But the inhabitants of Brest (and the peoples of the greater Belarusian territories) had no interest in political expediency. In the eyes of many, the single consequence of this act was to bring about the rightful reunification of a single Belarusian nation under the constituency of the Belarusian SSR. Sadly, though, the grim reality was that the Nazis were soon to turn up in force on the western bank of the River Bug, almost at the same time as Soviet forces began to mass on the eastern side.

So it was that the peace was short-lived and the city was first in the line of fire when Hitler unleashed Operation Barbarossa on an unsuspecting and wholly unprepared USSR on 22 June 1941. Word of massive German troop movements in the vicinity of the border reached an increasingly panic-stricken Kremlin in the days before the attack began but Stalin did nothing, refusing to believe that the Molotov–Ribbentrop Pact was about to be torn up. The city itself fell within a few hours, but this was the start of the most stirring period of history for the fortress. The unparalleled feats of heroism and courage of its defenders in the weeks that followed have passed into legend. Not without good reason did a grateful nation subsequently bestow the title of 'Hero-Fortress' (the city also being granted the status of 'Hero City of the Soviet Union', one of 13 throughout the USSR to be honoured thus). Those soldiers who were first to feel the might and fury of the Nazi war machine somehow held out throughout the summer of 1941 in conditions of intense attrition. Their bravery and self-sacrifice in holding back the invasion for six long weeks (as supplies of food and drinking water dwindled to nothing) gave the rest of the Soviet Union just enough time to gather itself for the withering onslaught that was to follow. To see now the vivid red-brick walls of the fortress, pockmarked with shell damage and riddled with machine-gun fire, is to gain some understanding of the enormity of the unfolding events that summer. By the time the fortress finally fell, nearly all of the defending troops had been killed. With tragic poignancy and as an enduring mark of their ultimate sacrifice, one of the last of them had inscribed in large letters on the wall of one of the barracks, 'I am dying but not surrendering. Farewell, Motherland!' By this time, the fortress was deep behind enemy lines, almost all of Belarusian territory now under the yoke of Nazi oppression. The years of tyranny that followed were brutal in the extreme. Brest's Jewish population was all but wiped out during the course of 1942, as was the case throughout the whole country, before the Red Army liberated the city in July 1944. The latest chapter in the long history of this cosmopolitan city was begun in February 1945 at the peace conference conducted by the Western powers at Yalta, when it was formally restored to the sovereignty of the Belarusian SSR and the greater Soviet Union. Upon the disintegration of the USSR, Brest became part of the newly created independent nation state of Belarus.

GETTING THERE AND AWAY

BY AIR The local airport is 12km east of the city. Built in the 1970s, it used to operate weekly flights to Minsk and 15 cities in the old Soviet Union, including Moscow, Kiev and Novgorod. Today it operates only summer flights to and from holiday destinations in southeastern Europe. If air travel is your preferred option, take one of the scheduled routes either to Minsk, Vilnius or Warsaw, then complete your journey by train (see page 64 for more details).

BY TRAIN There is easy access from the West and Brest city finds itself on two major trans-European routes: Brussels to Irkutsk and Vienna to St Petersburg.

Furthermore, every single train from Berlin to Moscow stops here. Many visitors journey by means of the daily services that depart from the central railway station in Warsaw (including a sleeper service) for its equivalent in Brest (*5hrs; one-way ticket BYN30–70, sleeper compartment BYN130–170*). Alternatively, take a cheap local train from the Polish border town of Terespol. Within Belarus, up to 13 trains a day leave Minsk for Brest (*4hrs; from BYN15 one-way*); the journey time is 40 minutes shorter if the service is on the gleaming new rolling stock, with mobile charging points and in-seat catering, with one daily overnight sleeper.

The symbolic status of the city as a bridge between East and West, the old Soviet Union and the rest of Europe, endures in one very practical sense when it comes to rail travel into the country and beyond to the East. The wider-gauge tracks of the established rail network in Belarus and the Russian Federation mean that travellers by train from the West are delayed for several hours here while the bogies of their carriages are adjusted to fit the change in track width. There is a neat trick with the latest RZD Talgo rolling stock on some services on the Berlin–Moscow route, however, which does not need to go through the old gauge-changing process; it simply 'slides' from one gauge to the other in a mere 60 seconds! This makes it a particularly popular service.

Unfortunately the **central railway station** [203 B1] in Brest isn't very central and you will need to take a short cab ride into the heart of the city, or hop on any of the buses that pass right in front of the station, a large, Neoclassical building of archetypically pre-Revolutionary grandeur. Originally built between 1833 and 1866, when it was one of the largest railway stations in the whole of the Russian Empire, this fine building was reconstructed in the Stalinist style in 1956. It sits in the middle of a huge jumble of criss-crossing lines heading to all points of the compass (there are railway lines everywhere in this town) and is still one of the city's best-known buildings. It's an enduring image that features extensively on promotional material for the whole country. In its heyday, it was not only one of the biggest but also one of the most elegant and sumptuous railway stations throughout the Empire, before it metamorphosed to bear the mark of classic post-war Stalinist design. It is divided into northern and southern sections, for trains travelling westward and eastward respectively, with a large and very long station hall dividing the two. The standard of service here is excellent; I have heard of one visitor who didn't speak Russian being taken under the wing of an attendant with a fine commitment to customer care, who closed her ticket booth to escort the weary traveller to the currency exchange, where she helped him to buy currency for his trip. There is also a restaurant here with a surprisingly decent standard of cuisine. All of the facilities are billed as being available 'round the clock' but, in reality, it would be unwise to count on this much beyond nine in the evening. When I arrived at 05.45 one morning for the early train to Minsk, the concourse was in darkness and nothing was open.

Red tape is a painful experience because of the proximity to the national border and of course, every passenger on a service crossing the state border from here must go through customs and immigration before proceeding on to the platform. When leaving the station through the 'main' exit, just be careful not to become disorientated, because this splendid building actually gives the impression of being turned to one side at an angle of 90 degrees; the imposing frontage with its iconic hammer-and-sickle fresco actually faces the railway tracks to one side. Do go outside and take a look at the delightful exterior from this angle (it's an excellent photo opportunity), then walk round to the left of the façade to access local transport. In fact, even if you're not taking a train, find an hour during your

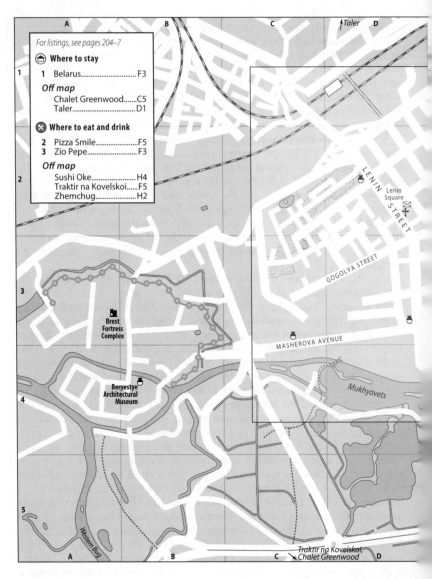

time in this city to have a wander around the station. See how many hammer-and-sickle motifs you can spot. The buildings are delightful inside and out and, as with so much of this border town, there's a real sense that this is a key location at the centre of a continent on the move. Just gazing at the arrival and departure boards is a thrill.

BY BUS Brest is situated on the main transcontinental coach route and there are buses to all points of the international compass but, although this is a cheap option, the journey times are long and uncomfortable. The **bus station** [203 C1] (*35 Mitskevicha St;* ✆*114 for information & to book tickets;* e *av@brest.by;* w *av.brest.by*) is situated in the middle of the city, 500m to the southeast of the railway station.

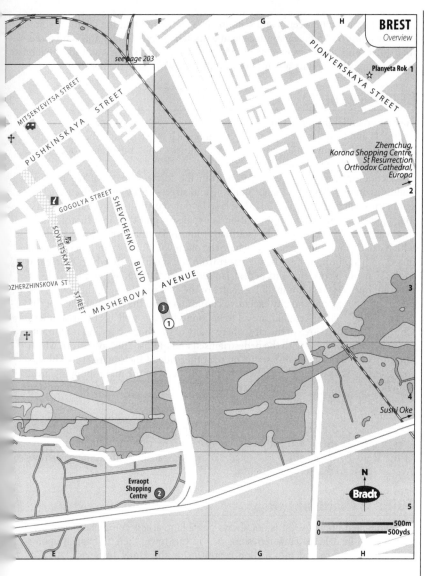

Planyeta Rok 1

*Zhemchug,
Korona Shopping Centre,
St Resurrection
Orthodox Cathedral,
Europa*
2

Sushi Oke

Evraopt
Shopping
Centre 2

MITSKYEVITSA STREET

PUSHKINSKAYA STREET

STREET

GOGOLYA STREET

SOVETSKAYA STREET

DZHERZHINSKOVA ST

SHEVCHENKO BLVD

MASHEROVA AVENUE

PIONYERSKAYA STREET

N

Bradt

0 ————— 500m
0 ————— 500yds

There are four buses a day from Minsk (*4hrs 30mins–5hrs 15mins; BYN22*) and at least two daily buses from Warsaw (*5hrs 20 mins–7hrs 30mins inc border formalities; BYN45*).

BY CAR There *should* be easy access by car on the main highway that crosses the border here. The Brest crossing is located at the Warsaw Bridge just out of town on the major pan-European highway but it is a place of some notoriety, for no other reason than the seemingly capricious nature of the guards. Unexpectedly long delays can be experienced, entirely without warning and apparently at the whim of the border guards on duty. Some of the tales told by travellers are approaching legend and waits of up to 12, 24 and even 36 hours have been reported, although the average

4

wait appears to be between 2 and 6 hours. It is rumoured that the guards are not immune to the odd monetary inducement to hasten the process, but this is no more than gossip and, in any event, is singularly not advised. Just sit tight and admire the view of a line of stationary and immobile vehicles snaking into the distance.

GETTING AROUND

There is no underground system in Brest, but the city centre is compact and most of the sights and facilities are within easy reach of each other, though the walk to the fortress and the railway museum will test your fitness. Cabs, buses and trolleybuses are all cheap, efficient, plentiful and easy to use.

Orientation is relatively easy. Apart from the fortress, many of the pre-war buildings are inevitably no longer standing and streets in the city centre were laid out in the trademark chequer-board style so favoured by post-war urban planners. The square in front of the train station is expansive and the large thoroughfare that leads out of it in a straight (southerly) line is Lenina Street, halfway along which can be found Lenin Square, where the old revolutionary continues to stand guard on his plinth, just across the street from the square itself, which is actually in the shape of a crescent. This pedestrianised street, attractively laid in bricks of different hues, is the administrative centre of the city: the House of the Soviet, the offices of the regional and city executive committees and the regional office of the National Bank of the Republic are all to be found here, as well as St Christopher's Church. The tourist area of the city, where many of the shops, bars and restaurants are to be found, begins with the pedestrianised end of Pushkinskaya Street, which runs directly opposite Lenin's statue on the other side of the square. Three blocks to the east is Sovyetskaya Street, which is in the heart of the main shopping area, also home to many bars and street cafés. The long process of pedestrianising Sovyetskaya itself is happily complete, to match sections of other streets in the area, and this part of town is now pleasing on the eye. The entire scene has been transformed by the addition of attractive lighting, paved areas and furniture. Most sites of interest are located within the compact centre, with the notable exception of the Hero-Fortress, which is located 2.5km away at the bottom of Masherova Avenue, close to the railway museum.

TOURIST INFORMATION

As highlighted previously, it is not always possible to access comprehensive tourist information in Belarus. How refreshing it is in this town, then, to happen upon a state tourism office and information centre inside the **Hotel Intourist** [203 C4] (*15 Masherova Av;* ℡ *20 52 61;* e *tur_intourist@mail.ru;* w *brestintourist.by;* ⏱ *09.00–19.00 Mon–Fri, 09.00–13.00 & 13.30–17.30 Sat*). Turn immediately right as you enter the lobby and take the stairs in the corner to the first floor. What a find it is! The staff are extremely accommodating and only too pleased to help with bookings for guided excursions around the town, oblast or anywhere in the country. Excellent English is spoken and there is a good stock of tourist literature (in English) on the city and region. English-speaking guides are also on hand to lead any excursions and visits that you might arrange. Any visit to the city really should start here.

There is also a **Brest Trans-Frontier Information Centre** [203 C2] (*46 Sovyetskaya St;* ℡ *21 00 58;* e *infocentrbrest@mail.ru;* w *tric.info;* ⏱ *08.30–17.30 Mon–Fri*), a trans-border initiative originally part of a European Union TACIS programme that aimed to increase co-operation and infrastructure integration

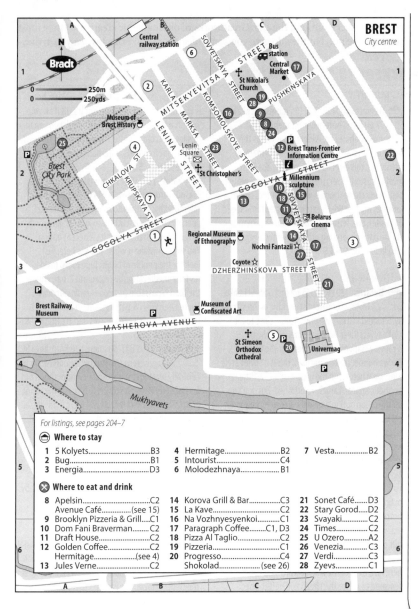

Bradt

0 ———— 250m
0 ———— 250yds

Central railway station

Bus station

Central Market

St Nikolai's Church

Museum of Brest History

Lenin Square

St Christopher's

Brest City Park

Brest Trans-Frontier Information Centre

Millennium sculpture

Belarus cinema

Regional Museum of Ethnography

Nochni Fantazii

Coyote

Brest Railway Museum

Museum of Confiscated Art

St Simeon Orthodox Cathedral

Univermag

Mukhyavets

SOVYETSKAYA STREET
KARLA MARKSA STREET
MITSKEYEVITSA STREET
KOMSOMOLSKOYE STREET
PUSHKINSKAYA
LENINA STREET
CHKALOVA ST
KRUPSKAYA ST
GOGOLYA STREET
SOVYETSKAYA STREET
DZHERZHINSKOVA STREET
MASHEROVA AVENUE

For listings, see pages 204–7

🏠 **Where to stay**

1	5 Kolyets	B3
2	Bug	B1
3	Energia	D3
4	Hermitage	B2
5	Intourist	C4
6	Molodezhnaya	B1
7	Vesta	B2

✖️ **Where to eat and drink**

8	Apelsin	C2
	Avenue Café	(see 15)
9	Brooklyn Pizzeria & Grill	C1
10	Dom Fani Braverman	C2
11	Draft House	C2
12	Golden Coffee	C2
	Hermitage	(see 4)
13	Jules Verne	C2
14	Korova Grill & Bar	C3
15	La Kave	C2
16	Na Vozhnyesyenkoi	C1
17	Paragraph Coffee	C1, D3
18	Pizza Al Taglio	C2
19	Pizzeria	C1
20	Progresso	C4
	Shokolad	(see 26)
21	Sonet Café	D3
22	Stary Gorod	D2
23	Svayaki	C2
24	Times	C2
25	U Ozero	A2
26	Venezia	C3
27	Verdi	C3
28	Zyevs	C1

in the border region. Primarily dealing with economic issues under the strapline 'contacts without borders', it is also a useful source of local information and the website is a good start before you arrive.

Additionally, a great many national and local tourist agencies have offices in the city, with new ones appearing all the time. They will all be able to book local excursions for you. Before you leave home, you might find it useful to browse the site **w** brest.by, which has some helpful English information on Byelovezhskaya Puscha National Park and the heroic fortress siege. Extremely well written, they tell the story in great detail, with some excellent photographs. There is also a large 'photo album' of numerous scenes around the city. Great works of photographic creative art they most certainly are not, but they do give you some idea of what to expect when you arrive.

WHERE TO STAY

UPMARKET

 Hermitage [203 B2] (55 rooms) 7 Chkalova St; 27 60 00; e hotel@hermitagehotel.by; w hermitagehotel.by. Widely regarded as the best hotel in town, close to City Park & many of the sights, this offers a touch of class & a high level of customer service. The elegantly decorated bedrooms are spacious & well appointed, while facilities inc free Wi-Fi, excellent restaurant (see opposite), bar, terrace, karaoke club, spa, gym & secure parking, among others. Themed events are also held here. **$$$$**

MID-RANGE

Belarus [201 F3] (153 rooms) 6 Shevchenko Bd; 22 16 48; e bresttourist@tut.by; w bressturist. by. Situated in a picturesque location close to the Mukhavyets River (45 mins' walk from the bus & railway stations) & convenient for the Warsaw Bridge frontier crossing by road, this is a Soviet-style functional hotel with the usual facilities & little aesthetic appeal. Largely refurbished, but don't go for the cheap option where the decorators have not yet been. Facilities inc free Wi-Fi, parking on site, restaurant, café & bar, & a casino & bowling alley are located next door. **$$$**

Intourist [203 C4] (139 rooms) 15 Masherova Av; 20 20 83; e int@brest.by; w brestintourist.by. Located on one of the city's main thoroughfares leading to the fortress, this functional, post-Soviet high-rise monolith is a 25min walk from the bus & railway stations but convenient for the Warsaw Bridge border crossing. There has been a significant makeover here but, as with the Hotel Belarus, don't be tempted to go for the cheap non-refurbished rooms. There is a cavernous restaurant, 2 bars (one of them ⌚ 24hrs), free Wi-Fi & an ATM in the lobby, while on the 1st floor is the city's excellent tourist information centre & travel agency. There is an extra charge for parking nearby in a secure area. English is spoken. The new website is slick, informative & very helpful. **$$$**

Molodezhnaya [203 B1] (38 rooms) 6 Komsomolskaya St; 21 63 76; e molodezhnaya@ tut.by; w molodezhnaya.by. Reasonably central & handy for train/bus stations, this modest hotel is functional & without frills, but it's OK if all you want is a bed & some b/fast (although you can buy this level of comfort elsewhere in the city for less). Services inc free Wi-Fi, café-bar, secure parking & 24hr reception. **$$$**

Taler [200 D1] (17 rooms) 88b Krasnogvardyeskaya St; 245 01 45; e admin@ talerhotel.by; w talerhotel.by. This small hotel, open since 2013, is a little way out (2.5km north of the railway station) but it's a decent option. You won't mistake it when you get here; just look for the jumble of bright blue roofs. Inside it's faux-medieval in the restaurant & bar, where the food is passable (⌚ noon–midnight daily). There's free Wi-Fi & parking, but no lift for the 3 floors. Not lavish by any means, but it's friendly & comfortable. **$$$**

Vesta [203 B2] (58 rooms) 16 Krupskaya St; 20 75 33; e hotelvesta@tut.by; w hotelvesta.by. Centrally located in a peaceful neighbourhood not far from City Park. The concrete box exterior is not promising, but don't let this put you off; inside, all is rather quaint & cosy. Significantly refurbished, much of it is fresh, if a little unexciting. If you can, get one of the older rooms, with faux wood panelling & 1920s-style décor. Facilities here are somewhat limited, though there is a sauna, hairdresser, café, small 'banquet room', 24hr lobby bar & free Wi-Fi. **$$$**

BUDGET

✳ **5 Kolyets** [203 B3] ('5 Rings'; 21 rooms) 9 Gogolya St; 20 84 95. Located within the football stadium at the Brest sports complex & handy for all the sights in town, this is my preferred option for cheap & cheerful budget accommodation in Brest. Follow the signs from the stadium precinct to find the reception desk on the 3rd floor. Staff are very friendly & the cost of the room is paid up front in cash. All is new & clean, spick & span & very basic, but it's fantastic value for money. B/fast is served in the small café (⌚ 08.00–23.00 daily, closed 1st Mon of the month). Dynamo Brest play football at the stadium & if you're lucky there will be a home fixture while you're in town. A schedule of forthcoming matches is on the display board outside the ticket office. **$$**

🏠 **Bug** [203 B1] (72 rooms) 2 Lenina St; 📞27 88 00; e reservation@hotelbug.by; w hotelbug. by. Only a 3min walk from the railway station, this imposing building (named after the river, one hopes!) matches the station itself for faux grandeur, but despite the significant refurbishment in recent times it's all rather dark & gloomy inside, with old-style Soviet service matching the old-style Soviet décor. The restaurant here is unspectacular & b/fast isn't inc in the price of your stay. An acceptable budget option, although the proximity to the station is its only true redeeming factor. Free Wi-Fi. **$$**

🏠 **Energia** [203 D3] (28 rooms) 58 Dzherzhinskova St; 📞21 35 59. Handily located for Sovyetskaya St but not easy to find as it forms part of a shared block, this is basic, cheap & reasonably cheerful. Services inc small café-bar, ATM, billiard

room, Wi-Fi (4th & 5th floors only, not free) & parking. **$$**

OUT OF TOWN

🏠 **Chalet Greenwood** [201 F5] (22 rooms, all with private decking terrace) Beloe Ozero village; m 44 500 0172; e chaletgreenwood@gmail.com; w chaletgreenwood.com. Located 35km south of Brest & 3km off the P94 road, this is a pleasing alternative if nature holds greater appeal than the city. Open since 2013 & close to the Polish border in a beautiful forest location with 2 charming lakes nearby, it offers a full range of outdoor activities & comfortable, well-appointed rooms. Everything here is done to a very high standard, inc service, with free Wi-Fi, excellent restaurant (Italian food a speciality), bar, lounge area, secure parking, pool & bathhouse. City transfers available & kids are particularly welcome. Good English spoken. Picnic lunches made to order. **$$$$**

✖ WHERE TO EAT AND DRINK

Brest is a cosmopolitan city with a direct and very large window overlooking the West. The diversity of food emporia reflects this, with eateries in significant supply particularly in and around the pedestrianised area of Sovyetskaya Street. Most establishments are of a similar standard in terms of quality and cost, so do experiment. Head and shoulders above the rest is my very favourite restaurant in all Belarus, so do try to pay the Jules Verne a visit and show the guys there your copy of this book!

RESTAURANTS

✖ **Dom Fani Braverman** [203 D2] 53 Sovyetskaya St; 📞21 12 11; ⏲ 11.00–23.00 Mon–Thu, 11.00–23.30 Fri–Sat, 11.00–22.30 Sun. Opposite Prodtovari supermarket & La Kave bar, this reincarnation of Art Café has an elegant exterior that is not quite matched by the interior décor, but the food is good & the service relaxed & efficient (though you will pay for the privilege). **$$$$**

✖ **Hermitage** [203 B2] 7 Chkalova St; 📞27 60 11; ⏲ 07.00–11.00 (b/fast), noon–23.00 (lunch & dinner), 07.00–03.00 (drinks) daily. The restaurant at the fine hotel of the same name, it's open to non-residents & is well worth a visit. Staff are helpful & friendly, the varied menu is of high quality & the overall experience here is a very positive one. Just bear in mind that it's popular for weddings & special events, so check first before you go. **$$$$**

✳ ✖ **Jules Verne** [203 C2] 29 Gogolya St (at the junction with Karla Marksa St); 📞20 93 27;

⏲ 17.00–01.00 Mon–Thu, noon–01.00 Fri–Sat, noon–midnight Sun. My personal favourite in town & indeed, the whole country, this restaurant is a joy. As you might expect from the name, the décor is pure Victoriana, with dark wood panelling, mock oil lamps & sepia etchings on the walls. But it's all very tastefully done & the food is excellent. Self-billed as offering 'world cuisine', with northern European (particularly German & Scandinavian) plus Indian & Thai food on offer in a comfortable & relaxed setting. The menu is available in English & there is even a special menu for children. First-class service & very professional, smiley staff complement the experience. On my first visit with Olya in 2007 we chose Indian & my chicken massaman with vegetables & garlic chilli nan was outstanding. Seven years later in spring 2014 I chose mutton biryani & cauliflower gobi, which was exquisite. I had with me the bill & the notes I wrote from that first visit, which I shared with the staff to their great amusement! In 2017 my mutton biryani was still delicious & Natasha's chicken tikka masala was equally as good. This place gets better with age. $$$$

✕ Sushi Oke [201 H4] 37a 28th July St; ☎48 06 67; ⏰ 14.00–midnight Sun–Thu, 14.00–02.00 Fri–Sat. Southeast of the city centre across the river, its exterior is unimposing & inside you get what you would expect: Japanese décor & decent sushi. Take-away service available to pre-order. $$$$

✕ Traktir na Kovelskoi [201 F5] 36 Kovelskaya St; ☎28 04 79; ⏰ noon–midnight Mon–Thu, noon–03.00 Fri–Sun. South of the river on the P17 road out of town, so you'll need to make a specific trip here (just look for the row of old cars out front). The décor is olde world & retro gimmicky, the food is decent & the service is friendly. Give it a try if you have your own transport, perhaps on an anti-clockwise loop from the city centre after a visit to the Railway Museum & Hero-Fortress. $$$$

✕ U Ozero [203 A2] On the shore of Upper Lake, Brest City Park; ☎20 93 30; ⏰ noon–23.00 daily. In a lovely spot right by the side of the largest ornamental lake in City Park, this café nestles among the trees & in the summer you can sit on the terrace sipping chilled Baltika beer as you watch your shashlik cooking on the BBQ. The décor is faux Belarusian village but it's done well, with a wood fire indoors for the winter, when all is cosy & inviting. The menu has a wide variety of cuisine, inc traditional Russian dishes. The food & service are good. $$$$

✕ Zhemchug [201 H2] 125 Bogdanchuka St; m 29 125 27 27; e info@zhemchug.by; w zhemchug.by; ⏰ noon–midnight Sun–Thu, noon–02.00 Fri–Sat. Away to the southeast of the city centre in a lovely riverside location, this is another place to try if you have your own transport. The décor is elegant, the food is interesting Asian/European fusion & the service is OK, though known to be brusque on occasion. Worth a visit in summer for the outside terrace. There's a 30% discount off the lunch menu (⏰ noon–16.00 Mon–Fri). Then later there's karaoke ... $$$$

☀ ✕ Pizzeria [203 C1] Pushkinskaya St (just beyond the junction with Sovyetskaya St); ⏰ 11.00–23.00 daily. Another favourite of mine is this basement hang-out. It's nothing special but the pizzas are good & unless you know it's there you probably wouldn't venture in, so it's a great place to escape tourists & the hustle & bustle of the city. Olya & I found it while researching for the 1st edition. I've returned a number of times since &

I've never been disappointed. To find it, go to Zyevs (see opposite) & it's right next door. $$$

✕ Zio Pepe [201 F3] 4 Shevchenko St; ☎20 50 52; ⏰ noon–05.00 daily. Standard pasta & pizza restaurant, but it's cheap & open all night, largely because it shares the premises with a nightclub & casino. There is also a bar. $$$

CAFÉS

To complement the project to pedestrianise much of the tourist part of the city centre, new cafés are opening all of the time. I particularly noticed big changes on my last research visit. All of the following are worthy of your attention for a coffee while you amble, but you can also get a decent meal in most of them too. Each hits an acceptable standard; thereafter, qualitative assessments are entirely subjective. Expect to find more new venues when you visit.

☕ Avenue Café [203 C2] 50 Sovyetskaya St; ☎21 65 33; ⏰ 11.00–midnight daily. Sharing the same red-brick building as La Kave, this place serves staple dishes to a decent standard & is popular. I prefer La Kave, but that's just my view.

☕ Brooklyn Pizzeria & Grill [203 C1] 23 Pushkinskaya St; ☎222 22 14; ⏰ noon–midnight daily. Just round the corner from Sovyetskaya, the food here is decent but unremarkable. Decent atmosphere & reasonably popular.

☕ Paragraph Coffee [203 D3] 66 Sovyetskaya St; ☎52 88 52; e office@paragraph. by; w paragraph.by; ⏰ 08.00–23.00 Mon–Fri, 10.00–23.00 Sat–Sun (also at 32 Karbisheva St [203 C1]). Decent coffee & desserts, relaxed & refined. Another good option for a pit stop mid-wander. Popular with students, so don't be surprised to walk in on an impromptu poetry or classical music recital. I like both of these venues.

☕ Pizza Al Taglio [203 C2] 55 Sovyetskaya St; ☎20 83 36; ⏰ 11.00–23.00 daily. A tiny pizzeria opposite Avenue Café & a good choice for quick & tasty pizza on the hoof while you're wandering, especially if time is tight.

☕ Pizza Smile [201 F5] 11 Warsaw Highway; ☎50 11 40 (395 59 55 for deliveries); ⏰ 11.00–23.00 daily. If you're on the road & simply in need of calories & sustenance by way of a pit stop en route through Brest, then this is an OK bet for pizza & sushi, either to eat in or take away. It's located within the Evraopt shopping centre.

💻 **Progresso** [203 C4] 17 Syentyabra St (around the corner from Intourist Hotel); m 25 777 70 00; ⏰ 07.00–midnight daily. I stumbled across this venue one Sun morning when taking a stroll from my hotel after b/fast. Billed as belonging to the Intourist 'complex', it's a fast-food venue, modern & without frills, but the coffee is good & it makes for a decent escape from the city.

✳ 💻 **Shokolad** [203 C3] 63 Sovyetskaya St; ☎ 328 18 44; ⏰ 10.00–21.00 daily. Opened in spring 2017, this friendly & eager-to-please place serves very good coffee, desserts & confectionery. Natasha & I were offered chocolates with a horseradish filling; we were sceptical but pleasantly surprised. Unpretentious & understated. I like this place.

💻 **Sonet Café** [203 D3] 110 Sovyetskaya St; ☎ 22 14 63; ⏰ 09.00–midnight daily. Good coffee, fine desserts & the ideal place to hang out with refreshments while you wait for the lighting of the kerosene lamps at dusk (page 215).

💻 **Svayaki** [203 C2] 5 Pushkinskaya St; ☎ 95 95 55; ⏰ noon–23.00 daily. Traditional Belarusian décor & cuisine close to Lenin Sq. Recommended by tourist contacts as 'a taste of old Belarus' so go with caution & expect visitors from abroad. Still, give it a try but don't expect too much.

💻 **Times** [203 C2] 30 Sovyetskaya St; ☎ 20 71 76; ⏰ 08.30–23.00 Mon–Fri, 11.00–23.00 Sat–Sun. In a prime location towards the top of Sovyetskaya, the outside terrace is a great spot for people-watching. The food (European) & service are excellent & it's popular with locals. It opens early on w/days & I hear it's a good bet for b/fast. One of my correspondents describes it as 'a little slice of Soho'.

💻 **Venezia** [203 C4] 5 Internatsionalnaya St; ☎ 20 33 49; ⏰ 11.00–23.00 daily. Good Italian cuisine, competitive pricing & a pleasing setting. Very popular with families; there are play areas inside & out for children.

💻 **Zyevs** [203 C1] 20 Pushkinskaya St; ☎ 61 98 98; ⏰ 11.00–22.00 daily. Excellent coffee bar next to Brooklyn Pizzeria (see opposite).

BARS

Brest has a wide choice of bars & increasingly, decent quality beer (especially non-filtered) can be found all over town. The following is but a small selection, & there will be others I haven't yet tried out that are equally worthy of mention. The upmarket & mid-range hotels listed on page 204 also have bars available to non-residents, as do most of the cafés listed opposite.

✳ 🍷 **Draft House** [203 C2] 57 Sovyetskaya St; ☎ 53 09 93; ⏰ noon–01.00 daily. Excellent location & top choice for good-quality craft beer. The menu is standard pizza, burger & staple pub grub, but the service isn't great & the wait for food is long. Natasha & I spent an evening here alfresco updating the new edition & gave up on the delay. To accompany our scribbling we settled for a selection of hot beer snacks instead, which came much quicker & did the job. Noisy, busy & popular, which is fine if you're in the mood. Sit outside on the street if you aren't. I actually like this place, delays notwithstanding.

🍷 **Korova Grill & Bar** [203 C3] 73 Sovyetskaya St; ☎ 20 92 08; ⏰ noon–02.00 daily. In a great location halfway down Sovyetskaya, this place is for you if you like meat grilled over the fire. Come early if you haven't booked. Noisy, busy & popular with locals. The food is decent (especially the burgers) & the beer is good; there's a top night out to be had here. The outdoor decking area is pleasing in the summer & there's a separate eating space out on the pedestrianised street.

🍷 **La Kave** [203 C2] 50 Sovyetskaya St; ☎ 53 27 80; ⏰ 10.00–23.00 daily. Located towards the top end of Sovyetskaya in a pleasing red-brick building with outside seating for the summer, this is a good option for decent food & beer. Not much else to say. There's a lot on the menu (which isn't always a good sign) but the staples are done well enough.

ENTERTAINMENT AND NIGHTLIFE

Clubs do not open until around 20.00, but you can dance the night away until at least 04.00.

☆ **Coyote** [203 C3] 14/1 Dzherzhinskova St; ☎ 823 64 64; ⏰ 16.00–midnight Sun–Thu, 16.00–03.00 Fri–Sat. Brash Americana, decent food & a top selection of excellent beers. Very popular at the w/end, when there's live music from quality bands & the place really buzzes.

Recommended if you're in for a late night of partying.

☆ **Nochni Fantazii** [203 C3] 73 Sovyetskaya St; ⊕ 21.00–04.00 Wed–Sun. Formerly City Club, all of the usual nocturnal facilities are on offer here & it's apparently popular with the locals, though no-one I know has been there. Centrally located in the heart of the town, so it should be a decent bet for a late night out.

☆ **Planyeta Rok** [201 H1] 48 Pionyerskaya St; 📞 46 64 83; w planetrock.by; ⊕ 19.00–05.00 Wed–Sun. As befits the name, this is a loud, brassy venue with thumping music as a constant backdrop. Relaxing it isn't, but it's ideal if you're in the mood to burn off some calories on the dance floor with gassy beer for refreshment. There's also a café & games room. The location, on the northeastern fringe of the city centre, is not ideal.

☆ **Solo Karaoke Club** [203 B2] 7 Chkalova St; 📞 104 00 22; ⊕ 20.00–04.00 Mon–Thu, 20.00–05.00 Fri–Sat, 20.00–midnight Sun. The karaoke bar at the Hermitage Hotel. You might fancy a visit if you're staying here, but it probably isn't worth a trip out if you're not.

☆ **Zio Pepe** [201 F5] 4 Shevchenko St; 📞 20 50 52; ⊕ 20.00–04.00 Wed–Sun. The nightclub & casino arm of the Italian restaurant (page 206) has little to complement your pizza. Standard club fare.

SHOPPING

Look no further than the central area bounded by Lenina, Gogolya, Kyubisheva and Mitskevicha streets for most of your purchasing requirements. Sovyetskaya Street runs north–south through it. Most of the best of the city's stores and boutiques are here and the convenience of a single, easily navigable location is too good to miss. On Sovyetskaya itself (on the left heading south, just beyond the Church of St Nikolai) is a children's store selling clothes and toys. Elsewhere in this area are many outlets selling fine sweets, presents, souvenirs, fashionable clothes and beauty products. To recharge your batteries, there are many bars and cheap eateries where you can obtain fast but tasty food and refreshments. There is also the excellent **Central Market** [203 C1] on Pushkinskaya Street, with a wide range of fresh produce and other goods.

SHOPPING CENTRES

Evraopt 11 Warsaw Highway, 8 Komsomolskaya St, 44 Laktyonova St, 6A Yasyenevaya St, 5 Gvardeiskaya St, 150 Raduzhnaya St, 2 & 37 Yuzhny Gorodok, 123 Skripnikova, 24 Respubliki Av, 342 Moskovskaya St & 50 Orlovskaya St. If you're in need of everyday essentials & everything under one roof, try these hypermarkets run by the ubiquitous chain retailer scattered across the city.

Europa [201 H2] 202 Moskovskaya St

Galereya Grand [203 C1] 15 Kyubisheva St

Korona Shopping Centre [201 H2] 210 Moskovskaya St

Univermag shopping complex [203 D4] Masherova Av. I have it on good authority from 2 reliable sources, which include my friend Olya, that this outlet, 200m east of the Hotel Intourist, is an excellent source of good-value shopping. Clothes, beauty products, traditional souvenirs & other 'present material' are all available here at very competitive prices, Olya tells me.

OTHER PRACTICALITIES

Currency-exchange bureaux are easy to find in this border town and as it is a free economic zone, foreign currency is in plentiful supply. A useful tip is to have not only Belarusian roubles and US dollars with you, but also small supplies of euros and Polish zloty. After all, Poland is only a short walk away! There are lots of **banks** and **ATMs** all over town. There is also an excellent **post office** [203 B2] at the top of Pushkinskaya Street (at the Lenina Street end), on the left-hand side as you enter Lenin Square.

BREST FORTRESS ❋ [200 A3] (*Брэсцкая Крэпасць/Брестская Крепость; Masherova Av;* \20 03 65, 20 00 12; ⊕ *08.00–midnight daily;* w *brest-fortress.by; site admission free*) The largest and most popular visitor attraction in the city, this is one of the truly 'not to be missed' visits to be had during your stay in Belarus, let alone your limited time in Brest. To do it full justice, you will need to give yourself at least 4 hours to see everything. The walk here from the city centre will take around 45 minutes; alternatively, the local bus service stops at points along Masherova Avenue, the main road running straight and true past the Hotel Intourist.

The location was very well chosen by the planners, because the complex holds a strategically important position at the confluence of the Bug and Mukhavyets rivers. It occupies a huge site, its diameter being around 1km, although much of the outer defence line was obliterated in the terrible fighting that took place here in 1941. The stronghold within occupies a small island in the centre of the river, which is connected to the remainder of the structure by three small bridges.

Construction began in 1838 and took four years. There is one single piece of architecture still standing in its midst from pre-1838 Brest, when the town centre stood here: the beautiful **Byzantine Church of St Nikolai** (not to be mistaken for its namesake on Sovyetskaya Street). It was severely damaged during the 1941 siege and reduced almost to rubble. While the exterior has been mostly renovated, its golden dome being a particularly striking feature, much remains to be done to the interior, although services are regularly held here. For now, the walls are bare brick and plaster (there are neither friezes nor murals), but this throws into even sharper relief the beautiful icons that are mounted in many places. And right in the centre of the church is its most beautiful feature: a huge golden chandelier, delicately suspended from the ceiling almost to head height, adorned with icons and ceremonial rushniki. As you pass through the main door, turn immediately right to view the small but informative pictorial display in black and white that reveals the church at various stages of splendour and misery through its cyclical periods of construction and destruction. It is something of an oddity to find such a sanctuary of reverence and piety in this location, when all around speaks of conflict and bloodshed. Devotional objects such as small icons and candles are available for purchase inside in the right-hand corner immediately after you enter.

The fortress had an important defensive role to play in World War I, after which it was used mainly for housing soldiers in the 1920s and 1930s. In 1941, it came to the attention of the world during the first six weeks of Operation Barbarossa, when the Nazis threw everything they could at it to break the resistance of the defending forces. The Germans took the entire town in the first few hours of their attack. Around 90% of the city was destroyed in a furious and relentless barrage of withering artillery fire. The fortress suffered severe damage too, but those garrisoned inside held out. The Nazis turned the focus of their strategy from attack to attrition and so it was that the siege began. Elsewhere, the German advance eastward was gathering pace by the day. Six weeks later, they had almost taken Smolensk, deep into Russian territory, before the resistance of the defenders of the fortress was finally broken. Much of it was in ruins and only a handful of men had survived but, in the context of the wider conflict, an invaluable job had been done. Citizens all over the USSR had been inspired by the daily news bulletins they received from the front line, telling of the heroism of the small band of Soviet troops striving valiantly against their Nazi aggressors. Stalin had been given just enough time to plan his campaign, so that when he issued his rallying call to every citizen of the Union to defend the Motherland to the death, the vast empire at his command swung into action in a patriotic fervour of almost spiritual intensity. Little wonder, then, that the 1939–45 global conflict is still referred to throughout the countries of the former USSR as the Great Patriotic War. At the end of hostilities, the decision was taken not to rebuild the fortress, but instead to turn it into a huge shrine, a giant monument to commemorate all that transpired here. Exactly the same thought process informed the concept and design of the deeply affecting state memorial at Khatyn (page 186).

A walk around the complex Bear all of the history in mind as you enter the complex. The approach along Masherova Avenue is long, straight and slightly downhill, with sculptures in the shape and colour of the Soviet flag lining the route, upon each of which is embossed an image of the head and shoulders of one of the defending troops. On the left is a memorial to the heroes of the siege. Also on this side and adding nothing to the scene is an ugly and incongruous factory with an enormous red-and-white striped chimney, while on the right is the city's railway museum (page 212). At various points along Masherova Avenue and particularly in the vicinity of this museum, enormous works of construction are under way, both residential and commercial. There have also been massive road improvements hereabouts, the main border crossing at Warsaw Bridge being not far away. At the bottom of the avenue there used to be a huge car park for the fortress complex with space for over a thousand vehicles. On my first visit in 2007 it contained six cars. That car park is now much reduced in size to accommodate the expansion of the highway. As you cross the new road and begin the long walk towards the fortress, your eye is drawn to the first iconic sight, over 100m in front of you, where an enormous concrete block, grey and sombre, rests on the remains of the outer wall, into which has been cut a gigantic star. This is the entrance. Just inside is a small booth, where explanatory information in English is now available, and at least one of the duty rota staff speaks faultless English. As you walk through, tape recordings are playing of the wireless broadcast that first broke the news of the invasion, laid over stirring military music and the sounds of battle. As you come out of the tunnel and walk another 150m ahead, the eye is immediately drawn to a massive, glistening bayonet obelisk, 100m high, near to which is an astonishing concrete sculpture (entitled *Courage*), into the top of which has been carved the head of a grim-faced defender. It is almost 34m high and the reverse side has carvings depicting various scenes from the heroic defence. At the foot of the obelisk is the inevitable eternal flame, guarded round the clock by four teenagers from the Corps of Pioneers. The vaguely comical ceremony of the changing of the guard does little to enhance the sanctity of this hallowed place; and if, like me, you ever witnessed the same process at Lenin's mausoleum in Moscow during the days of the Soviet Union, you will understand what I mean here. Next to the flame are three rows of symbolic tombstones bearing the names of the fallen heroes.

All of this awaits in the middle distance. For now, take a slow stroll along the paved pathway, past a row of tanks on the left, all the while admiring the beauty and the many species of tree that line the walkway on the edges of the river beyond on both sides. The willows are particularly beautiful. As you reach the end of the path and enter the circle within, pause for a moment to look around. Immediately to your left is a grim but moving sculpture, starkly entitled *Thirst*. It depicts a soldier, near to exhaustion or even death, lying on his side and half crawling, his right hand holding a machine gun and his left imploringly holding out a helmet for water. Legend has it that this depicts the last soldier left in the garrison when it was finally taken. He (and the handful of his comrades who remained) had gone without food or water for 40 days, so the story goes, and when the Nazis finally broke the resistance of the last survivors, so moved were they by this man's endurance and heroism, that they let him go. This tale may have been embellished in the telling over the years but, like all such stories, much of it is likely to be true.

I last visited here on a Sunday morning. In this area I saw youngsters parading in uniform, bearing arms, under the stern supervision of their drill sergeant. Other youngsters were practising drills in civilian clothes, some of them considerably less enthusiastic than others. Then I spotted a wedding party at the eternal flame. Behind the *Thirst* sculpture and all the way around this inner section lies an incomplete circle of two-storey buildings, the former barracks, most of which are still intact. Those to the left house a number of **galleries for art and literature** (⊕ *10.00–18.00 Tue–Sun*). The work of individual artists and writers is frequently on display here. In front of these bullet-riddled buildings are displays of military equipment. The centre ground is taken by the sculpture *Courage*, with the eternal flame, obelisk and symbolic tombstones. If all of this were not enough to paint a bleak tableau, piped choral music, sombre and doleful, plays constantly at a number of locations. Behind is the Church of St Nikolai and to the right, the brick remains of the **White Palace** can be seen, with most of the building's exterior intact. Entrance into the shell is forbidden, however, presumably for reasons of safety. It was here that Lenin pulled off his masterstroke of political expediency in 1918, when he negotiated the Treaty of Brest-Litovsk with the invading Germans. Further to the right is the **Defence of Brest Fortress Museum** (✆ *20 03 65*; ⊕ *09.00–18.00 Tue–Sun; admission BYN2.50*), one of three on the site, all of which are well worth a visit. Neatly arranged exhibits tell the story of the construction and history of the fortress, as well as graphically depicting the conditions of the siege. Particularly impressive are the items and memorabilia recounting the human side of the terrible events that occurred here. Explanatory information boards with English text are now on display at every exhibit.

The White Palace represents one of the entrances to the central stronghold and a small bridge behind it leads to the final small island at the centre. When you get there, it is worth gazing around you; the view of the battle-scarred red-brick **Kholmsky Gate** is one of the iconic images that you may have seen in books.

You should now take time to retrace your steps back through the entrance, pausing *en route* to look at the many plaques positioned throughout the site, on which a date appears in large letters, followed by a brief description of the key events at each location (sadly in Russian only). And for refreshment and reflection, turn left immediately after you pass the museum and walk down a short but beautiful tree-lined avenue to the Café Citadel (⊕ *10.00–23.00 daily*), housed in a series of vault-like rooms in a low, red-brick building; soft drinks, alcoholic beverages and snacks are available cheaply. Expect to find more staff there than customers. Toilets are also available here.

Do remember that the grounds of the complex are open until midnight. A promenade here at dusk is particularly atmospheric. And to prepare you for your visit before you leave home, spend some time on the English pages of the excellent website (page 209). It's packed with contextual and historical detail.

MUSEUMS AND HISTORICAL SITES
Beryestye Archaeological Museum ✳ [200 B4] (*Археалагічны музей «Бярэсце»/Археологический музей «Берестье»*; ✆ *20 55 54*; ⊕ *Nov–Feb 10.00–17.00 Wed–Sun; Mar–Oct 11.00–18.00 Wed–Sun, last entry 30mins before closing; admission BYN1.20, with extra charge of BYN0.50 to take photographs*)

Situated south across the river from the fortress and with access from inside it, this large modern building was constructed around an excavation site. Now open again after extensive renovations, the vast single-storey canopied hall is home to more than 40,000 artefacts in 14 galleried exhibit areas from the 11th to the 14th centuries, all relating to the original settlement here a thousand or so years ago. Most were discovered in the course of the extensive excavations that have been ongoing for 40 years and, in one or two locations near to the museum, current archaeological digs can still be seen. The exhibits line the walls of the hall, while the enormous floor space is taken up with a sunken reconstruction of the original town as it stood in the second half of the 13th century. In total, the remains of more than 30 buildings are available for viewing and there's also a scale model of how it would have looked when first constructed. All in all, this museum offers a welcome respite from the sombre experience of cruel and bloody modern warfare that has assaulted you thus far in this place. There's also a souvenir stall by the ticket desk near the entrance. But do tread carefully around here and do not stray on to any path other than to the museum. After all, you are pretty close to the border with NATO at this point! On my last visit I went for a modest wander and it didn't take me long to come up against barbed wire and high fences, with the remains of an old watchtower from the days of the Soviet Union close by. I backed off immediately when a police car appeared from nowhere.

Brest Railway Museum ✳ [203 A4] (*Брэсцкі чыгуначны музей/Брестский железнодорожный музей;* \26 37 64; ⊕ *Oct–Apr 08.30–17.30 Tue–Sun; May–Sep 09.00–18.00 Tue–Sun; guided tours bookable 09.00–17.00; admission BYN2.50*) On the left-hand side of Masherova Avenue as you leave the fortress (200m beyond the car park and across the new road) is the open-air railway museum, a place of boundless joy for railway enthusiasts. Opened in 2002, it displays historical steam locomotives from the 1930s and 1940s, together with a staff carriage dating from 1915 and diesel engines from more recent times. All of them are in full working order and have been beautifully maintained. The iconic Soviet red star is everywhere to be seen and there are some splendid photo opportunities. Some of the engines can be mounted to experience the driver's perspective. It is only when you are up close to these magnificent feats of engineering that you truly understand their vast size. I'm no railway geek, but I was entranced for several hours when I came here. The site is compact and the rolling stock is lined up on parallel rows of tracks. Guided tours for up to 20 people can be arranged in advance for an extra charge. The grounds and exhibits are frequently used for shooting films and as the location for festivals.

Museum of Brest History [203 B2] (*Музей гісторыі горада Брэста/Музей истории города Бреста;* 3 Levanyevskaya St; \23 16 25; ⊕ *10.00–18.00 Wed–Sun; admission BYN2.50*) As might be expected, artefacts and exhibits tell the story of the city through the ages, providing useful background information for the student of local history. And it's in a quaint building in a pleasant location.

Regional Museum of Ethnography [203 C3] (*Брэсцкі абласны краязнаўчы музей/Брестский областной краеведческий музей;* 60 Karla Marksa St; \23 91 16; ⊕ *10.00–18.00 Tue–Sun; admission BYN2.50*) Linked to the Museum of Brest History and located in a charming historic building (a 19th-century former hotel and theatre), this museum focuses more on society and culture. There are extensive collections of artefacts from the region, rare books and archival antiquities.

Museum of Confiscated Art [203 B3] (Музей «Выратаваныя мастацкія каштоўнасці»/Музей «Спасённые художественные ценности»; 39 Lenina St; ✎ 20 41 95; ⊕ 10.00–17.00 Tue–Sun; admission BYN2.50) Known locally as the 'Museum of Salvaged Artistic Valuables', this quirky concept displays rare pieces of fine art from around the world. The factor of added interest is that they were all confiscated from would-be art thieves by customs officials at the nearby border!

CHURCHES AND CATHEDRALS
St Christopher's Church of Exaltation of the Holy Cross [203 B2] (Касцёл Узвышэння Святога Крыжа/Церковь Воздвижения Святого Креста) This church was constructed in 1856 from the bricks of Catholic churches and monasteries that previously existed in the Old City. Within is the renowned 17th-century icon *Our Lady of Berestye*, richly decorated in gilt and precious stones. Services are held in both Polish and Belarusian. The acoustics of the building are of the very finest quality. This archetypical example of Catholic architecture is located just off Lenin Square, where the man himself remains on duty, ever alert. A nice contrast of belief and ideology.

St Nikolai's Church [203 C1] (Царква Святога Мікалая/Церковь Святого Николая) Situated on the northeastern side of Sovyetskaya Street (close to the junction with Mitskevicha Street), this delightful church is one of the most beautiful in the whole of the city. Built between 1904 and 1906 in the pseudo-Russian style to commemorate the end of the Russo-Japanese War, it is a stunning example of Orthodox décor, both outside and in. The deep blue cupolas decorated with gold stars are particularly striking, especially in the sunshine. Closed during the time of the Soviet Union, it was only restored and returned to its parish in the 1990s.

St Simeon Orthodox Cathedral [203 C4] (Свята Сімяонаўскі кафедральны сабор/Свято-Симеоновский кафедральный собор) This lovely example of 16th-century Orthodox architecture is situated on the south side of Masherova Avenue, right next to the Hotel Intourist and on the way to the fortress; its exterior is lime green in hue. *Very* lime green. You may be reminded of a highly decorated cake at first glance. Much of the current construction dates from 1865 and this is the only place of worship in the city that has never once closed its doors, whatever the prevailing circumstances outside. Inside and right of centre as you walk in is a tomb that is said to contain some of the earthly remains of the city's Father Superior and martyr Aphanasye, who was tortured to death for his Orthodox beliefs in 1648. His statue was erected and sanctified just outside the grounds of the cathedral in 2005.

St Resurrection Orthodox Cathedral [201 H2] (Свята-Васкрасенскі сабор/Свято-Воскресе́нский собо́р) On the way out of the city in an easterly direction, at the junction of Partizansky Avenue and Moskovskaya Street, stands the imposing St Resurrection Orthodox Cathedral. Its silver domes are particularly eye-catching. Built only in 2003, its altar was sanctified by His Holiness Alexei the Second, Patriarch of Moscow and All Russia. Below ground level is a special vault to honour the renowned icon *Our Lady of Kazan*.

PARKS AND RECREATION
Brest City Park [203 A2] (Брэсцкі гарадскі парк/Брестский городской парк) Originally laid out by Russian soldiers who were stationed near here in 1906, the park is only 10 minutes' walk from the railway station on the right-

4

After the privations of World War I, the few who survived in the Jewish community found themselves living in terrible conditions. Many were homeless and took refuge in the city's synagogues for shelter. In 1921, a relief programme initiated by American philanthropist Felix Warburg financed the construction of a new Brest suburb to accommodate homeless Jewish war veterans, their families and the many orphans of the community. Close by was a large Jewish cemetery that had been established in the 1830s. During the Great Patriotic War the Jewish community suffered abject brutality. Before the 1941 invasion by the Nazis the population of Brest was 52,000, half of whom were Jews. After hostilities ended only 19 Jews remained. The cemetery was desecrated and vandalised by the Nazis, then after the war it was ransacked by the Communists, who stole the gravestones and used them in construction projects. Some of the stones were used by ordinary people of the city to pave gardens at their homes and their dachas. In recent times, news of the discovery of some of these stones reached the ears of the Jewish community. Now over 1,200 of them have been recovered and are presently stored under the arches of the Hero-Fortress, awaiting a decision as to a permanent home.

Some of the original Warburg houses were still standing only a few years ago, though sadly the last of them is now gone. Two were bulldozed to make way for a new supermarket and the last five on Pyervy Minsky Lane have also been flattened. During the works of demolition and the digging of the new supermarket foundations many gravestones were unearthed, while the site of the old Jewish cemetery is now a disused sports field and running track. All that remains is a hidden plaque marking the burial site of the great Rabbi Josef Dov Soloveitchik, from the Rabbinic dynasty that gave rise to the Brisk Yeshiva that exists today in Jerusalem. There are plans within the Brest community to create a memorial at the cemetery, but there are issues about the need for permission

hand side of Lenin Avenue. The original area of 4ha has been redesigned and significantly expanded to some 50ha. It reopened to visitors on 1 May 2006 and, not unsurprisingly for a former Soviet republic, its official title is now 'First of May Culture and Entertainment Park'. It is the largest in the city and a beautiful place to walk and meander, with dozens of species of trees that are not normally to be found in this part of Europe. There are also two delightful ornamental ponds, called the Upper and Lower lakes, which are connected by a canal through which water lazily flows. Newly built bridges of decorative iron span the canal, with another bridge linking the island in the centre of the Upper Lake to the shore. Two fountains complement the overall ambience. There are also tennis courts and many attractions for children. To complete your self-restoration, visit the lovely café U Ozero ('By the Lake'; page 206). When refreshed and relaxed, try your luck in the amusement park, listen to a performance at the open-air concert stage, or perhaps visit the large disco club (or then again, perhaps not!). Many refreshment kiosks are also situated throughout the park.

Sovyetskaya Street and its environs ✳ When I first visited Brest in 2007, works of pedestrianisation along Sovyetskaya and the streets off it where in full swing. Subsequent visits always saw progress, and I'm happy to report that everything is now pretty much done. That's not to say, of course, that the from the authorities and also funding. The clock is ticking for this important slice of Jewish history in Brest.

A model of the original Warburg colony is displayed at the city's tiny **Holocaust Museum** in the Brest Jewish Community Centre (*Музей «Яўрэі Брэста»/Музей «Евреи Бреста»; 32 Gogolya St;* ⊕ *no set opening hours, so arrange your visit in advance; admission free*). Small it may be, but it provides a very informative history of Jewish Brest. Among the exhibits are Nazi records revealing that on one single day in 1941, almost 17,000 Jews were murdered. On Kubysheva Street not far from the junction with Gogolya stands the **bust of Menachem Begin**, the sixth Prime Minister of Israel, who was born in Brest in 1913. On a wall nearby is a plaque acknowledging that the building here was once the school he attended as a boy. Indeed, within the city boundaries stand a number of **Jewish memorials** at key locations of historical significance. Perhaps the most poignant site of all is the location of the foundation stones of the **original synagogue** within the curtilage of the **Belarus cinema** [203 C2] (*62 Sovyetskaya St*). From the outside it is still possible to see the shape of the original walls because, incredibly, the cinema was built *around* the synagogue! And inside, the arch of the original building still forms part of the architecture of the new. Enter the cinema through the main entrance and go down the stairs as you would if going to use the conveniences. You may have to explain to the attendant that the usual fee is not appropriate in this case. Then down in the basement area you will find row upon row of the original foundation stones. There is no plaque to mark their significance.

For further information on anything concerning Jewish Brest, to arrange access to memorial sites, to meet members of the current community or to arrange a museum visit or local tours with Russian- or English-speaking guides, contact British sustainable development charity **The Together Plan** (page 116) or Belarusian NGO **Dialog** (page 38).

city's planners won't have new ideas to enhance the environment further. It's an attractive sight and a fine place for meandering, with lots of appealing street furniture. At the same time though, there's a real sense that this is a frontier town. The ambience is decidedly Western, which I guess is purely a matter of geography. There are countless numbers of bars and flashy shops, with money, money, money everywhere to be seen. After all, the European Union is literally a short walk away. Everything on Sovyetskaya speaks of capital and the West. When I was last here I found myself a little morose at the extent to which Western commercialism is steadily subsuming much of the old. I turned on to Pushkinskaya Street where I saw a little old lady, arms weighed down with tatty old carrier bags. She was sorting through the rubbish in the gleaming new bins. It was quite some metaphor. At the junction with Gogolya Street is a small square where you will find the attractive **millennium sculpture** [203 C2], with tablets at the base displaying summaries of key events in the city's history. Just above these tablets are attractive friezes depicting those events. From here, look to spot the cinema built around the **old synagogue** (see above).

One final not-to-be-missed experience awaits your attention before you leave Brest, and for this you need to be standing at the bottom of Sovyetskaya Street before dusk, to witness the ceremonial **lighting of the kerosene lamps**. The attractive street furniture in the pedestrianised area includes a collection of historic lamps,

4

each of which is lit by hand every evening by an elegant gentleman sporting a peaked cap and vintage uniform with shiny buttons (it is good luck to rub them). He carries a stepladder in one hand and a lighter in the other. It's a thoroughly charming vignette, though you are likely to share it with a number of jostling tourists snapping pictures and posing for selfies. Don't be put off. Dusk is such a wonderful time of day wherever you are and whatever you are doing. This is one experience in the gloaming you are unlikely to find anywhere else. An information board displays the anticipated times of ignition week by week.

FESTIVALS If you find yourself in Brest at the end of July, look out for the **city's birthday celebrations**. The official date is the 28th, but festivities take place over a number of days, culminating in the main event on the final Sunday of the month. Activities include parades of revellers in fancy dress, particularly knights of old, street theatre, concerts and sports events. Visitors come from all over the country to watch and take part, as the whole city swings into party mood in a dazzling display of colour, light and sound.

Then in October, Sovyetskaya Street is the scene for the **Autumn Fair**, a celebration to give thanks for the bounties of the harvest. The thoroughfare overflows with an abundance of natural produce, in a symbolic display of the enduring relationship between the people and the land.

OUTSIDE BREST

PINSK (Пінск/Пинск) Some 180km east of Brest on the M10 motorway stands Pinsk, the ancient capital of the lands of the **Polyesye**, with a history enveloped in mysteries and mists. Its appeal and significance over the centuries have been shaped by the geographical location of the town. Formerly surrounded by swampland, it's little wonder that this has always been called 'the land of woods, bogs and fogs'. But the town's strategic position at the western end of the Polyesye, on a bend of the mighty Pripyat River and at the confluence of the Pinya and Strumen, quickly ensured that it gained power and influence as a major stopping-off point along the ancient north–south and east–west trade routes. Nowadays, it is a town with a population of over 128,000 and its significance as a fertile centre of agriculture is assured. There is also a small but specialist industry here manufacturing boats that sail the local rivers.

History The historical settlement of Pinesk, named after the Pina River that flows through the modern town, was first established over 900 years ago. This makes it one of the oldest Slavic settlements in the country. In strategic terms, it held an uneasy position between warring principalities. Although declaredly neutral, its sympathies were with the Novogrudok princes, and not surprisingly it was taken under their patronage in 1320 and subsumed within the Grand Duchy of Lithuania. In 1569, after the creation of the Polish-Lithuanian Commonwealth, its strategic importance was recognised when it became the administrative centre of the province of Brest. Then in 1581, this status was further enhanced when the town was granted rights of self-determination and government under Magdeburg Law. Its significance and influence continued to grow exponentially as it developed into a large residential settlement. Only the commonwealth's capital Wilno (now Vilnius) was a more important town.

But the period 1640–1706 was a time of abject misery for the townspeople. Successive invasions and sackings on the part of Cossacks, Poles, Ukrainians and

Russians decimated the population, destroyed much of the town's architecture and wiped out the community's infrastructure. Miraculously and in spite of almost relentless conflict, the city not only survived as a settlement, but also managed to flourish. From 1793 until 1939, it came under the jurisdiction of first the Russian Empire, then Poland after the Polish-Soviet war and finally the Soviet Union. At the outbreak of World War II, the Jewish community comprised over 90% of the town's total population and, during the tyranny of the Nazi occupation from 1941 to 1944, all were interned in concentration camps, most of them never to return. Records are incomplete, but it is believed that as many as 30,000 Pinsk Jews perished during 'the final solution', including 10,000 in just one day. It was liberated by the Red Army and returned to Soviet ownership in 1944, before finally coming under the jurisdiction of the Republic of Belarus in 1991, upon the creation of the new state.

 Where to stay and eat There are several hotels and restaurants in town.

Pripyat Hotel, Restaurant and Café Complex (229 rooms) 31 Dnyeprovskaya Flotilla St; ☎ 165 65 96 33; e info@andre.by. As might be expected, the largest hotel in town is a multi-storey concrete edifice that is archetypically Soviet, though the location is lovely, with delightful views across the nearby park & the river. It is located on the bank of the Pina River, east of the St Francis Monastery. Facilities inc a restaurant (☎ 382 88 88;

🕐 07.00–01.00 for b/fast, lunch & dinner; $$$), bar, open-air café, disco, ATM, unattended car parking & helpful tourist office, from where tours can be booked. **$$**

✘ Restaurant Taverna 12a Korzha St; ☎ 32 29 50; 🕐 noon–01.00 daily. This rustic wooden taverna serves excellent shashlik, & there's a pleasant outdoor terrace if the weather is good. **$$**

What to see and do The best way to make the most of a visit here will be on an organised tour from Minsk or Brest with one of the state tourist agencies. There is much to see. Two of the most interesting visitor attractions can be found within walking distance of each other, not far from the banks of the Pina River. The first of these is the **St Francis Monastery and the Assumption of the Blessed Virgin Roman Catholic Church**, constructed between 1712 and 1730. Founded in 1396, this was one of the oldest religious sites in the Grand Duchy of Lithuania. The original wooden church was looted and burned many times before the Baroque structure of stone that replaced it was completed in 1730. Inside are seven ornate altars, together with myriad sculptures and carvings, all the work of master craftsman Jan Schmitt. There are also several beautiful paintings and frescoes. In the grounds is a belfry constructed in 1817.

On the other side of the road bridge (but on the same bank) is the **Jesuit Collegium**, built between 1635 and 1648. It is an imposing three-storey building, with Baroque and Renaissance features, walls that are 2m thick and impressive vaulted ceilings. In its day, it was an educational institution for both religious and secular teaching. The crypt contains the relics of the Jesuit martyr Andrei Babolya, who was murdered by Cossacks in 1657 and canonised in 1853. The library was emptied of its valuable collection of works in 1940 in anticipation of war. They were taken to Leningrad (now St Petersburg) and have never been returned. Today the building houses the **Belarus Polyesye Museum** (музей Беларускага Палесся/ музей Белорусского Полесья; 22 Lenin Sq; ☎ 165 35 93 72; 🕐 10.00–18.00 Tue–Sun; admission BYN2).

There is also a more modern structure worthy of a visit at the junction of Gorky and Pervomayskaya streets, north of the river. It is the **Consistory and the Resurrection Slovuschy Orthodox Church**. A wooden church built in 1668 originally stood on this site, before the stone building that replaced it in 1778 was destroyed during the Great Patriotic War. After the war, a cinema was built here, but the ground was subsequently reconsecrated and a new church built in 1995. Its black domes are especially striking, particularly under snow.

BYELOVEZHSKAYA PUSCHA NATIONAL PARK AND BIOSPHERE RESERVE

✳ (*Нацыянальны Парк Белавежская Пушча/Национальный Парк Беловежская Пуща; Каменуику, Kamenyets district;* \ *163 15 63 98;* e *npbpby@ rambler.ru, beltour7@mail.ru;* w *npbp.by*) First established as a national park in 1939 (although a 'park' has existed here since the Middle Ages), it joined the list of UNESCO World Heritage Sites on 14 December 1992, then in 1993 it was granted the status of Biosphere Reserve, affording unique opportunities for specialist ecological study. There are conference and library facilities here, together with accommodation for up to 100 visiting scientists.

Today, the park is an integral and important feature of around 1,700km² of ancient primeval forest within Belarusian borders, although the woodland stretches across the border into Poland, which jointly administers the park with Belarus. Deeply worrying tales have reached my ears in recent times that extensive logging is in progress on the Polish side. This must be resisted, because the forest here is all that now remains of a vast canopy that once covered the whole of the huge northern European plain, the former home and playground of Polish princes and Russian tsars. In fact, the last private owners of the forest were the tsars of the Russian Empire, from 1888 to 1917. After the Revolution, it was nationalised and brought under the jurisdiction of the state. More than 900 plant species have been recorded, including 26 tree and 138 shrub species. Almost two-thirds of them are indigenous to the area. A number of the mighty oaks may be over 650 years old. One of them, 'the Solitary Oak', is specifically signposted within the park.

Today life here is calm and the reserve is home to around 212 species of bird, including corncrake, eagle owl, white stork and white-tailed eagle, along with 59 species of mammal, including wild boar, wild horse, roaming elk, beaver, lynx, fox, deer, wolf, otter, badger, mink, ermine, marten and, most famously, bison. By 1920, the European bison was almost extinct. Once to be seen roaming the great continental plain in their thousands, only a handful remained. But with careful management and controlled husbandry in the intervening years, numbers have increased to more than 2,500 in eastern Europe. Several hundred are known to inhabit the park and can readily be seen from the roads and paths.

In 2009, the park celebrated its 600th anniversary. To mark such an auspicious event, the celebrations included an upgrade for many of the facilities here. The Museum of Nature is well worth a visit, and there are four decent hotels with a range of restaurants, cafés and bars. Extensive tourist trails have also been established throughout the park for the walker, horserider and cyclist alike. And children of all ages can pay a visit to the 'real' Grandfather Frost in the 'real' wooden fairy-tale house that he calls home, where he lives with his granddaughter Snyegoruchka, the Snow Maiden. Interestingly, Grandfather Frost is to be found

VISA-FREE BYELOVEZHSKAYA PUSCHA

In 2015 a presidential decree permitted visa-free entry to the park for visits of up to 72 hours, subject to conditions and an application procedure that was at least as complex as the visa application itself! By further decree in January 2018 this period was extended to ten days. See page 54 for further details.

here in full regalia all year round. I met him in April! The reserve is also home to around 4,000 people in scattered communities, most of whose livelihoods are agriculturally based.

Getting there and away The park is located around 70km north of Brest and 20km from the nearest town, Kamenyets. Several buses a day run from Brest to the park gates and back again, both direct and around the houses via Kamenyets and Kamenyuky. The direct service out of Brest and back again means that if time is at a premium, it's possible to head to the park from Brest for a day trip, though a longer stay is to be recommended. There is no transport within the park itself, other than that arranged by official tour operators. As there are small communities within the park it is technically possible (just) to drive your own car around, but the state guards this natural treasure very jealously indeed and there are many red-tape hoops to jump through before a permit is granted. Also, this is border country, so security is high. Every time I've been, lorry loads of frontier guards could regularly be seen driving around. At one point on a licensed drive around the park, we came to the very border itself with barbed wire fencing and armed guards, the road turning sharp left at the very last moment. Even the wild animals don't get to cross back and forth. It's far better to come here with your own vehicle, which you then leave at the car park immediately outside the gates, or else on an organised tour, which can be arranged through staff at the Hotel Intourist in Brest (page 202), or any other agency there. If you want to deal with the arrangements elsewhere in the country, perhaps in Minsk, note that all tourist agencies within Belarus market a number of very comprehensive tours to this and other sites. Someone else then takes care of the driving and the itinerary; you can just sit back, admire the view and take in the sights. Either way, a large sign marks the crossing of the park territory boundary as you pass through the village of Kamenyuky, before the gates to the park proper appear ahead and the road just stops. Cars park to the left of the barriered entry and coaches to the right, and there are souvenir and ticket kiosks here too.

Where to stay and eat This is a really lovely place, with nourishment and regeneration for the soul. All is beautifully calm and quiet, with constant birdsong near and far as the backdrop to your wanderings. The park's three small **hotels** (numbered 1, 2 and 3) and the one outside the park gates but less than 1km away in the village of Kamenyuky (number 4) all date from the Soviet era and were more than a little tired and shabby until they were all upgraded as part of the 600th-anniversary celebrations, although their appearance is still a tad dated. My view is that this adds to the charm of the place. A visit here is all about getting back to nature, and I always find the standard of the facilities to be commensurate with that aim. All of the rooms are neat, clean and with en-suite facilities. For my first visit I had booked a twin room with my travelling companion, but we turned out to be the only guests and were given a room each at no extra charge.

If you're travelling solo and without Russian, the process of getting installed in your pre-booked hotel is challenging. Walk through the barriered gates (you won't be challenged), past the war memorial and towards the large building facing you. This is the restaurant with Hotel Number 3 above. Walk to the left and enter the reception of Hotel Number 4. This is the main reception area for all three of the hotels within the park itself. If you're booked into Hotel Number 3, retrace your steps to enter the door facing you, immediately under the sign for Hotel Number 3. Walk straight down the long corridor to the desk at the end, show the piece of paper you were given in the main reception area, and collect your key. It's as simple as that …

Restaurant and café facilities in the park are all decent. If you're staying in any of three hotels at the park gates, breakfast is taken in Café Sosni, the wooden chalet on the left as you walk from the hotel area. The main restaurant (☉ *noon–midnight daily, closed 1st Mon of the month; $$$*) is the large building you see first as you enter through the gates. It's a cavernous place with an enormous central room on the ground floor and smaller rooms off and upstairs. Dark wood abounds and a constant companion to your dining is piped Russian music. On a March Tuesday evening when I was first here, my companion and I had the large room all to ourselves except for one other family, although we still had to wait an hour after ordering for our dinner to be served. The menu offers such dishes as 'forester's dream salad', 'hunter's sausages', 'royal meat with garnish' and 'stewed wild game with vegetables', though I settled for some variety of cutlet/burger with salad, fries and a delicious mushroom preparation, all of which was not only edible but tasty, perhaps the more so for the wait.

What to see and do
Visitor facilities are collected together at this site just inside the park gates. They include a number of cafés and restaurants, a sauna, swimming pools, bicycle hire and sports courts/pitches for those so inclined. The first-class **Museum of Nature** (*admission BYN3.50, guided tours BYN5 maximum 10 persons*) is also located here, where exhibits are displayed in four halls on the second floor of the building. You might want to visit here first before venturing into the park itself for a general overview, not least because an English audio tour is available for only BYN3.50. There is a commendable level of detail in the displays and the audio guide enables the visitor to dip in and out as preferred. My favourite exhibit is the scale model of the hunting palace built by Alexander III, the fate of which graphically illustrates the ping-pong nature of conflict, statehood and ownership in this part of Europe over the centuries. On the ground floor a video is shown (only in Russian, though) and you can also find here the library, teaching room, informative display boards and a small shop for souvenirs and books, some of them in English. The opening hours for the shop are advertised as 09.00–18.00, but it's all a little hit and miss and depends largely upon whether or not there's anyone around to open up. That said, every staff member is unfailingly helpful and will go the extra mile to offer help and assistance. On my last visit Natasha and I were the only visitors there.

Head out of the museum and walk straight ahead to find the **Valeri animal enclosure** (*admission BYN3*). I've documented elsewhere in this book my disquiet over animals being restricted in pens. The opportunity to see wild creatures up close simply does not justify the denial of their freedom, in my view. Others may see it differently. I first took the 4km circular walk around the cages in 2014 and I found it a very uncomfortable experience. True, there is a wide variety of wildlife to see. Bison, deer and wild boar have sizeable enclosures in which to roam, but others, notably wolf, lynx, racoon, fox and birds of prey had little room to move and all looked decidedly stressed and unhappy when I was there. The animals were pacing up and down, backwards and forwards, never at rest and perpetually anxious. The birds repeatedly battered their wings on the fences around their enclosure. Worst of all was the fate of the two brown bears, who sat morosely on old rubber tyres in their secure metal box measuring just 10m x 5m. It was very sad to witness, and was my only negative experience in this otherwise delightful place. Things were considerably better when I visited in the autumn of 2017, with the smallest cages now empty of their former inmates, though I was unable to ascertain their fate, and I didn't venture as far as the bear cage. The larger compounds were still in use, but the residents at least had a decent amount of space in which to meander.

Perhaps these are more enlightened times. All around is the sound of birdsong and at the right time of year, a cacophony of woodpeckers at work. At the top of the circular walk is an area of swamp beyond the path, and visitors in the spring should take care to avoid stepping on the dozens of frogs that cross at this point. I had never seen blue frogs before, but I did here, in abundance.

Tickets for bus tours, the museum and the Valeri animal enclosure are bought at the kiosks just outside the park gates. **Bus tours** of differing duration are advertised at a range of prices in the region of BYN10, but on my first visit in the spring of 2014 only the Grandfather Frost tour was running, costing BYN8.50. I was feeling suitably festive, so went along for the ride. The audio commentary on the bus is only available in Russian, unfortunately, as is the walking tour to meet Grandfather Frost himself, but even without speaking the language I reckon it would still be worth doing and I enjoyed every minute of it. The ride deep into the forest takes about 20 minutes, before the bus reaches a fenced enclosure where a costumed handmaiden is waiting to escort the party around. There are tacky souvenir chalets at the entrance, as well as a café, and then the tour proper begins. It's all rather drawn out, with endless scenes and carvings from Belarusian folklore for you to see while the handmaiden recounts fairy tales and myths, enthusiastically encouraging audience participation in legend-laden ritual at various points on the walk. But the man himself is there, and when those assembled shout loudly enough, out he comes for a chat and to present the opportunity to be photographed with him. On my tour, when he found out that two Englishmen were in the audience the opportunity for some fun was too good to miss. 'Arsenal!' he shouted, thumbs up, followed by 'Juventus', thumbs down. Finally, after peeking into Snyegoruchka's bedroom and being photographed on the great man's throne, there's a gift for everyone, but you will have to go yourself to find out what it is. The whole experience is a glimpse into the legend, myth, superstition and ritual of the country and even if it's a manufactured and clichéd one, you somehow don't mind. Then on the ride back we saw not only bison and boar in the wild, but also a number of border guards in their natural environment. The tour lasts 2 hours from start to finish.

A number of **bicycle routes** ranging from 10km to 27km in length have been laid out, all clearly marked. Maps are available, as are the services of a guide to lead you around if required. There are also a number of **walking routes** of modest length, including to 'the Tsar's Glade' and 'Forest Mysteries'. A number of the ancient oaks have their own name, including the 'Emperor of the North' and the 'Tsar Oak'. Some of the signposting is in English to help you find them. One of my correspondents describes a pleasing circular walk of around 6km in length from the rear of the Valeri animal enclosure, through the edge of the forest itself and past three pretty ponds. Specialist photographic safaris can also be booked.

Increasingly, the state and its expanding tourism industry are coming to recognise the significance and value of this unique environment. Tour operators within and outside the country are tapping into the growing constituency of wildlife tourists, such that more and more people are getting to know and experience the bounteous riches that are waiting to be discovered here. One time passing through Minsk-2 National Airport, I met a group of around a dozen British travellers who return to the park year on year. They were wary of sharing their experiences too widely, lest the trickle of visitors grows to a deluge. It might just pay to get here sooner rather than later. I love it here and never tire of returning. Whether standing on the Alexander III bridge to watch and listen as the trees sigh in the breeze, crouching at the edge of a lake at dusk under heavy skies as the gods unexpectedly open the clouds for the sun to peep through, embracing the Solitary Oak and feeling the majesty of its spirit and longevity, or sampling samagon at the small Museum of Old Living deep in the forest, there is restorative energy to be felt all around.

KAMENYETS (Камянец/Каменец) This town is located on the road from Brest to the national park and is only 20km or so from its southern boundary. Chronicles show that in 1276, Duke Vladimir Vasilkovich dispatched his architect Olexa to the area to find a suitable location to construct a fortress to defend his lands and house a settlement within its defences. By 1289, its construction had been completed. It was built on the motte and bailey principle though only the tower is now left, the famous **Byelaya Vyezha** (**White Tower**), while the settlement itself grew over time to become the town of Kamenyets as it is today. Sitting atop a mound of earth surrounded by a ditch, this cylindrical tower, 30m high and over 13m in diameter, isn't actually white anymore, but notwithstanding the inaccuracy of the name (which endures to this day), it is a splendid architectural monument in outstanding condition. It's visible from all directions as you approach the town; park at the top of Lenina Street outside the Bel-Maris shop and café (⊕ *10.00–19.00 daily*) if you're travelling under your own steam. Here you will see the statue of the Duke's architect Olexa with attendant bison. The delightful Church of St Simeon behind and to the right is well worth a look. Next cross the road, pausing to view the war memorial, before proceeding into the paved square in front of you, at the head of which stands the tower. It is said that underground passages were built beneath it at the time of original construction leading to the nearby river, presumably as a means of escape in times of attack. Today the White Tower houses a really interesting **museum** ✷ (⊕ *10.00–17.15 Tue–Sun; admission BYN2*). The ticket kiosk is to the right as you enter the square, separate from the tower, and the entrance is through a small door at the bottom of the steps at the base of the tower. The basement and four floors above it house enchanting displays of exhibits, pictures and information boards, including a model of the fortress as originally built. The renovations, both inside and out, have been done extremely well. As in so many museums and places of historical interest in this country, we were the only visitors when I was last here, and an attendant followed us the whole way round. A visit to this lovely museum is highly recommended, either during your stay in the national park or as an excursion from Brest.

STRUVE GEODETIC ARC (Геадэзічная Дуга Струвэ/Геодезическая Дуга Струве) For those with a penchant either for ticking items off a list or for Fiennesian exploration (perhaps both), Brest oblast has evidence of this impressive 19th-century wonder of geometrical surveying in three locations. Between 1816 and 1855, scientist and mathematician Friedrich Georg Wilhelm Struve (originally of German extraction but based in Russia) conducted a series of surveys along the line of the present 26th meridian extending south to the Black Sea from Norway. Acting under the patronage of Tsar Alexander I of Russia and with the intention of determining as precisely as possible the size, shape and circumference of the planet, Struve laid out a chain of 258 triangulation points over a distance of 2,820km. Thirty-four of the original points were added to the UNESCO List of World Heritage Sites in 2005, five of which are to be found in Belarus. Spread over ten modern-day countries, the 34 listed points are marked by small monuments of differing design, size and shape, mostly in isolated rural areas, though in Belarus each monument is the same: an inscribed, black rectangular monolith topped with a sphere representing the globe. They are not easy to locate and even more difficult to access. Geocaching it isn't, but it's still fun to track them down. Three of the five can be found in the Ivanova district of Brest oblast, the other two being sited in the districts of Oshmyany and Zelva in Grodno oblast. For further information, go to the informative Russian website w struve.by, which has useful photographs as well as precise co-ordinates for the location of each point.

ELSEWHERE The territory of Brest oblast is rich in culture, with around 120 historical parks and estates and over 2,000 buildings and monuments of historical interest. Among the oldest of the sites is the settlement of **Beryestye**, which has buildings dating from the 11th and 12th centuries, while many churches are worthy of note, including the Roman Catholic church in the original 'Belarusian Gothic' style in the village of **Ishkold** (Baranovichy district), the Roman Catholic Renaissance church in the village of **Chyernovchytsy** (Brest district), the Monastery of the Cartesian Order in **Beryezha** and the Church of St George in the village of **Synkovichy** (Lunynyets district). Also of interest are the part-ruined remains of the 17th- to 18th-century Sapyegazh Palace in **Ruzhany**, with its imposing façade of columns and elegant galleries. The village of **Kossava** also has a spectacular ruined castle, along with a museum dedicated to the life of Tadeusz Kościuszko, a Belarusian-Polish aristocrat born near here who fought with George Washington in the American War of Independence, and later became a citizen of the United States.

FOLLOW US

Use **#belarus** to share your adventures using this guide with us – we'd love to hear from you.

 BradtTravelGuides
 @BradtGuides & @NigelRoberts23
 @bradtguides
 bradtguides
 bradtguides

Brest City and Oblast   OUTSIDE BREST

4

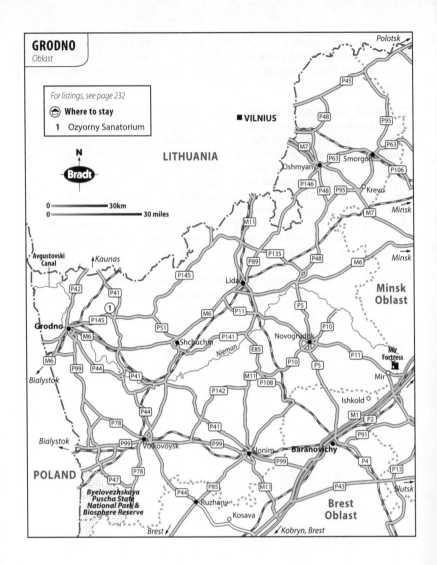

For listings, see page 232

GRODNO
Oblast

For listings, see page 232

⊖ Where to stay
1 Ozyorny Sanatorium

N
Bradt
0 ————— 30km
0 ————— 30 miles

POLOTSK

VILNIUS

LITHUANIA

P45
P48
P95
P63
M7
P63 Smorgon
Oshmyany P106
P146 Krevo
P48 P95
M7 Minsk

M11
P135
P89 P48 M6 Minsk

Avgustovski
Canal
Kaunas
P42 P145
P41
P145
Lida
P89
Grodno
M6
M6 P51 M6 P11
Shchuchin P141 P5
P99 P44 Nieman E85
Bialystok P41 M11 P108
P44
P78 P142
Bialystok P99 P41
Volkovoysk P99
POLAND P78
P47
Byelovezhskaya
Puscha State
National Park &
Biosphere Reserve
P44
Brest Ruzhany
Kosava

Minsk
Oblast

Novogrudok P10
P11
P10 P5 Mir
Fortress
Mir
Ishkold
M1 P2
P91
Slonim Baranovichy
P99 P4 P13
Slutsk
M11 P43 Brest
Oblast
Kobryn, Brest

5

Grodno City and Oblast
Гродна/Гродно

Telephone code 152

The region of Grodno is situated in the northwest of Belarus and has borders with both Poland and Lithuania. The administrative and cultural centre of the region is the city of Grodno itself, with a population of 365,610. Situated 278km west of Minsk and just 294km east of Warsaw, it is only 20km from Poland and 40km from Lithuania. Records indicate that the city has been in existence for almost 900 years. Not surprisingly, given its location, it has a significant Polish and Lithuanian heritage.

The greatest wealth of the Grodno region consists of the leafy groves forming the magnificent tract of natural forestation that occupies more than one-third of its territory to the northeast and southeast of the city, either side of the historic town of Lida. Comprising both coniferous and mixed woodland, it is pleasing to see that pockets of the ancient virgin forests that once covered this whole continent have survived more or less intact here.

This is also a land rich in lakes, large and small, but all of them picturesque, with a reputation for crystal-clear waters. The renowned Avgustovski Canal also runs through the northwestern corner of the region for 22km on its meandering way to Poland. The charms of the canal and the many leisure services attendant upon it are promoted vigorously by the local tourism industry, which is particularly well geared up for incoming visitors from abroad.

The geographical proximity of the oblast to western Europe is not of itself the reason for this. Were it so, then Brest would be similarly advanced in its preparation for foreign visitors (and it is not). The real reason, acknowledged by the tourism industry and confirmed by increased visitor numbers, is that since the passing of a presidential decree in 2016, it has been possible (subject to conditions) to visit much of the oblast visa-free for up to five days, a period that has now been extended to ten days (see box, page 228). There is little doubt that the key motivation for these initiatives was the internationally marketable site of interest that is the section of the Avgustovski Canal passing through the oblast.

The history of the region, characterised first by conflict and then by the ensuing peaceful coexistence of Baltic and Slavonic peoples, has left its mark on the territory. The original fortress of Grodno, built on the banks of the Nieman River in the 11th century, has now evolved into an elegant, thriving, bustling, energetic and cosmopolitan modern city, where more examples of Classical architecture have been preserved than in any other city of Belarus. Indeed, the national state government has declared the historical centre of Grodno a special architectural zone under the protection and jurisdiction of the state itself. Of the country's major cities, it is perhaps Vitebsk and Grodno that best lend themselves to an appreciation of their charms, apparent if you meander through the streets at a leisurely pace, gazing at the richness of the buildings that surround you.

There are also many fine examples of architecture in the region, most notably the beautiful 16th-century fortress of Mir, the dramatic ruins of Novogrudok's 14th-century castle and a number of unusual military churches. During the 15th and 16th centuries, many of the Eastern Orthodox churches were required to serve the dual purposes of worship and as places of fortified refuge against the attacks of aggressors, and many of those that are still standing look more like towered castles. The best examples of these fortress-churches can be seen in the villages of Synkovichy (built 1407) and Murovanka (1524). In Smorgon, the 16th-century Calvinist cathedral is well worth a visit. And for students of topography and geometrical surveying, two of the points of the Struve Geodetic Arc (page 222) included in the five within Belarus on the UNESCO World Heritage List are to be found within the oblast, in the districts of Oshmyany and Zelva.

In short, this is a land full of ancient towns and villages that repay the close attention of admiring visitors many times over. Hand in hand with the easing of visa regulations here is a consequential (and significant) improvement in the quality of tourism services. There is a palpable change in mindset on the part of those charged with promoting tourism, from strategists at the top down to the personnel who will be your direct contacts for services. My ministry sources tell me that the Grodno experience is now being held up as best practice, and other regions are encouraged to observe and to learn and to implement new ways of marketing and promotion.

HISTORY

The town of Grodno is believed to have been founded as an important strategic, military and trade centre on the northwestern border of Kievan Rus, although evidence of Palaeolithic settlements dating back over 10,000 years has been discovered in the vicinity of the modern city. Between 1000BC and AD1000, the territory is thought to have been inhabited by confederations of Baltic tribes, but by the middle of the 11th century, the Slavic Krivichi and Dryhavichy tribes had begun a policy of expansionist colonisation in the area. It gained its first mention in the *Primary Chronicle* in 1127 and it is clear that by this time, the geographical location of this Slavic settlement at the crossroads of many trading routes had enabled it to attain the status of capital of an independent principality, possibly as long ago as the 10th century.

Economic and cultural development was swift, such that later in the 12th century the city had its own architectural school, as evidenced by the splendid Kolozhskaya Church of St Boris and St Hleb (page 237). By 1280, Grodno had been subsumed into the mighty Grand Duchy of Lithuania. Indeed, under the rule of Grand Duke Vitautis, from 1376 to 1392, the town acquired equal status with Vilnius as a second state capital. Conflict with knights of the Teutonic Order lasted into the 15th century and it was from here that Vitautis led the forces of the duchy to victory in the famous Battle of Grunwald. Even today, this battle is still regarded as a major landmark in the development of modern Belarus. Then in 1496, charter rights of self-determination under Magdeburg Law were granted. The King of Poland and Grand Duke of Lithuania Stefan Batory established his main residence in Grodno during the 16th century for more than ten years. His influence can be widely seen today in much of the city's architecture. From the second half of the 17th century, in the time of the influential Polish-Lithuanian Commonwealth, meetings of sejms (a branch of government with delegated powers) were regularly held here, as a result of which the town's influence on regional and national politics grew. The last ever of the commonwealth's sejms took place in 1793, before the final Rzeczpospolitan monarch Stanislas Augustus Poniatowski resigned the crown in 1795, leading to the Third Partition of Poland. Thereafter, the city passed into Russian hands, in which it served a key municipal function as the seat of a local administration, one of the most advanced in the whole empire. In 1859, the Warsaw to St Petersburg railway was completed through Grodno, which thus became an important junction on the line.

The start of the 20th century saw much revolutionary activity at key locations throughout the empire, most notably the revolution of 1905. At the same time, Belarusian nationalism was developing. Grodno played its part, with the first Belarusian periodicals being printed here. The city and its environs were once more a war zone during the 1914–18 conflict and German forces were in occupation from 1915. As a consequence of outrageously callous (though perhaps necessary?) political expediency on the part of Lenin to end Russian involvement in the war, these territories were formally ceded to Germany by the Bolsheviks under the Treaty of Brest-Litovsk in 1918, following which the first Belarusian nation state was allowed to come into existence.

It did not endure for long. Between 1919 and 1921, the area changed hands many times. Units of the Red Army established Soviet power on two separate occasions, with claims to sovereignty also being made by the newly created Polish state and by Lithuania. Then finally, the Riga Peace Treaty of 1921 incorporated Grodno region into Poland. The city of Bialystok, 100km to the southwest, became the capital of the region and Grodno's economic significance fell into decline, although it had risen again by 1930 with the growth of the Jewish population. Military units stationed here were pressed into action when the Nazis invaded Poland in 1939, then when the country was shamefully carved up by Nazi Germany and the USSR under the terms of the notorious Molotov–Ribbentrop Pact of Non-Aggression, a significant engagement took place in and around the city between the Red Army and Polish troops, as the Russians marched westward to establish a buffer to protect the sovereignty of Soviet national borders. Fighting was brutal and bloody. To this very day, each side continues to deny the claims of the other in terms of actual losses, although one fact has now been established without ambiguity. As accepted at long last, thousands of Polish officers who had been taken prisoner were subsequently murdered by the NKVD acting under Stalin's direct orders and buried in mass graves, most notably those discovered in relatively modern times in the forests of Katyn. When Grodno passed into Soviet hands as part of the Belarusian Soviet Socialist Republic, much of the Polish population was dispersed elsewhere within the USSR, before the city once more fell to the Germans in 1941 after the start of Operation Barbarossa. Liberation by the Red Army in July 1944 came too late to save Grodno's Jews, the majority of whom died in Nazi concentration camps. At the end of the war, Soviet sovereignty was restored. This endured until the breakup of the Soviet Union, when Grodno became one of the key cities of the newly established nation state of Belarus.

Today, the grace and charm of the historical centre conceals a competitive commercialism in the wider area. The oblast is probably the best developed in the entire country in terms of industrialisation: components of buses, tractors, combine harvesters, cars, agricultural machinery, radios and television sets, plastics, fertilisers, manmade fibres and threads, furniture, textiles, shoes and tobacco goods are all produced here in significant quantity, while a favourable climate and fertile soil have helped to promote agriculture as a key component of the local economy.

All in all, this is a very classy city indeed. It's hip and sassy, but at the same time, relaxed and comfortable. Even the high-rise suburbs have a certain elegance. I have stayed in crumbling Soviet-style apartment blocks in five of the six major cities and the urban scene here is by far the most attractive. Certainly, the concrete is still crumbling, but the design and exterior of the blocks is a cut above, with wide swathes of tree-lined parkland in-between. I was with my Belarusian travelling companion on her very first visit to Grodno. We've covered much of the country together and she was very impressed indeed. And like everywhere else, impressing the locals is no mean task. And it is also a truly multi-cultural city, renowned for its tradition of tolerance and inclusivity. Refuge has been given to Tatars, Jews and Prussians (among others) in times gone by. Today, communities of over 80 different nationalities exist somewhere in the oblast. One-third of the population classes itself as being Polish or of Polish descent, while there are also significant Russian, Ukrainian and Lithuanian communities. It's no surprise to find, then, that the city is home to the biannual Festival of National Cultures in June, when the streets become one giant stage for the performing arts. Anyone lucky enough to be in the city when the festival is on has a treat in store. As well as performances, dishes of many national cuisines are in evidence, along with national crafts, dances and music in different languages. There are fireworks and ornamental water displays. The grand finale takes place in the town's central square and continues until dawn. It's a most impressive spectacle. In the autumn of 2017 it was my good fortune to be in the city on the day it celebrated its 890th birthday, with flags, bunting, street theatre, performing arts, craft stalls and pop-up cafés filling the streets. And of course, the statue of Lenin was still there to hold court, the old Bolshevik maintaining his steely gaze while all below was a riot of colour, noise and partying.

GETTING THERE AND AWAY

BY AIR The airport is situated 18km southeast of the city. It has all the facilities necessary to handle national and international traffic, but although state airline Belavia operates charter flights to destinations in Russia and further afield (for

VISA-FREE GRODNO

As of 1 January 2018, visitors are allowed access to Grodno oblast without a visa for up to ten days, subject to a long list of preconditions. Everything the visitor needs to know about coming to Grodno visa-free is contained within the comprehensive English pages of the informative website w grodnovisafree.by. Like so many things in this country the procedure is not without complexity and is subject to certain conditions. For example, there are geographical limits to the area within the oblast covered by the regime. Critically, you will also need to book a package of tourism services in advance. Visits are largely confined to the western half of the region, though this does include Avgustovski Canal. Only two land crossing points originally permitted entry into the country (one in Poland and one in Lithuania) when the regime was first announced by presidential decree in 2016, but a subsequent decree increased the number of entry points with effect from January 2018. The list of 'dos, don'ts and must haves' before you even get here (and then when you arrive, in terms of things to produce at the border) is depressingly long. But do persevere as there is much to see and experience here, and the acts of successfully conquering the bureaucratic monolith involved in planning your trip, getting here and then getting home again are monumental achievements all of their own. Even if you don't need or wish to avail yourself of the visa-free concession, the website still contains a mine of useful tourist information. See page 54 for more details on where you can find information regarding the visa situation.

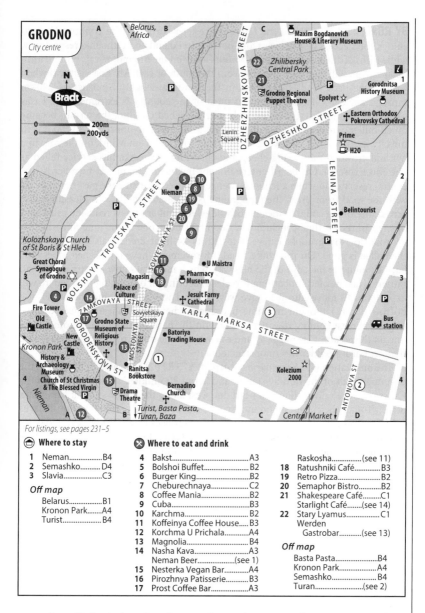

GRODNO
City centre

Belarus, Africa

DZHERZHINSKOVA STREET

Maxim Bogdanovich
House & Literary Museum

Zhilibersky
Central Park

Grodno Regional
Puppet Theatre

Epolyet

Gorodnitsa
History Museum

OZHESHKO STREET

Eastern Orthodox
Pokrovsky Cathedral

Lenin
Square

Prime
H2O

Nieman

LENINA STREET

Belintourist

Kolozhskaya Church
of St Boris & St Hleb

BOLSHOYA TROITSKAYA STREET

SOVYETSKAYA ST

Great Choral
Synagogue
of Grodno

U Maistra

Pharmacy
Museum

Jesuit Farny
Cathedral

Magasin

Palace of
Culture

ZAMKOVAYA STREET

Fire Tower

Sovyetskaya
Square

KARLA MARKSA STREET

Old
Castle

GORODENSKOVA ST

Grodno State
Museum of
Religious
History

New
Castle

MOSTOVAYA STREET

Batoriya
Trading House

Bus
station

Kronon Park

History &
Archaeology
Museum

Ranitsa
Bookstore

Kolezium
2000

ANTONOVA ST

Church of St Christmas
& The Blessed Virgin

Nieman

Drama
Theatre

Bernadino
Church

Turist, Basta Pasta,
Turan, Baza

Central Market

For listings, see pages 231–5

Where to stay

1	Neman	B4
2	Semashko	D4
3	Slavia	C3

Off map

Belarus	B1
Kronon Park	A4
Turist	B4

Where to eat and drink

4	Bakst	A3
5	Bolshoi Buffet	B2
6	Burger King	B2
7	Cheburechnaya	C2
8	Coffee Mania	B2
9	Cuba	B3
10	Karchma	B2
11	Koffeinya Coffee House	B3
12	Korchma U Prichala	A4
13	Magnolia	B4
14	Nasha Kava	A3
	Neman Beer	(see 1)
15	Nesterka Vegan Bar	A4
16	Pirozhnya Patisserie	B3
17	Prost Coffee Bar	A3

	Raskosha	(see 11)
18	Ratushniki Café	B3
19	Retro Pizza	B2
20	Semaphor Bistro	B2
21	Shakespeare Café	C1
	Starlight Café	(see 14)
22	Stary Lyamus	C1
	Werden Gastrobar	(see 13)

Off map

Basta Pasta	B4
Kronon Park	A4
Semashko	B4
Turan	(see 2)

example, to Turkey), there have been no internal commercial passenger arrivals or departures within Belarus for some time now.

BY TRAIN The train station (*37 Budenyi St; ☏ 73 44 41*) is situated 2km northeast of the city centre. Four trains a day arrive from and depart for Minsk (a one-way ticket starts at BYN12). Daytime journeys are at least 5 hours in length, with night-time services significantly longer. The service to Brest and Vitebsk is much less frequent, but one consequence of the easing of visa regulations here is that more trains and buses than before cross the border from Poland and Lithuania.

BY ROAD Tucked away in the far northwestern corner of the country, Grodno enjoys good access by road west and north into Poland and Lithuania respectively, while Minsk (due east) is less than 4 hours away on the M6 motorway. From within Belarus, you will approach the city from the south or east. My first visit was when I drove the back roads from Brest in the south, a delightful journey of 240km through ancient villages. Given that most of the country is extremely flat, I was surprised to find that 100km or so before I reached Grodno, the terrain became much hillier, with extensive panoramic vistas opening up unexpectedly. So it is in the city itself. My last visit was also by road, this time from Minsk on the M6, in a hot and crowded minibus (a cheap and cheerful marshrutka bus service billed as 'the M6 Express'). On-board entertainment included a bumpy U-turn across the central reservation when a fellow passenger realised we had gone past her stop. As with the road from Brest, the topography is moderately hilly, with pleasing views across the rolling countryside on both sides. A number of new roadside cafés have opened in recent times, including a decent 24-hour one at the junction with the P5 road to Novogrudok. I haven't tested its 24-hour credentials yet, but I hear the coffee is good. On this route, road improvements have established a periodic hard shoulder at the edge of the highway, which means it's now a faster drive than hitherto. Just be alert: oncoming vehicles executing an overtaking manoeuvre will expect you to move into it to give way. When I was once behind the wheel of a borrowed car, I thought my time had come when 500m ahead appeared three wagons abreast coming towards me, one on the hard shoulder on the other side, one on the adjacent carriageway and one on my side of the road. It was just as well that my hard shoulder was unobstructed …

The bus station (*7A Krasnoarmeiskaya St;* \75 82 02) is located in the east of the city, due south of the railway station and about 20 minutes' walk from the centre. Cross over the railway line and head due west along the arrow-straight Karl Marx Street. Today, the cheapest and most convenient way to get around within Belarus is by means of the intercity bus routes: many services leave Grodno every day for destinations in Russia, Ukraine, Lithuania, the Czech Republic, Poland and Latvia, stopping off at the major centres of population within the country *en route*. At least one bus an hour leaves for Minsk, with a one-way ticket starting at BYN16. The proximity of the Lithuanian border means that the daily morning bus departing Kaunas, where the airport there is served by budget airline Ryanair, is one option for cheap travel into Belarus, with a one-way ticket costing around BYN40.

GETTING AROUND

ON FOOT Unlike Brest, Grodno's attractions are more widely spread over a larger geographical area, although it is possible to cover a good proportion of the main sites in one walkable sector of the town (see box, page 241). Unusually for a Belarusian city, the urban scene is particularly hilly, especially in the centre. Elsewhere, only Vitebsk matches its topography. This gives it an airy, lofty feel, with big skies and surprisingly impressive panoramas when you least expect them, especially from the northern bank of the river. This does mean that walking has its dividends.

BY BUS AND TROLLEYBUS Buses and trolleybuses are rather old and generally very full, but they are a great way to see the city and you will feel like a local in the process. A trolleybus ride is one of those experiences that is so totally eastern European, and very evocative. Best of all, they are incredibly cheap: a single ticket anywhere in the city will you set you back no more than BYN0.45, a handful of pence only. Tickets are available from the driver or at kiosks located at many stops. Just don't forget to punch your ticket when you get on. Checks are frequent from plain-clothes inspectors and fines for violations are rigidly enforced.

BY MARSHRUTKA Travel by marshrutka is also an option. The price is a little higher but, at BYN0.90, still very cheap. Just expect to be crammed in and not to have the most comfortable of journeys. Either pay the driver when you get in, or else pass your cash over the heads of your fellow passengers if it's really crowded. A tap on the shoulder is most likely to be the next passenger behind you doing the same thing. If you sit on the front seat, you will be expected to act as the conductor! Children travel free, as long as they sit on an adult's lap.

BY TAXI As everywhere else, cabs are readily available for more bespoke journeys. Expect to pay around BYN11 for a 15-minute ride. On local networks dial 107, 135, 155, 156, 158, 161, 163, 181, 183 or 252 for service.

TOURIST INFORMATION

The city now has a **tourist information centre** [229 D1] (*38 Ozheshko St;* \ *77 36 06;* e *grodnortss@gmail.com;* w *tourgrodno.by;* ⊕ *09.00–13.00 & 14.00–18.00 Mon–Fri*), though sadly, sharper marketing has not yet addressed the absurdity of it being closed over lunchtime and at weekends. Subject to this glaring omission, however, Grodno is easily the best prepared of all Belarusian cities to welcome visitors from abroad, with the exception of Minsk itself. Information display units with comprehensive notes in English are to be found throughout the city centre. At every site of interest there is a large board with a barcode for you to download key information if your phone has the technology, a project funded by the European Union. You will also be able to buy maps, postcards and some guides (mostly in Russian) from the kiosks present in each hotel, but again, hours of opening are whimsical and wholly unpredictable. The state tourist agency **Belintourist** has a branch office at 13 Lenina Street [229 D2] (\ *75 04 01, 77 33 99*), where the helpful staff will be ready to arrange excursions for you, and there are several other agencies in town offering similar services.

WHERE TO STAY

Despite its charm and the beauty of the architecture, Grodno was not (until quite recently) a great city to find attractive hotels; then came the Semashko, the Kronon Park and the Slavia. If you have a yearning for it, you can still sample the clichéd experience of knowing what it was like to travel around the Soviet Union in its heyday at the Turist or the Belarus, but if you can afford to go upmarket, then your stay in this delightful city is going to be the better for it. And a stay at the Neman is a decent compromise between the two ends of the scale. For a different experience altogether, sample the clean air and calm of the Ozyorny Sanatorium, 30km outside the city.

UPMARKET

🏠 **Kronon Park Hotel** [229 A4] (15 rooms) Pishki Park, Pishki district; \ 73 98 00; e info@ kronon.by; w kronon.by. Situated on the western fringes of the city in beautiful woodland, this 2-storey boutique hotel is a real charmer, its

picturesque location easily compensating for the lack of proximity to the main sights in town. The exterior is pseudo-Baroque & inside, the décor is sumptuous & elegant. The bedrooms are well furnished & benefit from all mod cons. In terms of facilities, it gives the Semashko a good run for its money & there is also a transfer shuttle to the railway station. Like the Semashko, the restaurant is worthy of a visit on its own (see opposite). It's rated by many as one of the best hotels in the country, & in every respect the standards to be found here are high, though expect to pay a premium for everything. **$$$$**

⌂ **Semashko** [229 D4] (41 rooms) 10 Antonova St; ☎ 75 02 95, 75 02 99; e sem-hotel@tut.by; w hotel-semashko.ru. Located close to both bus & train stations & just a 10–15min walk from the sights, this privately owned hotel (the first to be opened in the city) offers an altogether different experience. The décor is shiny, fresh & bright (if just a little on the gaudy side; check out the bridal suites!) & the service extremely slick. Opened in 2003, with facilities spread over 3 buildings, all of which are equipped to Western standards & well appointed, following an extended renovation in 2008–09. These inc a very good restaurant (see opposite), café, bars, swimming pool & sauna, free Wi-Fi & on-site parking. It's very popular with wedding parties, so check ahead as to what is going on here before you arrive. The excellent service so in evidence at this hotel extends to the preparation of picnics for guests leaving very early in the morning on tours out of town. The hotel website incorporates useful English pages on the city's tourist sites. **$$$$**

⌂ **Slavia** [229 C3] (24 rooms) 1 Molodyozhnaya St; ☎ 77 35 35; w hotel-slavia.by. Opened in 2009, this hotel's real selling point is the excellent location, close to many of the city's facilities & historical sights. Everything on offer here also matches what's available at the Semashko (excluding pool & sauna), inc picnics for departing visitors, although the restaurant has not been tested. **$$$$**

MID-RANGE

⌂ **Belarus** [229 B1] (189 rooms) 1 Kalinovskova St; ☎ 74 07 84. The city's biggest hotel & like so many in this country, another concrete block. Quite frankly it's a grim & dismal place. The lobby is awful: it's like the waiting area of a bus station, only with less charm. But it's an OK alternative if everywhere else is booked up.

Just keep your expectations low. The bus & railway stations are both around 2km away. **$$$**

✴ ⌂ **Neman** [229 B4] (66 rooms) 8 Stefan Batory St; ☎ 79 17 00; e info@hotel-neman.by; w hotel-neman.by. My favourite hotel in the city for its all-round ticking of boxes. It lacks the charm of the upmarket places, but the location is good (on the edge of Sovyetskaya Sq), the décor is bright & shiny, the staff are cheerful & friendly (many speak good English), the beer restaurant is decent (see opposite) & the beds are the most comfortable I've slept in on my travels in Belarus. Services inc parking front & rear, free Wi-Fi, sauna, spa, ticket agency, restaurants (⊕ noon–midnight Sun–Thu, noon–02.00 Sat & Sun), bar & ATM. Excellent value for money. I reckon the hotel & beer restaurant combo make for a good choice. **$$$**

⌂ **Turist** [229 B4] (129 rooms) 63 Yanki Kupala Av; ☎ 54 57 96; w tourist.grodno.by. Located 3km southeast of the city centre (3km from the railway station & 1.5km from the bus station) in a suburb across the river, this is another drab & gloomy 1980s concrete box. All rooms are adequately appointed & clean, but tired. There is a decent range of facilities inc currency exchange, spa & solarium, restaurant, café & snack bar. **$$$**

OUT OF TOWN

✴ ⌂ **Ozyorny Sanatorium** [map, page 224] (350 rooms) 231753 Ozyory; ☎ 79 85 00; e ozerny@ozerny.by; w ozerny.by. The global rise in health & well-being tourism has not passed Belarus by. This modern complex, built in 2003 & 30km east of the city on the P41 road, is one of a growing number of facilities offering a full range of medical treatments & wellness programmes. As an alternative to a stay in a city centre hotel, it also works if you just want a room & a meal. There's a shuttle bus to & from the train station in Grodno, & the informative website tells you all you need to know about facilities & prices. Everything is bookable online. I can't speak for the treatments, but at BYN60 for a comfortable bed & a tasty breakfast, I was more than satisfied. All rooms are well appointed, while the peace, calm & fresh air of the place come free. **$$$**

✗ WHERE TO EAT AND DRINK

Now that the pedestrianisation of Sovyetskaya Street is complete there's a decent choice of eateries in town, while three of the hotels (Semashko, Kronon Park and

Neman) have restaurants that are worth a visit. Explore the main drag at leisure, starting at the Drama Theatre and continuing up past the House of Culture on your left, then down to the bottom of the pedestrianised area. Take a look down the side streets if you have time. There are many decent places to take in a meal, hang out for a beer or two, or to watch the city go about its business over a coffee. Some I have tried for myself, while others came recommended when I asked among local people in town.

RESTAURANTS

✳ ✖ **Bakst** [229 A3] 21 Zamkovaya St; ✆ 888 43 50; e bakstgrodno@gmail.com; w bakst. rest; ⏱ noon–midnight Sun–Thu, noon–01.30 Fri–Sat. This sprawling restaurant at the bottom of Zamkovaya, near to the fire station & opposite the Choral Synagogue, only opened in February 2017. Inside all is themed on the work of Grodno's own Leon Bakst, the renowned artist & theatrical designer. This is an elegant eatery, with a menu of mixed European cuisine (including a number of Jewish dishes) to match. The outside terrace has decent views across the river & there is live music at w/ends. Background jazz during my visit was just a little too loud, but this is a trifling criticism. **$$$$**

✳ ✖ **Karchma** [229 B2] 31 Sovyetskaya St; ✆ 74 35 63; ⏱ 10.00–midnight daily. Centrally located at the bottom of Sovyetskaya St, this is one of the best in town. Hip & crowded, it's a fine venue for a night out & the locals love it. The rustic décor is tastefully done & the whole package, from appearance to ambience, is classy. European & Belarusian cuisine is served & the standard is good (with decent service to match), but do get there early or you won't secure a table. **$$$$**

✖ **Korchma U Prichala** [229 A4] 14 Zavodskaya St; ✆ 74 20 45; ⏱ noon–midnight Mon–Fri, noon–02.00 Sat–Sun. Probably the best thing going for this place is the riverside location & the summer terrace. The menu is Belarusian & European, but you can probably eat better elsewhere in town. That said, there are few better places for a cold beer on a warm evening. Live music at the w/end. Do bear in mind that smoking is permitted here. **$$$$**

✳ ✖ **Kronon Park** [229 A4] Pishki Park, Pishki district; ✆ 73 98 00; w kronon.by; ⏱ 07.00–10.30, 12.30–16.00 & 18.00–01.00 Mon–Fri, 07.00–01.00 Sat–Sun. The restaurant at the hotel of the same name (page 231) is a delight. Excellent food & service are complemented by the gorgeous setting in forested parkland, though you will pay for the privilege. If the weather is right,

dine alfresco on the terrace. Everything here is sophisticated & understated. The only downside is the distance from the city centre, but the overall quality here more than compensates for the need to take a cab ride. **$$$$**

✖ **Semashko** [229 D4] 10 Antonova St; ✆ 75 02 80; w hotel-semashko.ru; ⏱ 07.00–02.00 daily. The restaurant at the hotel of the same name (see opposite) serves Belarusian & European cuisine. All is slick, classy & stylish but, as with Kronon Park, you will pay the corresponding premium. **$$$$**

✖ **Stary Lyamus** [229 C1] 1A Dzherzhinskova St; ✆ 77 09 65; e markiza_todo@mail.ru; w markiza.by; ⏱ noon–02.00 daily. Situated right on the edge of Zhilibersky Park & close to Lenin Sq, this serves Belarusian & European dishes to the accompaniment of live music & floor shows. Standards (both cooking & service) are very good, while the interior (pseudo-rustic) is relatively well done & pleasing on the eye. It gets noisy after 22.00 when the nightclub crowd arrives & it's used by national tourist agencies (presumably to give their foreign clients a taste of 'Old Belarus'). This is a good endorsement in terms of quality, but might not be an attractive feature if you particularly want the company of locals. That said, the quality factor edges it for me, so give it a try. **$$$$**

✖ **Basta Pasta** [229 B4] 35 Pobyedy St; ✆ 310 03 10; ⏱ noon–midnight daily. Acceptable décor, helpful staff, decent pizza, pasta & sushi. You can do better in town than this, but it does the job for calories & sustenance if you're clubbing at the adjoining Baza nightclub (page 235). **$$$**

✳ ✖ **Neman Beer Restaurant** [229 B4] 8 Stefan Batory St; ✆ 79 17 73; w hotel-neman. by; ⏱ noon–midnight Sun–Thu, noon–02.00 Fri–Sat. The beer restaurant at the hotel of the same name (see opposite) is another of my favourites. If staying at the hotel, turn right out of the front door & right again, then down the steps. Soft lighting, elevator music & rustic décor with a surfeit of dark wood panelling greet the visitor but don't be put off, not even by the screens showing sport & cartoons. The staff are attentive, prices are good & all is relaxed here. After a long day on the streets the ambience is welcoming, the beer is cold & you can later fold straight into one of the most comfortable beds in the country if this is your hotel. Last time I chose the pork steak in a cream, mushroom & garlic sauce with fries & sauerkraut. My travelling companion went for fillet steak. Neither of us were disappointed. **$$$**

* **✕ Nesterka Vegan Bar** [229 A4] 35 Mostovaya St; m 33 336 18 71; e nesterka. bar@gmail.com; f @nesterkabar; ☺ 16.00–midnight Mon–Thu, 16.00–02.00 Fri, 14.00–02.00 Sat, 14.00–midnight Sun. The only vegan restaurant in Grodno when I was last in the city. Located at the Drama Theatre, the menu is ambitious & the food beautifully presented. **$$$**

✕ Retro Pizza [229 B2] 31 Sovyetskaya St; \74 00 56; ☺ noon–01.00 Sun–Thu, noon–02.00 Fri–Sat. Right next door to the Karchma & sharing the same address. The fare is standard pizza-style, but tasty. It's a useful consolation prize if you intended to eat at the Karchma but got there too late for a table. Pizzas are made to order from a wide variety of toppings. I especially rate the 'Mexicana' here, & a good range of salads, pasta & meat dishes is also available. The décor is relatively pleasing on the eye, although just a little too orange for my liking. The low ceiling gives it a vault-like appearance, so it can be noisy, but the tables are thoughtfully laid out. Service is understated & efficient. **$$$**

✕ Turan [229 B4] 15a Klyetskava Av; \51 00 51; e reyn.grodno@mail.ru; w turan.by; ☺ noon–02.00 daily. Located in a southeastern suburb, this newish venue is an OK bet if you're staying in this part of town, but probably isn't worth a trip out if you're not. The pizzas are decent, though. **$$$**

* **✕ Bolshoi Buffet** [229 B2] 18 Sovyetskaya St; \77 17 80; e bigbuffet@mail.ru; w bigbuffet. by; ☺ noon–midnight daily. Located on the top floor of the Nieman department store on Sovyetskaya, I love this place. OK, so haute cuisine it may not be, but it's cheap & it's certainly very cheerful. A hot dish, salad & a soft drink from the self-service buffet costs around BYN6, so for a pit stop mid-meander along Sovyetskaya it can't be beaten. Check out the 'how it works' plan on the website for a giggle; it's in Russian but the graphics tell all you need to know! **$$**

CAFÉS & BARS

In addition to those below, other places I've spotted on Sovyetskaya but never had time to try include **Ratushniki Café** at the top end, close to the cab rank [229 B3] (☺ 09.00–21.00 Mon–Fri, 10.00–19.00 Sat–Sun), **Pirozhnya Patisserie** a short way down [229 B2] (☺ 09.00–21.00 daily) & **Semaphor Bistro**, a little further down still & on the same side [229 B2] (\45 02 48; ☺ noon–midnight Sun–Thu, noon–01.00 Fri–Sat). Give them a try & let me know. There's even a **Burger King** [229 B2] here now. I couldn't possibly comment.

☕ **Cheburechnaya** [229 C2] 1 Ozheshko St; \77 13 48; ☺ 10.00–22.00 Mon–Sat, noon–22.00 Sun. Just around the corner at the bottom of Sovyetskaya St, you'll find cheap fast food, snacks & coffee here.

☕ **Coffee Mania** [229 B2] 31 Sovyetskaya St; \72 34 11; ☺ 09.00–21.00 Sun–Thu, 09.00–23.00 Fri–Sat. Sharing the same address as the Karchma restaurant & Retro pizzeria. It's sandwiched between the two.

☕ **Cuba** [229 B3] 12 Kaluchinskaya St; \77 33 00; ☺ noon–23.00 daily. Located just off Sovyetskaya St. I feel I've missed out by not sampling the coffee & cocktails here, because whenever I ask for a recommendation in Grodno, this is always the first name I hear. Opened in 2013 & now very popular. Give it a try & tell me what I'm missing.

☕ **Koffeinya Coffee House** [229 B3] 5 Sovyetskaya St; m 29 781 02 53; ☺ 10.00–23.00 daily. This small coffee bar next to Raskosha (see opposite) is easy to miss, but it's one for the coffee enthusiast (especially if you want to avoid crowds).

♀ **Magnolia** [229 B4] 31 Mostovaya St; \72 00 87; ☺ noon–midnight Sun–Thu, noon–02.00 Fri–Sat. Situated on the edge of Sovyetskaya Sq & virtually opposite the Neman Hotel, so expect alcohol, bright lights & dancing. Enough said, but the central location (it couldn't be more central!) makes getting there & back very easy, especially if you're staying at the Neman.

* ☕ **Nasha Kava** [229 A3] 11 Zamkovaya St; m 44 585 42 45; ☺ 09.00–23.00 Sun–Thu, 09.00–01.00 Fri–Sat. I do like this place, very much. Tucked away down Zamkovaya yet really central, it's quiet, understated & first rate. I sat here for an hour or 2 last visit as I updated the manuscript for the latest edition of this guide, the attentive staff ferrying regular coffee to my table.

✳ 🖵**Prost Coffee Bar** [229 A3] 18 Zamkovaya St; m 44 553 77 63; ⏰ 10.00–22.00 daily. On the corner of Zamkovaya & Gorodyenskova, this small bar serves decent coffee (& cakes) & the outside seating area is perfectly positioned to witness the daily blast from the top of the Fire Tower (assuming you haven't picked the trumpeter's day off). It's a busy road, but the vista also includes the old & new castles as well as the choral synagogue. One of my favourite spots in town for reflection & to people-watch.

🖵**Raskosha** [229 B3] 7 Sovyetskaya St; ✆72 11 52; ⏰ 09.00–midnight daily. This elegant café at the top of the pedestrianised area, quiet & relaxed, has a courtyard out back offering a pleasant spot for coffee, cake & a chat.

🖵**Shakespeare Café** [229 C1] 1 Dzherzhinskova; m 29 537 55 19; ⏰ 11.00–23.00 daily. This cosy little café, hidden away in the basement of the Puppet Theatre, is a real gem. Come before a performance, or just come with a book to escape the hustle & bustle of the city.

🖵**Starlight Café** [229 A3] 11 Zamkovaya St; m 29 257 75 77; w starlightcafe.by; ⏰ 09.00–23.00 Mon–Thu, 09.00–midnight Fri–Sun. Adjoining Nasha Kava (see opposite), it's a worthy alternative. I love the pizza here, but anything on the menu is good.

🍷**Werden Gastrobar** [229 B4] 31 Mostovaya St; m 29 254 04 54; w werden.by; ⏰ 08.00–midnight Sun–Thu, 08.00–04.00 Fri–Sat. Handily located at the bottom of Sovyetskaya Sq close to Ranitsa Bookstore & in the same building as the Magnolia (see opposite), this popular venue attracts a strong local following. Service is good & the staff are friendly. The menu is interesting & varied, punctuated with a quirky dish or 2 that may raise an eyebrow. Be bold.

ENTERTAINMENT AND NIGHTLIFE

If you have your dancing shoes and fancy a late night, try the following.

☆ **Africa** [229 B1] 1a Vrublevskava St; m 29 744 17 44; ⏰ 20.00–03.00 Sun–Thu, 20.00–05.00 Fri–Sat. Guess the theme. Loud & brash, noisy & popular; grab a pizza or burger here when energy levels dip in the small hours.

☆ **Baza** [229 B4] 35 Pobyedy St; ✆333 13 33; w clubbaza.by; ⏰ 22.00–06.00 Fri–Sat. I'm no judge, but people tell me this club south of the river is the best in town.

☆ **Epolyet** [229 D1] 30 Ozheshko St; ✆44 83 42; ⏰ 22.00–06.00 Thu–Sun. It's brash & noisy, but also a fun night out, I hear.

☆ **Kolizeum 2000** [229 C4] 31 Karla Marksa St; ✆75 34 88; w kolizey2000.by; ⏰ noon–06.00 Mon–Fri, 18.00–06.00 Sat–Sun. Interchangeable with others in the genre, but still popular.

☆ **Prime** [229 D2] 2 Studencheskaya St; m 33 356 63 81; ⏰ 17.00–02.00 Mon–Tue, 17.00–05.00 Wed–Sun. I don't know anyone who has been to this club north of the river. Give it a try & let me know.

SHOPPING

Confine your shopping expeditions to Sovyetskaya Street (page 239) and you won't go far wrong, but if you can't find what you're looking for there, you could try one of the following; just don't expect to find anything else that you didn't find on Sovyetskaya, though. For unusual gifts of quality, wander into any of the small and utterly charming galleries dotted around the city. All exhibit and sell a variety of unusual arts and crafts. My personal favourite is **U Maistra** ✳ [229 B2] (*8 Kirova St*; ✆*74 09 70*; e *umaistra@gmail.com*; w *ymaistra.com*; ⏰ *10.00–19.00 Mon–Fri, 11.00–18.00 Sat*). When last in the city I popped in for browse and the artist whose work was then on display was in residence. She took great pleasure in patiently showing me around and describing each item for me.

Batoriya Trading House [229 B4] 10 Stefan Batory St, in Sovyetskaya Sq, 150m down from Farny Cathedral; ☎72 39 18; e batoriagrodno@ mail.ru; w batoria.grodnotorgservice.by; ⊕ 08.00–22.00 Mon–Fri, 09.00–22.00 Sat–Sun. The pavement outside this little shopping centre is widely used as the place to meet before a night out, especially by young people, or for friends to just hang around together.

Central Market [229 D4] 6 Poligrafistov St; ☎75 22 34; ⊕ 08.00–16.00 Tue–Sun. For the hustle & bustle of market trading Belarusian-style.

Ranitsa Bookstore [229 B4] 33 Mostovaya St; ☎72 17 65; ⊕ 10.00–18.00 Mon–Fri, 10.00–17.00 Sat, 10.00–15.00 Sun. It's the best bookshop in town but others run it close, particularly the one on Sovyetskaya St.

OTHER PRACTICALITIES

There are many **banks** and **currency-exchange bureaux** in the centre of town, with **ATMs** in increasing numbers all over the city. Two **chemists** (⊕ *until 20.00 Mon–Sat & 19.00 Sun*) can be found on either side of Sovyetskaya Street. The city's **post office** [229 C4] is at 29 Karla Marksa Street off Sovyetskaya Square.

WHAT TO SEE AND DO

Because the city is located so close to the border with Poland and Lithuania, it has one of the largest concentrations of Roman Catholic worshippers in the whole of Belarus. It is also a centre of Polish culture, with the majority of ethnic Poles in the country residing in the city and its surroundings.

CHURCHES ALONG THE NIEMAN It is hardly surprising that Catholicism dominates much of the architectural heritage. One of the iconic landmarks of the city is the 17th-century Roman Catholic **Jesuit Farny Cathedral** ✴ [229 B3] (Кафедральны касцёл Святога Францішка Ксаверыя/Собор Святого Франциска Ксаверия) at the top of Sovyetskaya Square. The construction of this fine and imposing example of high Baroque architecture, over 50m in height, was begun in 1678 by Stefan Batory at the same time as he was redesigning the Old Castle 300m or so to the southwest. As if these activities were not enough to keep a man engaged, he was also busy leading the mighty Polish-Lithuanian Commonwealth in a series of continuous and uninterrupted military campaigns at the time. So it was that the cathedral was not actually consecrated until 27 years after work began, in the exalted presence of Peter the Great and Augustus the Strong. Further additions were made in the early part of the 18th century and its late-Baroque frescoes and magnificent altars were not finally completed until 1752. The interior is simply stunning. In all, there are 14 altars, the primary of which is unique: at 21m high, it was the tallest in all Rzeczpospolita. On my last visit, I sat in quiet contemplation at the front, waiting for a service to begin. Outside, autumnal dusk was descending. It was difficult to appreciate the splendour of the main altar in the gathering gloom, but then someone flicked a switch to illuminate it from top to bottom. The sight took my breath away. To appreciate the grandeur of the exterior, walk across the square in front of the cathedral all the way to the steps of the House of Culture, then look back. The effect is particularly impressive by night.

At the bottom of the square to the left is **Bernardino Church and Seminary** [229 B4] (Бернардынскі касцел/Бернардинский костел). This 16th-century Roman Catholic complex stands in its own extensive grounds, 200m to the south of the Farny Cathedral, on a hill on Parizhskoi Kamuny Street overlooking the Nieman

River. Originally of Renaissance design, it was substantially altered in both 1680 and 1738. It is archetypical of the styles that flourished in the 17th century, from Gothic to Baroque. The interior is considered a masterpiece of so-called Wilno (Vilnius) Baroque. The church suffered some damage during the Great Patriotic War, but renovations were later sympathetically completed. Today, the oil paintings, lavish décor, alabaster statues and displays of relics and other artefacts might lack the splendour of those to be found in Farny Cathedral, but they have a beauty all of their own. The large grounds are host to a number of other monastic buildings, including cloisters, a charming wooden two-storey dormitory, a convent and a Dominican monastery. When you leave by the front door, walk to the end of the garden for an excellent view of the unusual drama theatre (page 239) directly across the road. If you get the chance, try to do so at sunset. The quality of the light at this time of day is particularly impressive for both backlighting the theatre and also bathing the front of the church in a rich luminescence, especially when set against a deep blue, cloudless sky.

To the right of the theatre, on the other side of Gorodyenskova Street, is the delightful Orthodox **Church of St Christmas and the Blessed Virgin** ✳ [229 A4] (Свята-Раства-Багародзіцкая царква і кляштар базыльянак/Рождество-Богородичный монастырь). Constructed between 1721 and 1750, its whitewashed walls beautifully showcase the deep blue roofs and magnificent domes of matte black adorned with shimmering golden stars. The courtyard is pretty and the interior of the church is well worth a look.

Just under a kilometre along the riverbank beyond the Old and New castles (page 238) as the crow flies but further by road given the topography of this part of town, atop a hill of its own on the edge of neat parkland in a delightful suburb of old wooden houses, stands the oldest remaining building in the city: the **Kolozhskaya Church of St Boris and St Hleb** ✳ [229 A3] (Барысаглебская царква, Каложская царква/Борисоглебская (Коложская) церковь). Do try very hard to visit this special place. Three-quarters of the original stone sections remain from the 12th century, the south wall having collapsed in the landslide of 1859. This is hardly surprising. The high hill on which it is precariously perched stands right above the Nieman River. First mentioned in *Chronicles* in 1183, this church is the only surviving example of the ancient style of 'Black Ruthenian' architecture, which can be distinguished from the style employed in the design of other Eastern Orthodox churches by the use of stones of blue, green or red hue, arranged to form crosses and other images on the wall. Inside and outside it is stunningly beautiful. After enjoying the enchanting design of the crosses on the exterior, take a look inside. The original stone walls and pillars are whitewashed and without frieze or other embellishment, but everywhere to be seen, hanging from pillar and wall, or just propped up in alcoves and corners, are countless icons, incense burners and gilt candle holders. I was lucky enough to visit on one of the special holy days of the Orthodox calendar, when a service of commemoration was in full flow. It was spine-tingling. As the officiating priest recited the holy incantations, a dazzling shaft of sunlight arrowed from the high window, diagonally to the floor at his feet, while incense swirled and danced in the beam. All the time, the choir sang a cappella and the parishioners seemed held rapt by the majesty of the occasion, some standing, some kneeling to kiss the floor, all incessantly crossing themselves and bowing. It was impossible not to be moved. When you have finished exploring within, go back out of the door, turn to the left, walk to the rail at the edge and lean for a while to take in the view. Far to the left is Farny Cathedral, and from this perspective you have a true idea of just how enormous its façade really is.

CASTLES AND OTHER HISTORIC BUILDINGS From Farny, sweep your gaze westward (to the right) to see the old **Fire Tower** [229 A3] (Пажарная каланча/ Пожарная Каланча), built in 1912 as a belated response to the great fires of 1885 that destroyed around 600 houses, half of all the city's buildings. Next can be seen the New and Old castles. You have a good perspective of the hill on which they are built from here. To complete the panorama, you have a fine view upriver to the forests beyond the city boundary. If you have time, take a stroll down to the riverside along the new ornamental pathways that have been laid out to the right of the church. The gradient of the steps is gentle. Turn left at the bottom, all the while gazing up at the church above or taking in the view up and downriver, then to complete a short circuit back up to the church, take the first path on your left. It's steep but there's a handrail. If you're in a mood to amble further afield, continue towards town along the dirt track by the side of the river. The first road on your left will take you up to the Fire Tower; alternatively, keep going to climb the ornamental steps to explore the Old and New castles, and the Drama Theatre. If you have transport at the church, take a short stroll into the park before you leave to inspect the impressive monument to the foundation of the city. If you're a Tolkien fan, images of Middle Earth will come to mind.

Now retrace your route and head back towards the Drama Theatre. Before you get there and just as you pass the Fire Tower, look right to find the **Stari Zamak** [229 A3] (Стары замак/Старый замок) and the **Novi Zamak** [229 A4] (Новы замак/Новый замок) (Old and New castles) perched side by side on the hillside overlooking the river. This lofty position enables them to dominate the southwestern quadrant of the city and they can be seen for some distance, particularly from south of the river. The **Old Castle**, which is located on the site of an earlier fortress, was built of stone in the 14th century to the orders of Grand Duke Vitautis. It was then thoroughly overhauled in the late 17th century in the Renaissance style by the Italian architect Scotto at the behest of Polish king Stefan Batory, who made the castle his principal residence. He died there seven years later and is interred in Grodno. Several modifications have been made since, but the attractive 17th-century stone arch bridge linking the castle with the city to the east still survives.

The main building, which dates from 1678, contains part of the city's **History and Archaeology Museum** (*Гродзенскі дзяржаўны гісторыка-археалагічны музей/ государственный историко-археологический музей*; \ *72 18 51*; e *grodno_ museum@tut.by*; w *museum-grodno.by*; ⊕ *10.00–18.00 Tue–Sun, last entry 17.00; admission BYN2*). The collection is extensive, and to do it justice you will need at least 2 hours. When you leave, walk down the brick-paved path from the entrance and pause to look over the wall. To the left, you will see cut into the hillside to separate the Old from the New an elegant set of ornate steps going all the way down to the riverside. There are pleasant gardens and walkways to be found here, along with a small cafeteria built in the medieval style, with an attractive outdoor seating area. Along the river to the left lies the bustle of the commercial city and to the right in the distance, extensive forests. In-between are attractive old wooden houses set in extensive green parkland on the opposite bank. If you look over to the right of the bridge, you can see the Fire Tower again. Before you move on, go back through the archway, bear round to the right and, when you reach the building in front of you, walk behind it to find the remains of the old castle walls. If you have the right footwear and a head for modest heights, pick your way across the top for some splendid views up and down the river. Note to self: next time, don't leave reading glasses perched on top of head while scrambling. It's a long way down to retrieve them …

Now retrace your steps back through the archway and continue to the end of the paved path. Pass through the double wrought-iron gates to find the **New Castle**, built in the Rococo style by architect Karl Pepelman between 1737 and 1742 as a summer residence for King Augustus III, who had ascended the throne of Poland in 1734. It suffered major damage during the Great Patriotic War, but over time the extensive rebuilding programme has restored much of the original Baroque elegance. The exterior looks a tad shabby, although inside the works of restoration are most impressive. The lack of attention to detail outside is in strict contrast to the manner of reconstruction elsewhere throughout the western territories of the former Soviet Union in the post-war period. Today, the section facing the river houses a library, while at right angles to it is the other section of the city's **History and Archaeology Museum** (↘74 33 60; ⊕ 10.00–18.00 Tue–Sun, last entry 17.30). As with the old section, the exhibits here are well worth a couple of hours of your time. Returning outside, you will see that the courtyard is neatly laid out and populated with trees of different species.

Before you leave this part of town, take a small detour back to the **Fire Tower** for a look at the magnificent mural at its base. Also, be sure to spot the life-size figure in fireman's uniform leaning on the balustrade of the lookout platform at the very top. On my last visit I was taken to witness the unusual spectacle of a serving fireman lustily blowing a trumpet fanfare from this platform. Apparently the ceremony is performed every day at noon, and the requirement is a feature of the firefighter's job description. Sadly my visit seemed to coincide with his day off. I hope you have better luck. The adjoining buildings house the functioning fire station and the city's museum of firefighting history. On the other side of the road is the magnificent structure of the **Great Choral Synagogue of Grodno** [229 A3] (*Вялікая харальная сінагога/Большая хоральная синагога; Museum of Jewish History;* ↘297 82 61 14; ⊕ 10.00–18.00 daily; admission free). Originally built in 1578 and once one of the most beautiful in all of Europe, the structure and façade in recent times were in need of significant repair. Work to the exterior had restored the building to much of its former glory, before a catastrophic fire in November 2013 caused significant damage to the interior. Ambitious plans to re-establish this important centre for the local Jewish community are currently in the course of being developed and realised. For now it remains a building site, but access is still possible. Despite advertised opening hours, the entrance to the 'museum' itself was locked on my last visit, though a knock on the door of the administration office was answered by the head of the city's Jewish community, who was delighted to show us around the interior. It's still work in progress, but display boards (in Polish and Russian text only) have been erected to recount relevant historical details. Such restoration work as has already been completed is exquisite, though much remains to be done. For further information, go to w jewishgrodno.com. Today the synagogue marks the location of the significant ghetto here during the Nazi occupation. A simple but moving memorial and commemorative plaque is sited at the point where once stood the former entrance to the ghetto on Zamkovaya Street, on the left-hand side as you head up towards Sovyetskaya Street from here.

AROUND SOVYETSKAYA STREET Standing directly between the New Castle and Bernardino Church is the unusual and slightly unnerving design of the **Drama Theatre** building [229 B4] (*Гродзенскі абласны драматычны тэатр/Гродненский областной драматический театр; 35 Mostovaya St;* ↘72 34 27 (reservations); e dramagr@mail.grodno.by; w drama.grodno.by). Looking like something modelled on the coronet of a Middle Earth monarch (your second Tolkien image in this city!), it was clearly intended to speak of opulence and wealth but, when I first came here in 2007, it didn't pay to look too closely. The exterior was shabby and in need of a whole new coat of paint. The intended effect was further prejudiced by the proliferation of empty beer bottles littering the pavement around the outside. It was all really disappointing. But I'm happy to report that when I returned in the spring of 2014, the theatre's fascia had received a major facelift and the walkways around it had been upgraded. There was not a single empty beer bottle to be seen. The eye-catching design of the theatre is now displayed in all its glory and it takes its place as one of the leading images of the city at last. The ticket kiosk is tucked away to the left of the main entrance. Tickets can also be booked online; the informative website will tell you all you need to know about the schedule of performances, and the site's historical notes are worth a read too. As with the castles next door, the view across the river from the walkway behind the theatre is magnificent. It is also worthy of mention at this point that the view from the south bank is equally splendid, although the perspective is reversed, of course. As you drive or walk on to the bridge crossing the river, look up to see all of these buildings towering above you.

The theatre stands on a major traffic junction at the bottom of a vast pedestrianised area bordered by Mostovaya and Stefan Batory streets with **Sovyetskaya Square** [229 B3] (Савецкая плошча/Советская площадь) at the top. Stand with your back to the tank on its plinth and look uphill across the square. Immediately on your left is the **Ranitsa Bookstore** (page 236), where you can find a good selection of English material. Walk on past it to find an ATM, with decent views of the Fire Tower beyond and to the left. Next is the city's **Palace of Culture** [229 B3] (палац культуры/Дворец культуры). The pedestrianised area here is a skateboarder's paradise (as are the environs of the Drama Theatre). Look across the square at this point to locate (from left to right) Farny Cathedral, Batoriya Trading House, Neman Hotel, Tsentralny Store and the Bernardino Church and Seminary.

Keep going through to the top of the square and into **Sovyetskaya Street**, which is regarded as the main thoroughfare and centre of activity, particularly since it's now fully pedestrianised. The shopping streets of Minsk are now starting to look like those that we recognise in the West, with vulgar neon and shouty billboards, but elsewhere in Belarus things remain a little calmer and more understated. In Grodno and particularly on Sovyetskaya Street, small specialist shops, bookstores, cafés and bars nestle unassumingly behind pastel façades. There are also Western designer stores here, but advertising is almost non-existent. There are buskers in abundance, with street stalls and souvenir kiosks seemingly taking up every available plot on the pavement. At the top end on the right is one of the city's main department stores, **Magasin** [229 B3] (🕐 09.00–20.00 daily), selling all manner of things on two floors. Some of the items appear to be quite luxurious and will probably be some way beyond the means of the average local resident. You can also buy some reasonable souvenirs here, especially ceramics, textiles and straw-crafted goods. As you pass down the street, there is also a cinema, halfway down on the right-hand side. Pause here to inspect the tablets laid into the footpath commemorating notable milestones in the history of Belarusian cinema, as well as the pretty mural and the military bust on the other side of the street. Then, a little further down on the left, is the **Nieman** department store [229 B2] (🕐 10.00–20.00 daily). Relatively new, it is bigger and fresher than Magasin. There is also a delightful street café right outside bearing the same name, selling soft and alcoholic drinks and snacks to customers at tables on the pavement under umbrellas. At the bottom of the street turn right and walk past the Oblast Executive Building (see if you can spot the plaque commemorating the visit of Felix Dzerzhinsky and the founding of the

A HISTORICAL WALKING TOUR

To take in a good selection of the best sights in town, you might like to try this circular walk. If you include shopping time and also stops for refreshments, you could spend a whole day on it. Begin at the Old and New castles [229 A3/4], including a walk around the two museums there. Visit the Church of St Christmas [229 C4] and head east past the Drama Theatre [229 B4], before crossing the road to Bernardino Church [229 B4]. When you leave the church, turn right along Stefan Batory Street, one of the boundaries of Sovyetskaya Square [229 B3]. Pay a visit to Batoriya Trading House [229 B4] for some souvenirs, before continuing on to Farny Cathedral [229 B3]. Upon leaving there, walk across the square, through the pleasant ornamental gardens and turn right down Sovyetskaya Street to the end, browsing and people-watching as you go. At the bottom, turn right and proceed into Lenin Square to see the old fella keeping watch. If you're feeling energetic, cross over the street for a promenade around lovely Zhilibersky Central Park [229 C1], before retracing your steps back to Sovyetskaya Street. Walk back up it on the other side and through the square, the attractive paved area of which is much favoured by promenaders and skateboarders. Turn right down Zamkovaya Street just before you reach the Palace of Culture [229 B3] to pass the memorial marking the former entrance to the ghetto on the right. On the left at the bottom of the street is the Museum of Religious History [229 A3]. Across the main road is the Fire Tower [229 A3], with the Great Choral Synagogue [229 A3] to your right and the New Castle [229 A4] diagonally opposite. Stroll down to the riverside and rest on a bench in the gardens there. You will have deserved it!

Grodno revolutionary war committee in 1920) to enter Lenin Square, where the old revolutionary still stands guard.

EASTERN ORTHODOX POKROVSKY CATHEDRAL [229 D1] (Свята-Пакроўскі кафедральны сабор/Свя́то-Покро́вский кафедра́льный собо́р) This cathedral should not be missed if you have the chance to see it. Located on the corner of Ozheshko and Lenina streets beyond Zhilibersky Central Park and only a few hundred metres from the railway station, this Russian revivalist extravaganza of pale pink stucco, red roofs and matte black onion domes is a gem. Dating from 1907, it was built to commemorate the city's army officers who lost their lives in the 1904–05 Russo-Japanese war.

GORODNITSA HISTORY MUSEUM [229 D1] (*Музей гісторыі Гарадніцы/Музей истории Городницы; 37 Ozheshko St; ☎ 72 16 69; ⏲ 10.00–18.00 Tue–Sat, last entry 17.30; admission BYN1.90*) Themed on the activities of the city's former Gorodnitsa trading district but with displays and artefacts relating to the history of the city generally, this museum incorporates a small but very attractive wooden building that is well worth a visit in its own right. Only 8m by 9m and one of a number of master craftsmen's houses built along this street in the 1760s as far as the site of the modern-day Lenin Square, this is the only one left and is of considerable historical significance.

PHARMACY MUSEUM ✱ [229 B3] (*Аптэка езуітаў/Аптека-музей; 4 Sovyetskaya Sq; ☎ 74 00 81, 74 36 66; e muzeum@biotest.by; w am.biotest.by; ⏲ 09.00–19.00 Tue–*

Sun; admission free, BYN1 to take photographs) Situated right next door to Farny Cathedral, the building in which this unusual museum is housed was constructed by Jesuits in 1687, specifically for pharmaceutical research. The charming pharmacy itself (⊕ *08.00–21.00 Mon–Sat, 09.00–18.00 Sun*), one of the oldest in Belarus, is well worthy of a few moments of your time, not least for the sights and odours of carbolic and antiseptic that are so evocative of childhood! There is also a comprehensive range of fine herbal teas available for purchase. The tiny museum is in an adjoining room. Opened in 1996, it is the only one in the country dedicated to the history of pharmaceutics. Finding it open, however, is a very hit-and-miss process; on every occasion that I've visited within advertised hours, it has been closed. The plaque outside the building even shows different times to those displayed inside, but there is usually someone on hand to open the locked gate and supervise your visit. An attractive souvenir booklet can be purchased for BYN2.

MAXIM BOGDANOVICH HOUSE AND LITERARY MUSEUM [229 C1] (*Музей Максіма Багдановіча/Музей Максима Богдановича; 10 Pyervaya Maya St;* ✆ *72 22 54;* w *bogdanovich.grodno.by;* ⊕ *10.00–18.00 Tue–Sun, last entry 17.30; admission BYN1.55*) The famous Belarusian poet lived with his family in this house between 1892 and 1896. It opened its doors as a museum dedicated to his life in 1982 and exhibits include family photographs, personal belongings and collections of poetry. Some of the rooms recreate the interior of the house as it would have been when the family was in residence.

GRODNO REGIONAL PUPPET THEATRE ✳ [229 C1] (*Гродзенскі абласны тэатр лялек/Гродненский областной театр кукол; 1/1 Dzherzhinskova St;* ✆ *74 59 30 (reservations);* e *grodnolyalka@gmail.com;* w *grodnolyalka.by*) Located in a charming building of pastel stucco in a lovely park, performances here are a real delight. Featuring works of Pushkin and Kupala, Wilde and Shakespeare, there is something for small children, teenagers and adults alike. The website tells all you need to know about schedules and includes some interesting historical notes.

GRODNO STATE MUSEUM OF RELIGIOUS HISTORY [229 A3] (*Гродзенскі дзяржаўны музей гісторыі рэлігіі/Гродненский государственный музей истории религии; 16 Zamkovaya St;* ✆ *74 25 13;* e *muzey-religii@tut.by;* w *muzej.by;* ⊕ *10.00–18.00 Tue–Sun, last entry 17.30; admission BYN2*) Located in a charmingly restored nunnery at the bottom of Zamkovaya, just around the corner from Prosto Café, this interesting museum charts the social and religious history of the country. Individual events, lectures, concerts and expositions are hosted from time to time.

ZHILIBERSKY CENTRAL PARK [229 C1] (парк Жылібера/Парк Жилибера) Only a short walk from Pokrovsky Cathedral on one side and Lenin Square on the other, this park was once shabby but has received a major facelift in recent years, such that it has been transformed into a really lovely oasis of green within the city. Today it is a place for quiet reflection and gentle promenading. There is a lake, ornamental bridge and lazy meandering stream with attractive statuary throughout, while the walkways are illuminated by night. Cross the road out of Lenin Square and enter by the steps on either side. If you then cross the wooden bridge to the right and pass under the road overhead, you come to a quieter, more secluded area of the park. Less populated than the main section, it's a delightful backwater. Here you have a first view of the delightful Pokrovsky Cathedral. Climb out of the park on the right-hand side, past the buildings of Yanki Kupala University, cross the road and pay the

cathedral a visit. Before retracing your steps, treat yourself to a coffee from the H20 café next door.

OUTSIDE GRODNO

AVGUSTOVSKI CANAL ✻ (Аўгустоўскі Канал/Августовский Канал) This site is something of a jewel in the crown for the local tourism industry and the state has invested some US$28 million in its infrastructure, three times the amount spent on Njasvizh Castle in Minsk region, one of the country's top five international attractions. It's been included since March 2006 as a preliminary submission for the UNESCO World Heritage List, and construction work on the canal linking a series of natural lakes was completed in the 19th century. Originally used for commercial transportation but now a leisure facility, this fine example of hydraulic engineering was twice bombed to destruction in two world wars, with the 22km Belarusian section rebuilt between 2004 and 2006. The countryside hereabouts is beautiful, and there are ample opportunities to enjoy a full range of outdoor activities including walking, cycling, horseriding and kayaking. Tours by motorboat serve the less energetically inclined. All can be booked via travel agencies in Grodno and elsewhere, though pointing your own transport north out of the city on rural back roads and accessing facilities direct when you reach the canal has enormous appeal. First take the P42 road north out of Grodno for 20km, broadly following the line of the Nieman River. At Gozha look to turn left across the river in the general direction of Sapotskin. After 12km (4km before you reach Sapotskin) take a right turn and drive a further 5km to the village of **Nemnovo** at the eastern end of the canal. Nemnovo is on a direct bus route from the city and services run twice a day (Wed, Fri, Sat & Sun). It has an interesting museum charting the canal's history and you can also visit the old lock keeper's house nearby, built in 1830 in Russian classicist style. The canal's largest sluice is situated here. For a rural overnighter, ecotourism is developing fast in the area. Several farmsteads offer accommodation, including Avgustovski Zakutok, Anneta, Tartak, Lya Svyatska, Hatu u Staha and Garadzensky Mayontak Karobchytsy. The Association of Rural and Ecotourism 'Country Escape' (page 51) can assist with bookings. A number of campsites, a 'tourism complex' and 'recreation zones' are currently being established in the area and it may be a good idea to come here sooner rather than later. Once a year in August, a festival of culture takes place around the Dombrovka sluice, featuring ethnic craftsmen, folk musicians and performing troupes from Belarus, Poland and Lithuania.

LIDA (Ліда/Лида) Lida is the second-largest town in the oblast. Situated 160km due east of Grodno on the M11, it suffered greatly in the chequered history of warfare that dominated the area in the Middle Ages, then again in the Great Patriotic War, when it was extensively damaged. Once upon a time the mighty structure of the **castle** (*Komsomolskaya Bd;* m *29 158 70 79, 25 987 09 71;* ⊕ *10.00–18.30 Tue–Sun; admission BYN3/2.50/2 adults/students/children*) must have completely dominated the town, though now it is dwarfed by a hideous apartment block right next to it. Under massive works of renovation and reconstruction for years, the castle is now open for business again. This includes an annual historical festival of pageantry in September when the Middle Ages come to life once more with jousting tournaments and battle re-enactments as a huge celebration takes over the entirety of the castle's grounds to mark the occasion of Dozhinki (harvest). Happily, the renovation work has restored the exterior elevations to much of their former glory, such that the dominance of the Soviet apartment block next door has been much reduced.

This is one of the biggest castles in the whole country, measuring 80m by 80m. Made of stone and brick, the design and style are very similar to that employed in the building of Mir Fortress (page 246). Construction began in the middle of the 14th century, then in the centuries that followed it was sacked and plundered a number of times. In 1953, it was included in the state's List of Protected Monuments and in 1976 works of restoration began. They have been ongoing ever since. The repairs to the exterior of the two corner towers and the massive walls appear to be complete. There is also a high-level walkway inside and there is a plan for the towers to house a museum. Don't be surprised to find further works in progress when you visit. Although it's possible to appreciate the importance of the castle simply by reference to its size, it lacks the charm of other historical sites such as Mir and Njasvizh (not least because the massive interior is little more than a cavernous empty space, except when populated with craft and souvenir stalls on festival days). This means that whereas Mir and Njasvizh are worthy of excursions in their own right, Lida is not. Put another way, pop in if you're in the area, but don't spend a day on a specific expedition from somewhere else.

If travelling by car, take the M11 road off the M6 from Minsk. About 2–3km after entering the town, look for the Great Patriotic War train with its iconic red star, mounted on a plinth on the right-hand side of the road, and the castle will soon appear. Go past it and turn immediately right to park on the road outside the huge iron doors of the entrance. If there is no room for your vehicle here, retrace your steps back to the large car park at the bottom of the boulevard. Across the road from the main entrance is the **tourist information centre** (*8 Zamkovaya St;* \52 55 03; ⊕ *Apr–Oct 08.00–17.00 Tue–Sat; Nov–Mar 08.30–17.00 Tue–Sat*). No English is spoken here, but the staff are extremely helpful and eager to please and the centre is well stocked with leaflets and guides, some of them with significant English text. If you can make yourself understood, ask for the excellent map and mini-guide to the sites of interest in the town, which includes text in English. **The Exultation of the Holy Cross Roman Catholic Church** is another of the town's main symbols. Built between 1765 and 1770 in the Baroque style, the interior is exquisite. The town also has a **museum of local history and art** (*37a Pobyedy St;* \53 22 94; e *lixmuseum@ mail.ru;* w *lixmuseum.by;* ⊕ *10.00–19.00 Tue–Sun; admission BYN1/0.70/0.50 adults/students/children*) and there are various monuments commemorating events in the Great Patriotic War, including the eternal flame complex with the tomb of the Unknown Soldier, a sculpture honouring the partisans and soldiers who liberated the city, and the memorial stone marking the mass grave of over 5,000 Jews murdered by the Nazis on a single day in May 1942. Other than these sites, the town has little to commend it, being a typically charmless post-war urban planning nightmare.

🏠 **Where to stay and eat** According to staff in the TIC, the best place in town for an overnight stay is the **Hotel Kontinent** (*8 Kirova St;* \56 73 66; **$$$**). Alternatives are the **Hotel Equator** (*4 Kirova St;* \53 01 01; **$$**) and **Hotel Lida** (*1 Grunvaldskaya St;* \52 69 95; **$$**), next door to the castle. For a truly authentic Soviet-style experience, leave the castle by the main entrance, cross the boulevard to the hideous apartment block opposite and pay a visit to the **canteen** (⊕ *10.00–17.00 Mon–Fri*) to be found on the ground floor in the right-hand corner (see box, opposite).

MIR ✳ (Mip/Мир) Some 200km east of Grodno via the M6 motorway (and only 90km southwest of Minsk but just within Grodno oblast, 15 minutes off the main

LONG LIVE THE WORKERS' CULINARY REVOLUTION!

'There's a canteen in the apartment block opposite; would you like to try it?' I wasn't sure if Olya was joking or not. We were in Lida, and had driven hard from Grodno that morning, without breakfast or even refreshment *en route*. It was now almost 14.00 and both of us were hot, thirsty and hungry. Looking around, we didn't seem to have an abundance of choice. We strolled over, entered by the small, tatty door and stepped into a whole new world. Turning right up the stairs, we followed a line of local people into a freezing, cavernous hall with monstrous, nightmarish décor straight from the Soviet Union of the 1960s and the cheapest furniture and furnishings imaginable. We joined a silent queue shuffling towards a doorway through which could be seen a line of serving dishes, with the kitchens beyond. I was reminded of the early industrial scenes in David Lean's majestic movie of Pasternak's epic novel *Doctor Zhivago*. The smell of overboiled vegetables was unmistakable. The parallel with school dinners was also impossible to miss. I chose pork and mashed potato, liberally smothered with a sauce of indistinct origin, accompanied by a side salad of beetroot and potato, with watery tomato juice to drink. Olya went for fish and the same additions as I chose. The bill came to BYR6,500 in the old currency; around US$3 for the lot. And it was surprisingly tasty. Around us, our fellow diners ate in silence. When we had finished, we took our empty plates on our cheap plastic trays and placed them on the rickety, noisy conveyor at the end of the room, where they were transported with a judder directly to the kitchens. We went to the take-away hatch to buy two half-litre bottles of fizzy soft drinks for the rest of our journey. We chose two well-known American brands, which were plonked unceremoniously on the hatch by a scowling waitress who had snatched the wad of tatty notes from my hand without even a glance, let alone a word or acknowledgement of our presence. These drinks cost more than our lunch. We left in silence, glad to be returning to the warmth of the sun from our foray back in time. When I returned seven years later, nothing had changed. Not even the décor. If you're ever in the vicinity, then don't miss out on a truly memorable experience.

M1 motorway to Brest) stands the small museum town of Mir and its beautiful 16th-century fortress.

The settlement of Mir was looted and burned by invading crusaders in 1395. By 1434, it had fallen into the ownership of the 'big baron' Radzivili family, whose patronage ensured a steady increase in the significance of the settlement, as it grew first into a township and then into the administrative centre of Mir county. In the late 16th and early 17th centuries, earthen walls were built around the township and it became a fortress. Four corner gates, the foundations of which have now been excavated, gave access from the four main roads that originally met here. In 1579, the township was granted rights of limited municipal self-determination and government, so that it very quickly attracted craftsmen and tradesmen of various nationalities, including Belarusians, Tartars, Jews and ethnic travelling people. Indeed, the extravagant duke Carol Stanislav Radzivili bestowed upon a certain Jan Martsynkyevich the grand title of 'King of the Gypsies' of the great principality of Lithuania in 1778, also declaring Mir to be their capital.

Naturally, the mixture of cultures and ethnicities had a defining influence on the community that was established here. It is for this reason that a Roman Catholic church, Eastern Orthodox church, synagogue and mosque were built in close proximity. Very quickly, the township began to attract merchants and their goods from all corners of Belarus, Poland, the Baltic states and Russia.

Getting there and away Given that Mir is much closer to Minsk than to Grodno, you are more likely to visit from the capital city. By car, take the main M1 motorway from Minsk towards Brest and take the turn north on to the P64 road (signposted to Mir) for 8km. The town is situated on the bus route from Minsk (departing from the central bus station) to Novogrudok and the journey takes around 2 hours (tickets BYN5–6 each way).

 Where to stay and eat The 16-room hotel within the Fortress itself (⟍ *159 62 82 92, 159 62 83 73;* e *reception@mirzamak.by*) has a range of singles, twin rooms, apartments and suites, which can be booked direct. Also here is restaurant Knyazhesky Dvor (⟍ *159 62 82 94;* e *knyjeski_dvor@tut.by;* ⊕ *09.00–23.00 daily*), serving decent Belarusian cuisine in a 'traditional' vaulted environment.

What to see and do
Mir Fortress (*Мірскі Замак/Мирский Замок;* ⟍*159 62 82 70;* e *info@mirzamak. by;* w *mirzamak.by;* ⊕ *10.00–18.00 Mon, Wed–Sun; admission BYN12/6 adults/ students & children Mon–Fri, BYN14/7adults/students & children Sat–Sun*) Shortly after turning off the motorway on the P64 road, the fairy-tale castle of Mir comes into view. Situated on the edge of the town in a delightful setting overlooking a serene lake and built largely of stone and red brick, it is not only a powerful monument to the influence of the princes who commissioned its construction, but also very pleasing on the eye. Since 2000, it has been designated a UNESCO World Heritage Site, one of four in the country.

The walls and towers of the castle (still known today as the 'medieval flower') first appeared in the 1520s, followed by the construction of the Renaissance palace itself between the late 16th and early 17th centuries. After a battering during the war with Russia in 1655 and the later Northern War, it gradually fell further into disrepair, before a revival in the 1730s when a portrait gallery and ornate banqueting hall were added, together with a beautiful Italianate garden containing citrus, fig, myrtle, cypress, box, mahogany and laurel trees. The scent on the breeze of summer evenings must have been extravagant and intoxicating. Latterly, the complex suffered extensive damage in the Great Patriotic War, when a Cossack regiment was stationed here and a number of engagements took place in the vicinity. A very significant programme of restoration is now complete and this beautiful walled structure of five towers (after the first four, a fifth was added for security purposes in the centre of the west wall facing the road to Vilnius as the only means of access by drawbridge and portcullis) and a courtyard accommodates a small hotel, conference hall and traditional restaurant in addition to the museum of exhibits housed in various rooms throughout the building. Caution is needed when negotiating the steep, narrow and winding staircases which permit access to those parts of the castle that are open to the public, with some of the steps being quite large. It is possible to climb to the very top of the southwestern tower, the best-preserved of the five, from which there are extensive panoramic views over the town and surrounding countryside. The five floors currently house works of fine art.

The panorama as you walk around the castle walls by the lakeside towards the fortress is magnificent. This stretch used to host souvenir stalls, some tacky, but some with attractive artefacts and books at reasonable prices, though all have now been moved to the adjoining small car park (where you will also find a café). My own preference is not to use this car park, but to use the much bigger one further up the hill. It's only a short walk to the fortress, but the view to it over the lake from this point is majestic. In the castle grounds stands a pretty chapel of Modernist style (built in 1904) that served as a burial vault. Across the lake are remains of the former estate buildings, surrounded by 16ha of landscaped park, established at the same time as the chapel. There are many varieties of trees and a wooden bridge that accesses a small islet in the lake. This is an excellent spot to take photographs of the castle and is frequented by newlyweds as part of their 'grand tour' (page 175).

From the top car park, walk to the left of the castle to enter through the main gate. After purchasing your ticket, the self-guided tour begins when you mount the stairs in the left-hand corner of the reception area. Audio guides are available. The works of restoration are truly impressive. Pause to examine the exhibits and display boards (some in English) in the first rooms, then mount the steep stairs into the dining room. The ceiling here is exquisite. At this point you must also put slippers over your shoes from the supply in the corner and if you don't, you will be sternly told off! Continue to follow the markers around the rooms on your self-guided tour. When you emerge from the exhibition, the small hotel is on the left-hand wall, while on the other side is a souvenir shop. Diagonally opposite is the start of the walk around the ramparts and towers, which in places is extremely steep and narrow. You should think twice before tackling the climb if your knees and joints are not in the best of order but if they are, it's a glorious adventure indeed. When you're ready, leave the fortress by the gate through which you entered and turn left around the castle to walk up to the family chapel, where you will be asked to show your castle entry ticket. There is a simple iconostasis with examples of icons from Russia and Mir itself.

Other sites in Mir To complete your visit, take a stroll into the small town. Retrace your steps towards the bottom car park, cross the river and walk along the road and up the slight incline. Ahead of you and left of centre is the 16th-century Renaissance Roman Catholic Church of St Nikolai, currently undergoing reconstruction (although it's still possible to take a look inside), as is the Castles Road café. A little further along the road on the right-hand side is the town's modest square, with market stalls in the centre. Like the castle, much of the town was destroyed in the war, so these buildings are reconstructions rather than originals, albeit painstakingly and lovingly restored. A clockwise stroll will take you past Café Rageda (closed on my last visit for a refit), a small shop and then Mir Hotel, where there is an ATM. Look behind the hotel to spot the original architecture of the **Jewish quarter**. Dating from the early 19th century, here stood the *kahal* (the self-government building), two synagogues and the *yeshivah* (a rabbinic academy for the study of Holy Scriptures), though now only part of the late 19th-century synagogue remains, next to the new one presently in the course of construction. Near here is a small **museum** (✎ *159 62 34 70; admission BYN0.50*) dedicated to the Jewish history of the town, which one of my correspondents describes as 'rather ramshackle but charming'! Opening hours are less than reliable, so call ahead before you arrive. On the far side of the square is the attractive 16th-century **St Trinity Church**, then you complete your circuit by walking past a number of shops and banks (also with ATMs) sandwiching the tiny bus station. For a different (and equally beautiful) panorama of the castle, look for the track between the first bank on this side and the bus station, which takes you back down towards the river through rows of old residential homes. It's not difficult to find your way and I do like circular perambulations! If you have the time, head behind the trees some way to the north of the castle to see the **monument** to Jewish victims of the Holocaust and an old Jewish cemetery. A total of 1,600 Mir Jews were executed on 9 November 1941 and a further 850 were imprisoned in the ghetto that was later established in the castle, all of whom were murdered on 13 August 1942. Also a little way out of town beyond St Trinity Church is a **Muslim cemetery**, and there is an Orthodox one at the **Church of St George**. If you're going on to Njasvizh in Minsk region under your own steam, turn left out of the top car park and keep going for around 30km.

NOVOGRUDOK ✳ (Навагрудак/Новогрудок) In the 13th century, Belarus was the nucleus of the great principality of Lithuania and, when Mindaug was crowned Grand Duke of All Lithuania here in 1253, Novogrudok was named the Great Duchy's capital. The town is dominated by a hill on which the ruins of a 14th-century castle stand.

Getting there and away Situated around 40km northwest of Mir on the P11 road, Novogrudok can be visited by way of a detour from your excursion to Mir although, as with a trip to Njasvizh in Minsk region, this will make for a long though fascinating day. A stop off on the M1 journey from Brest to Minsk is also a possibility. The M1 is a good road, as befits its status as a major pan-European highway, with pleasing views, and even though it's one of the most significant routes across the continent, I've rarely seen much traffic on it! Take the P5 at Baranovichy, signposted Novogrudok. Roads off the main routes in this country are almost always empty of cars and it is still possible to experience the joy of motoring here. Five kilometres after you turn off the M1, look for the imposing Catholic church in need of repair at Stalovichi before you pass through the attractive rolling hills around Gorodishcha. Fifteen kilometres further on, beyond the village of Porechye, is lovely Lake Svityaz and its sanatorium. Another 6km further is the very attractive church at Valyevka. You will cross the ring road shortly after this point. Regular buses run from Minsk central bus station (*one-way ticket BYN9*) and there are also marshrutka services (*BYN7*).

 Where to stay and eat If you're in need of refreshment, pause for coffee at **Bar Rhum** (*9 Lenina Sq;* ☎ *1597 20 9 70;* ⊕ *Mar–Nov 07.00–01.00 daily; Dec–Feb 07.00–midnight daily*), located just to the right of the pale orange-stuccoed House of Culture. **Hotel Panski Dom** (*3 Grodnenskaya St;* ☎ *1597 25 3 85;* **$$**) is a little further down the road leading to the Cathedral of St Nicholas, with **Café Stary Gorod** (☎ *1597 24 7 78;* ⊕ *noon–midnight Mon–Thu, noon–01.00 Fri–Sun*) right next door.

What to see and do
The castle This is the highlight of a visit to Novogrudok. Little of its structure remains today but, at the height of its influence, the seven imposing towers made it the largest and most significant fortress in the country, as befitted the town's status. At 323m above sea level, the castle hill is one of the highest points in the country and the views over the town and surrounding Nieman River, with a radius of 15–20km, are singularly impressive. At the height of its powers, the town enjoyed extensive trade links with the countries of central Europe, the Baltic, Scandinavia and Byzantium. It also made a huge contribution to the development of the ideas

of the Reformation in Belarus. Inevitably, conflict and war gradually weakened its position, so that today only traces of its former greatness remain. From 1654 to 1667, the castle itself suffered very significant damage during the war between the armies of Russia and Rzeczpospolita, and then between 1700 and 1721 it was all but destroyed by the Swedish army during the Northern Wars. Just two ruined towers and a portion of the exterior wall remain atop the bluff, although the Farny Transfiguration of the Lord Roman Catholic Church remains towards the bottom of the hill. Originally founded as a place of worship by Grand Duke Vitautis in 1395, the current church was built in 1723. It is a fine example of the 'Sarmat' Baroque style, which is characterised by a fortress-like appearance.

There is a ring road around most of the town and, whatever the direction from which you approach, you will find yourself looking upwards. Approaching from the north gives a much better impression of the strategic importance of the town and the dominance enjoyed by the castle. I have come from the direction of Mir from the southeast and from Baranovichy to the south, and in either case the castle isn't easy to find. As you enter the town, look for the water tower on the horizon and keep heading upwards until you can go no higher, then the castle is relatively easy to spot. Leave your vehicle in the car park just off Lenin Square. Walk towards the right as you leave the car park and head into the castle grounds, past the Mitskevich statue on the left. The earthworks are massive. The Barrow of Immortality is on the left, and you should climb to the top to admire the magnificent 360-degree panorama. Again, it's easy to appreciate the significance of the strategic location of the defences. The Farny Cathedral is below and to the left of the two ruined towers, some way down the hill. The town itself is in the other direction, with fine views of the Cathedral of St Nicholas and the Church of Sts Boris and Hleb.

Other sights in Novogrudok The great Belarusian poet Adam Mitskevich was born in Novogrudok and was christened in the Cathedral of St Nicholas. Other sites within the town relating to the poet include the nearby **Barrow of Immortality** mound, at the foot of which is a memorial stone; the **sculpture** close to the mound on the other side of castle hill; and the location of the **house** where he was born in the square, where there is now a **museum** (*1 Leninskaya St;* \ *1597 24 3 40;* ⏰ *09.00–18.00 Tue–Sun; admission BYN2.10/1.80/1.40/free adults/students/ children/disabled visitors*) dedicated to his life and work. In the grounds, certain outbuildings of the original house have been recreated.

Just off the square is a **history museum** (*2 Grodnenskaya St;* \ *1597 22 3 95;* ⏰ *09.00–18.00 Tue–Sun; admission BYN1.50/1 adults/students & children*) with excellent and moving exhibits relating to the fate of the Jewish community and the activities of the partisans led by the Bielski brothers who were active in the forests around here resisting the Nazi oppression in the Great Patriotic War. The Jewish community in the town before the war was a very significant one. The Nazis murdered nearly everyone and the small number who survived were deported for slave labour. There is now a small but deeply affecting **museum of Jewish resistance** (*66 Minskaya St;* \ *1597 21 4 70;* ⏰ *09.00–18.00 Tue–Sun (but call first to arrange an appointment); admission BYN1.50/1 adults/students & children*) on the road out of town to Minsk, where once the town's ghetto stood. Housed in one of the original barracks, the exhibits are poignant and moving. The entrance to the tunnel dug by the prisoners during the occupation is still there, in the corner of the first room. Outside stands a charming memorial, recently unveiled, with a story to melt the heart (see box, page 250). Four other places of worship, two of them Eastern

Novogrudok, Tuesday. It is warm as we get out of the car and I want to drop to my knees to kiss terra firma. We've just driven 145km from Minsk. Naturally we set off over an hour late, but Boris the Charioteer cut the deficit to a handful of minutes. I was the front-seat passenger and I was very, very scared. (You can read more about Boris on my blog 'Nigel Roberts: To Belarus and Beyond'; **w** nigelroberts23. wordpress.com.)

I'm travelling with good friends from The Together Plan (a British charity; page 116) for the unveiling of a new monument to the Jews from the Novogrudok ghetto murdered by the Nazis in four punitive operations between August 1942 and September 1943.

First we visit the tiny but moving museum housed in a former barracks on the site of the ghetto. The small rooms contain artefacts and information boards displaying sepia photographs of the families imprisoned here. Lives brutalised, lost, but not forgotten. In 1943 the prisoners dug a tunnel, 70cm x 70cm and 250m long, which helped over 100 escape before the tunnel was discovered. Those who were still crawling through were gunned down as they fled. Four of the escapees are still alive. The tunnel entrance is in the corner of the museum and later we walk the line of it, though we are unable to see where the prisoners broke earth to flee. The exit from the tunnel is now in a private garden. It took four months of back-breaking toil to dig out the escape route and we walk it, very slowly, in less than 2 minutes.

People begin to arrive for the unveiling ceremony in twos and threes. Local folk, schoolchildren, council officials, the *chargé d'affaires* from the US Embassy and his staff. Survivors from the Minsk ghetto arrive by bus, and soon a few dozen attendees swell to many hundreds. There aren't enough chairs. A solemn and solitary violin is playing as the ceremony begins. It's a beautiful, bright sunny day with a strong breeze that carries an edge.

A camera drone buzzes only metres above the crowd as five guys in dinner jackets and open-necked shirts step up to sing *Hava Nagila* in Hebrew, a cappella. There are speeches, mournful songs and a deeply affecting recital from a young

---

Orthodox (the 18th-century Cathedral of St Nicholas and the 16th-century Church of Sts Boris and Hleb), one Roman Catholic (the 18th-century Church of St Michael the Archangel) and one a 19th-century mosque, are also all worthy of a visit. During the months of summer, the bloody history of the region is regularly recreated for the tourist through battle re-enactments, which attract very large crowds.

Retrace your steps back into Lenin Square, where once the old market stood. There's a **tourist information centre** (*4 Patchtovaya St;* \15 972 77 47; **e** novtic@tut. by; **w** tourgrodno.by; ④ 09.00–18.00 daily) where a deal of helpful information and a good number of informative booklets are available, some of them with English pages. The staff are very pleased to see visitors, though no English is spoken here. The TIC itself is tucked away and is not easy to find. Head down Patchtovaya, a small street leading to the Church of Sts Boris and Hleb out of the back of the square. You first spot a green 'i' sign on the wall; go past it and turn right into the yard, through the door and up the stairs into the darkness. Turn left and knock on the door to the left.

OTHER TOWNS IN THE REGION Finally, there follows a selection of smaller picturesque towns and villages that can be found in the greater Grodno region. There are many others, equally as pretty and with similar attractions, which have not made

woman with a huge yellow star on the breast of her old and worn overcoat. She carries a battered suitcase. With help and support, the Minsk ghetto survivors walk slowly to the memorial to remove its cover.

Now the sun gleams on the enchanting statue of a young girl, Michle Sosnovsky, dressed in costume to celebrate the Jewish festival of Purim. On a day like today in 1943, she and a young friend disguised themselves to escape from the ghetto but were recognised and denounced by a former neighbour. They were arrested, taken to the police station and shot.

The story of how Michle was chosen for the memorial is extraordinary. A battered old photo album from the 1930s contains her picture. That album belongs to a British Jewish family with ancestral roots in Novogrudok, and they have now established a link by friendship between Michle and old family connections. The statue replicates her photograph. Two generations of the British family are guests of honour at today's ceremony. It's a tale of tragedy, redemption and ultimately an affirmation of life and survival.

We share Soviet champagne and a buffet with the Minsk survivors before we are driven to another memorial, in a deep depression at the side of the road marking the spot chosen by the Nazis for mass murder. Then we visit a beautiful lake a little way down the road, where the battalion of Estonian police who committed the atrocities went to wash the blood from their hands and clothes. The Nazis enjoyed enlisting others to help with the dirty work, not that the Estonians needed too much encouragement, it seems.

Seventy-four years on, memories have not dimmed and the visceral pain remains. But little Michle has at last returned home.

Jeannette Josse (the British connection to Michle Sosnovsky) has self-published a wonderful book of photographs telling the family story and explaining the extraordinary course of events leading to the founding of the new memorial. Further details are available from Jeannette direct (e jdjosse@aol.com).

it into the list. If you're feeling ambitious, acquaint yourself with the oblast's public transport system and hop on a bus to explore. If not, and if you don't have your own transport or a local friend who can drive you, the only option is to book yourself an excursion through one of the tourist agencies in town. You will at least get to see something of the natural beauty and architectural splendour of this lovely region.

Oshmyany (Ашмяны/Ошмяны) Oshmyany, a small, 14th-century town that was once a fortress of the Grand Dukes of Lithuania, is situated northeast of Lida, just 20km from the border with Lithuania. It boasts the beautiful St Mikhail Archangel Roman Catholic Church, originally constructed in the early 15th century and rebuilt between 1900 and 1906 in the renowned Vilnius Baroque style. Also here is the brick-built Orthodox Church of the Resurrection; together, both buildings frame the historical town square. The well-known Belarusian painter Korchevsky (1806–33) was born in the town. He studied in Vilnius and St Petersburg, before leaving the country for Italy in 1829.

Krevo (Крэва/Крево) Along the M7 road in the direction of Minsk, 30km to the southeast of Oshmyany is Krevo, with its ruined remains of a 14th-century castle in the style of Lida, Mir and Novogrudok, all of which were part of the same defensive line that was constructed to repel Crusaders. As with many of the castles along this line of fortification, it suffered extensive damage during the Northern Wars (1700–21). Its final destruction was all but complete during a three-year period in World War I, when Krevo found itself on the front line between the opposing armies of Germany and Russia.

Smorgon (Смаргонь/Сморгонь) Some 30km northeast of Krevo on the P106 road, Smorgon is an ancient town standing close to the Viliya River, surrounded by scenic countryside. The powerful Radzivili dynasty that so influenced the historic towns of Mir and Njasvizh had many connections here. Napoleon's long retreat from the gates of Moscow in 1812 passed directly through the town and the emperor himself made a last stop before passing over command to Marshal Murat and escaping to Paris with only his personal guard. The 19th-century Roman Catholic Church of St Mikhail has an extremely unusual structure, comprising an eight-sided base alongside a multi-tiered belfry with a hipped roof and octagonal drum at the apex.

Shchuchin (Шчучын/Щучин) Some 60km due east of Grodno on the road to Lida lies the town of Shchuchin, with its rare fortress-church that dates from the 16th century. Near to the town's enormous central square, 100m by 200m, stand the Roman Catholic Church of St Theresa (built in the Classical style in 1827), the Orthodox Church of St Mikhail the Archangel (constructed in the second half of the 19th century) and some traders' houses dating from the late 18th to early 19th centuries.

Slonim (Слонім/Слоним) Down in the southeastern corner of the oblast (on the north–south M11 motorway, 101km due south of Lida and 142km southeast of Grodno) stands Slonim with its majestic Great Synagogue, now sadly in a state of very considerable disrepair. It is said that Jews first settled here in 1388, while the synagogue itself was built between 1642 and 1648. The inventor responsible for running water in Belarus, Hirsch Kunitza, was Jewish, and the first homes in the country with running water were in Slonim. Michael Marks, Jewish co-founder of retail giant Marks and Spencer, was born here. Today the Jewish community in Slonim is small and in need of support to help re-establish itself; British charity The Together Plan (page 116) is looking to initiate a restoration project to restore the synagogue to its former glory.

6

Vitebsk City and Oblast
Віцебск/Витебск

Telephone code 212

Bordering Lithuania, Latvia and Russia, the Vitebsk region is situated in the north and northeastern part of Belarus and occupies almost one-fifth of the country's total territory. The administrative centre of the oblast is the charming and elegant city of Vitebsk, birthplace and long the home of artist Marc Chagall, with a population of around 378,000. Situated on the Western Dvina River (where the Vitba and Luchosa rivers also converge) and famed for its rich cultural and scientific traditions, it's one of my favourites of the country's six cities.

This whole area is the country's lakeland, with 11 out of the 19 major lakes of Belarus being found here. It is a region of delightful natural beauty and charm, of deep blue lakes and stunning pine forests, famed way beyond the country's national boundaries. The most precious gem in the entire area is undoubtedly the collection of Braslav Lakes, 50 of them in total, covering a surface area of 130km², all incorporated into a national park, with rare species of plants and wildlife preserved in their natural environment. And situated in the southwest of the region is the stunning Berezinsky Biosphere Reserve, over 85% of which is primeval virgin forest.

The concept of sustainable ecotourism is one that the country has been striving to promote for some years now, with limited success until recently insofar as visitors from outside its borders are concerned. Things are now on the up as the country gradually increases its preparedness for incoming tourists; and probably more so than in the other oblasts, there is real potential for truly developing ecotourism here in a manner that complements the natural resources existing in abundance, while at the same time securing their protection into the future.

The oldest town in all Belarus, Polotsk, is also in this region. Founded in AD862, this Slavic settlement is known to have been the centre of Christianity during the time of Rus, the first Russian state. Do try very hard to visit this delightful town. You won't be disappointed.

Vitebsk is widely regarded as being second only to Minsk as the cultural capital of the country and then not by much. It is the location of the popular and much-loved Slavianski (Slavic) Bazaar (see box, page 256), an international song and culture festival that takes place annually in the open air in late July and early August. Most of the musical programme is devoted to a celebration of ethnic Slavic music. As well as the bazaar, the city also hosts 27 other annual festivals celebrating the performing arts, including modern dance and chamber music. At times, it seems the entire city morphs into festival mode. And the original School of Arts founded in 1919 by Marc Chagall continues to thrive. Overall, there is little doubt that the reputation of Vitebsk as an international centre for the promotion of the performing arts and fine art is assured.

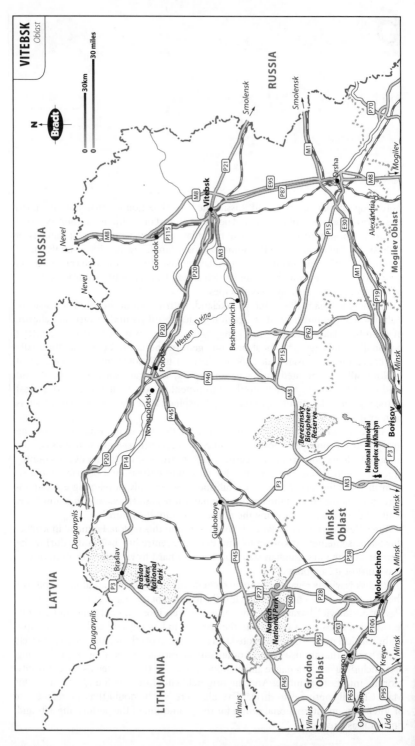

It nicely fits the character of the city of Vitebsk (as a place where artistic temperament can flourish) that its foundation is based on the romance of legend. It is said that while travelling through the region in the year AD974, Princess Olga of Kiev was so impressed by the beauty of the hill at the junction of the Western Dvina and Vitba rivers, marking the site of an old Slavic settlement of the Krivichi tribe, that she ordered a city to be founded in that very spot. At best this tale is apocryphal and at worst a manufactured fiction, but so attractive it is that 974 is the official year of the foundation of the city! In reality, it is likely to have first been settled by the Vikings exploring south during their migration from their Scandinavian homelands in search of trade with Greece.

Whatever the true story, the existence of Vitebsk as a fortified centre of trade and commerce is recorded in *Chronicles* dating from the 11th century. At this time, trade links with the Russian cities Kiev and Novgorod, with Byzantium and with western Europe were already in existence along the Dnieper and Dvina. Unfortunately (but not surprisingly), this marked the territory as being prime for invasion and subjugation on the part of warring princes and foreign armies. It became part of the Grand Lithuanian Duchy early in the 14th century and then, on 15 July 1410, significant numbers of Vitebsk citizens helped the combined armies of Lithuania, Poland and the Czech kingdom to defeat the Teutonic Order at the famous Battle of Grunwald. In 1597, limited rights of self-determination under Magdeburg Law were granted, only to be taken away when all of the town's Orthodox churches were closed in 1622 following the assassination of Uniate archbishop Kuntsevich during the course of a riot in the city. Then, between 1700 and 1721, Vitebsk suffered considerable damage to both fabric and infrastructure in the Northern Wars that set Sweden against the Russian Empire. The town was almost completely destroyed by fire in 1708 and, over time, trade fell away as the population diminished.

Vitebsk was annexed by Russia in 1772, leading to limited revival of the city's wealth, but when Emperor Napoleon invaded the country on 24 June 1812, Vitebsk found itself directly in the line of the march to Moscow. Napoleon had bought the loyalty of the noblemen of Vitebsk by promising to restore the right of self-determination that had been the privilege of the city in its time as an administratively autonomous region of the former Polish-Lithuanian Commonwealth. However, the peasants of the region were mobilised en masse by the Russian imperial army; and we all know who won in the end. On 11 July, the Russian army was billeted here on the retreat from Polotsk and then, over a three-day period from 13 July, there was very heavy fighting involving tens of thousands of troops on the western fringes of the city. At the conclusion of the engagement, the Russians were forced to retreat eastward. On 16 July, Napoleon entered Vitebsk. He established his headquarters in the Governor's Palace, high on the bank of the Dvina, but his stay was only a short one. The emperor had more pressing business in Moscow but as history tells, things didn't end well for him there.

In the meantime, incessant war had taken its toll on the city. By 1825, the population was fewer than 17,000 and it was not until the emancipation of the serfs throughout the Russian Empire in 1861 that its fortunes began to revive, greatly assisted by the construction of two major rail links (Moscow–Riga and St Petersburg–Kiev) that crossed here. The census of 1897 shows that the population was then over 66,000.

In 1892, the famous Russian painter Ilya Repin took up residence in the city. This was the start of its golden age as a spiritual home for notable painters, including

'It is perfectly in order to shoot the President when he is on the stage,' said the man sitting behind us at the concert. It was an unusual conversational gambit. Do we really look like potential assassins? Our informant explained that President Lukashenko is a bit touchy about being photographed, but would not mind at all if we clicked away while he was up front on the stage. Dozens of photographers shot the President of Belarus as he duly opened the Vitebsk festival on a sultry summer evening.

Every year since 1992, the city of Vitebsk in the northeast corner of Belarus has hosted an extravagant festival of music, art and culture known as the Slavianski Bazaar. If Marc Chagall could be conjured up from the grave, he would not recognise much of suburban Vitebsk with its ranks of apartment blocks. Chagall lived in the town's Jewish quarter for over 20 years. The old centre of Vitebsk has been handsomely restored, and the city on the banks of the Western Dvina always charms the crowds who attend Vitebsk's week-long festival in July each year.

Presidential words, fraternal greetings from Slavic brothers in Kiev and Moscow, drum rolls and genuine applause for the president presaged a spectacular evening of heavy bass, diamante thongs, clever acrobatics and folksy dance ensembles. Pop and rock aplenty with some jazz and classics thrown in. President Lukashenko evidently enjoyed the spectacle from the presidential box, and we enjoyed watching Lukashenko. Plenty of security chaps, whispering regularly into their lapels, kept a watchful eye on the crowd.

Down on stage, singers and dancers from all over the Slavic world performed to polite applause. Guests from other countries too: among them Germany, Belgium, Latvia, Croatia and Kazakhstan. In 2009, it took a kid from Norway to really get things going. Alexander Rybak, winner for Norway of that year's Eurovision Song Contest, happens to be Belarusian by birth, so Vitebsk was a kind of homecoming for the local boy made good. No-one worried that Rybak hailed from Minsk, not Vitebsk, and left Belarus when he was just nine years old.

Chagall himself, Kazimir Malyevich, Mstislav Daburzhynsky and others. Further, many masters came to teach at Chagall's school. It must have been an exciting time to be around, with the streets being turned into one enormous art studio, where buildings and the sights of the city were brought to life on canvas. Much of the substantial body of work that was created then is still to be found in the city, a rich representation in tableau form of life here early in the 20th century.

Always a multi-faith city, Vitebsk prior to World War I was over 50% Jewish, with Yiddish in wide use as a common means of communication. During the war, the town became a military garrison close to the front line and the population was swelled by a significant refugee contingent. In the climate of unrest and dissatisfaction that prevailed, Bolshevik propaganda was widespread. The town's soviet was established only two days after Lenin took power in the country, but there was more misery in the civil war that ensued. Little by little, things began to improve and the revival continued apace during the intensive industrialisation of the Soviet Union under Stalin, although the population suffered just as much as the rest of the country by reason of the infamous and brutal ideological purges of the 1930s.

The latest phase of industrial prosperity came to an end with the Nazi invasion in 1941. Only days after it began, bloody engagements were taking place in the vicinity of the city. Thanks to heroic rearguard action on the part of the Red Army

For a week each July, Vitebsk is consumed by culture high and low. Offering everything from poetry to pop, artists from more than two dozen nations present themselves to attentive crowds. Of course, the locals love anyone with a Belarusian connection. 'Literature is the conscience of the nation,' proclaimed Yevgeny Yevtushenko gravely at a reading at the 2009 Slavianski Bazaar, a thought that was politely noted by the poet's devoted admirers. What really won their hearts, though, was the revelation that the Siberian-born poet (remember *Zima Station?*) has a local connection. Yevtushenko's grandfather was born in Belarus. In 2010, Georgian singer Lasha Ramishvili won the hearts of the Vitebsk crowd by astutely choosing to sing a traditional Belarusian folk song.

The city so intimately associated with Marc Chagall sparkles at festival time. The sun usually shines, there are barbecues and beer tents aplenty, and a diligent army of orange-clad litter collectors keep the city impressively clean. In a city that is always intimate, it is easy to get close to the performers. I learnt a little about fandom too, as a group of starstruck girls pressed around the doors of a smart hotel, anxious to catch a glimpse of their favourite pop idols. Men muttering into their lapels kept the minimally skirted crowd at bay.

As I walked with friends through Vitebsk after the 2009 opening ceremony, we heard a symphony of police sirens behind us on the main road. Loudspeakers then proclaimed that the road must be cleared. We watched and waited and then a cavalcade of limousines slid by, heading out of town. Were I at home, I might have been tempted to take a quick pic or two. But then I remembered Belarusian etiquette. The President may only be shot when he is on stage.

Nicky Gardner is co-editor of hidden europe *magazine. Find out more about her work at* w *hiddeneurope.co.uk; see ad, page 118.*

on the western bank of the Dvina River, a significant proportion of the population and most of the industry was evacuated and moved far to the east. But it was only a matter of time before the town fell. The Germans established a huge garrison and those residents who remained in and around the city were brutally repressed, not least as punishment and reprisal for the large-scale underground and partisan activity that was established here. The Red Army returned to claim the city once more in June 1944, but only after the fiercest of battles, often involving hand-to-hand fighting in the suburbs. Only 15 of the city's more significant buildings and 186 civilians survived from a pre-war population of 170,000, 30,000 of whom had been Jews. Nearly a quarter of a million of the region's inhabitants had either been killed in action or murdered in Nazi concentration camps. It was not to be until the end of the 1960s that the city's population reached that of 1939. For over 500 years, no war in this part of Europe has passed the city by without plunder, looting and destruction, such is the strategic importance of its geographical location.

Today, the region is home to some of the country's largest industrial and scientific plants, as befits the area's scientific heritage, while cultural life and the arts are also flourishing. The great traditions begun by Repin and Chagall continue to be upheld, and this cosmopolitan city can indeed be said to represent a nexus of the old and the new.

6

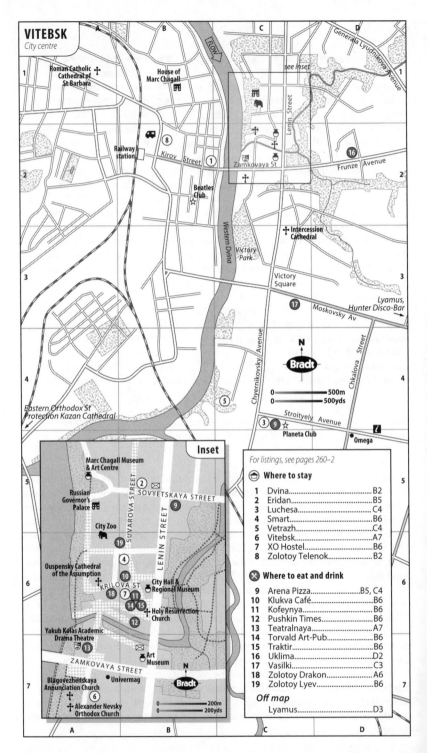

VITEBSK
City centre

FLOW

Generala Lyudnikova Avenue

Roman Catholic
Cathedral of
St Barbara

House of
Marc Chagall

see inset

Lenin Street

Railway
station

Kirov   Street   ①   ⑧

Zamkovaya St

Frunze   Avenue   ⑯

Beatles
Club

Western Dvina

† Intercession
Cathedral

*Victory
Park*

Victory
Square

Chvernikovsky Avenue

*Lyamus,
Hunter Disco-Bar*

⑰   Moskovsky Av

Chkalova Street

N
Bradt

0 ═══ 500m
0 ═══ 500yds

⑤

*Eastern Orthodox St
Protection Kazan Cathedral*

Stroitely Avenue

③ ⑨
Planeta Club

Omega

Inset

Marc Chagall Museum
& Art Centre

Russian
Governor's
Palace

② ✉
SOVYETSKAYA STREET

SUVAROVA STREET

LENIN STREET

⑨

City Zoo
⑲

Ouspensky Cathedral
of the Assumption

④

⑩

KRILOVA ST
⑱ ⑦ ⑪
⑭ ⑮

City Hall &
Regional Museum

† Holy Resurrection
Church

⑫

Yakub Kolas Academic
Drama Theatre
⑬

ZAMKOVAYA STREET

✉

Art
Museum

N
Bradt

Blagovezhenskaya
Annunciation Church
⑥

Univermag

† Alexander Nevsky
Orthodox Church

0 ═══ 200m
0 ═══ 200yds

GETTING THERE AND AWAY

BY TRAIN Vitebsk is located at the crossroads of major pan-European rail links north–south and east–west. The splendid station building is located in a square of pleasant gardens at the western end of Kirov Street. There are several 'express' trains a day to Minsk (*4–5hrs; BYN15 one-way*), while within the country there are also slower and less frequent services to Brest and Grodno (*both around 12hrs overnight; BYN32 one-way*). Several trains a day call at Polotsk (*1hr 30mins; BYN6 one-way*). Leaving the station, it's a straight 15-minute walk east to the Kirov Bridge and the town centre, where you can take your bearings for all of the city's major sites.

BY BUS There are 12 buses a day to and from Minsk (*5hrs 30mins; BYN11 one-way*), and the bus station is located 10 minutes on foot to the northeast of the railway station. You can also get a marshrutka from Minsk (*4hrs; BYN10 one-way*); services are hourly and always busy, so booking in advance is strongly recommended (**w** *v-minsk.by*). There are also regular bus and marshrutka services to Polotsk (*2hrs; BYN5–6 one-way*). Tallinn in Estonia can also be reached by coach and although this is an interesting way to enter the country, it is rather long.

GETTING AROUND

ON FOOT The city certainly repays exploration on foot, although the sites of interest are spread over a large geographical area. It's a very hilly place and there are climbs between the key locations. Come suitably shod and be prepared for some leg work! A number of sights are located on either bank of the Dvina River, in the vicinity of the Kirov Bridge. On a bright and sunny day late in autumn, a stroll along the river here, through the splendid wooded gardens, is a real delight. The other advantage of walking is that it affords an opportunity to enjoy the pre-war architecture at leisure, such as remains, though there is a rich diversity of attractive architecture generally. Look particularly for examples of the low red-brick buildings so prominent in the works of Marc Chagall. And the upside of the topography is that there are expansive views to be had all over, with big skies and a real feeling of loftiness. Unexpected ravines hide lovely parks that are perfect for promenading, especially by the Vitba River. The best vantage point (and one of the finest urban views in all six of the country's cities, in my opinion) is from the edge of the square at the front of the stunning Ouspensky Cathedral at the end of Krilova Street (off Suvarova), high above the east bank of the river. So, if the weather is fine, don't give yourself too onerous a task by trying to cram in an extra museum or two; plan to tick less off your list and spend more time ambling. Many people will tell you that the best time to visit is when the Slavianski Bazaar is on, and it's certainly true that the dazzling array of colour and activity is irresistible. I have a friend, a local writer and journalist, who always encourages me to come at festival time, when the bars are full. I'm not so sure: my favourite time to meander the lovely streets is out of season, in spring and autumn; if you're lucky with the weather, it's a wonderful opportunity to stroll unhindered and appreciate the elegance of the city with very few people around.

BY PUBLIC TRANSPORT Otherwise, take advantage of the cheap, cheerful and plentiful (but overcrowded) supply of **buses**, **trams** and **trolleybuses**. Most rides, however long, should not cost more than BYN0.50. The tram system is one of the oldest in this part of Europe, second only to Kiev's. It was first constructed to facilitate the carriage of goods, materials and supplies, on the basis that the city was too hilly for horses! **Marshrutka** services also operate and there are plenty of **taxis**; no fare anywhere in the city should be more than BYN25, but be sure to agree the price in advance.

TOURIST INFORMATION

As in previous chapters, please allow me again to mention that every effort has been made to establish comprehensive and corroborated information on opening times of restaurants, museums, bars and clubs, but occasionally you may find that reality appears to fly in the face of ostensibly reliable published data available from a number of sources. Wherever you can, do check ahead. Increasing numbers of tourist agencies, both state and private, can now be found in the city, but be sure to establish their credentials first. The best source of information is the Tourist Information Centre for Vitebsk region [258 D4] (*10 Stroityely Av;* ☎ *58 95 13;* e *tour-vit@mail.ru;* w *tourvitebsk.gov.by;* ⊕ *08.00–13.00 & 14.00–17.00 Mon–Fri*). A word of caution; at the time of writing, news reached me that the centre had plans to relocate, though information as to when and where to was disappointingly unavailable. If you can, check ahead before you visit. A decent map with good graphics (although in Cyrillic) can be purchased for BYN9.50 at booksellers, stalls and retail outlets in the city, including at the railway station. Before you arrive, visit w vitebskcity.by for a useful range of tourist and visitor information.

WHERE TO STAY

UPMARKET

🏠 **Eridan** [258 B5] (26 rooms) 17/21 Sovyetskaya St; ☎ 60 44 99; e hotel-eridan@mail.ru; w eridan-vitebsk.com. Handily located for the Marc Chagall Museum & Art Centre in a 19th-century building on the corner of Sovyetskaya & Suvarova, this friendly boutique hotel is rated the best in the city, though the Smart is now running it close. It's just a tad shiny, but with good service to match. Facilities inc lobby bar, restaurant (⊕ *07.00–midnight daily;* $$$), sauna & pool (separate charge), free Wi-Fi & secure parking (separate charge). **$$$$**

🏠 **Smart** [258 B6] (8 rooms) 11 Suvarova St; ☎ 64 40 00; e smartvitebsk@gmail.com; w smartvitebsk.com. This is a small but charming hotel, centrally located in another lovely fin-de-siècle building. Sadly it's not disability friendly; there are 3 floors & no lift. Facilities inc decent European/Mediterranean restaurant specialising in seafood (⊕ *07.00–23.00 daily;* $$$), 24hr reception services, free Wi-Fi & free secure parking to the rear. All rooms are well appointed & standards of service are good. **$$$$**

MID-RANGE

🏠 **Luchesa** [258 C4] (146 rooms) 1 Stroityely Av; ☎ 29 85 00; e reception@luchesa.by; w luchesa.by. This is a concrete Soviet-style monolith with décor to match, but it does have the advantage of being at the intersection of major routes, although some way to the south of the city centre but with easy access to the sights by public transport. It is 3.5km to both the railway & the bus station from here. There's a passable restaurant serving Russian & European cuisine (⊕ *07.00–23.00 daily;* $$), while other facilities inc a bar, travel & excursion bureau, hairdresser, solarium, currency exchange & a kiosk selling souvenirs & newspapers. **$$$**

🏠 **Vetrazh** [258 C4] (147 rooms) 25/1 Chyernikovsky Av; ☎ 27 22 75. Built in 1989 & located not far from the Luchesa on the eastern bank of the Dvina River, to the south of the centre. With rooms on 8 floors, it's pretty standard, Soviet-style stuff: functional, modest, but relatively cheerful. An upsurge in prices has placed this hotel in the mid-range bracket, though sadly there has been no corresponding increase in quality, notwithstanding some modernisation. In-house advertising pitches strongly for the youth market. Services inc restaurant, bar, snack bar & a very noisy disco! **$$$**

BUDGET

🏠 **Dvina** [258 B2] (56 rooms) 41 Ilinskava St; ☎ 35 91 73. Located on the western bank of the Dvina River close to the Kirov Bridge (& therefore very central), this hostel-like hotel has the usual choice of rooms, along with a restaurant, disco & secure parking. Cheap & cheerful. Pets are also welcome! **$$**

🏠 **Vitebsk** [258 A7] (201 rooms) 5/2A Zamkovaya St; ☎ 64 32 80; e info@hotel-vitebsk.by; w hotel-vitebsk.by. In the city centre, 1.5km from the railway & bus stations, the hotel is on 12 floors with a range of rooms & suites, plus restaurant, bar, travel & excursion bureau, currency exchange, conference room, hairdresser – & lots of concrete. Don't expect too much here, but it will serve a functional purpose at a competitive price, especially as it's well situated for easy access to the city's sights. **$$**

✳ 🏠 **XO Hostel** [258 B6] (56 beds in 6 dorms & 2 twin rooms) 10/2 Suvarova St; ☎ 61 96 06; m 29 618 45 54; e post@xostel.by; w xostel. by. For cost, location & value for money this clean & cheerful hostel cannot be beaten, but it's difficult to find. At the junction of Suvarova & Krilova, look for an arch with a modest 'Hostel' sign above on the south side of Krilova. Pass through it & you'll find a door with an even smaller & more unassuming sign, round the corner on the right. Run by a husband-&-wife team who are both friendly & cheerful, it has no frills, but the common areas for cooking & washing are perfectly acceptable & the sleeping arrangements do the job. Free Wi-Fi available. Another selling point is the location, which is first class. Metres from Ouspensky Cathedral & a range of eateries, it's the perfect base for your stay in this delightful city. **$$**

🏠 **Zolotoy Telenok** [258 B2] (25 rooms) 6a Belaruskaya St; ☎ 64 03 64. This is a small hotel/hostel within easy walking distance of both bus & railway stations. Amenities inc café, bar, secure parking, hairdresser, billiards & bowling. **$$**

✖ WHERE TO EAT AND DRINK

The city's reputation has more to do with culture and the arts than fine dining, but some restaurants are worthy of note and are listed below. The restaurant at **Eridan Hotel** (see opposite) enjoys a good reputation for excellent food and service, but it is expensive. At the other end of the scale there is now a McDonald's in town, but don't tell anyone I told you. As an alternative dining experience if you are **self-catering**, the huge supermarket Omega [258 D5] (on the corner at the junction of Stroityely Avenue and Chkalova Street) has delicious ready-cooked meals that are good to go; or try the excellent **take-away menu** at the gastronome on the west side of Chkalova Street, between Moskovsky and Stroityely avenues. Additionally, most branches of the supermarket chain Vesta have a good selection of meals to go.

RESTAURANTS

✖ **Teatralnaya** [258 A7] 2 Zamkovaya St; ☎ 33 63 98; w teatralnoe.by; ⏱ noon–04.00 daily. This used to be a trendy venue with a large artsy clientele; not surprising really, as it's located beneath the Yakub Kolas Theatre. But I hear things have nosedived here. Latest reports are that the vaults are empty every night & that all is dingy now, from service to food to ambience. I haven't been for a while. Do take a look, but go without expectations & with a Plan B to hand. After the restaurant closes, the venue becomes a nightclub, well into the small hours. **$$$$**

✖ **Arena Pizza** [258 B5] 57/4 Lenin St; m 33 305 20 22; also at 3/3 Stroityely Av [258 C4]; m 33 305 25 08; w arena-pizza.by; ⏱ 10.00–23.00 daily. These 2 related emporia serve standard but decent-quality pizza in a mock Italianate café setting. There's a particularly fine vegetable pizza on the menu & a delivery service is available until 23.00 (m 29 714 71 47, 29 715 71 57). Very good value. **$$$**

✳ ✖ **Lyamus** [258 D3] 1 Pobyedy Av; ☎ 57 59 08; ⏱ noon–23.00 daily. A little way from the sights & in the southeast of the city centre, this fine restaurant & micro-brewery is nevertheless recommended. Don't be put off by the unappealing exterior; inside, the traditional Belarusian décor is well done, the beer is very good & the food is decent, with friendly service to match. **$$$**

✖ **Pushkin Times** [258 B6] 4 Tolstova St; m 29 733 66 00; ⏱ noon–02.00 daily. Centrally located,

6

the vaulted interior makes for a cosy dining experience. Good food & decent service. **$$$**

✗ Traktir [258 B6] 2 Suvarova St; ☎35 83 83; w vtraktir.com; ⊕ noon–midnight daily. Long regarded as the best restaurant in town both for atmosphere & the quality of its menu. The halo may have slipped just a little but many still rate it highly. Well located, close to the City Hall & in one of the older, more attractive streets in the whole city. Give it a try. **$$$**

✗ Uklima [258 D2] 10 Frunze Av; ☎35 91 54; ⊕ 10.00–midnight daily. There are 2 dining rooms here; both are pub-style cosy & the food is good. **$$$**

✗ Vasilki [258 C3] 9 Moskovsky Av; m 29 557 42 73; ⊕ 10.00–23.00 daily. An outpost of the Vasilki chain in Minsk; expect faux-old Belarusian décor & traditional cuisine. Cheerful service & decent food. **$$$**

✱ **✗ Zolotoy Drakon** [258 A6] 8–10 Krilova St; ☎65 30 00; ⊕ noon–midnight daily. Located near Ouspensky Cathedral, serving good-quality Chinese food at reasonable prices. **$$$**

✗ Zolotoy Lyev [258 B6] 20/13 Suvarova St; ☎35 81 11; ⊕ noon–midnight daily. On the same street as Traktir but further up the hill between Ouspensky Cathedral & the Marc Chagall Museum

& Art Centre, near the entrance to the zoo, this is one for the summer months when good shashlik can be enjoyed alfresco on the terrace, though inside is recommended too. I haven't tried it but good friends have & they like it. Decent value, & regular live music. **$$**

CAFÉS & BARS

⊑ Klukva Café [258 B6] 3 Krilova St; m 33 395 30 35; ⊕ 09.00–22.30 daily. Formerly Biskvit café, all is bright & friendly here with good coffee & desserts to match. Decent b/fast too.

⊑ Kofeynya [258 B6] 2 Suvarova St; m 29 137 07 30; ⊕ 10.00–23.00 daily. Retro & homely inside, with a decent terrace for the summer – & the coffee is good. Stop off here for a mid-wander rest.

✱ **♀Torvald Art-Pub** [258 B6] 1 Tolstova St; m 29 712 11 11; ⊕ noon–04.00 daily. Hugely popular with locals, this relatively new pub in a top location at the bottom of Suvarova offers a lively atmosphere, decent food, good range of beer, very friendly service & live music. The proprietor is quite a character. It's *the* place to go in Vitebsk says one of my correspondents, who tells me it's rammed every night. Enough said.

ENTERTAINMENT AND NIGHTLIFE

Vitebsk has a greater than usual number of higher-education establishments for a city of its size and has a substantial student population. Not surprisingly, then, youth culture is reasonably well catered for. This means that you might expect to find a wide choice of bars, and you won't be disappointed, especially at the lower end of Suvarova Street and its environs. This is a good opportunity for you to undertake some exploration of your own. Most of the bars are open from late morning until 23.00 or midnight, while those that are also clubs will stay open until well into the small hours for you to dance the night away.

☆ **Beatles Club** [258 B2] 12 Kastrichnitskaya (Oktyabrskaya) St; m 29 514 02 09; w beatlesclub.by

☆ **Hunter Disco-Bar** [258 D3] 7a Tereshkovoi St; m 33 301 50 50; ⊕ 18.00–04.00 Sun–Thu, 18.00–06.00 Fri–Sat. Located away in the

southeast of the city centre & beyond Lyamus. Come here for a very loud & very late night after dinner for a few beers. Regular themed nights. Popular with locals.

☆ **Planeta** [258 C4] 3 Stroityely Av; m 29 719 99 03; ⊕ 18.00–06.00 Fri–Sat

SHOPPING

Vitebsk is famed more for its status as a centre of fine art than for the quality of the shopping experience it offers. Chagall-related paraphernalia is omnipresent, but that apart, there is nothing here that you cannot find elsewhere in the country.

Since 1992 Vitebsk has hosted the 'Slavyanski Bazaar' festival, a glorious celebration of international song and culture that attracts artists primarily from Belarus, Russia and Ukraine, though there are also guests from a significant number of other countries, both Slavic and non-Slavic. For one glorious week in high summer, the entire city turns into a gigantic street party, with 5,000 artists performing at significant and fringe events, seemingly on every street. The English-language website w fest-sbv.by/en is a mine of colourful facts and information on the history of the festival and current practical arrangements. The main events take place at the purpose-built 6,500-seat domed amphitheatre on Frunze Avenue in the middle of town, just along from the junction with Lenin Street. Now 25 years old, it's a sizeable concrete bowl and an enduring image of the city. Over three million people have attended events since it was built.

The **Univermag department store** [258 B7] on Zamkovaya Street has a reasonable array of traditional Belarusian handicrafts on offer (as does the railway station and the open market situated close by). The town's distillery produces some of the highest-quality vodka in the whole country and bottles aimed at the tourist market (in other words, just a little kitsch) are available in shops throughout the city.

OTHER PRACTICALITIES

There are **banks** and **currency-exchange bureaux** aplenty here, particularly on Lenin Street, although these do tend to close early. **ATMs** are now located all over the city. There are two **post offices** on Lenin Street [258 B5/B7] (*32 & 52/16*) that are both open until 19.00 on weekdays, as well as other branches throughout the city.

WHAT TO SEE AND DO

Of the six major cities in Belarus, Vitebsk has been fortunate to be able to retain a palpable and living sense of history (much more so than any of the other five), notwithstanding the widespread destruction wrought in the Great Patriotic War. To varying degrees, the prevailing influence and atmosphere in those five is certainly the more recent Soviet past, but not so here. Whatever the reason, there is a delicate sense of refinement in this elegant town.

MUSEUMS AND GALLERIES In terms of the arts, it will be no surprise that Marc Chagall's presence dominates the city.

Marc Chagall Museum and Art Centre ✳ [258 C1] (*музей Марка Шагала і Арт-цэнтр/музей Марка Шагала и Арт-центр; 2 Putna St;* ☏ *48 55 68 (also for booking guided visits);* e *chagall@chagall.belpak.vitebsk.by;* w *chagal-vitebsk.com;* ⊕ *Apr–Sep 11.00–19.00 Tue–Sun, last entry 18.30; admission BYN2.50*) Opened in 1992, this fine building is situated in an especially green part of town that is pleasing on the eye, where a major European collection of 300 original works of art consisting of dreamy lithographs, xylographs, etchings and aquatints is displayed on two floors. The collection also owns a series of illustrations to Nikolai Gogol's novel *Dead Souls*. Note that photography is not allowed, but each work has an identifying label in

6

English. I especially like *La ville* from 1968, with its depiction of the single-storey wooden houses to be found all over town a hundred years ago. The ground floor is devoted to works of the artist, while the second floor is used as an exhibition space. Displays of works of different artists are on show from time to time.

House of Marc Chagall ✻ [258 B1] (*дом-музей Марка Шагала/Дом-музей Марка Шагала; 11 Pokrovskaya St;* ✆ *66 34 68;* ⊕ *Apr–Sep 11.00–19.00 Tue–Sun, last entry 18.30; admission BYR2.50*) The artist's father built this house at the end of the 19th century and it's an archetypically eastern European red-brick Jewish home. Chagall spent his formative years here; indeed, his earliest scribblings as a child were committed to paper as he lay above the fireplace in the kitchen. He also painted the view from the lounge window many times, subsequently recalling this period of his life with great affection in his autobiography. Opened to visitors at the same time as the museum, it displays articles and relics of Jewish family life from the late 19th and 20th centuries, though only the medicine cabinet and spice grinder in the kitchen are Chagall family originals. There are also copies of archive documents, photographs and works of art on the walls detailing the life of the artist and his family in the city. Look for *The Street* (1920), showing this very house, and also *Small Shop in Vitebsk* (1914), an image of the front room, which was used as a workshop and stall for selling everyday essentials to supplement the family income. Chagall's uncle was a self-taught violinist, though not a particularly good one. His grandfather's favourite perch was on the very roof of the building, and Chagall combined both into the fiddler on the roof image in *Death* (1908), also to be found on display. The house is very small (11 people lived here!), but it's well worth a visit. Many of the exhibits have labels in English and there's a small selection of souvenirs and books at the entrance desk.

Outside in the back garden is an attractive statue of the artist. Walk out of the yard and turn left along Pokrovskaya Street. In a few hundred metres you will come to another Chagall monument at the point where a number of roads converge. This used to be the market square, and a number of red-brick buildings of the time survive. His father worked as a fishmonger here. The statue was erected in 1992 to commemorate the artist's 150th birthday and it depicts his wife Bella floating above Chagall himself, who sits holding his hand to his forehead. The image of someone floating is classic Chagall. The artist's pose is something of an enigma, though locals say that his demeanour thus results from the location of his seat directly in front of the large Socialist mural opposite. Decide for yourselves.

Art Museum [258 B7] (*Віцебскі мастацкі музей/Витебский художественный музей; 32 Lenin St;* ✆ *33 63 01;* ⊕ *10.00–18.00 Tue–Sun; admission BYN4*) Many of the artists featured here were natives of the region, including Ilya Repin, who is widely regarded as being the founder of the art movement in the city.

Yakub Kolas Academic Drama Theatre [258 A7] (*Нацыянальны акадэмічны драматычны тэатр імя Якуба Коласа/Национальный академический драматический театр им. Я. Коласа; 2 Zamkovaya St;* ✆ *(box office) 62 63 81*) Built in the Classical style and once adorned with the same pale orange stucco as the City Hall and Russian Governor's Palace (it's now yellow), this theatre is home to a company that enjoys an enviable international reputation. It is one of only a small number in the whole country that presents performances exclusively in the Belarusian language. This should not be seen as a bar for foreign visitors, however, because presentations are usually so vividly striking and avant-garde in nature that language is only one

Vitebsk has many sons and daughters of repute whose fame is well known within the country, but perhaps the most internationally renowned of them all is the 'brilliant dreamer', the Surrealist painter Marc Chagall (1887–1985). He was born into a family of Hasidic Jews, one of ten children, and some of his best works display a charming nostalgia both for his devout upbringing and for the city of his birth. Life was difficult for the family, his father being a menial worker in the local fish factory, although it is clear from the artist's autobiography that his childhood was a happy one, in which he was allowed to endlessly roam the suburbs of the city and the surrounding countryside. But where Chagall was a dreamer, his father most certainly was not. In the absence of support from his parents to pursue his great passion for art, he left the city that he so loved in 1906 to study in St Petersburg. He moved to Paris in 1910 under the patronage of lawyer Max Vinaver. There he was befriended by Robert and Sonia Delaunay, in whose circles he found inspiration to develop Cubist ideas. He returned to Vitebsk prior to the outbreak of war in 1914 and married his fiancée Bella, who was to be a major influence on his later work. After the 1917 Revolution, he was appointed Commissar of Art for Vitebsk, a role that did not come easily to him. He also founded, directed and taught at the School of Arts in the city, but he moved to Moscow in 1920, then back to Paris in 1922. His work was denounced by the Nazis and, at the outbreak of war, the family moved to the south of France and then to the USA. When Bella died in 1944, Chagall was overcome with grief at the loss of his muse. He stopped painting for quite some time, although his subsequent relationship with Virginia Haggard (they had a son together) brought a return to creativity. Returning to France in 1947, he subsequently married Valentine Brodsky (in 1952). In the 1960s, he was commissioned to design stained-glass windows for the Hadassah University Medical Centre in Jerusalem, work that profoundly impacted upon his faith. Further commissions for murals and costume design followed in France and America. He died in 1985.

Influenced by Cubism and Surrealism but always an independent artist of unique style, Chagall referred to Vitebsk as 'my second Paris' (although some claim that he actually called Paris his 'second Vitebsk'), and cameo sketches of the city as it was in the early 20th century are reflected in many of the works of this great master. In January 1991, Vitebsk celebrated the first Marc Chagall Festival, then in June 1992 a monument to him was erected on his native Pokrovskaya Street, with a memorial inscription being placed on the wall of his home at the same time. The small wooden house is now open to the public and the city also has a first-class Chagall Museum (page 263).

part of the experience. Stand outside the front on the right-hand edge of the building (with your back to it) and walk towards Kirov Bridge to admire the view uphill and right of the Ouspensky Cathedral. On the left-hand edge a glorious vista of the city's architecture unfolds across the lower and upper parts of the city.

CHURCHES Most of the churches in the city (particularly those from the time of the Polish-Lithuanian Commonwealth) were destroyed, either in warfare or under the communists. At one point there were 60 churches and almost the same number of synagogues in this city of hills. Many of the churches have been restored or rebuilt with

6

glorious attention to detail, but all that is left of the synagogues is the ruined frontage of the one where the Chagall family worshipped, close to the old market square. Lean on the balustrade at the edge of the square outside Ouspensky Cathedral and, from your lofty perch, gaze over the lower city and count how many churches you can see. A splendid array of style and design awaits. Many are within walking distance of this point. Plot your route and away you go. Here is but a selection to tempt you:

Ouspensky Cathedral of the Assumption ✳ [258 A6] (Свята-Успенскі кафедральны сабор/Свято-Успенский кафедральный собор) Situated on the end of Krilova Street, high above the Dvina River on the eastern bank, this is an absolute delight. Originally constructed in 1777, little of the original building survived Stalin's demolition in 1936 and full reconstruction works were only completed in 2000. The interior is a vast open space, but the décor is most

---

FREE AS A BIRD   *Nicky Gardner*

Marc Chagall, born Moyshe Shagal in Vitebsk in 1887, died in exile in France in 1985. He left Vitebsk in 1922. The artist never returned to his native city. But scenes from Chagall's early life in the Vitebsk region continued to feature in his art to the very end of his life. His images, which dramatically defy the laws of physics, poignantly record the lost Jewish life of Vitebsk. Only Chagall, the master of metaphor, could capture all the colourful children of Israel in one sack.

> *Si je n'étais pas juif je n'aurais pas été un artiste*
> (Were I not a Jew, I would not be an artist at all)
> Marc Chagall, *Ma Vie* (1931)

Frayvia foygl. Free as a bird. That was Moyshe. Local boy. Nice kid. His pa was in the herring business. The man reeked of fish. And Moyshe's ma, well she ran a shop. Groceries, that sort of thing. They lived out near the railway line. Brick house on Pokrovskaya. Simple, nothing fancy. Like most folk round these parts, they were a hard-working family. Quiet, I'd say. Observed shabbat of course. The Torah and trade make good partners. *Toyre iz di beste skhoyre* – that's the way they saw it. And that's the way I see it.

Hey, look at that man sitting up there on that pointed gable. So high. He goes up there every morning, perches on the roof and eats *tzimmes*. Cannot be so comfy right up there.

Anyway, I was telling you about Moyshe. He stopped going to the synagogue after his Bar Mitzvah. Until then, he'd gone to *heder* with the other local lads. Moyshe had a fine teacher at the *heder*, a good man who taught the boys the prayer book and took them down to the steam bath (*banya*) on Fridays. The talk was that Moyshe's Hebrew wasn't up to much, but he really lapped up all those old Yiddish tales of how life once was in these parts. Of course, it's all changed now.

See all those wooden houses across the way? The little grey house. That's my place. Typical Vitebsk. You can see the domes of the cathedral beyond, over on the side of the river where the Russians live. Looks like that fella over there is carrying his house on his back. All our people are on the move. *Di shtot geyt.* The whole town is leaving. Leaving for ever. All except the fella up on the gable. Not sure about him. Not quite right in the head, I'd say. Or just a *luftmentsh*. Just like Moyshe himself. He grew up to be a bit of a *luftmentsh*.

Young Moyshe often went out to Liozna. The family hailed from there. A smallish spot on the road to Smolensk. You probably know it. Last of the Jewish *shtetls* in the Pale. The end of our world. Moyshe's Uncle Zusya still had a place out there. A barber, I think. They had a shop

266

sumptuous. Not only is the cathedral extremely pleasing on the eye inside and out, it is also ideally located for a fine meander. From the balustrade on the edge of the square, the view to the Kirov Bridge and beyond across the lower city is delightful, although the beauty of the vista hides dark deeds. On the other side of the river to the right of the bridge is old **Jewish Vitebsk** and there was a large ghetto here during the Nazi occupation, one of several across the city. Twenty thousand Jews were murdered in 1941 alone, up to 800 a day. Many were put on boats and drowned in the river. Reflect for a moment on the obscene disparity between the charm of the view today and the horrors that occurred here only decades ago. When you're ready to move on, the landscaped walkways down to the river and back are definitely worth exploring in every direction. Climb back up to the square and it's now a stroll of only a few hundred metres north high above the river to the Russian Governor's Palace and the Marc Chagall Museum

too. Moyshe was good at art. Sort of taught himself. He showed me a sketch once that he'd done on one of those trips out to Uncle Zusya's place.

When I was young, there were two parts to my world. There was my Vitebsk. Safe, Jewish. My dad used to take me round to the home of the *rebbe*. And then there was the Russian part of town. That was a different Vitebsk. It had churches and cathedrals, but I didn't know any Russians. They came and went. St Petersburg, Moscow. Always with the *ayznban*. The train made Vitebsk part of Russia. The train is Russia. Not my world.

After Moyshe stopped going to the *shabbat* service, his ma took him out of *heder* and sent him to the Russian school. Odd really. That sort of thing never happened in my day. They must have slipped the teacher something to get the boy in. The Russian school didn't normally accept Jewish lads. Everyone called him Moysey then. I guess it sounded a bit more Russian. Anyway, he must have done well because he went on to art college in St Petersburg, then moved to Paris.

You know, I didn't hear much of him for years. Then there was the Revolution, and next thing I knew Moyshe was back in town and one of the bigwigs. Grand title. Commissar for Art in Vitebsk. He founded the People's Art College, the local museum and got involved with the theatre. All good party stuff. By then he had married Berta. Local girl. You know her family, of course. The Rosenfelds. They had a jewellery store near the town hall.

Did I tell you about the green violinist? The fiddler on the roof? No, not yet? But that's not a tale for now, as dusk is falling. Strange, strange … look up by the church. There's a man flying over there. He has a sack over his shoulder. *Kol Israel, eyn torbe*. All the children of Israel in one sack. There'll be none of us at all left in Vitebsk soon. Good that Moyshe drew us all before he and Berta moved to France for good. There's even a picture of me, they say. I dunno if it's true. But a friend told me that Moyshe gave me a red beard in his painting. The red Jew. Keep a lookout for me, won't you?

C'est de cet instant (1911) que la métaphore, avec lui seul, marque son entrée triomphale dans la peinture moderne.
(It was at that instant (1911) and through him alone, that metaphor made its triumphant entry into modern painting)

The French poet André Breton writing in 1941 about the work of Marc Chagall.

Nicky Gardner is co-editor of hidden europe *magazine. Find out more about her work at* w *hiddeneurope.co.uk; see ad, page 118.*

and Art Centre, with the **City Zoo** [258 A6] in-between. The zoo itself is nothing special, though the old red-brick entrance building is a fine example of the early style once found all over the city. At any point of your choosing when you've seen enough, head east away from the river until you reach Suvarova Street. It has been attractively paved and pedestrianised, with a wide choice of coffee bars, restaurants and cafés for when you're in need of sustenance.

Just along from the cathedral on Krilova Street is Zolotoy Drakon (page 262), while Zolotoy Lyev (page 262) is next to the zoo's entrance building on the corner of Suvarova and Yanki Kupala. When refreshed, head downhill along Suvarova Street and explore the sights along Tolstova and Pushkina leading down to Zamkovaya Street, including City Hall, the Pushkin statue, Yakub Kolas Theatre and a number of beautiful churches.

Holy Resurrection Church [258 B6] (Васкрасенская царква/Воскресенская церковь) Situated at the bottom of the hill on Suvarova Street, this is probably my favourite of the city's churches. Built between 1772 and 1777 but substantially reconstructed in 2009 after virtual destruction in 1936, the exterior murals are justly famed. Also impressive are the twin bell towers.

Intercession Cathedral [258 C3] (Пакроўскі сабор/Покровский собор) Located on Shubina Street near the junction with Lenin Street and a short walk north from Victory Square, this beautiful 19th-century cathedral has lovely exterior murals worthy of your attention.

Alexander Nevsky Orthodox Church [258 A7] (Храм святога дабравернага князя Аляксандра Неўскага/Храм святого благоверного князя Александра Невского) Situated on Zamkovaya Street, close to the Western Dvina River, just across the road from the Yakub Kolas Academic Drama Theatre and within the grounds of the reconstructed Blagovezhenskaya Annunciation Church (described below), this is a tiny but strikingly beautiful reconstruction in wood of the 10th-century church that originally stood on this spot.

Blagovezhenskaya Annunciation Church [258 A7] (Дабравешчанская царква/Благовещенская церковь) A church has been standing on this site in Zamkovaya Street since the middle of the 12th century, but the original building, which had been extensively renovated in the 14th and 17th centuries, was reduced to rubble by the communists in 1961. Then in 1992 it was fully restored to its original appearance and magnificence (or at least, to how the architects imagined it to have been). The design technique, limestone blocks separated by two rows of brick, with the exterior being covered with a thin layer of stucco, is classically Byzantine and, with the exception of this church, there is evidence of only one other (at Novogrudok) north of the Black Sea. Sadly, the church at Novogrudok was never actually completed and now lies in ruins. Work on both of them was probably undertaken by the same team of Byzantine architects and builders.

Eastern Orthodox St Protection Kazan Cathedral [258 A4] (Царква Казанскай іконы Божай Маці/Церковь Казанской иконы Божией Матери) Erected in 1760 with elements of Baroque and early Classical, the white plaster of the exterior and the matte black of the cupolas splendidly enhance the glittering gold domes and crosses above. It is to be found on Maxim Gorky Street on the western bank of the Dvina River, away to the southwest of the city centre.

Roman Catholic Cathedral of St Barbara [258 A1] (Касцёл Святой Барбары/Собор Святой Барбары) Built between 1884 and 1885 on the site of an earlier church established in 1785, this cathedral on Leningradskaya Street in the northwest of the city centre was built in the Neo-Romanesque style of architecture. It's very red indeed and is perhaps best described as 'Gothic' with a capital G.

OTHER BUILDINGS   Other historical buildings worthy of your attention include:

City Hall [258 B6] (Ратуша/Ратуша) Located just along Lenin Street from the Art Museum and built in 1775, it has been extensively renovated. The current building replaced the original from 1597, when Magdeburg rights were granted. The beautifully ornate Baroque clock tower is an especially entrancing feature. Incorporated within is the **Regional Museum** (☏66 05 87; w *ratusha.by;* ⊕ *10.00–18.00 Tue–Sun; admission BYN1*), where relics, artefacts and memorabilia detailing the history of the city and region are displayed, with a particularly impressive collection devoted to the city's privations during World War II.

Russian Governor's Palace [258 A5] (Губернатарскі палац/Губернаторский дворец) Built in the early 1770s and located in the pretty square to the right of the Marc Chagall Museum and Art Centre, this was the place chosen by Napoleon in 1812 to celebrate his 43rd birthday during the long Russia campaign. A contemporary building of the City Hall, the pale orange stucco and Classical style make both of them pleasing to the eye. Later, during the October Revolution in 1917, this palace was home to the Military Revolutionary Committee that declared Soviet power in the city and oblast. Outside in the square is the stone **obelisk** commemorating the centenary of the Russian victory over Napoleon's forces, topped by the iconic double-headed eagle, interestingly gazing north and south instead of east and west as is usually the case! Look for the missing chunk of stone, shot off the monument during the first military engagement in 1941. Close by is the monument to the liberating forces of the Red Army, constructed on the line of the front where fierce engagements took place over a nine-month period in 1943–44. The ravine of the Western Dvina River is especially precipitous here.

Victory Square and Victory Park [258 C3] (Плошча Перамогі/Площадь Победы and Парк Перамогі/Парк Победы) Said to be the biggest square in the whole of Belarus (I haven't paced it out but I'm not sure if this claim can be right), it's a vast block-paved area used for public events on a grand scale. You'll find the complex at the bottom of Lenin Street south of the Kirov Bridge. The park contains the three-bayonet monument built in 1974 to represent the three Red Army fronts that liberated the city from Nazi occupation in 1944. Also here is the eternal flame and four separate memorials symbolising each of the four years of occupation, the whole commemorating the Soviet heroes of the Great Patriotic War – military, civilian and partisan. This is a fine location for promenading and, if you amble north along the bank of the Western Dvina, you will come to the Blagovezhenskaya Annunciation and Alexander Nevsky churches (see opposite) at the top of the park.

OUTSIDE VITEBSK

POLOTSK ✳ (Полацк/Полоцк) After Vitebsk itself, this is the region's second-largest town (85,000 inhabitants) and one of the most attractive in all Belarus. On its doorstep is the urban sprawl of the larger and much less attractive town of

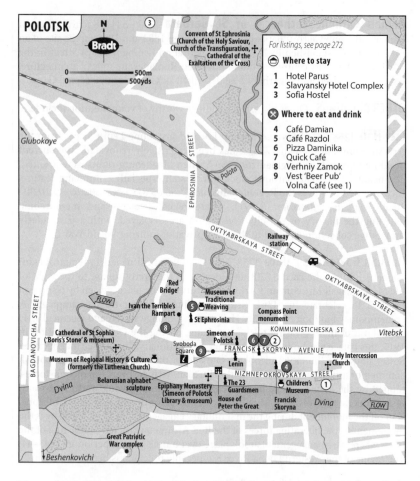

POLOTSK N

Bradt

0 ———— 500m
0 ———— 500yds

Convent of St Ephrosinia
(Church of the Holy Saviour,
Church of the Transfiguration, ✝
Cathedral of the
Exaltation of the Cross)

For listings, see page 272

🛏 **Where to stay**
1 Hotel Parus
2 Slavyansky Hotel Complex
3 Sofia Hostel

❌ **Where to eat and drink**
4 Café Damian
5 Café Razdol
6 Pizza Daminika
7 Quick Café
8 Verhniy Zamok
9 Vest 'Beer Pub'
Volna Café (see 1)

③

Glubokoye

EPHROSINIA STREET

Polota

OKTYABRSKAYA STREET

Railway
station

OKTYABRSKAYA STREET

FLOW

'Red
Bridge'

Ivan the Terrible's
Rampart

Museum of
Traditional
Weaving

St Ephrosinia

Compass Point
monument

KOMMUNISTICHESKA ST

Vitebsk

BAGDANOVICHA STREET

Cathedral of St Sophia
('Boris's Stone' & museum)

Museum of Regional History & Culture
(formerly the Lutheran Church)

Belarusian alphabet
sculpture

Simeon of
Polotsk

Svoboda
Square

FRANCISK SKORYNY AVENUE

Lenin

NIZHNEPOKROVSKAYA STREET

Holy Intercession
Church

Epiphany Monastery
(Simeon of Polotsk
Library & museum)

The 23
Guardsmen

Children's
Museum

House of
Peter the Great

Francisk
Skoryna

Dvina

FLOW

Dvina

Great Patriotic
War complex

Beshenkovichi

Novopolotsk ('New Polotsk', population 102,000), constructed in 1958 as a base for the local oil industry. There's nothing for you to see there but happily, lovely Polotsk has riches to spare. Located 105km northwest of Vitebsk along the A215 road, this historic settlement (one of the oldest cities in the whole of eastern Europe) has a beautiful riverside location on the Western Dvina, which also flows through Vitebsk. It is often referred to as 'the city of all Belarusian cities', with a rich literary heritage. Poet, translator and teacher Simeon of Polotsk was born here, as well as the great humanist and translator of the Bible, Francisk Skoryna. This is an especially pleasant town to meander and explore on foot, and many people regard it still as the spiritual cradle and first capital of modern Belarus. This includes my good friend Larissa Yatskevich, a tour guide and former university lecturer, who told me once, 'It all started here for Belarus!' Interestingly, it was only after the collapse of the Soviet Union that people began to learn of such things; until then it appears that only post-1917 history was taught in schools.

History The name of the town is derived from the Polota River, which flows into the Western Dvina here, at the foot of the magnificent Cathedral of St Sophia (page 273). In fact, Polotsk was one of the earliest of the major settlements of the Slavic tribes and is widely regarded as having been the first independent 'Belarusian' state. It was first referred to in the *Primary Chronicle* of AD862 and it featured significantly in Viking incursions from the north. Norse sagas describe the city as the most heavily fortified in all of Kievan Rus.

Between the 10th and 12th centuries, the greater principality of Polotsk emerged as the dominant centre of influence in all of the lands now recognised as Belarus. It continually asserted its sovereignty over other powerful settlements and administrations of Kievan Rus to become not only a political capital, but also the episcopal see and the controller of certain subservient western lands occupied by Baltic tribes. In fact, its influence stretched from the shores of the Baltic Sea in the west to the area of Smolensk in the east. Its most powerful ruler was Prince Vyseslav Bryachislavich ('The Sorcerer'), who was believed by the people to be a magical shape-shifter, with the ability to assume the form of any animal at will. To this day there remains a statue of him in the town wearing a wolf skin and with eagles on his back. You can find it outside the market on the road to the Convent of St Ephrosinia, on the left. He reigned from 1044 to 1101 and an inscription commissioned by his son Boris in the 12th century can still be seen today on the huge boulder placed near to the Cathedral of St Sophia, which was built between 1044 and 1066 as a symbol of the power and independence of the city.

The town became part of the Grand Duchy of Lithuania in 1307. It is believed that its geographical location and the extent of its influence and power made it the most significant trading centre in the whole of the duchy. It was granted self-determination and the right to govern under Magdeburg Law in 1498, but was sacked by Ivan the Terrible in 1563, before being returned to Lithuania in 1578. This signalled the start of a long period of settled affluence and it was granted the status of regional capital in the Polish-Lithuanian Commonwealth until partition in 1772. Cyclical warfare in the region eventually took its toll and the city slipped into a gradual process of steady decline. After partition, it was relegated to the status of a small provincial town of the Russian Empire, then during the invasion of Russia by the French in 1812 two decisive battles were fought here.

In 1897 the population of the town was 30,000, 12,000 of whom were Jews. But on 21 November 1941 the Nazis murdered every single surviving Jew (around 8,000) following the establishment of the first ghetto in the centre of town, the ghetto having been later relocated towards the Convent of St Ephrosinia (page 276). In 1995, a monument to the dead was erected on the P20 highway on the edge of town in the vicinity of the site of the second ghetto. The monument is modest, but no less moving in its impact. It is believed that the murders took place in the woods across the other side of the highway. Since the war the Jewish community in the town has slowly begun to re-establish itself, but the wounds will never heal.

Getting there and away There are several daily **trains** to Polotsk from Vitebsk (*2hrs; BYN5 one-way*), and you can also get here direct from Minsk, but the journey is long (up to 8 hours, although it can be quicker, dependent upon the service). The **bus** station is only 100m from the railway station, with several daily buses running to Vitebsk and Minsk. Marshrutkas depart from Minsk metro station Pervomayskaya on the hour (and half hour during the day) (*4hrs; BYN7 one-way*); full details can be found at **w** polotsk-minsk.by. It's a popular service, so do book ahead. To get the best out of a visit here, arrange an excursion from Vitebsk (or even Minsk, which is 250km southwest on the M3 'motorway'), but do try to stop over at least one night in town as there's too much to cover in a single day's excursion.

Where to stay and eat *Map, page 270*

⌂ **Slavyansky Hotel Complex** (110 rooms) 13 Francisk Skaryny Av; ☎42 22 35; e slavanskycomplex@mail.ru; w slavanskiy.by. Also known as the Hotel Dvina & located 1.5km east of St Sophia Cathedral, 1km from the railway station & 1.5km from the bus station, this is the largest hotel in town. Rooms consist of sgls, dbls & suites. The design of the building is repro-Classical, with a richly ornate & multi-pillared entrance, but inside it's nothing special, with the bedrooms showing their age. It's acceptable & clean, the staff are reasonably friendly & it works as an adequate place to rest your head for the night. The Slavyansky restaurant (*☉42 07 97; ☉ noon–midnight daily; $$$*) is part of the complex & is of a similar standard. **$$$**

✳ ⌂ **Hotel Parus** (50 rooms) 50A Nizhni-Pakrovskaya St; ☎42 51 70; w parus-polotsk. by. Built in 2011 on the Western Dvina at the eastern end of Nizhni-Pakrovskaya, this is my own preference in Polotsk. It is part of a complex that also inc a rowing club. There are no frills, all is cheap & cheerful, but it's clean & functional. **$$**

⌂ **Sofia Hostel** (13 rooms) 20 Schmidt Lane; m 29 559 88 08; e sofiahotel2014@gmail.com; w sofiahostel.by. Some 4km north of the river, so not best placed for the sights (with the notable exception of the Convent of St Ephrosinia, 1km east), this friendly hostel is nevertheless great value for money. Services inc free Wi-Fi, bicycle hire & bathhouse (additional charge). **$$**

✗ **Pizza Daminika** 11 Francisk Skaryny Av; ☉ 10.00–23.00 daily. Located just to the west of the Slavyansky restaurant, this is a pretty good pizzeria, a reliable source tells me, with a vegetable pizza on the menu sporting an unusual but tasty bean topping. **$$**

☕ **Café Damian** 41B Nizhni-Pakrovskaya St; ☎42 87 66; w damian.by; ☉ noon–midnight daily. It's yet another tired recreation of a medieval fortress, but the service is good & the food, though unspectacular, is wholesome & reasonably priced. The eating area is to the rear of the bar. There's enough here for me to keep returning.

☕ **Café Razdol** 15 Tolstova St; ☎46 04 33; w razdol.com; ☉ noon–midnight daily. Located next to the Weaving Museum, there are no frills here, but it's adequate & cheap.

☕ **Quick Café** 13 Francisk Skaryny Av; m 29 619 50 09; ☉ 09.00–22.00 Mon–Thu & Sun, until midnight Fri–Sat. Adjoining the Slavyansky complex, this is a decent spot to pause for a coffee & a rest while you're on my historical walking tour of the town (see opposite).

☕ **Verhniy Zamok** 6 Zamkoviy Lane; ☎42 01 26; ☉ 10.00–23.00 Mon–Thu & Sun, until midnight Fri–Sat. Situated beyond Svoboda Sq on the way to the Cathedral of St Sophia, it's nothing special but the food is wholesome & you'll feel like a local.

✳ ☕ **Volna Café** Adjoining the Hotel Parus; ☎45 81 73; ☉ noon–midnight Sun–Wed, noon–02.00 Thu–Sat. Service is slick & courteous, the food is simple but tasty (I had very passable lemon chicken with blinis & sour cream), but the décor is hideous, & I do mean truly vile. It's a throwback to the old Eastern Bloc of the 1970s, perhaps 1972 Albania or 1974 Bulgaria. There are pink drapes, bright orange plastic lamp shades, tiny mirror balls with coloured lasers, & everything gleams like polished steel. Astonishingly loud cabaret to the accompaniment of electric keys & a boom box, followed by a disco, complete the scene. When last I was there, the final tune of the night was *Ra Ra Rasputin* by Boney M at alarmingly high volume. It's so awful that you simply *must* give it a go. I loved every second. The photo gallery on the Hotel Parus website will tell you all you need to know.

🍷 **Vest 'Beer Pub'** 14 Francisk Skaryny Av; ☉ 10.00–23.00 daily. It says outside in English that it's a 'beer pub', & that's what you get, although snacks & light meals (blinis, pancakes, etc) are also served.

What to see and do Two parallel roads, Francisk Skaryny (formerly Karl Marx) Avenue and Nizhni-Pakrovskaya (formerly Lenina) Street run east–west through town, and most of the things I describe in this section are to be found there. You will also find a number of other bars/cafés and shops and, on Francisk Skaryny, several banks with ATMs, including one immediately to the left of the Slavyansky Restaurant, where you will also find a display board of helpful tourist information in English. The area bounded by these two roads is very much the main drag and together they form the centrepiece of my suggested historical walking tour.

A historical walking tour With the exception of the complex at the Convent of St Ephrosinia (page 276), all of the other sights in the town can be visited as part of an enchanting single circular tour on foot. And many of them have an information board outside with a short description in English. Further, the recently upgraded street furniture includes directional signs that are also in English, with larger information boards (again in English) at a number of strategic points along the way.

Along the riverbank Your meander begins at the magnificent **Cathedral of St Sophia** (Сафійскі сабор/Софийский собор), which is situated in an elevated position just beyond the western end of Nizhni-Pakrovskaya Street (from which it dominates the town), but you can pitch into the walk at any point you choose. When first built between 1044 and 1066, this glorious cathedral was a direct rival of those bearing the same name in Novgorod and Kiev. A rich library was maintained here that included the *Polotsk Chronicle*, but everything disappeared without a trace during the 16th-century Livonian Wars. On the orders of Tsar Peter the Great it was blown up by retreating Russian forces in 1710, before being rebuilt by the Poles between 1738 and 1750 as a Baroque Roman Catholic cathedral. Today, only the eastern elevation and some of the basement walls are the originals, but when first built its seven towers must have been a particularly imposing sight. Further restored in 1985, it now houses a **museum** (*1 Zamkovaya St*; \ *42 53 40*; e *sophia.polotsk@museum.by*; w *sophia.polotsk. museum.by*; ⊕ *10.00–17.00 Tue–Sun; admission BYN5*) dedicated to its history. There is also a concert hall seating over 300. Festivals of chamber music are held in April and November, with organ recitals every Sunday.

Just outside, between the cathedral and the river, is the huge boulder of **Boris's Stone** (Барысавы камяні/Борисовы камни), upon which Vyseslav Bryachislavich's son Boris carved the inscription, 'Dear Lord, please help Boris, your slave' in the 12th century, along with a cross and other Christian symbols. There are splendid views up, down and across the river here. To the right, the Western Dvina is joined by the smaller Polota River. On the south side of the river, directly opposite the cathedral, lies a complex dedicated to the Great Patriotic War, with a grassy pyramidal **memorial** (the 'Mound of Immortality') and a decent **museum** (*1 Tusnabolova-Marchenka St*; \ *46 93 20*; e *war.polotsk@museum.by*; w *war.polotsk.museum.by*; ⊕ *10.00–17.00 Tue–Sun; admission BYN2*), with exhibits dedicated to the defence, occupation and liberation of the town, as well as stories relating to its inhabitants.

If so inclined, you can slightly extend this circular tour beyond the cathedral by walking away from the town and down a steep bank to cross a rickety bridge into a lovely settlement of delightful wooden houses. Correspondent Alastair Watson alerted me to this charming diversion when he returned from his Belarusian adventure in the autumn of 2017. Without speaking any English the villagers are really friendly, he says; and on his way back to the cathedral, he came across an elderly couple scrumping apples from someone else's orchard …

Whether you add in this extra loop or not, take the steps down towards the river from Boris's Stone and you soon come to a tatty plastic pipe in a rather scruffy little area, with a trickle of water coming from it. This is actually a spring. The water has been tested and shown to be pure, such that the faith of local people in its recuperative powers is absolute. That being the case, it really needs something of a facelift. If you carry on down to the riverside, looking east along Nizhni-Pakrovskaya on the left-hand side of the street is the former **Lutheran church**, a stone and red-brick Neo-Gothic building constructed at the beginning of the 20th century. No longer a church, it now houses the **Museum of Regional History and Culture** (*Нацыянальны Полацкі гісторыка-культурны музей-запаведнік/Национальный Полоцкий* *историко-культурный музей-заповедник;* ✆ *42 27 15;* e *local.polotsk@museum. by;* w *local.polotsk.museum.by;* ⊕ *10.00–17.00 Tue–Sun; admission BYN3)* A short walk further along the street, on the right-hand side and with a lovely river frontage, is the beautiful **Epiphany Monastery** (Богаяўленскі манастыр/Богоявленский монастырь). Founded in 1582 and originally constructed of wood, it burned down in 1761 and was reconstructed in 1788 under the patronage of Catherine the Great. The primary centre of Orthodox worship and teaching in the town, it was closed after the October Revolution of 1917 and was not restored to full use until 1990, the extensive works taking nine years to complete. In 1994, part of the complex was opened as the **Simeon of Polotsk Library and Museum** (*Музей-бібліятэка Сімяона Полацкага/Музей-библиотека Симеона Полоцкого; 22 Nizhni-Pakrovskaya St;* ✆ *42 57 25;* e *simeon.polotsk@museum.by;* w *simeon.polotsk.museum.by;* ⊕ *10.00– 17.00 Tue–Sun; admission BYN7*), the only museum devoted solely to book printing in the whole country. There is also a reading room with seating for ten. Simeon is an important literary figure in the history of this country. Poet, writer, playwright, translator and all-round enlightener, he is known to have lectured here in the second half of the 17th century.

If you look along the riverbank to the left from the rear of the museum, you will see the **Monument to the 23 Guardsmen**, erected in 1989 to commemorate the heroism of soldiers of the First Baltic Front who lost their lives when the Nazis blew up the only bridge across the river (a wooden one) at this location on 3 July 1944. Across the road from the printing museum and a little to the right is the **House of Peter the Great** (*Дом Пятра Першага/Дом Петра Первого; 33 Nizhni-Pakrovskaya St;* ✆ *45 81 16;* w *walk.polotsk.museum.by; admission BYN2*). Built in 1692 as a small apartment building with elements of Baroque style, it was the residence of the Tsar throughout the summer of 1705 while he commanded the Russian imperial army in the Northern Wars that were raging at the time. It now houses a permanent exhibition ('A Walk Along Nizhni-Pakrovskaya Street'), access to which is available by contacting the museum direct in advance.

Around Svoboda Square Turning away from the river at the Epiphany Monastery and in towards the town, you very soon reach the central **Svoboda Square**. It's a vast, brick-paved open space with pale stucco buildings all around, with the exception of the Brutalist Soviet apartment blocks immediately behind the war memorials, on the site of a former Catholic monastery blown up in 1963. An image of the monastery has been painted on the side of the Art School building directly opposite. The first war memorial is the Napoleonic War monument, built in 2010 as an exact copy of the original melted down in the Great Patriotic War for arms. Immediately behind is the monument commemorating the liberation of the town in 1944. To the left you will see the former Russian Governor's house (now a bank), with the town's administrative offices next left. Also here is the **tourist information centre** (*8 Francisk Skaryny Av;* ✆ *42 69 49;* e *tic_polotsk@belladvina.com;* w *belladvina.com;* ⊕ *09.00–17.00 Mon–Fri, 10.00–15.00 Sat, Sun closed for lunch 13.00–14.00 daily*), where some information is available in English. On the opposite side of the square is a colonnaded yellow stucco building of some charm, which houses the oblast administrative offices. It's a copy of the original flattened by the Nazis. The oak tree outside the building to the left is colloquially regarded as a place of remembrance for those murdered during Stalin's purges.

Proceed out of the square to the right of the apartment blocks and past the bar dispensing fearsome beer brewed on the premises (I haven't sampled it but local friends advise extreme caution) and notice first the 18th-century Jesuit seminary on the left. Constructed during the days of the Grand Duchy of Lithuania, it became a military school during the subsequent Russian occupation. It was later a hospital and is now a university. If you can, visit between 08.00 and 14.00 to observe the chiming of the attractive clock built into the opposite wall as you enter the courtyard, immediately above the well (which is 29m deep). It's quite a performance. As the clock strikes the hour, piped music heralds a procession of figures from the town's history around the base, led by St Ephrosinia. If you've also visited Prague's clock there will be strong resonance for you here, though Polotsk people think theirs is better!

Retrace your steps out of the courtyard and immediately opposite are two sides of the ramparts built by Ivan the Terrible, 600m in length. Nothing remains of the former eight-tower fortress inside (it's now the site of a sports stadium), which was once a symbol of Ivan's brutal reign. He occupied the town for 16 years from 1563, during which time 3,000 Jews were murdered. If you head uphill to the left of the ramparts and then round to the left, you will be back at the stunning **Cathedral of St Sophia** (page 273). I only mention it again here to help you get your bearings and because, as you walk towards it, a glance below to your left brings into view a fine example of a Russian red-brick building from the 19th century. Now retrace your steps back into Svoboda Square, with Ivan the Terrible's ramparts on your left this time.

A short detour along the road out of the northwestern corner of the square adjacent to a pretty landscaped area, downhill and under the ramparts, pausing briefly outside the oblast administrative offices to take a look at the **Monument to St Ephrosinia** on the right-hand side (the first woman to be canonised by the Orthodox Church and also the country's first saint), brings you to the grimly named '**Red Bridge**' over the Polota River. It was thus named to commemorate the bloody battles that took place near here in October 1812 during the Napoleonic campaign, when around 14,000 soldiers lost their lives, in equal numbers on both sides. The original bridge was a wooden one. This road takes you to the **Convent of St Ephrosinia**, but other than for those with time to spare and a high level of fitness it's too far to walk, with little to see on the way other than the statue of Prince Vyseslav Bryachislavich described earlier.

Now return up the hill towards Svoboda Square. On the left before you get there, between the bridge and the statue of St Ephrosinia, stands the small **Museum of Traditional Weaving** (*Музей традыцыйнага ручнога ткацтва Паазер'я/ Музей традиционного ручного ткачества Поозерья; 1 Voikova St;* ✆ *42 30 41;* e *tkach.polotsk@museum.by;* w *tkach.polotsk.museum.by;* ⏰ *10.00–17.00 Tue– Sun; admission BYN2*). Three rooms trace the history of this activity, so critically significant to the culture of the country, in relation to the Vitebsk region. Visitors receive explanations (Russian only, sadly) about the holy symbolism of images that feature in designs, along with the ancient myths that are encoded in ostensibly simple patterns. This museum is well worth a visit if you have a translator with you. Gaze around as you leave the museum. The landscape includes the faded glory of an imposing multi-colonnaded stucco building on one side (now in need of urgent and significant repair) and the might of Ivan the Terrible's ramparts on the other, with the road to the Red Bridge cutting through below. Suitably shod, it's possible to pick your way up, over and along the ramparts. The views through the trees make it worth your while.

Along Francisk Skaryny Avenue Back in Svoboda Square, head diagonally across to the left and enter Francisk Skaryny Avenue. It is long, straight and almost 100m wide, with delightfully landscaped gardens, pathways and seating through the middle, which makes it ideal for my favourite pastime in Belarus: promenading and watching the world pass by. Join the locals in a meandering amble. You first come to a literary symbol of some importance to the Belarusian language, the small **sculpture** placed here in 2003 to celebrate the 22nd letter of the Belarusian alphabet. The inscription reads 'from Ephrosinia, from Skaryna, from Polotsk has the world emanated'.

Walk on past shops and a bank with ATMs to reach the ubiquitous **Lenin statue**, then head left across the avenue to the **statue of Simeon of Polotsk** in a lovely little square. Also erected in 2003, it's another important symbol of the country's literary heritage. Continue down the avenue, past the **souvenir shop** at number 11 selling traditional gifts, and **Pizza Daminika**, to reach the **compass point monument** sited at the *exact* centre of the continent of Europe. It must be the exact centre point, because Belarusian scientists have precisely calculated it to be so, though it is understood that other scientists of equal renown lay claim to the very same distinction in Ukraine. The information boards here are especially useful; the text is only in Russian, but the photographs will help you to orientate yourself. Walk on past the **Slavyansky Hotel and Restaurant** and into **Skaryny Square** to find the imposing **statue of Francisk Skaryna**, deep in thought.

Back down to the river Back on to the avenue, it's a short walk to the **Brutalist Soviet monument** with its affecting images of Red Army soldiers, while down to the right, close to the road bridge over the Western Dvina, is the **Holy Intercession Church** (Свята-Пакроўская царква/Храм Покрова Пресвятой Богородицы), the history of which included conversion into a chocolate factory in the 1950s. It was standing outside this church that I experienced a David Lean moment on my last visit. The bridge road sits on a steep escarpment behind the church and, as I gazed up at it, with only a vast steel grey sky above and behind, I watched as a babooshka moved slowly, almost painfully, on the skyline. My eyes followed her all the way along the escarpment, a huge tableau of earth and sky, upon which this single point of solitary and almost imperceptible movement was the only other feature. Between the church and the river is a small children's amusement park, and to the right is the **Hotel Parus and Volna Café** (page 272). Continue west past the hotel along Nizhni-Pakrovskaya Street to the **House of Peter the Great** (page 274) and your historical circuit is complete. Shortly after the hotel on the left at number 48 is an archetypical red-brick building from the 19th century. There's another further along on the same side at number 26, just after the modest but attractive pink stucco apartment building of similar vintage at number 30. At this point look across the river to see the **19th-century Catholic monastery** and to its right, the delightful **Catholic church** with its blue roof and towers. *En route*, be sure not to overlook the quirky **Children's Museum** at number 46 (*дзіцячы музей/Детский музей;* \ *42 45 58;* e *children.polotsk@museum.by;* w *children. polotsk.museum.by;* ⊕ *10.00–17.00 Tue–Sun; admission BYN2*) with its 19th- and 20th-century artefacts for 21st-century children to play with, including old cameras, typewriters and sewing machines. The two **sculptures** (front and back) have idiosyncratic charms of their own. See also a little further on the **Monument to the 23 Guardsmen** (page 274). And at any point along Nizhni-Pakrovskaya are opportunities to drop down for a riverside stroll.

The Convent of St Ephrosinia (*Спаса-Ефрасіннеўскі манастыр/Спасо-Ефросиниевский монастырь; 89 Ephrosinia Polotskaya St;* \ *42 14 29;* ⊕ *09.00–17.00 Tue–Sat; admission free*) This is the last of the sights in this lovely town, and one not to be missed. In the 12th century, Polotsk was the capital of a hugely significant principality (Minsk being no more than a small town in its shadow). St Ephrosinia was the daughter of Prince George and Princess Sophia of Polotsk. She shunned riches and refused all proposals of marriage, instead running away to become a nun against her parents' wishes. Legend has it that she was ordered in a vision to build a place of worship, and thus the **Church of the Holy Saviour** was established. It faces you within the complex as you pass under the belfry. Built and consecrated in 1161, it is one of the best-preserved examples of early church architecture in the whole country. On the outside, some of the original red brick from the 12th century has been left exposed. To the right are the graves of several nuns. Enter the church to see on the right a portrait of the saint bearing the sacred cross that she commissioned herself from skilled local craftsman Lazar Bogsha. This exquisite six-armed golden cross, decorated with enamels and precious stones, has seen many adventures. After being stolen for the first time it subsequently turned up in Smolensk, then disappeared again in mysterious circumstances in 1941 during the evacuation of the museum where it was stored. At the time, the cross is said to have incorporated a number of holy relics of enormous spiritual significance. It was never seen again and doubtless now sits in a private collection somewhere. A replica was made in 1992 and is displayed every Saturday and Sunday between the hours of 09.00 and noon. It remains a powerful and mystical symbol of the spirituality of true believers within the Orthodox community in Belarus. Continue on into the body of this small church, where a sight to take away your breath awaits. Every wall and pillar is adorned with 12th-century frescoes of exquisite beauty. Already long in the process of restoration since 1995, the repairs are still ongoing, but even as work in progress the impact is stunning. Every available space has its own fresco. In the 19th century, these beautiful images were covered in a layer of cement with oil paintings on top. No longer are they hidden from view. The original floor is also being restored. St Ephrosinia died in 1173 while on pilgrimage to Jerusalem. Her relics were later taken to Kiev before being returned to this lovely church by Tsar Nikolai II in 1910. Interestingly, they were exhibited in museums all over the Soviet Union after the Revolution, miraculously surviving the destruction of Vitebsk during the war. Now kept at the convent complex, they are currently in the process of restoration before being displayed once more in the church founded by the saint herself.

Outside to the left is the slightly larger **Church of the Transfiguration** (built in 1842). To the right stands the imposing, black-domed 1897 **Cathedral of the Exaltation of the Cross.** Lavishly ornate inside, this is the present location of St Ephrosinia's holy relics. The whole makes for an extremely pleasing excursion. Ladies should note that heads must be covered and if wearing trousers, you will be required to put on a skirt over the top of them. Scarfs and skirts may be borrowed from the collection stored in the metal wardrobe on the right of the belfry.

GORODOK JEWISH CEMETERY Some 39km north of Vitebsk on the P115 road is the town of Gorodok, site of an important **Jewish cemetery** dating back to 1700. It is significant because it remains largely intact and is thus an uninterrupted physical record of the burials of a Jewish shtetl over a continuous period in excess of 300 years. This makes it an important site for archival research. Covering an area approximately 760m square, there are estimated to be 5,000–8,000 graves there. It remains in use for burials to this day. The Jewish community in the town is relatively small but is committed to securing the necessary funding for remedial work and improvements under the auspices of an international appeals committee, to ensure this site of major historical record is protected for the future. Two important Holocaust sites are also to be found in the vicinity. Elsewhere in the country, Jewish cemeteries have largely been destroyed as a result of the neglect, vandalism and destruction that have followed wholesale victimisation of communities, resettlement and mass murder across the centuries. This makes securing the future of the Gorodok cemetery all the more important. For further information and to arrange a visit, contact the UK sustainable development charity **The Together Plan** (page 116) or Belarusian NGO **Dialog** (page 38).

OTHER TOWNS AND VILLAGES IN VITEBSK OBLAST Nestling in various locations throughout the Vitebsk oblast are many small towns and villages that are worthy of your time. The **church architecture** of this region (both Orthodox and Catholic) is particularly impressive, with stunning examples to be discovered all over the area. You will also find a number of romantic ruins of castles, palaces and fortified manor houses. Sadly, access by public transport is not easy unless you can speak the language and have lots of time to sit on a rattling bus, so unless you have your own transport the best advice is to arrange a tour or excursion through one of the state agencies. Those following are but a tiny selection of the many things you might want to visit and see. Some 50km due west of Vitebsk on the A245 road is the town of **Beshenkovichi** (Бешанко́вічы/Бешенко́вичи), an administrative centre that was first mentioned in 1460. Located on the Dvina River, noteworthy sites include the 18th-century palace and extensive parkland, together with the beautiful Orthodox Church of St Elias, built in 1870. Some 85km southwest of Polotsk on the A235 is the 16th-century town of **Glubokoye** (Глыбокае/Глубокое). Numerous buildings in the Baroque style are to be found here, together with the stunning 17th-century Orthodox Church of the Nativity and the 18th-century Holy Trinity Roman Catholic Church. Established towards the end of the 11th century and located 70km due south of Vitebsk, at the crossroads of two major intercontinental routes east–west (the M1) and north–south (the M8), the town of **Orsha** (Орша/Орша) is one of the oldest in the country. And as well as being a key port on the Dnieper River, it is also a major junction on the Minsk–Moscow railway line. The station is a glorious building, housing shops and an excellent restaurant. Also here is the beautiful Holy Epiphany Kuteinsky Monastery, originally home to a renowned 17th-century printing house, and, in a lovely riverside location, the beautiful walled Orthodox Church of St Ilia is a 'must see'.

BRASLAV LAKES NATIONAL PARK ✳ (*Нацыянальны Парк Браслаўскія Азёры/ Национальный Парк Браславские Озера; 1 Dachnaya St, Braslav;* \ 215 36 77 07; e *braslav_by@tut.by;* w *braslavpark.by; see also* w *braslav.com*) With the sprawling town of Braslav within its boundaries, this beautiful park of 70,000ha is located close to the border with Latvia, about 250km north of Minsk and slightly less northwest of Vitebsk, through Polotsk along the P14 road. Established in 1995, it is famed for the unique nature of its aquatic ecosystems. The southern part of the park is mostly lowland marsh and forest, while the central and northern parts consist of beautiful blue lakes interconnected by a labyrinth of hundreds of rivers and streams set in picturesque rolling hills. No fewer than 189 species of bird live here, including black stork, osprey, tern, bittern and ptarmigan. It is also possible to spot elk, wild boar, roe deer, beaver, fox, racoon, badger and wolf roaming free in their natural environment, although all are of course shy and evasive. There are also complexes consisting of large pens for closer study, although do bear in mind that these are enclosed spaces. Animals are not free to wander without boundaries and as a matter of principle, the difficulties of this concept speak for themselves. Inhabiting the lakes are 28 species of fish, such as eel, whitefish, whitebait, zander, pike, catfish, carp, bream, chub, turbot, tench, perch, gudgeon, loach, ruff and stickleback. The park is rich in flora (more than 800 species). The areas of forestry include birch, pine, fir, black elder and aspen. All in all, the march of time has largely bypassed this delightful area and, as a sanctuary to step off the world in search of some inner peace and calm, there are many worse places to choose.

Visitors can dip into various organised tours on horseback or by car, as well as on the water or by foot, lasting from one to several days. The pastimes of hunting and fishing are particularly well served. One of the most delightful trips is by launch across the limpid lakeland waters.

The journey by road from Minsk to the town of Braslav is long and tiring (though the scenery gets better the further north you travel), while the journey from Vitebsk is shorter and on better roads. Several buses a day leave for the town from Minsk and Vitebsk.

Where to stay and eat In terms of facilities, the five main leisure complexes are listed here. There are also campsites at other locations within the national park area, as well as farmsteads offering overnight stays. Accommodation can be booked direct via the official websites (see opposite), while stays, tours and excursions to and around Braslav Lakes (including travel, accommodation and all ancillaries) can be arranged via most of the state and privately owned tourism companies, all of which will offer a range of options to suit all tastes.

Braslav Lakes Hotel (16 dbls, 8 bungalows & 3 summerhouses) 53 Leninskaya St, Braslav; 215 36 00 00. Located lakeside. Services here inc parking, free Wi-Fi, floating sauna on the lake, BBQ area, sports facilities, routes for walking & cycling, hunting & fishing, equipment hire, boating, private beach area, bar & restaurant (⊕ noon–20.00 Sun–Thu, noon–midnight Fri–Sat). **$$**

Drivyaty tourist centre (Sleeps 74; 2 4-storey buildings containing 29 twins & 8 suites) 215 36 22 46. On the outskirts of the town of Braslav, on the shore of Lake Drivyaty itself. Facilities on site include secure parking, children's area, summerhouses, campfire, bathhouse & lakeside beach. **$$**

Leoshky tourist centre (Sleeps 55 in 18 cottages) 25km from Braslav on the shore of Lake Severny Volos. Services inc parking, 2 summerhouses, limited Wi-Fi, sports facilities,

hunting & fishing, cycle & boat hire, BBQ area, 2 piers & private beach area, with a bathhouse nearby. The waters are particularly clear here. **$$**

Slobodka tourist centre (Sleeps 16 in 8 summerhouses) 12km from Braslav on the shore of Lake Potyekh, near the village of Slobodka. Facilities inc secure parking, bathhouse, BBQ area & lakeside beach. A 2.5km-long designated path runs from here along the Sloboda ridge, with excellent views over the surrounding area. **$$**

Zolovo tourist centre (Sleeps 14–18 in 4 lakeside summerhouses) 25km from Braslav in a forest location near Lake Zolovo. Secure parking, walking & bicycle routes, picnic area, bathhouse, swimming pool, fitness centre, fishing & boating facilities, as well as open-air pens for wildlife, but do bear in mind my earlier caveat concerning enclosed spaces for animals. **$$**

BEREZINSKY BIOSPHERE RESERVE (*Бярэзінскі Біясферны Запаведнік/ Березинский Биосферный Заповедник; Domzheritsy Building, 3 Tsentralnaya St;* 213 22 63 18; e *tourism@berezinsky.by;* w *berezinsky.by*) Now part of UNESCO's World Network of Biosphere Reserves, this special place was originally opened in January 1925 to preserve and nurture another splendid natural environment, as well as to conserve and protect the valuable wildlife living there, notably beaver. Covering around 85,000ha and attracting around 20,000 visitors per year from within Belarus and abroad, this is a substantial area of wilderness. Here is a land of virginal primeval forests (mostly pine and spruce), marshland (one of the largest in Europe) and lakes, rich in diverse flora and fauna, sitting right in the middle of the watershed of the Baltic and Black seas. The areas of marshland are particularly beautiful. Small wooded islands rise above marsh plains as far as the eye can see. Thousands of years ago they were proper islands, washed by the waves of the vast glacial lake that is buried now under a thick and impenetrable layer of rich peat. The largest and longest river, the Berazhina, is an integral link in the system that connects the Baltic Sea to the Black Sea. In times gone by it was a very important trade route. Today, trade has been replaced by leisure and the river is populated with visitors retracing the routes taken by Vikings and Greeks in history.

Around 52 species of mammal live here, including brown bear, elk, wolf, otter, wild boar, lynx, the once rare (but now flourishing) beaver and even the extremely rare European bison, along with 217 species of bird (including the golden eagle and the seldom-seen black stork), ten of amphibian, five of reptile and 34 of fish. And mosquitoes. Clouds of them. The vegetation is also richly diverse, with more than 780 herbaceous varieties being found in the reserve, as well as over 200 varieties of moss and lichen.

The reserve is situated 130km northeast of Minsk and the same distance southwest of Vitebsk, the M3 motorway between the two passing directly through it. There are several daily buses and marshrutka services from Minsk and Vitebsk.

🏠 **Where to stay and eat** Facilities for enjoying this special place at leisure are reasonably good. For people who prefer to spend time much closer to nature, as well as the listed hotels there are also a few small but snug **wooden huts** located in the most picturesque areas of the park. These are situated at **Nivki** (accommodating ten people in five double rooms, with kitchen, bathhouse and picnic site; **$$**), **Domzheritskoye and Olshitsa Lakes** (accommodating six people each at lakeside locations, with kitchen, bathhouse, picnic site and piers; **$$**) and at **Plavno** (also accommodating six people in three double rooms, with kitchen, bathhouse, lounge and open fire, picnic site, pier, sports area and access to the beach; **$$**). This one is situated not far from the hotel of the same name.

Long accessible only by prearrangement with a state agency, accommodation, tours and the museum may now be booked direct via the informative website. For the less independently minded, most state and private tourist agencies will still offer various tours, ranging from weekends that include a visit to the nature museum and the open-air pens along prescribed ecological routes, to specialised longer-term environmentalist tours to observe between 120 and 150 species of wild animals in their natural habitat. The emphasis here is on providing enjoyment through education and the raising of awareness of important ecological issues. Visitors have the opportunity to take a close look at local ways of life and traditions, be entertained by ethnic folk troupes, sample local and national cuisine, experience traditional trades, visit sites of important historical and cultural heritage and learn more about the scientific study undertaken here, as well as watching films on an ecological theme, observing nature and taking part in environmental discussions. And to hunt, for those so minded.

🏠 **Hotel Plavno** (10 dbl rooms) 📞 213 22 63 00. Formerly a presidential residence much favoured by Alexander Lukashenko, incorporating a restaurant, billiard room, hall with cosy fireplace, picnic areas & bathhouse. The best of the rooms are in the attic, all with views over the lake & the woods. There is a beach nearby. If you picture a large wooden ski chalet, with wall-to-wall pine panelling, then you won't be far wrong. Because it's a former presidential residence, you can land your helicopter here! It's located lakeside within a forested area, so the setting is picturesque. **$$$**

🏠 **Hotel Serguch** (36 rooms) ☎ 213 22 63 00. This is part of a complex that inc a recently renovated nature museum, a new museum of mythology & the House of Ecological Studies with assembly hall seating 200 (for seminars & meetings), computer room, small cinema, café-bar, exhibition space & library. Facilities at the hotel inc restaurant, bar, banqueting hall, billiard room & bathhouse. There is also a 4km nature trail incorporating a number of routes for walkers & cyclists, as well as open-air pens for wildlife. **$$$**

UPDATES WEBSITE

You can post your comments and recommendations, and read feedback and updates from other readers online at **w** bradtupdates.com/belarus.

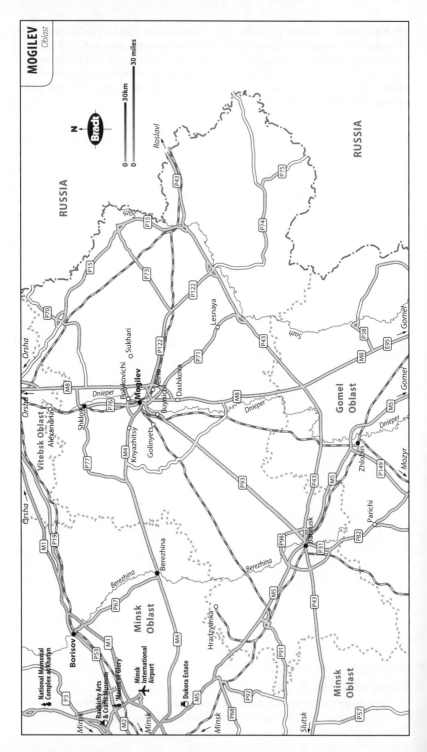

MOGILEV *Oblast*

7

Mogilev City and Oblast
Магілёў/Могилёв

Telephone code 222

Mogilev is a city of 380,000 inhabitants on the hilly western bank of the Dnieper River in eastern Belarus, around 100km from the border with the Russian Federation. It is the capital of a region that has excellent transport links, with main connections to Russia, Ukraine and the Baltic states crossing the territory by road and by rail. Mogilev itself is a major rail junction, and the three significant rivers that criss-cross the oblast, the Dnieper, Berazhina and Sozh, are still used for navigation and transport purposes. The city itself is one of the main economic and industrial centres of Belarus. At the end of the Great Patriotic War, an enormous metallurgy complex incorporating a number of steel mills was established here as part of Stalin's programme of mass rebuilding and reindustrialisation. There are also many other significant industrial complexes for the manufacture of cranes, tractors and cars, along with a vast plant for chemical production and many other light industries. Yet the economy of the region and its social infrastructure have been significantly prejudiced by the consequences of the Chernobyl catastrophe: 35% of the territory was contaminated by radioactive particles in the immediate aftermath of the explosion and there are still many areas forming hotspots of radiation that will remain out of bounds for a very long time. No fewer than 13 out of the 21 districts in the oblast are officially recognised as being in need of specialist measures. Agricultural land makes up over 50% of the territory and, between 1986 and 1991, some 47,000ha of previously arable but now contaminated lands were taken out of use.

This is all the more tragic because the region is known for its picturesque scenery, with forest covering over 30% of the area. Another 18% is occupied by predominantly low-lying meadows and marshland (not dissimilar to the region of the Polyesye in the south of the country, but less extensive), while the growing of crops (mostly rye, barley, buckwheat, oats and potatoes) plays a key role in the agricultural sector. Cattle breeding (both for meat and milk production) is also a feature, while in a number of districts there are fur, poultry and fish farms. At present, reorganisation of the agricultural sector is still under way. Production co-operatives, joint-stock companies and private farms are being established, while for now and for the foreseeable future, collective farms (*kolkhoz*), state farms (*sovkhoz*) and supporting enterprises also continue to operate.

The region has a long and interesting history. These lands have been ravaged many times by fierce battles, with only monuments remaining to tell the tale. For example, near the village of Lesnaya, 55km southeast of Mogilev on the P71 road, stands the memorial complex commemorating the 200th anniversary of the Russian army's victory over the Swedes, consisting of a chapel and a museum dedicated to the history of the region. And the memorial of Buynichskoye Field keeps alive the memory of heroes of the Soviet Union from the Great Patriotic War. Then in the context of contemporary history and current affairs, the village of Alexandria, just to the north of the town of Shklov (35km due north of Mogilev on the P76 road), is famed for being the birthplace of the first (indeed, only) president of Belarus, Alexander Lukashenko. You can visit the local museum in the village school, with its special section devoted to the President, see the location of his family home (2km away) and drink from the spring that can be found nearby at young Alexander's favourite childhood place. The Sports and Tourism Department of the Mogilev Regional Administration has marketed this as 'an unusual waterway route for canoe enthusiasts' under the strapline 'Paddle Your Way to President Lukashenko's Home Town'.

Today, Mogilev is a sprawling, noisy city of business and industry, the face of which presents a mixture of old and new, traditional and avant-garde. Nowhere is this better represented than Leninskaya Street. Now renovated and restored, with the enigmatic stargazer street sculpture on display in Star Square, it's regarded with affection by residents and visitors alike. As Mogilev has less for the visitor to see than any of the other five cities, a walk along Leninskaya is a must.

Each year, Mogilev is home to two very different festivals: Zolotoy Shlyager (the 'Golden Hit Parade'), featuring retro-pop, in November, and Magutny Bozha ('Almighty God'), dedicated to sacred music, in July and August. There is also an annual animation festival.

HISTORY

Mogilev can boast many connections with famous visitors who have spent time here. The people of the city turned out en masse when Russian Tsar Peter the Great arrived by boat on the Dnieper in 1706; Catherine the Great famously met with the Austrian Emperor Joseph II here in May 1780; Russian poet Pushkin spent time in the city, as did writer Gogol; and, from 1915 to 1917, Emperor and Tsar Nikolai II and his family were in residence for significant periods of time, right up to the point of his abdication. The headquarters of the vast Russian imperial army were located in Mogilev (due to its favourable geographical position) and he was of course supreme (and self-appointed) commander-in-chief. In every respect, therefore, the city can be said to have been the final residence of the last tsar of Holy Mother Russia. There are references to the royal family all over the city and oblast.

This and other towns in the area such as Mstislavl and Krichev were founded in the 12th and 13th centuries, although Slavic tribes of the Krivichi and Radzimichy had first established settlements in the region in the 10th century. The city itself was founded in 1267 by around 200 settlers, although local archaeological excavations have suggested that there were early Iron Age settlements on the site of the current town, specifically where Gorky Park now stands. From the early 14th century, it was a constituent part of the Grand Duchy of Lithuania. After the Union of Lublin and the creation of the Polish-Lithuanian Commonwealth, it was transferred to new royal owners. There followed a period of strong growth in the local economy, owing to the advantageous geographical location of the city right at the centre of major trade routes from north to south and from east to west. Crafts such as weaving, metalwork, woodwork, leather processing, gun-making and the art of jewellery manufacture were all developing intensively here. In the 15th century, the city also became a pottery centre. Trade in many different crafts was so significant that it acquired a customs office of its own. Then in 1577, it was invested with new rights of self-government and granted city status by King Stefan Batory under Magdeburg Law. This was a golden age for the city. It was a large river port, more prosperous than Minsk, and many trade ships were to be seen moored here. By the end of the 17th century, there were 15,000 residents of the city living in 3,000 houses. At the same time, Mogilev became a very significant centre for Eastern Orthodoxy, the largest in all Belarus. There were many substantial congregations and a theological seminary was established to protect the faith. Meanwhile, congregation schools promoted the 'development of education', while printing houses published literature in the Belarusian, Greek and Latin languages. Around this time, the Orthodox Church of St Nikolai, the Epiphany Orthodox Cloister and the Jesuit Roman Catholic Church were built.

During the Northern Wars between 1700 and 1721, the Swedes sacked and destroyed more than half of the city's houses, while Peter the Great himself ordered that it be razed to the ground in 1708. After the First Partition of Poland it inevitably fell into the hands of imperial Russia, but continued to flourish as the administrative centre of the region. Then, during the war against France in 1812, French forces under Marshal Davoilt captured and plundered the city.

When serfdom was abolished in 1861, the social and economic development of Mogilev accelerated exponentially. The city's museum was founded in 1867. July 1883 saw the first issue of the *Mogilev Eparchy News*. In 1885, there were only 124 business enterprises employing 270 workers, but just 15 years later there were 220 businesses employing 790 workers. The first theatre was built in 1888 (it is still standing and worthy of your attention if you're in town – see page 292) and by 1897 the population had swollen to over 43,000, nearly half of whom were literate. In the early part of the 20th century, there were three types of credit institutions relating to commerce, land and small debtors, together with three printing houses and a number of mechanical workshops. Indeed, the city was widely regarded at this time as being the most developed and affluent of all the European cities of the Russian Empire.

However, internal economic crisis, the global depression of the early 20th century and emerging revolutionary ideas widened the gulf between the classes, and Mogilev's economic prosperity and social cohesion soon began to unravel. The year 1901 saw the first significant strike by workers at the dairy plant, followed by workers in the rag trade in 1903. Political rallies took place on 1 May from 1901 to 1904, and in late May 1905 there was a strike in the bakery, followed by a walkout of railway workers in December 1905. Demands for improved working conditions continued and in May 1906 hairdressers, shoemakers and tailors downed tools to demand that the working day be reduced to 9 hours. At the beginning of World War I, martial law was imposed throughout the region. On 22 March 1917, in the aftermath of the February Revolution, the City Deputy-Council of Workers and Soldiers was formed. And the power of the collective ensured that in the first half of 1917 Mogilev workers held a number of strikes, seeking various political and economic objectives.

After the ensuing October Revolution the city remained under anti-Soviet forces for a whole month until, on 18 November 1917, the Deputy-Council of Workers and Soldiers passed a resolution that accepted Soviet rule and took over the administration of Mogilev. There followed the start of a short period of intense instability, when on 18 February 1918 German forces occupied the city, followed by Polish troops on 12 March and then the German army again on 26 May. Finally, in 1919, it was overrun and captured by Red Army forces.

It is thought that up to 25,000 people from the oblast volunteered for the Red Army in the early days of the Great Patriotic War and, from 24 June to 3 July 1941, its Western Front headquarters were located in the city. By that time, a significant proportion of the major industrial plant and machinery had already been evacuated east.

7

But despite the frenzied construction of two encircling defensive lines in just seven days under the protection of the 172nd Division, Mogilev fell to the Nazis on 26 July 1941, after 23 days of intense and savage fighting. A cruelly oppressive regime was immediately established by the invaders. Five concentration camps were created in the region and during the period of the war, over 70,000 citizens of the city died and a further 30,000 were taken to Germany as slave labour. Most of them were Jews. Then, on 6 April 1943, the Mogilev partisan army was formed. It very quickly grew to comprise 34,000 active volunteers.

In June 1944, the Red Army launched its Belarusian offensive operation and on 28 June the city was finally liberated by troops of the 2nd Belarusian Front. On 25 April 1980, Mogilev was awarded the Order of the Great Patriotic War (First Class) for the bravery and resilience displayed by its citizens during the oppression of the war years.

After the war, the city was reconstructed at an astonishing pace and by 1959 the population had spiralled to 122,000 people. New housing estates and 'micro-districts' were springing up all over town and new bridges were built over the Dnieper to cope with the increasing demands on the city's infrastructure. Today, Mogilev's position as a major (and modern) industrial city contributing significantly to the economy of the country is assured.

GETTING THERE AND AROUND

Mogilev is well appointed in terms of transport links, with major rail and road routes passing through the city. In terms of getting around, the usual mixture of **bus**, **tram**, **trolleybus** and **taxi** is on offer, all cheap and all reliable, but you are unlikely to need to go far in this city as most of the sights are located on the western bank of the river, in a fairly small and compact area around Leninskaya Street. Walking is thus the best option, though when you need it, the integrated infrastructure for public transport is particularly impressive in this city.

BY TRAIN Built in 1902, the main railway station is a most attractive building, adorned in pastel stucco. It is located 2km north of the city centre, at the western end of Grishina Street. There are plenty of local trains serving towns in this and adjoining regions. Mogilev is also a stop on several main-line routes serving Minsk (several trains a day), Gomel, Brest, Grodno and Vitebsk within Belarus, and international destinations such as Moscow, St Petersburg, Vilnius and Kiev. The journey time from Minsk is around 4 hours and the cost of a one-way ticket starts at BYN5.

BY BUS There is also a bus station close by, with varied and alternative routes throughout the oblast. Several services also arrive from and depart for Minsk every day. As with the train, journey times are around 4 hours and the price of a one-way ticket starts at BYN7. The town is located midway between the cities of Vitebsk and Gomel on one of the country's major routes north–south (the M8). Journey times and ticket prices are broadly the same. Minsk lies 203km to the west along the M4.

TOURIST INFORMATION

A useful compendium of civic, cultural, historical, tourist and administrative information for visitors and residents alike can be found on the English pages of the excellent website maintained by the city's executive committee (**w** *mogilev.gov.by*).

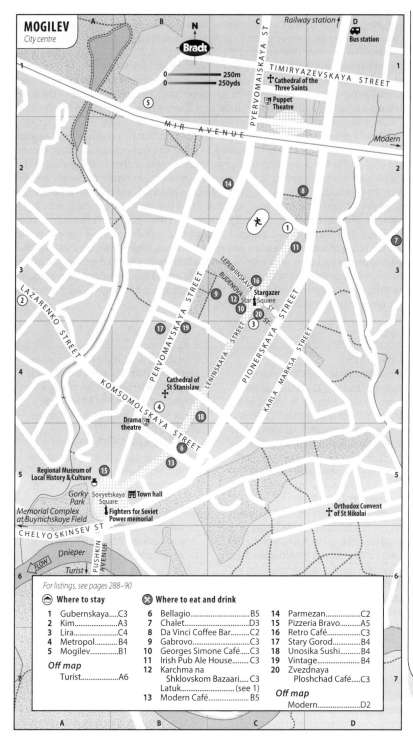

MOGILEV
City centre

N

Bradt

0 —— 250m
0 —— 250yds

A | B | C | D

LAZARENKO STREET

MIR AVENUE

PERVOMAYSKAYA STREET

KOMSOMOLSKAYA STREET

CHELYOSKINSEV ST

PYERVOMAISKAYA ST

TIMIRYAZEVSKAYA STREET

LEPESHINSKAYA
BUDENOVA
LENINSKAYA STREET
PIONERSKAYA STREET
KARLA MARKSA STREET
PUSHKIN AVENUE

Railway station

Bus station

† Cathedral of the
Three Saints

Puppet
Theatre

Modern

Stargazer
Star Square

Cathedral of
St Stanislaw

Drama
theatre

Regional Museum of
Local History & Culture

Gorky Park Sovyetskaya
Square   Town hall
Memorial Complex   Fighters for Soviet
at Buynichskoye Field Power memorial

Orthodox Convent
† of St Nikolai

Dnieper
FLOW
Turist

For listings, see pages 288–90

⌂ Where to stay

1 Gubernskaya.......C3
2 Kim.......................A3
3 Lira........................C4
4 Metropol............B4
5 Mogilev..............B1

Off map
   Turist....................A6

✗ Where to eat and drink

6   Bellagio................................B5
7   Chalet..................................D3
8   Da Vinci Coffee Bar..........C2
9   Gabrovo...............................C3
10 Georges Simone Café.....C3
11 Irish Pub Ale House........C3
12 Karchma na
     Shklovskom Bazaari.....C3
     Latuk............................(see 1)
13 Modern Café.....................B5

14 Parmezan....................C2
15 Pizzeria Bravo............A5
16 Retro Café..................C3
17 Stary Gorod...............B4
18 Unosika Sushi............B4
19 Vintage.......................B4
20 Zvezdnaya
     Ploshchad Café.....C3

Off map
   Modern......................D2

But even though it does contain some architectural features of interest to the visitor, Mogilev is not yet geared up for the international tourist trade. In this context, it is the least developed of the country's six major cities. Given that it's an industrial centre, most of the focus is on facilities for businesspeople. Indeed, sites of interest to the traveller or leisure visitor are not well promoted at all, with only a few tourist agencies in town offering excursions. The best of them is the state **Intourist agency**, handily located on the first floor of Hotel Mogilev (*6 Mir Av;* ✆70 70 28; e *mog-intourist@mail.ru;* w *intourist.by;* ☺ *09.00–18.00 Mon–Fri, 10.00– 15.00 Sat (spring & summer)*). It is thus easy to find, but by no means easy to gain access to its services. When I enquired as to its whereabouts on my first visit to the city, staff at the hotel reception desk directed me to a door in the corner of the lobby, where a jobsworth told me I wasn't allowed in. Another jobsworth arrived after I pressed the issue, but he directed me to offices along the street, before the hotel receptionist marched over to order them crossly to let me in! Once I'd got upstairs and into the office, the staff there couldn't have been more helpful. English is spoken and some printed material in English is available, though not much, but a wide range of tours and excursions can be booked. Otherwise, far and away the best option is to fix a stay as part of an organised tour, arranged before you arrive in the country or from the capital Minsk, with one of the accredited state agencies or international operators (page 50). In truth, there's not enough to keep you here for more than a day and a night at most.

WHERE TO STAY

UPMARKET

⌂ **Gubernskaya** [287 C3] (46 rooms) 56/6 Leninskaya St; ✆22 26 19; e gubernsky@ gubernsky.by; w gubernsky.by. Located centrally in one of the city's refurbished late 19th-century buildings & open since 2007, this hotel is aimed at the business market. Rooms are spacious but the décor will not be to everyone's taste. Staff are friendly & eager to please. Facilities inc free Wi-Fi, free monitored parking, café-bar, currency exchange & ATM. **$$$$**

✱ ⌂ **Kim** [287 A3] (9 rooms) 27 Lazarenko St; ✆22 91 13; e info@kim-hotel.by. Located just out of the city centre, this small hotel offers the best value & comfort in town, though without frills. It's of European standard, with all rooms being well appointed. The staff are attentive & keen to please, while the modest size of the establishment gives it a homely & cosy feel. Facilities inc free Wi-Fi, free monitored parking, café, 24hr reception & travel booking service, but there is no lift serving the 3 floors. The railway station is 4km away & the bus station 3km. **$$$$**

✱ ⌂ **Lira** [287 C4] (8 rooms) 45 Leninskaya St; ✆25 25 43. This is another small hotel that comes highly recommended. Opened in 2003 but significantly refurbished since then, it is located

in the heart of the city just metres from Star Sq, all of the rooms are comfortable & the service is good. Facilities inc free Wi-Fi, free parking, 24hr reception, café, billiard room & travel booking service. Small swimming pool, sauna & spa are adjacent. **$$$$**

✱ ⌂ **Metropol** [287 B4] (53 rooms) 6 Komsomolskaya St; ✆70 70 51; e reception@ metropol.by; w metropol.by. Only open since Dec 2013, it's a decent attempt at creating the sort of hotel visitors from elsewhere in Europe will recognise, & its reputation is already high. Expect the staff to go the extra mile. Located centrally between the Drama Theatre & St Stanislaw Cathedral, it offers free Wi-FI, restaurant, free parking, business & travel services, pool, spa, sauna & steam room. **$$$$**

MID-RANGE

⌂ **Mogilev** [287 B1] (356 rooms) 6 Mir Av: ✆73 88 88; e hotel_mogilev@mail.ru; w mogilev. amaks-hotels.ru. Another example of the omnipresent concrete monolith so favoured by the Soviet Union in the 1970s. Located downtown & 3km from the railway station (3.5km from the bus station), the rooms, ranging from sgls to suites, are exactly what you would expect:

functional but without charm. It was built in 1972, so the concrete is past its best, especially on the balconies. Don't look down … Notwithstanding regular refurbishment, it always looks tired & drab. Last time I chanced a non-refurbished room to save on cost. Don't do it. These rooms may be cheap, but they are hideous. Facilities inc Wi-Fi (fee payable), monitored parking (fee payable), self-service café & separate bar (both extremely avg), ATM & currency exchange. Despite its modest charms this is my hotel of preference here, largely because of the delightful walk into town along the bank of the Dubrovenka River. You emerge at the bottom

of Sovyetskaya Sq, one of the key sites of the city & the start of your promenade along Leninskaya St. **$$$**

🏠 **Turist** [287 A6] (134 rooms) 6 Pushkin Av; ✆ 48 56 55; **e** mogilevtourist3@mail.ru; **w** mogilevtourist.by. Built in 1986 & situated downtown in a park on the banks of the Dnieper, the adequately appointed rooms of this concrete block are on 7 floors, ranging from sgls to suites. Services inc Wi-Fi (fee payable), monitored parking (fee payable), exchange bureau, restaurant, bar & snack bar. **$$$**

✖ WHERE TO EAT AND DRINK

I've spent less time in Mogilev than in any of the other five cities in Belarus, such that my personal experience of the charms of its restaurants, bars and cafés is limited. That said, I've asked trusted contacts in the tourism industry and local people about the establishments I've listed here, which means that a degree of local intelligence from corroborating sources has been garnered to assist in the presentation of information. This should give you enough base data to undertake your own road test with a degree of confidence. My advice is that your best option will be to reconnoitre along Leninskaya Street and within its vicinity, where locals and visitors alike are wont to spend leisure time in surroundings that are known to be safe, pleasing and easy on the eye. It's where you are going to be spending most of your time anyway. Do please let me know how you get on. To assist with your research in advance, visit the very informative listings site **w** nightmogilev.com, though sadly it's in Russian only.

RESTAURANTS

✖ **Bellagio** [287 B5] 21 Leninskaya St; ✆ 23 08 08; ⊕ noon–23.00 daily. Everyone tells me this is probably the best restaurant in town, ideally located towards the bottom of Leninskaya St. Expect Italian fine dining in a relaxed setting; standards are consistently high & it's always busy, with award-winning chef Luigi Pomata running a tight ship. Definitely recommended, but not cheap. **$$$$**

✖ **Chalet** [287 D3] 4 Darvina St; ✆ 70 71 23; **w** shale.by; ⊕ 11.00–23.00 daily. I stumbled across this restaurant while trying to find the Convent of St Nikolai on foot. It's out of the town centre in a plush residential location &, judging by the size of the SUVs in the car park, it's a haunt of the well-to-do. Shorts & T-shirt rendered me way too underdressed to sample its delights, but the décor is sumptuous, the menu imaginative, & when I asked elsewhere I was told that everything about this place is impressive. Extensive grounds provide ample opportunity for comfortable

alfresco dining. Whenever you go, expect to pay for the experience. **$$$$**

✖ **Gabrovo** [287 C3] 31 Pervomayskaya St; ✆ 22 28 54; ⊕ 10.00–02.00 daily. Reasonably centrally located, this stock 1970s Russian-style eatery & nightclub specialises in Belarusian & Bulgarian cuisine. There's also live music every night except Mon. **$$$**

✖ **Karchma na Shklovskom Bazaari** [287 B5] 13 Budenova St; ✆ 22 23 46; ⊕ 11.00–23.00 daily. Just off Star Sq, the décor is clichéd medieval & the food is standard European. There are probably better choices in the immediate vicinity, but if you're feeling adventurous, give it a go. **$$$**

✖ **Latuk** [287 C3] 56/6 Leninskaya St; ✆ 25 28 16; ⊕ 07.00–midnight daily. Located at the Gubernskaya Hotel, this serves standard European fare. **$$$**

✖ **Modern** [287 B5] 12 Korolyeva St; ✆ 79 07 56; **e** restmodern@mail.ru; **w** restoran-modern. by; ⊕ 11.00–midnight daily. Cosy & relaxed, with good service, but it's off the main drag & probably not worth the trip unless you're close by. **$$$**

✳ ✖ **Parmezan** [287 C2] 34/1 Pervomayskaya St; ✆ 40 84 08; w parmezan.by; ⊕ 09.00–23.00 daily. Long established & one of the most pleasing of the city's café-restaurants. It's another Italian, but it's done to a decent standard & there is also a take-away & delivery service. It's strollable from the centrally located hotels & the website is informative for a browse before you try. **$$$**

✖ **Pizzeria Bravo** [287 A5] 2 Sovyetskaya Sq; ✆ 20 40 40; ⊕ 11.00–23.00 daily. Located in the corner of the square next to the Regional Museum of Local History & Culture, it's standard pizza fare, but this is a handy option for the start or finish of your amble along Leninskaya. **$$$**

✖ **Unosika Sushi** [287 B4] 23A Leninskaya St; ✆ 21 88 88; w unosika.by; ⊕ 10.00–22.00 daily. For good-value sustenance on the hoof, this sushi bar & take-away is a decent option. The menu on the website tells you all you need to know, inc prices. **$$**

✖ **Vintage** [287 B4] 29 Pervomayskaya St; ✆ 25 76 12; ⊕ noon–19.00 Mon–Tue, noon–midnight Wed–Thu, noon–02.00 Fri–Sat, 14.00–midnight Sun. Centrally located & offering European, Russian & Belarusian cuisine (as well as its own confectionery range), this is a decent shout if you're in the mood for Soviet-style dining & karaoke. **$$**

CAFÉS

🖵 **Da Vinci Coffee Bar** [287 C2] 68 Leninskaya St; ✆ 31 31 95; ⊕ 10.00–23.00 daily. Right at the top of Leninskaya & thus a little off your likely beaten track, but the coffee is good & the desserts are decent.

🖵 **Georges Simone Café** [287 C3] 44 Leninskaya St; ✆ 31 15 18; w simone.by; ⊕ 10.00–23.00 daily. Unsurprisingly, given the name, Parisian in theme & décor, it's directly opposite Zvezdnaya Ploshchad Café & seems to suffer by comparison. It's never as busy as its rival.

🖵 **Modern Café** [287 C3] 15 Leninskaya St; ✆ 25 94 94; ⊕ 09.00–23.00 daily (08.00–11.00 1st Mon of the month). A pleasant bistro at the bottom of Leninskaya, with good coffee & decent ice cream.

🖵 **Retro Café** [287 C3] 16 Lepeshinskava Street; ✆ 22 13 00; ⊕ 11.00–23.00 daily. Tucked away just off Star Sq, it's unpretentious & easy to overlook, so less busy than others. It's worth a try.

🖵 **Zvezdnaya Ploshchad Café** [287 C3] 45 Leninskaya St; ✆ 22 39 62; ⊕ 08.00–23.00 daily. Splendidly located right on Star Sq, this is bustling & very popular.

BARS

🍷 **Irish Pub Ale House** [287 C3] 61 Leninskaya St; ✆ 72 27 62; e info@ale-house.by; ⊕ noon–23.00 daily. I have Irish antecedents, so this may be a less than objective view, but there's Guinness, football & loud music here; so what's not to like?

🍷 **Stary Gorod** [287 B4] 16 Pervomayskaya St; ✆ 22 46 21; ⊕ 19.00–05.00 nightly. I'm told the food here is delicious & the service is excellent. Given that it's well located & ideally placed for you to be able to see & do other things in the vicinity, this should be a great place to recharge before continuing with your explorations. Give it a try.

OTHER PRACTICALITIES

There are no specialist shopping facilities here that cannot be found elsewhere, although the shop at the Regional Museum has some interesting souvenirs. The best place to browse and to purchase, not surprisingly, is along Leninskaya and other streets in the vicinity. Beware tacky souvenirs, though. There are plenty of banks, currency exchanges and ATMs in town.

WHAT TO SEE AND DO

In all probability, your first visit to Mogilev is likely to be on a tour or excursion from Minsk, perhaps with an overnight stay. The area simply is not geared up for independent leisure travel, but the infrastructure for tours via the state agencies is excellent. This will not be to everyone's taste of course, but until such time as the tourism *industry* develops to match the breadth and quality of the tourism *product* in this country, a guided excursion is going to be the only way for visitors to gain their first sight of the riches on offer in the more remote areas. When you return next time, armed with the knowledge you will have acquired first time around (and, preferably, some of the language), it will be a different story. For now, just relax and let someone else do the work while you soak up some local knowledge and climb on to that learning curve.

Here are the best of the sights that you are sure to see:

CASTLE SITE (GORKY PARK) [287 A5] The original castle was built of wood in 1267 when the city itself was established by around 200 settlers. It was then enlarged and considerably modernised between the 16th and 18th centuries. Today all that remains of the castle itself is an archaeological dig, but it is still possible to appreciate the strategic importance of the location, high above the confluence of the Dnieper and Dubrovenka rivers. Now Gorky Park, an Orthodox church was built here on the site of the old castle at the end of the 20th century, and it's only a very short walk along the top of the escarpment to Sovyetskaya Square, through the pleasant grounds of the park.

SOVYETSKAYA SQUARE ✳ [287 A/B5] Another Belarusian city, another square on the grandest of scales; and it's usually empty. When I was last there (in the height of summer) I had it all to myself, apart from a handful of Belarusian tourists. Associated with trade and government since the founding of the city, the lofty perch affords fine views from the edge of the escarpment across the Dnieper into the lower town and beyond. I like to sit on the balustrade with my back to the square to ponder the meaning of life and to gaze south into the distance across the urban sprawl. Below is a major road junction and bridge across the Dnieper, the noisy traffic and constant movement of humanity a sharp contrast to the quiet solemnity of the square behind me. Wherever your point of entry into the square, your eye is immediately drawn to the magnificent **memorial** entitled 'The Fighters for Soviet Power'. Dedicated to the glory of the 23-day defence of the city in 1941, the statue itself is an impressive Motherland metaphor. Murals and displays abound, with images of heroism and of residents and soldiers individually honoured for their contribution to the cause. Also here is the splendid **town hall**. Sadly it's a reconstruction. The original 17th-century building was considered one of the finest examples of civil architecture, but it was significantly damaged during the Great Patriotic War and later demolished in 1957. Rebuilt and finally opened in 2008, it's a fine commemoration of the civic prosperity of the city and an interesting visual counterpoint to the image of Soviet might on the other side of the square. An observation platform halfway up the tower affords excellent views, and it's also possible to climb higher, into the clock tower, for an even better view. The building houses a small **museum** dedicated to the history of the city (*1A Leninskaya St;* ☎*24 50 11;* e *ratusha.mogilev@gmail.com;* w *ratusha-mogilev.com;* ⏰ *10.00–18.00 Wed–Sun, last entry 17.30*). The website is particularly informative on the history of the town hall and the city in general.

REGIONAL MUSEUM OF LOCAL HISTORY AND CULTURE [287 A5] (*Музей гісторыі Магілёва/Музей истории Могилёва; 1 Sovyetskaya Sq;* ☎*22 01 20;* e *kraimog@list. ru.;* ⏰ *09.30–17.30 Wed–Sun, last entry 17.00; admission BYN6*) The first history museum was founded in the city in 1867. It survived a number of privations, revolution not the least of them, and was reincarnated more than once. Then at the outset of war in 1941, its treasures were hidden in an apparently secure facility. At some point during the Nazi occupation they disappeared and the search for them still goes on. After the war, it took many years for new collections to be amassed. Happily the museum is now open for business once more in a fine stucco building located between the war memorial and the town hall, on the left-hand side of Sovyetskaya Square. On display are over 300,000 artefacts, consisting of archaeological finds from the region, coins and treasures, icons and other holy relics, paintings, ethnographic displays, historical documents, war memorabilia and articles of everyday life from the 19th and 20th centuries, all collected since the liberation of the city in 1944. The reassembled historical collection from 1917 to 1945 is particularly interesting, consisting of four exhibitions in 18 rooms. Great historic events and significant periods of time are covered in considerable detail, including the 1917 Revolution, mass industrialisation, Stalin's purges, the Nazi occupation and subsequent partisan insurrection. Walking excursions of 45 minutes' duration, lectures on the move about history and the environment, can be booked for groups of up to 25 people, but only in Russian, although with advance notice an English speaker of sorts might be available. The museum's website is a treasure trove of information, though sadly only in Russian. Well worth a visit.

LENINSKAYA STREET ✳ Running from Sovyetskaya Square, on the left of the town hall, this street is worthy of a leisurely promenade – if you can shut out the noise of the city, that is. The architecture has been substantially renovated and the thoroughfare pedestrianised, with imaginative street furniture to complement the whole effect. The **drama theatre** and **Cathedral of St Stanislaw** are both close by. The buildings have attractive pastel-coloured stucco fronts in pale yellow, orange and lime green. But although the restoration work is very professionally done and the intention to recreate Mogilev of old is to be commended, it's all just a little twee, and somehow lacking the charm of similar projects in other cities, notably Brest and Vitebsk. It's probably because everywhere else in this city you'll find the noise and constant movement of business, industry and commerce, such that even though Leninskaya is made for promenading, it doesn't feel like a relaxed or relaxing environment, which is something of a disappointment. There's even a vague whiff of Disneyland about it all, down to the land train that chugs back and forth along the street, with the few tourists that come here on board. Still, there are some fine pavement cafés and a few shops that are worth a browse. And in the central **Star Square** [287 C3], directly outside the Radzima cinema, stands the enigmatic **bronze sculpture of a stargazer** pointing to the heavens, in the middle of 12 bronze high-backed chairs arranged in a semicircle representing the signs of the zodiac. All around, sculpted into the pavement, are stars and symbols. It is the work of a modest and unassuming artist, the sculptor Vladimir Zhbanov, a veteran of the Afghan conflict. His work is to be found all over Minsk. It's urban art at its best. Do check out the stargazer, but take the time to look elsewhere in the square too. The sculpture is the obvious highlight, but there's also an interesting array of buildings. Look for the USSR mural from 1953 on the wall above Colin's store, as well as fine examples of 19th-century red brick among the pale stucco. If the rest of Leninskaya is a tad noisy and brash, all is generally calm and classy here.

DRAMA THEATRE [287 B4] (*Магілёўскі абласны драматычны тэатр/ Могилёвский областной драматический театр; 7 Pervomayskaya St;* ✆*31 00 45;* e *info@mdrama.by*) Built in May 1888, this charming red-brick building is worth a visit in architectural terms alone. It now specialises in contemporary drama, but works of masters such as Gorky, Chekhov and Kupala are also performed here. When I was last in the city a revival of the French farce *Boeing Boeing* was on offer!

A night at this theatre was a favourite pastime of the last tsar Nikolai II and his family. Look for the charming bronze sculpture of an 18th-century lady and her dog at the bottom of the front steps. It's another work of Vladimir Zhbanov. Further along the street and not far from the Cathedral of the Three Saints is the popular and famed children's **Puppet Theatre** [287 C1] (*73 Pervomayskaya St;* ✆ *32 66 90*).

ROMAN CATHOLIC CATHEDRAL OF ST STANISLAW [287 B4] (Касцёл святога Станіслава/Костел святого Станислава)
Built between 1738 and 1752 in the Baroque style and fronted by four majestic colonnades, this cathedral is beautifully decorated with many exquisite murals depicting the entire cycle of the Scriptures. Magnificent though it is, the exterior of the building is a tad shabby and in need of some tender loving care. Organ recitals are regularly held here and it is also the location of the annual Magutny Bozha ('Almighty God') festival of sacred music in July and August.

ORTHODOX CONVENT OF ST NIKOLAI [287 D5] (Свята-Мікалаеўская царква/ Свято-Николаевская церковь)
This walled monastic complex has preserved the structure of its magnificent Baroque cathedral, which was constructed in 1668, including the bell tower, walls and gates, together with the original (and quite stunning) four-tiered iconostasis and some magnificent frescoes in dazzling colours from the 17th and 18th centuries on the exterior of the elevations. It was much frequented by Nikolai II, including after his abdication, and an icon portrait of the Tsar is on display. It's a little way out of the city (I once set off to walk here but was defeated by the heat and topography of the land, which makes it difficult to find and keep one's bearings), but don't be put off; try very hard to organise transport for a visit to this beautiful place.

CATHEDRAL OF THE THREE SAINTS [287 C1] (Царква Святой Тройцы/Церковь Святой Троицы)
Located at the junction of Pervomayskaya and Timiryazevskaya streets, this splendid cathedral was constructed between 1903 and 1914 to honour three saints (Basil the Great, Gregory the Theologian and John Chrysostom). It is a fine example of retro Russian design. The most significant place of Orthodox worship in the city (and often frequented by Tsar Nikolai II), this is one of its architectural gems.

MEMORIAL COMPLEX AT BUYNICHSKOYE FIELD (Мемарыяльны комплекс Буйніцкае поле/Мемориальный комплекс Буйничское поле)
Located southwest of the city centre and 2km beyond the main conurbation on the P93 road, just to the west of the small village of Buynichi (on the right of the highway as you leave the city, with the village to the left), it is here that a hugely significant military engagement took place in the early weeks of the Great Patriotic War. For 23 long days and nights, shortly after Operation Barbarossa began, this place was the scene of a heroic defence action on the part of Red Army soldiers of the 388th Infantry Division, who delayed the capture of the city (and thus slowed up the advance on Moscow) long enough to buy Stalin time and for the Soviet Union to gather its strength and resources for the defence of the greater part of the Motherland. The heroism displayed by regular Red Army soldiers and partisans here has passed into legend and the Regional Museum of Local History and Culture in Mogilev's Sovyetskaya Square has an excellent feature on the engagement. The complex is open to the public between 1 April and 31 October, though on many days of the year hero veterans of the Red Army can be found here, taking part in official ceremonies

of remembrance or else visiting in small numbers to honour the memory of their fallen comrades. It is a sad, solemn, but ultimately uplifting place. After passing through a triple archway of simple but affecting design, the visitor comes to the chapel of remembrance and adjacent to it, the memorial Lake of Tears. There are also displays of tanks and military equipment, together with a memorial stone upon which are inscribed verses of the renowned war correspondent, writer and poet Konstantin Simonov, a veteran of the battle who documented its events. Upon his death, his ashes were scattered over the field in accordance with his last wishes. There is an excellent English-language website (w *simonov.co.uk*) devoted to the life and work of this esteemed writer and some research before you visit will help to set the scene for you. Also close by in the village of Buynichi is an interesting **open-air ethnographical museum and centre for handicrafts** recreating life in a 19th-century Belarusian village. It houses a reconstructed mill and a number of traditional workshops and buildings showcasing rural trades, plus a café and play area for children. Adjoining it is the **Zoological Garden** established in 2004, incorporating enclosures for a variety of wild animals. There's even a Siberian tiger. My own view on the morality of animals imprisoned in cages is well documented in the pages of this book, but you must judge for yourselves.

OUTSIDE MOGILEV

Even though the surrounding countryside is attractive, particularly on and around the rivers that cross the region, access by public transport is difficult for two reasons: first, you're going to need to be able to speak the language and second, the infrastructure is not geared up for visitors who want to explore, but for local people who need to get from their homes to work, to market and to school or university. But some of the excursions arranged by the state agencies will include a tour of the rural areas, particularly if you arrange an overnight tour from Minsk. Noteworthy architectural monuments of the district include the attractive 18th-century **town hall** in the town of **Shklov** (Шклоў/Шклов), 35km north of Mogilev on the P76 road; the 19th-century **Church of the Protection of the Virgin** in the village of **Veino** (Вейна/Вейно), 5km east of Mogilev on the P122; the early 20th-century **Assumption Church** in the village of **Golinyets** (Галынец/Голынец), 10km southwest of the city on minor roads; the 19th-century **outhouse** of the Zhukovsky estate, used as a military hospital for the Russian army during the 1812 campaign in the village of **Dashkovka** (Дашкоўка/Дашковка), 15km due south of the city on the E95 road; a **Dominican church** built in 1681 in the village of **Knyazhitsy** (Княжыцы/Княжицы); and the early 20th-century **Assumption Church** in the village of **Sukhari** (Сухары/Сухари), 20km northeast of the city on the P96 road. Finally, there is a small but interesting **military history museum** in the village of **Polykovichi** (Палыкавічы/Полыковичи), just to the northeast of Mogilev on the P123 road. There is also a **well and thermal spring** here, much revered in folklore since the 16th century for its supposed powers of healing. Tsar Nikolai II visited many times with his family for the young Tsarevich Alexei, a haemophiliac, to take the waters. Tourist agencies market it thus to this very day. This is a good reflection of the sites to be seen on an organised tour through the oblast, but there are many others further afield that are worthy of your attention. Come back with your own transport and explore one day.

8

Gomel City and Oblast
Гомель/Гомель

Telephone code 232

Gomel is the second-largest city of Belarus and the main administrative centre and capital of Gomel oblast. With a population of 535,229, it is located high above the western bank of the Sozh River, in the southeastern part of the country, 300km from Minsk and close to the borders with Russia and Ukraine. The city is a large and significant transport junction at the centre of a rail and road crossroads that connects the rest of the country to the west (and thence to the countries of western Europe beyond), the Baltic states to the north, Russia to the east and Ukraine to the south. Historically the Sozh River was once a major trading route, with the journey downriver to Kiev taking around 6 hours. The port at Gomel continues to operate on a limited commercial basis. Today, modern Gomel shares with Mogilev the accolade of being one of the largest industrial centres of Belarus. The region's southern position and mild climate also mean that conditions for the development of agriculture are most advantageous.

Away from the city, the countryside is particularly attractive: a land of forests and picturesque riverbanks, with low marshland in-between. Here is the eastern end of the Polyesye, the unique land of 'fogs and bogs'. In the days of the Soviet Union, the fragile balance of nature here was disturbed, as marshes, peat bogs and lakes were artificially dried up with the aim of increasing the proportion of land available for cultivation. Happily, the topography and ecology survived (while the USSR itself did not) and much of the area was preserved in its natural state and condition. Today, Pripyatsky National Park affords visitors the opportunity to admire this rare environment in circumstances where the ecological balance, the animals that live here and the plants that thrive are nurtured and protected.

In addition to the natural delights to be enjoyed, there are also many manmade creations of great interest. Architectural delights in the region include the recreated castle complex and St Michael the Archangel Orthodox Church in Mozyr, the 18th-century church and Jesuit college in Kalinkovichy, the early 18th-century Church of St Nicholas in Petrikov and the beautifully restored church at Zhelizniki (in Vetka district), believed to be the oldest in the entire region (and one of the oldest in the country). In the school at Nyeglubka (also in Vetka district), students are taught the art of weaving on wooden looms constructed exactly as they were many hundreds of years ago, to preserve the old and traditional ways. Many bitter engagements were fought on these territories in the Great Patriotic War; for example at Khalch, on the road from Gomel to the town of Vetka, there was great loss of life as the Red Army fought to cross the Sozh, with Gomel itself almost completely flattened under fierce bombardment. Monuments to heroism and sacrifice are everywhere to be found in this oblast.

The region is also only 120km or so from the deserted Ukrainian city of Pripyat, where the ill-fated nuclear plant at Chernobyl was situated, and this region suffered

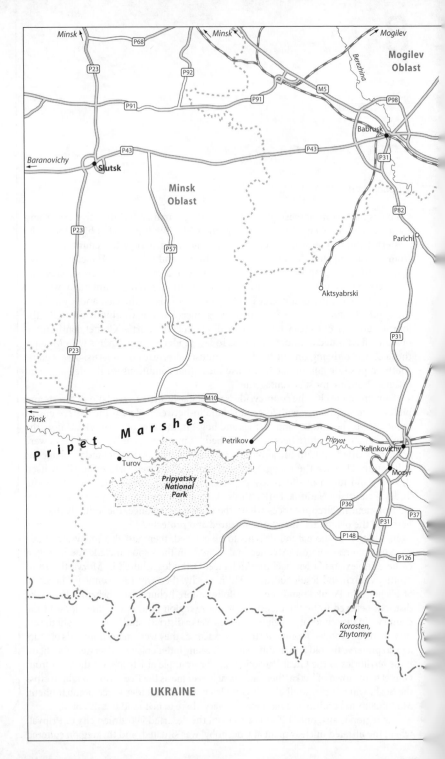

Mogilev

Mogilev

Roslavl

**Mogilev
Oblast**

P93

P43

M5

Dnieper

P43

RUSSIA

M5

M8

Zhlobin

P38

Zheliznik

P149

P30

Nyeglubka

Svetlogorsk

Dnieper

M5

Bartolomyeyevka
(abandoned village)

Sozh

P30

E271

Khalch

Vetka

Gomel City
Airport

P82

M5

Gomel

Rechitsa

M10

M10

Dnieper

P32

Sozh

M8

Chernihiv

M10

P33

Khoiniki

P35

UKRAINE

Pripyat

*Polyessky Radiation
and Ecology Reserve*

N

Chernobyl nuclear
power station

Pripyat

0 ——————— 30km

0 ——————— 30 miles

Kiev

Wherever they occur in the world, one consequence of disasters, manmade or natural, is that history thereafter is divided into 'pre' and 'post' periods. The catastrophic explosion at Chernobyl was one such event, and nowhere is the 'before and after' factor more acutely articulated than in Gomel region.

The damage to Belarus as a whole is almost beyond measure. Analysts believe that the cost has totalled in the vicinity of US$235 billion; put another way, this equates to 32 annual state budgets of the pre-tragedy period. Practically all spheres of human activity have been affected in the regions, particularly those in the southeast. Farmland and pastures have been excluded from agricultural use, while the use of forest, mineral, organic, fuel and other resources is subject to restrictions. Among other losses suffered in the regions are the closure of enterprises and companies, output reduction, significant expenditure for the resettlement of whole communities, and the cost of ensuring safe living conditions and social security for residents of the contaminated regions, including their medical care and recuperation. In particular, the cost to the social and community infrastructure is incalculable. And the effect of the 'Chernobyl factor' on the lives of individuals and families continues to manifest itself in all sorts of unexpected ways. The existence of real and readily diagnosable medical problems and conditions is an irrefutable fact, with evidence and data to back up the claims. More difficult to analyse and articulate are the consequences of the despair and lack of hope that follow in the aftermath of such cataclysmic events.

Gomel oblast took the biggest hit and bore the brunt of the disaster. In the country as a whole, more than 135,000 people from 470 townships and villages, two-thirds of which were in Gomel oblast, had to leave the worst-affected territories and resettle to safer regions of the republic and beyond, into the wider area of the Soviet Union. My own adoptive family in Vetka were forced to move many hundreds of kilometres east into the Urals, almost without notice. It was years before they were permitted to return.

In the aftermath of the disaster, the oblast developed a system of radiation monitoring and control, as well as a series of protective measures in agro-industrial production, which is financed from the state budget. The region continues to roll out measures aimed at improving medical services to the victims of the catastrophe. The Polyesye Radiation and Ecology Reserve was also set up in the oblast to study the effects of exposure to radioactive material and to undertake

the worst contamination in all of Belarus, with subsisting levels of radiation still very high in some areas of its countryside. There are a number of 'no go' areas in the region to which access is available only by means of official pass. Additionally, strict rules remain in force about the production and distribution of foodstuffs, together with strong government advice about what to eat and drink in terms of natural products.

HISTORY

First mentioned in *Chronicles* in 1142, the original settlement here was established at the place where the Gomeyuk Stream flows into the Sozh River. Today, this point is marked by the ornamental swan lake at the bottom of a ravine in the Rumyantsev-Paskevich Park, as well as a relatively new sculpture depicting one of the first strategic thinking to assist with the development of long-term planning for the affected areas to address ongoing social issues.

Various foreign charitable organisations from Germany, Great Britain, Ireland, Japan, Italy, Austria, Belgium, the USA and other countries render significant support to Gomel in mitigating Chernobyl's consequences. They supply drugs and medical equipment, organise learning and development opportunities for Belarusian doctors in Western clinics and arrange recuperation visits to foreign countries for children from the most contaminated regions. More recently, on the initiative of the United Nations and the World Bank, the oblast launched projects aiming to promote the rehabilitation of the contaminated territories, insofar as that can be safely achieved. These projects seek the support of the international community in two ways. First, in securing loans for developing the industrial infrastructure and creating new jobs in the affected regions, thus providing an opportunity for local people to raise their level of social security themselves; and secondly, in the transference of skills to local people to enable the country itself to rebuild its infrastructure according to its own perception of where the need really lies.

The trouble with radiation pollution is that you can't see it, smell it or taste it. For the most part, everything looks exactly the same. The consequences are there to be seen, in terms of abandoned villages, derelict homesteads and signs by the side of the road displaying the familiar radiation logo barring access down some of the woodland tracks and old roads, but not the radiation itself. It is for this very reason that many people, particularly the elderly, have gradually moved back to their former homes in areas where it is still unwise to live, eat the fruits of the forest and drink water from the local streams.

In this region of great natural beauty, radiation is all around: in the water, in the food, in the ground and in the air that people breathe. In autumn 2017, good friends of mine went mushroom-picking in the forests outside Gomel. A check at a local testing centre revealed contamination six times the level of normally expected background radiation. They threw the mushrooms away. Radiation is part of the way of life and it won't be going away for a very long time. The challenge is to combat its consequences while making the safest and best use of natural resources, without compromising the health and well-being of all who live here.

settlers. A number of different Slavic tribes seem to have coexisted peacefully in the area and, as with so many other communities in these lands, Gomel's geographic location was extremely favourable when it came to developing trade, because of the river routes connecting northwest and southeast Europe.

Originally included in the estate of Prince Rostislav Mstislavich, it subsequently shared the fate of most Belarusian towns, passing through the hands of one conquering warlord after another, from princes of Kievan Rus to Ivan the Terrible. In 1335, it was ceded to the Grand Duchy of Lithuania and in the 16th century its castle held a strongly fortified position high above the Sozh River in major engagements against invading Tatars from the Black Sea. Then, in 1670, a significant step in the development of the region came with the grant of rights of self-determination and governance under Magdeburg Law. As in earlier times, tradesmen and merchants were encouraged to return once again as the commercial

I remember my first visit to the region in 2001 for two particular reasons. First, while visiting a large school I asked the headmaster to explain the purpose of a digital display in the entrance hall, the numbers on the readout constantly changing, apparently in random fashion. He told me that it was a monitor showing the level of radiation pollution in and around the school (this monitor has now been removed). Then later that day, I visited a kindergarten. I passed from room to room, smiling fondly at the accoutrements of the toddlers and small children that were all around: toys, books, clothes and, in one room, a series of cupboards, the drawers of which were tiny beds for the littlest tots to take an afternoon nap. It made me miss my own children very much. And in this place of youthful innocence and apparent safety and security, my gaze fell on an object resting on the window ledge. When I went over to take a closer look, I saw that it was an old-fashioned Geiger counter.

On a later visit to the oblast, I was given the opportunity to spend a day in the restricted zone with two senior local officials, one an elected deputy and the other an ecological expert. On a warm spring day, we took the road from Vetka that leads towards Svetilovichy and then onward to the Russian border. It is a long, straight and flat road, with extensive silver birch forests on either side, just beyond the tarmac. Not far out of Vetka was the permanent militia post that was then manned 24 hours a day to monitor those who passed through this area. Unsurprisingly, we encountered no difficulty here. It is now manned no more. Some 5km further on is a road to the left and just before you reach it, you notice the first half-derelict property of the now lost village of Bartolomeyevka. As you turn in, there stands the telltale sign warning of dire consequences if you enter, the sinister international radiation logo leaving you in no doubt as to the violation of the natural order that lies beyond. We got out of the car to walk for a while. The sun was shining, birds were singing and everywhere we looked were the signs of new life, of growth and regeneration in the hedgerows and trees. Except that all around us, the insidious, creeping and degenerative radiation

prosperity of the city and its satellite villages grew. Yet for the next hundred years or so, short periods of economic stability were followed by debilitating conflict as the strength and power of Gomel's warring neighbours waxed and waned.

It passed to Russia after Poland was partitioned in 1772, and then in 1775 Catherine the Great gifted the town to one Count Rumyantsev. A brave soldier as well as a tactically astute militarist, he was not only a hero of the people, but also a personal favourite of the Empress herself. His loyalty to her was rewarded with many lavish gifts that included (among other things) extravagant jewels, military decorations, ornate silver trinkets and works of art. Emancipation of the serfs was still almost a century away and so the gift of the town also included 5,000 peasants living in the area. Finally (and most significant of all), she gave him 100,000 roubles to build a palace. It took him five years to replace the old wooden castle with a magnificent mansion of stone. It was designed by Rastrelli, the architect responsible for the Winter Palace in St Petersburg.

Gomel quickly began to take on the architectural characteristics of a major European city. In 1834, Rumyantsev's younger son Sergei sold the palace and grounds to Count Paskevich, who added further features, built the nearby tower and designed the ornamental gardens that are still there today. In 1850, permeated the very ground on which we walked. The most obvious sign of incongruity was in the form of the buildings that we passed, all with the windows and roofs bulldozed by the authorities to prevent people from living there. The remains of the large village school were particularly poignant. We were assured that it was perfectly safe for us to be here on a short-term basis and indeed, the advice of medical experts sought prior to the visit had confirmed that this would be so. We drove further into the contaminated zone, passing another manned checkpoint as we crossed a small stream. Every time we stopped, I got out of the car to scan our surroundings. The countryside here is stunningly beautiful. Rivers, streams, woodland, marsh and meadow are punctuated by small villages of delightful wooden houses. All empty, or at least, most of them. Very occasionally, we would pass individual dwellings with smoke spiralling from the chimney and a babooshka tending the crops in the garden outside. The state turns a blind eye to these people. On the face of it, produce from the land here cannot be sold. Regular checks on the radioactivity of fruit and vegetables are supposed to ensure that this is so. I couldn't help wondering, though.

On another occasion, I got to understand the extent to which limitations on access into the zone are rigidly enforced. I was in the second of two cars *en route* back to Vetka from a visit to a farm in Vyeliki Nyemki, a small hamlet north of Svetilovichy where I and others had been working on sustainable development projects. The state officials accompanying us on the visit were in the first car and I was travelling with colleagues who had never before seen the abandoned village described above. We slowed and turned in, the first car pulling away into the distance. We had only just got out of the car when it returned at high speed, one of the officials leaping out to shepherd us back into our vehicle. I was later told by a colleague who was travelling in the first car that as soon as the officials realised we had turned off, the driver performed a high-speed U-turn to fetch us back. Genuine regulation for all the right reasons, or just bureaucracy? I still can't decide.

the first telegraphic communication line in all Russia was established between St Petersburg and Simferopol on the Black Sea, passing through Gomel. At the same time, the city found itself on the new highway between St Petersburg and Kiev. By 1888 it had become a major rail junction. This was a time of great prosperity, with trade, industry and culture developing rapidly. Another major road route was completed by the construction in 1857 of a bridge erected over the Sozh. By 1913, the town's population had soared to over 104,500, including a large and influential Jewish community.

The early part of the 20th century saw much revolutionary activity in Russia, and in 1917 the empire fell at last. The first Soviet was established in Gomel in December 1917, and then in April 1919 the administrative area was incorporated into the newly independent but short-lived republic, which then became part of the Soviet Union. By 1926, it had become one of the most significant regions in the Belarusian SSR. Indeed, the 1920s and 1930s saw massive and rapid economic growth in terms of the industrial and infrastructural development of the town. Huge industrial enterprises were established. By 1941, the town was able to boast 264 of them, along with 144,200 inhabitants. Indeed, Gomel ranked third at this time in the whole of the republic in terms of industrial output.

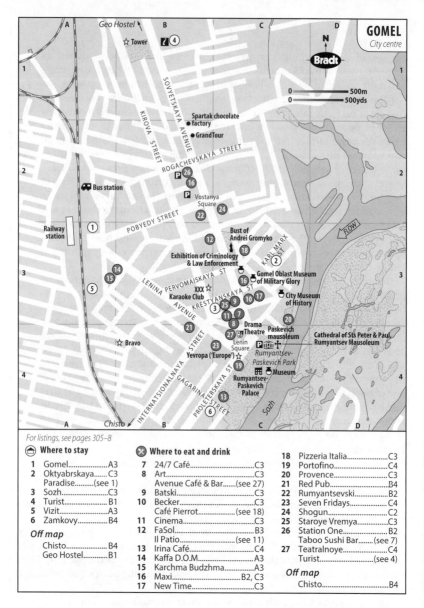

GOMEL
City centre

Geo Hostel

☆ Tower

SOVYETSKAYA AVENUE

KIROVA STREET

ROGACHEVSKAYA STREET

Spartak chocolate factory

GrandTour

Bus station

Railway station

POBYEDY STREET

Vostanya Square

LENINA PERVOMAISKAYA ST

AVENUE

KRESTYANSKAYA ST

Bust of Andrei Gromyko

Exhibition of Criminology & Law Enforcement

XXX ☆ Karaoke Club

KARL MARX ST

Gomel Oblast Museum of Military Glory

City Museum of History

☆ Bravo

INTERNATSIONALNAYA STREET

GAGARINA STREET

PROLETERSKAYA ST

Drama Theatre

Paskevich mausoleum

Lenin Square

Cathedral of Sts Peter & Paul, Rumyantsev Mausoleum

Yevropa ('Europe') ☆

Rumyantsev-Paskevich Park

Rumyantsev-Paskevich Palace

Museum

Sozh

Chisto

FLOW

N

Bradt

0   500m
0   500yds

For listings, see pages 305–8

Where to stay

1 Gomel........................A3
2 Oktyabrskaya.........C3
   Paradise..........(see 1)
3 Sozh...........................C3
4 Turist.........................B1
5 Vizit...........................A3
6 Zamkovy....................B4

Off map
   Chisto.......................B4
   Geo Hostel..............B1

Where to eat and drink

7 24/7 Café...................C3
8 Art...............................C3
   Avenue Café & Bar.......(see 27)
9 Batski..........................C3
10 Becker........................C3
   Café Pierrot.......(see 18)
11 Cinema.......................C3
12 FaSol...........................B3
   Il Patio.............(see 11)
13 Irina Café..................C4
14 Kaffa D.O.M..............A3
15 Karchma Budzhma...............A3
16 Maxi.......................B2, C3
17 New Time..................C3

18 Pizzeria Italia.............C3
19 Portofino....................C4
20 Provence.....................C3
21 Red Pub.....................B4
22 Rumyantsevski...........B2
23 Seven Fridays.............C4
24 Shogun.......................C2
25 Staroye Vremya.........C3
26 Station One................B2
   Taboo Sushi Bar.......(see 7)
27 Teatralnoye................C4
   Turist.................(see 4)

Off map
   Chisto.......................B4

By the time of the Nazi invasion in July 1941, the Jewish community had increased to around 50,000, approximately one-third of the city's total population. Some managed to flee in the early days of Operation Barbarossa but, after the city fell on 19 August 1941, those who could not or would not leave were confined to conditions of unspeakable barbarity. In the final analysis, over 100,000 people from the oblast were to die in five concentration camps and four ghettos, or after having been transported to Germany as slave labour. The city itself was virtually flattened, with 80% of buildings destroyed. The Nazis stripped the town of all industrial equipment, food reserves and stocks of raw materials for transportation back to Germany.

The region was a major centre for resistance activities of the partisan movement and, on 26 November 1943, the town was liberated by forces of the Belarusian Front of the Red Army. In 1946, the process of restoration and reconstruction of Gomel began, based on the preservation of original features in strategic planning terms. By 1959, the population had climbed to 168,000 and in 1962 the first trolleybuses appeared on the streets. Little by little in the four decades that followed, Gomel developed once more into a major European city, full of hustle and bustle, as significant new projects were completed, including newly established residential areas and the construction of a pedestrian bridge over the Sozh from the Rumyantsev Park. At the end of the 1990s, the works of construction for the new suburban railway station, another new river crossing and the impressive 'Ice Palace of Sports' (a huge facility for public sports use) were finished, as befitted the country's second city. And today, ambitious programmes of residential development are in the course of being realised, bringing whole new micro-districts into existence. Gomel's future looks to be a bright one.

GETTING THERE AND AWAY

BY AIR Situated 8km from the city, Gomel Airport is the second largest in the country, though its primary purpose currently is the movement of freight. The Belarusian state airline Belavia operates some passenger services to a number of cities in the former Soviet republics, but it is no longer possible to fly to other destinations within Belarus. Don't be disappointed. You're not missing out. My only experience of flying down to Gomel from Minsk (with the now defunct airline Gomelavia) was a particularly scary one, which must remain a tale for another occasion.

BY TRAIN The main railway station is located on Privakhsalnaya Square at one end of Lenina Avenue [302 A3] and only 15 minutes' walk from the city centre. There are frequent trains each day to and from Minsk (*3hrs; BYN15 one-way*), the introduction of gleaming new rolling stock with excellent on-board facilities substantially reducing journey times. There is also an overnight sleeper service on older rolling stock (*7–8hrs*).

BY BUS The bus station [302 A2] is situated just a few hundred metres away from the railway station (turn left out of the main exit). There are several daily services to Minsk (*6hrs; BYN12.50 one-way*) and regular routes also operate north and west to the major centres of population within the country and south and east into Russia and Ukraine. Local bus services also depart from here and the coverage is excellent, both in terms of frequency and also the number of destinations served.

BY CAR The M5 motorway heads northwest from here to Minsk and, all along the route, major works of upgrading are in the course of being implemented. This means the journey is currently not without delay or adventure, but when complete the new dual carriageway will render it much less arduous than ever it was on single carriageway. The ring road around the city of Babrusk (almost halfway between Gomel and Minsk) has already made a big difference. Journey times are generally around 5 hours at present if the traffic is heavy, but should fall to around 3½ hours when all upgrade works are complete. Other major roads will take you west via Mozyr to Brest and then into western Europe, north via Mogilev to Vitebsk and then into the Baltic states and, finally, east and south into Russia and Ukraine.

GETTING AROUND

The main thoroughfare heading north to south within the city is Sovyetskaya Street. The gradient rises as you head south and at the very top is Lenin Square, where you-know-who still presides over the city from his lofty perch on a granite plinth. Behind is the park where the palace and cathedral are to be found, then beyond and some way below the park is the Sozh River. Lenina Avenue leaves the square from the same side as Sovyetskaya, but in a northwesterly direction and at an angle of around 45 degrees. It's then a straight 15-minute walk to the railway station. To access the bus station, turn left out of the main entrance/exit of the railway station and walk straight ahead for 200m. There are plenty of taxis to be found around here, particularly right outside the main entrance to the railway station.

The **bus, tram** and **trolleybus** services are plentiful and cheap, if overcrowded. Directly in front of you out of the railway station is Pobyedy Avenue and a straight 10-minute walk along here will bring you back to Sovyetskaya. Turn right to complete the triangle back up to the park. The centre is compact and all you will want to see can be easily accessed on foot.

Everything you need to know about transport in this city can be found on w gomeltrans.net, though sadly only in Russian.

TOURIST INFORMATION

As with previous chapters, please bear in mind that in spite of continuing checks, regular corroboration with trusted sources and repeated personal visits, the still-developing nature of tourism in this country and the sometimes random (and inexplicable) divergence between readily available data and reality means that the information provided in these pages on opening hours, telephone numbers and prices for restaurants, bars, clubs, museums and the like will be occasionally different from what you find when you hit the ground. Actually, I reckon this adds to the charm of travelling here!

The city of Gomel has a number of tourist agencies, most of them on Sovyetskaya. The **national state agency** (under the guise of the agency 'GrandTour') [302 B2] (*61 Sovyetskaya St;* ✆*60 04 00;* e *grandtour.gomel@gmail. com;* w *grandtour.by,* w *belarustourism.by;* ⊕ *09.00–19.00 Mon–Sat*) offers a range of information materials (some in English) and you'll be unlucky if no English speaker is available when you visit. It is also possible to book tours here and make all the usual tourist arrangements. Otherwise, the reception desks at the larger hotels will have limited amounts of information. The agency **Gomeltourist** operates from a base in the Hotel Turist on Sovyetskaya (see opposite), offering a full range of visitor facilities, including tours around the city and out-of-town excursions. There is now also a small **tourist information centre** [302 A2] within the main railway station.

The oblast executive committee's website (w *gomel-region.by/en*) is packed with information; it's primarily aimed at members of the community, but you can pick up some very useful intelligence about facilities and infrastructure nonetheless. The city executive committee's website (w *gomel.gov.by*) is also a very good source of practical information, particularly with regards to hotels, restaurants, clubs, cafés and bars, as is the website w hi-gomel.by. For informative notes on history and the towns of the area, the best resource is w goldring. gomel-region.by.

UPMARKET

✳ 🏠 **Zamkovy** [302 B4] (42 rooms) 6 Gagarina St; ✆ 75 04 60; e zamkovyj@yandex. ru; w zamkovyi.com. Only a few years old, this is the best hotel in town. Cheap it isn't, but it's decent value for money. Ideally located next to Lunacharsky Park, mere metres from Café Irina, everything about it oozes quality & high-end service. Everyone I know in Gomel, from friends to staff at tourist agencies, say so without hesitation. It's difficult to disagree. The theme is faux medieval (even the billiard room!), but it is done well. Good English is spoken & the staff always go the extra mile. Services (some of them at additional cost) inc free parking, restaurant, bar, beauty salon, pleasing gardens, billiards room, car hire, travel services & sauna. **$$$$**

🏠 **Chisto** [302 A4] (37 rooms) 4a Bratyev Lizyukovikh St; ✆ 232 30 73 73; m 29 173 73 73; e hotel@4isto.by; w 4isto.by, w chistohotelgomel.connectotels.com. Also new & very shiny, this bright & bubbly hotel in its own complex consistently scores highly with visitors. Located west of the city (& 10mins from the railway station by car) the location in an industrial suburb is not the best but facilities are good, standards of service are high (good English is spoken) & prices are extremely competitive. The green spaces of Festivalny Park are a 15min walk away. Facilities inc 24hr reception, a decent (& lively) beer restaurant (🕐 noon–01.00 Sun–Thu, noon–03.00 Fri–Sat), bar, ATM, fitness centre, sauna, free Wi-Fi, free parking, on-site mini-market & complimentary b/fast. A packed lunch service is also available. I have yet to stay here but all indications are promising. Just bear in mind, though, that more than one guest has reported it can be noisy late at night. **$$$**

MID-RANGE

🏠 **Gomel** [302 A3] (91 rooms) 1 Privakhsalnaya Sq; ✆ 71 67 25; e gost_gomel@gomel-hotel.by; w gomel-hotel.by. Formerly in the same ownership as the Hotel Sozh, Gomel has seen significant refurbishment, but it's still a sterile, soulless place. Services inc restaurant, café, gym, ATM & currency exchange. Its big advantage is location: it's the first high-rise you see on your left as you exit the railway station. B/fast extra. **$$$**

🏠 **Paradise** [302 A3] (34 rooms) 1 Privakhsalnaya Sq; ✆ 71 25 26, 77 41 11; e info@ gomelparadise.com; w gomelparadise.com. A small but significantly refurbished hotel, situated in the same building as the Hotel Gomel. The reception area is wall-to-wall pseudo-marble & it's tacky. There's a small buffet restaurant & café here of acceptable standard, serving European, Russian & Belarusian cuisine, plus secure parking, currency exchange, ATM, laundry, hairdresser & shop. Rooms range from sgls to apts & all are functional, but no more. Decent value, though, & with more foreigner-friendly service than the Gomel. **$$$**

🏠 **Sozh** [302 C3] (132 rooms) 16 Krestyanskaya St; ✆ 75 61 99; e info@hotelsozh.by; w hotelsozh. by. This passable 4-storey hotel was built in 1960 & has been refurbished a number of times. It's centrally located just off Sovyetskaya (close to the top end) in the heart of the city. Facilities inc restaurant (it used to be highly rated by the locals but standards have slipped significantly), 2 24hr bars, currency exchange & secure parking. Beware the economy rooms – they are cheap, but to describe them as basic is something of an understatement. All in all, the location is probably the best thing going for this place. **$$$**

🏠 **Turist** [302 B1] (172 rooms) 87 Sovyetskaya St; ✆ 57 49 51; e info@gomeltourist.com; w gomeltourist.com. Built in 1986 & substantially refurbished in 2004, there's no escaping that this is an archetypical Soviet concrete block, situated 2km from the railway station & 2.5km from the bus station. With rooms spread over 7 floors, you pretty much get what you might expect: drab décor, little warmth in terms of atmosphere, but adequate & functional facilities, inc currency exchange, Gomeltourist travel bureau (✆ 57 49 49), restaurant spread over a number of rooms (all of which offer live music or evening cabaret; page 307), café, bar (🕐 24hrs) serving excellent coffee, sauna & massage room. Rooms range from sgls to 3-room suites. All in all, it does the job, but at a price. My very first night in Belarus was spent here in 2001. Conference attendees & businessmen (national & international) use this hotel, so be wary of the unofficial 'services' that will be on offer, ie: the knock on the door & the late-night phone call after you turn in (see box, page 78). **$$$**

🏠 **Vizit** [302 A3] (87 rooms) 6 Kisilyeva St; ☏ 77 37 75; e spir_ros_aspekt@mail.ru; w gomel.amaks-hotels.ru. A very shiny hotel in the Amaks chain, it's only a few hundred metres from the railway station. Services inc free parking, limited travel facilities, bar, café, ATM & car hire. After a full refurbishment in 2013, the standard of materials & workmanship is not great, but the staff are very helpful (most speak English) & if you don't expect too much, it's decent value for money. **$$$**

BUDGET

🏠 **Hostel Geo** [302 B1] 1d First Krupskoi Lane; m 44 584 22 55; w hostel-geo.by. Located north of the city centre in a residential suburb, this friendly & spotlessly clean hostel is excellent value for money. There are dorms, family rooms & twins, with facilities for laundry & cooking. There is also a pretty garden (& BBQ area), free Wi-Fi & parking. Children & families welcome. **$$**

🏠 **Oktyabrskaya** [302 C3] (145 rooms) 1 Karl Marx St; ☏ 77 68 91. Not far from the river & at the right end of town for most of the sights, there are sgls, dbls & suites on 6 floors. There's a bar & a café, plus a few other basic facilities, but b/fast is not inc in the price of the room. This hotel is more or less constantly in a process of refurbishment, so only a proportion of the 145 built rooms will be available at any given time (in autumn 2017, the number was 42). It's cheap, but not very cheerful; a last-resort option. **$$**

✖ WHERE TO EAT AND DRINK

RESTAURANTS

✖ **Provence** [302 C3] 1 Bilyetski St Lower; m 44 773 03 03; ⊕ noon–midnight daily. 'There's a new restaurant in town that I want to show you. I think it's the best.' Thus spoke Olya when I visited Gomel in 2014. When I was last in the city in the autumn of 2017, many of my other Gomel friends agreed it's one of the best restaurants in town, if expensive. A 2-storey establishment, right on the bank of the Sozh River, it has excellent views from the terrace up & down the river. To find it, walk down to the riverbank from the rear of the Rumyantsev Palace, locate the sculpture of the first settlers, & keep going riverside under the footbridge that crosses to the other bank. You soon come to the restaurant. It serves French & Italian cuisine to a high standard, the décor is tasteful & everything about this place is a cut above the rest. There's also a bar on the 1st floor that is very popular with Gomel's student population. **$$$$**

✖ **Café Pierrot** [302 C3] 14 Pushkina St; ☏ 71 71 37; e cafepierrot@mail.ru; w pierrot. by; ⊕ 11.00–23.00 daily. Look for the puppet theatre & there you will find this pleasing café. The menu is European of decent quality, & the theme, unsurprisingly, is classical French. Homely, relaxed & friendly, the service is particularly good. I haven't eaten here but friends in town give it the thumbs-up (especially the puddings). **$$$**

✖ **FaSol** [302 B3] 36 Sovyetskaya St; m 44 790 33 33; ⊕ noon–23.00 daily. 'FaSol' as in 'doh, reh, me', etc, so guess the theme! The interior is pleasing Victoriana & the service is particularly good. The menu is varied & it's available in English. Quality is good & the prices are reasonable. The ambience is tarnished somewhat by the ubiquitous music screens & by night it's a very popular karaoke bar, when you should expect to queue to get in. My preference is to go in the afternoon, when it's relaxed & you'll probably have it all to yourself. It's the personal favourite of good friend Liza & Olya also likes it here, as do her friends, & I can see why. Recommended, though not if you have a smoking phobia, as the non-smoking section is just half of the area where everyone else is lighting up. **$$$**

✖ **Il Patio** [302 C3] 6 Kommunarov St; ☏ 70 15 55; ⊕ noon–01.00 daily. Situated within the 'Continent' entertainment complex & next door to a cinema towards the top end of town, this is a chain restaurant but the décor, quality of food & service are all acceptable. It's nothing special, but there's a wide variety of Italian classics, 20 or more pizzas & a salad bar. My friend Veronika reckons the pizzas here are very tasty. **$$$**

✳ ✖ **Irina Café** [302 C4] Lunacharsky Park, 3 Gagarina St; ☏ 70 36 44; ⊕ 17.00–01.00 Mon, 13.00–01.00 Tue–Thu & Sun, noon–03.00 Fri–Sat. Very close to the impressive Zamkovy Hotel, the park location is near to perfect. The dining area inside is small & quite ordinary, but outside is an attractive terraced eating area under cover of a huge awning. There are patio heaters for chilly evenings, plus a large BBQ. The cuisine is Belarusian & European from a varied menu.

Service is excellent & the food is of a very high quality. It's my personal favourite in town. $$$

✳ ✗ **Karchma Budzhma** [302 A3] 3 Privakhsalnaya St; ☎ 33 31 81; 🕐 11.30–23.00 daily. Located near to the railway station, this is a worthy attempt at creating something traditional. The interior is modelled on a village dwelling of old, with all the attendant trappings & adornments that you might expect. Classic Belarusian dishes (inc draniki & machanka of course) are served with unusual & extravagant drinks, inc kvas flavoured with mint & a very tasty honey liqueur infused with herbs. The menu is extensive & is available in English. My only word of warning is not to over-order, as the portions are huge. I once came here in a group of 5, & 3 meals between us would have been more than adequate in terms of volume. Good value & an entertaining night out. Locals like this place, & I like it too. $$$

✗ **Pizzeria Italia** [302 C3] 14 Pushkina St; ☎ 77 67 55; 🕐 noon–midnight daily. Handily located towards the top end of town. Decent Italian cuisine is served in 2 dining areas – the veranda is the nicest. Very good value for money. $$$

✗ **Portofino** [302 C4] 2 Lenin Sq; ☎ 55 77 77; 🕐 noon–midnight daily. Located within the Europe Entertainment Centre, this serves European & Japanese cuisine. A business lunch menu is available noon–16.00, & there's even a kids' menu. Actually, it's all done rather well, from the décor to the food to the service. $$$

✗ **Shogun** [302 C2] 29a Sovyetskaya St; ☎ 20 50 50; e info@shogun.by; 🕐 noon–midnight Sun–Thu, 01.00 Fri–Sat. This relatively new teppanyaki grill & sushi bar is a big hit with the locals. Situated next to the circus & incorporating Kelly's Bar (🕐 noon–02.00, 04.00 Fri–Sat), it's bright, shiny & the food is good. Worth a try. $$$

✗ **Staroye Vremya ('Old Times')** [302 C3] 14 Krestyanskaya St; ☎ 26 07 57; w staroevremya. by; 🕐 noon–01.00 daily. It's very popular with out-of-town visitors, especially from abroad, but don't let that put you off. My Gomel friends like it too, especially Viktor. As you might guess, it's an attempt to recreate days of yore, including the Soviet era. Spread over 4 rooms, each with its own theme entirely unconnected with the others (inc the USSR, football & a bucolic idyll). There's even a full-size section of a trolleybus for a bar! It's gimmicky, but the décor is never less than interesting & the food is decent value. $$$

✗ **Taboo Sushi Bar** [302 C3] 12 Sovyetskaya St; m 44 575 75 75; 🕐 noon–23.00 daily. Decent sushi. $$$

✗ **Turist** [302 B4] 87 Sovyetskaya St; ☎ 57 49 85; 🕐 07.30–midnight daily. Situated at the Hotel Turist, there are 3 restaurants in this complex, all serving Belarusian & European cuisine to a decent standard, although the service is not the fastest & it's a little frosty too. The rooms are cavernous & it's all very shiny & rather noisy. Live floor shows while you eat will take you back to the days of 1970s-style cabaret. $$$

✗ **24/7 Café** [302 C3] 12 Sovyetskaya St; m 29 604 53 12; 🕐 10.00–23.00 daily. Cheap & cheerful fast food. $$

✗ **Batski** [302 C3] 12 Sovyetskaya St; m 44 595 95 95; 🕐 11.00–23.00 daily. This one is a little left-field, but as a budget option & something different it can't be beaten. It's a self-service café, where you choose from the range of hot & cold dishes laid out before you. The décor, dark & medieval, is better than you might expect, the quality of the food is good & the prices are very reasonable. There's a pleasant outside terrace on Sovyetskaya for you to watch the world go by. If time is tight, it does the job. $$

✳ ✗ **Station One** [302 B2] 2 Rogachevskaya St; ☎ 77 71 16; 🕐 noon–01.00 daily. My good friend Oxana lives close by & she eats here all the time. Nothing is too much trouble for the hospitable Palestinian owner, who consistently serves up good, tasty food at a very good price. There's an on-street terrace for the summer. It's another one of my favourites, not least because the music is so good! $$

CAFÉS

🖳 **Cinema** [302 C3] 4 Kommunarov St; ☎ 74 08 88; 🕐 noon–02.00 Sun–Thu, noon–05.00 Fri–Sat. This decent café, not surprisingly, is located at a cinema, the one next door to the 'Continent' entertainment complex where Il Patio pizzeria is found. The location is good & it's a functional venue for a coffee stop.

✳ 🖳 **Kaffa D.O.M.** [302 A3] 34 Lenina Av; ☎ 71 80 60; 🕐 08.00–midnight daily. The coffee is good here & the staff are always eager to please. Relaxed & comfortable, it's good friend Liza's favourite haunt in town for coffee & a chat with mates. I agree.

⌂ Maxi [302 B2] 46 Sovyetskaya St; ☎71 72 13; ☉ 08.00–23.00 daily. Olya says that the cakes, ice cream & coffee here are among the best in town, although not the cheapest. I like it too. Pavement seating is available & there's another Maxi that looks & offers the same further up Sovyetskaya on the opposite side of the road [302 C3], just after the mural depicting the history of the city, though it's not as good as this one.

⌂ Rumyantsevski [302 B2] 38 Sovyetskaya St; ☎29 76 29; ☉ 11.00–midnight daily. Gomel friends have little to say about this place, other than that it's OK, which matches my own assessment. The décor is shiny & the food is acceptable, as are standards of service.

⌂ Teatralnoye [302 C4] 3 Lenina Av; ☎75 77 95; ☉ noon–midnight daily. I rather like this place, tucked away just off Lenin Sq. Just up from Seven Fridays cocktail bar (see right) on the opposite side of the road, it's a decent alternative if you're looking for something a little quieter!

BARS

♀ Avenue Café & Bar [302 C4] 3 Lenina Av; m 44 754 01 00; noon–02.00 Sun–Thu, noon–05.00 Fri– Sat. A worthy rival to both New Time & Red Pub for dancing & a top night out, my sources tell me. Come earlier in the day for decent food. The shashlik is good & in the summer the outside dining area is pleasant. It works for coffee, cake & a chat too.

♀ Becker [302 C3] 2 Sovyetskaya St; ☎75 72 71; ☉ noon–midnight daily. Handily placed, the beer & ambience are good here. It's always popular; my Gomel friends don't rave about it, but it's a decent option for a good night out.

♀ Chisto Pivnoi [302 B4] 4a Bratyev Lizyukovikh St; ☎93 93 93; ☉ noon–01.00 Sun–Thu, noon–03.00 Fri & Sat. Located away to the west of

the city centre at the Chisto hotel complex (page 305), so very handy if you're staying there. There's live music nightly.

♀ New Time [302 C3] 17 Langye St; ☎23 04 08; ☉ 11.00–02.00 daily. The owners of Staroye Vremya ('Old Times') on the other side of Sovyetskaya also run this bar for the younger generation & they seem to have the formula right. The Burakov family are good friends of mine & dad Viktor likes the former, while daughter Veronika is a regular at the latter! It's busy, lively & noisy, so perfect for the city's youth. I can't speak from personal experience, but I'm told this is the place to come for dancing. The food here is pretty good, too.

♀ Red Pub [302 B4] 10 Lenina Av; m 29 955 55 22; ☉ noon–23.00 Mon–Thu, noon–05.00 Fri, 14.00–05.00 Sat, 14.00–23.00 Sun. Very popular for dancing & live music, though neither the food nor the service will win too many awards. That said, more than one person in my circle reckons this place is a decent alternative to Avenue & New Time for a late night on the tiles.

✻ ♀ Seven Fridays [302 C4] 6 Lenina Av; ☎26 61 01; e 7evenfridays@mail.ru; w 7fridays.by; ☉ noon–02.00 daily. My good friend Alicia raves about this American cocktail bar & grill. Don't come for a quiet night out, but if Americana is your style & you're in the mood for a long night of eating & drinking in a lively atmosphere, then you're in luck. Alicia tells me its reputation brings young people from far & wide, & that it's heaving on Fri & Sat nights. The party nights are legendary. The cocktails are excellent & the bartenders love to put on a show, so recline on one of the plush Chesterfields & take it all in. The food is also standard Americana & the quality is decent. Beware the loo, however. It has a challenging mirrored floor & ceiling, so only venture in when sober.

ENTERTAINMENT AND NIGHTLIFE

Gomel is home to a larger than average number of excellent universities and higher-education facilities, as befits its status as the country's second city. In fact, the State University, with over 10,000 students alone, is actually located on Sovyetskaya Street. With so many students in residence, the bar and club scene is thriving. And as you might expect, there is a wide choice of establishments. As in the other major cities, the coffee-bar culture that was lost in the West decades ago continues to thrive here.

The establishments on Sovyetskaya and Lenina, the main hub of activity, tend to be lively. There are lots and lots of cheap and cheerful Soviet-style bars and cafés on both sides of each road, all the way up to Lenin Square at the top. Be adventurous and walk in to any that take your fancy. The most chic street is Pobyedy, so bars here like to think of themselves as being a cut above.

☆ **Bravo** [302 B4] 1a Rechitskaya St; ☎ 75 49 89; ⏲ noon–05.00 daily. Once popular, though some think its better days are over.

☆ **Hollywood Nightclub** [302 C3] 6 Kommunarov St; ☎ 74 15 47; ⏲ 13.00–05.00 daily. Centrally located & popular, not least for the karaoke.

☆ **XXX Karaoke Club** [302 B3] 9 Kirova St; ☎ 22 07 07; ⏲ 18.00–04.00 daily. Right in the heart of

the city, garish décor & an open microphone await, as does your audience.

☆ **Yevropa ('Europe')** [302 C4] 2 Lenin Sq; ☎ 77 88 00; e club@europaclub.by; w europaclub.by; ⏲ noon–05.00 Tue–Sun. Brash & loud, there's plenty to keep you amused long into the small hours at this entertainment complex.

OTHER PRACTICALITIES

A gentle amble up Sovyetskaya Street towards the park will take you past a variety of shops in increasing numbers, including two very good bookshops, one on each side of the road, and a number of small department stores that are worth a browse. The classiest shops are to be found in Pobyedy Avenue, off Sovyetskaya Street. An alternative place for purchases is the cathedral, which has two stalls at the rear selling posters, cards, beeswax candles and very cheap artefacts (such as images of icons for your wallet, desk or car) that make excellent souvenirs.

Incidentally, if you visit the GrandTour agency at 61 Sovyetskaya (page 304), cross the road and drop in to the **Spartak chocolate factory** [302 B1] (*63 Sovyetskaya St;* ☎ *30 15 59;* e *ouk@spartak.by;* w *spartak.by*). The chocolate produced here enjoys a particularly impressive reputation both within Belarus and outside its borders. Do visit the shop and sample its wares, as well as treating yourself to a drink of hot chocolate at the adjoining cafeteria. It's rich, viscous, full of sugar and utterly irresistible. Just around the corner is the Spartak restaurant, serving passable European food ($$).

As befitting the country's second city, **banks** and **currency exchanges** are to be found all over the town centre, with **ATMs** in increasing numbers.

WHAT TO SEE AND DO

There is much in this city for the visitor with an enquiring mind, and happily almost all of the sites of interest are within walking distance of each other. I have grouped them into a single walking tour but if you aim to cover everything in one go it will take most of the day (and be a strenuous one at that). The choice is yours; either see it as a challenge to experience everything in one hit, or else take things at a more leisurely pace and meander; dip in and out as suits you best once you have a feel for the layout of the city.

WALKING TOUR
Along Sovyetskaya Street One of my favourite pastimes in the whole of Belarus is to take a stroll along Sovyetskaya Street, with its fine 19th- and 20th-century architecture, and into the park. If you begin on the eastern side of the street at **Vostanya Square** [302 B2], opposite Pobyedy Street, take a look first at the **tank** mounted on a granite plinth on your left. It's a monument to the Red Army heroes who liberated the city in 1943. Also here, incorporating the Top Tour travel agency (⏲ *09.00–19.00 Mon–Sat*) is a pale-orange stucco building that was a hospital in the Great Patriotic War, and later a Nazi prison where up to 100,000

were incarcerated. On the wall heading up to the football stadium are two **plaques**; the first commemorates those who lost their lives here and the second marks events in this square during the October Revolution. Head up Sovyetskaya past the circus and its fountains, where at the weekend families bring their children to promenade and to ride in the battery-operated cars. In the pretty park that you now reach, close to the pavement, look for the **bust of Andrei Gromyko** [302 C3]. He was the Soviet Union's foreign minister in successive governments for an incredible 28-year period that spanned four decades, notably under Leonid Brezhnev. Gromyko first entered government under Stalin and he was unquestionably one of the giants of Cold War diplomacy. He was born in a small village near here. This park also now features models of some of the world's iconic sites, such as the Eiffel Tower, Brest Hero-Fortress and Moscow's Kremlin. Exhibitions in miniature seem to be de rigueur in Belarus these days.

Further along, you will pass a series of **murals** depicting key events in the history of the city, beginning with its foundation in 1142. You very soon emerge into **Lenin Square** [302 C4], a vast area of tarmac with the **drama theatre** to your right and, in front of you, the **statue of Lenin**, high on its plinth, gazing magisterially over the entire city.

Rumyantsev-Paskevich Park and Palace ✳ If you enter Rumyantsev-Paskevich Park to the left of Lenin's statue, you will find that you are standing directly in front of the early 19th-century **Cathedral of Sts Peter and Paul** [302 C4] (Сабор Святых Пятра i Паўла/Собор Святых Петра и Павла). Built to Classicist design, it is an imposing building, but its real delights are to be found inside, for the iconostasis and walls display a wonderful collection of icons. Daily services are held at 08.00 and 17.00 from Monday to Saturday. On Sundays, they take place at 06.30, 09.00 and 17.00.

Turn right out of the cathedral, then right again towards its rear aspect and you find yourself standing in front of an oddity: the pseudo-Classical **Paskevich mausoleum** [302 C4] (маўзалей Пашкевіча/мавзолей Пашкевича), an excellent photo opportunity. A few steps back in the direction of the cathedral is the entrance down to the crypt containing the tombs of family members. This is well worth a moment of your time, for the vaults have been beautifully restored. Emerging back up the steps, carry on past the mausoleum towards the railings and pause to take in the view over the Sozh. The countryside to the east stretches away in front of you beyond the river. On the far bank are wide groves of trees that come almost to the water's edge, leaving a strip of sandy, light-coloured soil that could almost be a beach. This is exactly the purpose that it serves for local people in the months of summer, though Olya never comes here: 'much too busy', she says.

Now turn your back on the Sozh, lean on the railings and take in the panoramic view across the **park**. The initial layout was commissioned at the end of the 18th century by Count Pyotr Rumyantsev around the palace (see opposite) that was built upon his orders on the site of the former medieval castle. It was subsequently acquired by Russian general Ivan Paskevich in 1834 and thereafter significantly renovated. Among others, the renowned British architect John Clark worked extensively on the project. Here is an exquisite example of Classical park design. Covering 25ha high above the Sozh, various species of tree have been deliberately arranged into groups that enhance their features. There is Belarusian maple, ash and chestnut, together with eastern white pine, northern white oak and Manchurian walnut. Standing away to your left, in the middle of the park, beautifully complemented by the woodland all around it, is the palace itself. This isn't the best perspective from which to view its charms; a better one soon awaits you. Head diagonally back towards Lenin Square and make for the ornamental fountain, with benches all around it. Beyond the fountain, along a path, is another seating area. From here, the view of the palace is at its best and by now you will have noticed the light classical music that is constantly relayed over speakers situated all over the park.

Now concentrate your attentions on the magnificent **Rumyantsev-Paskevich Palace** [302 C4] (*Палац Румянцавых-Паскевічаў/Дворец Румянцевых–Паскевичей;* w *palacegomel.by;* ⏰ *see website; admission price based on exhibitions, English audio guide available*). It was reduced to little more than a shell by extensive bombardment during the Great Patriotic War, and the subsequent commitment to rebuilding the palace and reassembling its collections is truly impressive. The standards of workmanship and attention to detail are extraordinary, such that today the décor and adornments are exquisite. When the Nazis came in 1941, 2,000 artefacts were shipped east to Stalingrad, then further east into the Soviet Union as Stalingrad itself came under threat. Sadly only 300 items found their way back to their original home. Look specifically for several candelabras that lean and twist extravagantly, the legacy of the battering they took during the course of their wartime journeys back and forth. Meander the rooms at leisure to see furnishings, portraits, busts, artefacts and sculptures recounting the history of the palace and its owners. See how many portraits you can identify in the Golden Dining Room. A new exhibition of religious items had been established when last I visited in the autumn of 2017, including holy books, icons, plates, relics, cups, chalices, robes and crosses. One of the galleries also contained a fascinating collection of old Soviet posters to mark the 100th anniversary of the October Revolution.

Treat yourself to a final stroll around the park, for this is such a romantic location! I recall walking here one winter's day in watery sunshine, with snow on the ground, wrapped in scarf, gloves, heavy overcoat and hat, listening to the music playing over the tannoy, watching the sunbeams slanting down through the bare trees and deep in thought. I looked up to see an elderly couple. They were clasped in a tender embrace, dancing to the music, gazing deeply into each other's eyes as they twirled around and around, smiling and laughing gaily. I've walked these paths in each of the four seasons and there's always something to admire. It's one of my favourite places in all the world for reflective perambulation and deep thought. If you head across the front of the palace and follow the gradient of the path downwards, you find yourself entering a ravine. If you look up to the left, you will see the imposing 39m **tower** added by Count Paskevich after the original palace was constructed, while below you and to your right is Swan Lake, an ornamental pond with its resident swans. You have two choices now: you can either climb out of the other side of the ravine (eliminate the inclines by crossing the new bridge if you prefer) and head through the woods until you reach a rickety tower, pay the attendant BYN1.5 and then climb the even more rickety spiral staircase until you emerge on a wobbly platform high above the treeline. The view over the city is simply fantastic, but your perch is a lofty one and it really does wobble quite dramatically. Or, if heights don't suit you, take a turn around the pond and head for the railings by the river, then stroll at your leisure by the side of its fast-flowing waters. At regular points along the riverbank and throughout the park are small café-bars serving soft drinks, alcoholic beverages and light snacks. You can also take a 40-minute cruise along the river from here, with some lovely views across the lower town.

There are several points at which you can turn away from the river and climb back into the park. When you do, take a stroll across the high pedestrian bridge to the other side of the river and back, with splendid views on either side.

Museums If you still have room for more history, walk back into the park and turn left along the railings above the river in the direction of the palace to visit first the small **museum** [302 C4] (⊕ *10.00–18.00 Tue–Sun; admission BYN1.50*), a branch of the Vetka Folk Arts Museum (page 315), which contains a selection of traditional artefacts (including ancient books and rushniki) to be seen more extensively in Vetka. Then retrace your steps to leave the park beyond the cathedral towards Pushkina Street to find the **City Museum of History** [302 C3] (*гарадскі гістарычны музей/Городской исторический музей; 32 Pushkina St;* ❱75 58 43; e *mushistory@tut.by;* w *gomelhistory.museum.by;* ⊕ *10.00–18.00 Wed–Sun, Tue pre-booked tour groups only; admission BYN3.30/2.35/1.90 adults/students/children*). Originally built as a hunting lodge for Count Rumyantsev, this elegant building is now a repository for exhibits, works of art, temporary exhibitions and recreations of various rooms from 19th-century townhouses of the type found in this part of the city. Snapshots from the times of Rumyantsev and Paskevich come to life here, and a visit thus complements your earlier tour of the palace.

To understand more about the impact of warfare on the lands and people of the region, particularly the privations of the Great Patriotic War, visit the **Gomel Oblast Museum of Military Glory** [302 C3] (*Гомельскі абласны музей ваеннай славы/Гомельский областной музей военной славы; 5 Pushkina St;* ❱77 57 41; e *gommilmus@tut.by;* ⊕ *May–Sep 11.00–19.00 Mon–Fri; Oct–Apr 10.00–18.00 Mon–Fri; admission BYN1.65*). I've been several times, and on each visit it was virtually empty of visitors. Several rooms tell the story of the region in armed engagements across the centuries, through the medium of exhibits, models, uniforms and military hardware. The exhibits concerning the terrible events that occurred here from 1941 to 1944 are deeply affecting. Outside is a display of vehicles, guns, planes, helicopters and a huge steam locomotive proudly displaying that iconic red star (it's a brilliant photo opportunity). Try to find the time to visit – you won't regret it.

For an unusual experience that is no less interesting, visit the linked **Exhibition of Criminology and Law Enforcement** [302 C3] (*Выстава крыміналогіі і праваахоўнай дзейнасці/Выставка криминологии и правоохранительной деятельности; 1 Pushkina St;* ❱71 23 79; e *gommilmus@tut.by;* ⊕ *May–Sep 11.00–19.00 daily; Oct–Apr 10.00–18.00 daily; admission BYN0.70/0.50/0.40 adults/students/children*). Two rooms house exhibits relating to the fight against crime and the work of various law enforcement agencies from 1917 to the present day, including with regard to 'post-revolutionary terrorism'. There is also a corner devoted to the work of investigators preventing the removal of antiquities without the necessary papers; hence my concern about Sergei Nikolaevich's Old Believers' bible (page i).

OUTSIDE GOMEL

VETKA ✳ (Ветка/Ветка) This small town, 22km northeast of Gomel and founded in 1685 by 'Old Believers' who had fled from Russia, has been my Belarusian home since my very first visit in 2001. It has also made a huge contribution to my own personal development and, in spiritual terms, it has a very special place in my heart. It's a mix of provincial Mother Russia and the revolutionary CCCP at their finest, where the golden cupolas of the Orthodox church dazzle in the sunlight, the concrete of the 1960s Soviet apartment blocks continues to crumble and Lenin gazes with majesty and fortitude across recently renovated Red Square. Indeed, there is new build on a significant scale throughout the town, largely residential, and a huge new supermarket on the outskirts. The street where I live when I'm here, and my home in Belarus for the last 17 years, is Karl Marx Street. Part tarmac, part sand and rutted with pot-holes, it is to be found in the old part of town. Number 42 is halfway down on the right, with the small shop that Valeri built with his own hands to one side. Between them, members of the family staff it from 08.00 until 19.00, every day of the week. If I'm in town, I wander in around 18.00 to share a beer and some dried fish with Valeri and his mates. Dexter the dog lounges on his old sofa on the front porch next door. Valeri and I took him out for a walk one night and inevitably ended up in a bar. We forgot to bring him home, much to Tanya's outrage, but he wandered back several days later, none the worse for the experience. Valeri says he's a street dog, and that the whole town is his home. We're good mates, Dexter and me. Richard the family cat spent 14 years at a contemptuous distance before he finally accepted me as part of the household. For all that time he had barely given me a glance, then he unexpectedly relented and each night we shared the divan in the parlour. He had more room than me. Sadly Richard is no more. But like Dexter, I continue to wander the streets of this town in all seasons and all weather, by day and by night. There's something about it that keeps drawing me back that I can't articulate. We just fit, I guess.

Located on the banks of the Sozh River, Vetka is surrounded by forest and marsh. The name is assumed to have been derived from an island of the same name in the river. It was twice burned to the ground by the tsar's troops, in 1735 and 1764, with its residents being forced to resettle to the outer provinces of eastern Russia. At the time, it was widely known for the unique style of icon painting that was practised here. There was also a specialist school for woodcarving. In 1772, the town was annexed to the Russian Empire and in 1852 it became part of the Gomel administrative region.

In 1880, Vetka is known to have counted around 6,000 inhabitants, 994 wooden and 11 stone buildings, six windmills, a rope factory and a tannery. Anchors were produced at local forges and ships were constructed at the shipyard on the Sozh from 1840. There is still a wharf there today. In the middle of the 19th century, the richest of the town's merchants had their own steamships. During the war years from August 1941 to September 1943, Vetka was under the occupation of the Nazis, who murdered 656 of its residents, the majority of them Jews.

In 2017 the town received something of a facelift, with significant improvements to roads and the general infrastructure (including a new bus station) in anticipation of a visit from the country's president on the anniversary of the Chernobyl catastrophe. Sadly he didn't come, but at least local people now have the benefit of a considerably spruced-up environment. Vetka is also home to the Children's Correction Centre, which was the focus of WOVA's charitable works for some time (see boxes, pages 112 and 114).

Getting there and away By car from Gomel city centre head north down Sovyetskaya Street away from Lenin Square and continue almost to the city limits. At the plinth-mounted single-seat aeroplane, turn right on to the P30 road and continue for 20km, crossing the Sozh River just before you enter Vetka. Regular bus and marshrutka services depart Gomel bus station for Vetka bus station (on the town's western fringe).

Where to stay and eat There is a small hotel here, a decent pizzeria, a number of bars, a bank with an ATM and shops serving everyday needs. The **Sozh Restaurant** on the main square (⏰ *10.00–20.00 Mon–Thu, noon–midnight Fri, 18.00–midnight Sat;* $$) serves traditional Belarusian fare. It's a vast, cavernous room that is almost

When I first visited Vetka in 2001, the focus for the Orthodox congregation was a small wooden church on one of the roads out of town. It was badly in need of repair. The priest told me that work had started on a new construction in the middle of town, but that the project had come to a halt when the source of funds dried up. Each time that I returned, the half-built shell and surrounding building site felt like a metaphor for all of the infrastructural problems that beset the people of this country. And then, out of the blue, I arrived in town after an absence of 12 months to find the church complete, its golden domes glinting in the sunshine. It was to be consecrated during my visit by the head of the Orthodox Church in Belarus, none other than the Metropolitan Filaret of All Belarus himself, and when I went to see the Chief Executive of Vetka Executive Committee, Viktor Burakov, to update him on developments with our joint sustainability programmes, I was humbled to receive an invitation to attend.

The day of the ceremony dawned bright, with a cloudless blue sky. We made our way to the church and were greeted by a mass of local people. As we were led through, our eyes fell upon two trails of wild flowers, freshly picked, that lay along the sides of the path from the entrance gates, up the steps and into the church itself, leading all the way to the iconostasis. The riot of colour and the heady aroma presented a glorious living display. Inside, people were crammed shoulder to shoulder, and together we waited over an hour for the Filaret's entourage to arrive. Then, without any warning other than a series of urgent whispers that reached us in a wave from the gates, the invisible choir in the gallery above burst into life with a soaring, a cappella Divine Liturgy that sent a tingle all the way up my spine and made my heart want to burst with joy.

There was a huge surge as the procession came into view, with priests in ascending order of seniority and bedecked in astonishingly ornate robes to match their status, all of them with huge spade beards, extravagantly swinging incense

always empty and always cold, but the food is nourishing and good value. On two separate occasions, I have seen it alive with colour and noise. On my first visit, I was honoured to be invited to the wedding of the daughter of a senior local official here. The second time was the lavish lunch given on the occasion of the consecration of the recently completed church (see box, above).

What to see and do
Jewish Vetka Behind the locked gates of a farm enterprise on the edge of town stands the recently and privately commissioned **memorial** to the Jewish dead of the district, 200 of whom were murdered in this very location. The atrocity was long rumoured to have taken place, but a mass grave was only discovered when building work was being undertaken at the farm. It is believed that some bodies are yet to be discovered. In recent times, the local newspaper has published the names of the collaborators who it alleges were involved in the murders. Even now, old wounds are being reopened in this community. On the other side of town, unseen behind a petrol station, is the site of the old Jewish **cemetery**. Once there were over 1,000 graves here, but all that remains today are a few broken stones and some rusted railings. Valeri took me to see it once and told me how, 45 years ago, he and his friends used to play hide and seek between the gravestones as children. Over time all fell into disrepair and the cemetery was gradually taken apart by the Communists,

holders as if their lives depended upon it, responding to the liturgy with chants of their own. Constantly and urgently, people all around me were muttering, bowing their heads, eyes to the ground and crossing themselves incessantly, almost obsessively. It was impossible not to be caught up and swept away by the tide of mysticism and ancient, holy ritual that was washing over us all. Then the Filaret himself appeared, head high, exuding sacred power and influence, his gaze slowly passing over every corner of the congregation. Wherever his gaze rested, if only for an instant, people crossed themselves even more frantically than they had before (if that were possible), while His Holiness periodically responded with the slightest of inclinations of his head.

The entire process of consecration took almost 2 hours. At one point, the filaret blessed each of the walls with holy water flung from the bristles of an enormous brush, like something a decorator would use. At least twice, he changed his robes. To do so, he stood in the middle of the congregation, on a slight dais, while junior priests solemnly and reverently removed each layer of robe for him and replaced it with another. Once, he reached inside and produced a magnificent comb with a flourish, before proceeding to preen his flowing beard, deliberately, slowly and with more than a slight air of superiority.

When it was all over, we accompanied him to the local restaurant, where the tables were creaking under the weight of food and vodka. The priests came too. At various points throughout the meal, they broke into spontaneous, soaring a cappella harmonies, delivered ever louder and with more gusto as each empty vodka bottle was replaced by another full one. The celebration lasted long into the afternoon, until the Filaret decided it was time to go. In an instant he was out of his seat and, after blessing all those assembled before him, he swept out of the room like a ship in full sail, his entourage trailing behind. An extraordinary day.

who used the stones to build roads. **School Number One** in Vetka has a display of materials and documents concerning the Jewish community of the town together with a splendid **museum** of artefacts and information relating to local history. Items on display include hand-drawn Red Army maps from nearby engagements in the Great Patriotic War, Soviet Union memorabilia and rare religious treasures. The school's history teacher, Sergei Nikolaevich Perepelyuk, is the curator, as well as a very dear personal friend and a particular fount of local knowledge. There isn't much he doesn't know about this region. During the war years, engagements took place all over the district, and remains of the fallen are still being found. Only recently, building work at School Number One uncovered the bodies of a number of German soldiers. Valeri tells me this is happening all over Belarus.

A London-based foundation, the Belarus Holocaust Memorials Project (w *belarusmemorials.com*), has a mission to place memorials at the location of each of the 400 known sites of Nazi massacres of the Belarusian Jewish Community. As the Vetka experience shows, there are likely to be further sites yet to be identified. By the summer of 2017, 99 memorials had been erected through the good offices of this worthy cause.

FolkArtsMuseum ☀ (*музей народнага мастацтва/музей народного искусства;* 5 *Red Sq;* ☎02 26 70, 02 14 49; e *vetkamuszejj@rambler.ru;* w *vetka.museum.by;* ⏰ 09.00–

Historically, Vetka was renowned as a centre for Старовери ('Old Believers'), the religious group that eschewed the reforms of Patriarch Nikon in the 17th century and suffered disenfranchisement and persecution as a result. Most fled or were forced to resettle, notably under Catherine the Great, who banished significant numbers to Siberia. Indeed, the group was still suffering prejudice and oppression into the 20th century, to the extent that members were forced to hide from the police and pass themselves off as mainstream Orthodox believers. As a result, Old Believer communities exist today in far-flung locations around the world and estimates as to the number of followers vary from one to ten million worldwide. Many Old Believer churches still exist throughout Gomel region, including in the city itself.

The most visible divergence is that Old Believers will make the sign of the cross with two fingers only instead of three, as officially recognised by Orthodoxy. They continue to use the older Church Slavonic translation of the sacred texts. The performance of Baptism is only accepted through three full immersions; anything else, for example the pouring of water over the forehead, is wholly rejected. There are also many essential differences in church services. There is an Old Believers cemetery in Vetka, where the crosses on the graves are markedly different from those found in other Orthodox cemeteries. I have a number of very good friends in Vetka who are descended from Old Believer families, including Natasha and her mum, fourth- and fifth-generation believers. They practise the old ways still. They tell me they have interesting stories to tell, but I'm still waiting …

18.00 Tue–Sun; admission BYN2) Prior to the Chernobyl catastrophe the population of the district exceeded 40,000, but after a massive resettlement programme to take people away from the areas of radiation pollution, this number had shrunk to only 7,200 by the first anniversary of the disaster. On 1 November 1987, a splendid museum was opened here, with high-quality exhibits displaying the unique historical and cultural features of the region. Located in a former merchant's house, its ceremonial entrance doors have beautiful wooden carvings worked by the founder and his assistants. The items on display, including ancient artefacts, icons, books, manuscripts, traditional costumes and woven rushniki (many from the unique weaving school in the nearby village of Nyeglubka) are simply stunning. This is particularly true of the icons. Most of the ones exhibited here were crafted by Old Believers in the 17th century in the style of those on display in Moscow's cathedrals. The founder of the museum was Fyodor Grigorievich Shkliarov, a native of Vetka and a fervent promoter of local culture. He began to assemble artefacts in the 1960s and continued to enlarge his collection into the 1980s. Public interest began to be engaged over the years and these items laid the foundation for the museum. Sadly, Shkliarov died the year after it opened. His portrait hangs there still, showing him surrounded by many of the items in his own collection. Today, the museum has a national reputation as an artistic educational centre, where research is undertaken into the study of traditional Belarusian culture. A visit here is highly recommended. I have encouraged a number of foreign visitors to come to experience the charms of this museum, and none have been disappointed.

Located just off Red Square, the recently renovated **church** is well worth a visit. Inside, it is bright and airy. Painted on the iconostasis is a fresco depicting the fate of the victims of Chernobyl. Directly outside is the **memorial stone and church bell** dedicated to the memory of those who died in the immediate aftermath of the Chernobyl explosion, along with the lost villages in the uninhabitable zone whose residents were required to leave their homes for good.

KHALCH (Хальч/Хальч) This small village in Vetka district, located high on the western bank of the Sozh, is notable for its **19th-century manor house** that is occasionally open to visitors on an ad hoc basis (major works of renovation have been on the go for years) and its small wooden **church**. As you cross the Sozh on the road from Gomel to Vetka and just before you enter the town, look up to your left. The brightly coloured blue church is situated high atop a bluff, looking down over the river towards Vetka. A heroic and bloody engagement took place here in 1943 as the Red Army, supported by groups of partisans, fought to cross the river to liberate Gomel.

There is a regular bus service to Khalch and Vetka from Gomel. If you are driving, take the road that runs directly from the bottom end of Sovyetskaya. It's a straight road, heading in a northeasterly direction. Khalch is situated 18km along it, just before you cross the Sozh. Vetka is on the opposite bank.

MOZYR (Мазыр/Мозырь) Some 130km southwest of Gomel on the western bank of the Pripyat River (and only 10km off the M10 motorway connecting Gomel with Brest) stands the town of Mozyr, 'the Belarusian Switzerland'. It is rare to find gradients in this country but the ridge high above the river here is a notable exception. Mozyr was first mentioned as a township in *Chronicles* in 1155, but the original wooden citadel (destroyed by fire in the 15th century) was recreated over a period of four months in 2006 as part of the celebrations to commemorate the town's 850th birthday. Limited information as to design and style was gleaned from historical records, and a significant degree of guesswork was also involved. The result is today's compact **castle complex** (⏲ *10.00–18.00 daily; admission BYN1.60*), which is worthy of a visit notwithstanding the passing nod to a Disneyesque interpretation of medieval history. Souvenir stalls abound, while characters in period costume roam the towers, ramparts and small church, and musicians serenade as you wander. When I was last here in the autumn of 2017 their repertoire of 'traditional Belarusian music' included 'Loch Lomond' and 'The Sailor's Hornpipe', with a dash of Mike Oldfield for good measure. My view of this attraction may have been coloured by the backdrop of slate grey skies dumping rain in stair rods, so you might want to keep an open mind before you visit. Whatever your judgement, worth taking in is the panorama from the edge of the escarpment. Down below in the foreground (riverside) is the town's central square, where Lenin continues to preside, of course, with Sovyetskaya Street stretching away into the distance. To the right lies the river itself, with flatlands beyond to the horizon.

A short stroll downhill from the complex stands the small **Polesskaya Veda Museum** (*Музей «Палеская веда»/Музей «Полесская веда»; 15 Kamsamolskaya St;* ☎ *236 32 46 62;* e *mozyr_muzey@mail.ru;* w *mozyr.museum.by;* ⏲ *10.00–18.00 Tue–Sun; admission BYN1*), dedicated to the archaeology, history, traditions and folk culture of the area. A visit here nicely complements your tour of the castle complex.

Further down the hill is the **Orthodox Church of St Michael the Archangel**. The exterior was clad in scaffolding when last I visited in 2017, but do persevere and step over the threshold. Originally constructed as a Catholic church in the late 17th century, then converted to Orthodoxy around 1870, it is built in late Baroque style.

Inside, the iconostasis and its adornments are impressive in themselves, but the real joy is the ceiling's stunning decorative work. Turn left as you leave the church to find steps down to the crypt, a separate and distinct place of living worship. Used as a prison in the 1930s, this is well worthy of a visit. It is believed that up to 2,000 of those incarcerated here were murdered between 1936 and 1937 during the height of Stalin's notorious purges. The sanctified remains of several victims are contained in two caskets with glass panels at the furthest extremity of the crypt.

For sustenance, try the **Stary Gorod restaurant** (*1 Oktyabrskaya St;* \236 20 24 94; e *sputnik-mozyr@tut.by;* w *sputnik-m.by;* ⊕ *noon–midnight Mon–Fri, noon–01.00 Sat–Sun*). Part of the Sputnik entertainment complex, which is flashy, glitzy and just a little hideous, it serves very decent food. My lunch of salad, borsch and draniki was delicious.

If travelling from Gomel by car, take the M10 motorway west out of the city in the direction of Brest for 120km. At Kalinkovichy turn left on to the P131 road for 10km into the centre of Mozyr. There are regular train, bus and marshrutka services from Gomel.

NYEGLUBKA (Неглюбка/Неглюбка) Located on back roads 45km northeast of Vetka, this is another small village that is pretty but unremarkable, other than in respect of the **village school** there. For it is here that the descendants of traditional weavers are taught the skills and crafts of their forebears on intricate wooden looms crafted in exactly the same way as the originals. The headteacher is pleased to welcome visitors and always eager to showcase the skills of her students. It's difficult to find, but the tourist route devised by the local executive committee includes a visit here and tourist agencies in Gomel will be more than pleased to book you a place on the tour.

Only a few kilometres to the west of here is the tiny hamlet of **Zhelizniki**, where the restoration of one of the oldest Orthodox churches in all Belarus has now been completed. I have visited it several times at various stages of the works and it is a joy to be able to report that all is now complete. A visit here is also included on the locally devised tour.

PRIPYATSKY NATIONAL PARK ✳ (*Нацыянальны Парк Прыпяцкі/Национальный Парк Припятский; agricultural town Lyaskovichi, Petrikov district;* \2350 57 0 02; e *lyaskovichi@npp.by;* w *npp.by*) On the western fringes of the oblast is the Pripyatsky National Park. Deep within the mystical Polyesye region and covering 82,529ha, it was established in the marshy lowland area and floodplains between the Pripyat, Stivha and Ubort rivers to protect and preserve the unusual ecological systems that are to be found in this area, along with its landscape and biological diversity. The tract of primeval oak forestation here is one of the largest in Europe, and the park is of particular interest to ornithologists: around 265 species are registered, including the greater and lesser heron, common crane, eagle owl, serpent eagle and marsh owl. Since 1987, the European bison has been reintroduced and there are now believed to be 67 individual animals within its boundaries.

To wander the woods and marshes of this special place is to reconnect with the natural world in a way that is becoming increasingly difficult to do in modern times. My last visit was in the autumn, the colours predominantly golden with punctuations of red and russet. The day before had been ceaselessly rainy, so mist clung everywhere in the air. I followed deer tracks, glimpsed fox and squirrel and elk, and I stood; stood to listen and to watch. In spring the landscape is completely different. The winter snows have melted and, in places, the water level rises by around 2m. Try very hard to experience these precious lowlands, whatever the season, but be sure to leave all the baggage of life in the West behind before you arrive.

Specialist travel companies in the English-speaking world offer guided tours around this and other national parks in Belarus, including Naturetrek (w *naturetrek. co.uk*). Tours from one to ten days in the park can be arranged through a variety of tourist agencies within the country. The English pages on the park's website contain useful information about all there is to do here, as well as practical details concerning accommodation and facilities. Alternatively, access information and services via the park's department of tourism (\ *291 25 00 95; e travel-npp@tut.by*). There is no admission fee for entry to the park per se; visitors pay for those specific services they choose to access, including tours, entry to museums, fishing and a range of other leisure activities.

If travelling independently by car, head either to Turov (page 320) as a jumping-off point or to the village of Lyaskovichi (see below), the location of the park's administrative centre and other local facilities. The P23 road runs due south from Minsk for 192km to the junction with the M10 motorway connecting Gomel with Brest, the main arterial road link running east–west and border to border in the south of the country. Take the M10 east in the direction of Gomel for 28km to the town of Zhitkovichi, before turning south on the P88 road for 30km to reach Turov. If feeling adventurous, leave the P23 road 20km south of Slutsk and meander the P55 and P57 back roads towards Zhitkovichi. Cross the M10 and take the H4003 minor road for 24km to reach Lyaskovichi. The country's main rail link running east–west between Gomel and Brest follows the line of the M10. Zhitkovichi is a stop on the line and the town also has regular bus and marshrutka services. Transport into and around the park can be sourced locally.

Where to stay and eat Accommodation in the town of **Turov** (page 321) makes an ideal base for roaming the park, though an alternative is to stay in the 'Nad Pripyatyu' accommodation complex (a hotel and three wooden lodges) in the village of **Lyaskovichi** on the banks of the Pripyat River. It stands east of Turov and a waterborne meander between the two is a delight. The journey on minor roads is much less direct but the terrain hereabouts lends itself to an experience of comparable charm. The hotel opened in 2009 and it's very shiny, but the rooms are well appointed, the service is good and there is a small restaurant (⊕ *07.00– midnight daily*) offering decent Belarusian cuisine. I have stayed in the hotel and other than my immediate party, it was empty. One advantage of staying here is that the park's fine **Museum of Nature** (\ *2350 98 2 41; ⊕ 08.30–17.30 Tue–Sun; admission BYN4*) is directly opposite on the other side of the road. Taxidermy is not to everyone's taste, of course, but the stuffed animals on show represent only a portion of all you can see, and the exhibits are well presented. Helpful information boards in English on flora, fauna and ecology are in every room. A stop here for an explanation of all the visitor needs to know about the history and ecology of the area is a particularly useful precursor to your ambles *en plein air*.

Another tourist accommodation centre is found deep in the forest at Khlupinskaya Buda, consisting of four smaller lodges, and there is camping elsewhere at the Kabachok and Cheretyanka centres, on the banks of the river and by Cheretyanka Lake respectively. There are even motorboats moored on quays at various locations, with accommodation in a small number of cabins; others are used for day trips. Tourist agencies within Belarus have all the information necessary for informed choices to be made, but do your own research first via the park's informative website.

Turov ✳ (Турaў/Туров) This small, well-manicured town, on the southern bank of meandering tributaries of the Pripyat River, is the park's main centre of population and spiritual heart of the Polyesye. As soon as you pass the town's sign you notice straight away that the road, buildings, gardens and fences are all well maintained. You almost feel you've entered a historical theme park. First mentioned in *Chronicles* in AD980, it was the capital of a province that included the historic towns of Slutsk, Njasvizh and Pinsk. Indeed, some historians believe that Turov was second in importance only to Kiev in Old Russia. Mystery and legend abound in the Polyesye, no more so than in this town. A number of stone crosses are to be found here, imbued by legend with great magical powers of healing and protection from harm, Turov being their final resting place after a journey (it is said) floating along the river and against the current from Kiev. See how many you can find.

The town was also home to 12th-century theologian, preacher and writer Saint Kirill (Cyril), one of the most significant figures of Kievan Rus. In 1993 a striking 7m **monument** was erected in his honour as part of the commemorations to mark the 1,000-year anniversary of the town's founding. Standing atop castle 'hill' above the Pripyat River (actually a modest mound), it dominates the town. Just a few steps away is the archaeological exhibition '**Ancient Turov**' (⊕ *10.00–14.00 & 15.00–17.00 Tue–Sun; admission BYN2*) on the site of the original 12th-century temple. Only the foundations remain and this is very much a live archaeological dig, but you can circle the perimeter on a raised walkway, where display boards and cabinets tell the story. There are also two souvenir stalls. A very short walk away is the **cemetery of Sts Boris and Hleb**, a place of pilgrimage, with travellers arriving from far and wide to worship at the site of two of the magical crosses that miraculously grow from the ground by a few millimetres each year, apparently. Non-believers might be tempted to conclude, however, that their continuing growth could be explained by more natural causes; this might just be an ancient burial ground that is slowly subsiding. Visitors are encouraged to kneel on the mats provided at each cross to touch the stone. Apparently they feel warm or cold, as determined by the cross itself. When I took my turn, it felt pretty much as I was expecting stone in the ground to feel. My cynicism was not all-consuming, however; there is certainly a feeling, difficult to articulate, that this is a special place.

A short stroll away and riverside is the town's **main (Red) square**, with a choice of accommodation and eateries. It's a good place to start your meanderings around the town, with the river, a number of war memorials and the Pripyatski restaurant to draw your attention. From the quay, boat trips along the river as far as Mozyr can be arranged. The state tourism agency Turovschina has something of a monopoly here (*152 Leninskaya St;* ✆ *235 37 93 19;* e *turovtur@tut.by, turovschina@mail.ru;* w *turovschina.by*) and visitors are encouraged to avail themselves of its services for all bookings. Although in Russian only, the website is a mine of information on prices and facilities, with a detailed gallery of photographs to help you make your choices.

Also worth a look in town is the early 19th-century wooden **Church of All Saints** (*99 Leninskaya St*), which has remained standing (though significantly renovated) despite the ravages of war in these parts. Two more of the magical stone crosses can be found here, as well as the icon of St Nicholas, which is said to weep tears. I haven't witnessed this phenomenon myself. Adjacent is the more recent **Cathedral of Sts Cyril and Lawrence** (*97a Leninskaya St*), completed in 2013, where another of the magical crosses has found a home.

All in all Turov is a fine place to base a tour of Pripyatsky National Park. Holy relics abound and await your close attention, though one priceless artefact you won't see is the Turov Gospel, one of the earliest and finest examples of Slavonic manuscript. Written in the 11th century, it was removed to Vilnius in 1865 (where it still resides).

Where to stay and eat Moored on the edge of the main square is the **Polyesye floating hotel** (m *29 395 80 18;* **$**), a barge with cabins (doubles and twin bunks) that are modest, though cosy and comfortable. Also here is the modern and well-appointed **Turov hotel and restaurant** (*235 37 51 64;* **$**). Away from the square and riverside in an easterly direction is the **Strumen hotel complex** (*3 Richevskaya St;* *235 37 62 14;* **$**), which includes two lodges (**$$$$**) and separate sauna.

Appendix 1

LANGUAGE

Editorial discipline dictates that the scope and ambit of this small appendix on language can be no more than the briefest of introductions, though it should be enough to get you started. To move beyond the basics I strongly advise readers to pursue further learning via the many media for study that are available today (page 81). **Russian** and **Belarusian** have equal status in Belarus as national languages, both of which have alphabets based on the Cyrillic script. Both of them are of eastern Slavonic origin and they share a great deal in terms of grammar and syntax, but have broad variances in vocabulary. The ear and eye of non-linguists will discern little difference between the two languages. Everyone speaks Russian, while Belarusian is becoming increasingly more widely used throughout the full range of media as interest blossoms in the promotion of a distinct identity for Belarus.

I have replicated the Russian alphabet below in its entirety and added the Belarusian equivalent for the few characters that are written differently. Most people are utterly daunted by the Cyrillic alphabet and in a sense this is perfectly understandable. When all is said and done, you're going back to school to learn how to read all over again! But perseverance pays huge dividends. Your pronunciation of words will be greatly facilitated if you can acquire a degree of familiarity with each letter and its sound. When you master the basics of being able to pronounce a few words you will be surprised by how much you can begin to understand in a very short time.

I have included some words and phrases in Russian to help you along the way. Wherever you travel in the world, faltering but earnest attempts at communicating in the language of your hosts are generally well received. This is certainly the case in Belarus. The people here think theirs is the forgotten country of Europe; and the rest of Europe (and indeed the world) might be on a different planet, given the paucity of interaction between most Belarusians and people in the West. So take a very deep breath and give it a go. You will always be greeted with a smile. Don't forget though; English is widely taught in schools from an early age and young people especially will be keen to try out their own (enviable) language skills on you.

If you are starting from scratch it may be overly ambitious to attempt a full language course before you go, and to take grammatical texts and a dictionary on your travels will probably serve no useful purpose. But I do strongly recommend that you take a phrasebook, and the best two on the market are those published by Lonely Planet and Rough Guides. There is nothing to choose between the two in terms of quality and both balance just the right amount of academic detail with practical expediency.

THE CYRILLIC RUSSIAN ALPHABET

Russian		Phonetic pronunciation
А	а	a, as in far
Б	б	b, as in bill
В	в	v, as in violin
Г	г	g, as in go
Д	д	d, as in do

Е	е	ye, as in yellow
Ё	ё	yo, as in your
Ж	ж	zh, as in pleasure
З	з	z, as in zebra
И	и	ee, as in eaten
Й	й	y, as in coy
К	к	k, as in kitchen
Л	л	l, as in lantern
М	м	m, as in my
Н	н	n, as in never
О	о	o, as in open
П	п	p, as in pillow
Р	р	r, as in growl (but roll your tongue extravagantly!)
С	с	s, as in suspense
Т	т	t, as in tea
У	у	oo, as in moose
Ф	ф	f, as in face
Х	х	pronounce loch like a Scot!
Ц	ц	ts, as in fits
Ч	ч	ch, as in cello
Ш	ш	sh, as in shampoo
Щ	щ	shsh, as in fresh shampoo
Ъ	ъ	hard sign, to keep a consonant hard
Ы	ы	i, as in mill
Ь	ь	soft sign, to soften a consonant
Э	э	e, as in envelop
Ю	ю	u, as in usurp
Я	я	ya, as in yam

For the purpose of rudimentary learning to enable you to read the basics of Belarusian, you need to know that from the Russian language, the letter И и is replaced by I i and that there is an additional letter Ў ў pronounced like a 'w', as in 'how'.

The main challenge with English as a foreign language is that the frighteningly large number of rules is only exceeded by an even larger number of exceptions to those rules. This problem doesn't exist with Russian. It's a much more phonetic language, so when you've cracked the Cyrillic alphabet, the only thing left to worry about is locating which syllable in a word carries the emphasis. In the following pages, underlining shows which syllable to stress. For your first visit, though, none of this should be a problem; if you set your expectations at a level appropriate to your likely interactions with local people, you won't have too much difficulty in being able to read and understand the odd word or two, which should give you the confidence to utter a few words and simple phrases that will be readily understood. Try these for starters:

FIRST MEETINGS AND NICETIES

Hello (formal)	Здравствуйте	*Zdravstvoitye*
Hi (casual)	Привет	*Preevyet*
Good day	Добрый День	*Dobri Dyehn*
Good morning	Доброе Утро	*Dobroye Ootra*
Good evening	Добрый Вечер	*Dobri Vyeicha*
Yes	Да	*Da*
No	Нет	*Nyet*
Thank you	Спасибо	*Spaseeba*

You're welcome	Пожалуйста	*Pazhalsta*
Please	Пожалуйста	*Pazhalsta*
Excuse me	Извините	*Eezvenitye*
What is your name?	Как вас зовут?	*Kak vas zavoot?*
My name is …	Меня зовут …	*Minya zavoot …*
Pleased to meet you	Очень приятно	*Orchin preeyatna*
How are you?	Как дела?	*Kak dyela?*
Good	Хорошо	*Hurashor*
Excellent!	Отлично!	*Atleechna!*
Bad	Плохо	*Plorkha*
Very	Очень	*Orchin*
Do you speak English?	Вы говорите по-английски?	*Vy guvareetyeh pa angleeski?*
Do you understand?	Понимаете?	*Punimahyetye?*
I don't speak Russian	Я плохо говорю по-русски	*Ya plorkha guvareyoo pa rooski*
I don't understand	Не понимаю	*Knee puneemaiyoo*
Repeat, please	Повторите, пожалуйста	*Puvhtareetye, pazhalsta*
I like …	Мне нравиться …	*Minye nrahvitsa …*
I don't like …	Мне не нравиться …	*Minye ni nrahvitsa …*
I love …	Я люблю …	*Ya lyooblyoo …*
See you again	До встречи	*Da fstryechi*
Goodbye	До свидания	*Dos sveedanya*
Bye	Пока	*Paka*
Good night	Спокойной Ночи	*Spakoinoi Norchi*
Bon voyage!	Счастливого пути!	*Shistleevava puti!*
All the best!	Всего хорошего!	*Fsevor harrorshiva!*

KEY WORDS

What?	Что?	*Shtor?*
Who?	Кто?	*K-tor?*
Where?	Где?	*Gdyeh?*
How?	Как?	*Kak?*
Why?	Почему?	*Puchyemoo?*
On the left	На лева	*Na lyeva*
On the right	На права	*Na pravha*
Straight ahead	Прямо	*Preeyarma*
near	Не далеко	*Knee dalyekor*
far	Далеко	*Dalyekor*

SHOPPING

How much does this cost?	Сколько это стоит?	*Skorlka ehta stoyit?*
What is it?	Что это?	*Shtor ehta?*
A lot	Много	*M-norga*
A little	Чутьчуть	*Chootchoot*

FOOD AND DRINK

bread	Хлеб	*Khlyeb*
cheese	Сыр	*Syrr*
meat	Мясо	*Myasa*

fish	Рыба	*Reeba*
fruit	Фрукти	*Frookti*
vegetables	Овощи	*Orvashee*
mushrooms	Грибы	*Greebi*
potatoes	Картошки	*Kartoshki*
water	Вода	*Vada*
milk	Молоко	*Malakor*
juice	Сок	*Sok*
sugar	Сахар	*Sakhar*
tea	Чай	*Chai*
coffee	Кофе	*Korfye*
beer	Пиво	*Peeva*
vodka	Водка	*Vordka*
breakfast	Завтрак	*Zavhtrak*
lunch	Обед	*Abyed*
dinner	Ужин	*Oozhen*

ADJECTIVES

big	Большой	*Balshoi*
small	Маленький	*Marlenki*
hot	Горячий	*Grryachi*
cold	Холодный	*Khorladni*
new	Новый	*Norvee*
old	Старый	*Staree*
beautiful	Красивый	*Krasseevi*
delicious	Вкусный	*Ffkoosni*

NUMBERS

0	Нуль	*Nool*
1	Один	*Ahdjeen*
2	Два	*Dva*
3	Три	*Tree*
4	Четыре	*Chyetearye*
5	Пять	*Pyats*
6	Шесть	*Shhehst*
7	Семь	*Ssyem*
8	Восемь	*Vorsyem*
9	Девять	*Dyevyats*
10	Десять	*Dyesyats*
20	Двадцать	*Dvahdsahts*
50	Пятьдесят	*Pyatdyesyat*
100	Сто	*Stor*
500	Пятьсот	*Pyatsort*
1,000	Тысяча	*Teesyatchsa*

DAYS, SEASONS AND TIME

yesterday	Вчера	*Vcherra*
today	Сегодня	*Sivordnya*
tomorrow	Завтра	*Zavhtra*
Monday	Понедельник	*Ponyedyelnik*
Tuesday	Вторник	*Vtornik*

Wednesday	Среда	*Ssreda*
Thursday	Четверг	*Chetvyerg*
Friday	Пятница	*Pyatnitsa*
Saturday	Суббота	*Sooborta*
Sunday	Воскресенье	*Voskresyenye*
What time is it?	Который час?	*Katory chass?*
now	Сейчас	*Saychass*
hour	Час	*Chass*
minute	Минута	*Minoota*
spring	Весна	*Vyesna*
summer	Лето	*Lyeta*
autumn	Осень	*Orsyen*
winter	Зима	*Zeema*
day	День	*Dyenn*
morning	Утро	*Ootra*
afternoon	После обеда	*Porslye abyeda*
evening	Вечер	*Vyeacha*
night	Ночь	*Norch*

Wanderlust
travel magazine

Appendix 2

FURTHER INFORMATION

Unsurprisingly for a country that continues to be so little known or understood in the West, not much has been written in English about Belarus directly. But if you search hard enough, there are some gems to be found, and those that I list are but a selection. I do urge you to read as widely as you can before you go, because any insight that you can gain into the history of this country and its people will only be of benefit to you as you travel around and forge relationships along the way. Just bear in mind that it's really difficult to find works of balance, proportion and moderation that are written with objectivity by those with detailed personal knowledge of what actually goes on in this fascinating country. Against that background, easily the best starting point has to be *That's Belarus, Babe!* (page 330). I have also added reference to a few of the best books on the Chernobyl catastrophe; although it occurred outside the national borders of Belarus, no traveller and student of the issues facing Belarusian society today can hope to be prepared for the deeply affecting experiences to be gained from a visit here without at least a rudimentary knowledge of what occurred on that fateful spring night in 1986.

BOOKS
Travelogues and memoirs

Applebaum, Anne *Between East and West: Across the Borderlands of Europe* Papermac, 1995. An account of a journey from the Baltic to the Black Sea made in 1991, in which the author describes her encounters not just in Belarus, but also Lithuania, Russia and Ukraine. That it is a subjective work adds significantly to the fascination of the tales that are recounted in these pages, and anyone who has travelled in this part of Europe will recognise much from their own experiences with great fondness.

Duffy, Peter *The Bielski Brothers* Harper Collins, paperback, 2004. This tells the courageous story of the brothers who saved the lives of countless hundreds of Jews in the forests of Belarus from the early days of the Great Patriotic War all through the Nazi occupation, at the same time creating, shaping and leading a ruthlessly efficient partisan fighting force whose contribution to repelling the invaders and delivering the ultimate liberation of the occupied territories is impossible to overstate.

Guterman, Norbert (introduction), Chagall, Bella (author) and Chagall, Marc (illustrator) *Burning Lights* Random House USA Inc, 1989. An affectionate remembrance of Jewish life in pre-Revolutionary Vitebsk. Beautiful drawings by the famous Belarusian artist delightfully illustrate the memoirs of his wife.

Hobson, Charlotte *Black Earth City: A Year in the Heart of Russia* Granta Books, 2002. This book contains only passing references to Minsk but, like Thubron (page 328), Hobson has a deeply perceptive eye for humanity. The characters she describes paint a rich tableau of life for ordinary people in a provincial Russian town against a backdrop of major political upheaval as the Soviet Union broke apart. The beautiful cameo illustrations of the warm relationships within the author's circle of friends in Russia are charming vignettes that might very easily describe those that I have been fortunate to be able to experience over the course of my time in Belarus.

Kagan, Jack *We Stood Shoulder to Shoulder* Arima Publishing, 2010. Based on extensive Belarusian archives, this is another first-hand account of life as a partisan with the Bielski brothers in the forests of Belarus. Kagan has a particularly understated narrative style that only adds to the potency of the stories he relates. It was the same when I met him in the spring of 2014 to hear harrowing first-hand tales of extraordinary courage in the face of barbarity (all recounted in a calm, matter-of-fact way), including the astonishing tale of his own escape from the ghetto. Then in October 2017 I found myself in Novogrudok, standing at the mouth of the very tunnel through which he and others made their escape (see box, page 250). This remarkable man is sadly now deceased. How I wish I could have spent longer in his company.

Kagan, Jack and Cohen, Dov *Surviving the Holocaust with the Russian Jewish Partisans* Vallentine Mitchell & Co Ltd, 2001. More deeply moving stories of heroism and tragedy from the Nazi occupation of Jewish territories in Belarus, with detailed factual information taken from Belarusian archives.

Marsden, Philip *The Bronski House* Harper Perennial, 2005. This unusual and moving blend of history, tragedy, romance and travel writing is a real delight. Based on a journey shared with exiled poet Zofia Hinska returning to the Belarusian village of her birth, it recounts an ensuing 'rites of passage' experience that was to link the history of this troubled region to a poignant family tale. It's a fine illustration of the effect of momentous events in shaping the national psyche that endures to this day. Highly recommended.

Tec, Nechama *Defiance* Oxford University Press, 2008. This covers much the same ground as *The Bielski Brothers* (page 327), and is the better known of the two. It also spawned the highly successful film of the same name and if you ignore the worst excesses of 'the Hollywood treatment' (including some of the actors' accents), the film is a very powerful dramatisation of a truly inspiring story of resilience against the odds. I suggest you read the book first and then see the film.

Thubron, Colin *Among the Russians* Vintage, 2004. A splendid memoir of the journey taken by the author across the Soviet Union in the 1980s, when he drove 16,000km from the Baltic to the Caucasus and then to the far east of the Soviet Empire in an old Morris Marina. Only the first chapter is about Belarus (his point of entry into the USSR), but the poignant tales that follow about the people he met along the way could easily have been written about Belarusians.

Yaffe Radin, Ruth *Escape to the Forest* Harper Collins, 2000. A children's book that tells the story of a young Jewish girl living with her family in the town of Lida at the start of the Great Patriotic War. Based on a true story (but also part fiction), it describes life under the Nazis before she and her family fled into the forest to join the band of partisans resisting the occupation and saving Jewish lives.

Other eastern European guides For a full list of Bradt's eastern European guides, see

w bradtguides.com/shop.

Evans, Andrew *Ukraine* 2013.

Taylor, Neil *Estonia* 2014.

Politics, history, economy and society

Bazan, Lubov *A History of Belarus* Glagoslav Publications Ltd, 2014. A decent attempt at placing modern Belarus in its historical context, though some scholars question the premise upon which the author (a native Belarusian with an impressive CV) draws some of her conclusions. This need not trouble the reader seeking an introductory brushstroke history.

Bennett, Brian *The Last Dictatorship in Europe: Belarus Under Lukashenko* C Hurst & Co Publishers Ltd, 2012. Written by the UK's Ambassador to Belarus from 2003 to 2007, it is an intriguing assessment of the man responsible for shaping this post-Soviet nation state. Not everyone who knows the country will agree with the conclusions drawn, but it remains an interesting read for observers and commentators.

Beorn, Waitman Wade *Marching into Darkness: The Wehrmacht and the Holocaust in Belarus* Harvard University Press, 2014. An important contribution to the shameful story of Nazi oppression and brutality in this part of Europe that has long waited to be told. Essential reading for an understanding of the events that significantly contributed to the national psyche of this country and its people.

Coombes, Anne *Culture Smart! Belarus* Kuperard, 2008. This series of guides to countries all over the world (from Afghanistan to Vietnam), sets out to cover the basics of custom, belief, culture, history, politics, home life, business, society and sensitive issues in a standard format. Practical, sensible, easy to read and accurate, this slender tome slips easily into a pocket and will be a helpful companion on your travels.

Gross, Jan T *Revolution from Abroad: The Soviet Conquest of Poland's Western Ukraine and Western Belorussia* Princeton University Press, 2002. A scholarly tale of life in this part of Europe under the yoke of Soviet oppression in the period between the end of World War I hostilities and events prior to the Great Patriotic War, leading to the tragic consequences of the resultant clash of opposing totalitarian ideology in the West and the East of the continent.

Ioffe, Grigory *Understanding Belarus and How Western Foreign Policy Misses the Mark* Rowman & Littlefield Publishers Inc, 2014. A perceptive and timely assessment of the many challenges faced by this country in the course of its complex relationships with the West and with Russia.

Kaliada, Yuri *Belarus Free Theatre: New Plays from Central Europe* Oberon Books Ltd, 2014. Original works of drama translated into English by a close associate of *Belarus Free Theatre*, an independent company styling itself as 'the executive arm of the Ministry of Counterculture' (now based in London and performing underground in Belarus where and when able). The works collected here are the winners from 523 plays submitted to the company's 2014 International Contest of Contemporary Drama. See also *Belarus Free Theatre: Staging a Revolution (New Plays from Eastern Europe)* (2016) and *On Freedom: Powerful Polemics by Supporters of Belarus Free Theatre* (2015), both published by Oberon Books.

Marples, David *Belarus: A Denationalized Nation* Routledge, 1999. Now somewhat dated, but it retains its legitimacy as a commentary on the Soviet-style politics in evidence in the country at independence and throughout the 1990s.

Parker, Stewart *The Last Soviet Republic: Alexander Lukashenko's Belarus* Trafford Publishing, 2007. Much of what is written and broadcast in Western media about this country is characterised by ignorance and an unwillingness to look beyond clichés. This knowledgeable and approachable book will help to counterpoint the misinformation with a sense of proportion and balance.

Silitski, Vitali and Zaprudnik, Jan *Historical Dictionary of Belarus* The Scarecrow Press Inc, 2007. Accessible and brimming with facts, this welcome update of the 1998 edition contains much here to inform the reader intent on discovering all there is to know about this country.

Snyder, Timothy *The Reconstruction of Nations: Poland, Ukraine, Lithuania, Belarus, 1569–1999* Yale University Press, 2004. A scholarly work of analysis into the turbulent history of these eastern European countries, whose past and present are inextricably interwoven.

Wilson, Andrew *Belarus: The Last European Dictatorship* Yale University Press, 2011. An approachable tome that attempts to place the realities of modern Belarus in their historical context. As with the Bennett work (see above), there will be those with personal experience of life in this fascinating country who will beg to differ with the conclusions drawn, but this should not detract from the worth of its contribution to the debate.

Zaprudnik, Jan *Belarus: At a Crossroads in History* Westview Press Inc, 1993. Also a little dated, but it remains a powerful commentary on the complexities of the country's history and its impact on political and social life in the immediate aftermath of independence. The fact that the author has Belarusian antecedents lends gravitas to his observations.

Chernobyl

Alexievich, Svetlana *Chernobyl Prayer* Penguin Classics, 2016. A collection of intensely moving remembrances from those who lived through the nightmare. These heartbreaking reminiscences are not easy to read but their story is one that richly deserves to be told. Alexievich is one of the finest of today's Belarusian authors. Awarded the Nobel Prize for Literature in 2015, her works of non-fiction expose the reality of life in the final years of the Soviet Union and after its collapse. Anything she writes is worthy of close attention.

Dowswell, Paul *The Chernobyl Disaster (Days That Shook the World)* Hodder Wayland, 2003. A short (64 pages) but informative, no-nonsense resumé of the 24-hour period in which the explosion occurred. Aimed at the teenage market, it's a simple (but not simplistic) introduction to the key issues. If your time is limited, this is the one to read.

Mycio, Mary *Wormwood Forest: A Natural History of Chernobyl* Henry (Joseph) Press, 2005. This splendid book addresses the consequences of the disaster from a different angle; that of the natural world's wildlife sanctuary evolving in the radioactivity of the exclusion zone.

Petrucci, Mario *Heavy Water: A Poem for Chernobyl* Enitharmon Press, 2004. Based on first-hand accounts from people who were there, this is a work of great dignity and impact displaying powerful humanity and insight.

Roche, Adi *Chernobyl Heart* New Island Books, 2006. This book is an excellent contribution to the story of the fine work undertaken by children's charities to help alleviate the plight of those whose lives have been so affected by the insidious radioactive fallout. Adi's selfless commitment is already well documented elsewhere and the stories recounted here are both tragic and uplifting all at once.

Belarus today

Cheriakova, Masha and Chernova, Marta *Heta Belarus Dzietka! (That's Belarus, Babe!)* 2016. 'Our book is a celebration of Belarus from within with an outsider's view', say the authors on their excellent website (w *etobelarusdetka.com*), a summary that beautifully captures the spirit of this charming book. Written in both English and Belarusian (presented side by side on the page) with locals and visitors from abroad in mind, the witty and chatty style incorporates a commendable sense of self-parody. Those who know the country will recognise much within its pages and for those coming to the subject for the first time it offers an excellent introduction to people and society in today's Belarus. Every Belarusian I know (particularly among the younger generation) thinks this book is a gem. I absolutely agree. The authors are also closely associated with the splendid website w hifivebelarus.com.

Health

Wilson-Howarth, Dr Jane, *Bugs, Bites & Bowels* Cadogan, 2009

Wilson-Howarth, Dr Jane, and Ellis, Dr Matthew *Your Child Abroad: A Travel Health Guide* eBook, Bradt Travel Guides, 2014

Magazine

hidden europe Available by subscription via the website of the editorial bureau, based in Berlin and run by Nicky Gardner and Susanne Kries (w *hiddeneurope.co.uk*), this periodical is an absolute gem. Showcasing travel writing of the highest quality, it focuses on those cultures and communities of Europe that seem to evade other writers and observers, as well as the means of slow travel that connect them. Several pieces on Belarus have found their way on to the pages of various editions. See ad, page 118.

WEBSITES New websites are appearing all the time, but the list below showcases some of my favourites.

General information
w **34travel.me/gotobelarus** Independent site with an accessible, informative style.
w **belarus.by** The country's official website.
w **belarusdigest.com** An extremely interesting independent source of objective information aimed at the English-speaking world.
w **belarusfeed.com** Independent, chatty and newsy.
w **belarusguide.com** An independent virtual guide to the country.
w **belarustoday.info** For news, current affairs and culture.
w **belarustourism.by** The state's national tourism agency.
w **etobelarusdetka.com** Closely linked to hifivebelarus and an equally fine source of insider information, particularly within the site's blog posts.
❋ w **hifivebelarus.com** Maintained by young, vibrant, local experts with a passion for promoting their country.
w **visitbelarus.net**

Region-specific information For information on specific areas, go to the sites of the oblast executive committees (all of which have English pages). Additionally, the executive committees of the six cities all have English pages on their own sites; in each case, type the name of the city into your browser followed by the suffix '.gov.by'. Many Belarusian tour agencies have informative websites in English, with operators speaking good English at the other end of a phone line or computer terminal to take care of your needs directly.

w brest-region.gov.by
w minsk-region.gov.by
w mogilev-region.gov.by
w gomel-region.gov.by
w grodno-region.gov.by
w vitebsk-region.gov.by

Index

Page numbers in **bold** indicate major entries; those in *italic* indicate maps.

INDEX OF ADVERTISERS